THE CORRESPONDENCE
OF
EDWARD
YOUNG

1683–1765

Edited by

HENRY PETTIT

OXFORD
AT THE CLARENDON PRESS
1971

Oxford University Press, Ely House, London W.1

GLASGOW NEW YORK TORONTO MELBOURNE WELLINGTON
CAPE TOWN IBADAN NAIROBI DAR ES SALAAM LUSAKA ADDIS ABABA
DELHI BOMBAY CALCUTTA MADRAS KARACHI LAHORE DACCA
KUALA LUMPUR SINGAPORE HONG KONG TOKYO

PRINTED IN GREAT BRITAIN
AT THE UNIVERSITY PRESS, OXFORD
BY VIVIAN RIDLER
PRINTER TO THE UNIVERSITY

ABBREVIATIONS

Barbauld	*The Correspondence of Samuel Richardson* . . . [with] *A Biographical Account* . . . By Anna Laetitia Barbauld. 6 vols., 1804.
Bath	Historical Manuscripts Commission, *Calendar of the Manuscripts of the Marquis of Bath preserved at Longleat, Wiltshire.* Vol. i, 1904.
Climenson	Emily J. Climenson, *Elizabeth Montagu, the Queen of the Blue-Stockings: Her Correspondence from 1720 to 1761.* 2 vols., 1906.
Colorado MS. (Pettit)	From the editor's library.
Croft	Herbert Croft, 'Young', in *Lives of the Most Eminent English Poets* . . . By Samuel Johnson. Vol. iv, 1781.
Dapp	Kathryn Gilbert Dapp, *George Keate, Esq., Eighteenth Century English Gentleman.* 1939.
Elwin–Courthope	*The Works of Alexander Pope*, ed. W. Elwin and W. J. Courthope. 10 vols., 1871–89.
Halsband	*The Complete Letters of Lady Mary Wortley Montagu*, ed. Robert Halsband. 3 vols., 1965–7.
Hartford MS. (Williams)	From the library of Ralph M. Williams of Trinity College, Hartford, Connecticut.
Llanover	*The Autobiography and Correspondence of Mary Granville, Mrs. Delany*, ed. Lady Llanover. 6 vols., 1861–2.
Longe	Julia G. Longe, *Martha Lady Giffard: Her Life and Correspondence.* 1911.
Longleat MSS.	From the collections of the Marquis of Bath in Longleat, Wiltshire.
McKillop	*James Thomson 1700–1748: Letters and Documents*, ed. Alan McKillop. 1958.
Montagu	*The Letters of Elizabeth Montagu*, ed. Matthew Montagu. 4 vols., 1809–13.
Moy Thomas	*The Letters and Works of Lady Mary Wortley Montagu*, ed. Lord Wharncliffe with additions [etc.] by W. Moy Thomas. 2 vols., 1898.
New Haven MSS. (Osborn)	From the collections of James M. Osborn of New Haven, Connecticut.

New Jersey MSS. (Hyde)	From the collections of Donald and Mary Hyde in Somerville, New Jersey.
New York MSS. (Houghton)	From the collections of Arthur A. Houghton, Jr., of New York City.
Nichols–Doran	*The Complete Works . . . of the Rev. Edward Young . . . to which is prefixed, A Life of the Author,* by John Doran, ed. James Nichols. 2 vols., 1854.
Osborn	Joseph Spence, *Observations, Anecdotes, and Characters of Books and Men,* ed. James M. Osborn. 2 vols., 1966.
Pettit	Henry Pettit, *A Bibliography of Young's 'Night-Thoughts'.* University of Colorado Studies, Series in Language and Literature, No. 5, 1954.
Reading MSS. (Collins)	From the collections of Edward T. Collins of Reading, Berkshire.
Sale	William B. Sale, Jr., *Samuel Richardson: A Bibliographical Record of His Literary Career.* 1936.
Shelley	Henry C. Shelley, *The Life and Letters of Edward Young.* 1914.
Sherburn	*The Correspondence of Alexander Pope,* ed. George Sherburn. 5 vols., 1956.
Surrey MSS.	From the collections of Major-General Sir Eustace F. Tickell, K.B.E., of Cobham, Surrey.
Swedenberg	'Letters of Edward Young to Mrs. Judith Reynolds', ed. H. T. Swedenberg, Jr., in *The Huntington Library Quarterly,* ii (October 1938), 89–100.
Thomas	Walter Thomas, *Le Poète Edward Young (1683–1765): Étude sur sa vie et ses œuvres.* 1901.
Tickell	Richard Eustace Tickell, *Thomas Tickell and the Eighteenth Century Poets (1685–1740).* 1931.
Tickell Letterbook	Transcription of correspondence in the collections of Major-General Sir Eustace F. Tickell, K.B.E., of Cobham, Surrey.
Williams	*The Correspondence of Jonathan Swift,* ed. Harold Williams. 5 vols., 1963–5.

THE CORRESPONDENCE OF EDWARD YOUNG

16.		[?April 1723]	Alexander Pope	[no ltr.]
17.	[?London]	[Th.] 2 May [?1723]	Alexander Pope	
18.		F. [?7 February 1723/4]	Lady Mary Worley Montagu	
19.		[?10–21 February 1723/4]	Lady Mary Wortley Montagu	
—	Thomas Clutterbuck to Young.	London. [Sa.] 20 June 1724		*unpd.*
20.	Haslemere, Surrey	[M.] 3 August 1724	Thomas Tickell	
21.	Chiddingfold, Surrey	[Su.] 20 September 1724	Thomas Tickell	
22.	[Sheen, Surrey]	[Sa.] 10 October 1724	Thomas Tickell	*unpd.*
23.		[?October 1724]	Henrietta, Duchess of Marlborough	*unpd.*
24.	[?Sheen, Surrey]	[?Tu. 20 October 1724]	Thomas Clutterbuck	[no ltr.]
25.	[Sheen, Surrey]	[Tu.] 20 October 1724	Thomas Tickell	*unpd.*
26.		[Sa. 24 October 1724]	Thomas Tickell	*unpd.*
27.	Chiswick, Mdx.	[M.] 16 November [1724]	Thomas Tickell	*unpd.*
28.	Chiswick, Mdx.	[W.] 2 December 1724	Thomas Tickell	*unpd.*
29.	Chiswick, Mdx.	[M.] 14 December 1724	Thomas Tickell	
30.	London	[Tu.] 2 March 1724/5	Thomas Tickell	
31.		[Sa.] 3 July 1725	Thomas Tickell	[no ltr.]
32.		[Tu.] 27 July 1725	Thomas Tickell	*unpd.*
33.	Chiswick, Mdx.	[F.] 3 September 1725	Thomas Tickell	*unpd.*
34.	London	[W.] 29 December 1725	Thomas Tickell	*unpd.*

56.	[?Oxford]	[?Sa. 26] July 1729	Edward Kinaston [no ltr.]
57.		M. [?April–June 1730]	Henrietta Howard
58.		[?1734–1736]	Alexander Pope [no ltr.]
59.	Welwyn, Herts.	[F.] 23 February 1738/9	John Williams
60.	Welwyn, Herts.	[Su.] 25 November 1739	John Williams
61.	Welwyn, Herts.	[F.] 7 December 1739	Edmund Curll
62.		[Tu.] 18 December 1739	Edmund Curll
63.	[?London]	M. [?4 or 11 February 1739/40]	Lady Oxford *unpd.*
64.	[?London]	Tu. [?5 or 12 February 1739/40]	Duchess of Portland *unpd.*
65.	East Sheen, Surrey	[W.] 20 February 1739/40	Duchess of Portland *unpd.*
66.	Welwyn, Herts.	[W.] 21 May [1740]	Judith Reynolds
67.	[East Sheen, Surrey]	[Th.] 29 May [1740]	Judith Reynolds
68.	East Sheen, Surrey	[Su.] 1 June [1740]	Judith Reynolds
69.	East Sheen, Surrey	Th. [?5 June 1740]	Judith Reynolds
70.	East Sheen, Surrey	[Tu.] 10 June 1740	Judith Reynolds
71.	East Sheen, Surrey	[?Su. 15] 5 June 1740	Judith Reynolds
72.		[?W. 18 June 1740]	Judith Reynolds [no ltr.]
73.	Tunbridge Wells, Kent	[W.] 2 July 1740	Judith Reynolds
74.	[Tunbridge Wells, Kent]	[M.] 21 July [1740]	Judith Reynolds *unpd.*
75.	[Tunbridge Wells, Kent]	[Su.] 3 August [1740]	Judith Reynolds
76.	Tunbridge Wells, Kent	[M.] 4 August 1740	Edmund Curll
77.	Tunbridge Wells, Kent	[F.] 15 August [1740]	Duchess of Portland *unpd.*
78.	[Tunbridge Wells, Kent]	[Su.] 17 August [1740]	Judith Reynolds

79.	[Tunbridge Wells, Kent]	[F.] 22 August [1740]	Judith Reynolds
80.	Tunbridge Wells, Kent	[M.] 25 August 1740	Duchess of Portland
81.	[Tunbridge Wells, Kent]	[M.] 1 September [1740]	Judith Reynolds
82.	[Tunbridge Wells, Kent]	[W.] 10 September 1740	Duchess of Portland
83.	[Tunbridge Wells, Kent]	[F.] 19 September 1740	Judith Reynolds
84.	Ditchley, Oxon.	[M.] 13 October [1740]	Duchess of Portland
85.	Ditchley, Oxon.	[Tu.] 14 October [1740]	Judith Reynolds
86.	[Ditchley, Oxon.]	[M.] 3 November [1740]	Judith Reynolds
87.	[?Ditchley, Oxon.]	[F.] 7 November 1740	Duchess of Portland
88.	Bulstrode, Bucks.	Th. [20 November 1740]	Judith Reynolds
89.	London	[Tu.] 25 November 1740	Duchess of Portland
90.	[London]	Th. [?4 December 1740]	Duchess of *unpd.* Portland
91.	Barnet, Herts.	[Tu.] 9 December 1740	Judith Reynolds
92.	Welwyn, Herts.	[Sa.] 20 December 1740	Duchess of Portland
93.	[Welwyn, Herts.]	Su. [?January 1740/1]	Duchess of Portland
94.	London	[W.] 14 January 1740/1	Judith Reynolds
95.	London	[?Th. 15 January 1740/1]	Duchess of Portland
96.	London	Su. [?18 January 1740/1]	Duchess of Portland
97.	London	[Tu.] 27 January 1740/1	Judith Reynolds
98.	[London]	[?Th. 29 January 1740/1]	Duchess of Portland
99.	Welwyn, Herts.	Su. [?1 February 1740/1]	Duchess of Portland

121.		[August 1742]	John Potter, [no ltr.] Archbishop of Canterbury
122.	Tunbridge Wells, Kent	[Sa.] 21 August 1742	Duchess of Portland
123.	Welwyn, Herts.	[F.] 1 October 1742	Duchess of Portland
124.	Welwyn, Herts.	[F.] 15 October [1742]	Duchess of *unpd.* Portland
125.	Welwyn, Herts.	[W.] 17 November 1742	Duchess of *unpd.* Portland
126.	Welwyn, Herts.	[Sa.] 20 November 1742	Sir Thomas Hanmer
127.	Welwyn, Herts.	[Su.] 12 December 1742	Duchess of Portland
128.	Welwyn, Herts.	[Th.] 13 January 1742/3	Duchess of Portland
129.	[Welwyn, Herts.]	F. [?18 March 1742/3]	Philip Yorke
130.	[?Welwyn, Herts.]	[Su.] 20 March 1742/3	[?Richard [no ltr.] Mead]
131.	[Welwyn, Herts.]	[?April 1743]	Duchess of *unpd.* Portland
132.	Welwyn, Herts.	[Th.] 2 June 1743	Duchess of Portland
133.	Gubbins, Herts.	Su. [?11 June 1743]	Duchess of Portland
134.	Welwyn, Herts.	[Su.] 10 July 1743	Duchess of *unpd.* Portland
135.	[London]	[W.] 20 July [1743]	Duchess of *unpd.* Portland
136.	Welwyn, Herts.	[Th.] 25 August 1743	Duchess of Portland
137.	Welwyn, Herts.	[W.] 14 September 1743	Duchess of *unpd.* Portland
138.	[?Welwyn, Herts.]	[?M. 25 September 1743]	Duchess of Portland
139.	London	[Sa.] 29 October 1743	Duchess of Portland
140.	[London]	[Su.] 20 November 1743	Duchess of Portland
141.	Welwyn, Herts.	[Sa.] 10 December 1743	Duchess of Portland
142.	Welwyn, Herts.	[Tu.] 17 January 1743/4	Duchess of Portland

143.	[London]	[March 1743/4]	Duchess of Portland *unpd.*
144.	Richmond, Surrey	[M.] 19 March 1743/4	George North *unpd.*
145.	[Richmond, Surrey]	[March 1743/4]	Duchess of Portland *unpd.*
—	Duchess of Portland to the Duke of Newcastle	[M.] 14 May 1744	*unpd.*
146.		[Tu.] 29 May 1744	Duchess of Portland
147.	Welwyn, Herts.	[F.] 1 June [1744]	Duchess of Portland
148.	[?Welwyn, Herts.]	[W.] 20 June 1744	Samuel Richardson
149.	[London]	W. [?27 June 1744]	Duchess of Portland *unpd.*
150.	Welwyn, Herts.	[M.] 9 July 1744	Samuel Richardson
151.	Welwyn, Herts.	[M.] 23 July 1744	Duchess of Portland
152.	[Welwyn, Herts.]	[Su.] 29 July 1744	Samuel Richardson
153.	London	[Tu.] 30 July [1744]	Duchess of Portland *unpd.*
154.	Welwyn, Herts.	[Su.] 16 September 1744	Duchess of Portland
155.	Welwyn, Herts.	[Su.] 18 November 1744	Duchess of Portland *unpd.*
156.	Welwyn, Herts.	[Su.] 25 November 1744	Duchess of Portland *unpd.*
157.	Bulstrode, Bucks.	[Sa.] 8 December 1744	Samuel Richardson
—	Richardson to Young	London [*c.* W. 12 December 1744]	
158.	[Bulstrode, Bucks.]	M. [?17] December 1744	Samuel Richardson
159.	[Watford, Herts.]	[?December 1744]	Duchess of Portland
160.	Welwyn, Herts.	[Th.] 3 January 1744/5	Robert Dodsley [no ltr.]
161.	Welwyn, Herts.	[Th.] 17 January 1744/5	Duchess of Portland
162.	[London]	Su. [?3 March 1744/5]	Duchess of Portland *unpd.*
163.	[London]	Su. [?14 April 1745]	Duchess of Portland *unpd.*
164.	Welwyn, Herts.	[Th.] 2 May 1745	Samuel Richardson

No.	Place	Date	Correspondent	
9.	Welwyn, Herts.	[Th.] 10 September 1747	Duchess of Portland	
o.	Welwyn, Herts.	[Th.] 8 October 1747	Duchess of Portland	unpd.
I.	Welwyn, Herts.	[F.] 16 October [1747]	Robert Dodsley	
2.	[Welwyn, Herts.]	[Su.] 25 October [1747]	Duchess of Portland	unpd.
—	Duchess of Portland to Young	Bulstrode, Bucks. [W.] 4 November 1747		unpd.
3.	Welwyn, Herts.	[Su.] 8 November 1747	Duchess of Portland	unpd.
—	Richardson to Young	London [Th.] 19 November 1747		
4.	Welwyn, Herts.	[Su.] 22 November 1747	Duchess of Portland	
5.	Welwyn, Herts.	[Tu.] 24 November 1747	Samuel Richardson	
6.	Welwyn, Herts.	[Su.] 29 November 1747	Duchess of Portland	unpd.
7.	Welwyn, Herts.	[Su.] 6 December 1747	Duchess of Portland	unpd.
8.	Welwyn, Herts.	[Su.] 27 December 1747	Duchess of Portland	unpd.
39.	[Welwyn, Herts.]	[?January 1747/8]	Samuel Richardson	
40.	London	[W.] 27 January [1747/8]	Duchess of Portland	unpd.
41.	[Welwyn, Herts.]	[March 1747/8]	Duchess of Portland	
42.	Welwyn, Herts.	[Tu.] 12 April 1748	Duchess of Portland	
43.	[Welwyn, Herts.]	[Sa.] 30 April 1748	Samuel Richardson	
44.	Welwyn, Herts.	[Sa.] 4 June 1748	Duchess of Portland	
45.	Welwyn, Herts.	[Su.] 25 September 1748	Duchess of Portland	
46.	Welwyn, Herts.	[Su.] 30 October 1748	Duchess of Portland	unpd.
47.	Welwyn, Herts.	[Th.] 3 November 1748	Caroline Lee Haviland	unpd.
48.		[?November 1748]	Caroline Lee Haviland	[no ltr.]
49.	Westminster, Mdx.	[Tu.] 22 November 1748	Duchess of Portland	

No.	Place	Date	Correspondent	
—	Duchess of Portland to the Duke of Newcastle	Westminster [F.] 17 May 1745		unpd.
165.	[Welwyn, Herts.]	[Su.] 19 May [1745]	Duchess of Portland	
—	Duchess of Portland to the Duke of Newcastle	Westminster [Early] June 1745		unpd.
166.	[Welwyn, Herts.]	[Tu.] 11 June 1745	Samuel Richardson	
—	William Murray to the Duchess of Portland	[Tu.] 18 June 1745		
167.	Fulham, Mdx.	[Tu.] 9 July [1745]	Duchess of Portland	unpd.
168.	Fulham, Mdx.	[W.] 10 July 1745	Duchess of Portland	unpd.
—	Duchess of Portland to the Duke of Newcastle	Welbeck [M.] 15 July 1745		unpd.
169.	[London]	Su. [?18 August 1745]	Duchess of Portland	unpd.
170.	Tunbridge Wells, Kent	[W.] 21 August [1745]	Duchess of Portland	
171.	[Tunbridge Wells, Kent]	Sa. [?14 September 1745]	Samuel Richardson	
172.	Tunbridge Wells, Kent	[Tu.] 17 September 1745	Duchess of Portland	
173.	[Tunbridge Wells, Kent]	Tu. 17 September 1745	Samuel Richardson	
174.	Fulham, Mdx.	[F.] 25 October 1745	Duchess of Portland	
175.	[?Fulham, Mdx.]	[Early November 1745]	Duchess of Portland	unpd.
176.	[?Fulham, Mdx.]	[?W. 20 November 1745]	Duchess of Portland	unpd.
177.	Bulstrode, Bucks.	Tu. 26 November 1745	Samuel Richardson	
—	Richardson to Young	London [Tu.] 3 December 1745		
178.	Welwyn, Herts.	Su. [8 December 1745]	Duchess of Portland	
179.	Welwyn, Herts.	[Tu.] 10 December 1745	Samuel Richardson	

180.	Welwyn, Herts.	[Th.] 19 December 1745	Samuel Richardson
181.	Welwyn, Herts.	[Su.] 2 February 1745/6	Duchess of Portland
182.	Welwyn, Herts.	[Tu.] 18 February 1745/6	Samuel Richardson
183.	[Welwyn, Herts.]	[?February 1745/6]	Samuel Richardson
184.	[Welwyn, Herts.]	[?Tu. 4 March 1745/6]	Mrs. Grace Cole [no ltr.]
185.	Welwyn, Herts.	[Tu.] 4 March 1745/6	Samuel Richardson
186.	[Welwyn, Herts.]	[W.] 19 March 1745/6	Samuel Richardson
187.	Welwyn, Herts.	[Su.] 6 April 1746	Duchess of Portland
188.	Welwyn, Herts.	[Su.] 20 April 1746	Samuel Richardson
189.	Welwyn, Herts.	Su. [?4] May 1746	Samuel Richardson
190.	Welwyn, Herts.	Su. [?1 June 1746]	Duchess of Portland *unpd.*
191.	[Welwyn, Herts.]	[Th.] 12 June [1746]	Duchess of Portland
192.		[F.] 4 July 1746	Duke of Newcastle
193.	[Welwyn, Herts.]	[Th.] 17 July 1746	Duchess of Portland
194.	Welwyn, Herts.	[Th.] 17 July 1746	Samuel Richardson
195.	[?Welwyn, Herts.]	[?July–August 1746]	Samuel Richardson
196.	Welwyn, Herts.	[Su.] 10 August 1746	Duchess of Portland *unpd.*
197.	Welwyn, Herts.	[Su.] 17 August 1746	Samuel Richardson
198.	[Welwyn, Herts.]	[Tu.] 23 September 1746	Duchess of Portland
199.	[Welwyn, Herts.]	[?October 1746]	John Grover [no ltr.]
200.	[?Welwyn, Herts.]	[Th.] 16 October 1746	Duchess of Portland
201.	Welwyn, Herts.	[Tu.] 28 October 1746	Duchess of Portland
202.	Welwyn, Herts.	[Tu.] 11 November 1746	Samuel Richardson
203.	Welwyn, Herts.	[Su.] 16 November 1746	Samuel Richardson
204.	Welwyn, Herts.	[Su.] 23 November 1746	Duchess of Portland
205.	Welwyn, Herts.	[Tu.] 2 December 1746	Samuel Richardson

206.	Welwyn, Herts.	[F.] 5 December 1746	
207.	[London]	[W.] 17 December 1746	
—	Richardson to Young	[London] [W.] 24 December 1746	
208.	Welwyn, Herts.	[Su.] 28 December 1746	
209.	Welwyn, Herts.	[Su.] 11 January 1746/7	
210.	Welwyn, Herts.	[Su.] 11 January 1746/7	
211.	[Welwyn, Herts.]	[Sa. 17 January 1746/7]	
212.	Welwyn, Herts.	[Tu.] 20 January 1746/7	
213.	Welwyn, Herts.	[Tu.] 3 February 1746/7	
214.		[February 1746/7]	
215.	[London]	[?M. 23 February 1746/7]	
216.	[London]	F. [?27 February 1746/7]	
217.	[London]	[Tu.] 3 March 1746/7	
218.	Welwyn, Herts.	[Th.] 9 April 1747	S
219.	Welwyn, Herts.	[Th.] 16 April 1747	D
220.	Welwyn, Herts.	[Su.] 3 May 1747	S
221.	[Welwyn, Herts.]	[?Mid-May 1747]	D
222.	Welwyn, Herts.	[Su.] 17 May 1747	S
223.	Welwyn, Herts.	[M.] 1 June 1747	D
224.		[?June 1747]	S
225.	Welwyn, Herts.	[Su.] 5 July 1747	S
226.	Welwyn, Herts.	[Su.] 19 July 1747	D
227.	[Welwyn, Herts.]	[W.] 5 August 1747	S
228.	[Welwyn, Herts.]	[?August 1747]	D

250.	Welwyn, Herts.	[Su.] 18 December 1748	Duchess of Portland
251.	Welwyn, Herts.	[Su.] 8 January 1748/9	Caroline *unpd.* Lee Haviland
252.	Welwyn, Herts.	[Su.] 29 January 1748/9	Duchess of Portland
253.	[Welwyn, Herts.]	[Th.] 9 February 1748/9	Samuel Richardson
254.	Welwyn, Herts.	[Th.] 9 February 1748/9	Mary *unpd.* Delany
255.	Welwyn, Herts.	[M.] 20 February 1748/9	Duchess of Portland
256.	[Welwyn, Herts.]	[Su.] 26 February [1748/9]	Caroline *unpd.* Lee Haviland
257.	Westminster, Mdx.	[March 1748/9]	Sir William Bunbury
258.	[Westminster, Mdx.]	[Sa.] 25 March 1748/9	Sir William Bunbury
259.	Welwyn, Herts.	[Su.] 9 April 1748/9	Caroline Lee [no ltr.] Haviland
260.	[Welwyn, Herts.]	[?Sa. 6] May 1749	Samuel Richardson
261.	Welwyn, Herts.	[Su.] 7 May 1749	Duchess of Portland
262.	[Welwyn, Herts.]	[W.] 24 May 1749	Samuel Richardson
263.	[Welwyn, Herts.]	[Su.] 9 July 1749	Samuel Richardson
264.	Welwyn, Herts.	[M.] 10 July 1749	Caroline Lee *unpd.* Haviland
265.	Welwyn, Herts.	[Tu.] 3 August 1749	Duchess of Portland
266.	[Welwyn, Herts.]	Tu. [?22 August 1749]	Duchess of *unpd.* Portland
—	Richardson to Young	[London] [Sa.] 9 September 1749	
267.	[Welwyn, Herts.]	[Su.] 10 September 1749	Samuel Richardson
268.	Welwyn, Herts.	[Su.] 17 September 1749	Duchess of Portland
269.	Welwyn, Herts.	Th. [21 September 1749]	Duchess of *unpd.* Portland
270.	Welwyn, Herts.	[Su.] 8 October 1749	Duchess of Portland
271.	Welwyn, Herts.	[Su.] 15 October 1749	Samuel Richardson
272.	Welwyn, Herts.	Tu. [?24 October 1749]	Duchess of Portland

273.	Welwyn, Herts.	[Sa.] 28 October 1749	Samuel Richardson
—	Richardson to Young	London [?Tu. 31] October [1749]	
274.	Welwyn, Herts.	[Su.] 5 November 1749	Samuel Richardson
275.	Welwyn, Herts.	[Th.] 16 November 1749	Duchess of Portland *unpd.*
276.	Welwyn, Herts.	[Tu.] 12 December 1749	Samuel Richardson
277.	Welwyn, Herts.	[Tu.] 26 December 1749	Duchess of Portland
—	Richardson to Young	London [M.] 1 January 1749/50	
278.	Welwyn, Herts.	[Su.] 7 January 1749/50	Samuel Richardson
279.	[Welwyn, Herts.]	[Tu.] 27 February 1749/50	Duchess of Portland *unpd.*
280.	[Welwyn, Herts.]	[Tu.] 10 April 1750	Samuel Richardson
281.	Welwyn, Herts.	[F.] 20 April 1750	Duchess of Portland
282.	[Welwyn, Herts.]	[Su. 8 July 1750]	Arthur Onslow [no ltr.]
283.	[Welwyn, Herts.]	[Su.] 8 July 1750	Samuel Richardson
284.		[Spring or Summer 1750]	Edward Cave [no ltr.]
—	Richardson to Mary Hallows	London [W.] 5 September 1750	
285.	[Welwyn, Herts.]	[Su.] 16 September 1750	Samuel Richardson
286.		[Early October 1750]	Arthur Onslow [no ltr.]
287.	Welwyn, Herts.	[Tu.] 16 October 1750	Samuel Richardson
288.	Welwyn, Herts.	[Su.] 21 October 1750	Duchess of Portland
289.	Welwyn, Herts.	[Su.] 4 November 1750	Duchess of Portland
290.	[Welwyn, Herts.]	[M.] 10 December 1750	Samuel Richardson
291.	Welwyn, Herts.	[Th.] 13 December 1750	Samuel Richardson

—	Richardson to Young	London [W.] 2 January 1750/1	
292.	Welwyn, Herts.	[Su.] 6 January 1750/1	Duchess of Portland *unpd.*
293.	[Welwyn, Herts.]	January 1750/1	Samuel Richardson
294.	Welwyn, Herts.	[Su.] 20 January 1750/1	Duchess of Portland
295.	Welwyn, Herts.	[Su.] 27 January 1750/1	Vincenz Bernhard Tscharner
296.	[Welwyn, Herts.]	[Su.] 10 March 1750/1	Samuel Richardson
297.	Welwyn, Herts.	[Tu.] 19 March 1750/1	Samuel Richardson
298.	[Welwyn, Herts.]	[Th.] 26 March 1751	Samuel Richardson
299.	[Welwyn, Herts.]	[Tu.] 9 April 1751	Samuel Richardson
300.	[Welwyn, Herts.]	[Late] April 1751	Samuel Richardson
301.	Welwyn, Herts.	[Sa.] 20 April 1751	Vincenz Bernhard Tscharner
302.	Welwyn, Herts.	[F.] 26 July 1751	Duchess of Portland
303.	Welwyn, Herts.	[Tu.] 30 July 1751	Samuel Richardson
—	Richardson to Young	[London] [Th.] 1 August 1751	
304.	[Welwyn, Herts.]	[W.] 7 August 1751	Samuel Richardson
305.	[Welwyn, Herts.]	[Tu.] 3 September 1751	Duchess of Portland
306.	[Welwyn, Herts.]	Th. [12 September 1751]	Duchess of Portland *unpd.*
307.	[London]	[Su.] 29 September 1751	Duchess of Portland
308.	[?London]	Th. [?October 1751]	Duchess of Portland *unpd.*
309.	[?Welwyn, Herts.]	[?M. 11 November 1751]	Theophilus Leigh [no ltr.]
310.	[Welwyn, Herts.]	[Sa.] 23 November 1751	Samuel Richardson
311.	[Welwyn, Herts.]	[Su.] 1 December 1751	Duchess of Portland *unpd.*
312.	[Welwyn, Herts.]	[Su.] 8 December 1751	Duchess of Portland *unpd.*
313.	[Welwyn, Herts.]	[Tu.] 10 December 1751	Samuel Richardson

333. [?Welwyn, Herts.]	[Tu.] 18 December 1753	Samuel Richardson
334. [?Welwyn, Herts.]	[F.] 21 December 1753	Joseph Warton
— James Elphinston to Young	Brompton, Mdx. [M.] 24 December 1753	
335. [Welwyn, Herts.]	[Tu.] 1 January 1754	James Elphinston
— James Elphinston to Young	Brompton, Mdx. [M.] 7 January 1754	
336.	[Th.] 14 March 1754	Samuel Richardson
— Benjamin Fletcher to Charles Reynolds, Chancellor of Lincoln	Welwyn, Herts. [F.] 19 April 1754	*unpd.*
337. [Welwyn, Herts.]	[Tu.] 25 June 1754	Duchess of Portland
338. [Welwyn, Herts.]	[Su.] 14 July 1754	Samuel Richardson
339. [Welwyn, Herts.]	[Su.] 21 July 1754	Samuel Richardson
— Richardson to Young	[London] [W.] 24 July 1754	
340. [Welwyn, Herts.]	[?Su. 28 July 1754]	Arthur Onslow [no ltr.]
341. [Welwyn, Herts.]	[Su.] 28 July 1754	Samuel Richardson
342. [Welwyn, Herts.]	[Th.] 1 August 1754	Samuel Richardson
— Richardson to Young	[London] [M.] 5 August 1754	
343. [?Welwyn, Herts.]	[M.] 5 August 1754	Samuel Richardson
344. [?Welwyn, Herts.]	Su. [11 August 1754]	Samuel Richardson
— Richardson to Young	London [W.] 14 August 1754	
345. [Welwyn, Herts.]	[Su.] 3 November 1754	Duchess of Portland *unpd.*
346. [?Welwyn, Herts.]	[?November 1754]	[?Charles Douglas]
— Richardson to Young	London [Tu.] 17 December 1754	
347. [?Welwyn, Herts.]	[M.] 30 December 1754	Duchess of Portland *unpd.*
— Richardson to Young	London [Tu.] 21 January 1755	
348. [Welwyn, Herts.]	W. [?22 January 1755]	Samuel Richardson

349.	[Welwyn, Herts.]	Su. [?26 January 1755]	Samuel Richardson
350.	[Welwyn, Herts.]	[W.] 5 February 1755	Mary Delany
351.	[Welwyn, Herts.]	Th. [?13 February 1755]	Samuel Richardson
352.	[Welwyn, Herts.]	[Th.] 6 March 1755	Samuel Richardson
353.	[Welwyn, Herts.]	[Su.] 23 March [1755]	Samuel Richardson
354.	[Welwyn, Herts.]	[Su.] 30 March 1755	Samuel Richardson
355.	Welwyn, Herts.	[Su.] 6 July 1755	Bennet Langton *unpd.*
356.	[Welwyn, Herts.]	[Su. 10 August] 1755	Samuel [no ltr.] Richardson
357.	Welwyn, Herts.	[Su.] 10 August 1755	Robert Dodsley
358.	[Welwyn, Herts.]	[Su.] 7 September 1755	Duchess of Portland
359.	[Welwyn, Herts.]	[Su.] 20 September 1755	Samuel Richardson
360.	[Welwyn, Herts.]	[Su.] 9 November 1755	Joseph Warton
—	Richardson to Young	London [F.] 23 April 1756	
361.	[Welwyn, Herts.]	[Tu.] 27 April 1756	Samuel Richardson
362.	[?Welwyn, Herts.]	[Tu.] 27 April 1756	Duchess of *unpd.* Portland
363.	[Welwyn, Herts.]	[Su.] 2 May 1756	Mary Delany
364.	[Welwyn, Herts.]	[Tu.] 6 July 1756	Samuel Richardson
365.	Welwyn, Herts.	[Su.] 11 July 1756	Samuel Richardson
366.	[Welwyn, Herts.]	[Th.] 29 July 1756	Duchess of Portland
367.	[Welwyn, Herts.]	[Tu.] 17 August 1756	Duchess of *unpd.* Portland
368.	[Welwyn, Herts.]	[Su.] 12 September 1756	Samuel Richardson
—	Dodsley to Young	[London] [Th.] 7 October 1756	
369.	[Welwyn, Herts.]	[Th.] 14 October 1756	Robert Dodsley [no ltr.]
—	Richardson to Young	[London] [Th.] 4 November 1956	
370.	[Welwyn, Herts.]	[Tu.] 9 November 1756	Samuel Richardson

371.	[Welwyn, Herts.]	[Tu.] 21 December 1756	Samuel Richardson	
—	Richardson to Young	[London] [Late December 1756]		
372.		Su. [2 January 1757]	Samuel Richardson	
—	Richardson to Young	London [F.] 7 January 1757		
373.	Welwyn, Herts.	[Su.] 9 January 1757	Duchess of Portland	*unpd.*
374.	[Welwyn, Herts.]	[Th.] 13 January 1757	Samuel Richardson	
—	Richardson to Young	[London] [F.] 14 January 1757		
375.	[Welwyn, Herts.]	[Th.] 20 January 1757	Samuel Richardson	
376.	[Welwyn, Herts.]	[Th.] 24 February 1757	Samuel Richardson	
377.	[Welwyn, Herts.]	[Sa.] 26 March 1757	Samuel Richardson	
—	Richardson to Young	London [Tu.] 10 May 1757		
378.	[Welwyn, Herts.]	[Th.] 12 May 1757	Samuel Richardson	
379.	[Welwyn, Herts.]	[Su.] 15 May 1757	Samuel Richardson	
380.	[Welwyn, Herts.]	[Su.] 22 May 1757	Samuel Richardson	
381.	[Welwyn, Herts.]	[Su.] 29 May 1757	Samuel Richardson	
—	Richardson to Young	London [Tu.] 19 July 1757		
382.	[Welwyn, Herts.]	[Th.] 21 July 1757	Samuel Richardson	
—	Richardson to Young	[London] [Tu.] 26 July 1757		
383.	[Welwyn, Herts.]	[Sa.] 30 July 1757	Samuel Richardson	
384.		[Su.] 11 September 1757	William Slade	
385.	Welwyn, Herts.	[Tu.] 27 September 1757	Samuel Richardson	*unpd.*
386.		[Su.] 23 October 1757	Samuel Richardson	
—	Richardson to Young	[London] [M.] 24 October 1757		
387.	Welwyn, Herts.	[Th.] 27 October 1757	Friedrich Gottlieb Klopstock	

388.	[Welwyn, Herts.]	[Tu.] 1 November 1757	Samuel Richardson
389.	Bath, Somerset	[F.] 30 December 1757	Friedrich Gottlieb Klopstock
390.	[Bath, Somerset]	[Tu.] 3 January 1758	Samuel Richardson
—	Richardson to Young	[London] January 1758	
391.	[Bath, Somerset]	[?January 1758]	John Jones [no ltr.]
392.	[Welwyn, Herts.]	[Su.] 30 April 1758	Samuel Richardson
—	Richardson to Young	[London] [Tu.] 2 May 1758	
393.		[Su.] 14 May 1758	Samuel Richardson
394.	[Welwyn, Herts.]	Su. 28 [May 1758]	Samuel Richardson
395.	[Welwyn, Herts.]	[Su.] 4 June 1758	Samuel Richardson
396.		[?1–7 July 1758]	Thomas Secker, [no ltr.] Archbishop of Canterbury
—	Thomas Secker, Archbishop of Canterbury, to Young	London [Sa.] 8 July 1758	
397.	[Welwyn, Herts.]	[Su.] 9 July 1758	Duchess of Portland
398.	Welwyn, Herts.	[W.] 12 July 1758	Duke of Newcastle
399.		[Th.] 7 September 1758	Duchess of Portland
400.		[Su.] 8 October 1758	Samuel Richardson
—	Richardson to Young	London [W.] 11 October 1758	
401.	[Welwyn, Herts.]	[W.] 6 December 1758	Samuel Richardson
402.	[Welwyn, Herts.]	Su. [?17 December 1758]	Samuel Richardson
—	Richardson to Young	[?London] [M.] 18 December 1758	
403.	[Welwyn, Herts.]	[?W. 20 December 1758]	Samuel Richardson
—	Richardson to Young	[?London] [F.] 22 December 1758	
—	Richardson to Young	[?London] [Tu.] 26 December 1758	
404.	[Welwyn, Herts.]	[Su.] 7 January 1759	Samuel Richardson
405.	[Welwyn, Herts.]	[Th.] 11 January 1759	Samuel Richardson

—	Richardson to Young	[?London] [W.] 24 January 1759	
406.	[Welwyn, Herts.]	[W.] 7 February 1759	Friedrich Gottlieb Klopstock
407.	[Welwyn, Herts.]	[?April 1759]	Samuel Richardson
408.	[Welwyn, Herts.]	[Sa.] 14 April 1759	Duchess of *unpd.* Portland
409.	[?Welwyn, Herts.]	[Late] April 1759	Samuel Richardson
410.	[Welwyn, Herts.]	Su. [?Early May 1759]	Samuel Richardson
411.	[Welwyn, Herts.]	Tu. [22 May 1759]	Samuel Richardson
—	Richardson to Young	London [Th.] 24 May 1759	
412.	[Welwyn, Herts.]	[F.] 25 May 1759	Samuel Richardson
—	Richardson to Young	[London] [Tu.] 29 May 1759	
413.	[Welwyn, Herts.]	[?Th. 31 May 1759]	Samuel Richardson
414.	[Welwyn, Herts.]	[?Early June 1759]	Samuel Richardson
415.	Welwyn, Herts.	[Th.] 21 June 1759	Samuel Richardson
416.	[Welwyn, Herts.]	[Su.] 29 July 1759	Duchess of *unpd.* Portland
417.	[Welwyn, Herts.]	[Sa.] 11 August 1759	Samuel Richardson
418.		[?August 1759]	Samuel *unpd.* Richardson
—	John Jones to J. Waller	Welwyn, Herts. [Tu.] 4 September 1759	*unpd.*
—	J. Waller to John Jones	St. Neots, Hunts. [Th.] 20 September 1759	*unpd.*
419.	[Welwyn, Herts.]	[Su.] 28 October 1759	Duchess of Portland
420.	Welwyn, Herts.	[Th.] 20 December 1759	Duchess of *unpd.* Portland
421.	[Welwyn, Herts.]	[Th.] 10 January 1760	Duchess of *unpd.* Portland
422.	[Welwyn, Herts.]	[?February–April 1760]	Samuel Richardson
—	J. Waller to John Jones	St. Neots, Hunts. [Th.] 10 April 1760	*unpd.*
—	J. Waller to John Jones	[St. Neots, Hunts.] [M. 14 April 1760]	*unpd.*

423.		[April–May 1760]	John Scott
424.	[Welwyn, Herts.]	[Th.] 29 May 1760	George Keate
—	J. Waller to John Jones	St. Neots, Hunts. [F.] 25 July 1760	*unpd.*
425.	[Welwyn, Herts.]	[Th.] 7 August 1760	Duchess of *unpd.* Portland
426.	[Welwyn, Herts.]	[M.] 11 August 1760	George Keate
427.	[Welwyn, Herts.]	[M.] 8 September 1760	Samuel Richardson
—	J. Waller to John Jones	St. Neots, Hunts. [Th.] 11 September 1760	*unpd.*
428.	[Welwyn, Herts.]	[W.] 5 November 1760	The Trustees of the Welwyn *unpd.* Charity School
429.	[Welwyn, Herts.]	[Th.] 20 November 1760	Duchess of Portland
430.	[Welwyn, Herts.]	[Tu.] 20 January 1761	Duchess of Portland
431.	[London]	[February 1761]	Duchess of *unpd.* Portland
432.	Welwyn, Herts.	[Su.] 22 February 1761	George Keate
433.	Welwyn, Herts.	[Su.] 15 March 1761	George Keate
434.	[Welwyn, Herts.]	[Th. 9 April 1761]	Elizabeth Montagu
435.	[Welwyn, Herts.]	[Su.] 12 April 1761	Friedrich Gottlieb Klopstock
436.	Welwyn, Herts.	[Su.] 12 April 1761	Count Christian Günther Stolberg
437.	Welwyn, Herts.	[Su.] 3 May 1761	Elizabeth Montagu
438.		[Tu.] 26 May 1761	Elizabeth Montagu
439.		[Tu.] 2 June 1761	Elizabeth [no ltr.] Montagu
440.	[Welwyn, Herts.]	[Su.] 7 June 1761	Johann Arnold Ebert
—	Ebert to Young	[June 1761]	
441.		[Tu. 16 June 1761]	Andrew *unpd.* Millar
442.	Welwyn, Herts.	[M.] 29 June 1761	Johann Arnold Ebert
443.	Welwyn, Herts.	[Th.] 2 July 1761	Elizabeth Montagu
444.	[Welwyn, Herts.]	[Tu.] 21 July 1761	Elizabeth Montagu

445.	Welwyn, Herts.	[Th.] 30 July 1761	Elizabeth *unpd.* Montagu
446.		[1761]	Frances, Lady Boscawen
447.		[W.] 2 September 1761	Elizabeth Montagu
448.		[W.] 2 September 1761	Unknown *unpd.*
—	John Jones to Joseph Spence	[Welwyn, Herts.] [Th.] 3 September 1761	
—	Catharine Talbot to Young	Southwark, Surrey [Th.] 3 September 1761 *unpd.*	
449.	[Welwyn, Herts.]	[Tu.] 6 October 1761	George Bubb Dodington, Lord Melcombe
450.	[Welwyn, Herts.]	[Sa.] 17 October 1761	George Bubb Dodington, Lord Melcombe
451.	[Welwyn, Herts.]	[Su.] 18 October 1761	Duchess of *unpd.* Portland
—	Baron Melcombe (Dodington) to Young	Hammersmith, Mdx. [Tu.] 27 October 1761	
452.		[Th.] 29 October 1761	George Bubb Dodington, Lord Melcombe *unpd.*
453.	[Welwyn, Herts.]	[Su.] 28 February 1762	George Keate
454.	[?Welwyn, Herts.]	[?Spring 1762]	George Keate [no ltr.]
455.	[Welwyn, Herts.]	[Su.] 14 March 1762	Duchess of *unpd.* Portland
456.	[Welwyn, Herts.]	[Th.] 27 May 1762	Duchess of Portland
—	John Jones to Young	[?Welwyn, Herts.] [Th.] 27 May 1762 *unpd.*	
457.	[Welwyn, Herts.]	[Tu.] 1 June 1762	Duchess of Portland
458.	Welwyn, Herts.	[Tu.] 27 July 1762	Duchess of *unpd.* Portland
459.	Welwyn, Herts.	[Tu.] 3 August 1762	Duchess of *unpd.* Portland
460.	[Welwyn, Herts.]	[Tu.] 24 August 1762	Duchess of Portland
461.	Welwyn, Herts.	[Tu.] 2 September 1762	George Keate
462.	[Welwyn, Herts.]	[?Autumn 1762]	Duchess of *unpd.* Portland

463.	[Welwyn, Herts.]	[?September 1762]	Mrs. Anne Brett	
464.	Welwyn, Herts.	[Su.] 19 September 1762	Mrs. Anne Brett	
465.	Welwyn, Herts.	[Th.] 25 November 1762	Thomas Newcomb	
466.	[Welwyn, Herts.]	[Th.] 2 December 1762	George Keate	
467.	Welwyn, Herts.	[Su.] 2 January 1763	Duchess of Portland	unpd.
468.	Welwyn, Herts.	[Tu.] 4 January 1763	George Keate	
469.	Welwyn, Herts.	[Th.] 13 January 1763	Duchess of Portland	unpd.
470.	Welwyn, Herts.	[Su.] 6 February 1763	Thomas Broughton	unpd.
471.	Welwyn, Herts.	[Su.] 27 February 1763	James Elphinston	
472.	[?Welwyn, Herts.]	[Spring 1763]	Earl of Bute	[no ltr.]
473.	Welwyn, Herts.	[Th.] 24 March 1763	George Keate	
474.	Welwyn, Herts.	[Th.] 14 April 1763	George Keate	
475.	Welwyn, Herts.	[Th.] 28 April 1763	Andrew Millar	unpd.
476.	Welwyn, Herts.	[Th.] 3 May 1763	George Keate	
477.	Welwyn, Herts.	[W.] 1 June 1763	Johann Arnold Ebert	
478.	Welwyn, Herts.	[Th.] 2 June 1763	Duchess of Portland	
479.	Welwyn, Herts.	June 1763	Trustees of the Welwyn Charity School	unpd.
480.	Tunbridge Wells, Kent	[Tu.] 19 July 1763	Duchess of Portland	unpd.
481.	[Welwyn, Herts.]	[Su.] 11 September 1763	George Keate	
482.	Welwyn, Herts.	[M.] 7 November 1763	Earl of Bute	unpd.
483.	Welwyn, Herts.	[Th.] 29 December 1763	Johann Arnold Ebert	
484.	Welwyn, Herts.	[Su.] 12 February 1763	George Keate	
485.	Welwyn, Herts.	[Tu.] 13 March 1764	Duchess of Portland	
486.	Welwyn, Herts.	[Su.] 18 March 1764	George Keate	
487.	Welwyn, Herts.	[Th.] 22 March 1764	George Keate	
488.	Welwyn, Herts.	[Tu.] 3 April 1764	George Keate	

LIST OF PLATES

Reproduction of Young's letter to Robert Dodsley   p. 285

(between pp. 328–9)

Joseph Highmore's portrait of Edward Young, aged 71 years (see Samuel Richardson's letter to Young of 17 December 1754). Reproduced by permission of the Warden and Fellows of All Souls College, Oxford

An engraving by Joseph Brown of Christian Friedrich Zincke's enamel portrait of the Duchess of Portland, aged 25 years

Joseph Highmore's portrait of Samuel Richardson, aged 61 years. Courtesy of the National Portrait Gallery

'Avenue of Chesnut trees in the garden (of Guessens) formerly belonging to the Revd. Dr. Edward Young at Welwyn, Herts.' From a series of pen and wash drawings of Welwyn in the Hertfordshire County Record Office, made by J. C. Buckler (1794–1894) in the years 1832–4. Courtesy of the Record Office and W. Branch Johnson

INTRODUCTION

For a full century after its appearance in the years 1742–6, *The Complaint; or, Night-Thoughts on Life, Death & Immortality* gave the name of Edward Young household currency throughout the Old World and the New. The story of the author's life, especially as it related to circumstances giving rise to the poem, was spun into legend emphasizing the importance to the creative act of a personal commitment, what Young himself spoke of as 'the strong impulse of some animating occasion'. It was a legend few dared challenge. Even the slayer of myth, Samuel Johnson, old in years and seasoned to the public temper, resorted to another's hand when it came to the account of Young, the only one of the fifty-two *Lives of the English Poets* not written by Johnson himself. Johnson's wisdom, if not his courage, was vindicated by the protests the unsympathetic life of Young provoked at its publication in 1781. Not until 1854 was the aura of sanctity which had come to surround Young dispelled by the defiant and youthful George Eliot. Owing as much to the impotence of criticism as to the undisciplined will to believe, little regard was had to biographic actualities and it was not until George Eliot's classic attack, 'Worldliness and Other-Worldliness: The Poet Young', that considered attention began to be paid to the poet's life. It was as though the question of artistic sincerity raised by the poet's major achievement had eclipsed the historic values of the very active and extended life of a respected literary giant who had been on familiar terms with distinguished contemporaries as far removed from one another in time as Joseph Addison who died in 1719 and Joseph Warton who lived until 1800.

Whatever the reasons, the letters of Edward Young have been remarkably slow to surface. A scattered few have appeared in print from time to time. Others have come up for sale only to disappear among the papers of private collectors. The only substantial lot to appear in print before the twentieth century was a collection of 111 letters to Richardson from 1744 to 1759. These were among a series published in the *Monthly Magazine* in the years 1813–19 as 'Memoirs and Remains of Eminent Persons: One Hundred and Fifty Original Letters between Dr. Edward Young, Author of Night Thoughts, and Mr. Samuel Richardson, Author of Clarissa, Grandison, &c.' The manuscripts of this collection have almost entirely disappeared. Comparison of the eight surviving originals (letters 304, 325, 336, 349, 354, 395, 413, 417) with their transcriptions in the *Monthly Magazine* breeds confidence in the essential authenticity of the remaining printed letters. Unfortunately, this publication escaped the attention of Young's biographers and editors from James Nichols and John Doran in 1854 to Henry C. Shelley as late as 1914. On the other hand, twenty-one of Young's letters to Richardson fabricated by Mrs. Anna Letitia Barbauld in 1804 with no regard to editorial integrity continued to haunt the Young legend until their forgery was exposed in 1942.

In 1901, in the most definitive life of Young up to the present, Walter Thomas published the seventeen letters of 1760–4 to the poet George Keate that had come to the British Museum at the death in 1878 of Keate's grandson, John Henderson. In 1904, moreover, one of the greatest caches was found at Longleat among the papers of the Marquis of Bath, namely, Young's letters of 1740–65 to Lady Margaret Harley, wife of the second Duke of Portland. The letters had come to Longleat through the marriage of the Duchess's daughter to the Viscount Weymouth in 1759. Of the 182 letters in the collection, 106 were published by the Historical Manuscripts Commission in the first volume of a *Calendar of the Manuscripts of the Marquis of Bath*, enough to show the richness of the material, even though an index to the letters up to 1753 shows that eight letters having to do with the Duchess's efforts to get preferment for Young in the Church had been excised.

When Richard Eustace Tickell published a life of his ancestor, the poet Thomas Tickell, in 1931, he included nineteen of Young's letters written between 1715 and 1728 as he found them transcribed in Tickell's Letterbook. He missed eleven others which were not in the Letterbook but which are among the family papers. The latest addition to the canon is a batch of twenty letters to Judith Reynolds in the years 1740–1. These letters, like those to the Duchess of Portland, were accompanied with a list as if they had been prepared for publication, and as with the Portland letters the list mentions letters no longer in the collection. In this instance, the editor, John Fenn, who had acquired the letters through family connections, thoughtfully dated his work on them, 23 November 1781, at the height of interest in the life of Young done by Herbert Croft for Johnson's *Lives of the Poets*. Perhaps Fenn found no publisher brash enough to reflect on the public image of Young by revealing that he was courting within months of his wife's death. More likely, though, Fenn was restrained from involving his family in indecorous publicity. In any event, it would be intriguing to speculate on the effect this kind of typical eighteenth-century 'worldliness' would have had on either the Victorians or their severest critics. As it was, the letters remained hidden until their sale in 1911, or more properly until publication in 1935 on their rediscovery in the Huntington Library. When they appeared they only added to the humanizing portrait of Young which had begun to take form with the Portland letters.

At this time, though, it is not for the view of Young himself so much that his letters are important as it is for the panorama of English familiar life that opens to the reader. Beneath the archaic gallantry and elaborate affectation of Young's letters—never written for publication—it is possible to feel closer to another age and time than in many of the more justly celebrated correspondences of the century that brought the familiar letter to the level of literary art. This common touch, if it may be so called, of Young's letters helps explain why they have been so slow to come out. It may also explain why so few altogether have survived. Where, for instance, are his letters to his wife's family, the Earls of Litchfield; to his close friends, Colley Cibber and Aaron Hill; to the politicians, Bubb Dodington and Speaker

Onslow; to his son-in-law Henry Temple; to the D'Arandas of Putney or the Coles of Chelsea; or to his lifelong friends, Thomas Newcomb of Richmond or Thomas Colborn of Ely? Perhaps they are lost for ever. In any event, it seems time to put into order what letters are at hand.

EDITORIAL PRACTICE

In the present edition, Young's letters, including records of lost letters (excepting those of the Portland and Richardson correspondence as these are reasonably complete), are arranged chronologically and numbered in sequence for convenience in identification. Letters to, or closely connected with, Young are distributed in order of appearance to provide continuity and appropriate context for Young's letters. These letters to or about Young are not numbered. Every letter, however, is headed with the place of origin, date, and name of person addressed. All matters supplied by the editor, here as elsewhere, are within square brackets ([ ]) accompanied by a mark of interrogation (?) where the interpolation is conjectural. This three-part heading is followed immediately by outside address and postmark in the few instances where these items are present in the manuscript. Endorsements, notably on letters to public officials showing date of receipt or of filing, are not recorded except where they supply information not otherwise evident. The last part of the heading of each letter names the place where the manuscript is preserved or is marked 'not traced' where it has not been found. The heading closes at this point if the letter has not been previously published, or by reference to the chief books or periodicals where it is known to have appeared in print. With some modification the heading of each letter follows that put into practice by R. W. Chapman in his *Letters of Samuel Johnson* (1952).

The text, whether from manuscript or printed source, follows the original as faithfully as modern typography allows. Spelling, punctuation, capitalization, cross-outs, and interlineations are all kept as they were found. The only intentional exceptions are (1) the use of the curved letter 's' in place of the older upright letter resembling the lower case 'f', (2) the reduction to the normal line of letters commonly raised half a line for terminal abbreviations in manuscript, (3) use of ampersand (&) for Young's frequent plus sign (+), and (4) the use of italics where words are underlined in handwriting. Beyond these exceptions the editor has scrupulously tried to remark in the notes on any doubtful handwriting or questionable typography. Any 'silent corrections' are wholly unintentional. All postscripts, even the most trivial, are included as in such occasional instances the context of the letter is often most tellingly revealed. Undated letters, particularly of the Portland, Richardson, and Reynolds groups, are kept in the order of their appearance in the collections unless there is substantial evidence otherwise. Annotation is designed to identify references and apparent allusions wherever possible, particularly of persons, books, and 'dated' circumstances. There is an Index of Correspondents and a General Index. Entries under personal names do not include conventional greetings and remarks.

ACKNOWLEDGEMENTS

In preparing the letters, the editor has had the help of so many persons and institutions over so long a time that his records are undoubtedly incomplete and he regrets the omission of names from even the extensive list that follows. The demanding search for accuracy, which is a staple of editing, accustoms one to austere impersonality. For that reason alone, the warm personality of scholarly association in the common pursuit is the more gratefully remembered by the editor as the lasting reward of his labours.

First of all, the editor must acknowledge the trust confided in him for publication of 332 letters from manuscript, 127 for the first time, by the following: the Marquis of Bath (182), the British Museum (41), the Tickell family (30), the Huntington Library (21), Dr. Williams's Library and the Bodleian (10 each), Yale University Library (8), the Historical Society of Pennsylvania (4), Edward T. Collins of Reading (3), the Burgerbibliothek Bern, A. A. Houghton, Jr., of New York, Mrs. Donald Hyde of New Jersey, and the libraries of Harvard and the Victoria and Albert (2 each), as well as 13 more held singly by the Birmingham Public Library, Cambridge University Library, the City of

Cardiff Public Library, the University of Colorado Library, the Folger Shakespeare Library, the library of the University of Leeds, the Morgan Library, the National Library of Scotland, the library of the University of Nottingham, the Princeton University Library, Wellesley College Library, Ralph M. Williams of Hartford, and the editor himself.

In addition to the persons and institutions already mentioned, extraordinary help has come from the directors and staff of the following institutions: Bath Municipal Libraries, the Museum Calvet of Avignon, Trinity College Library of Cambridge, the Honnold Library of the Claremont Colleges, Guild Hall Library, the Hampshire County Archives, the Handel-Museum of Halle-Saale, the Hertfordshire County Archives, Lambeth Palace Library, the Lincolnshire Archives Committee, the London County Archives, the London Library, the National Portrait Gallery, the National Register of Archives, the New York Public Library, the Oxfordshire County Records Joint Committee, the Prerogative Court of Canterbury in Somerset House, the Public Record Office, Westminster Public Library, and the Library of Windsor Castle.

For special favours and encouragement the editor is also heavily indebted to the following persons: Gordon T. Banks of Goodspeed's Bookshop in Boston, A. C. Baugh of the University of Pennsylvania, Revd. E. C. E. Bourne of the Hedgerley Rectory in Slough, Miss J. M. M. Burgess of McGill, the late Professor John Butt, Wolfgang Butzkamm of Münster, John Carter of Sotheby's, Frank Cattell of the Gosling's branch of Barclays Bank, James L. Clifford of Columbia, Miss Dorothy Coates sometime curator of the Bishop Ken Library in Longleat, J. E. Congleton of Findlay College, Brian Connell of London, Miss Elsie Corbett of Spelsbury, Arthur Crook of *The Times Literary Supplement*, the late Percy J. Dobell of Tunbridge Wells, Horst W. Drescher of Münster, Charles Duffy of the University of Akron, Revd. Cyprian de Marmion Dymoke-Marr of the Clewer Rectory in Windsor, T. C. Duncan Eaves of the University of Arkansas, G. B. Fergusson of the New Bond Street Branch of the National Provincial Bank, John F. Fleming of New York, Charles E. Frank of Illinois College,

Robert Greaves editor of Bishop Secker's autobiography, the late Professor R. H. Griffith, Robert Halsband of Columbia, Harlan W. Hamilton of Case Western Reserve, Edward L. Hart of Brigham Young University, Frederick W. Hilles of Yale, Revd. R. S. Hook of St. Luke's Rectory in Chelsea, Robert D. Horn of the University of Oregon, Ben Kimpel of the University of Arkansas, Lewis M. Knapp of Colorado College, Louis A. Landa of Princeton, William G. Lane of the University of North Carolina, Wilmarth S. Lewis of Farmington, Bryant Lillywhite of Haslemere, Roger Lonsdale of Balliol College, Alfred B. Mann of Rutgers, Dr. F. L. Mars of Nice, Robert F. Metzdorf of the Parke-Bernet Galleries, John H. Middendorf of Columbia, Will S. Moore of St. John's in Oxford, Francis Needham sometime librarian of Welbeck, Lady Constance Osborn of Moor Park, James M. Osborn and Frederick A. Pottle of Yale, Mrs. Mark B. Packer of the Houghton Library in Harvard, the late Professor Frederick Clark Prescott, Miss Fannie Ratchford of the University of Texas, C. J. Rawson of the University of Newcastle, E. E. Reimer of the University of Winnipeg, André Rousseau of the Faculté des Lettres in Aix-en-Provence, William B. Sale, Jr., of Cornell, J. Burke Shipley of the University of Illinois, John Sparrow of All Souls, D. Stafford of St. George's Church Vestry in London, J. A. Stargardt of Marburg, Colton Storm of Arizona, Major-General Sir Eustace Tickell of Surrey, the late Geoffrey Tillotson of London University, the late Professor Chauncey Brewster Tinker, Miss Margaret Triggs of London, E. Jackson Webb of Prescott College, Cdr. H. B. Webb of Lord Mountbatten's staff, Miss Lelia Winsborough of Texas, Miss Marjorie Wynne of Yale, R. W. Zandvoort of Amersfoort, and Colorado colleagues: Richard Chadbourne, Karl K. Hulley, the late Professor Leslie L. Lewis, Miss Mary Elizabeth Nelson, and Paul and Dorothy Thompson, as well as those faculty members who made possible release of time for the editor.

For direct financial aid the editor thanks the American Council of Learned Societies, the American Philosophical Society, and the University of Colorado.

For devoted work on the manuscript, the editor thanks

Mrs. Mary Jane Hampton, Miss Helen Leek, Mrs. Eloise Pearson, Miss Joyce Thompson, and Miss M. A. Hennings who compiled the indexes. The work of editing has been lightened immeasurably by the repeated laborious attention and contributions towards its progress by Edward T. Collins of Reading, Harry Forster of Woodstock, the W. Branch Johnsons of Welwyn, and James R. Sutherland of London University. The attentive patience of the Clarendon Press staff has removed many a blunder. Finally, the editor returns loving thanks to his wife for her day-to-day practical help and her good sense and endurance. As Young said of Lady Betty, 'She spoke me comfort.'

1.[1] [?Salisbury, Wilts.] [F. 10 August 1705].[2] Samuel Reynolds.[3]

Not traced.—Algernon Graves and William Vine Cronin, *A History of the Works of Sir Joshua Reynolds*, 1901, iv. 1682 (in a section entitled: 'Concerning the Parentage and Kinsfolk of Sir Joshua Reynolds' by Sir Robert Edgcumbe).

Dear Sam,
    Yesterday morning I lost (pardon if grief and confusion want address) the best of fathers. My affliction is so great I know not yett how to wrestle with it. My greatest relief is making my complaint to my friends and pleasing myself with the thought that they will condole with me if they really are so. I would but can no more.
                            Your afflicted humble servant,
                            E. Young.

1a. Chiddingfold, Surrey. [M.] 9 June [?1707].[4] Thomas Turner.[5]

Address: To ye Rev. Dr. Turner / President of Corpus Xty / College / In / Oxford. *Postmark*: 14/iv [June]. *Seal*: Harris arms.
Bodleian Library (MSS. Rawl. Letters 92, ff. 220–1).

Revd Sr
    Twas with yr Leave I left Oxford, butt haveing been
                                                                it
absent much longer yn Usiall, I thought ∧ my Duty to beg

---

[1] Discovery and transmittal of this letter by the tireless research and generosity of Edward Collins came when the present edition was in proof-state.

[2] In its printed form the letter is dated at the end: '12 *Aug*., 1705', doubtless from an endorsement of its receipt, as Young's father died on the morning of 9 August. He was buried in Salisbury Cathedral of which he was dean.

[3] Samuel Reynolds (1681–1746) was a member of Young's Oxford college, Corpus Christi. He later became master of Plympton Grammar School in Devonshire and father of the famous portrait-painter, Sir Joshua Reynolds (1723–92).

[4] The year 1707 is the most likely of three possibilities during Young's residence in Corpus Christi from the fall of 1703, when he transferred from New College, to

[Notes 4 and 5 cont. *overleaf*]

a continuance of ye Same: I hope my Absence has not Forfeited my Title either to yr Society or Favour; my Circumstances make it more Convenient for me to be in ye Country; Yett if there is Any thing I can do either in my Absence, or by Returning for a time to Oxford¹ which You think will Become me as a Member of ye University, and You'l please so far to Favour me as to find means to lett me know of itt, I shall Number itt to ye many other Kindnesses conferd on

Sr

Your Obligd

& most humble Servant

Edward Young.

June 9th
Chiddingfold by
Haslemire²
 in Surry

[in left margin] My Mother gives her most humble Service.³

the winter of 1708, when he became a Fellow of All Souls. The years 1705 and 1706 are eliminated by entries in College Buttery books showing Young's presence in College on the 9th of June of both years. The year 1708 is unlikely as Young's absence during the year was definitely not 'longer than usual'. The year 1704, for which records are missing, must remain a possibility, since the letter is found among papers of 1704, 'arranged in chronological order' in the Bodleian Library, and also since the message from Young's mother in the postscript might be explained by her husband's presence in Bristol at the time. Evidence seems stronger, however, for the year 1707. Young's father's death on 9 August 1705 would explain his mother's being in Chiddingfold where her daughter lived. On 9 June 1707 Young had been absent from College seven months, from 5 November 1706, almost certainly 'longer than usual'.

⁵ Thomas Turner (1645–1714), D.D., President of Corpus Christi College, Oxford, since 1688. His acquaintance with Young's father, Edward (1642–1705), was presumably of long standing. On 12 September 1678 Francis Turner (1638?–1700), then Vice-Chancellor of Oxford (later Bishop of Ely), wrote from The Hague to his brother Thomas commending the elder Young as 'a discreet, learned and devout . . . chaplain' to the General of the British forces, Thomas Butler (1634–80), Earl of Ossory (Bodleian Library, MS. Tanner Letters 39, f. 97). On 13 October 1703 the elder Young addressed Thomas as 'My Honoured Friend' (Bodleian Library, MSS. Rawl. Letters 92, f. 169).

¹ College records show that Young returned on 14 August 1707, remaining there until 21 November.

² Chiddingfold, in the extreme south-west of Surrey, adjoins the Sussex border, four miles north-east of Haslemere, a 'chapel of ease' to Chiddingfold and served by the same rector or his vicar.

³ This is the only reference the poet makes to his mother, Judith (1645–1714), in his extant letters. On the death of her husband, 9 August 1705, when he was serving as Dean of Salisbury, she had moved into Chiddingfold to be with her only

2

2. [Oxford].[1] [W.] 8 June [1715]. Alexander Pope.[2]

Address: To Mr Pope / at Mr Jervas's / In Cleaveland Court / St James / London. *Postmark*: 9/IV [June].
British Museum (Add. MSS. 4807, f. 86).—Elwin–Courthope, x. 117; Sherburn, i. 294.[3]

Dear Sr

Just now I receivd ye Homers,[4] wh wth that You design for ye publick Library (of wh I will take ye Care desird) are in Number but Eleven, whereas ye List You sent was of ~~for~~ Twelve.

I am DrSr
Yr most Affectionate
Humble Sert EYoung

June 8th

The mistake was Easie, nor wd I have You give YrSelf farther trouble I will Expect mine at leasure.[5]

surviving daughter, Anne (1684–1714), wife of John Harris (1682–1759), Rector of Chiddingfold and later (1718) of Ash in Surrey. Judith continued to live in Chiddingfold until her death on 8 December 1714. In the churchyard of St. Mary's, Chiddingfold, was formerly to be found the inscription on her tombstone: 'Here lyeth the Body of Judith widow of the Revd Edward Younge, late Dean of Sarum [Salisbury], dyed December ye 8th in the 69th year of her age, Anno Domini 1714' (Thomas, p. 52). The death of Anne, Young's sister, occurred on 23 March of the same year.   [1] The place and year of this letter are clear from the contents.

[2] This is the first of the only two extant letters Young is known to have written to Pope. It suggests that they are already on somewhat familiar terms. Croft (iv. 372) thought they were not acquainted as early as 27 August 1714 when Pope reported there were no Oxford panegyrics ready to welcome the new monarch, failing to mention Young's verses (*On the Late Queen's Death, and His Majesty's Accession to the Throne*) soon to be published. Thomas (p. 51), however, thought their acquaintance was earlier since both had dedicated poems to Lansdowne in 1713 and both had moved in the same literary circles. In a letter to Gay 4 May 1714, Pope spoke slightingly of Young's 'tragic majesty' in reading his own verses, and it may have been about this time that the acquaintance began.

[3] Sherburn's record of the address in his publication of this letter (Sherburn, i. 294) is mistaken, probably as a result of taking the wrong cover sheet in the binding of the manuscripts as the original conjugate leaf. Paper, watermarks, and handwriting confirm the cover sheet with the proper address. It is the kind of mistake easily made from microfilm readings without immediate access to the manuscripts.

[4] Pope's translation of the first book of the *Iliad* was published 6 June 1715. The next letter supplies further details on the number of copies Young received and of his disposition of them.

[5] Previous editors have boggled this last word: 'leasure', Elwin–Courthope making of it 'Crupes' and Sherburn 'Wasses'. The omission of an expected 'yr' before the word may have been misleading (see Helen Leek, 'An Illegible Word in a Letter from Young to Pope', *Notes and Queries*, xv, June 1968, 211).

3.[1] [Oxford]. [?June 1715]. Bernard Lintot.

Address: To Mr Bernard / Lintot / at ye Cross Keys [remainder of address cut away].

British Museum (Grangerized copy of Byron's *Poetical Works*, 1839, vol. 29), c. 44. f.

[Top of letter cut away].

1. The Publick Library.
2. All Souls.
3. Maudlin.
4. Pembroke.
5. Corpus Xti.
6. Queens.
12 7. New Coll:
8. Dr Adderly.[2]
9. Mr Bridgman.[3]
X. Dr Evans.[4]
11. St Johns Coll.
12. The Gentleman whose receipt I sent.[5]

Thus You see ye Twelve are Disposd of, & no One remains for my self, though Mr Popes Letter says yt He orderd One for my self also to be sent.

Yr Sevt
E Young

---

[1] This letter clearly belongs close in time to the letter to Pope of 8 June. The circumstance that the opening has been cut away suggests that this may be one of two untraced letters which Spence recorded in the following anecdote: 'Tonson and Lintot were both candidates for printing some work of Dr. Young's.—He answered both their letters in the same morning, and in his hurry misdirected them.—When Lintot opened that which came to him, he found it began, "That Bernard Lintot is so great a scoundrel, that, &c."—It must have been very amusing to have seen him in his rage, he was a great sputtering fellow.' (Osborn, 1966, i. 342).

[2] Robert Adderley (1678–1717), D.D. (1714), Fellow of All Souls College.

[3] Roger Bridgeman (1701–50), B.A. (1722), M.A. (1724/5), D.D. (1736), Oriel College.

[4] Abel Evans (1679–1737), D.D. (1711), St. John's College.

[5] Perhaps Richard Harrison (b. 1677) of New College, of whom Young speaks in his letter to Tickell of 28 June as having compared the Pope and Tickell versions of the *Iliad*.

4. [Oxford].¹ [Tu.] 28 June [1715]. Thomas Tickell.²

Address: To Mr Tickell / at Buttons Coffee-House / In Covent Garden / London.³
Surrey MSS. (also Tickell Letterbook, pp. 69–70).—Shelley, pp. 33–4; Tickell, pp. 43–4.

J[un]e 28
[in another hand] 1715

Dear Tickell

Be assurd I want no new Inducement to behave my self like Yr Friend. To be very plain, ye University almost in General gives ye preference to Popes Translation;⁴ they say his is written wth more Spirit, Ornament, & Freedom & has more ye Air of an Original. I enclin'd some, Harison⁵ &c: to compare the Translations with ye Greek, wh was done; it made some small alteration in their Opinions, but still Pope was their man. The bottom of ye Case is this, they were strongly prepossest in Popes favour, from a wrong notion of Yr Design, before ye Poem came down; & ye sight of Yrs has not had force enough upon theem to make theem willing to to [*sic*] contradict theemselves, & own they were

¹ The place and year of this letter are established by the topics discussed.
² Tickell, a member of Queen's College, Oxford, from 1701 and a Fellow from 1710, was to become one of two under-secretaries to Joseph Addison when he was made Secretary of State in 1717.
³ Button's Coffee House, Russell Street, Covent Garden, had been set up in 1712 or 1713 by Daniel Button (d. 1731), a former servant of the Countess of Warwick who was to marry Joseph Addison in 1716. It became associated with Whig literary and political activities.
⁴ Tickell's translation of the first book of the *Iliad* had been published by Tonson on 8 June, two days after Pope's translation had been published by Lintot. Tickell, aware of his rival's popularity, anticipated a public preference for Pope's translation in the preface to his own version: 'I Must inform the Reader, that when I began this first Book, I had some Thoughts of Translating the whole Iliad, but had the pleasure of being diverted from that Design, by finding the Work was fallen into a much abler Hand. I would not therefore be thought to have any other View in publishing this small Specimen of Homer's Iliad, than to bespeak, if possible, the Favour of the Public to a Translation of Homer's Odysseis, wherein I have already made some progress.'
⁵ Richard Harrison and his brother William (1688–1713) were sons of a 'master' of St. Cross near Winchester and may have been known to Young before he himself went up from Winchester to Oxford. Young had entrusted William with the manuscript of his *Poem on the Last Day* (1713) in March 1710/11 and had memorialized his friendship with William, 'Partner of my Soul', in *An Epistle to Lord Lansdown* (1713).

in ye wrong, but they go far for Prejudict persons & own
Yrs an excellent Translation, nor do I hear any Violently
affirm it to be worse than Popes, but those who look on Pope
a[s] a Miracle, & among these to Yr Comfort Evans is ye
                even
First Anding these Zealo[ts] /[verso]/ allow yt you have
outdone Pope in some Particulars. E.g. The speech
Begin[nin]g

> 'Oh sunk in Avarice &c:
> And leave a naked &c:
> &c:[']

Upon ye whole I affirm ye Performance has gaind You
much Reputation, & when they compare You wth wt they
shd compare You, wth Homer only, You are much admird.
It has given, I know, many of ye best Judges a desire to see
ye Odyssies by ye same hand, wh they talk of wth pleasure,
& I seriously beleive Yr first Piece of yt will quite break
their partiality for Pope, wh yr Illiad has weakend, & secure
Yr success. Nor think my Opinion groundlesly swayd by
my wishes, for I observe as Prejudice cools, You grow in
favour, & You are a better Poet Now, than when Yr Homer
first came down. I am persuaded fully yt Yr Design cannot
but succeed Here, & it shall be my Hearty Desire & Endeavour that it may. Dear Tickell Yrs most Affectionately
                                                    EYoung
My Humble service to Mr Addison
& Sr Rich[ard][1]

1 Young's acquaintance with Joseph Addison (1672–1719) and Sir Richard
Steele (1672–1729) began as early as 1713. His lines 'To Mr. Addison on The
Tragedy of Cato' (13 April 1713) had been published with the play. Steele in turn
had welcomed *A Poem on the Last Day* by Young in the 15th number of *The Guardian*
(9 May 1713), and an essay in *The Englishman* of 29 October 1713, attributed to
Addison, praised the poem and reported that Young was at work on a play of his
own. In 1714 Young inscribed to Addison his verses: *On The Late Queen's Death and
His Majesty's Accession to the Throne*.

5. Haslemere, Surrey.[1] [Su.] 26 May 1717. Edmund Curll.[2]

Not traced.[3]—*An Ode . . . to the Memory of . . . the Countess of Berkeley . . .* by Mr. Newcomb, London: Printed for E. Curll, 1717;[4] *The Weekly Journal; or Saturday Post*, 31 August 1717;[5] London *Evening Post*, 3 and 19 September 1717;[6] George Sherburn, 'Edward Young and Book Advertising', *Review of English Studies*, iv (1928), 414–17;[7] Helen Leek, 'The Edward Young–Curll Quarrel', *The Papers of the Bibliographical Society of America*, lxii (1968), 321–35.[8]

Mr. CURLL,

I have perus'd the POEM which you receive with this, with much Pleasure, and I believe you will find your Advantage considerable in Printing it.

Yours, &c.

Haslemere,   E. YOUNG
May 26, 1717.

[1] Young passed the summer here in the company of his brother-in-law, John Harris, and not as Thomas (p. 66) guessed, in Ireland.

[2] At the time of this letter, Curll had published two of Young's poems: *The Force of Religion; or, Vanquish'd Love* (1714 and 1715) and the third edition (first London) of *A Poem on the Last Day* (1714).

[3] The text of this letter, which became the subject of bitter public dispute, is that which Curll printed on the back of the title-page of Newcomb's *Ode*, advertised in the *Post Boy* of 23 July. Two other versions of the letter appeared in print (see Curll's public letter to Young of 31 August and notes to Young's letter to Tickell of 19 September).

[4] Thomas Newcomb (1682 ?–1765), chaplain to the Duke of Richmond (1672–1723), had been a fellow student with Young in Corpus Christi College, Oxford, 1703–4. The Countess of Berkeley (1694–1717), daughter of the Duke of Richmond, had died 12 January 1716/17 (*The Weekly Journal or British Gazetteer* of 19 January).

[5] See Curll's letter to Young of 31 August.

[6] For that of the 3rd see notes to Young's letter to Tonson of [?9–12 September] and for that of the 19th see notes to his letter to Tickell of 19 September.

[7] In Sherburn's publication of this letter, he concludes: 'Perhaps unwittingly, Young was a party to what in twentieth-century America might be called "a publicity stunt" ' (p. 417).

[8] Having access to the unpublished letter from Young to Tickell of 14 September, which was not available to Sherburn, Miss Leek establishes Addison's opposition at this time to policies of the Earl of Berkeley and argues that Young 'denied writing [the letter] because its printing placed his political career in jeopardy'. His 'panic', she concludes, '. . . is understandable, and his subsequent defense nothing more than an inadequate effort to justify his initial rash act' (p. 335).

6. Haslemere, Surrey. [Th.] 27 June [1717].[1] Thomas Tickell.

Address: To Thomas Tickell Esq.
Surrey MSS. (also Tickell Letterbook, pp. 41–2).—Tickell, pp. 64–5.

Dear Tickell

I am satisfied yt ye Advise You give me does, as You tell me, proceed from perfect Friendship; it were most base in me after such Instances of Yr goodwill to want Words to convince me of it. Since my First Method was not Adviceable give me leave to make You my Patron, wh I am ye more willing to do because what I send You has much ye Advantage of anything with wh I have had to do; And I am pleasd it shd be a Publick monument of my Gratitude to my 2 best Friends.[2] Besides suppressing it, is withholding from You & Mr Addison an Excuse for shewing me Favour beyond my Merit when Occasion offers. As to Mr A——n I have no Title to his Favour, what He does is of his pure Goodness, & You know how Indulgently some Consture[3] Attempts of this Nature. Beside I have had no Opportunity before of Complimenting ye Government.[4] I Flatter myself ye Thing is capable of receiving Your Favour, & yt with it, it will be no Enimie to my reputation in Verse; and wt is much more Reputation it will tell ye World yt I am (wh is most True) Dear Sr

Yr most Obligd
&Affectionate Humble Sevt
EYoung

         not
I have   taken ye Liberty of Your or Mr A——n's Name, nor shall presume to do it without Yr leave, wh I hope will

---

[1] The year of this letter is from Tickell's endorsement on the back of the first leaf.

[2] There is no trace of this poem. After Addison's death (17 June 1719) Young paired the two names in *A Letter to Mr Tickell occasioned by the Death of the Right Hon. Joseph Addison, Esq.*

[3] A variant of *construe*; Bailey's *Dictionary* (1736) gives *conster*.

[4] Young had, however, embraced publicly the Revolution Settlement on the death of Queen Anne by welcoming the Hanoverian king in a verse epistle: *On the Late Queen's Death and His Majesty's Accession to the Throne*, inscribed to Joseph Addison, as Secretary of the Regency, and published between the Queen's death 1 August 1714 and the arrival of George in England 18 September.

be granted. I wd willingly hear soon from You it being late
in ye Year besides an Occasionall Thing[1] will suffer by
being Tardy & loosing ye season
Haselmore in Surry.
June 27.
/[verso]/ [In the hand of Tickell] Haselmore in Surry
June 27

1717
Mr Young
/[conjugate leaf]/[2] As You read I desire You to mark wt
You think fit to be alterd & then if You think proper let
Mr Philips[3] know I beg ye same favour of Him for on such
a subject I wd be Correct as possible.

The Design of my Papers is to give a sketch of Mr
A——ns life. I warm myself to ye Undertaking by first
touching on some particula[r] Circumstances of it, & fall
into a profest Attempt of ye Whole. This is a Design in wh
I cannot Despair of Yr best Assistance, & a Design yt has
carryd me beyond my former Abilities; Possibly some particulars of Mr A——s life may Occur to you wch [I] ought
not to have omitted if so pray let me know theem, I shall
think no time or pains too much in finishing a Piece of such
a Subject.

7. [?Haslemere, Surrey]. [?Th. 29] August 1717.
Thomas Tickell.

Not traced.[4]

[1] The epithet, 'Occasionall Thing', almost certainly indicates that the verses were
to celebrate the appointment of Addison as Secretary of State (16 April 1717) and
of Tickell as one of his under-secretaries (20 April). Since Tickell's appointment
had stirred some jealousy in party ranks, it may be that Young was advised not to
contribute to the arousing of bitterness.

[2] This paragraph and the next, although in Young's handwriting, are not transcribed in the Letterbook and as a result do not appear in the biography of Tickell.

[3] By 'Mr. Philips' (the bearer of Young's letter to London ?), Young probably
refers to Ambrose Philips, the poet and politician who served as secretary of the
Hanoverian Club formed at Queen Anne's death to assure the Hanoverian succession
over competing claims of the Stuart followers.

[4] Evidence of this letter is Young's statement in his letter of 14 September 1717:
'About 3 weeks agoe I sent You a Peice of Job.'

Edmund Curll to Young [London]. [Sa.] 31 August 1717.

Not traced.[1]—*The Weekly Journal; or Saturday Post*, 31 August 1717.

To Mr. Young at Chidingfold in Surrey. Aug. 31, 1717.

Sir,

It having become a Fashion of late, to let our private Affairs make a Part of the publick Occurrences, I am obliged in my own Defence, to apply to you in this manner, with relation to a rude and false Advertisement[2] inserted in the Evening-Post of Saturday last in the following Words—Whereas Mr. Curll the Bookseller has published an Ode, as recommended by Mr. Young. This is to give Notice, that Curll was not authorized so to do by Mr. Young; and that the Letter prefix'd to the Ode was not written by him.

The Matter of Fact you know to be thus. On the 26th of May last, you sent me a Poem inclosed in a Cover, under the following Title. An Ode sacred to the Memory of that Truly Pious and Honourable Lady, the Countess of Berkeley; and with it two Letters, one from the Author, and another from your self; yours, which I have now before me; I here transcribe it verbatim.—Mr. Curll, I have perused the Poem of the Reverend Mr. Newcomb, which you receive with this, with much Pleasure, and I believe you will find your Advantage considerable in printing it. Yours, E. Young.

The first charge against me in the Advertisement, is, That I have published this Ode as recommended by you. Pray, Sir, is it not a Recommendation when you acknowledge the great Pleasure you received in reading it. 2dly. I was not authorized so to do by you. Nor was I prohibited by you from doing it; and I had the Author's Consent to what I did. 3dly The Letter prefix'd to the Ode was not written by you. Certainly, Sir, this Advertiser keeps a Jesuit in his Family, who by a gross evasion has advised him to assert, that the

---

[1] The original of this letter was probably never sent to Young.

[2] The advertisement, as quoted by Curll, appeared in the London *Evening Post*, 27–9 August.

Letter was not writ by you because in the printed Copy, the Parenthesis of the Author's Name is omitted.

I believe, Sir, Mr. Newcomb will not thank the Advertiser for this Treatment, and whatever Bolt was levelled at me by this ridiculous Procedure, I freely forgive it, and sincerely assure you, that I will always keep clear of incurring that vile Scandal of denying my own Hand. Yours, &c. E. Curll.

8. [Haslemere, Surrey]. [(?M. 9–Th. 12) September 1717]. [Jacob Tonson].

British Museum (Add. MSS. 28275, f. 500),—*Review of English Studies*, iv (1928), 415–16.

Some time in May ye Revd Mr Newcomb read to me an Ode of his on ye Ldy B. & desird me to direct him to a Bookseller; I gave him a Letter to Mr Curl, wh I designd shd go no farther than himself. When ye Ode was Publisht I saw a Letter prefixt wth my name,[1] but Differing from yt I sent. I, on this, to avoid ye Censure of assuming ye Prerogative of Judging for ye Publick, an Office above me, gave notice yt Mr C—— was not authorized to publish any thing of mine to yt purpose, & yt ye Letter prefixt was not mine.[2]

a Letter
Mr C—— instead of asking pardon for publishing under my name without my leave, charges me wth denying my Hand; & two Witnesses attest ye Truth of ye Charge.[3]

[1] i.e. Young's letter to Curll of 26 May.

[2] i.e. the advertisement reproduced in Curll's letter to Young of 31 August.

[3] Curll had published statements of two witnesses, as follows: 'An Ode, Sacred to the Memory of that truly Pious and Honourable Lady the Countess of Berkley. This Poem I receiv'd in Manuscript from Mr. Young with the following Letter, Mr. Curll, I have perus'd the Poem of the Reverend Mr. Newcomb, which you receive with this, with much Pleasure, and I believe you will find your Advantage considerable in Printing it. Yours E. Young. Haslemere, May 26. 1717. This Letter I prefix'd to the Poem, (not without Mr. Newcomb's Privity,) Mr. Young neither Authorizing, nor forbidding the contrary; but since in a rude and false Advertisement, inserted in this Paper last Thursday, it is said, Mr. Young did not write this Letter, I hereby give Notice that any Gentleman may see the Original, and likewise desire no farther Correspondence with Mr. Young, since he is pleas'd to deny his

The Letter publisht was thus

(Viz) Mr C—— I have purusd ye Poem You receive wth this wth much pleasure, & believe You will find Yr Advantage considerable in printing it.

The Letter I sent ran thus

(Viz) Mr C—— I have perusd ye Poem of ye Revd Mr N—— wh You receive wth this wth much Pleasure; *He enquird of me after a Bookseller & I directed Him to You*; & I beleive You will find Yr Advantage in printing it.

When one 3d of a Letter is omitted, & yt Omission makes a Material alteration in ye Import of ye Whole, I conceive yt Letter [no] longer ye Same as it was at first; & therefore I denyd ye *Publi*[sht Letter was] Mine.

[verso] But Mr C—— may say this Omission is not Material; I reply yt it [is] Material, & yt I cant conceive any reason why Mr C—— left it out, i[f not] because He knew it to be so; for had yt Omission not been made the Letter wd   have   lookt (as I designd it) as a recommendation to ye Bookseller, not to ye World; but yt Omission being made, it is otherwise.

If ye Part omitted was not Material even in Mr C——'s Opinion, I cannot Imagine why He Omitted it. He cd not overlook it, for tis in ye middle of ye Letter, & a 3d part of it; 3ce [thrice][1] He has printed yt he calls my Letter, & if he mistook once, He cd not so often; He got Witnesses to attest yt ye *Printed* Letter was mine, who sure wd not attest it without Reading ye Original Letter at ye very time; it being a Point in wh Honest men wd be very Punctual: I

own Hand. E. Curll. N. B. The above mention'd is a true Copy of Mr. Young's Letter. Witness my Hand. R. Francklin' (*Evening Post* of 31 August–3 September 1717).

'Kirdford, Sept. 4. 1717. Being call'd upon by Mr. Curll the Bookseller, to detect the Falsity of an Advertisement inserted in this Paper of August the 29th I think my self oblig'd in Justice to Mr. Curll, to Attest, that the Letter he printed before my Ode on the Death of the Countess of Berkeley, was, (as far as it had any Relation to the Poem) Genuine; and I cannot but stand amaz'd at Mr. Young's denying it, as well as at his ungenerous Treatment of me, without giving me the least Intimation of his unkind Design, and in Regard to my own Reputation, I think I am not to be blam'd in endeavouring to make my own Vindication reach as far as his Scandal has done. Tho. Newcomb' (*Evening Post* of 5–7 September 1717).

[1] i.e. in (1) the volume containing the *Ode*, (2) *The Weekly Journal* of 31 August, and (3) the *Evening Post* of 3 September.

conclude yrefore Mr C—— cd not be Ignorant of this
Omission; If He thought it Material, He shd have ~~inserted~~
continud in
  yt Part. If He thought it Immaterial, He ought at least,
(when He chargd me wth so foul a Crime as yt of denying
my Hand, & yt so often, & so vehemently,) to have Signifid
yt there was indeed some small omission in ye Lr printed ~~of~~
                                               thought
~~wt was in ye Original,~~ but such as He ⁀ made no alteration
in ye Import of it.
P. S. As Mr C—— omitted ye part above Noted, so I verily
think He Added also ye word *Considerable* to Advantage at
ye End of ye Letter.[1]

9. Haslemere, Surrey. [Sa.] 14 September [1717].
Thomas Tickell.

Address: To Thomas Tickell Esqr. / at Whitehall / London.
Surrey MSS.

                [in another hand] Haslemore Sept 14 1717?
Dear Sir,
  It is possible You may have seen my name lately asperst,
if so I beg You to look on Fridays Evening Post for my
Vindication;[2] & if You are satisfid by it of my Innocence, to
stand by my Reputation as You have Oppertunity; especially
if by accident it has reacht Mr ——.[3] You know how greatly
it is my Concern to be Cleard to Him.
  I shall be very anxious till You are so kind to let me hear
how clear I stand of ye scandall of *yt Villain* in Your own
Opinion, & wheather I suffer in His, on whose good
Thoughts my greatest Hopes rely.
  Though I know I shall clear my self to ye World in
general yet I can not but be very sollicitous & impatient to
know the sense of Those Persons whose Good Opinion I am

---

  [1] See Young's letters to Tickell of 14 and 19 September for the aftermath of this
incident.
  [2] Young was under the impression that his letter to Tonson of [?9–12 September]
would have appeared in the paper this weekend.
  [3] i.e. Addison.

Particularly concerned to secure; I beg therefore, at yr first leasure to hear from You.—About 3 weeks agoe I sent You a Peice of Job.—[1]

I am Dear Sir
Yr most Obligd Humble Sevt
EYoung.

Wt I say in ye Evening Post, if Curl has ye Impudence to deny it, I can shew under his own hand, & Newcomb (who Recants) will take his Oath of it.—But as You are my Friend, if You think proper, call on Curl, as You p[ass] yt way for a sight of my Original Letter, wh he has promist to any Gentleman, & yt will convince You all at once. This wd be a very great Friendship for then you will have it in Yr Powr to be Confident in my Defence.

My Humble Service to Mr Philips.
I beg it particularly of You to do me Justice to
Mr ——. Sr Rich: Steel. & Mr Philips.
Haselmore Sepr 14th

10. Haslemere, Surrey. [Th.] 19 September [1717].
Thomas Tickell.

Address: To Tho: Tickell Esqr. / at Whitehall / London.
Postmark: 21/SE [September].
Surrey MSS. (also Tickell Letterbook, p. 40).—Tickell, p. 80.

Sepr 19. [in another hand] 1717
Haselmore
In Surry.
Dear Sir.
On 2d thoughts I'm wholly of yr Opinion as to Curl, but supposing yt ye Advertismt I sent Mr Tonson lay unprinted because Mr Tonson was out of Town, I sent anothe[r] wh I fear tis too late to recall;[2] but I shall go no farthe[r].

[1] Young published *A Paraphrase on Part of the Book of Job* in 1719.

[2] The other draft, differing from that sent to Tonson, appeared in print as follows: 'Some Time in May last the Rev. Mr. Newcomb read to me an Ode on the Death

I am glad to hear there is anything right in my *Verse*,[1]
I beg You mark wt Places Mr A—— wd have alterd & to
let it find ye Advantage of being in Your hands. I shall be
exceedingly Obligd & pleasd to find Yr corrections in it
when I wait upon You in Town wh I propose to do next
month.

I am Dear Sir
Yr most Obligd
& Affectionate Humble Sevt
EYoung.

Pray my most Humble Duty
& Thanks.

of the Ldy B. and desir'd me to direct him to a Bookseller; I gave him a Letter to
Mr. Curll. Soon after the Ode was publish'd, and a Letter prefixt with my Name to
it, but differing from that which I sent.

'On this, that I might not be censur'd for assuming the Prerogative of Judging
for the Publick, which is an Offence above me, I advertis'd that Mr. C—— was not
authoris'd by me to publish any Recommendation of the Ode, and that the Letter
prefix'd was not writ by me.

'On which Mr. C——, instead of asking my Pardon for printing a Letter which
he call'd mine without my Leave, he charges me with denying my Hand, and main-
tains his Charge with two witnesses.

'My Letter ran thus (viz.)

'Mr. Curll, I have perus'd the Poem of the Rev. Mr. Newcomb which you receive
with this, with [much] Pleasure, [He enquir'd of me for a Bookseller, and I directed
him to you] I believe you will find your Advantage in printing it.

'The Part inclos'd thus [ ] is omitted in the Letter publish'd, which Omission
makes the letter look like a Recommendation to the Publick (as Mr. C—— wou'd
have it) not to the bookseller (as it was design'd by me) and therefore the whole
Drift of the Letter being thus alter'd by that Omission, I deny'd it to be mine.

'If Mr. C—— had thought the Omission material, he should not have made it, if
he thought it not material, he shou'd at least (when he accus'd me of so foul a Crime
as that of denying my Hand, and that so often and so violently) have own'd that
there was indeed a small Alteration in the Letter publish'd from the Original, but
such as he thought of no Consequence to the Meaning of the Whole.

'But this Omission is not all, as far as I can recollect my Letter, I do most firmly
believe he added also (much) to Pleasure, and (considerable) to Advantage. E.
Young.' (*Evening Post* of 17–19 September).

[1] For the context of this paragraph, see Young's letter to Tickell of 27 June 1717.

11. February 1718/19. Martha Lady Giffard.[1]

British Museum (Egerton MSS. 1717, f. 58).—Thomas, pp. 581–2.

To the Lady Giffard on the Countess of Portland's[2] being
ill of a fever.

Severest Fate! must Portland Droop,
And on the Bed of pain decay,
When on undeserving throngs
A Blooming health is thrown away?

Ye Guardian pow'rs! with outstretch'd Wings,
Her Couch propitious hover o'er;
And chide the Tumult in her Veins,
And bid her Spirits burn no more

But if a Single Life seems small,
And you neglect our Trivial pray'r
Oh think upon her Royal Charge,
And let Three Kingdoms be your Care[3]

Nay, farther still our Ardent Vows
To Your Compassion to commend,
Know 'tis not only Portland's Life;
But 'tis the Life of Giffard's Friend.

For that we sue, and find a Dawn
Of hope, that glimmers thro' our Tears;
For Giffard proves, Transcendent Worth
Is sometimes crown'd with Length of Years.

How does her Matchless Strength of Mind,
Superior Triumph over Time!
When ere She Speaks, we lose her age
And Listning, wonder at her Prime.

Like her and like the Deathless Bays
May *Portland* too in Winter bloom
Advance in years, nor feel their Weight
The *Giffard* of an Age to come.

---

1 Martha, *née* Temple (1639–1722), sister of Sir William Temple (1628–99), and widow of Sir Thomas Giffard (d. 1661).

2 The Countess of Portland, Jane Martha Temple (1672–1751), a niece of Lady Giffard, was the widow of William Bentinck (1649–1709), first Earl of Portland.

3 In 1718, when George I deprived the Prince of Wales of custody of his children, the Countess of Portland was appointed governess of the three daughters: Anne (1709–59), Amelia (1710–86), and Caroline (1713–57).

Ye Sacred, Ye Celestial Choir!
Ah give your threatned Purpose o'er!
Ah, do not take her *All* away!
Her Virtuous Soul was Yours *Before.*

I am,
Madam,
With the truest respect,
Your much obliged
& most Obedient Servant
Edward Young

Febr. 1718/9.

12. Oxford. [Su.] 22 November [1719].¹ Martha
Lady Giffard.

Address: To the Honble / Lady Giffard, / at her house in Dover Street,
London.

Not traced.²—Longe, pp. 304–5.

All Souls,
Nov. 22.

Madam,—This letter is not to acknowledge the Receipt of
ye Cabola³ I have not yet had time to look into it, being very

---

¹ The year of this letter, as of the two that follow, is determined by the reference
to Lord Burghley in the letter of 6 February [1719/20]. Young tutored Burghley
from the fall of 1719 to the spring of 1720. The first date appears from a report in
a letter from Maurice Johnson to Dr. William Stukeley of 14 October 1719: 'Mr.
Young, now LL D. [i.e. D.C.L., 10 June 1719], who wrote the poem on the Last
Day, and Busiris, is taken into the Earl of Exeter's family as tutor to his lordship's
eldest son Lord Burleigh, & is going to travel with him' (*Biblio. Topog. Brit.* No. II,
Part II, 1781). The second date is that of Young's entering the service of the Duke
of Wharton. An indenture of 10 July 1722 (Public Record Office, C 54/5218, No. 2)
between the Duke and Young cites a deed poll of 24 March 1719/20 made over to
Young by the Duke and speaks of Young's having left the service of the Exeter
family at the Duke of Wharton's request 'sometime past', presumably at the date
of the deed poll, and certainly before the young Lord Burghley had succeeded his
father as Earl of Exeter in 1721.
² The manuscript of this letter was listed in Maggs Bros. catalogue no. 737 of
the year 1944 as item No. 1085. Efforts to locate it have been unavailing.
³ Probably not a true cabala, as assumed by Julia Longe in her discussion of the
Young–Giffard letters, but rather some version of the political *Cabala* (1653) for
help on the tragedy of the Earl of Essex on which Young was working at this time.
It may have been *The Prince's Cabala; or Mysteries of State* of 1715.

warmly engaged in a Pursuit[1] which probably Mr. Cary[2] has or will mention to yr Ladyship. I give you joy of yr winter quarters, I hope the Town will pay for the loss of sweet air and quiet you left behind at Sheen. I will now dress my Heroe[3] by that assistance you have been pleased to send me, so that I shall look on Him (if he deserves that honour) as partly yours. This I assure your Ladyship without a compliment I am much better pleased with him than I was before since I find I have you for a rival in my esteem of him. I think him the truest Englishman I ever knew, for he is bold, generous, and indiscreet. I beg my humble respects to all your Ladyships Relations wh I have the Honour of knowing in Town. I have allmost finished the Second Act which shall wait on you.—I am Madam with All Respect Yr Ladyships much obliged & ever Dutiful Humble Sert. E. Young.

13. Oxford. [Su.] 17 January [1719/20]. Martha Lady Giffard.

Not available.[4]—Longe, p. 303; *Letters of English Authors from the Collection of Robert H. Taylor: A Catalogue of an Exhibition in the Princeton University Library May 13 to September 30, 1960.*

[1] i.e. Young's engagement as tutor to Lord Burghley.

[2] The Rt. Hon. Walter Cary (1686–1757) would have been known to Young from their student days together in both Winchester and New College, Oxford. At his marriage 4 January 1716/17 he was described as a resident of West Sheen, Surrey, and St. James's, Westminster (*Herald and Genealogist*, 1871, vi. 30). His wife was Elizabeth, daughter of Anthony Sturt of London and widow of John Jeffreys who had acquired property in Sheen formerly under lease to Sir William Temple (Daniel Lysons, *Environs of London*, 1792, i. 451). On 20 June 1717, Tickell had written to George Bubb (Dodington): 'Mr Cary, who is just returned to town from a survey of his lady's jointure in Wales, tells me that Mr Young has promised to pass part of the summer with him at Sheen, where Sir William Temple, was our friend's predecessor' (British Museum, Egerton MSS. 2174, f. 310). From Young's correspondence during the summer of 1717 it does not seem likely that he visited Cary before the fall of the year, but perhaps it was on one such visit that he first met Lady Giffard, as she continued to maintain a residence in Sheen as well as in London.

[3] The Earl of Essex (1566–1601), if one may judge from this and the two letters that follow, though nothing further is known of the play in which he was to figure.

[4] The manuscript of this letter was exhibited at the Princeton University Library in 1960 by Robert H. Taylor. All but the first paragraph and the last sentence of the letter was reproduced in the catalogue of the exhibition and has been followed in forming the text here reproduced. It differs in some respects from that printed in the Longe volume but appears to be a more faithful transcription of the original which has unfortunately not been available.

All Souls,
Jan. 17.

Madam,—I had long since answered ye Favour of yr last had I not proposed waiting on yr Lyship when I received it in a few days which Design Accidents drove of[f] till last Week at which time I endeavoured to pay my Respects to yr Ladyship but not so fortunate as to find you at Home nor to have time enough in Town to make a second Visit leaving it early the next morning. I endeavoured likewise to wait on Mr. Temple¹ in St. James Square but He was out of town on an occasion which I am sorry for.

*Rutland*² wh yr Ladyship is pleased to enquire after, is I believe a perfect Creature of Mr Banks, & I followd Him implicitly in it; but if the Case is as you represent it, if the Earl marryd ye Widow of Sr P. Sidney, & she had that mark of Distinction from ye Queen which you mention, it will do infinitely better for my purpose. I wish, Madam, you would refer me to any Authority in Print or Manuscript to Confirm it.

I have, Madam, been so hurryd of late, as Men often are, with doing of Nothing that I have not found time to transcribe the Second Act; but as soon as it is Fair it shall wait upon you, for after ye Present of a first Act, all the others are a Debt. Essex's Mistress being Sr Pps Widdow, Walsinghams Daughter³ & being termed by ye Queen her Ægyptian are all Peculiar*ys*⁴ of beautifull Consequence to my Design. I thank yr Laysp for the Information and am with ye greatest and truest respect—Madame yr Ladyships Most faithfull Humble Servt.

E. Young

¹ Henry Temple (1676–1757), created 1st Viscount Palmerston in 1723. The London house, which he had taken in 1716, was situated on the east side of St. James's Square, the second house north of the entrance to Charles Street (Arthur Irwin Dasent, *The History of St. James's Square and the Foundation of the West End of London*, 1895). His eldest son, Henry, was to marry Young's stepdaughter, Elizabeth Lee (?1718–36), 18 June 1735, and to be made the prototype of Young's 'Philander' ('For twenty summers [1720–40] ripening by my side') (*Night-Thoughts*, ii. 586).

² The widowed Countess of Rutland, secret wife of the Earl of Essex in *The Unhappy Favourite; or, The Earl of Essex* (1682), a tragedy by John Banks still popular on the London stage at this time.

³ Lady Frances, wife of Sir Philip Sidney (1554–86), daughter of Sir Francis Walsingham (1530–90).   ⁴ For this word, Longe prints 'potentialities'.

14. Oxford. [Sa.] 6 February [1719/20]. Martha Lady Giffard.

Bodleian Library (MS. Eng. letters d. Y4).—Longe, pp. 303–4.

                                        Feb: ye 6th
                                        Allsouls. Oxon.

Madam

It is ye peculiar Happiness of some Persons that whatever they do is most Agreeable; of wh Truth Yr Ladyship gave me a very extraordinary Instance in Yr Last, where You make even the shortning of Yr Letter to me an Obliging Action, by the kind motive You assign for Yr doing it; & if Yr Yr [*sic*] Ladyship can make a Thing of that Nature Agreeable, I Know nothing which You may not make so to me.

I am Now, Madam, th[o]roughly satisfid of ye Truth of Yr Ladyships Information with relation to ye *Egyptian*,¹ & hope in some measure to deserve the favour You have done me in acquainting me with it, by making some tolerable Use of it, wh/[verso]/ without ye least shadow of a Compliment, is the most direct way I know to shew my Gratitude for such a Favour to such a Nature as Yours.

I have lately, Madam, been a little Alarmd; Ld B——y² having seen a Lady in This Place, who has given Him ye Palpitation of the Heart; I design therefore soon to leave this Place, & if possible the Thoughts of ye fair Lady behind Us: Though his Lordship is at present so true a Lover as to Vow Wretchedness for Live [*sic*], the Wretchedness either of Despair, or Possession, for she is much beneath his Quality: but This is a Secret. To amuse his Ldship for ye last ten Days I have had Him about ye neighbouring Country to see Sights; but I was not able to find any Prospect, or Building sufficiently beautifull to Rival Mrs —— in his Thoughts. I am Honord Madam,

                with ye greatest Truth & Respect
                yr Lyships most Obedient Humble Sevt EY.

¹ An epithet applied to Lady Frances Sidney, 'Walsinghams daughter', in Young's last letter to Lady Giffard. What it was that may have satisfied Young's interest in its substantiation, however, is not known.

² John, Lord Burghley (d. 1722), whom Young was tutoring.

/[conjugate leaf]/ I hope, Madam, all Yr Relations are well, to whom I give my best Respects when You see them.

15. [Oxford]. [Tu.] 1 March [1719/20]. Thomas Tickell.

Surrey MSS. (also Tickell Letterbook, pp. 66–7).—Tickell, pp. 77–8.

March ye 1st

Dear Tickell

I have now with me some Gentlemen of Maudlin who giving an Account of Dr Faryr's Funeral[1] (who is succeeded in his professorship by Dr Bertie of this College) say Tom Collins made an affecting speech over Him, & among other points dilated on his being a means of discovering Mr Addisons Genius[2] & Improving it by Exercises Imposed on Him, wh Exercises He sayd in express Terms He hopd ye Gentlemen now publishing yt Great Mans Works[3] wd search after, as being much too valueable to be neglected. I askd ye Gentlemen if they cd guess in wt Hands those Exercises might possibly be, who sayd Tom Collins was ye man to be consulted—Green[4] is this moment come in, who says He has writ to this purpose before, excuse therefore Dear Sir

Yrs most faithfully

EYoung.

16. [?April 1723]. Alexander Pope.

Not traced.[5]

[1] James Fayrer, a Fellow of Magdalen College from 1683 and Professor of Natural Philosophy from 1706, had died on the 23rd. The funeral address on the 25th was given by Thomas Collins (?1643–1723), Master of Magdalen School. Fayrer was succeeded by Charles Bertie (1679–?1741) of All Souls College by election on the 26th. [2] Addison had died 17 June 1719.
[3] Tickell was engaged in editing Addison's works, which he published in September 1721.
[4] Samuel Green became a Fellow of Queen's College 13 March 1714/15 (J. R. Magrath, *The Queen's College* ii. 312).
[5] Evidence of this letter is Young's reference in his letter to Pope of 2 May [?1723] to 'that instance of Yr Fdship I mentiond in my last'.

17. [?London]. [Th.] 2 May [?1723].[1] Alexander Pope.

Address: To Mr Pope / at Twitnam. *Postmark*: 2/MY[May]. British Museum (Add. MSS. 4809, ff. 25ᵛ, 26ᵛ).—Croft, iv. 407; Elwin-Courthope, x. 117; Sherburn, ii. 171.

May 2d

Dear Sr

Having been often from home I know not if You have done me ye favour of callg on me but be yt as it will, I much want that instance of Yr Fdship I mentiond in my last, a Friendship Im very Sensible I can receive from no One but Yr self. I shd not urdge this thing so much, but for very par:lar reasons; nor can you be at a loss to conceive how a *Trifle of this Nature*[2] may be of serious moment to me & while Im in hope of ye great Advantage of Yr advice abt it, I shall not be so absurd as to make any farther Step without it. I know You are much engagd, & only hope to hear of You at Yr entire liesure.

I am Sr
Yr most faithfull
& Obedient Sert
EYoung

1 Of the year of this letter, Sherburn said: 'On this letter Pope translated a part of Bk III of the *Odyssey*, and consequently the letter cannot be dated later than 1723. It is possible, but not probable, that the letter was written before 1723' (Sherburn, 1956, ii. 171).

2 Nichols footnoted this phrase in the proofs to Croft's biography of Young: 'It was to request a Prologue to one of his Tragedies' ('Proof Sheets of Dr. Sam: Johnson's Lives of the English Poets with Manuscript Corrections in his own Hand-Writing', Victoria and Albert Museum, Forster Collection 298). As Young is soliciting Pope's 'advice', however, Johnson's informant must have been mistaken. A more likely explanation is that Young is asking Pope's advice about relinquishing hopes of making a career in literature for the security of a place in the Church. The possibility of this interpretation rests somewhat on the credence that may be given to an anecdote reported as coming from Pope's editor, William Warburton (1698–1779): 'When he [Young] had determined to go into orders, he addressed himself, like an honest man, for the best directions in the study of theology. But to whom did he apply? It may, perhaps, be thought, to Sherlock or Atterbury; to Burnet or Hare. No! to Mr. Pope: who, in a youthful frolic, recommended Thomas Aquinas to him. With this treasure he retired, in order to be free from interruption, to an obscure place in the suburbs. His director hearing no more of him in six months, and apprehending he might have carried the jest too far, sought after him, and found him out just in time to prevent an irretrievable derangement' (Owen Ruffhead, *Life of Alexander Pope*, 1769, p. 225 n.).

18. F. [?7 February 1723/4].¹ Lady Mary Wortley Montagu.

Not traced.²—Moy Thomas, ii, 13–14; Shelley, p. 65; Halsband, ii. 34–5.

Madam,—The more I think of your criticisms, the more I feel the just force of them: I will alter which [*sic*] are alterable: those that are not I beg you to make a secret of, and to

¹ The date of this letter is estimated on the assumptions that the letter precedes Young's letter to Lady Mary of [?10–21] February 1723/4 and that it concerns the first rehearsals of *The Brothers* rather than those of the next theatrical season when the play was put forward once again and finally withdrawn from production on Young's taking clerical orders. There is evidence of its having been in rehearsal early in 1724 in two accounts in the *Universal Journal* dated from Button's Coffee House. The first, of Tuesday, 31 December 1723, spoke of 'a new Play next *Tuesday*, written on a *Persian* story; by Mr. Gay: After which a new Play of Dr. Young's, the Author of *Busiris* and the *Revenge*, will immediately be put into Rehearsal.' Gay's play, *The Captives*, played in Drury Lane from Wednesday, the 15th of January, until the 22nd. The second account is dated Saturday, 8 February, 'past 2 at Noon', and deserves quotation in full:

'All the Company has left this Place; the Room is now quite empty, and I have a little Leisure to reflect on what I have heard. For these two Hours past, the conversation has been turned upon *The Brothers*, a new Tragedy of Dr. Young's, now rehearsing. It is Impossible to guess at the Success of it, so very uncertain is the Judgement of the Town; and as for my part, I have very little Hopes of it; there's never a Ghost, never a flying Dragon, nor so much as one poor Windmill throughout the whole Play. I am surprised the Doctor should be so little acquainted with the prevailing Humour of the Town; the poor Man confides wholly in strong masculine Sense, with which his Play abounds; and I believe him as old fashioned, as to think himself writing in good Queen Bess's Days, when such a Fellow as Shakespear could be relished. The History on which the Plot is founded, is doubtless a good one. I am not in a Story-telling Humour, and must therefore refer my Reader to Livy, who will give him a long Account of Philip of *Macedon*, the good Friend and Ally of *Hannibal*, and Father to *Perseus* and *Demetrius*. In the same Author, he may find a long Detail of the Difference between these young Princes, which are the chief Subject of the Play. Livy has given us their orations before the King, to purge themselves of the reciprocal Accusation, of designing to murder each other; and Mr. *Young* has followed him so close, as to bring the Princes upon the Stage, before the King and Council, the one clearing himself of the foul Crime; the other artfully endeavouring to cast all the Villainy he had been guilty of upon his Brother. *Horatio* did not hesitate to say he thought it as fine a written Scene as had appeared upon the Stage for these many Years, and had good Reason to believe it would be as well acted; and Mr. *Young* seems to depend very much upon that Scene: but doubtless he'll be mistaken for I am credibly informed, the M–n–ger of the New House, has formed a Resolution, that it shall be acted to an empty Pit and Boxes, there being a new Entertainment in *Grotesque* Characters getting up there, entitled, *The Cruel Uncle*: Or, *The Children in the Wood*, so very artfully contrived, that at the instant *Perseus* and *Demetrius* are entring upon that Scene, the Ruffians, represented by *Harlequin* and *Scaramouch*, will be making their appearance at the Other House. The Consequence of this is easily foreseen, *Booth* and *Cibber* will preach to

[*Notes 1 and 2 cont. overleaf*]

make an experiment on the sagacity of the town, which I think may possibly overlook what you have observed, for the players and Mr. Dodington,[1] neither of whom were backward in finding fault, or careless in attention, took no notice of the flaw in D.'s honour, or Erixene's conduct, and I would fain have their blindness continue till my business is done; the players are fond of it, and as it has been said on a point of a little more importance, *si populus vult decipi, decipiatur.*[2]

I am, Madam,

Your most obedient and most humble servant.

[Postscript.]—Madam,—Your alteration in the fifth act will be of exceeding advantage in more views than one. I will wait on your ladyship with it as soon as I have done it, which will be, I believe, Monday morning. But that I'm satisfied you want no inducement to assist me as much as you can, I should add that I have more depending on the success of this particular piece than your ladyship imagines.[3] Friday noon.

bare Walls, whilst *Lanyon* and *Dupre* dance before a full Audience; and lest Mrs. Old[fiel]d's Name should sway some few unfashionable Wretches, they have contrived a very musical Robin-Red-Breast, which is to have more Melody in its Song, than there can possibly be in all the mournful Accents of the unhappy *Erixene.*'

² The original of this letter was sold by Sotheby's 25 July 1903, No. 577.

---

¹ George Bubb (1691–1762) had taken the surname of Dodington on the death of an uncle of that name in 1720. Young's letters from November 1724 to September 1725 are written from Dodington's homes in Chiswick and Covent Garden.

² 'If the people want to be deceived, let them be deceived.' Cardinal Carlo Caraffa, Legate of Pope Paul IV, referring to the Parisians (cf. Jacques Auguste de Thou, *Historia Sui Temporis*, i. 17). This is an adaptation of an old Latin proverb: 'Qui vult decipi, decipiatur', or as expressed by Robert Burton (*The Anatomy of Melancholy*, 1621, III, IV. i. 2) in his treatment of religious melancholy: 'Si mundus vult decipi, decipiatur.'

³ It seems likely that Young has in mind here his choice of profession either as a man of letters or a clergyman.

19. [?10–21 February 1723/4].[1] Lady Mary Wortley Montagu.

Not traced.[2]—Moy Thomas, ii. 11; Shelley, pp. 64–5; Halsband, ii. 35–6.

MADAM,—A great cold and a little intemperance has given me such a face as I am ashamed to show, though I much want to talk with your ladyship. For my theatrical measures are broken; Mariamne brought its author above £1,500, The Captives above £1,000, and Edwin, now in rehearsal, has already, before acting, brought its author above £1,000.[3] Mine,[4] when acted, will not more than pay for the paper on which it is written; but the moment I get abroad I will wait on your ladyship, and explain further. Only this at present, for the reason mentioned, I am determined to suppress my play for this season at least. The concern you showed for its success is my apology for this account, which were otherwise very impertinent. I am madam,

Your ladyship's much obliged
And most obedient humble servant.

[1] The date of this letter is estimated from Young's references to current plays and by its apparent relationship to the letter to which the date Friday the 7th of February has been tentatively assigned.

[2] The original of this letter was sold by Sotheby's 25 July 1903, No. 578.

[3] Elijah Fenton's *Mariamne* was first produced 22 February 1722/3 and continued to hold the stage on several occasions during the spring of 1723/4; John Gay's *The Captives* was on the stage from 15 to 22 January 1723/4; George Jeffreys's *Edwin* first appeared 24 February 1723/4.

[4] The withdrawal from rehearsal of *The Brothers* is noticed by a writer in the *Universal Journal* of 25 March 1724 who began an essay on the contemporary theatre with the following remarks:

'I am surprized that you should leave the Town so long in Ignorance, and the Expectation of a new Play, which they'll not have this Season. In a former you took Notice, that there was a Tragedy of Mr. *Young*'s rehearsing; and by the Character you gave of it made several impatient to see it brought upon the Stage. But Mr. Young, I am informed, has taken the Play from the House, and put it off till next Winter.

'Several doubtless will be surprized at a Poet's deferring his Benefit for near a Twelve Month, and some I know blame him for it; but for my particular Part, I very much applaud his Conduct. Who that had any Talent for Dramatick Poetry, would venture a good Tragedy at a time when nothing but Farce and Puppet Shows will go down with the Town? At [a] Time when should Shakespear himself rise from the Dead and appear in his Hamlet or Othello, he would be deserted for Harlequin and Scaramouch? What I am most surprized at, is that the Author should talk of venturing his Play amongst us next Winter, as if we were to recover our Senses by that time; but I am afraid he is not over well skill'd in Physick, else he wou'd soon find that such Epidemical Frensies are not of so short a Duration.'

Thomas Clutterbuck[1] to Young. London. [Sa.] 20 June 1724.

Surrey MSS.

Sir

Tho' I am extremly concern'd at Your misfortune,[2] yet I have some comfort in thinking it may possibly be in my power to be serviceable to You. It wou'd by no means become me to give advice in this matter, but if Your resolution to take orders is fixt, & You are determin'd to do it, I have from /[verso]/ My Lord Carteret, to tell You that he will immediately make You one of his Chaplains, & provide for You, as soon as he has taken care of three persons who are now upon his hands. A Lord Lieutenant has frequent opportunity's of obliging people this way; on the other side you know it is not an employment yt lasts very long; I think it incumbent /[conjugate leaf]/ upon me to give no encouragement beyond wt You may reasonably expect, & I answer for. Which ever way You determine You will always find me with great sincerity Sir

Your Obedient
Humble Servant
Tho: Clutterbuck.

Burlingtonstreet
June ye 20th
1724.

20. Haslemere, Surrey. [M.] 3 August 1724. Thomas Tickell.[3]

Surrey MSS. (also Tickell Letterbook, pp. 44–5).—Tickell, pp. 102–3.

[1] Clutterbuck, about whom little is known, is said to have been Member of Parliament for Liskeard, Cornwall (Tickell, p. 95), and more significantly was at this time first secretary to the newly appointed (3 April 1724) Lord Lieutenant of Ireland, John Lord Carteret (1690–1763).

[2] An allusion to his affairs with the Duke of Wharton (see note 1, p. 33, to Young's letter to Tickell of 20 October 1724).

[3] Tickell had been sent to Ireland in May as secretary to the Lords Justices to look after Carteret's interests until the latter's arrival in October.

Haselmore in
Surry Aug: 3
1724.

Dear Sr

What You take for Irresolution in me, is only Delay, Im absolutely determind to take Orders, but had reasons for defering it to the spring. However, on hearing again from You, I shall take orders immediately, if yt Delay in the least hurts my expectations from My Ld Carteret. He has allready promist me by Mr Clutterbuck to make me his Chaplain, & to provide for me after Three, wh are allready on his Ldships hands. You can infinitely better judge than I, to wt such a promise may amount, from your better knowledge of ye Preferments of ye Kingdom in wh You are, & of ye probable Duration of his Ldships powr There.

I am, I say, determind to take Orders, & if I cd I wd be Domestick to his Ldship, but He has two allready;[1] upon the whole I beg /[verso]/ Yr Assistance & Advice, & to know if there is any tolerable prospect of preferment in Ireland from ye Promise wh thro yr kind application Mr Clutterbuck has obtained for me.

I receivd Yrs This Hour, & determining to write ye same Day, (in order among other things to know if tis adviseable for me, immediately to take orders) I have but just time to ad yt I have ye truest sense of yr Friendship, & am most sincerely

Dr Sr
Yr much Obligd
& most obedient
Humble Sevt
EYoung.

Wt I apprehend is yt
his Ldship may consture my
delay a disrespect to his
favour; I shall do nothing
till Im so happy to hear from You.

[1] Presumably William Burscough, who was made Bishop of Limerick in 1725, and William Cotterell (d. 1744), who became Dean of Raphoe in 1725, and Bishop of Ferns and Leighlin in 1743.

21. Chiddingfold, Surrey. [Su.] 20 September 1724.
Thomas Tickell.

Surrey MSS. (also Tickell Letterbook, pp. 43–4).—Tickell, p. 102.

Chidingfold
in Surry.
Sepr 20. 1724

Dear Sr

I am perticularly unhappy yt the sea is between Us at
this time, for tho I hope You will not read ye satire¹ I send
without a Pen in yr hand, yet It must have receivd greater
Advantage if I was with You too. In this work I think I have
more than a common title to yr Assistance, since ye first Hint
of it came from You; tis my Last² & I'd have it as blameless
as I & my Friends can make it; That You are particularly
such I shall ever most gratefully own on many Accounts but
chiefly on ye Last, wh is a Friendship /[verso]/ of so high a
Nature as to make my Affection my Duty. The Instances of
false Friendship³ I have met with raises my value for the
True. Yrs has worn long & well with me, & if I can prove
my self worthy of ^it^ I will. Tis, You know, ["]part of a great
mans Character"⁴ yt his First Friendsps continud to be his
Last.

Im in Fields & Woods⁵ yt bear no News, All I can possibly
send You Hence in a Letter is sentiments of ye Head or

¹ A reference to *The Universal Passion* to which Young gave the general title
Love of Fame in its collected edition of 1728. At this time his intention was to publish it as a single satire inscribed to Lord Carteret, but by November he had decided
to divide the work into separate parts, which eventually numbered seven. The first
part was announced in *The Daily Courant* of 27 January 1724/5 as 'This Day . . .
Published'.

² By his 'Last', Young is not referring to the part of the satire later called 'Satire
the Last' but rather to his decision to give up a career in literature for one in the
Church.

³ One of the 'instances' was surely Young's unfortunate exploitation by the Duke
of Wharton.

⁴ Although the source of Young's quotation is not apparent, the 'great man' is
applied to Addison earlier, as it is also later in Tickell's 'Account of the Life' of
Addison prefixed to his edition of Addison's *Works* (1721).

⁵ Chiddingfold lies on the edge of the Weald among some of the most delightful
and richly wooded scenery of a county celebrated for its natural beauty.

Heart; my sincere gratitude where tis most Due is uppermost in ye Last. I am

Dear Sr

Yr most Obligd

& most Obedient Sevt

EYoung.

/[conjugate leaf]/

If Swift[1] & You Converse[2] I shd be glad if He saw ye satire too;[3] wh I desire You to return wth wt Benefit yr Affairs can afford it.

I send ye Copy by a Gentleman who says He shall be with You as soon as my Letter.

[1] Young's acquaintance with Swift commenced at least as early as 14 February 1712/13 when both men were at the deathbed of their mutual friend William Harrison. It was apparently renewed in the summer of 1720 when Young visited Ireland in company with the Duke of Wharton. That is the only time when Wharton was in Ireland during Young's service with him. Young's service began with a deed poll of 24 March 1719/20, made shortly before Wharton's visit to Dublin to liquidate his estate there. His movements were reported by Henry Downes, Bishop of Killala, in a letter of 5 July 1720 to William Nicolson, Bishop of Derry: 'Lord Wharton came over Sunday last [3 July], and has already sold all his estates in this Kingdom' (Nicolson's *Letters*, ii. 528). It has to have been on this visit that Wharton wrote the following note to Swift: 'Dear Dean, I shall imbarque for England tomorrow. It would be necessary for me to take leave of Ld Molesworth on many accounts & as Young is ingag'd in Town I must infallibly go alone unless yr charity extends it self to favour me with yr company there this morning I beg you would send me yr answer & belive me Sincerely yr faithful fri[en]d & Serveant, WHARTON. p. s. If you condescend so far come to me about Eleven of the clock' (British Museum, Add. MSS. 4806). Wharton's note, inscribed 'Monday morning', has been heretofore mistakenly assigned to the year 1718 in the absence of other evidence, but there can now be no doubt that it was written in 1720, and probably in the summer, perhaps shortly after Wharton's arrival.

It must have been during this visit of Young to Dublin that the famous incident occurred of Swift's making his prophetic statement of dying like a tree 'at top' which is recounted in Young's *Conjectures on Original Composition* (1759). In the spring of this year, Swift had been particularly bothered with prolonged attacks of deafness (Williams, 1963, iii. 348 n. 1).

[2] That Swift and Tickell were already acquainted is clear from Swift's letter to Charles Ford of 16 June 1724, soon after Tickell's arrival in Dublin, in which Swift wrote: 'We have got here a Poet for a Secretary, one Mr Tickell, born and famous since I left the World. We have mutually visited but neither of us at home; however I have dined with him at a third Place, and he is a Wit of as odd a Countenance as I have seen' (ibid. 15).

[3] It may have been at this time that Swift wrote his unflattering verses 'On Reading Dr. Young's Satires, called the Universal Passion'. Certainly if the verses, which were not published until 1734, had been written in 1728 or later, Swift would have used the newer title of 'Love of Fame'. Swift's modern editor, Sir Harold Williams, says only: 'Faulkner assigned this poem of Swift's to 1726, which is probably correct' (*The Poems of Jonathan Swift*, 1937, ii. 390.)

22. [Sheen, Surrey]. [Sa.] 10 October 1724. Thomas
Tickell.

Surrey MSS.
                                                      Octr ye 10th
Dear Sr   1724.
                        & Mr Clutterbuck
   My Lord Lieutenant   ∧   will be in Ireland
as soon as my Letter, I beg You to continue me yr friendship
with them. There has been yet no Ordination since the grant
of my Lord's favour to me. I hope therefore my not being
yet in Orders will not be imputed to me as a neglect, & now
I am going into Orders with all speed, so yt I humbly hope
that my Lords original promise, of wh I sent You an exact
Account, stands good to me. Or if my conduct is misunderstood, I beg You to interceed for me, & reestablish me in yt
Happiness You first obtained. /[verso]/ I had thoughts of
defering Orders till the spring, on Account of Affairs I was
to make up with D. Wharton, & a *subscription*[1] wh I thought
wd run better, before I was enterd into another way; But
I have thought better of it & will not defer it, having too
just a notion of ye very great Honor my Lord has done me
to delay Qualifying my self for it. If I can get a private
Ordination I will, if not, there is a publick one at Xmas wh
I will not omit. with my most humble Dutys to my Lord, &
most gratefull Respects to Mr Clutterbuck I am
                              Dear Sr
                                Yr most Obligd
                              & ever faithfull & most Obdt.
                              Servant   EYoung

Please to direct to Mr Carys
at Sheen near Richmond
              Surry.
I shall there abt a Month.

---

[1] No record of such a subscription or publication has been found. See his letter
of 2 March 1724/5 as well as the notes to his letter of 5 December 1726.

23.[1] [?October 1724].[2] Henrietta, Duchess of Marlborough.

Cambridge University Library (Rothschild Collection).

The

Dedication

To

Her Grace the Dutchess of Marlborough

Madam

I beg leave to dedicate the following Play to your Graces *Private* amusement. I *Publish* it to what I most Esteem in the World when I publish it to Yr Grace; & more is superfluous.

Nor do I less gratifie my Ambition, than my Gratitude in what I now do. I address myself to the Daughter of ye Duke of Marlborough, & to the Mother of Lady Mary. What a situation for Happiness is This? *Backward* yr Grace has the most Noble, & *Forward* ye most Beautifull prospect of any Person upon Earth. May You long, very long enjoy it; & so be as singular in your Happiness, as in your many Titles to it.

The Picture I have drawn in the following scenes of a Parents Affection, had been much more Perfect, had I had the Honour of sooner knowing the Charms of such a Daughter, & Yr Graces delicate sensibility of Heart.

Yr Graces exquisite relish for *Shakespeare*, is a Demonstration of yr Superior Tast in this kind of writing; Nor do I know any Exception to yr Graces refind Tast of real merit in every way, but Yr Partiality shown to me. Yet This is not without its Excuse, if the profoundest Veneration, & most peculiar Attatchment of Heart, may be allowd, with Generous minds, to hide a Multitude of Faults.

---

[1] The manuscript of this letter accompanies the manuscript of Young's play, *The Brothers* (1753), which came into the hands of Sir William Bunbury in 1748.
[2] The date of the letter is uncertain, but it could not have been before the birth of the Duchess's daughter, the Lady Mary (later Duchess of Leeds), on 23 November 1723, nor later than the year of the Duchess's death, 1733. Most likely it was written near the end of the year 1724 when Young withdrew his play from rehearsal.

Madam, A *Private Dedication* is, perhaps, without Precedent; & I am glad of it: For a Person possesed of so Peculiar a manner of Obliging, should, if possible, meet with as Peculiar a manner of Gratitude for it. I am for ever, with a Devotion You onely could occasion, & You onely can understand

Madam.

Yr Graces most Dutifull

& most Obedient

Humble Servt.

Edw: Young

24. [?Sheen, Surrey]. [?Tu. 20 October 1724]. Thomas Clutterbuck.

Not traced.[1]

25. [Sheen, Surrey]. [Tu.] 20 October 1724. Thomas Tickell.

Surrey MSS.

Oct 20.

1724

Dear Sr

I take ye Liberty of in[c]losing Mr Clutterbucks Letter, to You; both because I know not how to direct to Him, & because I would have You see, & second the Contents of it. When You have read it youll be so kind to seal it for me.

As I told You in my last I am absolutely determind to go into Orders, nor Did I defer it till this time out of any trifling Irresolution, or Views of another kind, but for ye reasons mentiond in my last, & I consulted Mr Clutterbuck about it who gave ye Answer wh I mention in his Letter, I therefore earnestly beg You to continue Your Friendship to me

---

[1] This letter was enclosed in the following letter to Tickell for his observation and forwarding. The London *Daily Post* for Monday, 19 October has the following item: 'Thos Clutterbuck set out for Ireland Friday last.'

in this Point of ye last Consequence, & I the more earnestly
/[verso]/ beg it because ye very great Injury I at present
suffer from ye Duke[1] might recommend me to ye kind
offices even of a stranger. I am with all truth & Love
Dear Sr
Yr most Obligd
& most Obedient Sevt
E Young

Please to direct to Mr Carys
at Sheen near Richmond
    Surry

26. [Sa. 24 October 1724]. Thomas Tickell.

Surrey MSS.[2]

Dear Sr
    [in another hand] Oct 24
    That You may the [more] see what grounds I have for the
Humble Re[ques]t I have made to You & Mr Clutterbuck
I will [pu]t yt whole Affair in one View.
    The Express prom[ise I ha]d from my Lord was, 'That
He would please to [make] me his Chaplain immediately, &
provide for me [after] three.[']³
    I did not take O[rders imm]ediately 1st Because I had
Three before me & [so I tho]ught there was no hast. 2ly for
the Reasons I h[ave] mentioned before relating to the Duke
of Wharton. B[ut] on these reasons I durst not defer Orders
without cons[ul]ting Mr Clutterbuck, who pleasd to write yt
'In that I could not do amiss; for yt He was persuaded my
Lords promise would stand good.['] I remember Sr I writ

---

¹ During the spring of 1724 the Duke of Wharton had backed the candidacy of
Sir John Williams for Sheriff of London in a hotly contested race which ended in
a court action awarding the office to his opponent, Edward Bellamy, on the 30th
of March. This event seems to have brought about the end of Wharton's political
ambitions in England and the 'injury' of which Young complains is no doubt his
failure to collect money owing to him, a debt which was to be settled only many
years after the Duke's death in 1731 and after prolonged hearings in Chancery.
² The manuscript of this letter is in bad condition, making conjectural supple-
ments necessary at some points.
³ See Clutterbuck's letter to Young of 20 June 1724.

You Mr Clutterbuck's answer very soon after; & indeed it had been absolute Madness in me, without ye Precaution mentiond, in ye least to have hazarded so great a stake.

/[verso]/ [What could be] there, Sr, in ye conduct Ive mentiond [to cause so v]ery severe a punishment as ye withdrawing My Lord's promise? If indeed my Lord imagind I set so little & unjust a value on it that I meant it only as a Refuge in case I cou[ld n]ot succeed elsewhere, twas most deservedly withd[rawn]n[.] But that This was by no means ye Case I [call you to] witness; & please to consider Sr how improbable [it is yt] it shd be so. For 1st my Lords patronage to on[e i]n my situation & at my time of Life is of in-[finite value] & I must be most Ignorant not to Know [this.] 2ly Had I other Patronages in View, I s[hould] not probably have spent that very Interval of Ti[m]e in forming Addresses to my Ld Carteret as I actu[a]lly did. One in Verse as a Dedication of a Satire I am about to Print,[1] wh Mr Clutterbuck thought as [w]ell let alone for yt my Ld was not fond of Poetical Compliments; Another in Prose craving his Lordships patronage to a Piece of Divinity wh I have finishd by me;[2] but Mr Clutterbuck sayd from my Lord that he was my Friend allready, & yt /[conjugate leaf] /I might make others by that Address.

But granting my Delay a Fault, please to confess what a Fault it was. I omitted but One Ordination & shall omit no more [af]ter I have withdrawn my Play,[3] & taken all other [step]s suitable to a determind resolution in ye point[. G]-ranting Sr, ye fault to be Great, is it [in] ye powr of repentance? if not, my repenta[nce I] am sure has been very sincere about it [and I ask] my Lords pardon in ye most humble manne[r if this con]duct is disaprovd of by Him.

This being truly ye fair state of ye whole case, I have great Hopes if my Lord was fully apprizd of it, by Yr & Mr

---

1 *The Universal Passion*, of which Satire I was published in January 1724/5, dedicated to the Duke of Dorset.

2 Unless the reference is to a work which has since disappeared, Young here probably refers to *A Vindication of Providence in which the Passions are Considered in a New Light*, which he delivered as a sermon at the death of George I in 1727 and published in 1728 with a dedication to Queen Caroline.

3 *The Brothers*, which was withdrawn about this time and not produced until 1753.

Clutterbucks Kind Intercession I should be quite reinstated
in his favour.

I therefore humbly & earnestly beg You & Mr Clutterbuck to joyn your Goodness to me in representing This to
my Lord; & I have great Confidence that ye Powr wh so
effectually Obtaind /[verso]/ my Lords Patronage & most
Indulgent Promise mentiond before will be able to secu[re
it] to me; unless I have been guilty of some misconduct wh
I think not of. With ye great[est Respect] & Regard I am
                    [Dear] Sr
                        [Your] most Obligd
                            [& most] Obedient Humble Sevt
                                    EYoung
Pray my most humble Duty
to My Lord & best respects
to Mr Clutterbuck, to whom
you'll communicate this at
your leisure.

27. Chiswick, Mdx. [M.] 16 November [1724].
Thomas Tickell.

Surrey MSS.

                                    Nov. 16. 1723[1]
                                    Mr Dodingtons
                                        at Cheswick
                                        Middlesex.
Dear Sr
    Yrs of ye 3rd I receivd this day.[2] Those Letters of mine
wh have since come to your hand will I humbly hope be
considerd by You & Mr Clutterbuck, for Sr I see in ye
News that Two of my Lords Chaplains are allready provided
for,[3] & what a Heartbreaking must it be to me who have a

---

[1] Young clearly wrote '1723', but all references in the letter show that it was a
mistake for 1724.

[2] Tickell's filing note on the back of Young's letter to him of 20 October,
'A[nswere]d. 3 Nov.', shows that the letters Young mentions in the next sentence
were already before Tickell when he wrote the letter Young is now acknowledging.

[3] Probably a reference to William Burscough and William Cotterell (see note
to letter of 3 August 1724).

promise to be provided for by his Lordship in ye Fourth place, wh is allready second, to be ye least in Doubt of yt Blessing, for all things considerd, I can give it no less a Term. Sr for God sake make my case your own, & pardon me if in a point of such exstream concern to me, & now so ripe & near an Event, in ye most warm but humble manner I sollicit You & Mr Clutterbuck to interceed with my Lord for me, on ye Account & for ye /[verso]/ Reasons wh with all submission I have written before.

And Mr Tickell for ye sake of yt long acquaintance & Friendship yt has been betwixt Us I entreat You (since it is a trouble yt cant return but is done once for all) yt You labour to bring things to a certainty (I mean as to ye knowledge of my Lords pleasure) for my Heart akes, & cant but ake at ye terrible suspence from knowing at such a Crisis on wt I can rely. Let me, Sr not be misunderstood I mean not by my Importunity to make my self troublesome to You & Mr Clutterbuck, but to ease ye necessary anxiety of my own Heart & make my humble Request in ye most ~~humble~~
Respectfu[l]
ʌ   manner, & I hope in God it will not be in vain.

One thing, Sr, I must mention to You in Confiden[ce] as my Friend apart & yt is This. In my Last Letter to You I mentiond a satire wh I would have Dedicated to my Lord Carteret but Mr Clutterbuck /[conjugate leaf]/ thought it not proper. That satire I have divided into distinct Epistles wh I propose publishing one after another directed to people of Fashion, for one of wh I have ye Offer of Mr Walpoles patronage;[1] wt I desire to know is if from so doing I can possibly hurt my self in ye least with my Ld Carteret; if so, be sure I shall not do it. For all I expect from Mr Walpole is a larger gratuity perhaps than from another person; wh in this Case You know is absolutely a Trifle. be not tender,

[1] Young was well advised to be cautious about dedicating to Walpole at a time when he was soliciting Carteret's help, as the two politicians were rivals for supremacy and Carteret's Irish appointment was largely an excuse for getting him out of London without wholly alienating him from the administration. Young eventually dedicated the 'last' part of *The Universal Passion* to Walpole, announced in *The Daily Post* of 17 January 1725/6 as 'This Day . . . published', and later, 29 January, in the *Dublin Weekly Journal*. Again, on 5 July 1726, *The Daily Journal* of London announced publication of Young's *The Instalment*, a celebration in verse of the induction of Walpole into the Order of the Garter.

Sr, of giving me yr Advice in this thing[.] I shall make no improper use of it, or be Indiscreet about it.

I most humbly beg ^an^ answer with the best speed yr Affairs will permit.—The last Point mentiond is a Trifle but as it concerns ye First; but as it relates to yt tis exstreamly material & therefore I trouble You about it.

I shall look on yr next Letter as ye /[verso]/ Ticket I have in yt Lottery of Life & shall Read ~on~ it with trembling. Pray my best respects & Thanks to Mr. Clutterbuck, of whom I ask a thousand pardons for ye frequent troubles I have given Him, but I humbly hope He will consider the great Occasion I am under. I am Dear Sr

Yr most Obligd
& most Obedient
Humble Sevt
EYoung

PS I press not for an Answer to This as wt will determin[e] me to Orders or not (yts resolvd at all Event) but ye Quiet of my Heart.

28. Chiswick, Mdx. [W.] 2 December 1724. Thomas Tickell.

Surrey MSS.

Mr Dodingtons[1]
at Chiswick.
Dec: ye 2. 1724

Dear Sr

This day I carryd my Testimonium from ye College for Orders to ye Bp of Whinchester, who will ordain me next Sunday sennight wh is Ordination Sunday.[2]

I desire You, Sr to acquaint Mr Clutterbu[ck] with This, & to renew ye humble request wh I have made in my late Letters to You & to Him, with all ye force You can. I can

---

[1] What the effect might have been on Young's hopes from Carteret of his writing from Dodington's is not clear. In April Dodington had been appointed a Lord of the Treasury and was thereafter to be closely dependent on Walpole.
[2] i.e. 13 December.

not add any thing material to ye Contents of my Last Letter
to You to wh I have not yet receivd ye favour of any answer;
I shall therefore only ask pardon for ye frequent troubles I
have given You, & beg to hear from You ye very soonest
You can; it being of ye greatest moment to me to know ye
Success /[verso]/ of your very kind endeavours for

Dear Sr
Yr most Obligd
& most Obedient
Humble Sevt
EYoung.

Pray my best Respects
to Mr Clutterbuck.

29. Chiswick, Mdx. [M.] 14 December 1724. Thomas
Tickell.

Surrey MSS. (also Tickell Letterbook, pp. 46–7).—Tickell, p. 105.

Mr Dodington's
Chiswick Dec: 14
1724.

Dear Sr
      This is to let You know yt I am in Orders,[1] the want of
making wh step was I presume ye Reason yt hitherto my
Lord has not declard his good pleasure concerning me. If ye
most humble requests wh I have made in former Letters are
(Thro yn continuance of yr Friendship to me) granted; I am
ready on ye very first notice of it to go for Ireland.
      I should be very glad to know if it is my good fortune to
make yt Journey soon, because if it is not there will be an
office vacant in ye College at Xtmas wh I would not let pass
by me. /[verso]/

[1] i.e. as a deacon. On the 19th he signed the Winchester Subscription Book
certifying to the Thirty-nine articles and the next day the Bishop recorded the
ordination as having taken place at his chapel in Chelsea (see H. B. Forster, 'The
Ordination of Edward Young', *English Language Notes*, 1963, i. 27).

Dr Cobb Warden of Winchester College is lately Dead[1]
& our Warden[2] has been so very ill yt we with reason think
of a successor.
Mr Cibber has lately been damnd. his Play is calld
Cæsar in Ægypt.[3] Tis a fit Production for ye banks of ye
Nile where there are monsters,[4] they say, half living & half
inanimate, for This is half Corneille[5] & half Cibber. I am
with ye greatest truth & gratitude

Dear Sr
Yr most Obligd
& most Obedient
Humble Sevt
EYoung.

30. London. [Tu.] 2 March 1724/5. Thomas Tickell.

Surrey MSS. (also Tickell Letterbook, pp. 47–8).—Tickell, p. 104.

Mr Dodington's
Covent Garden[6]
March 2st [*sic*]
1724/5

Dear Sr
When you are entirely at leisure it would be a very great
pleasure to me to hear how things stand in Ireland, Those
I mean in wh I have any concern; This is I grant too great
a curiosity, but very natural to one in my situation.

---

[1] John Cobb had died 25 November. His second wife, Sarah Stukeley (1684–
1760), may have been a first cousin of Young's (see note to letter of 5 June [1727]).
[2] Bernard Gardiner, Warden of All Souls, lived until 22 April 1726, when he
was succeeded by Stephen Niblett.
[3] Colley Cibber's play had opened at Drury Lane Theatre on the 9th and was
ridiculed in the newspapers and later by Pope.
[4] 'The stage carpenter had made plasterboard swans to swim on an imaginary
Nile. When drawn across the stage, they occasioned some ridicule among the
audience' (Alexander Pope, *The Dunciad*, ed. J. R. Sutherland, 1943, p. 416).
[5] The plot was that of Corneille's *La Mort de Pompée* (1642).
[6] Dodington's house in Covent Garden until 1726 was at the north-east corner of
the Great Piazza. It had been remodelled for Dodington in 1720 out of two houses,
one of which had been occupied in 1691 by the celebrated artist Sir Godfrey Kneller.

In yr last very kind Letter you say Dr Burscough[1] has not yet accepted of any preferment; our publick papers gave him a Bishoprick before Xmas, if He has it not pray wt is become of it? Since my Last to you I have set a subscription a foot,[2] wh perhaps it is proper for me to confine on This side the seas. /[verso]/ I wish I had any thing of amusement to communicate to you; but my comfort is, men so employd as you are stand in very little need of it. The Multitude is very angry yt E: Macclesfield[3] is to escape; He last night was at ye Princes court in his birthnight suit,[4] & they in their sagacity forsee yt ye Court is to protect Him.

I hope you will pay my Dutys to my Lord, & Mr Clutterbuck in the manner most proper for me to offer them, & I beg you to take share with them yrself in ye most sincere Esteem & gratitude of   Dear Sr

Yr most Obligd
& most Obedient Humble
Sevt [no signature, paper
torn away]

/[conjugate leaf]/

I write you a Letter of this nature not at all out of Im-[pud]ence, nor alltogether out of Curiosity, for [the] more light I have to conjecture at what is to be expected, the better I can direct my conduct in some particulars wh it is unnecessary to trouble you wth-all.

---

[1] William Burscough was appointed Bishop of Limerick on 31 May 1725 (*Historical Register*, 1725). Swift was to write to Carteret on 3 July 1725 urging the appointment and promotion in the Church of Ireland of men trained in the University of Dublin, an argument which may explain in part at least Carteret's failure to live up to his promise to Young (Williams, 1963, iii. 70–2).

[2] See letters of 10 October 1724 and 5 December 1726 (note).

[3] Sir Thomas Parker (1666 ?–1732), Earl of Macclesfield, had resigned as Lord Chancellor in January of 1724/5 as a result of an investigation which had revealed financial shortages in the Chancery. He was later found guilty and heavily fined. In 1719 Young had dedicated to him *A Paraphrase on Part of the Book of Job*, a pathetic, though unwitting, irony in view of these later circumstances.

[4] i.e. for the celebration of Princess Caroline's birthday, 1 March.

31. [Sa.] 3 July 1725. Thomas Tickell.

Not traced.[1]

32. [Tu.] 27 July 1725. Thomas Tickell.

Surrey MSS.

Dear Sr

'Tis now about a month since I writ to you in answer to
yr last Letter; & I am desirous of knowing how my expectations now stand: For if I have any Certainty or very great
probability of being provided for I could turn ye knowledge
of it to some account: & by yr saying that some Church
preferments have lately faln, (not mentioning how many)
I do not know but yt may be ye Case. At yr leisure therefore
I shd be very glad to hear from you. with all gratitude &
sincerity

                              Dear Sr
                    Yr most Obedient Humble Sevt
                                        EYoung.
July 27. 1725.

/[verso blank, conjugate leaf blank, verso]/ [in margin] Pray
my best services to Mr Clutterbuck.

33. Chiswick, Mdx. [F.] 3 September 1725. Thomas
Tickell.

Surrey MSS.

Dear Sr

In yr Letter to wh my last was an answer, You sayd yt my
Ld Lieut: thought it fit to give some preferments of Irish

---

[1] Evidence of a letter of this date appears in the annotation at the top of Thomas
Clutterbuck's letter to Young of 20 June 1724: 'From Clutterbuck. Enclosure in
Young's letter to Tickell 3 July 1725 (lost).'

gentlemen after his 2 English Chaplains were provided for.[1] and as the promise I had was to be provided for in ye *4th* place, I could not make that promise consistent with such an Intention of my Lords. Imagining therefore that my Lord might have forgot what promise He had been pleasd to make to me, to have Him reminded of it was all I meant, & if I sayd more I misrepresented my own Intention.

I am fully satisfid of yr sincere Friendship, & of yr taking the properest method to effect what you have so very kindly begun. I shall therefore give you no farther trouble on this head, but wait (as you advise) with patience for that /[verso]/ Event wh is to determine ye fortune of my life. I am Dear Sr

Yr most Obligd
& Obedient Humble Sevt
EYoung.

Pray my best Respects to
Mr Clutterbuck

Cheswick. Sepr ye 3d
1725.

34. London. [W.] 29 December 1725. Thomas Tickell.

Surrey MSS.

Dear Sr

Through fear of being importunate I fear I have been rude, in not paying my respect for so long a time; but, I hope, you'll easily beleive tis not thro want of Gratitude or Esteem. I should be much obligd if at yr leisure You let me know what condition my hopes are in; & if it is, now, proper for me to make any fresh Application to Mr Clutterbuck,

---

[1] Almost from the outset of his arrival in Dublin Carteret, abetted by pressure from Swift, made such a deliberate practice of preferring Irish residents to clerical posts, contrary to the policy of Hugh Boulter, Archbishop of Armagh and Primate of All Ireland, that by the renewal of his commission under George II in 1727, Carteret 'was specially excluded from the power of nominating deans' (Basil Williams, *Carteret & Newcastle*, 1943, p. 75).

for your Parliament is, I suppose near rising,[1] & I think at ye End of That you encouragd me to hope my Lord would take some notice of me. But whatever my Lords promises & Intentions /[verso]/ are, unless reminded He may forget; & if I mistake not I have seen four or five Church Vacancys in the publick papers. I am satisfied You have, & will do all yt is proper & kind. I beg you to give my best services & respects to Mr Clutterbuck, & to accept them your self for I am most sincerely

Dear Sr

Yr most Obedient

& faithfull Humble Sevt

EYoung

At Mr Vickers[2] a Stonecutter
o[']eragainst Burlington House
       Piccadilly.

Decem: 29th 1725.

35. [? January 1725/6].[3] Thomas Tickell.

Surrey MSS.

                        [In another hand] 1726

Dear Sr

If any of my Letters gave You occasion to think I imputed to You any negligence of my interest, they misrepresented my meaning[,] twas far from my Thought or apprehension; I only, (as was natural when my All lay at stake,) have taken liberty from time to time to put you in mind [h]ow much I stood in need of yr Friendship; I beg [y]ou therefore for god

---

[1] According to reports in the *Dublin Weekly Journal*, the Irish Parliament was adjourned from 24 December 1725 to 27 January 1725/6 and again adjourned on 8 March to 14 April. In the meantime Carteret is reported to have left Dublin on 28 March and to have arrived in England *en route* to London on 3 April.

[2] Rate books of the London Church and Market Division record payments by a 'Vickers' from 1721 to 1724 on a house in Portugal (later Piccadilly) Street. 'Bankrupts since our last List . . . Edward Vickers, of the Parish of St. James Westminster, in the County of Middlesex, Mason' (*St. James's Evening Post*, 4 August 1726).

[3] The exact date of this letter is conjectural. It was probably some time in January following the adjournment of the Irish Parliament on 24 December.

sake not to turn me over to *powerfull sollicitours* here, for I
have none of them, You & Mr Clutterbuck are all that I do,
or can rely on. I sent You my Ld['s] promise in Mr Clutterbucks own hand;[1] so that You know what my Hopes are &
ye Grounds of them. And it would be a great consolation to
me under my present circumstances to know that Promise is
still rememberd by my Ld; which his great concerns may
remove from his thought, nor can He, I presume, take it ill
to be put in mind of it. I sollicited to attend him before
/[verso]/ the meeting of your Parliament; in answer to wh
You sayd, twas proper I shd wait till the business of Parliament was over, & that acquiescence till then might recommend me the more afterward. That time is now come; I
therefore hope you'll not take it ill, if I humbly beg You
to let Him know
before my Lord leaves Ireland   what Hopes I
conc[eive] from his indulgent promise to me, & to recomm-
[end] me afresh to his Excellencys favour.

I am not so Idle as to think of [a] *ceremonious* Letter but
to know the Result of this would be a comfort to me; for I
am, & very justly, most anxious for ye event. I am with a
full sense of all your favours

> Dear Sr
> Yr most Obedient & Obligd
> Humble Sevt
> EYoung.

36. [Sa.] 12 February 1725/6. [?Thomas Tickell].

Not traced.[2]

[1] i.e. that of 20 June 1724, sent to Tickell in Young's letter of 3 July 1725.
[2] Evidence of this letter is its auctioning by Sotheby's 28 January 1875, as Lot
230: 'A. L. s. 1 page 4to. Dated Feb. 12, 1725. Probably to Tickell, in congratulatory terms.' The congratulations would almost certainly be on the forthcoming
marriage of Tickell.

37. London. [Tu.] 15 February 1725/6. Thomas Tickell.

Not traced.[1]

38. [London]. [Tu.] 1 March 1725/6. Lady Mary Wortley Montagu.

Hartford MS. (Williams) (also in facsimile, Bodleian Library, MS. Montagu, d. 1).—Moy Thomas, ii. 16; Thomas, pp. 591–2; Halsband, ii. 61.

Madam,
  I have seen Mr Savage, who is exstreamly sensible of the Honour yr Ladyp did him by me. You was I find too modest in your opinion of the present you pleasd to make him, if Mr Savage may be allowd to be a judge in the case.[2] Im obligd to go down tomorrow to *Wicomb Election*[3] wh is on Thursday, as soon as I return I will wait on yr Ladyp with the Trifle you pleasd to ask. wh I had done before but I have been & still

[1] Evidence of this letter is its auctioning by Sotheby's 9 March 1870, as Lot 76: 'A. L. s. to [Thomas Tickell]. Over against Burlington House. Feby. the 15, 1725–6.'

[2] The present was evidently some return Lady Mary was making for Savage's dedication to her of his *Miscellaneous Poems . . . by Several Hands*, a volume which Savage had ready for publication in February but withheld until September when it appeared with considerable change in its contents (see Moy Thomas, 1861, ii. 16, and Clarence Tracy, *The Artificial Bastard: A Biography of Richard Savage*, 1953, pp. 75–8). Young's acquaintance with Savage dated at least from 1724, according to Benjamin Victor's observation that he had been introduced to Young by Savage in that year (Benjamin Victor, *Original Letters, Dramatic Pieces, and Poems*, 1776, i. 268). In June 1725 the poem *The Authors of the Town*, now attributed to Savage, was 'inscribed to' Young as 'the author of The Universal Passion'. On 15 August 1726 Savage was to write of seeing Young at Twickenham: 'Since my retirement I have been visited by Dr. Young, who mentions you [David Mallet] often with an affectionate and uncommon ardor' (McKillop, 1958, p. 47). In the winter of 1727–8, Young was to visit Savage frequently during the latter's imprisonment.

[3] An election in Wycombe, Bucks., held 1 February 1725/6 to fill a Parliamentary vacancy had resulted in a contested election and a new one was ordered for 3 March eventually ending in the rejection of the candidate supporting the administration of Sir Robert Walpole. It has been argued that the campaign manager for the Walpole interests was Dodington and that Young's attendance was as his clergyman (Charlotte E. Crawford, 'Edward Young and Wycombe Election', *Modern Language Notes*, 1945, lx. 459–61).

am in all ye uneasiness a Cold can give. I am Madam with
great esteem
                         Yr Ladysp most Obedient & Obligd
                                 Humble Sevt EYoung.
March ye 1st
1725/6.

39. London. [Tu.] 1 March 1725/6. Thomas Tickell.

Surrey MSS. (also Tickell Letterbook, pp. 65–6).—Tickell, p. 106.

                                       At a Mason ag[ains]t[1]
                                        Burlington House
                                          March the 1st
                                            1725/6
Dear Sr
    The frequent trouble I am forct to give my friends by ye
pressure of my affairs I know will meet some indulgence
from you. my present request is, that you would apply to my
Lord Carteret for a grant of ye Deanery of Limmerick in
case it becomes vacant in his Lieutenancy. but that it will
not do, for ye present Dean is to hold it for a year & a half
after his arrival in ye Island of Bermudas, & He does not
propose leaving England till may.[2] my meaning therefore
in this request is, that it may serve me as a foundation to
make the same request to my Lord's successor.[3] wh may
possibly be of consequence to me. The /[verso]/ more
formally therefore this grant is made the more weight it will
        greater
have, & the   use it will be of to me. I shd not be thus
perpetually troublesome, but that the real truth is, that my

    [1] The 'Mason' was Edward Vickers from whose house Young wrote on 29 December
1725.
    [2] George Berkeley (1685–1753) was Dean of Derry, not Limerick, and had
received a charter for a college in America in June of the previous year. It was not
until 11 May of this year, however, that a grant of money was voted and not until
1728 that Berkeley actually left for America.
    [3] Carteret's successor as Lord Lieutenant of Ireland in 1730 was Lionel Cranfield
Sackville (1688–1765), first Duke of Dorset, to whom Young had dedicated the
first part of his *Love of Fame, the Universal Passion*, in 1725.

prudential motive for taking orders was my expectation
from my Lord, & but for that motive it had not been prudent
in me. if therefore I can secure nothing else during his
Administration, I would gladly secure a prospect, & the
method I humbly propose to yr Friendsp is the best, I
think, of doing so. I therefore earnestly entreat This favour
at yr hands wh shall be rememberd for ev[e]r by Dear Sr

Yr much Obligd
& most Obedient
Humble Sevt
EYoung.

Pray my best
respects to
Mr Clutterbuck &c:

40. London. [M.] 23 May 1726. Thomas Tickell.

Surrey MSS. (also Tickell Letterbook, p. 57).—Tickell, pp. 122–3.

At ye Golden & blue ball
in old Bond Street
May 23rd 1726.

Dear Sr
    My Ld Carteret has been so good to renew his promises
to me on Mr Clutterbucks application in my favour; so that
on any likelyhood of a Vacancy in the Irish Church I humbly
hope ye favour of yr quickest intelligences. I must take
leave Now of giving you joy of being Happy & in such
a Lady;[1] I wish I cd take your example in This; as I have
endeavourd to do in matters of less moment. The King has
been pleasd /[verso]/ to give me a pension of 200 ll. per an:,[2]

---

[1] 'The Honourable Tho. Tickell, Esq; was on Saturday last [the 23rd] married
to Miss [Clotilda] Eustace, Daughter to the Lady Eustace; a Lady of 10,000 l.
Fortune' (*Dublin Weekly Journal*, 30 April 1726). The service was performed by
Archbishop Boulter, Primate of Ireland.
[2] On 13 May Young had been granted a pension: 'George R.—Our will and
pleasure is, and we do hereby direct and require, that an annual pension of Two
Hundred Pounds be established and paid by you from Lady Day, 1725, unto
Edward Young, Doctor of Laws, during Our Pleasure, by quarterly payments, in
such and the like manner, &c, &c. Given at our Court at St. James's, the 13th day

which I think it my duty to let you know who have shown
so kind a concern for my wellfare. I am Dear Sr

        Yr most Obligd
         & most Obedient Humble Sevt
           EYoung.

My Lord & Mr Clutterbuck are well.
I beg my best respects & wishes to yr Lady.
Swift has just now entertained ye Town with an Irish Gal-
lantry of his own.[1] He has Rhyme for it &, /[conjugate
leaf]/ I hope, Reason. /[conjugate leaf, endorsement]/
London 23 May 1726
Dr Young.

of May, 1726, in the 12th year of our reign. By His Majesty's Command, /s/R.
Walpole, Will. Yonge, Wm Strickland. To our trusty and well-beloved Walter
Chetwynd, Esq.' (Public Record Office M., p. 529). In connection with this grant,
Thomas (p. 112) noticed in Thomas Hearne's diary (cxiii, 1) in the Bodleian
Library an excerpt from the *Reading Post or Weekly Mercury* for 18 July 1726 an-
nouncing the pension and describing Young as chaplain to [Caroline] the Princess
of Wales. *The London Journal* of 26 July confirms this report: 'His Majesty has
been pleased to grant to the Rev. Dr. Young, Chaplain to her Royal Highness the
Princess of Wales, and Author of the fine Satires, called, *The Universal Passion*, a
Pension of 200 L, per Annum, as an Encouragement to Poetry; which that gentleman has handsomely acknowledged in his Poem on the Instalment.' A further reference to the pension comes from the *Dublin Journal* of the same date: 'There is just
come to Hand a small Poem on Miss Harvey a Child of about a Day Old, in
Imitation of one by Mr. [Ambrose] Phillips on Miss C[artere]t, Written by D.
[*sic*] Young, Author of the Universal Passion, and other beautiful Poems, who for
his late excellent Performances hath obtain'd a Pension of 200 *l*. per Annum.' The
verses 'On Miss Harvey' are included among poems of doubtful authorship in *The
Poems of Alexander Pope* (John Butt, ed., 1954, vi. 441–2) and are reproduced from
a manuscript in the British Museum (Add. MSS. 32463). They were attributed to
Pope by Swift but denied by Pope, and the authorship remains in doubt. Their
playful tone is not characteristic of Young and the manuscript is not in his hand.

---

[1] Probably an allusion to *Cadenus & Vanessa*, which was published in London
on 19 May.

41. London. [M.] 5 December 1726.[1] Thomas Tickell.

Surrey MSS. (also Tickell Letterbook, pp. 64–5).—Tickell, p. 123.

> Boxes Coffee house[2]
> In old bond street
> Decem: ye 5
> 1726

Dear Sr

I have been very long in debt to you for a very kind letter, the advice of which I followd, but not with that success which I know you wishd. However when I waited on my Lord Leiutenant, He spoke very kindly in generals, & I hope still to find ye good effects of yr friendship to me. One reason I payd not my thanks for yr last before was, because I was willing to talk with Mr Clutterbuck first, who is not in town, to which I am just returnd having been absent all ye summer. /[verso]/

This very night the Lord Weighmouth is marryd to ye Duke of Dorsets oldest daughter,[3] wh makes a great noise. The thing is done in form, but ye partys are so young that the ye [*sic*] bridegroom is to travel.

Mr Niblet[4] whom you made interest for a few years agoe to come in fellow at Allsouls is now our Warden.—Jemmy More has a Comedy in rehearsal.[5]

---

[1] The date is clearly written in Young's hand in full. In the Letterbook, the day of the month was omitted, and in its first published version the '6th' was supplied.

[2] An advertisement in the *Daily Journal* of 18 February 1726/7 for a proposed edition of Young's works directed respondents to Boxe's Coffee-House: 'Dr. Young's Works being ready for the Press, such as please to subscribe, are desired to send their Names and first Payment, which is Two Guineas (for Three Volumes, in Quarto, the greatest Part of which was never yet published) to Boxe's Coffee-House, in Old Bond Street; or to Mr. Blandford's, at the London Gazette, Charing-Cross.' The advertisement was repeated on the 20th and 21st and appeared also in *The Daily Courant* and in *The Daily Post* of the same dates. Since there is no further record of such an edition, it must be concluded that this 'subscription' failed of its objective.

[3] Thomas Thynne, 2nd Viscount Weymouth, married Elizabeth Sackville, daughter of the Duke of Dorset.

[4] The names of Stephen Niblett and Charles Bertie had been submitted to the Archbishop of Canterbury who chose the former in the spring (*St. James's Evening Post*, 19 and 28 May 1726).

[5] *The Rival Modes.*

The marriage above mentioned has been carrying on for some time with great secrecy; & took no air till this very day when ye marriage made it not dangerous to be known. I am with ye most sincere esteem & gratitude.

> Dear Sir   Yr most affectionate
> & most obedient Humble Sevt EYoung

42. London. [Th.] 2 February 1726/7. Thomas Tickell.

Surrey MSS. (also Tickell Letterbook, pp. 54–5).—Tickell, p. 124.

Dear Sr

You know how the late vacancys in Church of Ireland are supplyd.[1] I waited on my Lord Carteret on this occasion, who told me twas removing people out of ye way which He must necessarily provide for. You know Sr what promises, by yr friendship, his Lordship favourd me withall, & know better than I how far it has been in his powr to make them good.

Mr Clutterbuck from ye first cautiond me not to go into Orders purely on prospects from my /[verso]/ Lord least they shd fail; but if I was in orders from my own determination, after 3 were provided for, my Ld would provide for me. his second Information was after 3 or 4 & yt He was commissioned by my Lord to give yt answer. Now whatever I shd otherwise have done, after I had such a promise from such a Patron, it was a rational motive to take ye step I took, & it was not in my powr to seperate it from my other considerations in yt matter. & if it had a weight in my determinations, I suffer, if ye promise fails me.

[1] Something of the extent of the 'late vacancys' is apparent in the following notice from the *Dublin Weekly Journal* for 21 January 1726/7: 'We are informed, that the Vacant Archepiscopal See of Cashel is appointed to be filled up with the Rt. Rev. Doctor Nicholson [William Nicolson, 1655–1727], Bishop of Derry; the Bishoprick of Derry with Dr. Downs [Henry E. Downes], Bishop of Meath; the Bishoprick of Meath with Dr. Lambert, Bishop of Dromore; the Bishoprick of Dromore with Dr. Carr, Bishop of Killaloe, who is to be succeeded by the Rever. Dr. Howard, Minister of St. Warbrough's in this City.' Robert Howard (1683–1740), a man of the same age as Young, was made Bishop of Elphin in 1729.

I speak this in excuse for my beging You to continue yr
good
ʌ   Offices to me, of wh Im exstreamlySensible. I know you
writ to my Lord on ye late occasion, & thank, & honour you
for it.

    /[conjugate leaf]/ When You write to Mr Clutterbuck,
if you thought fit to mention ye promises I have had perhaps
it would be of service to

Dear Sr

with ye truest respect & love,

Yr most Obligd

& most Obedient Humble Sevt

EYoung.

Boxes Coffee house
 Old Bond Street
  Feb 2d 1726.

43. [?London]. [Tu.] 21 February 1726/7. Thomas Tickell.

Tickell Letterbook,¹ pp. 55–7.—Tickell, pp. 125–6.

Feby 21, 1726.

Dr Sir/

    Mr Moores Play² is a bad one, yet met thro his Indescre-
tion worse Reception than as a first Performance it deserved.
His Circumstances are very bad, & too great an Eagerness
to mend them by the Profits of his Play made him so pressing
in the Methods he took to do it effectually that it disgusted
the Town.³ He got not £400 by it, which by no Means

---

¹ The original manuscript of this letter is no longer among the Tickell papers,
and its present whereabouts is unknown. The first paragraph was published by
Elwin and Courthope (1889, v. 221–2).

² James Moore Smythe's *The Rival Modes* had opened at the Drury Lane Theatre
27 January. A performance advertised 'For the Benefit of the Author' on the 30th
was called off and the tickets honoured at the sixth night, 3 February (*Daily Post* of
30 January and 3 February).

³ The following anecdote appears in an undated edition of *Joe Miller's Jests*
published by J. Barker: '. . . The late Mr. James Moor Smyth, inheriting some
portion of his mother's humour, undertook to write a comedy, which was called the
Rival Modes, against a third night of which he was very solicitous in disposing of
his benefit tickets, though he had just before a very handsome fortune left him by a

51

answers his Expectations, so that he talks of going abroad, thro the Necessity of his Affairs.

There were some Time since in our public Papers some very good Verses on Cadogans Death, which the Town gives to you.¹ His Sale which is now on Foot is one of the chief Entertainments of the Town. His vast Mass of Plate is for a private Man a wonderful Sight & is visited by all the Town as such.²

Sir Robert Walpole, & my Lord Bolingbroke have lately entertained us with some excellent Papers that publickly passed between them.³ We have had nothing good on the Stage this Season & little of any other Kind. There is a Piece, calld 'Summer'⁴ that has a Degree of Merit in it.

grandfather, but had been pretty free with it: and coming one day, dressed in black velvet, to a lady of his acquaintance, he was very earnest with her to take some, even though she had partly refused him before; Lord, Mr. Moor, said she, this suit of cloaths you have on looks very well, and who would have thought *it is only beggar's velvet*' (p. 102).

¹ According to Tickell's biographer, 'The death of Lord Cadogan . . . on 17th July 1726 . . . was the subject of one of the best of Tickell's poems, and Young's letter is the earliest mention of it which has been found. The full title is *On the Death of the Earl of Cadogan . . .*'. This poem has not been traced in print before 1748, when it appeared in Dodsley's *Collection of Poems* (Tickell, pp. 126 and 195). As the Commander-in-Chief of the army, William, 1st Earl of Cadogan had been a close ally of Carteret's in political struggles with the Walpole government.

² The sale by auction of Cadogan's 'rich Furniture, Pictures, Plate, Jewels, and other valuable Effects' was advertised in the *Daily Courant* and *Daily Post* from 8 February and took place on the four days beginning the 21st. The public was invited to view the 'Goods, Pictures, and Plate' daily and the 'Jewels' on Tuesdays and Thursdays.

³ *The Daily Journal* of 13 February carried the announcement of the exchange in these terms: 'This Day is published, The Occasional Writer, &c. Containing xxx's Letter, and a Reply to it, Paragraph by Paragraph.' A second letter was announced on the 17th and a third on the 24th. Tickell would have been aware of the acrimonious exchange, if not otherwise, through an account of it in *The Dublin Journa* of 21 February, which assigned the 'Reply' to Walpole himself.

⁴ Publication of this poem, eventually the second part of *The Seasons* (1730) by James Thomson, was announced in *The Daily Post* of 15 February as to be 'Tomorrow' and in the *St. James's Evening Post* of the 16th as 'This Day . . . published.' According to a story attributed to Thomson's friend David Mallet, its dedication to Dodington had been arranged by Young (Joseph Spence, *Anecdotes*, 1820, pp. 327–8). That Young was acquainted with Thomson as early as the summer of 1726 is clear from Thomson's mention of him to Mallet in a letter dated from London 2 August 1726 in which he wrote: 'I have racked my Brain about the common Blessing of the Sun You say is forgot, as much as ever S. did his in that elaborate Description of the Tooth-Ach, Dr. Young disconcerted, without being able to hit on it.' It is in this same letter that Thomson quotes Young's *The Instalment* with

Mr Voltaire, a French Author is publishing by an English Subscription an Epic on Harry the 4th of France,[1] as far as I can judge it has a polite Mediocrity running thro it & may be read with little Blame & less Admiration. Pope does nothing, but lives on his acquired Fame, as the Bear sucking on his Paws.—You have Swift with you & all his Wit, for I am one of those few, who think he left but little behind him in *Gulliver* [2] at least of that Kind which I most like.

Mr Pulteney plays a Paper calld the Craftsman[3] agst the Ministry, which for the most Part is very dull. Tho for the Sake of the great Equivalent, Scandal, much read. *Gay* is about some Fables for ye Use of Prince William[4] so that in a short time England will be able to repay Ireland for some . . . . . Poetry,[5] which some Time ago she receivd from thence.—I shall make the best Use of your Advice in your last. I am with the truest Affection & Gratitude Dr Sr &c. EYoung.

the observation that 'The Dr's very Buckram has run short on this Occasion: his affected Sublimity even fails Him, and down He comes with no small Velocity ["]A Star to us, a Comet to the Foe["]' [l. 38 of *The Instalment*] (McKillop, 1958 p. 41).

[1] Voltaire had come to England in the summer of 1726 and had been introduced to the King in January (*London Journal* of 28 January 1726/7). The edition of *La Henriade*, toward which the subscription mentioned by Young applies, appeared in March 1728. He became acquainted with Young, probably through his courting of Dodington, but whether or not the two had met by the time of this letter is not known.

[2] Swift's *Travels . . . by Captain Lemuel Gulliver* appeared 28 October 1726. Young's objections to it were detailed in his *Conjectures on Original Composition* (1759).

[3] *The Craftsman* began publication 5 December 1726. It was conducted by Nicholas Amhurst, with regular contributions by Bolingbroke and William Pulteney, and was designed to embarrass the Walpole administration.

[4] Gay's *Fables*, the first of which appeared in 1727, were inscribed to William Augustus, the six-year-old Duke of Cumberland and third son of George II (now still Prince of Wales). On the accession of George to the throne on his father's death in June 1727, Gay was appointed gentleman usher to the Princess Louisa, a post he declined.

[5] The omission in this sentence marked by five points by the copyist conceals the identity of the 'Poetry', which in all likelihood alludes to the pirated publication in Dublin in April 1726 of Swift's *Cadenus and Vanessa*.

44. London. [Th.] 20 April 1727. Thomas Tickell.

Surrey MSS. (also Tickell Letterbook, pp. 58–9).—Tickell, pp. 129–30.

Dear Sr

Next to sending You News, is to let you know that there is none to be sent; We have Nothing new but a Piece in Blank Verse on ye Death of Sr Isaac Newton, wh is not very extraordinary.[1] Our Weather (you see how I am reduced) is so very fine yt makes a great show of Ladys & Butterflies; last Sunday Kensington Gardens had all in it, yt had a mind to see or be seen; but to ye Dishonour of Christianity a Jewish Lady carryd away all ye Adoration of ye Place.

Our Friend Evans[2] has a Pleasant Parsonage in Surry, but is at odds wth all his Parish, & talks of Law, but is yet got no farther than Epigrams, of wh Apollo is content wth ye Tythe /[verso]/ nor is He in any danger of being su[e]d for the rest.

Mr Conduit Succeeds Sr Isaac Newton but there is some secret consideration of Dr Clarke of St James's ha[n]d in that affair.[3]

The Princess is making herself very fine at Richmond, with Canals, Plantations, Terrases & Popularity.[4]

There have [been] no new Geniuses risen in either of our Universitys since you left us. Sr John Vanbrugh left 3 Acts

---

[1] Sir Isaac Newton died 20 March and was buried on the 28th. The best-known elegy, in blank verse, was that addressed to Sir Robert Walpole by James Thomson (*To the Memory of Sir Isaac Newton*), but since Thomson's poem was not advertised for publication until 2 May (see Douglas Grant, *James Thomson*, 1951, p. 70), Young probably refers to one of several elegies which appeared at this time. Young was one of the Subscribers to Henry Pemberton's *View of Sir Isaac Newton's Philosophy* (1731).

[2] According to the *Dictionary of National Biography*, Abel Evans 'was presented by his college [St. John's, Oxford] to the rectory of Cheam, Surrey, a benefice which had been held by no less than six bishops'. Evans remained the rector until his death in 1737. To Evans is traditionally ascribed the epigram on Sir John Vanbrugh: 'Lie heavy on him, Earth, for he / Laid many a heavy load on thee.'

[3] Samuel Clarke, Rector of St. James's, Westminster, and disciple of Newton, declined the offer to succeed him as Master of the Mint and the post, said to have been worth £1,200 to £1,500 a year, went to John Conduitt, a nephew of Newton's by marriage to Katherine Barton.

[4] After a break with his father, George I, in 1718 the Prince of Wales took summer residence in Richmond where Caroline established a fashionable court. It was here that she built a grotto in 1735 and put Stephen Duck in charge. Young was now her chaplain.

of a Comedy behind him, to wh Cibber is ading 2 more to qualifie Their excellency.[1] Jacob Tonson hopes, He says, you have spent yr time well, He hopes to prey upon you at yr return.[2]

/[conjugate leaf]/ I have payd my constant Duty to my Lord Carteret, but fear ye late Vacancy will make no room for me.[3] What I most desire is to attend my Ld at his return, yr Advice, & Assistance in this will be most kind. with ye sincerest good wishes, gratitude & esteem

I am Dear Sr
Yr most Obedient
& most faithfull Humble Sevt
EYoung

Boxes Coffee house
  Old Bond Street
    Ap: 20th
     1727.

45. [?London]. [M.] 5 June [1727]. Thomas Tickell.

Surrey MSS. (also Tickell Letterbook, pp. 51–3).—Tickell, pp. 130–1.

June ye 5.

Dear Sr

Pope Swift & Arbuthnot are coming abroad in a Triple alliance of Wit.[4] ye work is now in ye Press—Pandit tria

---

[1] Sir John Vanbrugh (1664–1726) had died the year before (26 March). He left *The Journey to London* which was finished by Colley Cibber and renamed *The Provok'd Husband*. Its run of twenty-eight nights from its opening on 10 January 1727/8 is said to have set a record for the Drury Lane Theatre.

[2] Tonson published Tickell's poem: *On Her Majesty's Rebuilding The Lodgings of The Black Prince* in 1733.

[3] Presumably a vacancy produced by another shuffling of clerical appointments following the death on 14 February of William Nicolson shortly after his appointment as Archbishop of Cashel. In a letter of 13 May Swift wrote from England to Thomas Sheridan: 'I hear no News about your Bishops, farther than that the Lord Lieutenant stickles to have them of *Ireland*, which *W*[alpole] always is averse from, but does not think it worth his Trouble to exert his Credit on such Trifles.' Editing this, Sir Harold Williams said: 'Carteret urged the translation of Theophilus Bolton from Elphin, and Boulter, who was successful, the translation of Timothy Godwin from Kilmore' (Williams, 1963, iii. 207).

[4] According to R. H. Griffith's *Alexander Pope: a Bibliography* (1922), the first two volumes of *Miscellanies in Prose and Verse* were advertised as published in the *Evening Post* for 15–22 June 1727.

Cerberus Ora.[1] Swift is under mortifacation for not receiving ye first Visit from our Great men, wh He insists on, & they know their own Interest so little as not to comply, so yt He is like to return to Ireland for Homage, or his Ambition must starve.[2] Pope in his Part abuses Philips,[3] very intrepidly since ye sea is between them. Tompson of York[4] has rusticated his Lady for Gallantrys. Sr W. Yonge is propogating young Players on ye Body of Mrs Hern.[5] Conduit is writing ye Life of his Predecessor Sr Isaac Newton /[verso]/ who has left some Pieces of Divinity wh we expect with Impatience.[6] We have a dull paper calld ye Craftsman wh continues its fire on ye ministry but with little Execution, tho Pulteney, Chesterfeild & Bolingbroke are ye cheif Engineers. Our Universitys are asleep; & ye Church snores; Two or Three at most let their Lights shine before men, ye Rest are content with gloryf[y]ing &c: Gay has just given us some Fables 50 in number, & about 5 are tolerable; I wonder Pope can be so Dull. I wish He had Æsops Head as well as shoulders. Ld Baltamore[7] has been near Death by a Blow from a Tennis Ball to ye great affliction of ye Fair

1 Possibly a combination of two Virgilian expressions: *tenuitque inhians tria Cerberus ora* (*Georgics*, iv. 483) and *pandens tria Cerberus guttera* (*Aeneid*, vi. 421), in any event, meaning that Cerberus opens three mouths.

2 Swift was in England from 22 April this year to 18 September when he was called back to Ireland by the increasing concern of his friends for the health of Esther Johnson, who died 28 January 1727/8 (cf. J. Middleton Murry, *Jonathan Swift*, 1955, pp. 394–402).

3 Young evidently refers to the 'Character' of 'Macer', in manuscript entitled: 'A Short History of Am—— Ph——s,' but not first published until 1728 in the third volume of *Miscellanies*.

4 Edward Thompson (1697–1742), Member of Parliament for the city of York from 1722. When Sir George Savile consulted the Earl of Egmont in 1736 about his wife's behaviour, Egmont compared the situation with the earlier rustication to which Young refers, as 'the case of Mr. Thompson's wife; who being guilty in the same manner as Lady Savile, and sent by her husband to live in a distant place, he was obliged to bring her back to his house' (*Egmont Diary*, ii. 225).

5 Sir William Yonge (d. 1755), politician and playwright. By 'Mrs. Hern' Young refers to the actress Mary Heron of the Drury Lane Theatre company (d. 1736).

6 John Conduitt (1688–1737) collected materials for a life of Newton but left them undeveloped at his death. Two posthumous 'pieces of divinity' by Newton were *The Chronology of Ancient Kingdoms Amended* (1728) and *Observations upon the Prophecies of Daniel and the Apocalypse of St. John* (1733).

7 Charles Calvert (1699–1751), 6th Baron Baltimore, a nephew of Young's future wife, Elizabeth Lee, became Gentleman Usher to Frederick, Prince of Wales, in 1731.

/[conjugate leaf]/ who find no consolation under their misfortune but being beggard at ye Card Table; Money is all
the Dear man has left many of them to lose. I hope yr Irish
Ladys are more commendably employed; [*passage crossed
out which has been deciphered to read*: & yt you find One at
least a better excuse for breaking her Reste.] I never knew
so warm, so universal, & so expensive a pursuit of Pleasure
as at present among us; & yet I find not more Happy men
than formerly; wh confirms me in an opinion wh I have long
had, I mean, that Pleasure cheifly consists in well knowing
in what it is *not* to be found; as true Riches consist in knowing what /[verso]/ we do *not* want; & a great Part of Wisdom
is knowing what we need *not* Know. Painfull discussions of
ye mysterious Part of Religion, & strenuous Idleness in ye
Royal Society, have, I am satisfid given as much Intellectual
Deathbed repentance, as Drury Lane, & Exchange Ally
Repentance of another nature. There, & in Trade, a younger
Brother of Rashlys[1] has lately made a vast Fortune, & He
has bought ye Gainsborough Estate at Wickham in Hampshire, not far from Sr H: Stuckley's[2] yr old Friend. His
Daughter yt ^marryd^ Warden Cob, is since marryd to Mr St.
John of above 5000£ per an: who is a very handsom[e]
Fellow of 60. & she realy a fine woman of 50[.] Tis well for
you yt my Paper's no larger. I am D[ea]r Sr yr most obligd
& obedient H[umble] S[ervan]t EY.

[1] Jonathan Rashleigh (1693–1764), younger brother of Philip Rashleigh (d.
1736), married in 1728, and served in Parliament for many years as the representative
of Fowey, Cornwall.

[2] Sir Hugh Stukeley (d. 1719) of Hinton, Hants. His second wife, Mary, said to
have been the 'daughter of John Young Esq.' (Burke's *Dormant & Extinct Baronet-
cies*, 1844), may have been a first cousin of Edward Young. In any event, their
daughter, Sarah, widow of John Cobb, married Ellis St. John (d. 1729) in 1725 and
outlived a third husband, Captain Francis Townsend, to die in her 76th year at
her home in Winchester on 22 May 1760 (Somerset House, P.C.C. Lynch 407).

46. London. [F.] 17 November 1727. Thomas Tickell.

Surrey MSS. (also Tickell Letterbook, pp. 60–1).—Tickell, pp. 142–3.

Dear Sr.

I have been thus long silent not for want of Respect, but of Matter; We have had no Attempts of any note but Mr Voltare's Epic,[1] which is thought to have Considerable merit; the Author I know well, he[']s a gentleman, & of great Vivacity, & Industry, & has a good deal of Knowledge out of ye Poetical way. Mr Tompson a Scot is writting on ye seasons in blank Verse, tho no Imitator of Milton, what I have lately seen in Mspt, on ye spring[2] has an undoubted Tast, & Merit in it. I was last week at Oxford, where I saw your Friends of Queens, Green, Atkison &c:[3] they all value you as they ought. For want of others writings to amuse /[verso]/ you with, I have sent you a sermon,[4] wh I desire you to accept, & to convey a Copy to Mr Clutterbuck, & my Ld Carteret with my Duty. My Lord when I waited on him spoke not in such a manner as I wishd, & indeed expected; I mention not This either as a diminution of ye services you have done me, which, I am satisfd, are all in yr powr; nor to greive yr Friendship with my illsuccess; but only to let you know a Fact, ye knowledge of wh you will, I know, make ye best use of, you can, to my advantage. My Lord seems to disown that He has made _{any Promise} to patronize me, wh is severe.—/[conjugate leaf]/

We have Vanbrughs posthumous Play[5] in Rehearsal: & they that have seen it, speak of it favourably; Cibber has had ye management of it, & tamen vivit,[6] a great Proof of its excellent Stamina, nor can I give Sr John a greater praise.

---

[1] i.e. The *Henriade*.

[2] James Thomson's *Spring* was published in June 1728.

[3] Samuel Green (Fellow, 1715) and William Atkinson (Fellow, 1717) (J. R. Magrath, *The Queen's College*, 1921, ii. 312).

[4] Young's sermon, *A Vindication of Providence . . . preached in St. George's Church, soon after the Late King's Death* [11 June 1727], had just been published, according to *The Monthly Chronicle* for November.

[5] See note to letter of 20 April 1727.   [6] 'Nevertheless it survives.'

I shall not fail of leting you hear of things of this nature, from time, to time; & shall sincerely look on any new commands from you, as a favour to

Dear Sr

Yr most Obligd

& most Obedient Humble Sevt

EYoung

Matthews Coffee house
Old bond street. Nov: 17. 1727.

47. [?London]. [December 1727 or January 1727/8]. Richard Savage.

Not traced.[1]

48. [?1728]. James Brydges, first Duke of Chandos.[2]

University of Leeds (Brotherton Collection).—*Notes and Queries* (7 February 1863), 3rd series, iii. 109; Thomas, p. 109.

To his Grace the Duke of Chandos.

Accept, my Lord, the Satire wh I send
For who to *Satire* is so fit a Friend?
Others with censure will ye Verse pursue,
And just their hate, to give my Foes Their Due;

[1] Evidence of this letter is from Savage's letter to Theophilus Cibber (*A Collection of Letters and State Papers*, 1756, ii. 675–6), dated 'late December 1727, or early January 1728' (cf. Clarence Tracy, *The Artificial Bastard: A Biography of Richard Savage*, 1953, p. 88) in which Savage wrote: 'Dr. Young today sent me a letter most passionately kind.' Savage had been imprisoned 20 November 1727, tried for murder 7 December, sentenced to death soon after, and pardoned 6 January. *The Daily Journal* of 13 December 1727 reported that 'Mr. Savage and Mr. Gregory are visited daily by the Rev. Dr. Young, Fellow of All Souls College, Oxon.' Joseph Spence attributed to Young the story that 'Mr. Pope desired Dr. Young to forward five guineas to poor Savage, when he was in Newgate for the death of Sinclair; the doctor was so good as to carry it himself: and Mr. Pope afterwards told him that if Savage should be in want of necessaries, he had five more ready for his service' (*Anecdotes*, 1820, p. 356).

[2] James Brydges (1673–1744), first Duke of Chandos, had been mentioned favourably by Young in 1725 in the first part of *Love of Fame* and again in 1727 in *Cynthio*, an elegy on the death of Chandos's son, the Marquis of Carnarvon, who died 8 April 1727 in his 24th year of age. The manuscript is accompanied by the

You safely may support a Muse severe,
And praise Those talents wh You now can fear.
From other Great Ones I can tribute raise
Of *Vice* or *Folly*, to enrich my Lays,
But Chandos, an Unprofitable Thing,
Can nought on earth, but his *Protection*, bring.
                              [In another hand] E. Young

49. [?London]. [M.] 5 February 1727/8. Thomas
Tickell.

Surrey MSS. (also Tickell Letterbook, pp. 62–3).—Tickell, pp. 143–4.

Dear Sr
   Mr Pope is finishing a Burlesque Heroik[1] on Writers, &
ye modern diversions of ye Town, it alludes to Virgil &
Homer thro[ugh]out. The 5th book of Virgil is burlesqud

following letter of 6 December 1786 from Thomas Monkhouse, Provost of Queen's
College, Oxford, to Chandos's grandson: 'My Lord Duke, Having been for some
time in the Country, I could not give a more early reply to your Grace's very obliging letter of the 10th of last Month. I must in the first place beg your Grace's Pardon
for troubling you with such a trifle, and with a letter which was not sufficiently
explicit on the information it was intended to convey. What I meant to acquaint
your Grace with was, That the inclos'd Verses were written by the celebrated Dr.
Young, author of the Night Thoughts &c., and were intended as a general Dedication of his Satires to your Grace's Ancestor, the first Duke of Chandos. His Satires
were first publish'd in a Volume about the year 1730 [1728], and why these Verses
were not prefix'd I cannot inform your Grace, but the probable reason is, that his
Grace might not approve of it. Mr. Croft, the Author of the Life of Dr. Young in
Johnson's Lives of the Poets, who has many of Dr. Young's Papers, makes no doubt
of their originality. I have had them many years, and intended to have sent them
to your Grace long ago, as a small Family Anecdote that might not have come to
your Grace's knowledge, but they were casually mislaid. I inclose the Original for
your Grace's further satisfaction and in case your Grace wishes to preserve it, it is
much at your service, if not, it may be return'd to me. I must once more intreat
your Grace's indulgence for this liberty, and am My Lord Duke Your Graces most
faithful and most obedient humble Servant.' Accompanying the manuscript of
Young's play, *The Revenge*, in the Bodleian Library is a letter from Daniel Perkins,
dated 5 September 1747, in which he says in part: 'The Ms. of Dr. Young's play,
viz. The Revenge I likewise remember. It was amongst the Mss. at his Grace's house
in Cavendish Square [i.e. the Duke of Chandos].... I remember His Grace express
himself with great esteem of Dr. Young' (Rawlinson MSS. Poetry, 229). Young
dedicated his verse *Imperium Pelagi: The Merchant* (1730) to Chandos.

   1 Publication of *The Dunciad* was announced in *The Daily Post* of 18 May 1728.

into games, in wh Booksellers run for Authors, & Piss for
                                                    wise
Authoresses &c; as is like   part of ye 6th by a Vision of
Heroes in Dullness &c: tis near done, & what is done is
very correct. There is likewise in ye press a piece περι
βαθο[υ]ς,[1] wh I have not seen. There's lately published a
Piece calld Night,[2] but there is not in it one single star yt I
can find. The *Excursion*[3] a Poem in Blank verse is in ye verge
of Light; there is some merit in it. Tis by ye Author of
William & Margaret a Ballad.—

/[verso]/ The provokd Husband is now in its 23rd night,
& still in good Health; tho ye real merit of it is not great,
there is very little of Wit, or Humour, or Intreague [in] it,
but it well exposes ye present reigning Vice of ye Town, &
is admirably well playd.[4]

Gay's Beggars Opera[5] has a run, wh is well for him; He
might run if his play did not. Our Party papers wh abound,
have much more venom, than Wit. A pen seems not a
weapon proportiond to ye anger of either side; but no one
yet has been beaten but a poor Printer,[6] who has taken a very
fair Impression himself.

---

[1] The *Peri Bathous; or The Art of Sinking in Poetry* first appeared in the 'last'
volume of Pope's *Miscellanies* announced as published in *The Daily Post* of 8 March
1728.

[2] James Ralph's *Night: A Poem*, dedicated to the Earl of Chesterfield, was published 31 January 1727/8, according to *The Monthly Chronicle*.

[3] David Mallet's *Excursion* was published in March. Mallet had spoken of Young's
having read the first book the year before in May (cf. McKillop, 1958, p. 42).

[4] Young's reference to the 'reigning Vice' is summed up in a line in the play:
'The whole Town is agadding.' In the published version, the author Cibber said:
'The Design . . . [was] to expose, and reform the licentious Irregularities that, too
often, break in upon the Peace and Happiness of the Married State.'

[5] It had opened at Lincoln's Inn Fields on 29 January and was to set a record of
32 consecutive performances.

[6] This would appear to have been William Wilkins (d. 1751), described as 'the
favourite printer of the Whig party . . . [and printer of] *The Whitehall Evening Post*
and several other London newspapers' (Henry Plomer, *A Dictionary of Printers . . .
from 1668 to 1725*, 1922, p. 315). *The Monthly Chronicle* for January 1727/8 had the
following item under the date of 16 January: 'Three Persons sent out for Mr.
Wilkins, Printer of the *London Journal*, to the Crown Tavern in *West-Smithfield*,
and after some Words that pass'd, about an advertisement in a Paper printed by
him, they fell upon him, and beat him with Oaken Sticks, and then made off: Two
of them were taken, and carried before my Lord-Mayor, and appear'd to be *John
Gumley*, Esq; jun. and one *John Beeseley*; who were admitted to Bail for their Appearance at the next Sessions.'

Poor Steele[1] is laughing under a Mountain in Wales, it is all He can do, for he can scarce speak, & in such circumstances, it would be to ye Honor of a wiser man, to be able to do that. /[conjugate leaf]/

I beg You to accept favourably ye sermon[2] I send you (wh before I suppose miscarryd) & to beleive me with ye greatest sincerity

Dear Sr
Yr most Obligd
& most Obedient Sevt
EYoung.

Pray my most Humble Service
to Mr Clutterbuck &c:
Feb ye 5th
   1728.

50.[3] [?March 1727/8]. [?Lady Elizabeth Germain].

Historical Society of Pennsylvania MSS.

Madam.

I can not desire your Ladyships acceptance of ye Trifle I, now, send,[4] without remembering ye Last. I should not have presumd to have made use of your Name without your leave; Nor should I have sought your leave, if I had not had an honour for your Character; nor can I have an honour for your Character, without a concern for your Disapprobation;

---

[1] Steele, retired to Carmarthen, had suffered a paralytic stroke, from which he was to die in September of the next year. In a letter of September 1762, Benjamin Victor said he had been told Steele 'retained his chearful sweetness of temper to the last' (*Original Letters*, 1776, i. 330).

[2] A second edition of Young's *A Vindication of Providence* was published 27 January 1727/8, according to *The Monthly Chronicle*.

[3] This letter was described in Sotheby's catalogue of 12 May 1851 as addressed 'to a Lady on presenting her with Ms. copy of the "Revenge," a Tragedy'. The manuscript of the play accompanied the letter. From the contents of the letter, it is almost certain that the recipient was Lady Elizabeth Germain (1680–1769), to whom Young had dedicated the sixth part of *The Universal Passion*, published 24 February 1727/8.

[4] Unless indeed the trifle was the manuscript of the play, it would doubtless have been a copy of the collected satires under the new title: *Love of Fame*, published 18 March 1728.

which I am under a necessity of perceiving from your entire silence as to That Piece. The grounds of which disapprobation I do not comprehend.

But whatever ye grounds of it are, I shall be well satisfid, if they are consistent with that /[verso]/ real respect I meant to show by Addressing it to to [*sic*] You, & with an Unblameableness in my general Characters: And if it is not consistent with These I assure Yr Ladyship it is founded in a mistake. And You will do me infinite wrong, if You can think so meanly of me, as to imagine this Letter proceeds from any view, but a just concern for my Character, in general, & particularly for Yr Ladyships good Opinion, (not of ye writings) but of ye Integrity, & Respect of Madam

Yr Ladyships most Obedient
& most Humble Sevt
EYoung.

51. [March 1727/8]. Thomas Tickell.

Surrey MSS. (also Tickell Letterbook, pp. 49–50).—Tickell, pp. 144–5.

Dear Sr

The Birthday was very splendid, & full; the Riot & Throng of it was uncommon; but I hear of no mischeif occasiond by it, but ye Death of one gentleman who dropd down with his glass in his hand, & ye publication of two or three Panygericks; wh I dare say you will never see.[1]

Polly a wench yt acts in ye Beggars opera is ye Publica cura of our Noble Youth; she plays her Newgate-part well, & shows ye great advantage of having been born & bred in ye Mint; wh was realy her case. She, tis sayd, has raisd her price from one Gui[nea] to 100, tho she can not be a greater

---

[1] The following account without reference to anyone's death appeared in *The Daily Post* the next day: 'Yesterday being the Anniversary of her Majesty's Birth-Day, who then enter'd into the 46th Year of her Age, there was a numerous Court at St James's to congratulate their Majesties on that Occasion; at Noon the Guns were fired in the Park and at the Tower, and the Evening concluded with Bonfires, Illuminations, other Demonstrations of publick Joy throughout the cities of London and Westminster, and there was a fine Ball at Court.' The same paper of the first of March advertised 'Verses on her Majesty's Birth-Day' by Philip Frowde.

whore than she [was] before, nor, I suppose, a younger.[1]
/[verso]/

The ArchBp of Canterbury[2] who has been ill, sent his compliment to ye Queen on her Birthday by Dr Mead;[3] & let her know he was much better: but his Grace desird Dr Mead not to mention it to any of his Brethern *of ye Clergy,* because it was a day of Rejoyceing.

You see there are Jokes upon ye Bench, & that is all. Tillotson[4] is quite dead; Those among us who pretend to copy him, are like those, in Poesy, who pretend to copy Dryden, they have a little of ye Form but none of ye Powr. We seem content both with ye Genius, & ye Learning of our Predecessors. Nor do I see anything growing up thats [*sic*] threatens any Innovations amongst us. I have been lately at ye University where I wanted a man to converse with, tho our friend Digby[5] was Absent there. Who inverts /[conjugate leaf]/ Terrence: Absens, Presens ut sit.[6] This I mention to reconcile you to Ireland; You cd never be absent at a better time; at a better time I mean for yrself, nor consequently at a worse for me. But yr return will be ye more wellcome to

Dear Sr
Yr most Obligd
& most Obedient Humble Sevt
EYoung.

Pray My humble service
to Mr Clutterbuck &c:

---

[1] Lavinia Fenton (1708–60) played the part of Polly Peachum in Gay's *The Beggar's Opera*, which had opened in Lincoln's Inn Fields 29 January. She became the mistress and later (1751) the second wife of Charles Paulet (1685–1754), third Duke of Bolton. There is no support for Young's scandal. Gordon Goodway in the *Dictionary of National Biography* said: 'Both as a mistress and wife her conduct was commendably discreet.'

[2] William Wake (1657–1737), who had been in office since 1716.

[3] Richard Mead (1673–1754), physician to George II.

[4] John Tillotson (1630–94), Archbishop of Canterbury from 1691. In 1717 a biography of Tillotson was published based on materials left by Young's father, the Dean of Salisbury.

[5] Probably a son of William, fifth Baron Digby (1661–1752).

[6] A reversal of a phrase in Terence's *The Eunuch*: 'præsens, absens ut sies' (I. ii. 112). As Young uses it, it means that although he was away he was as though there in their conversation.

52. London. [Su.] 14 April 1728. Thomas Tickell.

Surrey MSS. (also Tickell Letterbook, pp. 67–8).—Tickell, pp. 145–6.

Dear Sr

I see some church preferment has been lately disposd of.
I know not what to say on that head, no promise could be
more express than that my Lord Lieutenant gave me. His
Lordship, ye papers say, is coming home.[1] If nothing more
material can be done, I humbly beg the favour of You to get
my Lord to make me his own Chaplain as Lord Carteret, on
his return, that I may be entitled to his favour as occasion
offers, on this side ye water.

I send two books[2] as a present to my Lord, ~~Car~~ if you
think such a present may do more good than harm; if you
think otherwise, I /[verso]/ desire ye books may rest with
you. pray my best respect to Mr Clutterbuck. I am with
all gratitude

Dear Sr
Yr most Obligd
& Obedient Humble Sevt
EYoung.

I have no manner of news, but that ye offended wits are
enterd into a club to take revenge on Swift & Pope for their
late Attack,[3] & yt hitherto they have justifid all yt can
be sayd against ym.

Aprill 14th
 1728
Matthews Coffee house
 Old Bond street.

---

[1] An entry in the *Dublin Weekly Journal* of 20 April 1728 under a London dateline of 13 March [?April] states that 'His Excellency, the Lord Carteret, Lord
Lieutenant of Ireland, hath obtain'd his Majesty's Leave to return home.' Carteret
was, however, delayed in reaching England until 23 May (*The Dublin Intelligencer*,
1 June 1728).

[2] Probably copies of Young's sermon: *A Vindication of Providence*, in the second
edition published 27 January, and *The Love of Fame in Seven Characteristical
Satires*, published 18 March.

[3] The third volume of the Pope–Swift *Miscellanies* had appeared in March.
It included the *Peri Bathous* which aroused much angry comment.

53. London. 1728. Unknown.

Not traced.¹

54. [Tu.] 1 April 1729. Joseph Spence.²

Huntington Library, R. B. 131213, ix. 389.—Joseph Spence, *Anecdotes*, 1820, p. 389; Nichols–Doran, *Works*, 1854, I. c; Austin Wright, *Joseph Spence*, 1950, p. 38; McKillop, 1958, p. 63.

Dear Sr
  I promised my Friend Mr. Tompson³ who is now finishing his Subscription in Oxford, all the advantages I could give him; for wch reason I beg leave to introduce him to so valuable an acquaintance as Yrs. Wch freedom I hope You will pardon in
                                          Dear Sir
                                          Yr most obedient
                                          and faithfull Servt
                                                E. Young.
April the first 1729.

55. [?Oxford]. [?F. 25] July 1729. Edward Kinaston.

Not traced.⁴

¹ The only known record of this letter is the ascription to Young in the Sotheby catalogue for 15 March 1888 of Lot 383: 'A. L. s. "The Author," to "My Lord," dated London, Golden Ball, Haymarket (1728). (Copy.)' The letter may have been addressed to Lord Carteret with Young's present of two books mentioned in his letter to Tickell of 14 April 1728, or it may have accompanied the verses to the Duke of Chandos (letter no. 48).

² Joseph Spence (1699–1768), Fellow of New College, Oxford, had been Professor of Poetry in the University from the preceding July. Young was to subscribe to his *Polymetis* (1743), and in 1759 (and probably again in 1765) to entertain him in Welwyn with numerous stories for what has become a source of literary history, his *Anecdotes, Observations, and Characters, of Books and Men. Collected from Conversation of Mr. Pope, and Other Eminent Persons of His Time* (edited by Samuel Weller Singer, 1820, and in 1966 by J. M. Osborn).

³ Proposals for printing James Thomson's *Seasons* by subscription had been first announced in January 1727/8; publication was accomplished in 1730. Spence 'enthusiastically supported the subscription', according to his biographer (Austin Wright, *Joseph Spence, A Critical Biography*, 1950, p. 38).

⁴ This and the next letter are known to have been written to Edward Kinaston (1679–1747) between 25–29 July 1729. Kinaston was an advocate of Doctors'

56. [?Oxford]. [?Sa. 26] July 1729. Edward Kinaston.

Not traced.¹

57. M. [?April–May 1730].² Henrietta Howard.³

British Museum (Suffolk Papers, MSS. 22626, 45 CH2).—J. W. Croker, ed., *Letters to and from Henrietta, Countess of Suffolk*, 1824, i. 284; Nichols–Doran, *Works*, 1854, i. li; Shelley, pp. 100–1.

Commons and a Fellow of All Souls College. On 24 July 1729 the Revd. John Aldworth, Rector of East Lockinge, Berkshire, died. The advowson of the parish being the property of All Souls and Young being a candidate to succeed to the living he wrote to acquaint Kinaston of the vacancy. Kinaston, in a letter of the 29th to Stephen Niblett, Warden of All Souls, wrote: 'Dr. Young first acquainted me with the Vacancy of Locking Living as likewise yt he was a Candidate to succeed, I told him I hoped matters would be made up among Yourselves. I had last post another pressing letter from Him in answer to Which, upon Your appearing for the Living, I have told Him my thoughts this post, that His turn may soon come again and that if I was He, I should this Time be easie And farther that if I was call'd upon as Fellow to act in this Affair I must declare for the Warden' (MSS. in the Archives of All Souls College). Niblett succeeded to the living 5 September 1729. Young must have been especially disappointed in the outcome as Lockinge was close to his ancestors' native pastures. In 1764 a special Act of Parliament annexed the living to the wardenship of All Souls. Toward the expenses of this Act Niblett gave £500, being at that time both the rector of Lockinge and the Warden of All Souls. *The Monthly Chronicle* for July 1730 reported that on 6 July 'The Rev. Dr. *Young*, Author of several Poetical Pieces, and Senior Fellow of *All-Souls* College, *Oxon*, was presented by the said College to the Lordship and Rectory of *Welling* [Welwyn] in *Hertfordshire*, worth about 300 l. *per Ann.*'

 ¹ Evidence of this letter is Edward Kinaston's statement: 'I had last post another pressing letter from Him [Young]. . . .' See notes to preceding letter.

 ² This letter was dated as early as 1727 by Croker and as late as 1733 by Thomas. There are numerous exceptions with either of these extremes, however, and the hypothesis of Shelley that it was written toward the end of 1729 or the beginning of 1730 has more to support it, as will appear in notes to various items mentioned in the letter. The year 1730 was an unusually active year in Young's life. On 26 January he published *Two Epistles to Mr. Pope, concerning the Authors of the Age*; in April he published *Imperium Pelagi, A Naval Lyrick Written in Imitation of Pindar's Spirit Occas[ione]d by His Majesty's Return, Sept. 1729, and the Succeeding Peace*. On 6 July he was given the rectory of St. Mary's Church, Welwyn, Herts., and on 4 August he married Lady Elizabeth Lee (Guildhall Library, MS. 4546, Register of Christenings, Marriages and Burials, St. Mary at Hill 1560–1812). In view of all this activity in Young's life, it seems highly likely that his appeal to Mrs. Howard for some preferment would have been made at this time, possibly between the time of the death of Lady Elizabeth's first husband (Col. Francis Henry Lee) on 26 March and Townshend's retirement in May (see postscript to letter).

 ³ Henrietta Howard (1681–1767), Countess of Suffolk (from 1731), notorious mistress of George II. She was a member of the royal household from before 1714 when George I came to England to her retirement in 1734. It is neither surprising

Moonday morng

Madam

I know his Majestys Goodness to his servants, & his Love of Justice in general, so well, That I am confident if His Majesty *knew* my Case, I should not have any cause to despair of his gracious Favour to me.

Abilities
Good Manners
Service
Age
Want
Suffering⎫
&⎬ for his Majesty.
Zeal⎭

These, Madam, are ye proper Points of Consideration in the Persons that humbly hopes his Majestys favour.

As to *Abilities*, All I can presume to say, is I have done the Best I could to improve them.

As to *Good Manners*, I desire no Favour, if any just Objection lies against them.

As to *Service*, I have been near 7 years[1] in his Majestys, & never omitted any Duty in it. Which Few can say.

As for *Age*, I am turnd of 50.[2]

As for *Want*, I have no manner of Preferment.

As for *sufferings*, I have lost 300 per an:[3] by being in his Majestys service, as I have shown in a *Representation*, which his Majesty has been so Good to read, & consider.

that Young should solicit her help nor, considering her strained relationship with the astute Queen Caroline, that the solicitation was not successful. It is wholly conceivable that this letter is the clue to the explanation of Young's never obtaining preferment under George II.

[1] It was in 1724 that Young took orders as a deacon in the Church, ostensibly for a promise of office in Ireland; it was in March 1725 that he became chaplain to Caroline as Princess of Wales. It was not until 1728 that he was appointed chaplain to George II.

[2] Young seems to have thought he was born in 1680 as he says in a letter to the Duchess of Portland of 2 January 1763 that he was then 'a person of 83'. Also, his death on 5 April 1765 is entered in the Welwyn church register as occurring 'in the 85th year of his age'. Thomas, however, found record of his baptism at Upham, Hants, 3 July 1683 (pp. 5–6).

[3] The £300 may have been as Thomas (p. 134) conjectured: 'sans doute pour avoir refusé un bénéfice offert par son Collège.'

As for *Zeal*, I have Written nothing, without showing my
Duty to their Majestys, & some Pieces are Dedicated to
Them.[1]

This, Madam, is the Short, & True state of my Case.
They that make their Court to ye Ministers, & not their
Majestys, succeed better. If my Case deserves some consideration, & You can serve me in it, I humbly hope,
& believe you will. I shall therefore trouble you no farther,
but beg leave to subscribe my self, with truest Respect,
& Gratitude

Madam
Yr most Obligd
& most Obedient
Humble Sevt
Edward Young.

Madam, I have some Hope yt my
Ld Townsend[2] is my Friend, if therefore soon, &
before He leaves ye Court, You had any
Oppertunity of mentioning me with yt favour
You have ever been so Good to show, I think
I would not fail of success; & if not, I shall owe You more
than any.

58. [?1734-6].[3] Alexander Pope.

Not traced.[4]

[1] 'Some Pieces' would include his sermon *A Vindication of Providence*, first
published in November 1727 and dedicated to the Queen; *Ocean, an Ode occasion'd
by His Majesty's late Royal Encouragement of the Sea-Service, to which is prefix'd,
An Ode to the King, and a Discourse on Ode*, published 8 June 1728; and *The Imperium Pelagi* of April 1730, which though dedicated to the Duke of Chandos is a
professed defence of the King's policies.

[2] Charles Townshend (1674-1738), second Viscount Townshend, shared power
with his brother-in-law, Sir Robert Walpole, until differences over foreign policy
in the spring of 1730 resulted in his resignation and retirement from office in May.
Young speaks as if he is already aware of the withdrawal of Townshend and this
adds to the probability of the conjectural dating of the letter.

[3] The date of the letter was probably soon after the publication of the fourth part
of the *Essay on Man* (1734). In the clamour over the authorship of the *Essay on Man*,
one Dublin publisher attributed it to Young, but there is nothing to show that the
circumstances ever came to Young's attention.

[4] Evidence of this letter is the statement of Joseph Warton in the second volume
of his *Essay on the Genius and Writings of Pope* (1782): 'Mr. Walter Harte assured
me, he had seen the pressing letter that Dr. Young wrote to Mr. Pope, urging him

59. Welwyn, Herts.[1] [F.] 23 February 1738/9. John Williams.[2]

Address: [Lyons, France].[3]

Not traced.—*Gentleman's Magazine*, lvii (May 1787), 371;[4] Nichols–Doran, *Works*, 1854, I. ci–cii; Shelley, pp. 110–11.

Wellwyn, Feb. 23, 1739.

Dear Sir,

Nothing can be more kind than the continuance of your friendship; nothing more unjust than your suspicion of my backwardness to embrace it. I esteem you for yourself, and the good company you keep. Homer was a very honest gentlemen, who talked of many gods, and believed but one. Horace says, *quanto tibi negaveris a Diis plura feres*.[5] Fenelon[6]

to write something on the side of Revelation, in order to take off the impression of those doctrines which the Essay on Man were supposed to convey' (quoted from the 5th edition, 1806, p. 143). Later, in his life of Pope prefixed to the *Works of Pope* (1797), Warton introduced essentially the same statement with the additional comment: 'There was always a friendship betwixt our Author [Pope] and Young; though Harte assured me, that Pope took amiss the pressing Letter Young conscientiously wrote to him', etc. (I. lv). Young paid tribute to Pope in the first of the *Night-Thoughts* and again, at his death, in the seventh 'Night'.

---

[1] Young had become Rector of St. Mary's Church in Welwyn, Hertfordshire, a village 25 miles north of London on the Great North Road, in July 1730. According to the Welwyn historian, W. Branch Johnson (*Welwyn, Briefly*, 1960, and *Welwyn, By and Large*, 1967), Young sublet the church rectory and himself occupied the more pretentious house, Guessens, opposite the church, at first by rental and in 1749 by purchase.

[2] John Williams had been secretary to Richard West, Lord Chancellor of Ireland, from 29 May 1725 to the death of West, 3 December 1726. He later married West's daughter.

[3] As reported in the *Gentleman's Magazine*.

[4] This letter and the following one to Williams were published as the first items in the *Gentleman's Magazine* for May 1787 with the following introduction:

'May 17.

Mr. Urban.

The two following letters of the famous Dr. Young were written to the same gentleman whose admirable letter was printed in vol. LIII p. 222, 3, 4, and are now communicated to you by   INDIGATOR.'

The 'admirable letter' was to the widow of Chancellor West, advising her on the education of her son Richard, poet and friend of Thomas Gray.

[5] Young is here adapting two lines from Horace:

> Quanto quisque sibi plura negaverit,
> Ab Diis plura feret. (*Odes*, Bk. III. xvi, 21–2)
> The more we to ourselves deny,
> The more the gods our wants supply. (Philip Francis).

[6] Fénelon would have been known to Young especially for his *Dialogues des Morts*.

was half an angel; and Newton[1] looked so far and so clearly into Nature, that he found himself under the necessity to clap a God at the head of it, in order to render any thing accountable. As to Voltaire, he is content with the contemplation of his own parts, without looking for any other immortality than they shall give him.

Thus, Sir, my sermon ends: But why this sermon? To shew myself qualified for the deanery or mitre you so kindly wish me. But these things are long in coming. If in your travels you should pick me up a little vacant principality, it would do as well; I am as well qualified for it, and as likely to succeed in it. Monaco would be a pretty sinecure; for, as I take it, the Most Christian King is so good as to do all the duty. I have brought you to the borders of Italy; I heartily wish you all pleasure in the land of Kantys.[2] But before that I hope to be *censured* by you in another letter, which would give me great satisfaction.

You enquire after writers. Here is a libel lately published, called *Manners*,[3] for which the author is fled, and the minister has been reprimanded: there are two or three things well enough said in it to balance a deal of gross abuse. The last publication I have read was about suicide, in which the author endeavours to persuade an Englishman not to hang himself when the wind is N. E.[4] Mustapha,[5] a new tragedy,

[1] Young was among the subscribers to Henry Pemberton's *A View of Sir Isaac Newton's Philosophy* (1728) and had a bust of Newton in his home (see Appendix B).

[2] Italy was the home of many celebrities with the surname of Conti: Antonio-Schinella (1677–1748), a philosopher who, as a visitor at the Court of George I during the years 1715–18 was probably known personally to Young; Joachim (1714–61), a singer who had been appearing in London about this time; Francesco (d. *c*. 1732), composer of the opera *Clotilde* which opened in London in 1709; Francesco (1681–1760), a painter; Ignazio, a composer active in the 1730s.

[3] By Paul Whitehead (1710–74). The *Gentleman's Magazine* (ix. 104) for February 1738/9 reported its publication as follows: 'Monday, 12. The Satire, call'd *Manners*, was voted scandalous, &c. by the Lords, and the Author and Publisher order'd into Custody, where Mr. *Dodsley*, the Publisher, was a Week; but Mr. *Paul Whitehead*, the Author, absconds: He says a certain *Peer* is run *military mad*; it seems he was *poetically mad*, and prophesy'd too true, in these *Lines*,

> Safe may Pope *dash the Statesman in each Line*,
> Those dread his Satire, *who dare punish mine.*'

Libel proceedings were delayed until September.

[4] Young's humorous allusion is too vague to know for certain to what piece he refers, but suicide was a popular subject of discussion at this time. Zachary Pearce had published a *Sermon on Self-Murder* in 1736, and the *Gentleman's Magazine* for

[*Notes 4 and 5 cont. overleaf*]

is treading the stage with some applause. Nothing shoots in
abundance this spring but divinity; a forward plant like the
snow-drop, but of little flavour. I desire you to re-enter me
into your little list of friends; and to be assured that, with
the most sincere affection and good wishes, &c. &c. &c. &c.

E. Young.

60. Welwyn, Herts. [Su.] 25 November 1739. John Williams.

Address: [Nice].[1]
Not traced.—*Gentleman's Magazine*, lvii (May 1787), 371–2; Nichols–
Doran, *Works*, 1854, i. ciii–civ; Shelley, pp. 112–13.

Wellwyn, Nov. 25, 1739.

Dear Sir,
    Letters from the dead[2] are so entertaining, that many wits
have lied their friends out of hell so agreeably, that mankind
has forgiven the imposition, for the sake of the pleasure.
    Next to letters from the dead, are those from the living
at a great distance, and, in some sense, inhabitants of another
world. But, as far as I can learn from your letter, *that other
world* I mean is itself *dead* since I was there, at least, much
out of order. Poor Sun! give him a glass of your pupil's
October,[3] to cure his November dumps; it will make him
gay, and dance as in our Rehearsal;[4] but leave a glass for

May 1737 had reprinted an article 'On English Suicide' from *Fog's Journal* of 14
May, and had published 'Lines against Suicide' by Joseph Smith in August 1738.
    [5] By David Mallet (1705 ?–65). It had opened at Drury Lane 13 February and
had run nightly until the day before Young's letter.

----

    [1] Nice, to which the *Gentleman's Magazine* says the letter was directed, was at this
time a dependency of the kingdom of Sardinia.
    [2] Young refers to a literary genre popular at this time. The publication in this
year of the *Miscellaneous Works* of Mrs. Elizabeth Rowe (1694–1737) may have
reminded him of her graceful dedication to him in 1728 of her *Friendship in Death
in Twenty Letters from the Dead to the Living.*
    [3] i.e. ale made in October. Williams's 'pupil' at this time is not known.
    [4] Buckingham's play, *The Rehearsal* (1671), had been revived at Covent Garden
Theatre in October and was enjoying a considerable success. It was advertised as
being accompanied 'With all the Music, Songs, Dances, Scenes, Machines, Habits,
and other Decorations proper to the Play [and] With Dancing by Mons. Poitier,
and Madam Roland' (*London Daily Post and General Advertiser* of 11 October).
Later performances were described as featuring a 'Grand Ballet', a 'Reprizal',
'English Sailor and Mistress', and a 'Tambarrine Dance called La Badinage de
Provence'.

his holiness the Pope; and, that it may go down with him
the better, you may let him know it is prescribed by the
Council of Nice.[1] When I was there,[2] I contracted a great
intimacy with the Mediterranean. Every day I made him a
solemn visit. He roared very agreeably; I hope our men of
war will soon learn his art for the entertainment of his
Spanish Majesty;[3] this is a kind of opera that will receive
no improvement from the loss of manhood.[4] If here you are
at a loss for my meaning (for I think I am a little obscure),
consult Mr. Patterson's[5] little wife; she will let you into the
secret; for I am mistaken, or our friend P. has taught her to
look on all eunuchs with high disdain, and to detest musick
for the execrable damages it has done the whole sex.

If you visit my quondam habitation, you will pass a solemn
assembly of cypresses; I have great regard for their memory
and welfare; they took up my quarrel against the Sun, and
often defended me from his insults, when he was much more
furious than you now represent him. You are so kind as often
to remember me with Mr. P. When you drink my health,
regard your own. I would have you eat my health, and I will

[1] Young may allude to either of two 'councils'. One was simply the municipal
council of representatives from the nobility, the craftsmen, the merchants, and the
common people. The other was an agreement reached between Francis I and the
Emperor Charles V in restraint of Pope Paul III on a visit to Nice in 1538, com-
memorated by a marble cross erected in 1568 in such a prominent position that it
is said no traveller by land would have missed seeing it.

[2] Young visited Nice in 1736 or 1737 when he had taken his stepdaughter,
Elizabeth Lee, bride of Henry Temple, to the Continent for her health only to have
to bury her at Lyons, 8 October 1736. Apparently he was still abroad on 19 January
1736/7 when the Vicar of neighbouring Furneaux Pelham, Herts., Charles Wheatly
(1686–1742), wrote to the antiquarian, Richard Rawlinson: 'Dr. Young I know
well. . . . I hear he is gone with his Lady to drink the waters at Aix la Chapelle
[Aachen, Germany]' (Bodleian Library, MS. Rawlinson Letters 29, f. 445).

[3] England had declared war on Spain 19 October 1739.

[4] Young's allusion is to the notorious Italian *castrati*. Charles Burney commented
on the practice as follows: 'I enquired throughout Italy at what place boys were
chiefly qualified for singing by castration, but could get no certain intelligence. . . .
The operation most certainly is against law . . . and all the Italians are so much
ashamed of it, that in every province they transfer it to some other' (*The Present
State of Music in France and Italy*, 1771, pp. 301–2).

[5] James Paterson (1692–1765), Scottish military representative of the King of
Sardinia in Nice. He is thought to have been in England from the summer of 1737
to the spring of 1738 and to have married Deborah Bowdler (1698–1782) of Bath
during this visit. Since Young could not have met Mrs. Paterson in Nice, it is
probable that he met her on his return, possibly at Bath which he is known to have
visited in 1737 or 1738.

drink yours: the north wants spirits; and the south, flesh; but take care you get not more than your own. There is great plenty in Italian markets, and it comes cheap; if any thing can be called cheap which may possibly cost a whole Roman nose.[1] I hope you have nothing of Rome about you but that noble feature; if you have, post away to his Holiness. No man makes more Protestants than the Pope, or more saints than the devil, when either of them is thoroughly known; for truth and virtue have no better friends upon earth than a near inspection and intimate acquaintance with the deformity and madness of their opposites. This, dear Sir, comes of your conversing with parsons; I forgot I was writing a letter, and was providing myself for next Sunday with a sermon against drinking, wenching, &c. &c. Pardon a friend's infirmity, and manfully bear your own calamity. May this be the greatest you meet with in your travels, and then you need not be in haste to return to your farm in Wales! My best wishes and services to Mr. P. &c. Lady Betty[2] sends compliments to you and Mr. P. &c. &c. I am, dear Sir, your obliged and affectionate humble servant,

E. Young.

61. Welwyn, Herts. [F.] 7 December 1739. Edmund Curll.

Bodleian Library (MS. Rawl. Letters 90, f. 72)—Shelley, p. 114.

Wellwyn
Decem 7th
1739.

Sr

I receivd the favour of Yours & have nothing more to say than This,[3]—You seem in the collection You propose to

---

[1] i.e. from syphilis.

[2] Young's wife, Lady Elizabeth Lee, died at her brother's London home in Hanover Square only two months later.

[3] The extraordinary bluntness of this letter is understandable in view of Young's public altercation with Curll in 1717. The present exchange of letters was unquestionably begun by Curll and includes, besides this letter, two others, those of 18 Decem-

have omitted what I think may claim the first place in it, I
mean a Translation from Part of Job printed by Mr Tonson.¹

I am Sr

Yr humble Sevt

EYoung

I am heartily sorry for
poor Mr Worrall.²

ber 1739 and 4 August 1740. The aftermath was the publication in January 1741
of *The Poetical Works of the Reverend Edward Young, LL.D.*, in two volumes,
'Printed for Messieurs Curll, Tonson, Walthoe, Hitch, Gilliver, Browne, Jackson,
Corbett, Lintot and Pemberton', dedicated by Curll to the Right Honourable Lord
Carpenter. An inscription 'To the Reader' stated: 'That this Collection of Dr
Young's Poetical Pieces, is published with his Approbation, and under his own
Direction, will sufficiently appear from his Kind Wishes, for its Success, expressed
in the following Letter, viz.

To Mr Curll,

Wellwyn, Dec. 9th, 1739.

Sir,

I received the Favour of yours, but am, at present, not at Leisure to review what
I formerly wrote*.

You seem in the *Collection* you propose, to have omitted what I think may Claim
the first Place *in it*, I mean, *A Translation from Part of Job*, printed by Mr *Tonson*.

I have no Picture†, or it should be at your Service; nor have I the *Epistle to Lord
Lansdowne*: If you will take my Advice, I would have you omit *That*, and the
Oration on Codrington: I think the *Collection* will *sell better without them.*‡

I heartily wish you Success in your Undertaking.

I *am, Sir,*

Your Humble Servant,

E. Young.

* A particular Friend of the Author's has reviewed and prepared all these Pieces
for the Press. †The Doctor was requested to let his Picture be engraven. ‡This we
cannot comply with, as rendering our Collection imperfect.'

The so-called letter from Young thus published in the collection of his works
will be seen to be a composition of extracts from the present letter and those of
18 December 1739 and 4 August 1740.

¹ *A Paraphrase on Part of the Book of Job* (1719) was included in the collection.

² Thomas Worrall (d. 1767) had published Elizabeth Rowe's *Friendship in Death*
(1728), dedicated to Young, as well as three of Young's own works: *A Vindication
of Providence* (1728), *Ocean, an Ode* (1728), and *An Apology for Princes* (1729). In
Literary Anecdotes of the Eighteenth Century (1812, iii. 740–1), John Nichols said
of Worrall that he 'unfortunately laboured under a mental derangement, which
terminated his life Sept. 17, 1767'. Young's expression of concern for him suggests
that Curll had reported Worrall's condition and perhaps his commitment to a mad-
house. This would explain the omission of Worrall's name from the congeries of
publishers listed under note no. 3 above.

62. [Tu.] 18 December 1739. Edmund Curll.

Bodleian Library (MS. Rawl. Letters 90, f. 73.)—Shelley, p. 114.

Sr

Be assurd I bear You no Illwill, I heartily wish you all success in yt undertakg, But am at present not at leisure to review what I formerly writ.[1]

I am Sr
Yr Humble Sevt
EYoung

Decem 18th
1739.

63.[2] [?London]. M. [?4 or 11 February 1739/40]. Lady Oxford.

University of Nottingham (Portland MSS.).

[In another hand] (1741)[3]

Madam

I very thankfully acknowledge yr Ladyship's kind Enquirys after me, under my Affliction: The compassionate

---

[1] Young's wife may already have been taken ill. Young was either in London at this date or about to go there. An extraordinary storm and cold spell struck England the day after Christmas. Young was absent from the vestry meeting of his church on 3 January and is known to have been with his wife at her death in London on the 29th.

[2] According to J. H. Hodson, Keeper of the Manuscripts in the University of Nottingham, this letter is 'filed amongst letters to the 2nd Duchess of Portland'. Without question, however, it was addressed originally to the Duchess's mother, Lady Henrietta Cavendish Holles (1693–1755), wife of Edward Harley (1689–1741), the second Earl of Oxford. It was obviously written soon after the death of Young's wife, and before Young left London for East Sheen, from where he wrote to the Duchess of Portland on Wednesday, 20 February.

[3] The added date is an apparent mistake for 1739/40, based on the erroneous dating of the death of Young's wife initiated by the article on Young in the *Biographia Britannica* of 1766 and perpetuated by innumerable citations thereafter. Notices of Lady Elizabeth's death appeared in the London papers for 30 January 1739/40, of which that in the *London Daily Post and General Advertiser* is an example: 'Yesterday died at her House in Hanover-street, Hanover Square, the Lady Elizabeth Young, Wife to the Rev. Dr. Young, and sister to the Right Hon. the Earl of Litchfield.' This date is also confirmed by an entry in the parish register of St. Mary's, Welwyn, for the year 1739/40, which reads: 'Janu[ary]: 29: the Right Honorable Lady Eliz[abeth] Yo[u]ng.'

regard of the Worthy is all the consolation Earth can give;
But Earth Alone will be found a poor Comforter under real
Distress. I am, Madam, preparing to leave in a few Days this
Place, in quest of That which I fear I shall not find: I go
not Home, I could no more bear the sight of that, than of
One whom *she* justly held as her Truest Friend,[1] & to whom

---

[1] The only known letter of Young's wife has recently turned up among manu-
scripts at Welbeck Abbey in possession of the Duke of Portland. It is addressed to
Lady Oxford in 1728 when Lady Elizabeth was the wife of her cousin, Francis
Henry Lee (1695–1730), as follows:

Agust ye 12/1728

Deare Madam
    when I had the pleasure of seeing you last, you desined to go to the bath the
latter end of this month, and I was in hopes of haveing the happyness of meeting
your Ladysp theire; but I am afraid I shall not have that pleasure; for I have bin
much better in my health since I came heare then I was and as my afairs are not
ended to my expectation so I am afraid I shall not go; it will be to expencive a
Jorney for me at this time; I am very sorry that I cant go because I proposed
agreable pleasure to my self in haveing agreable deale of deare Lady Oxfords
company; but I hope to heare that the bath has don your Ladysp agreable deale
of good and I have another wish which I belive your Ladysp may guess; I hope to
be in town by that time the bath season is over and to have the pleasure of seeing
your Ladysp theire but it is not quite certaine that I shall not be at bath; for I will
if posible; I live avery dull life heare I have bin oute but twice since I came; which
is aboute three months but I have the pleasure of keeping my sister company who is
confind being with child; my sister Litchfield [verso] is very ill of a fever last Letter
I received from Mr Lee he desird his humble Service to your Ladysp and he
d[es]ires to know if your Ladysp has any service to command in Scotland he proposes to be at home the Latter end of Sept I should be glad if your Ladysp would
be so good as to favour me a line and some commands being with the sincerest
affection

> Deare Madam
> your most obligd
> Humble Servant
> E Lee

pray give humble
service to my Lord
and Lady Margaret
if your Ladysp will be
so good as to direct for
me at Mr Brownes at
Kiddington neare Enston
    Oxfordshire

The 'Mr Browne' in the postscript was George (later Sir George) Browne, husband
of Elizabeth's sister Barbara (b. 1696). The 'Lady Margaret' was the only daughter
of the Earl of Oxford. She was now in her thirteenth year and was to become the
second Duchess of Portland six years later. Kiddington is adjacent to Ditchley, the
family home of Elizabeth and Barbara.

she bequeathed her tenderest Wishes: Such is my Weakness that I could not see Yr Ladyship, at present, without the greatest disorder. O Madam, God of his mercy preserve yr Heart from Sorrow: I am with a Respect and Gratitude which I shall not endeavour to express.

> Madam yr Ladyships
> most obedient, & ever faithfull
> Humble Sevt
> Ed Young.

I beg my Duty to my
  Lord
    Moonday morning.

64. [?London]. Tu. [?5 or 12 February 1739/40].[1] Duchess of Portland.[2]

Longleat MSS. (1) 5.

May It please Yr Grace
              a little way
    I am going   out of Town in hope of finding some releif from change of Place, but I could not go without returning Yr Grace & my Lord Duke my most humble Thanks for yr kind Notice of me in my Distress. God pre-
                                                  you
serve your Hearts from sorrow, & long continue   a
                                            a
mutual Comfort to each Other, wh is   Blessing Few know

---

1 This letter, like the preceding one, was obviously written shortly after the death of Young's wife on Tuesday, 29 January, and of course may have been written on the day of her death, and if so would have been written before the letter to Lady Oxford.

2 Margaret Cavendish Harley (1715–85) was the only daughter and heir of the second Earl of Oxford. As a child of six she had been addressed by Matthew Prior as 'lovely Peggy'. In 1734 she had become the wife of William Bentinck (1709–62), second Duke of Portland. She is the subject of Austin Dobson's 'Prior's Peggy' in the *National Review* for March–August 1913 (lxi. 701–17). Young could have known her either through his wife's acquaintance with her mother or through his own long acquaintance with the Temple family, as Henry Temple's aunt, Jane, was the second wife of the first Earl of Portland.

how sufficiently to value, till It is lost. I am with ye truest respect

> Madam
> Yr Graces most Obedient
> & Obligd Humble Sevt
> EYoung.

Madam I beg my
Duty to His Grace.
I shall take care of yr Graces Books.
    Teusday morning.
    [In another hand] 1739/40

65. East Sheen, Surrey.¹ [W.] 20 February 1739/40. Duchess of Portland.

Longleat MSS. (2) 6.

Madam

I had the Honour, & Consolation of your Grace's kind letter; The Notice of the Great is valueable; the Notice of the Worthy is Pretious. I shall certainly wait on Your Grace as soon as my Heart will permitt me. Madam I beg my most humble Respects to my Lord Duke, & to my Ld & Ly Oxford if You see them. May God allmightys blessing preserve your Grace, & Family in Health & Peace. I am with great Truth, Gratitude & Respect

> Madam
> Yr Graces most Obedient
> & Obligd Humble Sevt
> EdYoung.

East Sheen
Feb. 20th
[In another hand] 1739/40

¹ Young was visiting Henry Temple, presumably at the home of Temple's father, the first Viscount Palmerston (?1673–1757). Temple had married Young's step-daughter, Elizabeth Lee, 24 June 1735. He was now married (12 September 1738) to Jane Barnard, daughter of Sir John Barnard (1685–1764), recent Lord Mayor of London.

66. Welwyn, Herts. [W.] 21 May [1740]. Judith Reynolds.[1]

Address: To Mrs Reynolds.[2]
Huntington Library MSS. 22198.—Swedenberg, p. 91.

Wellwyn. May 21.
Dearest Madam.

I am detaind Here necessarily till Teusday next. On Wensday morning I propose the great Happiness of waiting on You in Norfolk street, And I hope in God we may then talk together to our mutual satisfaction, on the most importtant Point in human life. I wait with impatience for that Hour, wishing You, in ye mean time, All that Human Prudence, & Heavens favour can bestow. I am with the truest Affection & Esteem

            Dearest Madam
              Yr most Obedient
              & most Humble Sevt
              EYoung.

Pray my best Respects
to Mr & Mrs Godscall.[3]
I hope Miss[4] is better.

[1] Judith Reynolds (1690–1755), daughter of Robert Reynolds of Bury St. Edmunds, Suffolk, related through her mother to the Herveys of Ickworth. In 1781 she was described by an apparently biased member of her family as having been 'a Woman of good sense, but of a high spirit—charitable, if a promiscuous distribution of Money may be called Charity, but of an unforgiving Disposition towards those who had ever offended her & tyrannical to all in any manner dependant upon her' (Swedenberg, p. 91).

[2] The address shows the letter was not publicly posted.

[3] Nicholas (d. 1748) and Sarah (d. 1750) Godscall. In his will (Somerset House, P.C.C. Strahan 177), Nicholas called himself 'citizen and ironmonger of London'. The Godscalls lived in East Sheen near the Temples.

[4] The Godscall daughter Sarah (b. 1730) was to become (1750) a ward of her uncle, Sir John Barnard.

67. [East Sheen, Surrey].¹ [Th.] 29 May [1740].
Judith Reynolds.

Address: To Mrs. Reynolds at / Mr Townsends in / Norfolk Street / In the
Strand.² *Postmark*: Peny Post Payd Stone. Huntington Library MSS. 22199.
—Swedenberg, pp. 91–2.

                                                          May 29th
Dearest Madam.
 Be most assurd I have for You the truest Affection &
Respect; But I have some Difficulties which, at present,
much perplex me: & which I wish to see removd before You
mention to your Brother³ the Affair that is between us: As
You hourly expect Him, I thought it prudent to write This
before I left ye Town: As soon as the Difficulties are removd
I will let You know it: In the mean-time, I beg You to have
as favourable an Opinion of me as You can, till I have an
Oppertunity to Explain. With an infinite sense of the high
Obligation I lie under to You, I am from my soul
      Dearest Madam
       Your most Obedient
       & most Humble Sevt
       EdYoung.

 ¹ That Young wrote from East Sheen is known from the postman, 'Stone', whose
name appears regularly on letters from East Sheen.
 ² Rate books in the Westminster Public Library identify the house as that of
Joseph Townsend in Norfolk Street (St. Clement Dane Parish, 20 June 1740), just
off the Strand to the east of Somerset House. A Joseph Townsend, brewer, is listed
as a London voter, 7 December 1724 (*Daily Journal*).
 ³ James Reynolds (1684–1747) became secretary to Robert Walpole 1 July 1724
(*Daily Journal*) and three years later Lord Chief Justice in the Court of Common
Pleas in Ireland and Master of the Exchequer's office. Just a few weeks before Young's
letter it was reported that Reynolds was to be appointed a Baron of the Exchequer
(*London Daily Post and General Advertiser* of 16 April), an office with which he was
invested in June. He was knighted in 1745 and at his death in 1747 is reported as
having left a considerable fortune to his sister.

68. East Sheen, Surrey. [Su.] 1 June [1740]. Judith Reynolds.

Address: To Mrs Reynolds / at Mr Townsends next Door / to the Golden Key In / Norfolk Street / In the Strand. *Postmark*: Peny Post Payd Stone. Huntington Library MSS. 22200.—Swedenberg, p. 92.

June ye 1st
Mr Temples at
Eastsheen.

Dearest Madam

I know not if Mr Godscall told You, that on some Particular Accounts it is of the greatest moment to me that our Affair shd remain a secret, till a proper season: I want to explain to You my last Letter, which it is impossible to do sufficiently, but by talking with You: And yet I am afraid to visit You again, least our Acquaintance shd take air, in this curious World, sooner than It is Decent for me to have it Known.[1] However if You, Madam, ~~You think~~ that You cd apoint me at an Hour, when no Notice will be taken; please to let me know it, & I will be Punctual to a moment: If not, I must defer the Happiness of seeing You, & the Justice of explaining to You till I return from Tunbridge: But I had much rather, if I cd without giving suspicion, wait on You before I go. I beg the favour of a line from You as soon as possible, directed to This place; Please to let me know how yr Cold does; & if Yr Brother is arrivd.[2] All Here are pretty well. /[verso]/

I am just now come from Mr Godscall; Miss is Better.

I am Dearest Madam
with entire Esteem & Affection
Yr most Obligd
& most Obedient Sevt
EYoung.

Madam You know your own servants best; if They are not likely to suspect, tis certain No One else will. I leave ye

---

1 The allusion is patently to the death of Young's wife only three months earlier.

2 Reynolds arrived in London the next day, according to a report in the *Daily Advertiser* for 5 June.

Apointment therefore entirely to your Discretion: And shall
onely ad, that if it is Proper, It wd be to me ye greatest
Pleasure to wait on You soon.

69. East Sheen, Surrey. Th. [?5 June 1740].[1] Judith Reynolds.

Address: To Mrs Reynolds at / Mr Townsends in Norfolk / Street in the /
Strand. *Postmark*: Peny Post Payd Stone.
Huntington Library MSS. 22201.—Swedenberg, pp. 92–3.

                                                 Thursday
                                                 Eastsheen.

I receivd, Dearest Madam, your kind Letter with ye
greatest pleasure; & shall onely say to express my thanks for
it, That all Ladys have not ye same just, & indulgent sentiments with yrself.

Either, Madam, my Inclination imposes on my Judgment, Or I think, a *second* Visit can not give suspicion; I am
therefore determind on it, if You give me leave: Your
Brother is sometimes abroad, & his servants with him; If
his Motions are at all regular, You can chuse an Hour for
Our purpose. Please, Madam, to apoint ye Day & Hour, &
if it please God, I will be Punctual to it.

I desire You to direct your Letter to Mr Temple, & drop
a Blot (as thus •) on ye superscription, & I shall be sure to
have it unopend: And ye sooner I receive it, the Kinder it
will be to
                         Dearest Madam
                         Yr most Obedient
                         Obligd Humble Sevt
                         EdYoung.

        [1] The date is evident from the next letter.

70. East Sheen, Surrey. [Tu.] 10 June 1740. Judith Reynolds.

Address: To Mrs Reynolds.
Huntington Library MSS. 22203.—Swedenberg, p. 94.

Eastsheen
June 10th
1740.

Dearest Madam.

In return to ye favour of yours, I writ to You on Thursday last, but having receivd on answer, I suppose It might not come to hand. If It did I beg the favour of an Answer to it; & that You would direct it to Mr Temple, who will be sure to give it me Unopend, for I have showd Him yr superscription, & He will know your hand.

If You did not receive it, I beg You will apoint what Day & Hour I shall wait on You; For I apprehend I may make You one Visit more, without giving suspicion; especially, if at a time when your Brother is from Home. And I have the greatst desire of ye Happiness of seeing You before I leave You for so long a time. /[verso]/

That This, Madam, may be sure of coming to You, Mr Temple is so good as to deliver it Himself.

Whither what, I propose, of seeing you witht giving suspicion, be practicable, You, perhaps, are a better Judge than myself: If it is, I hope Youll be so good as to make me Happy in it. For I am most cordially

Dearest Madam
Yr most Obedient
& Obligd Humble Sevt
EdYoung.

71. East Sheen, Surrey. [?Su. 15] June 1740.[1] Judith Reynolds.

Address: To Mrs Reynolds at / Mr Townsends in / Norfolk Street In / The Strand. *Postmark*: Peny Post Payd Stone.
Huntington Library MSS. 22202.—Swedenberg, p. 93.

Dearest Madam It gives me pain that I can not see You. I kiss your Letter tho It brings that Ill news.

A cheif Difficulty that presses me, is a Fear least I expect more from You, than you may be willing to undertake. Madam, the Case stands thus; & Mr Temple told Mr G——ll[2] of it: I never yet had any hand in Family Affairs, & have no Turn for them: All Receipts & Payments of Money &c: was ye Province of my Wife: How far This may suit with your Temper or Inclination, I am at loss to know: & beg ye favour of You to write freely to me on this Point: For I think it not fair too desire anything of You after our meeting, which was unmentioned before.

Since, Dearest Madam, all the pleasure I can hope from You, for some time is by writing, I beg You to indulge me as much this way as You can: I mean by writing to me as soon, & as largely as You can.

/[verso]/ I thank You for the *Book*; & ye prudent Use You made of It: And I thank you still more for telling me yt your Health is mended, which will ever be most dear to

Madam
Yr most Affectionate
& most Obedient Sevt
EdYoung

Eastsheen
June 5th
1740.

---

[1] The letter is clearly dated June 5th, but since Young has now heard from Judith and goes on to explain a situation which he has only alluded to before, it seems probable that he accidentally wrote 5th for 15th.
[2] i.e. Godscall.

72. [?W. 18 June 1740]. Judith Reynolds.

Not traced.[1]

73. Tunbridge Wells, Kent. [W.] 2 July 1740. Judith Reynolds.

Address: To Mrs Reynolds / at Mr Townsends / In Norfolk Street / In the Strand / London. *Postmark*: 3/IY.
Huntington Library MSS. 6835.—Swedenberg, p. 94.

Tunbridge
Wells
July 2d
1740.

Dearest Madam

I was thrice at Mr Godscalls during yr stay at Sheen, in hopes of ye Pleasure of meeting You there; But being disapointed I hope ye Happiness of soon hearing from You. It will very particularly oblige me for I am, since I came hither, much indisposd, & I know no Consolation like hearing from a Friend. Was I not ill, I wd give You some account of our Company &c: But this I must defer till my next: I beg the favour to know how long You continue where You are; & to wt Place you make yr next Remove. For I hope ye favour of yr Correspondence, & that You will beleive me to be

Dearest Madam
Yr most Obedient & Affect:
Humble Sevt   EYoung.

[1] The eighteenth-century manuscript catalogue of the Young–Reynolds correspondence (Huntington Library MSS.) mentions a letter with the description: 'Tunbridge Journey put off for a few days.' It was offered for sale by the City [i.e. New York] Book Auction, 19 February 1949, but has since disappeared. The letter was said to have been dated 'Thursday 18th June', but Thursday fell on the 19th in 1740. Since Young almost never wrote both the day and the date, it would appear to have been a mistake of the cataloguer.

74. [Tunbridge Wells, Kent]. [M.] 21 July [1740]. Judith Reynolds.

Address: To Mrs Reynolds / at Mr Townsends in / Norfolk Street in The / Strand / London. *Postmark*: 23/IY.
Yale University Library (Osborn Collection).

Dearest Madam
　　I question not yr Address in the method of Applying to yr Brother. Tho Circumstances are commodious, the Happiness of Life must be cheifly owing to Prudence & Piety: Providence has taught me by long, & severe Experience that nothing can give real Happiness in this Life, but what will at ye same time promote our Happiness in the next. I much thank You for yr kind Wishes, but my Health is yet far from being reestablishd; But God is Gracious to ye Worst, & I despair not of his great mercys. It will be a great Comfort to me to hear from You at yr leisure. The Loss of a Friend[1] brought this Disorder on me, & I hope finding another may prove my Cure. With ye Sincerest good Wishes from

　　　　　　　　Dearest Madam
　　　　　　　　　Yr most Obedient & Obligd
　　　　　　　　　　Humble Sevt　EYoung.
July 21.

75. [Tunbridge Wells, Kent]. [Su.] 3 August [1740]. Judith Reynolds.

Address: To Mrs Reynolds / at Mr Townsends / In Norfolk Street In the / Strand / London. *Postmark*: 7/AV.
Huntington Library MSS. 22204.—Swedenberg, p. 95.

　　　　　　　　　　　　　　　　　　　　Aug. 3d
Dearest Madam.
　　I thank You for ye favour of yr last, & am sorry You was interupted; for the longer yr Letters are, ye Kinder; reading them is ye cheif Pleasure I have at this Place: What is a
Multitude to ᵃman of my Age? Indeed at any age all real

────────
[1] An allusion to his wife's death seems intended.

87

Happiness is from ye Commerce of Particulars. Are not You, Madam, of ye same opinion?

Methinks I grow better acquainted wth You by ye favour of yr Letters; & I am satisfid it ^{is} yr Interest to be as well known as possible. I propose staying Here till ye End of this Month, wh is longer than I designd, but as ye Waters have not yet answerd, I am willing by length of Time to give them fair Play: Mr & Mrs /[verso]/ Godscall are a Happy Pair, & Happiness gives Alacrity, & Alacrity is enterprizing, I shd not therefore much wonder if they went farther afield; their Hearts are at home in each other where ever they go. It is a Pleasure to me to see such Instances of Human Felicity: Perhaps You think they are Rare; It is true they are too Rare; but they are just a[s] common as *Prudence* & *Virtue*, in ye World.

We have had Here excessive Rains wch have given me a sorethroat. I hope You have nothing to complain of as to yr Health. It wd be a great Pleasure to me to hear my Hopes are not mistaken. I am wth all Affection & Esteem Dearest Madam

Yr most Obedt & Obligd
Humble Sevt   EYoung.

76. Tunbridge Wells, Kent. [M.] 4 August 1740. Edmund Curll.

Bodleian Library (MS. Rawl. Letters 90, f. 74).[1]—Shelley, p. 114.

Tunbridge Wells.
Ausgt 4th

Sr

I receivd not yrs till yesterday. I have no Picture,[2] or it shd be at yr service; Nor have I ye Epistle to Ld Lands-

---

[1] The manuscript of this letter shows Curll's editing of it for use in the composite letter he prefixed to his collection of Young's works in 1741, and not, as Thomas supposed (p. 143 n.), evidence of Young's disturbed state in writing it.

[2] Only two portraits of Young are known to have been painted: (1) before 1699, now unknown, willed to his mother by his aunt Catherine Young (Somerset House, P.C.C. 260 Smith, proved 6 November 1710), and (2) of 1754, now in the Dining Hall of All Souls College, Oxford, painted by Joseph Highmore at the request of Samuel Richardson.

downe:¹ But, if You will take my Advice, I wd have You omit That, & ye Oration on Codrington.² I think yr Collection will sell better without them—I wish you success & am

Yr Humble Sevt

EYoung.

77. Tunbridge Wells, Kent. [F.] 15 August [1740]. Duchess of Portland.

Longleat MSS. (3) 7.

Madam

During the severity of my Fever I begd Ly Frogmorton³ to let yr Grace know, yt I cd not write; nor can I now scarce guide my pen. I bless God I think ye Danger is over, but I am sunk to ye Lowest. I am not Madam ye person You You [*sic*] invited: If You will admit this poor Stranger whom You never saw before, I will wait on yr Grace as soon as I can crawll so far. My Duty to my Ld Duke. I am

Madam

Yr Graces most Obligd

& most Obedient Humble Sevt

EYoung.

Aug: 15

Tunbridge Wells.

[In another hand] 1740

¹ The *Epistle to . . . Lansdowne* (1713), said to be a second edition 'Printed from a correct Manuscript Copy' (which does not differ from the first edition) appears in Curll's collection, paged i–xxxii, over signatures a–b⁸, bound ahead of the remaining text in volume one, clearly an addendum to an otherwise already printed collection. George Granville (1667–1735), Baron Lansdowne, had been imprisoned for a time for suspected political complicity.

² The Codrington address, like the *Epistle*, was added to the already printed collection, on eight leaves signed a⁸, and paged i–xvi. It was bound at the end of the second volume.

³ Lady Catherine Throckmorton, the wife of Sir Robert Throckmorton of Weston, Bucks. Young's variant of 'Frogmorton' recalls William Cowper's later use of the familiar epithet of 'Frog' for the family.

78. [Tunbridge Wells, Kent]. [Su.] 17 August [1740]. Judith Reynolds.

Address: To Mrs Reynolds / at Mortlock[1] in / Surry. *Postmark*: 18/AV.
Huntington Library MSS. 22205.—Swedenberg, p. 95.

Dearest Madam
    Tho it has pleasd Allmy God in his great mercy to put at
last an end to my long fever, yet have I still a Blister on my
head,[2] & a weakness not to be expresd. Besides I am so
struck wth ye News of poor Mr Temple,[3] (who was taken
ill ye very same Day) yt I know not wt to do. Yr enquirys
[afte]r me are exstremely Kind, & shall ever be rememberd
wth ye greatest gratitude by

Dearest Madam
Most Yrs EYoung.

I can scarce guide
    my pen.
  Aug 17th.
My humble service
to Mr & Mrs G——ll

79. [Tunbridge Wells, Kent]. [F.] 22 August [1740]. Judith Reynolds.

Address: To Mrs Reynolds at / Mortlock in / Surry. *Postmark*: 23/AV.
Huntington Library MSS. 22206.—Swedenberg, p. 96.

Dearest Madam
    I bless God I continue free of my Fever; but am dispirited
greatly, nor can yet recover my Appetite or Sleep: but I trust
in God yt Time & These waters may reestablish my Health.
O Madam wt a loss is such a Friend?—But I take yr advice
& indulge myself no farther,[4]—My best services to Mr &

---

    [1] Mortlake is adjacent to East Sheen.
    [2] For 'a pleurisy' Dr. Mead recommended: 'a blister laid on the part affected in
order to draw forth the peccant humor', adding 'I have for many years past used
it with good success' (Richard Mead, *Medical Precepts and Cautions*, 1751, p. 45).
    [3] Henry Temple was to die the next day.
    [4] Henry Temple had died on Monday, and it is apparent that Judith had tried
to soften the blow to Young.

Mrs G——ll.—The tender Kindness of yr Letters takes fast hold of my Heart; & lays me under obligations wh shall never be forgot: Continue ye Charity of yr correspondence; Indeed I want consolation, & hearing from You is a Cordial to

Dearest Madam
Yr most Obligd & Affectionate
Humble Sevt   EYoung

Aug. 22

80. Tunbridge Wells, Kent. [M.] 25 August 1740. Duchess of Portland.

Longleat MSS. (4) 8.—Bath, p. 254; Shelley, p. 116.

Madam

I was exstremely ill when I writ my last Letter, & whither it was intelligible to yr Grace I can not tell. My Fever has left me under great weakness, for which I am advisd to drink these waters for a Fortnight longer, if It will then be convenient to yr Grace to admit an Invalid into so happy a Society, I shall pay my Duty at Bullstrode[1] wth ye greatest Pleasure. The Inducements Yr Grace is pleasd to mention, are very great; But none is greater, then ye Satisfaction I shall take in paying my Thanks for ye Honour You do to One so entirely unentitled to it. Madam I rejoyce that ye little Innocents[2] enjoy yt Health, wh they can not yet have possibly forfited by their Crimes; The Contrary of wh is generally the /[verso]/ Sting of those yt Suffer in a more advancd Age. I beg my humble Duty to his Grace, & my humble Service to ye Lady[3] yt is with You; Nor must She take ill my Liberty

[1] Bulstrode Park was the seat of the Dukes of Portland, near Gerrards Cross, Buckinghamshire, about 21 miles west of Whitehall on the road to High Wycombe and Oxford.

[2] At this time, there were four children, all under five years of age: Elizabeth (b. Oct. 1735), known as Lady Betty; Henrietta (b. early in 1737), known as Lady Harriet; William Henry (b. 14 April 1738), Lord Tichfield; and Margaret (b. 26 July 1739).

[3] Elizabeth Robinson (1720–1800). In a letter to her sister Sarah of 23 September she wrote: 'Dr. Young is coming soon. . . . He sends his compliments to me when he writes to the Duchess, and says he is perfectly acquainted with me, and all that

in doing so, for whatever she may imagine she is no Stranger
to me; wh I shall explain when I see Her. I am with all
possible respect & gratitude

> Madam
> Yr Graces most Obligd
> & most Obedient
> Humble Sevt
> Edwd Young.

Tunbridge Wells
Aug 25.
1740.

81. [Tunbridge Wells, Kent]. [M.] 1 September [1740]. Judith Reynolds.

Address: To Mrs Reynolds at / Mr Townsends in / Norfolk Street in the /
Strand. / London. *Postmark*: 3/SE.
Huntington Library MSS. 22207.—Swedenberg, p. 96.

Dearest Madam

 I thank God I have in a good measure recoverd my Appetite, but my sleep, strength, & spirits, still fail me; & how
far, at my Age, I shall ever be able to recover them, God
onely knows: to Him I pray for Patience, & Resignation;
of both wh I had a most eminent Example in my Dearest
Friend Mr Temple. My Physitians[1] tell me yt These waters,
Exercise, & Time, may do much; but alas! Madam, how
Little time have I to spare? Pardon me that I am so taken up
with my own Health as never to enquire after Yours: I beg
in yr next that You wd let me know how You do: For yr
Health & Happiness is very dear to Dearest Madam

> Yr most Affectionate
> Humble Sevt   EYoung

Sepr 1st

is the vision of a Poet, for I never saw him in my life . . .' (Climenson, 1906, i. 60).
Young had probably not seen her but doubtless had heard of her as a precocious
young lady under the tutelage of Conyers Middleton (1683–1750) of Cambridge,
whose first wife was Elizabeth's grandmother by an earlier marriage.

---

[1] One of these would have been Richard Mead to whom Young paid tribute in
the *Night-Thoughts* (ii. 38–44), though it is not known whether he was then at
Tunbridge Wells or had been consulted by Young while in London.

82. [Tunbridge Wells, Kent]. [W.] 10 September 1740. Duchess of Portland.

Longleat MSS. (5) 9.—Bath, pp. 254–5; Shelley, p. 117.

Madam

I have ye unhappy advantage of very sensibly condoling wth Yr Grace on yr present Complaint, labouring under ye Same myself, from a violent Cold, wh ye badness of ye Season has made Here, an allmost universal Complaint: The excessive Rains have washd away all our Company, all I mean yt came for Pleasure: They yt came for Health, are still fishing for it in these Waters: But ye Waters themselves now begin to be out of order. So yt I fear I shall scarce find what I sought: But I hope Yr Graces Park may give wt ye Wells deny me; For my Physitian tells me yt Steel & Riding are my onely Cure.[1] May God allmy restore, & preserve yr Health. With my humble Duty to his Grace, I am Madam

Yr Graces most Obligd
& most Obedient Humble Sevt
EYoung.

Sept 10th 1740.

83. [Tunbridge Wells, Kent]. [F.] 19 September 1740. Judith Reynolds.

Address: To Mrs Reynolds / at Mortlake in / Surry. *Postmark*: 20/SE. Huntington Library MSS. 22208.—Swedenberg, pp. 96–7.

Dearest Madam

Since You give me leave to take so great a Liberty, I beg the favour of waiting on You on Thursday Evening next, in Norfolk street; ye time of my being at Sheen being very

---

[1] For all 'species of consumption' Dr. Mead advised: 'a well regulated course of living, and *steel* medicines to strengthen the stomach, with laxatives at proper distances', and 'in all decays exercise . . . according to the patient's strength' especially 'riding on horseback' (Richard Mead, *Medical Precepts and Cautions*, 1751, p. 61). The filings of steel, known technically as 'Chalybis limatura', were a pharmaceutical staple, available at sixpence a pound (Gideon Harvey, *The Family-Physician and the House-Apothecary*, 1678, p. 129).

Uncertain, For I have business wh will keep me a Week at least in Town;¹ As ye Weather is fine I shd not have left this Place ~~so~~ till Michaelmas; (for ye Waters are my best Remidy) but ye Company has deserted me; & I am allready allmost alone. I am

> Dearest Madam
> Yr most Affec[tionate] &
> most Obligd Humble Sevt
> EYoung.

Sepr 19. 1740.

84. Ditchley,² Oxon. [M.] 13 October [1740]. Duchess of Portland.

Address: To Her Grace ye Dutchess / of Portland at Bullstrode. / Bucks.
Postmark: 15/OC Enston.
Longleat MSS. (6) 10.—Bath, p. 255; Shelley, pp. 117–18.

Madam

I thank yr Grace for ye late favours I receivd at Bulstrode:³ My Health I thank God is much better than before; but whither it is owing to ye Air, or the Conversation I shall not take on me to determine.

It is somewhat Odd, Madam, yt I should be better acquainted wth Miss Robinson since I left Her; But to unriddle I have met a Confident of One of her Admireror's;⁴

¹ Opposite the entry in the Administration Book in Somerset House, recording the swearing of Young to administer his wife's estate, is the notation 'Sept', suggesting that he had taken some action in the matter after his summer illness.

² Ditchley was the seat of George Henry Lee (1690–1743), 2nd Earl of Litchfield from 1716, brother of Young's late wife. It is in Oxfordshire, about 12 miles northwest of the city of Oxford.

³ On 8 October, Elizabeth Robinson wrote to her sister Sarah: 'The poetical Dr. Young is with us; I am much entertained with him; he is a very sensible man, has a lively imagination, and strikes out very pretty things in his conversation; and though he has satirized the worst of our sex, he honours the best of them extremely, and seems delighted with those who act and think reasonably.... [He] has got a terrible cold, to my great mortification; for he is hoarse, and can hardly be heard'(Montagu 1810, ii. 57–8).

⁴ The confidant was probably the Lord Quarendon mentioned in the postscript, George Henry Lee (1718–72), eldest son of the second Earl of Litchfield. Elizabeth Robinson's admirer, later referred to as 'Captain B', was undoubtedly the Hon. George Boscawen (1712–75) of Charlton Forest, Oxfordshire, and a neighbour of the Lees at Ditchley. He was a Captain in the Infantry, rising to Lieutenant-General before his death. In 1743 he married another lady.

who tells me his wounded Friend is in a very melancholy way; but as He is a Soldier, He is determined to behave in Character & rather to fall than fly: Your Friend, Madam, alone can tell whither tis adviseable for Him to make his Will.

I hope, Madam, the Little ones are as well as You wish them; & yr Grace as well as You deserve to be. I beg my Duty & best Thanks to my Ld Duke; & am wth ye truest Respect

> Madam
> Yr Graces most Obedient
> & Obligd Humble Sevt
> EdYoung

Ditchley Oct 13th
    1740.
Madam I beg my humble service
to Miss Robinson & Mr Achard[1] & Mr Hay[2]
Ld Quarendon his Friend is gone to the Bath.

85. Ditchley, Oxon. [Tu.] 14 October [1740]. Judith Reynolds.

Address: To Mrs Reynolds / at her House at / Mortlake / Surry. *Postmark*: 17/OC.
Huntington Library MSS. 22209.—Swedenberg, p. 97.

> Ditchley in
> Oxfordshire
> Octr 14.
> 1740.

Dearest Madam

This is ye first Post since I have been so fixd as to be able to put it in yr powr by giving a Direction, to give me ye Pleasure of hearing from You. My Ld Litchfield is at present at ye Bath but we soon expect his return; when I propose talking to him on our Affair: That I may do it ye more explicitely if You know more of your Brothers mind than when I saw You last, I should be glad to hear it. I bless God

---

[1] John Achard, the Duke's Swiss secretary and later tutor to the Portland boys.
[2] John Hay, a son of George Hay (d. 1758), 7th Earl of Kinnoull, and first cousin of the Duchess of Portland.

moving from Place to Place has improvd my Health. In
about a month I propose ye Happiness of waiting on You
in Town. In ye mean time I hope ye favour of your Correspondence; & You will do me great pleasure to let me hear
from You ye first Opportunity.

I am Dearest Madam

Yr most Obligd & Obedt
Humble Sevt   EYoung.

If You please my Humble
service to Yr Brother

86. [Ditchley, Oxon.].¹ [M.] 3 November [1740]. Judith Reynolds.

Address: To Mrs Reynolds in / Norfolk Street at Mr / Townsends In ye /
Strand / London. *Postmark*: 7/NO.
Huntington Library MSS. 22210.—Swedenberg, p. 97.

Nov: ye 3d

Dearest Madam

The approach of ye Parliament² & ye severity of ye
Weather, which like an unwellcome Guest is come before
it was expected, turns every bodys thoughts toward Town.
I hope, Madam, in ten days time to wait on You in Norfolk
street; In ye mean time I shall be too much in motion to have
an Oppertunity of ye Pleasure of hearing from You. I shall
go Hence to Oxford, Then to Bullstrode, then possibly to
Mr Wallers,³ & Thence to Town. We have frightfull

---

¹ That Young is still at Ditchley appears from the itinerary sketched in the letter.

² 'Tuesday 18 [November]. His Majesty went in State to the House of Lords,
and open'd the Session of Parliament with a most gracious speech' (*Gentleman's
Magazine*, x. 569).

³ Young's name is connected with three Wallers of High Wycombe, Bucks., from
time to time: Harry, Charles, and Richard. He had gone to Wycombe in 1726
during a Parliamentary election dispute which resulted in the seating of Harry
Waller (cf. Charlotte E. Crawford, 'Edward Young and Wycombe Election',
Modern Language Notes, 1945, lx. 459–61). In 1733 Charles and Richard Waller
begin to appear in Chancery reports in the suit against the Wharton estate, 'Styles
et al vs the Attorney General', to which Young was a party, as in the following
entry: 'Febry 2 paid Mr Chas Waller a Gratuity for his Journey and expenses in
inspecting into the State of the Mines in Yorkshire & examining into the management of the Agents there [£] 105—Aug 24 1733—by order of Mr Richard Waller'
(Public Record Office, C101/3229).

Prophecies about ye insuing Winter, but I will not yet despair of laughing at them. For tis sayd Nothing Violent can last: I beg my humble service to yr Brother, & am Dearest Madam

> Yr most Affectionate
> & much Obligd Humble Sevt
> EYoung.

87. [?Ditchley, Oxon.].[1] [F.] 7 November 1740. Duchess of Portland.

Longleat MSS (7) 12.—Bath, p. 255; Shelley, p. 118.

Madam

I am much obligd to yr Grace for ye Honour of yr letter; & still more for yr Desire of a Reply. If yr Grace designd onely a Compliment by it, You are fairly bit, for I am determind to think You sincere, & to value myself upon it accordingly.

As for Miss Robinson,[2] I am as much surprizd at her Ignorance in ye Particular I mentiond, as I am at her Knowledge in general; Both I am satisfid are very exstraordinary. However I have taken ye Hint she gave about providing agst Accidents; & a Friend has written to ye Gentleman at
—— yt He shd set his House in order with all convenient Expedition.

I am heartily sorry for Mr Hay,[3] & hope This will find him perfectly recoverd /[verso]/ I am Madam much obligd to my Lord Oxford for his kind remembrance of me. And as for ye Little Ones, yr Grace loves them ; But I do more; I consider Children as ye next Order of Beings to ye Blessed Angels; spotless Innocence is next in place to perfect Virtue; & I shall very shortly fly to their Protection: I beg my Duty

---

[1] The assumption of Shelley (p. 118) that this letter was written from Welwyn is mistaken as Young's letter of 20 December 1740 shows. Young may, however, have been in Oxford at this time.

[2] For the matter of this paragraph, see Young's letter of 13 October 1740.

[3] The Duchess's cousin, John Hay, was ill. Elizabeth Robinson said of him at this time: 'Hay is an auditor, as he cannot read himself' (Climenson, 1906, i. 61).

to my Lord Duke; my humble service to Miss Robinson,
Mr Hay &c: I am wth ye greatest Respect

> Madam
> Yr Graces much Obligd
> & most Obedient
> Humble Sevt
> EYoung.

Nov: ye 7th
1740.

88. Bulstrode, Bucks. Th. [20 November 1740].[1] Judith Reynolds.

Address: To Mrs Reynolds at / Mr Townsends in / Norfolk Street in ye /
Strand / London.
Huntington Library MSS. 22211.—Swedenberg, p. 98.

Dearest Madam.

I told You in my last yt I proposd being in Town in ten
days; but my Rambles have carryd me farther than I intended. I am very lately come to this place, where I shall
continue to Moonday or Teusday next, when I propose the
pleasure, if it please God, of waiting on You in Norfolk
street. Last moonday was the Day I first proposd, but I
could not comply with my own Inclinations in it. As
I remember You are, Madam, a lover of the Country; if so I
hope ye Town has payd You with Amusement for ye Loss
of your Retreat: I think to call at Sheen in my way to You,
& hope I shall find our Friends in good Health. I beg my
humble service to Mr Baron Reynolds & am

> Dearest Madam
> Yr most Obligd & Affectionate
> Humble Sevt   EYoung.

Bullstrode
Thursday Night.

1 The date of this letter is assumed from Young's saying he expects to be in
London 'Moonday or Teusday next' and his next letter, to the Duchess of Portland,
is from London, Tuesday, the 25th. On the 18th the Duchess had written from
Bulstrode to Mr. Achard in London, saying: 'Miss Robinson, Mr Potts & Doctor
Young desires their Service to you' (Portland MSS., University of Nottingham
Library, PwC40).

89. London. [Tu.] 25 November 1740. Duchess of Portland.

Longleat MSS. (8) 13.—Bath, pp. 255–6.

Madam

Your Grace may be assurd I should be glad to be out of Debt; But is it possible Yr Grace can accept a Letter from me in full for all Demands? I am therefore determind not to write: For is This writing? Yr Graces Correspondents give You a very different Idea of It. Heaven has blesd You with excellent Accomplishments; & wth a Relish for them in Others: Insomuch that It is scarce a greater Happiness than it is a Reputation to be among ye Number of yr Graces Friends: I know but One Instance where yr Goodnature has imposed on yr Understanding; & if Yr Grace (wh wd be Hard) shd be reproachd for a Single Fault, You are sure of me for yr Advocate, who am the onely gainer by it: But tho Madam, I can not ad to ye Briliancy of yr *Letter-Box*, I can ad to ye Variety of It. I present Yr Grace wth a Letter, wh /[verso]/ stands eminently distinguishd for all ye Rest; & defie You to show me Another in yr whole Collection, in which It had been a merit to be Short.

I am Madam
Yr Graces most Obligd
& most Obedient
Humble Sevt
EYoung

I beg, Madam, my best Respects
to my Ld Duke, to ye Ladys; to Mr
Hay, Mr Ashard & ye Little Ones
whom God for ever bless.

At ye 3 Golden Lyons
by Temple Bar
Nov: 25 1740.

90. [London]. Th. [?4 December 1740].[1] Duchess of Portland.

Longleat MSS. (9) 14.

Thursday night.

Madam

I design myself the Honour of waiting on the Dutchess of Kent[2] tomorrow morning: Yr Grace is so kind as to enquire if ye *Law* goes on to my satisfaction:[3] It goes on to my satisfaction, if I may be allowd to talk in the Language of fine Gentlemen; who are pleasd to say they have receivd satisfaction, when they are run thro ye Body.

Yr Grace says You *work*, *read*, & *turn*;[4] This, Madam, is giving a very modest account; Are You not discharging all ye Dutys of a Christian Life; & refuting (as far as in You lies) ye general Imputation yt falls on Persons of yr Rank? I know but one Irregularity wh I can fairly charge upon You, Which is begining Your Dissections at ye wrong end. Why ye *Wing* first?[5] I dare not call this a direct Immorality; But It is near it; It is a severe Reflection on ye Practise of all ye World beside.

But I do not beleive Yr Grace acts directly agst Yr conscience even in This; You have some salvo, some Jesuetical Distinction to make yt Heart /[verso]/ easie under it. Has Miss R——n[6] betrayd yr Grace into this Enormity? She is a Jesuit as far as accurate Distinction, & uncommon Discernment are Essential to that Character: Besides my Friend at ye B——th observes,[7] Her Spleen is leveld at ye Breast: & yt I therefore assent had He onely lost a Leg, He cd have born it like a Hero.

[1] The date is estimated from Young's intention of calling on the Duchess of Kent and from his having made the call by the time he wrote to the Duchess of Portland on 20 December from Welwyn where he had been since the 10th.

[2] Sophia Bentinck (d. 1748), widow of Henry Grey (?1664–1740), 11th Duke of Kent, aunt of the Duke of Portland.

[3] Young was party to a suit against the estate of the Duke of Wharton for non-payment of annuities granted him in 1719 and 1722.

[4] 'The Duchess of Portland was celebrated *for turning*. She turned in wood, jet, ivory, and amber' (Llanover, 1861, ii. 138).

[5] Apparently a playful reference to the Duchess's carving at table, the 'wing' begin a synecdoche for 'angel'.   [6] i.e. Elizabeth Robinson.

[7] Litchfield's eldest son, Lord Quarendon (see note to letter of 13 October).

But This, Madam, borders a little upon a Pun; & I know yr Grace starts as much at a Pun, as Mrs Pendarvess[1] at a spider: sweet animal! why shd It fright us? It was once a Pretty Girl, till *Pallas* gave her a rap wth her Thimble for embrodering as well as her self; & ye poor Girl having no Armbusade water at hand to heal ye Contusion,[2] her legs grew too long for her Body, (like Lady R——'s & Mrs G——ys)[3] yt's All: However, as I am much inclind to apologize for Mrs Pend——'s onely Fault; I will venture to say she has some excuse for her Antipathy; Since it is but Proper, yt she who inherits all the Polite Arts of that Goddess, should espouse her Qu^a rels.

And now, Madam, I hope Yr Grace is /[conjugate leaf]/ tird; if not You are very unreasonable: All ye News I can tell yr Grace, is, That a certain noble Peer[4] has not been half so wise as ye Honest Cits, wth whom I nightly, converse. He has blown aloud his own Horn; wh, (had He followed their wise example) He would have put in his Poket. I am with ye truest Gratitude & Respect

> Madam
> Yr Grace's most Obedient
> & Obligd Humble Sevt
> EYoung

I beg my Duty to my
Lord, & my humble service
to ye Ladys, & Gentlemen.

[1] Mary Granville (1700–88), widow of Alexander Pendarves (d. 1725). She had come to Bulstrode from Bath about the time of Young's second visit in November and had remained until early January. The transformation of Arachne by Pallas is from Greek mythology. Interestingly, just after this time, Mary sent her sister, Anne D'Ewes, a prescription for curing her child of the ague: 'A spider put into a goose-quill, well sealed and secured, and hung about the child's neck as low as the pit of his stomach' (Llanover, 1861, ii. 273).

[2] i.e. Arquebusade Water 'of the late Mons. de Raffore universally esteemed for its singular efficacy in curing Wounds, Cuts, Bruises, and Bleedings . . . to be had of his successor Mr. Ogle' (*The Gazetteer and London Daily Advertiser* of 26 April 1756). See 'Harquebusade' in the *Oxford English Dictionary*.

[3] Possibly Lady Romney, Priscilla Pym, wife of the 2nd Baron Romney, and Mrs. Grey, Susanna Hinton (d. 1774), second wife of Zachary Grey (1688–1766), both mentioned in the correspondence of Elizabeth Montagu.

[4] Either Lord Baltimore, who had spoken at length against the ministry in Parliament, or more probably an allusion to a self-proclaimed cuckolding.

91. Barnet, Herts. [Tu.] 9 December 1740. Judith Reynolds.

Address: To Mrs Reynolds at / Mr Townsends in Norfolk / Street in ye Strand / London. *Postmark*: 10/DE.
Huntington Library MSS. 22212.—Swedenberg, p. 98.

Barnet. Decemr
ye 9th 1740.

Dearest Madam

Last night Mr Lee my Son in Law[1] came to me from Wellwyn to call me thither on particular Occasion: Being obligd to go Early I cd not have ye Pleasure of waiting on You: How long I shall stay in the Country I know not yet; As soon as I return You shall know it: I dare not write to You from Wellwyn, for ye Mistris of ye Post[2] there, is a fine Lady & great Pryer into secrets; & I am not willing, this affair shd make a noise till it is more settled between us. All yr Friends at Sheen are well, & at yr service. I am Dearest Madam

Yr most Obligd
& Affectionate Humble
Sevt   EYoung.

Pray my humble service
to Yr Brother.

92. Welwyn, Herts. [Sa.] 20 December 1740. Duchess of Portland.

Longleat MSS. (10) 16.—Bath, pp. 256–7; Shelley, pp. 119–21.

Wellwyn in
Hertfordshire
Decemr 20th
1740.

Madam

I have been above ten days at this place; where my Memory is very troublesome to me & my Understandg is

---

1 Charles Henry Lee (*c.* 1721–44), actually Young's stepson, since 1732 Master of the Revels, gentleman usher to Princess Amelia, and either by now or soon to be a junior officer of the guard.

2 On the authority of W. Branch Johnson, historian of Welwyn, probably a Mrs. Ward of the Rose and Crown, who had been widowed in 1738 or 1739.

hard put to it to get the better of its severe impertinence.[1] I am heartily sorry for Mrs Elstob,[2] & hope in God she will not ad to ye great number of touching Admonitions Providence lately has been pleased to give me of my own Mortality: But You, Madam, are her Deputy; how worthyly are you employd? It is being Twice a Parent to bring Little Machines into Being, & then to inspire ym wth such an Understandg as shall make yt Being a Blessing to ym: How Hard is it yt a poor Whore, who murders her Child, shall be hangd, & a rich one, who neglects ye education of her Children, shall escape? The *First*, (tho she designs it not) makes an Angel; ye *Last*, makes a Legion of Devels if particular Providence does not interpose.

I had, Madam, ye Honour of waiting on ye Dutchess /[verso]/ of Kent; Who, in truth, for a Dutchess, is a very
              a
Odd one; she has   noble ambition of being allways in ye right; & either her Grace studies Propriety in all things; or
                     out
she is very Fortunate, as, witht   aiming at it, exactly to hit ye Mark:—wt I have hinted, Madam, concerng Dutchesses in general, is nothing to yr Grace; you are onely a Titular Dutchess, & have scarce one single Qualification for it; Insomuch, yt if You cd find in yr Heart to scratch ye Coronet out of ye Corner of yr Handkercheif, You might easily pass for a Lady of as sound a mind, & as good a Heart as any in Christendom. As for Miss R——[3] her Heart is hardend, & I find (by wt she says) yt she is determind, without any remorse, to carry her Face along wth her wherever she goes; but if yt may seem alltogether necessary, I humbly beseech her (sometimes at least) to leave her Understandg behind. Many an Honest Gentleman (tho born in Kent)[4] has done it, even when ye Wellfare of his Country was dependg.—I am glad to hear Mrs P—— is proud of her Weaknesses.[5] I shall now entertain some small hope yt I

---

[1] Young had been away from Welwyn since 27 May.

[2] Elizabeth Elstob (1683–1756), governess of the Portland children from 1738, an accomplished linguist and student of Anglo-Saxon.

[3] i.e. Elizabeth Robinson.

[4] Elizabeth Robinson was probably born at her mother's family home of Mount Morris in Horton, near Hythe, Kent.

[5] Mary Pendarves's disgust of spiders is her 'Weakness'.

may /[new sheet]/ not entirely be out of her Favour; But, Madam, since Mrs P——'s natural Antipathy is reenforced by her Pride, as You love Ingenuity, I beg You to keep some one Corner in yr House unviolated, least ye whole race of those admirable spinsters, who work without a wheel, may not entirely be destroyd. The Flys must be very fond of Mrs P. for routing their grand Enimies, but I am afraid she is not aware wth wm she is entering into so strickt an Alliance, for Beelzebub (ye Learned say) is King of ye Flys:[1] so yt wt I suspected before is now I think very Plain, (viz) yt Mrs P—— hates a Spider worse than ye Devel. wch I fear with ye Fair is no uncommon Case. If, Madam, ye Gentlemen will not take it ill, yt I put ym in such Company, I desire my humble service to ym; And particularly please Madam to let my Ld D. know yt I have a true & gratefull sense of ye Honour He does me by giving me a Place in his Remembrance.

As for ye Little Ones, He yt knows ym & does not love ym, is a Monster; & I wish He was a Monster wth six or eight hairy legs crawling on /[verso]/ Mrs P——'s work, yt she might justly wreck her full Vengeance on Him: But men in ye Shape of men let her spare, & set Miss R—— such an Example of Humanity, as may incline her to spend ye remainder of her Days in a Cloyster, wh is ye sole Expedient I can think of for her complying wth It. I am, Madam, wth ye truest Respect

Yr Graces most Obligd
& most Obedient
Humble Sevt
EYoung

Pray Madam, if yr Grace pleases
my best Wishes & humble Service
to Mrs Elstob.

I had allmost forgot to wish Yr Grace a Happy Xtmas; yt is, to wish you wd make Others as Happy as You can. For beleive me, Madam, 'They yt are most Social are most Selfish; &, but by giving Happiness to Others, we can not

[1] Traditionally the name of Lucifer's assistant had been formed of the two words: 'Baal' and 'bezub', literally meaning: 'Lord of the flies' (*New Century Cyclopedia of Names*, 1954).

receive it ourselves.'—I desire yr Grace to accept This Maxim as a New years Gift; for I never make but one a year. And This came into my Head for asking /[in margin of first page]/ myself how twas possible Yr Grace cd be so merry (as You say You are) in such weather as This: O yt I was a Salamander, & cd live in Flames! as poor Captain B———[1] has done for two years past: & will she not relent? I fear yr Friend loves her Flesh over-roasted. It may be wholesomer, but sure, Ladys, it is most Palatable with ye Gravy in it. But I grant meat witht *Bread* wont do.

93. [Welwyn, Herts.] Su. [?January 1740/1].[2] Duchess of Portland.

Address: To Her Grace ye Dutchess of Portland.
Longleat MSS. (27) 44.—Bath, p. 270; Shelley, pp. 141–2.

Madam

As I design myself ye Honour of waiting on yr Grace very Soon,[3] I shall not by Letter forestall wt I have to say as to ye Authors You mention:[4] Fiction may have a good Tendency, & History may have a bad one, wh I beleive to be ye Case wth regard to these two Writers of whom I shall say no more at present. I am much obligd to ye two Ladys for ye thousand fine things they did *not* say of me: But I take it a little Ill they did not make it ten thousand, since it wd have cost ym no more. Madam I beg my Love & Envy to ye Little ones; my real Duty to my Ld Duke, & my humble service to Mr Ashard: The Bear yr Grace mentiond in yr

---

[1] The suitor of Elizabeth Robinson mentioned in Young's letters of 13 October and 4 December.

[2] The date of this letter is established by Elizabeth Elstob's recovery from the illness referred to in Young's letter of 20 December.

[3] According to a letter of 20 December of Mary Pendarves the Portlands expected to be in London on 4 January (Llanover, 1861, ii. 139).

[4] One of these authors is almost certainly Samuel Richardson, whose *Pamela* had first appeared 6 November (Sale, 1936, p. 14) and, according to Mrs. Pendarves, was being read by the ladies at Bulstrode on 21 December (Llanover, 1861, ii. 138). The other author was certainly Conyers Middleton, Elizabeth Robinson's tutor and a close acquaintance of the Portlands. His 'history' of Cicero appeared about this time. On 27 October he wrote: 'Tully [Cicero] is now in ye Press at London' (British Museum, Add. MSS. 32457, ff. 70 and 143).

Last has stretched out his great Paw, & drags me to Town,
thro bad Weather; & gangs of Robbers, wh infest Enfield
Chace:[1] But wt can ye Fools expect from a man at Law? I
hope they will not beat me for my Poverty, for I can honestly
assure ym, that I have /[verso]/ parted wth my money to
Gentlemen who deserve hanging full as well as ymselves;
wh they can not take ill of me; at least, not so ill as if I had
foold it away in paying my Debts; or squanderd it in Charity.
I am, Madam, heartily glad to hear yt Mrs Elstob is restord
to her Health, & pleasing Province of sowing ye seeds of
Virtue, & Accomplishmt in so Happy a Soil: God preserve,
& encrease yr Graces peculiar Blessings; You know how to
make a right use of ym; nor need I say to yr Grace, wt I
might very properly to many—'Happy are They who are not
hurt by good things; Happy are They who have nothing on
Earth wh they hold Dearer than their Maker.' I am wth ye
truest Respect & Gratitude

Madam
Yr Graces most Obedient
& Obligd Humble Sevt
EYoung.

Wellwyn
Sunday Night

94. London. [W.] 14 January 1740/1. Judith Reynolds.

Address: To Mrs Reynolds / at Mr Townsends in / Norfolk Street in ye /
Strand. *Postmark*: Peny Post payd Shank.[2]
Huntington Library MSS. 22213.—Swedenberg, pp. 98–9.

Dearest Madam

I am just come from ye Country where I was detain too
long; And I should take it as a favour to know if You yet

[1] A portion of Middlesex between Hatfield and Barnet on the road halfway
between Welwyn and London, notorious for highwaymen.

[2] Rate books of St. Dunstan's parish for this period, preserved in the Guildhall
Library, show a 'Mrs. Shank' in Fleet Street near Temple Bar within a few doors
of the Tassel establishment mentioned below. According to Bryant Lillywhite
(*London Coffee Houses*, 1963, p. 382), John Shank is mentioned in 1695 as 'at Nan-
doe's Coffee House between the two Temple Gates' and in 1729 'Mr. Shank' is
described as 'Master of Nando's Coffee-house, Temple-Bar'. In a letter of 12 February 1764, Young says: 'Nandos was my Coffee house above three score years agoe.'

fully learnt what your Brothers Intentions are towards You;
If, Madam, You have not, I beg You would let me know as
soon as You can his final determination: I hope You have
enjoyd yr Health since I saw You, as I thank God I have
done. This is a bitter Day, but I hope it will not deprieve
You of ye Use of yr Pen if You have anything to communicate to me. I beg my humble service to yr Brother

    I am D[ea]rest Madam
     Yr most Obligd & Affectionate
     Humble Sevt EYoung.

Mr Tassels[1] just
within Temple Bar
Jan: 14 1740.

95. London. [?Th. 15 January 1740/1]. Duchess of
Portland.

Longleat MSS. (11) 18.—Bath, p. 257.

Madam
 I designd to have waited on yr Grace; but I find myself
obligd to hunt Money all This Day, as closely, as the
staunchest Hound this side Temple Bar. But what have I
to do with Money? Yr Grace promisd me what is much
more valueable; ye Friendship of Mrs Pendarves:[2] I thought
that long ere This I shd have known Her very well: But I
know her no more than I know yr Grace; And You Madam,
of all Female Riddles are ye most exquisite, & impenetrable:
Why was This favour so often promisd? Was It to try my
Philosophy, & see how well I cd bear a Disapointment, Or
was It to try my Tast, & see how I cd relish a Jest? The Jest
is too poynant for my Tast; ye Disapointment is too heavy
for my Philosophy: And therefore with sanguin Hope of

---

 [1] Benjamin Tassel (d. 1758), later identified as Young's 'townlandlord', was to
forward Judith's letters to him and thus circumvent the idle curiosity of the postmistress of Welwyn. Rate books of St. Dunstan's parish identify as Tassel's a building in Fleet Street near the Temple Bar.
 [2] From subsequent letters it seems clear that the Duchess was at work as a match-
maker. Mrs. Pendarves was later (1743) to marry Patrick Delany (?1685–1768),
the Irish clergyman remembered for his account of Swift.

better Treatment for the Future; & with profound Reverence of yr Graces Mysteries for ever

I am, Madam,
Yr Grace's most perfectly puzzled
& most cordially Devoted
Humble Sevt

EYoung.

From ye 3 Sphink's
Temple Bar.

96. London. Su. [?18 January 1740/1]. Duchess of Portland.

Longleat MSS. (15) 24.—Bath, pp. 260-1; Shelley, pp. 125-7.

Madam

On a review of Yr *Last* (for I read Yr Graces Letters more
than Once) I find You complain yt *Dullness & Illnature* prevails. I shall endeavour to cure You of that Displeasure, It
seems to give you.

If, Madam, we have no View in Company but of being
Diverted, or Improvd, our Disapointmts will be great; But
if we have a *Second* View; That, I mean, of paying a decent
regard to Society, by free, & frequent Intercourse wth It,
A Sense of discharging This Duty, will be like carrying our
own Stool wth us into Company & make us sit easie in it,
tho *Illnature* in ye Person of Mrs —— & Dullness in ye
Shape of Dr —— sat,[1] one on our right hand, & ye other
on our Left.

If This advice seems too Severe; Ill try to go still farther,
& show how This great Calamity may be turned into a perfect Diversion, by ye Help of a little Imagination in Us: If
then, Madam, Dr B—— & Mrs M shd visit us; Let us

---

[1] 'Mrs. M——' and 'Dr B——', as they are referred to below, may be a Mrs. More
and a Dr. Burton. The latter was used by Elizabeth Robinson as an example of a
tedious conversationalist: 'I have so many things to say that if I am not quicker of
speech than Dr. Burton, I should never get to the end of my story' (Montagu, 1810,
i. 292).

Oaf

suppose ourselves in the Theater, & yt ye Parts of an ~~Offe~~ ,
& a Vixen, were represented before us; how then shd we
admire ye wonderfull Talents /[verso]/ of ye Performers, &
swear every Word; Air, & Action, was acted up ye Life; &
thus steal from a Visit, ye best Dramatick entertainmt we
ever saw, without ye expence of a Crown.

If This, Madam, seems as *Phantastical*, as ye Former
Advice *Severe*, I will try a Third Expedient, wh is quite
Obvious, & Natural; & wh everybody, I beleive, makes use
of more or less: I mean, let us make use of Bad Company,
as a Foil to recommend the Good. We may, I think, justly
compare ye *Dullness* of the Doctor, to ye flat Insipidness of
Oyl; & ye *Illnature* of ye Lady, to ye Acrimony of Vinegar:
now might not These (well beat together) make excellent
sauce for Mrs P——; might they not give us a still higher
relish for ye charms of her Conversation?

And now, Madam, does not yr Grace think me bewitchd,
yt I talk thus to One, who cd tell me This, & ten times more?
—Madam, I do it out of pure goodhusbandry; I pick yr

a

Poket in order to make You   Treat; what I present to yr
Perusal, I steal from Your Example; while You, perhaps,
/[conjugate leaf]/ Madam, looking on ye Behavior I advise,
like Eve (in yr beloved Milton) looking into ye Lake,[1] fancy
You see an Angel, nor know It is Yourself.

And now, Madam, can You for yr soul imagine for wt
end & purpose I have written this long Letter? I have
written, as most of our Wits do, purely Madam, for a
Dinner, & humbly beg ~~yt~~ on *Teusday* or *Wensday* next (as
suits Yr Grace best) yt I may be admitted to yr Table, There
to make an Apology for ye trouble I now give You: If Mrs
P. was There she wd be so Charitable as to help me out. But
if she is there, I beg yr Grace to remember yt her Conversation will go down without Sauce: So yt you need not be at
ye Trouble of inviting either of ye Two *Cruets* mentiond

that

above. But   I may have ye Honour of being often in yr
Thoughts, I beg yt (for ye Future), whenever a Cruet of

---

[1] *Paradise Lost*, iv. 453–91.

                                    wd
either Kind comes to visit You, You   be so good as to
remember
                         Madam
                              Yr Graces most Dutifull
                                   Butler. EY.

As, Madam, Persons of the Character we have been /[verso]/
                of
speaking   may be calld *Cruets*; so there are Others, yt may
be calld *Salvors*, as They present us in Conversation wth all
yt is Delicious to ye most Elegant Tast. Will Yr Grace stand
Gossip to ye *Cruets*, or ye *Salvors*? If to ye *Last* It will, I
grant, be less trouble to You; But if to ye *First*, Yr Grace
will have ye Honour of being askd blessing by half ye Town.
—I beg, Madam, my Respects to ye *Salvors* of Yr Grace's
acquaintance; & please to let ye *Cruets* know yt if they
honour me wth a Visit I shall provide a *Sideboard* for Them;
yt they may not come too Forward in Company, wh they
are very apt to do.
    Madam I mention Teusday or Wenesday because To-
morrow I am necessarily engagd. I beg my Duty to my Ld
Duke & my humble service to Mr Achard.

Sunday, Temple Bar:

97. London. [Tu.] 27 January 1740/1. Judith Reynolds.

Address: To Mrs Reynolds at Mr Townsends / In Norfolk Street / In the
Strand / London. *Postmark*: Peny Post Payd Shank.
Huntington Library MSS. 22214.—Swedenberg, p. 99.

Dearest Madam
    I have now waited ten days in hopes of an Answer to my
last Letter, but have receivd none; The very great, & very
Just Esteem I have for You will not permit me to think any
part of yr Conduct is such, yt You can not perfectly justifie
it, if You please I shall therefore only say, yt I have, & ever
shall have ye deepest sence of yr many former favours, And

that I am, & ever shall be, wth ye sincerest Gratitude,
Respect, & Affection

Dearest Madam
Yr most Obedient
& most Humble sevt
EdYoung

Madam
If You please my
humble service
to Yr Brother.

Temple Bar
   Jany 27th
     1740.

98. [London]. [?Th. 29 January 1740/1]. Duchess of Portland.

Longleat MSS. (14) 23.—Bath, pp. 259–60.

Madam
    Money is ye Devil, & ever doing Mischeif, but It never
did me greater than Now, in denying me Honour & Pleasure
of waiting on Yr Grace before I leave the Town: But You,
Madam, who can confer Undeservd favours wth so great
facility; will I hope find no great Difficulty in excusing
Involuntary Faults: I had ye Delight & Reputation yesterday morning of waiting on Mrs Pendarvess: But what followd
—stands Candidate for a Place among yr Graces Mysteries;
& will not rashly be reveald by

Madam
Yr most Obligd & ever
Obedient Humble Sevt
EYoung.

I beg Madam my
sincerrest Duty to my Ld
Duke; & let Those yt are
Near & Dear to Yr Grace
divide my Heart between ym.

111

PS. But yr Grace is a Naturalist, I will therefore talk wth
You in yr own way: What so Flowery, & fragrant as ye Wood-
bine? Wt so Luxuriant & Fruitfull as ye Vine? How They
ravish our Senses? How They gladen ye Heart of Man?
How /[verso]/ divinely They inspire? Such Madam, is yr
Sex: But then, as You are made Exquisite like *These*; So,
like These, in Compassion to poor mankind, you are made
Feeble too: You were *Both* designd to give a tender Twine
around somethg Stronger than yrselves: The Vine & Wood-
bine, were not designd for Celebacy, but to mingle their
branches wth ye rough Oak, or Elm; Obliging, & Obligd;
receiving succour while they confer ye most perfect Ornament, & Delight.

Now, Madam, a Lady of Genius, yt abounds in Arts &
Accomplishmts; She can agreeably employ every Hour by
Herself; She can Stand Alone; She is free from ye Weakness
wh Lays other Ladys under ye natural Necessity of an
Embrace; & being Superior to her Own Sex, affects an
Independency on Ours. I wish yt This is not somewhat ye
Case of Yr Friend: If Yr Grace does me ye Honour of a
Line, You will assist in this Nice Speculation: I shd be glad,
for ye Sake of mankind to find myself mistaken about Her:
For realy, Madam, if She is made *onely* be to be admird, I
shall value Her no more than an Angel: And poor Angels
yr Grace knows, will meet wth many powerfull Rivals in so
wicked a World as This.[1]

99. Welwyn, Herts. Su. [?1 February 1740/1]. Duchess of Portland.

Address: To Her Grace.
Longleat MSS. (12) 19.—Bath, p. 258; Shelley, p. 121.

Madam
   It is my Duty to write, tho perhaps it wd be my Prudence
to forbear: For wt shall I write? Yet I will obey Yr Grace,

[1] The forthright Elizabeth Robinson said of Mary Pendarves: 'I know she would
not be guilty of such a grossièreté as having a child for the world: she is a perfect
Seraphim, all fine music and spirit' (Montagu, 1810, ii. 206).

& Disobey You at ye Same time, for pray wt Difference is there between *not* writing, & writing *Nothing*?—Since Yr Grace has layd me under an Obligation, & a Difficulty at ye Same Time by yr Kind Command; I will take my Revenge by being as severe on Yr Graces Letter as possibly I can. I am as ambitious to find faults in such a Correspondent, as yr Friends ye Natural Philosophers are to find spots in ye Sun: And I think I can do it effectually. You say, Madam, ye more Knowledge I have of Mrs P. the greater Esteem I shall have for her; Madam, You are mistaken, my Knowledge of Her may encrease, but I think, my Esteem for Her can not; at least I do no[t] desire It shd.—Again you say, Madam, That she has all ye Perfections of yr Sex, but none of ye Weaknesses: This Yr Grace designs as an Advantageous Character of yr Friend: But how far is It from it? I wish she /[verso]/ had a Fault or two I cd name, yt she might be ye more Valueable: By Perfection, Madam, in sublunary Things we mean such Qualities are [as] render them most agreeable to our own Purposes. Gold without Alloy will not work; It is quite Unfit for ye Mint; And I fear Mrs P. witht a little more of ye *mere mortal* in her, will hardly receive that Impression I am willing to make. Was Admiration our onely Passion the most shining Excellencies wd infallibly carry ye Day: But, Madam, there are Other Passions in ye Heart of man; & Those more importunate. —But wt Impudence is It in me to pretend to inform Yr Grace of wt lies hid in Ye Human Heart? You have often dissected It with ye most accurate Discernment; And I know but One Instance yt can call yr Judgment in Question, wh is Yr Graces undeservd Partiality to Madam

Yr Graces most Obligd
& most Obedt Humble Sevt
EYoung.

I beg Madam my
Humble Duty to my
Lord &c: Wellwyn Sunday Night.

100. [Early February 1740/1]. Duchess of Portland

Address: To Her Grace / the Dutchess.
Longleat MSS. (13) 21.—Bath, pp. 258–9; Shelley, pp. 122–4.

Madam

Notwithstanding my late Reproof Yr Grace can not forbear dwelling on ye Praises of Yr Friend. You say You are Happy in her Conversation; Had Pope been her Admiror, cd He possibly have praisd her more? Yr Graces endeavour to convince me of Her Worth is such another Attempt as if you shd strive to convince me of ye Truth of ye Christian Religion; Both are equally unne^ce^ssary; & equally imply ye Distrust of Judgement: But Yr Grace, like some Other celebrated Divines, ~~will dwell on a Point~~ ^preach eternally on a text^ yt needs no Comment; & leave quite Unexplained, wt is truly Mysterious: For Instance, Why has yr Friend in spight of several Advantageous Offers, devoted herself to ye criminal selfishness of a single Life, when she knows yt it is her Duty to diffuse Happiness as much as possibly she can? Why has she been weded to Musick, & ye Pencel; when she knows there is a Harmony far beyond yt of Sounds; & when Yr Grace by Example has convincd Her, /[verso]/ yt there is a way of furnishing her Apartments (without ye expence of Canvass) with a Variety of Beauties wh a Kneller[1] might be proud to reach:—But This Madam, is touching on too tender a Point; I see Yr Grace is under a decent Confusion, to find yr Friends justly admird Excellencies may be fairly turnd to her Reproach. Madam I shd not presume to take this Liberty had I not ye greatest Value for You Both; How then can I see wth Patience One committing a great Error, & ye Other flatterg Her in it? This must needs greive any Honest heart which knows how many singular Virtues You have to be tarnishd, & dishonourd, by This, single indeed, but Heinous Fault. Mend as fast as You can, & peradventure You may find Pardon: Boldly, Madam, as I speak, I an well aware, yt I have nothing but my *Age* to recommend

---

[1] Sir Godfrey Kneller (1646–1723), famed for his portraits.

my Advice; And indeed I shall be very Glad if It can recommend That, /[new sheet]/ For, alas! there is Nothing else yt can possibly be recommended by It. To conclude this melancholy Letter wth ye same Intrepid Integrity yt runs thro ye Whole, give me leave, Madam, to say, That as Well as You love yr Friend, & she yr Grace; as much as You are charmd wth each Others conversation; If yr Friend can not frame to herself ye Idea of any Conversation wh she cd like better, she deserves not ye blessing of Yours: To have a warm & elegant Tast for every good thing, but That wh Nature designd for her cheif Repast, is being, at best, an Illustrious Rebel to ye Schemes of Providence; wh, tho it may gain her ye Admiration of ye Weak, will make, on ye Discerning, but slight Impressions in her favour. I am wth ye truest Respect

Madam

Yr Graces most Obedient

& most Obligd Humble Sevt

EYoung.

Pray Madam
My best Respects to my
Lord; & humble service to
Mr Achard. I shall have
ye Honour of waiting on Yr Grace, & Mrs P. soon.

101. London. [Sa.] 7 February 1740/1. Judith Reynolds.

Address: To Mrs Reynolds at / Mr Townsends in / Norfolk Street / In the Strand. *Postmark*: Peny Post Payd Shank.
Huntington Library MSS. 22215.—Swedenberg, p. 99.

Feby ye 7th
1740.

Dearest Madam.

This moment I receivd ye favour of Yours & am most sincerely concernd for yr Indisposition: In answer to ye Contents of yr Letter, I told You Madam, in my last that I was sure You had good reason for all yr Conduct, & consequently stood not in need of any Excuse; And as to *thinking favourably of You*; I must do that if I think justly, wh I shall ever endeavour to do: I suppose yr Health permits You not, Madam, at present to give an Answer to that Letter of mine, wh was so long before It came to yr Hand. I have taken care yt any Letter, directed to Mr Tassells, shall be sure to come safe to me at Wellwyn: With most cordial, & fervent Prayr for your better Health I am

Dearest Madam
Yr most Obedient, Obligd &
Affectionate Humble Sevt.
EYoung.

102. Welwyn, Herts. [Th.] 18 February [?1740/1]. Duchess of Portland.

Address: Her Grace the Dutchess.
Longleat MSS (28) 46.

Wellwyn Feby 18
Six in ye Eveng

Madam

I this moment finishd ye History of *your* Pamela:[1] I am so very exstremely obligd to yr Grace, for introducing me to agreeable an Acquaintance; But This is not yr Grace's first favour of That kind: Is it not a shame at my Age to own myself Wiser, &, I hope, Better, for conversing with a little Minks of Fifteen?[2] If I had not had ye misfortune of coming into ye World half a Century too soon, I shd have strove to have formd my Life on Her Example: Yr Grace has nickd ye Time critically wth yr *Little Ones*: All ye Mischeif is, They will think ye credit of this amiable Performance, & Pamela's Character (I have good reason to hope) will be much less surprizing, when *They* are grown into Knowledge of ye World.—In a word tis an excellent Book; & ye Lady

---

[1] A second edition of *Pamela* had appeared on 14 February, according to Sale (1936, p. 14).
[2] i.e. the heroine of Richardson's novel.

yt feels no Impression from it, had best keep ye Secret: As
Mrs Jewks,[1] in comparison, will grow an Amiable Character.
                    I am, Madam, Yr Graces
                            most Obligd & most Obedt
                                Humble Sevt   EYoung.
Madam I beg my Duty to my
Ld Duke, & my best respects
to yr Good Company
/[in margin]/ PS. Pray, Madam, my Love to goodman
Andrews[2] when you see Him.

103. [Welwyn, Herts.][3] [F.] 27 February 1740/1.
Judith Reynolds.

Address: To Mrs Reynolds at / Mr Townsends in / Norfolk Street in ye /
Strand. *Postmark*: Peny Post Payd Shank.
Huntington Library MSS. 22216.—Swedenberg, p. 100.

                                            Feb: 27
                                              1740
Dearest Madam
    Thro the neglect of my Town-Landlord I receivd not ye
favour of Yours, till yesterday.
    I am heartily sorry for yr Brothers Inflexibility: Your own
Conduct thro this whole Affair has given m[e] ye highest
Esteem of Yr Virtue, & Prudence; & lays ~~me~~ me under
ye strongest Obligations to be to ye last moment of my life,
wth ye utmost Gratitude, Respect, & Affection
                                        Dearest Madam
                                        Yr most Obedient &
                                        most Humble Sevt
I hope in God that   EYoung.
yr pretious Health
is entirely reestablishd.

    [1] Pamela's custodian.
    [2] Young uses the name of Pamela's father apparently in playful allusion to some
one of the Duchess's circle of acquaintance.
    [3] Though the postmark shows that this, the last of Young's letters to Judith
Reynolds, was mailed in London, the reference to 'my Town-Landlord' (Benjamin
Tassel, near Temple Bar) suggests the probability that Young wrote from Welwyn
and sent the letter to London by a messenger to be posted there, thus avoiding the
attention of his local postmistress.

104. Welwyn, Herts. [Su.] 10 May 1741. Duchess of Portland.

Address: To her Grace.
Longleat MSS. (16) 26.—Bath, pp. 261–2; Shelley, pp. 127–8.

Madam

I beg Yr Grace to make my Complimts to Ly Isabella,[1] & pay her my Congratulations on her Conversation[2] to Xtianity: And please to let her know that if she is as good a Christian threescore years Hence, I will venture to promise Her infinitely more Admirers (& Those worth having,) than *this* World can afford her at fiveteen; tho she shd prove yr Fairest of her Race. Next to a *fine Person*, a *fine Understandg*, & a *greatness of Mind*, are, generally, the two cheif Objects of Human Pride; Now a *fine understanding*, is an Understandg of Compass, that takes in all things in wh we are much concernd, whether Present or Future, Seen or Unseen, in Fashion, or out: And a *great mind* is a mind yt has pwr to comply with ye Dictates of this *extensive View* in spight of all Temptations to ye Contrary.

Please, Madam, to let her Ladysp know, yt as she is just come into a World, where there are many very much inclind to impose upon strangers; I have taken ye Liberty, (as I wish her well,) to inform her of These Particulars: And now I give Her leave to be /[verso]/ as proud as she pleases of a Find Understandg, & a Great Mind, provided they are of ye right Sort.

me

If her Ladyship says she does not perfectly understand as having not yet learnt our Language, Tell her I desire her to copy her Mama, & then tis no matter whether she understands me or not.

I am Madam, Yr Graces
most Obedient & Obligd
Humble Sevt
Wellwyn May   EYoung.
ye 10th 1741.

---

[1] A Portland daughter, Isabella, had been baptized on the 5th (London *Daily Post* of 7 May). She had been born on 9 April 1741 and was to live only until 28 February 1743.

[2] An obsolete equivalent of 'conversion', the latest example cited in the *Oxford English Dictionary* being from the year 1570.

105. [London.] [Sa.] 30 May 1741. Duchess of Portland.

Longleat MSS. (17) 28.

Madam

I am just come to Town, & as Ill News flies apace, ye First thing I heard was that my Ld Duke was confind wth the Gout. I beg Madam, my humble Duty to his Grace & desire to know how He does: I hope Yr Grace feels no Pain but what is occasiond by my Lords. And to ballance That, I hope ye perfect Health of ye Little Family makes You some amends. I am wth true Gratitude & Respect

Madam
Yr Graces most Obedient
& Obligd Humble Sevt
EYoung.

May ye 30th
  1741.
I desire my humble service
  to Mr Ashard.

106. [London.] Su [?14 June 1741].[1] Duchess of Portland.

Longleat MSS. (18) 29.

Madam

I came to Town late last night, & return early Tomorrow morng, so that I am sorry I can do no more than enquire after Yr Graces Health, & that of Those yt are Dear to You.—I thank You, Madam, for your last kind Letter; tho

---

[1] The date of the letter is established from its apparent allusion to word of the critical illness of the Duchess's father, the Earl of Oxford. Oxford was taken ill on Saturday the 13th and was to die on the Tuesday following (letter of Mary Pendarves in Llanover, 1861, ii. 156–7).

It was by much the most melancholy Letter that was ever receivd, by

> Madam
> Yr Graces most
> Devoted & Obligd
> Humble Sevt
> EYoung.

I beg Madam my
Humble Duty to my Ld
& my Compliments
   to Mr Achard.

Sunday. [in another hand] 1741

107. Welwyn, Herts. [Su.] 12 July 1741. Duchess of Portland.

Longleat MSS. (19) 30.—Bath, pp. 262–3; Llanover, 1861, ii. 159;[1] Thomas, p. 593; Shelley, pp. 128–9.

Madam
   Could I have administerd any Consolation to Yr Grace,[2] & had forborn to do it; I then indeed had been quite Inexcusable: But I too well know yt ye first Agonies of real Sorrow have no ears; & that a man might as wisely talk wth his Friend in a Fever & desire his Pulse to lie still, as to Philosophize with a wounded Heart. These, Madam, are ye Strokes of Heaven, nor will They be defeated of their Effect; Nor indeed is It for our Interest that They shd: Of God Allmightys manefold Blessings to mankind, his Afflictions are the greatest. They will make us Wise, or Nothing will: We can not bare an uninterrupted Prosperity prosperously; we can not bear it without being a little Intoxicated wth ye Delicious Cup, wh will make our Virtue reel, if not fall: Hence an Antient sayd as wisely as wittily, No man is

---

[1] The editor of the Delany volumes thought Young's letter must have been given to Mrs. Pendarves. Slight variations in the text, however, show that what was published was a transcript of the original.

[2] i.e. on the death of her father, Edward Harley, 2nd Earl of Oxford. He was buried in Westminster Abbey on 24 June.

so Unhappy as He who never knew Affliction:[1] I therefore congratulate Your Grace on wt You suffer; nor let it sound cruel, or Harsh in yr ear; for in This I am but a little beforehand wth yr own self. For shortly You will bless God for this great Calamity, & find that ye Best may be betterd by ye Kind Discipline of Heaven. Heaven suffers nothing to happen to men but wt is for his Temporal or Eternal Wellfare: And our Tears have /[verso]/ as much reason to praise God, as our Triumphs: In what a blessed Situation are we then, Madam, under such a Being who does, who will do, who can do nothing but for our Good? What Passion in the Heart of man is half so Natural as ye Love of God, while man is in his right Senses? We have no motives of Love, but either ye Excellence of ye Thing itself, or its Benefit to Us; & in neither View has God any Rival, or Shadow of It. Now why is Divine Love so Natural to Us? & why is It enjoynd as ye First & great Command? Because, if This is complyd wth a Course of Duty will be a Course of Delight. We shall have ye same Pleasure in it as a fine Gentleman has in obeying ye Commands of a Favourite Mistriss: Love carrys ye whole Heart wth it, & when our Heart is engagd, among Toils & Difficultys we find Ease & Pleasure, & nothing is too hard for the great Alacrity of our Attempts.

But is not Love too familiar a Passion from such Insects towards ye King & Father of all Being? It seems to be so: But I beg yr Grace (for ye Bible is a pretty Book) to review ye Gospel for Whitsunday,[2] & to see wt a familiar Intimacy by that tremendous Powr is indulgd to men. I never read it but wth Astonishment. Nor is It possible /[conjugate leaf]/ for any one who reads it, to suspect that any of His Dispensations are realy Severe, who speaks to us in such Language, as ye fondest Father might make use of, & who will encourage no Expectations in us, yt shall not be far Surpassd by ye Event.

In a word, Madam, Heaven is as sollicitous for our Happiness Here, as is consistent wth its far Kinder Concern for our Happiness Hereafter: And our Afflictions (wh is saying much in their favour) plainly tell us we are Immortal:

---

[1] Seneca, *De Providentia*, iii. 3: 'Nihil . . . mihi videtur infelicius eo, cui nihil umquam evenit adversi.'   [2] St. John, 14:15-31.

Were we not, we shd be as Free from Cares, but then we shd be as Destitute of Hopes too, as ye Beasts that perish. May yt Powr *who bindeth up ye broken Heart, & giveth Medicine to heal its Sickness* be for ever yr Graces Comfort & Defence: And please to accept ye most cordial good wishes for ye reestablishment of yr Peace, & ye most sincere Respects for yt sole Foundation of It, yr Virtues, from

Madam

Yr Graces most Obligd

& most Obedt Humble Sevt

EYoung.

wt I write is not to Inform, but confirm yr Grace.
or rather to make my Court by showing yt in Points
of consequence I have ye honour to be of yr opinion.

Madam I beg my
humble Duty to my Ld
Duke &c:

Wellwyn July 12th
1741.

[verso] I beg my humble Duty to my
Lady Oxford when Yr Grace
sees Her.

108. Tunbridge Wells, Kent. [W.] 5 August 1741. Duchess of Portland.

Longleat MSS. (20) 32.—Bath, p. 263; Shelley, p. 130.

Tunbridge Wells

Madam

There are but Two Distempers, & Those very Different, yt bring People to this place: Either Redundancy, or Want of Spirits: The First makes people Mad, the Last Fools. The First, I observe, in this place, like Persons bit by ye Taruntula, Dance immoderately, till the Distemper flies off. The Last, like poor Jobs Friends, sit Silent for 7 Days together, till ye Water gives ym Utterance. The Virtue of ye Water is yet got no Higher than my Fingers ends, wh enables me to write; But when It will arrive at my Lips is uncertain, but when It does, I shall have ye Pleasure of conversing wth Yr Graces Friends, many of whom are Here, but all my Conversation wth ym has Hitherto been carryd on by Signs onely on my Part, for Sound to one in my state is too great an Expence.

/[verso]/ By This time Yr Grace begins to guess ye reason why I left ye Town witht taking leave: That was Rude, but I shd have been much ruder had I attempted it: To have made Yr Grace a Dumb Visit wd have been very unpolite; And at best, like Hamlets Ghost, I shd have been able to [illegible word stricken out] have spoke is [in] Dismal Monosyllables onely;[1] & therefore I humbly hope Yr Grace will pardon me for not frighting You out of your Wits. For I know no Lady on earth yt would have lost more by such an Accident wth ^{all} possible Respect & Gratitude I am ever

Madam

Yr Graces most Obligd

& Obedt Humble Sevt

EYoung

I beg my humble
Duty to my Ld Duke
&c: August ye 5
   1741.

109. [Tunbridge Wells, Kent.] Su. [?August 1741].
Duchess of Portland.

Longleat MSS. (21) 33.—Bath, pp. 263–4; Shelley, pp. 130–1.

Madam

Sr John Stanley[2] between ye Waters & a high relish of yr Graces regard to Him is so elevated, yt He talks of dancing at ye next Ball: Mrs Donollan[3] whom I have studid I

---

[1] The ghost of Hamlet's father repeats the single syllable 'swear' (*Hamlet*, I. v).

[2] Sir John Stanley (1659–1744), Commissioner of the Customs, married to Anne Granville, Mary Pendarves's aunt who had been Maid of Honour to Queen Mary II.

[3] Anne Donnellan, daughter of Nehemiah Donnellan, Lord Chief Baron of the Exchequer in Ireland. She was at Tunbridge Wells from the middle of July to the end of August. On 18 July Elizabeth Robinson had written to her: 'I hope Dr. Young will be at Tunbridge this season; he spends some time there. I believe you will find his thoughts little confined to the place; he will entertain you with conversation much above what one generally finds there, where they talk little but water,

find to be of an excellent Mind & Heart; I had once thoughts of drawing so amiable a Character at length; but I shall Abridge it in One Sentence wh implys All. 'She is worthy to be yr Grace's Friend.['] I am heartily sorry my Ld Duke has been in Pain,[1] but I hope by this time He is reaping the Advantage of It, in a quicker relish of Health: There is no One Here who have so Distinguished themselves either by their Wisdom or Folly, as to contribute to your Amusement by their History: Here is a Great Fortune,[2] wh is followd by a Pack of Noble Beagles, but wh will be ye Happy Dog no One yet can tell: I'm much obligd to /[verso]/ your Grace, & to ye D. & Dutchess of Leeds,[3] when I recover my own Country, I shall prevent the Honour of their sending to me. I proposd writing ~~to~~ ᵃ long letter, but Yr Grace is repreivd from ye execution of yt Design by ye Waters: I can neither stand, nor see, nor think, & if yr Grace can read wt I have allready written, His Majestys Affairs, at this Critical Juncture,[4] need not be at a Stand, for want of a Decypherer. I am, Drunk or Sober,

Madam

Yr Graces ever Faithfull
& Devoted Humble Sevt
EYoung.

I beg my best Wishes & humble Duty to my Ld Duke; & please to divide ᵐʸ Heart, like a Bisket, among ye little Ones.

Sunday.

bread and butter, and scandal' (Montagu, 1810, i. 247). On 1 September Mrs. Donnellan, in her turn, wrote: 'I conversed much with Doctor Young, but I had not enough to satisfy me. We ran through many subjects, and I think his conversation much to my taste. He enters into human nature, and both his thoughts and expressions are new' (Climenson, 1906, i. 85).

   1 The Duke suffered from gout.
   2 Young may be implying Anne Donnellan, as she had been given her sister Catherine's inheritance on the latter's marriage in 1728 with Robert Clayton.
   3 Thomas Osborne (1713–89), 4th Duke of Leeds, married (1740) to Lady Mary Godolphin, daughter of Francis, Earl of Godolphin.
   4 A hotly contested general election was in process following the dissolution of Parliament on 27 April. The new Parliament met on 1 December and Walpole's resignation came on 11 February in 1741/2.

110. Welwyn, Herts. [Th.] 17 September 1741.
Duchess of Portland.

Longleat MSS. (22) 34.—Bath, pp. 264–5; Shelley, pp. 132–3.

Wellwyn
Sepr 17 1741

Madam

To be courted by a Dutchess in my old age, is a very
extraordinary Fate. Should I tell it to my Parishioners, they
would never beleive one word I spoke to them from ye
Pulpit afterwards: I lie therefore under a terrible Dilemma;
I must either burst by stiffling this se^cret; Or make Atheists
of my whole Nighbourhood. Such scrapes as This, shd
teach ye World ye wholesome lesson of Humility, & never
to covet blessings yt are too great for them; which are very
apt to overwhelm them, or to betray; & while they gratifie
their Ambition, wound their Virtue, or their Peace.

But, Madam, I think it is in yr powr to make me some
amends for ye Injury You have done me; by standing my
Friend wth yr Graces correspondent Mrs Donollan; I should
be ashamd of not having ye truest regard for her accomplishments; & had I not passd thro London, like an Arrow out
of a Bow, I shd have *payd myself* ye Complement of waiting
on Her: wh I hope to do very soon.

As for ye Honour of waiting on Yr Grace, I have a
thousand Arguments against it, & ten thousand /[verso]/
Wishes for it; but Wishes & Arguments are a very unequall
match; tis therefore much to be feard I shall not have Virtue
enough to stay away.

As for yr Graces Letter wh has fallen into Mr Murrys[1]
hand, be not troubled; there were no secrets in it; had it
faln into ye Hands of my Ld Duke himself, it have done no
harm. I beg Yr Grace to be my Mr Murry, & in yr very
first Letter into *Bondstreet*,[2] to turn Advocate for me. This,

---

[1] William Murray (1705–93), later Lord Chief Justice of the King's Bench and
Earl of Mansfield, at this time a rising lawyer. As a student at Oxford in 1730 he had
made out an 'Outline for a Course of Legal Study' for the Duke of Portland. The
letter to which Young referred presumably was concerned with the Duchess's efforts
to obtain ecclesiastical preferment for Young.
[2] The site of Anne Donnellan's London home.

Madam, I repeat because it is realy some concern to me, for I am not onely indebted to Mrs Donollan, for ye credit of her acquaintance, but to her mitred Brother,[1] in a very particular manner. I am now reading some of his works not yet publishd, & that wth ye greatest Improvement, & Pleasure. He & I were Rivals at Tunbridge as to a marryd Lady, till her Husband in a jealous fit came from town, & snatchd her from ye impending Danger. But Yr Grace will keep ye secret.

/[conjugate leaf]/ I have heard Ly P———h's[2] character, & therefore am not at all surprizd to hear she is at Bullstrode. Her Lyship is nearly akin to yr Grace by a far nobler Relation than that of Blood: But what is That to me? I have a general Objection agst conversing wth Ladys: When Hats & Hoods meet, how naturally do they fall into mutual Flattery? The Vice, in yt case, seems to have obtain a general Toleration; ^nay^ It passes for an Accomplishment at Least, if not a Virtue: But if it is an Accomplishmt, Accomplishments can do mischeif. For this reason, I think for ye future, I shall converse wth no woman but yr Grace: not yt yr Graces [*sic*] never flatters; quite ye Contrary; but then You discover at ye same time so good an Understanding; that yr Flattery does no harm; tho our mouths water at it, we dare not swallow it, least while we accept of yr Compliment, we shd lose yr Esteem: for This we are sure of, we can not do wrong under yr Grace's eye, & pass Undetected: Thus, Madam, is yr Discernment our Rescue from yr Complaisance.

/[verso]/ If Yr Grace sees ye Ds of Kent, please to let her know that there was more Virtue in her enquiring after me than she perhaps imagines; That there is an unextinguishable ambition in man, wh is highly gratifid by such Honours, shown by some sort of Persons; & That I shall enter it, in that Short Inventory of Goods, wh Fortune allots me— 'That I was rememberd in absence by ye Ds of Kent'.

---

[1] i.e. her brother-in-law, Robert Clayton, since 1735 Bishop of Cork and Ross. The unpublished work was probably *A Replication . . . with a History of Popery* (1743).

[2] Lady Peterborough, Anastasia Robinson (d. 1755), famous dramatic singer and widow of the 3rd Lord Peterborough (1658–1735), an especially close friend of the Duchess.

And now, Madam, have I not writen a very long Letter?
And to show myself still more Generous, I have written such
a One, as can not possibly lay yr Grace under ye least
Obligation. This, Madam, is an Instance of Generosity, wh
I defie yr Grace to follow: Nor let This Frankness give You
ye least Disgust; For this is ye Onely Instance of Generosity,
in wh I presume on any share of Competition wth You. My
Ld Duke, ye Dear Little Ones, & Mr Achard—Yr Grace
knows my Meaning as well as I do; & can express it better.
The Sincerity of Heart will appear in its Birthday Suit, if Yr
Grace will vouchsafe to put it into Words; wh will much
oblige

Madam Yr Graces most Devoted
& ever Faithfull Humble Sevt   EYoung

111. Welwyn, Herts. [Th.] 29 October 1741. Duchess
of Portland.

Longleat MSS. (23) 36.—Bath, pp. 265–6.

Madam
Your Graces little Letter is a great Satyr; It is exstremely
Kind, & exstremely Severe; It pleases, & pains, Like a Bee
in a Blossom, from its ambrosial Entrenchment It stings me
home: Like my Ld B——[1] It bites, while it kisses.—Is
not Yr Grace tird? If not Ill run on till tomorrow, & outposie
that huge Waterpot of Flowrs, ye dropsical & facetious Ld
G——.[2] But I forget my Band. And therefore, Madam,
please to observe that all the Pleasures of man may be rankt
under ye following Heads.

1. Outward Senses
2. Imagination
3. Honour
4. Benevolence
5. Esteem
6. Selfapprobation

[1] If Young meant more than 'Lord Bee', the allusion is now lost.
[2] Unidentified.

7. Gratification of ye Will
8. Pain avoided
9. Hope.

You see, Madam, what a Monster Human Pleasure is, What a Hydra with a thousand heads? Which will your Grace please to chuse? That I suppose which is most like
your own; I mean, wh is most worth having of any   this *in* or any other, Assembly: /[verso]/ Now That, Madam, is *Benevolence*, (as I will prove at large when I have ye Honour of seeing You:) All the Other Pleasures, are *short*, or *precarious*, or mixt, as Those of *Sense, Imagination, Honour,* & *Esteem*; Or else *mortal*, as yt of *Hope*; or some way or Other inferior to ye Pleasure of *Benevolence*, as is even *Selfapprobation*, wh is onely a Consequence of *Benevolence*; & ye Cause is allways nobler than ye Effect.

Whether Yr Grace has examind this Truth as much as I have done, or no, I can not tell; but This I know that how little Acquaintance soever Yr Head may have made with it, It   *is* a great Intimate, & perfect Crony of yr Hearts, or ~~ed~~ Yr Grace cd not after my Behaviour be so Kind to me: But I dare say You had studyd, as well as *felt* it; else it wd be quite Impossible You shd be so great a Mistriss in it; I therefore must conclude by saying that Yr Grace is either a perfect Riddle, or a profound Philosopher. I am wth the truest Esteem, Madam,

Yr Graces most Obligd
& most Obedt Hble Sevt
EYoung.

/[conjugate leaf]/ I propose the Honour & Pleasure of waiting on You abt ye middle of next month, if Yr Grace permits. But I beg before I come down You wd turn ye
Ghost out of the Gallery.[1] Mr. Goldsmith[2] can do in a   *it*

---

[1] The 'ghost' of Bulstrode was legendary, said to have been that of the infamous Judge George Jeffreys (1648–89), for whom the house was built in 1686. At the time of Young's letter Elizabeth Robinson also spoke in a letter of 'the Daemons in Buckinghamshire'.

[2] A mistake for 'Grosmith', the Reverend George Grosmith (d. 1754), a Portland protégé, at the time Vicar of the neighbouring village of Dorney and a Minor

trice. But spare ye poor Red Sea, & send the Devel[1] to ye Spanish Squadron, or if You had rather send the Spanish Squadron to Him.

My Humble Duty to my Ld Duke.
My Love to ye little One[s].
My humble Service to Mr Achard.

Wellwyn Octr 29
    1741.

112. [Tu.] 17 November 1741. Duchess of Portland.

Address: To her Grace.
Longleat MSS. (24) 38.—Bath, p. 266; Shelley, pp. 134–5.

Madam
    Your Grace in your last has brought a very Severe Indict-ment against me, I can by no means plead guilty to it. On Friday[2] I propose rendering myself at yr Graces Tribunal; I shall not be content with holding up my hand, I will hold up my Heart at your Bar, & if You will promise not to prick it, You shall take it [in] your hand, & see if You can find out yt Fault wh You lay to my charge. I am very tender in this Point, for I know that not onely Good-manners, but Virtue

Canon of Windsor, and later, from 1746 to his death, Rector of the parish church of Hedgerly, which Bulstrode adjoins and where several of the Portland servants were buried. He is mentioned by Elizabeth Robinson about this time in connection with the following bizarre anecdote: 'A hatter of Windsor left £100 to a man on condition that he would bury him according to his desire under a mulberry tree in his own garden, 10 feet deep. The assistants to drink 12 bottles of wine over his grave, and French horns playing during the whole ceremony, and this was accord-ingly performed yesterday, to the great offence of Mr. Grosmith, who says he was not a Christian' (Climenson, 1906, i. 85).
    [1] Perhaps the 'Red Sea' and the 'Devel' were pictures in the Duchess's gallery.
    [2] It was during this visit that Young and Dean Alured Clarke of Exeter were together. Of them Elizabeth Robinson wrote: 'We have lost our divines [21 Decem-ber], whose company we regret; there is great pleasure in conversing with people of such a turn as Dr Young and Dr Clarke.' Of Young she added: 'There is nothing of speculation, either in the Terra Firma of Reason, or the Visionary province of fancy, into which he does not lead the imagination. In his conversation he examines everything, determines hardly anything, but leaves one's judgment at liberty' (Climenson, 1906, i. 91).

is concernd in the Violation of that Respect, wh I know is
your Graces Due, & especially from my self: But I think I
shall not fly to your Mercy, as an Asylum from your Justice;
Yr Justice season with a little spice of goodnature shall
acquit me: I would not, Madam, persist in my Vindication,
was it not /[verso]/ to rescue your Grace from a Mistake,
for a Mistake in Yr Grace is such a Novelty that for ought
I know, it might fright You into a fine Lady, & give yr
Grace an absolute Palpitation: As for myself, I can easily
own a Fault when I really commit it, as a Bankrupt is not
very tender of owning a Debt: Especially to Yr Grace I shd
freely make confession, for, (I know not how it comes to
pass) I find I could prefer a Pardon from Yr Grace before an
Acknowledgment from Another. I beg my humble Duty to
my Lord Duke & best Respects & Affection elsewhere.
I am

> Madam
> Yr Graces most Obedient
> but not abandoned, Criminal,
> & Humble Sevt
> EYoung.

Nov 17
1741.

113. Welwyn, Herts. [Tu.] 22 December 1741.
Duchess of Portland.

Longleat MSS. (25) 40.—Bath, p. 267; Shelley, pp. 135–6.

Madam
   As I write This to yr Grace on Horseback, You will forgive
the many Allusion[s] You meet with to that Animal. The
first I shall saddle is Mrs Pendarvess; I look on her Understanding to be very surefooted, & perfectly acquainted with
the Road; & tho Her Understandg cd show a good sheer
pair of Heels, & distance most companys it comes into, yet
is it wisely content not to rob others of their good humour
by seeing themselves Undone; thinking it enough yt it is in

[her] powr to give them the Spleen whenever she thinks fit.
As for Miss Robinson, her Understandg is of ye best blood,
& can carry any Plate she thinks good to put in for; But It
is sometimes rather pleasd to prance, than run, wh has this
advantage in it, that It   ^is^   done with more Grace, & less
Pains; & yet carrys in it a Demonstration at ye same time,
yt she can leave us whenever she will. As for Mrs Dews[1], my
Horse says He has no more similes, unless she will permit
me to say, That perfect Complainsance [*sic*] seems to be the
/[verso]/ Spur of her Conversation, & Discretion to hold
the rein. As for Yr Grace, your Understandg has been in the
Manage; Art & Nature cant adjust their rights about ~~about~~,
it; Each swears in Its turn, that she is yr greatest Benefactor;
& not being able to agree, they split the Difference, *Nature*
takes all that is most amiable in yr conversion, & *Art* all yt
is most prudent, yet even This does not end ye Dispute, for
they are forcd to call for grains & scruples to determine who
has the largest share.

Thus Ladies have I saluted You all round; & I am now
for binding You up in one Nosegay alltogether. Thus Incorporated pray Ladys wt are You? Are You the Graces or
the Muses? You are too many for ye *First*, & too Few for
the last, & yet there is a vast deal of both those Sisterhoods
in You. I will therefore fairly tell Yr Grace what I apprehend
to be [the] Case: Considering what a World we live in, &
that Wit & Beautie run both pretty low, Those 2 Societys
cd ~~not~~ no longer seperately subsist, & yt they might not
Both /[conjugate leaf]/ make an Absolute Break of it, One
somewhat like Yr Grace, & wiser than the Rest, proposd a
Coalition, & deputed You four Ladys as a little Committee
to mankind, to show that they still subsist, & to   ^do^   them
credit with ye World. But whether this be quite Honest in
those Jades calld Goddesses I leave to my Ld Duke [stricken

---

[1] Mrs. John D'Ewes (*née* Anne Granville), a sister of Mrs. Pendarves. In a letter to
her of 19 January following, Mrs. Pendarves remarked on her apparent expression of
distaste for some scandals about 'fine ladies': 'Our friend Dr Young, as you have
lately observed, has helped us much on these occasions; but if all the world were
prudent and regular in their behaviour, it would not be half so diverting as it is
now' (Llanover, 1861, ii. 167).

phrase] & Mr Achard to determine to whom I beg Duty
Respect & Service.

Wth the warmest sense of all Yr Graces favours particularly the last I am

Madam
Yr Graces most Obligd
& Obedt Humble Sevt
EYoung.

Wellwyn
Decem 22d
   1741.
Pray Mad[am]
My best respects
to the Committee
& Love to ye Little Ones.
Caroline[1] desires Yr Grace to accept of her Duty.

114. [Welwyn, Herts.]. [Tu.] 12 January 1741/2. Duchess of Portland.

Longleat MSS. (26) 42.—Bath, pp. 267–9; Shelley, pp. 138–9.

Madam

Your Graces Friend[2] has lately calld on me twice; He
passes to & fro like an Inhabitant of another world, &
tell[s] us the Deceast, the buryd in the Country, what is
doing upon Earth: I sent my Compliments to yr Grace by
Him, wh I was half unwilling to do, for tho we of these
lower Regions bear a good Regard to Virtue, yet since we
are quite incapable of doing any real Service, we are sparing
of verbal civilitys least It shd look like Compliment &
nothing else. If Miss Dashwood[3] is ye Creature You represent; I give your Grace joy of her, but I more congratulate

---

[1] Caroline Lee (*c.* 1727–49), Young's stepdaughter.

[2] Either William Freind (1715–66), Rector of Witney in Oxfordshire near
Ditchley, who had married a cousin of Elizabeth Robinson in 1739, or more likely,
his father, Robert (1667–1751), Headmaster of Westminster School and a Canon
of Windsor.

[3] Catherine Dashwood (d. 1779), one of the Duchess's circle especially acclaimed
for her beauty. She is said to have been courted by the poet James Hammond, who
died in the summer of this year. She never married.

Herself; All gain by good Qualities, but ye Possessor most: But be pleasd, Madam, to observe yt This possessor shd be possest: Fine women unmarryd, are like fine Diamonds in ye Jewellers Shop, gazd at by Multitudes, but Enjoyd by none, & if they stay there too long they are cheapend down below their real value: The Lady, & ye Ring should be Both worn; /[verso]/ The Ring when on ye finger is in its proper Situation, and answering ye End for wh It was made. Now I talk of marriage I will tell Yr Grace a piece of News, Sr Tho: Hanmer was marryd last Thursday to Mrs Pendar-vess,[1] This I heard in this Country but yesterday: I wish it be true, for I know they wd Both be Happier in yt State than singly they can possibly be; There is but One Objection against Marriage, & that is one wh ye wise world amongst its ten thousand Objections never makes; I mean that ye Hus-band & Wife seldom die in one Day, & then ye Survivor must be necessarily miserable.

But to return to ye delightfull Miss Dashhood [*sic*], Your Grace says she is exstremely Modest; I will let your Grace into a Secret, for I know Miss D—— well; I knew her Mother[2] before her, & I know her Daughter tho yet un-born: This Modesty is a lowly & successful Cheat: It seems to decline that wh It most desires; It proceeds from a love of Esteem, /[conjugate leaf]/ joynd to a Diffidence of our taking the most proper methods to gain it; This Diffi-dence creates yt inward uneasie Emotion, wh discovers itself in the Cheeks; A blushing Cheek who would not Kiss? But why? Because our own Pride tells us it carrys some Defference in it to our Judgment, & a Desire of our good Opinion; so yt ye Praise we bestow on this Virtue proceeds in some measure from our own Vice: Thus You see, Madam, yt I take ye Liberty of calling Yr Grace proud; But Madam take not offence at it; for if love of esteem is a Vice (wh is all

---

[1] The second wife of Sir Thomas Hanmer (1677–1746), from whom he had been estranged, had died in March of 1741. That Young was mistaken in what he had heard appears in his next letter.

[2] The blank in the couplet in Young's *Love of Fame*:

> Modern good-breeding carry to its height,
> And Lady D——'s self will be polite.

(v. 487-8)

which Dodsley said was either 'Lady Dashwood or Dysart' may be decided from Young's reference here as applying more certainly to the first of the two.

that I lay to your or Miss D——s charge) It is a Vice that is to be found in Other Angels, in those *Above*: Love of Esteem is planted in all created Rational Beings for excellent purposes, & it can never do harm, but when It is *conducted*, or *directed* amiss. Let none then be so Proud, & so foolish too at ye same time, as to say they have no Pride in them: I honour Miss D——s modest pride; It is ye onely Pride yt carrys its Point; Confident Pride defeats itself, & loses our Esteem by being too sure of carrying it. I dwell on This, /[verso]/ because about ten years agoe It was quite a Fashion with young Ladies to pretend to more Impudence than they had; And nothing cd put them so much out of countenance as to have it suspected that they [were] capable of blushing at anything: If Yr Grace knows any such please to tell them from me that They exstremely mistake their own Interest, if their designs are on mankind: Men are such impudent Rascals, but to their Honour be it spoken, so conscious of that their grand Defect, that they doat on Modesty whereever they find it, tho It shd happen to be in coaldust, & Tatters: Wt pretty company have I brought your Grace into? You see wt You get by desiring Letters from

Madam

Yr Graces most Obligd

& Obedt Humble Sevt

EYoung.

I beg my best Respects
to my Ld Duke &c:
Jan: 12th
1741.

115 [Welwyn, Herts.]. [Late February 1741/2].[1] Duchess of Portland.

Longleat MSS. (29) 48.—Bath, pp. 270-1; Shelley, pp. 143-4.

Madam

I humbly thank yr Grace for yr kind letter, but there are too many melancholy Articles in it to give all the Satisfaction

[1] The date is derived from the death of Young's neighbour mentioned in the latter part of the letter.

I cd wish. I hope my Lord Duke is perfectly recoverd of ye Gout, & that Lady Fanny[1] has likewise set yr Graces Heart at ease, as to her Disorder. But poor Dr. Clarke[2]—but why do I call him poor, I know no One whose Deathbed I shd envy more: He's a very Exemplary man, I love his Person, & I reverence his Character: I would write to Him, but that I fear might some way or Other prove troublesome; Yet I long to know how He does, & to hear better news of Him, than yr Grace sent me. If therefore You shd do me the Honour of writing, I beg Madam, a line or two concerning Him. I proposd much Satisfaction in his Acquaintance.

/[verso]/ It gives me great pleasure that Ld Quarendon[3] has yr Graces Vote, He certainly deserves it, & He has as certainly in it a proper Reward of great Desert. Ld Cornbury[4] I have not the Honour of knowing, but hope Yr Grace will introduce [me] to his Acquaintance; I know his Lordship's Character or I shd not desire this favour. When Persons of Quality have *Equall* merit with the most deserving of Those below them, they have really *Greater*; The Diamond is better set, & throws a brighter Lustre; I do not mean from their Fortune onely, but from their manner wh has often a Grace & Dignity in it Incommunicable to those of inferior rank. Since Yr Grace by yr own Authority has been pleasd to divorce Mrs P. & Sr T H.[5] they need not have the trouble of going to Doctors Commons. I propose Madam the Honour of waiting on yr Grace in Town /[conjugate leaf]/ about the 18th of next month. But if possible, & no great trouble to You, I shd be truly much ogligd if Yr

[1] Lady Frances, infant daughter of the Portlands, who died the next year. She had suffered a convulsion of which the Duchess had written to Elizabeth Robinson on 4 February.

[2] Alured Clarke (b. 1696), Dean of Exeter, whom Young had seen at Bulstrode in November. Like Young, Clarke was a Chaplain in Ordinary to George II and sued in vain for a bishopric. He died on 31 May.

[3] George Henry Lee (1718–72), Viscount Quarendon, served in Parliament for Oxford from 1740 to 1743 when he succeeded his father, Young's brother-in-law, the 2nd Earl of Litchfield.

[4] Henry Hyde (1710–53), Viscount Cornbury, had been re-elected to Parliament in 1741 for the University of Oxford.

[5] Referring to Young's mistaken report of Sir Thomas Hanmer's marriage with Mary Pendarves in his letter of 12 January: 'Doctors Commons' was the customary source of divorce at the time.

Grace wd let me hear of Dr Clarke long before. The Herse of Mr Hale my Nighbour, Friend, & a most eminently worthy young Gentleman, past by my Door for his own Seat, this very moment: He went to Town to provide for his marriage with One Miss Gilbert (whom I know well & admire) & dyd with her weding Ring on his Finger.[1] These things strike us, but most people are struck so often by them, that at last they seem to lose their feeling: When these Things cease to pain us, Heaven gives us up; It leaves us entirely to ye World to make ye most of it; the next step is, that ye World having us entirely its own begins to domeneer, & denys us our usual share of Pleasure, (wh is ye necessary case of ye Abandond) & then we are finely Bit. I beg my humble Duty to my Ld Service to Mr Achard &c: Yr Graces most Obligd & Obedt EY

/[in margin]/ Caroline gives her Duty.

116. [Welwyn, Herts.]. [Late February 1741/2]. Duchess of Portland.

Longleat MSS. (53) 90.—Bath, p. 281; Shelley, pp. 173–4.

Madam

I know what Pain is, & am heartily sorry for poor Mr Achard, & I wish I was more sorry still. We feel not enough for One another, considering who felt such Exstremitys for Us all. Afflictions, as your Grace most justly observes have their Use with regard to Another Scene: And give me leave to add, they have their excellent Use with regard to *this* Scene too; They soften the Heart, & make us more Humane; They Humble ye Heart, & make us sensible of Blessings in that Situation, which was Insipid to us before; The bare

---

[1] William Hale (b. 1713) of King's Manor, Walden (seven miles north-west of Welwyn), died in London on 16 February and was buried in Walden on the 28th. Nothing is now known of Young's acquaintance, Miss Gilbert. Hale's will (Somerset House, P.C.C. Trenley 88), made 10 February and proved 9 March, provides for a number of servants and friends but makes no mention of either a wife or a Gilbert. It does have a codicil bequeathing a £20 annuity to an otherwise unidentified Rebecca Howell.

Cessation of Pain, if Acute, gives us a Pleasure, Nothing else can give, & the bare Remembrance of it /[verso]/ is ye best Preservative against needless Disgust, & ye most Effectual Councellour for Prudent Caution, thro ye remaining part of our Lives.

Madam, I shall be proud of the Honour of being introduced to my Lord Cor[n]bury when I wait on your Grace in Town; When yt will be, I am yet Uncertain. As for Lady Andover,[1] she is a Person, every Good man would, I think, be glad to be acquainted withall, if for nothing else, yet for This, That Angels, those Beings of a nature so remote from, & unlike his Own, might give Him Hereafter ye less Surprize. This may look like a highflown Complement; What I mean by it is a plain & serious Truth, there is /[conjugate leaf]/ (if I mistake not) a sort of Unterrestrial softness, sweetness, Elegance, & Ease, in her Composition; *Painters*, for their Superior Beings, would steal such a Face, & *Philo-*
sophers to form the juster Notions of   their   Excellence, would Contemplate such a Mind.

I humbly thank yr Grace for yr Kind & welljudgd Advice with regard to yr excellent Cousin.[2] He is not ye man I meant. A less exceptionable Character is fitter for my Purpose. Yr Graces Time for speaking [stricken passage: ?to ye Duke?] is Mine; I absolutely acquiesce in your Goodness & Judgment, about it. But I should think that a *Promise*, is like *Money*, It carries Interest, & the sooner It is procurd, the Richer in Hope we should be.

/[verso]/ Madam I have the Honour to acquaint You
                                                is
Ladies in Town, that it   Spring in the Country; That every Day your Rivals, the Flowrs, exceedingly encrease; & threaten your Empire: But I beleive their Menaces are Vain. Mankind, who take upon them to hold the Ballance of powr between You, are too great Profligates to let rural Innocence prevail. They are not so much for Fair maids in February,

---

[1] Lady Mary Finch, daughter of Heneage Finch, 2nd Earl of Aylesford (1647 ?–1719), wife of William Howard, Lord Andover (d. 1757).
[2] The context makes certain that Young's reference is to the Duchess's politically powerful cousin, Thomas Pelham-Holles (1693–1768), Duke of Newcastle, who is credited with having exercised considerable control over Church offices.

as Fair maids round ye year. So yt I consider myself as an Unrivald Sultan, I am just now going to take a Walk in my Seraglio, & which will be the Happy Daisie I can not yet tell. I beg my humble Duty to my Lord Duke, & rejoyce the Little ones are well, & hope Mr Achard will share their Health, as well as their Hearts, & Innocence, in a Little time. I am Madam Yr Graces most Obedt & most H[umble] Sevt EY.

117. Welwyn, Herts. [Sa.] 10 April 1742. Duchess of Portland.

Longleat MSS. (31) 52.

Madam

I designd my self the Honour of waiting on your Grace in Town before this time, but I find myself Disapointed.[1] But I humbly beg Yr Grace not to let poor Caroline be disapointed too. She is at Lady Cathcarts[2] near You, in Westminster. She has sense enough to have an Ambition of being introduct to your Grace. I can not introduce, pray let your Servant supply my Place. When Yr Grace is disposd to do her the Honour of being admitted, please to let Her know it by yr Graces footman & she shall wait on You.

I have ^writen^ to Her about it.

I wish those of yr Graces high rank had more than two Advantages over Us beneath You but I can find no more. And they are Greater /[verso]/ Respect, [stricken word]; & more Oppertunitys of being Kind. The Last is in your own Powr, & yr Grace has securd it. But ye First depends on ye Justice of mankind. And are not they Unjust? If they are not, why did I not obey Yr Graces positive command to write a Month agoe?

¹ As Young was absent from a meeting of his vestry on the 20th, he apparently had gone to London by that time.
² Elizabeth Malyn (1691–1789), daughter of Thomas Malyn of Southwark, by her first marriage to James Fleet (d. 1733), had inherited a large house called Tewin Water in the village of Tewin, Herts., about three miles to the east of Welwyn. She had married a second husband, a Joseph Sabine of Tring, Herts., and in 1739 a third, Charles Cathcart (1686–1740), 8th Baron Cathcart.

Madam, my Lord Duke, in ye same letter that brought
that command, Enjoynd me not to mention One particular,[1]
wh, had I written at yt time, I knew not well how to avoid.
This, Madam, & my Purpose, at yt time, of being soon in
town on Carolines account, (as I told Yr Grace in a Letter)
was the real Occasion of yt seeming, but onely seeming Dis-
obedience to yr commands.

I hear, Madam, the Town is very Unhealthy. God allmighty preserve You & Yours. I beg my /[conjugate leaf]/
Humble Duty to my Lord Duke, & the Little Ones, & to
my Ly Oxford if in Town.

I am ever Madam
Yr Graces most Obedt
& Obligd Humble Sevt
EYoung

Wellwyn
Ap 10th
  1742.

/[verso]/ Pray

                &c
    my humble ser: to
    Mr Achard.

118. [Welwyn, Herts.]. [M.] 3 May 1742. Duchess of
Portland.

Longleat MSS. (32) 54.—Bath, pp. 271–2; Shelley, pp. 144–5.

Madam

                                             I
Such is my opinion of Your Graces goodness, that   can
chuse no Subject more agreeable to You than to speak of
your Friends: Last Week a neighbour of poor Dr Clarkes[2]
now in Huntingdonshire calld on me; He told me our

---

[1] Apparently something to do with the Portlands' efforts to get Young preferment in the Church, mentioned specifically in Young's letter of 1 August of this
year.

[2] This may have been John Jones (1700–70) who was to become Young's curate
in 1757. He was at this time Vicar of Alconbury, near Huntingdon.

Friend was still living, & that his Physitian sayd He might *possibly* live four or five years longer: That is in ye ever blessed will of God: After this melancholy account, I will give Yr Grace something more comfortable. The Doctor retains his spirits, & is chearfull under circumstances that fright ye Bystander. Now This wd be impossible, was there not an Indulgent Being who frights us with ye Appearance of remote Evils, in order to give entrance to his Fear into our Hearts; & when those Evils come supports us under them beyond our expectation, & more, /[verso]/ still beyond our Deserts. Dr. Clarkes Behaviour brings to my memory some Lines wh I have formerly read, whether it be in Fletcher[1] perhaps Your Grace can tell. After the Author has represented a good man who's name is *Philander* on his Deathbed behaving to ye Surprize of All about Him, He ads—

As some tall Towr, or lofty Mountains Brow
Detains the Sun, Illustrious from its Height,
When rising Vapours, & descending Shades,
In Damps, & Darkness, drown ye Spatious Vale,
Philander thus augustly reard his head
Undampt by Doubt, undarkend by Despair:
At that black Hour, wh general Horror sheds
On the low Level of Inglorious minds,
Sweet *Peace*, & Heavenly *Hope*, & humble *Joy*,
Divinely beamd on his exalted Soul,
With incommunicable Lustre, bright:

/[conjugate leaf]/ I hope in God, Madam, we may see our Philander[2] again, before These Verses are applicable to Him in their full extent. Heaven is pleasd to permit our Friends to be so very dear to us, That our parting with them (wh must necessarily be sometimes the case) might in some

degree losen that strong Hold, wh the   World   is apt to take

---

[1] The lines are Young's own, which with slight changes appeared at the conclusion of the second part of his *Complaint; or, Night-Thoughts* published about 1 December of this year.

[2] While these lines may apply to Clarke, the full description of 'Philander' in the *Night-Thoughts* is more applicable to Henry Temple.

on our Hearts: The most deplorable Case of all is, when the ye [*sic*] World so entirely fills our Hearts as not to leave Room even for our Friends. If such there are, Heaven keep your Grace as distant from Them, as your Disposition is from Theirs. I beg my Duty to my Lord Duke, & as many other real regards as Yr Graces family will please to accept from

Madam
Yr Graces most Obedt
& Obligd Humble Sevt
EYoung

May ye 3rd
   1742.

119. [Fulham or London]. [W.] 14 July [1742]. Duchess of Portland.

Longleat MSS. 134.[1]

Yr Graces most Courtly
& Obedient Humble Sevt.
EYoung.

I beg Madam my humble Duty to his Grace.

Next week Ld Litchfields second Daughter, Ly Mary will be Marryd to Mr Nevel of Leicestershire.[2] She has 6000 *l.* & His Fortune is 2000 *l.* per añ. & 50000 pound in money I saw the Weding cloaths.—But I ask pardon, This is not Philosophy but News.

July 14th.

----

[1] The top of this letter has been cut away.

[2] The marriage between Cosmos Nevill of Holt (1716–63) to Lady Mary Lee (1722–58) took place 31 July 1742 (John Nichols, *History . . . of the . . . County of Leicester,* 1795, 11, pt. 2, 729).

120. Tunbridge Wells, Kent. [Su.] 1 August 1742.
Duchess of Portland.

Longleat MSS. (33) 56.—Bath, p. 272; Shelley, pp. 149–50.

Madam

As this ^is^ a place where Books[1] are denyd us, as unwholsome; we must either read Human nature, in that pretty
Edition the good Company gives us of it, or read nothing
at all. I have read ye Company over & over, some Pages of
wh were very fair, & delightfull; Others were sullid, &
dogs eard wth ye cares & troubles of human life, & contributed more to the prevalence of ye Spleen, than the Waters
to ye cure of it.

Your Grace I know is curious to know ye general Contents of this Human Folio I have been reading; or what real
Knowledge I have gatherd from my perusal of it.

/[verso]/ Madam I fancy You have read it so often, & so
well understand it Your self, that all I can extract from it
will be nothing but a bad Copy of yr Graces own Thoughts.
However if your Grace has a mind to contemplate ye Difference between a Zinke[2] & a Signpost, I will send you my
Portrait of Human nature. But I must beg leave to defer
exposing myself till my next.

For really, Madam, tho there is no One on earth cd
sooner persuade me out of my Senses than your Grace; yet
I dare positively affirm yt my Head is gyddy; But whether
I stand on my Head or my Heels I will not presume to be
quite so Positive.

/[conjugate leaf]/ But, Madam, I hope I shall never be
so much indisposd, as to forget the great obligations I lie
under to your Grace & my Lord Duke, who has I plainly

---

1 That Young's mind is on books is not surprising as the first of his *Night-
Thoughts*, published anonymously at the end of May, had gone to a second edition
by the end of July.

2 i.e. a miniature by the celebrated Christian Friedrich Zincke (?1684–1767).
Zincke had done portraits of the Duchess and Mrs. Pendarves in the spring of 1740
(Climenson, 1906, i. 45). The will of the Duchess (Somerset House, P.C.C. Ducarel
436) assigns to Lady Andover her 'snuff-box with the four enamel portraits by
Zinke'.

find made so serious a Point of promotg my Interest wth their two Graces of Newcastle & Canterbury,[1] that I am scarce more obliged by his favour, than astonishd at his Singularity. I beg my humble Duty to Him, & wth sincere prayr for ye wellfare of [those] that are dear to your Grace,

I am, Madam,

Yr Graces most Devoted

Humble Sevt

EYoung

If yr Grace pleases, my
best Respects to my
Lady Oxford.

    Tunbridge. Aug. 1st
      1742.

Benjamin Victor to Young. [August 1742].

Address: To the Rev Dr Young at Tunbridge Wells.
Not traced.—*Original Letters . . . by Benjamin Victor*, 1776, 1, 75; Thomas, p. 624.

Dear Sir,

    Since I left you I have read a poem with a tremendous title, called The Complaint, or Night Thoughts on Death and Eternity.[2] A melancholly unfashionable subject—but the reading it gave me great pleasure; I found the thoughts quite new and Doctor Young written in large characters in every page.

    I found from your bookseller, Mr Dodsley, that you have carefully concealed your name, on purpose to try the force of your poem; but you are too good a writer to be able to conceal yourself from your admirers. I hear we are to have the happiness of reading two books more. If I was your bookseller I should greatly solicit you to add your name, because it would call the attention of those readers who are led by mode, consequently encrease the sale of the poem.

---

[1] i.e. the Duke of Newcastle and the Archbishop of Canterbury (John Potter ?1674–1747).

[2] The first of Young's *Night-Thoughts* was published 31 May 1742 and quickly went to a second edition, 31 July (Pettit, 1954, pp. 13, 16).

I hope to have the opportunity very soon of thanking you for this pleasure in London.

I am, dear Sir,
Your most oblig'd servant.

121. [August 1742]. John Potter, Archbishop of Canterbury.

Not traced.[1]

122. Tunbridge Wells, Kent. [Sa.] 21 August 1742. Duchess of Portland.

Longleat MSS. (34) 58.—Bath, pp. 272–3; Shelley, pp. 151–2.

Tunbridge Aug
21st 1742.

Madam

Your Grace is pleasd to write to me in so obliging, & in so sensibly affectionate a manner, that it, as it were chastises, while It confers ye greatest obligation, & gives me some pain to consider how little I deserve it at your hands. Your Grace is pleasd to ask pardon for giving me most kind & prudent Advice; Madam rather ask pardon, for Pardon askd; For that seems to imply a mean Opinion of my Gratitude or Understanding. As to my Ld Egmont[2] whose Character I honour, I thought I put myself in his way. It was not for me by making the first Advance to take his Lordsp into my patronage. But perhaps I was too shy. I assure yr Grace Ill endeavour to mend for ye future.

I hope in God, Madam, Yr Graces spirits are raisd by my Lady Oxfords perfect recovery. The Loss of a Friend is certainly ye severest stroke under Heaven. My Lady Bate-

---

[1] Evidence of this letter is Young's statement in his letter of 21 August to the Duchess in which he asks her to let the Duke know 'that on the receipt of his last kind Letter I immediately writ to ye Archbishop, as He advised'. None of Archbishop Potter's correspondence seems to have been preserved, at least among the relicts of his office now in Lambeth Palace Library.

[2] John Perceval (1683–1748), 1st Earl of Egmont, brother of Anne Donnellan's stepfather, Philip Perceval.

man[1] was Here /[verso]/ at that time she had appointed me
to drink Tea with her that afternoon, & when I came to ye
door I met ye sad News, wh denyd me that favour. I remember the time when I have trembled at ye sound of a Post-
horn, & was as much startled at ye sight of a Letter, as I
shd have been at a Warrant to seize my Person, & vast
Estate.

I congratulate yr Grace on Miss Robinsons marriage;[2]
bnt I will not congratulate her Spouse till I know He deserves
Her. But yr Grace knows my opinion of her allready. She
is a Surpri   zi   ng young Being, by wh I wd mean something of
a middle nature between Angel & Woman. Yr Grace will
naturally understand This better than Another.

But You it seems, Madam, are humbly content with
desiring a Portrait of mere Human Nature; This, Madam, I
promisd, & this (God willing) I will perform. But not now,
I do not design to trifle, but to be quite serious in it. Nor for
/[conjugate leaf]/ your Graces Information, but to rescue
You from Your Aversion, *News* & *Chitchat*, wh have by ye
cruel courtisie of England taken possession of ye Epistolary
Pen. But at present my thought is accidentally so much
engagd on Something else,[3] that I care not to enter on That
subject till I am more at leasure.

I beg, Madam, my humble Duty to my Lord Duke, &
please to let his Grace know, that on the receipt of his last
kind Letter I immediately writ to ye Archbishop, as He
advisd. It was such a Letter, as neither has receivd, nor
expected an Answer. I hope yr Graces Olive branches
flourish, & since the Spirit of Prophesie is on me, I will
foretell a miracle; they shall one day be turnd into Laurels,
& Myrtles. Prophesies Yr Grace knows are allways somewhat obscure, but if You consult Whiston,[4] or, perhaps, Mr

[1] Lady Anne Bateman, widow of Sir James Bateman (d. 1718), who had been
given lodgings in Windsor Castle in 1738 (Llanover, 1861, ii. 20).

[2] Elizabeth Robinson married Edward Montagu (d. 1775) on 5 August.

[3] Doubtless on the composition of his *Night-Thoughts*, the second and third parts
of which came out in December.

[4] William Whiston (1667–1752) was notorious for his lectures connecting
meteors, eclipses, and earthquakes with the fulfilment of prophecies. Since he made
a practice of lecturing at resorts such as Tunbridge Wells it may be assumed Young
had recently heard him.

Ashard,   (to whom my humble service)   He[']ll probably let You
into my meaning. I am ever, Madam,
                    Yr Graces most Obedt & Obligd
                    Humble Sevt EYoung.

/[verso]/ Madam I humbly beg my very best Wishes &
truest Respects to my Lady Oxford.

123. Welwyn, Herts. [F.] 1 October 1742. Duchess of Portland.

Longleat MSS. (34) 60.—Bath, pp. 273–4.

                                                    Wellwyn
                                                    Oct 1st
                                                    1742.
Madam
    Yesterday a Gentleman spent his day with me Here; &
He made the Day to me most agreeable, by an Entertainment I did not expect from Him. How He came by his
Intimacy with my Lady Oxfords Character I can not tell;
but He told me many particular Facts, most commendable
in it; of which I knew nothing before. I envy her Ladyship
the satisfaction she must receive from them. Wealth, &
Rank wh shine so bright, have two Rivals that outshine
them; I mean Wisdom & Virtue. Not to cant, But to speak
soberly, what I know to be True; These two Rivals give the
onely real Superiority, to any Person upon Earth. Wealth &
Rank will ever indeed gain Followers, & those the most
/[verso]/ Complaisant. But Bows & Smiles can subsist without Love or Esteem; & the Great Person that accepts them
with Joy, would often reject them with Disdain, if He saw
the Heart of his Admirer. But, Madam, with Wisdom &
Virtue, it is quite Otherwise. These compell our Esteem &
Love, we cant withhold them if we would: And it is certain
many would withhood [sic] them if they could: for All destitute of These Qualities, can not but envy that real & absolute
Superiority they give Others over them: And Envy hates as
much as ever she can; but in this Case Nature is against her
Hatred, & Love & Esteem will necessarily mix with it.

Thus, Madam, I have given your Grace a Key, by wh You may infallably understand the secret cause, of any Disrespect I may possibly /[conjugate leaf]/ show, or any Injurie I may possibly do, You, or Yours, Hereafter. You offer Violence, You compell, You extort, what Few are willing to part with, Admiration & Esteem. And I hate I [a?] Tyrant; & You I know hate Flattery; & therefore I have taken care
to
~~You~~ abuse your Grace as much as was in my Powr; & so much was in my Powr as would have killd half ye Dutchesses in this Kingdom; For I have fairly thrown your Coronet on the ground, & bid your Wisdom & Virtue tread it under their Feet.—I beg Madam my humble Duty, & best Respects to ~~to~~ my Lady Oxford, & my Ld Duke; my best Wishes & Affections to ye Little Ones, & my humble service to Mr Ashard.

> I am Madam, Yr Graces
> most Obligd & Obedt Hble Sevt
> EYoung.

Madam Caroline
desires You to accept
her Duty.

124. Welwyn, Herts. [F.] 15 October [1742]. Duchess of Portland.

Longleat MSS. (36) 62.

> Wellwyn
> Oct. 15

May it please your Grace
On the Tenth of this Month I set out for Bullstrode; & before I got to St Albans[1] was wett thro & thro: It rained so hard ye remainder of ye Day that I could not stir; And the
such
next morning I was seizd with   Pains in my limbs, as obligd me to return; I have since been under Discipline for a Fever, & got not on my Legs till Yesterday; my

---

[1] About ten miles from Welwyn, not quite half-way to Bulstrode.

Physitian tells me that in three or four Days I may take such a Journey; The moment I can I shall wait on your Grace with ye greatest Pleasure being exstremely sensible of the ye [*sic*] Honour done me by your kind Invitation, & many Other Indulgencies to

Madam
Yr Graces most
Obligd & most Obedt
Humble Sevt
EYoung.

16.
Madam I writ ye Above yesterday.
To day I am worse; I will, if it pleases
      wait on You
God I recover my Health if Your Grace
continues in the Country. I beg my Humble Duty to my Lord Duke &c.

125. Welwyn, Herts. [W.] 17 November 1742. Duchess of Portland.

Longleat MSS. (37) 63.

Madam
 I humbly thank Your Grace for a Letter which shows You to be no less Mistriss of a fine Pen, than of far better accomplishments. Madam I heartily condole with Your Grace for both the Persons Indisposd,[1] that are so near & dear to You. And I hope in a good God, that long ere This things are alterd for the Better. I have been long ill of a Fever (as I was this time twelvemonth at Bullstrode) & caught after just the same manner. This, Madam, is the reason I acknowledgd not the Honour of Yrs before. And which hinders

---

[1] The Duke of Portland and Lady Oxford, as appears from Young's letter of 12 December.

me now from being able to do more than subscribe myself
(with Carolines Duty to You)

Madam
Yr Graces ever Faithfull
& Obligd Humble Sevt
EYoung

I beg Madam my Duty to
  my Lord Duke & Ly Oxford
    Wellwyn Nov: 17 1742.

126. Welwyn, Herts. [Sa.] 20 November 1742. Sir Thomas Hanmer.

Not traced.—*Correspondence of Sir Thomas Hanmer*, ed. Sir Henry Bunbury, 1838, pp. 229–30.

Nov. 20th, 1742.
Wellwyn, Hartfordshire.

Honour'd Sr,

I have ordered Mr. Dodsley to wait on you with a thing called ye *Complaint*, & with ye second as soon as printed, wch will be soon.[1] I had Sr, sent it long before, but for reasons you shall know when I have ye honour of waiting on you.

As other parts are to follow, I beg the favour of your general advice. Something of that nature must occur to you, if you are at leisure to read what I send. I can not misunderstand any thing in that way; & I may reap great advantage from it. Tho' ever excellently qualified, your late amusements[2] must more peculiarly awaken, & make still more acute your discernment in things of this nature. Pardon Sr a freedom wch durst not have shew'd so bold a face, was it (not) conscious that it keeps company in my heart with the

---

[1] The first part of *The Complaint; or, Night-Thoughts on Life, Death, & Immortality* had appeared on 31 May and a second edition on 31 July. The second part was published on 30 November (cf. Pettit, 1954, p. 18).

[2] Hanmer had just completed work on an edition of Shakespeare which was published two years later in six volumes.

truest esteem for your signal worth, & ye most zealous wishes for yr wellfare.

I am, Hond Sr,
    Yr most obedt & faithfull Humble Servt,
        E. YOUNG.

Sr, I write this in confidence, for I do not own myself the writer of it.[1]

127. Welwyn, Herts. [Su.] 12 December 1742. Duchess of Portland.

Longleat MSS. (38) 64.—Bath, pp. 274–5; Shelley, p. 153.

Madam

I bless God my danger is over, but my Recovery is slow. The good news Your Grace sends me of my Ld Duke, & my Lady Oxford, will promote it. I never saw anything in Mr Hay[2] but what was a symtom of sound sense, I am not therefore so much surprizd, as pleasd, at ye account You give of his Sermon. If Your Grace sees Him I beg my humble service, & thanks for his late favour to me at Kensington. A good sermon is a most rational, & high entertainment to Those yt are so Happy as to have a relish for it, wh I am persuaded is your Graces Case. To keep Preaching a little in countenance with Those that have no very favourable Opinion of it, give me leave, Madam, to observe that ye Whole Creation preaches; I mean, that /[verso]/ we can make no just observation in any of ye Appearances in the Material World, but what will naturally have a moral good Effect on us. The sacred scriptures therefore are very justly

---

[1] How long Young kept his anonymity is not certain. As late as 4 December the Duchess of Portland wrote to Elizabeth Montagu asking her opinion of 'Night Thoughts', apparently without mentioning Young's name (Climenson, 1906, i. 133) and in reply Mrs. Montagu spoke of having read 'Mr. Hervey' in terms that suggest she was referring to Young's poem (Montagu, 1810, ii. 249).

[2] John Hay's brother Robert of whom the *London Morning Advertiser* for 27 December reported: 'We hear that the Rev. Mr. Haye, Son to the Earl of Kinnoul, and one of the Prebendaries of Carlisle, will succeed the Right Rev. Dr. Wills, Bishop of Landoff, as a Prebendary of Westminster.' He had apparently preached in Young's place at Kensington at this season during Young's illness.

considered as God Allmightys Second Volum[e], & Creation
as his First; Which speaks to ye same purpose, & if attended
to, ~~if~~ ^{is} ever bettering ye Human Heart. How Happy then,
& Wise is your Grace, who are fond of Both these Books?
Mr Hay, & Others, of Eminent talents for ye Pulpit, are
onely Commentors on them, or Panygerists, in their Praise.
Your Grace, by this time sees, there is something sacred,
as well as entertaining, in yr Drawers of Shells[1] &c: they
may be considerd as so many little Pages of that im-
mense Volum[e], wh God Allmighty has publishd in a most
pompous Edition, /[conjugate leaf]/ to induce his Rational
creatures to a ready, & constant Perusal of it. Proceed,
Madam, by your exemplary life, & behaviour, nay, even
by your Amusements, to preach to ye Preachers, & among
Others, to ye most attentive of your Congregation

Your Graces much Obligd
& most Obedt Humble Sevt
EYoung.

I beg Madam my humble
Duty to my Ld Duke & Ly
Oxford, & my love & respect
to ye little Ones.——Caroline
begs her Duty to yr Grace

Wellwyn Decemr 12
  1742.

128. Welwyn, Herts. [Th.] 13 January 1742/3. Duchess of Portland.

Longleat MSS. (30) 50.——Bath, p. 269; Shelley, pp. 140–1.

Madam
    What Yr Grace says of my Lady Oxford greives me, very
sincerely I speak it, for I honour & love, & ever shall, ye
Virtues of That Lady. Your Grace was so Good in your Last
letter as to pass a very handsome Compliment; had It been

---

   [1] Among the many hobbies of the Duchess was that of collecting shells.

more I should have had the Honour of waiting on You Here,
which I humbly hopd for a Week together, & put my House
in order. Caroline, whom Yr Grace is so Good as to remember will soon be in Town, & humbly ^{begs} she may be permitted the Honour & Pleasure of waiting on You. My
Lady Cathcart, our Nighbour, who has a House in Westminster is so good to take Her to Town for some time, that
ye Child may be curd of starting at a Human Face.

/[verso]/ I share Your concern, Madam, for her Grace of
Kent; I have as well great Obligations to Her; as a High
Opinion of Her.

Some, Madam, are apt to think that God Allmightys
Providence is indeed very particular, & Notorious, as to
Kingdoms & Nations; but as to Persons they imagine it is
somewhat more distant or remiss. The Truth, I conceive, is,
That ye Allmightys Providence & Inspection is equall as
to Both; All methods are taken with us, yt can be taken with
Free Agents in order to our Amendment. And tho allmost
every thing is an Instrument in ye Hand of Providence to
this End; Yet what seems to me to be peculiarly, & in ye
most eminent, & evident Degree Such, is, Our Friends.
With These Heaven can most Encourage, & most Chastise
us; These /[conjugate leaf]/ can give us ye greatest Pleasure;
& These, ye greatest Pain. I would by no means damp that
blessed & reasonable satisfaction wh arises from them in our
Days of Joy; Far from it; It is ^{not} onely our Prudence, but
our Duty, to Enjoy them. But then we shd sometimes consider, amid those most endearing & amiable Enjoyments,
that perhaps we are that moment wheting ye Arrow yt shall
wound us; for most sure it is ye more we Enjoy, ye more
we may Suffer from them; the more Severely we shall feel,
their Folly, their Misfortune, or their Loss.

Your Grace says You have a Disposition little Able to
support ye Loss or Misfortune of Yr Friends. Madam, I
never heard You commend yourself before. The Highest
/[verso]/ Character that can be given of a Human Creature
is 'A Being wth a feeling Heart'. Such a Heart I confess
runs great risque in ye present Scene; & yet Human

Prudence, & Divine Providence together, form an ampler
sheild for our Defence than is generally imagind. And when
arrows of Pain strike thro it, such a feeling Heart has This
to say to it self, 'That those very Pains well-born will entitle
it to a scene, where there is Nothing but Pleasure to be felt;
& where an Unfeeling Heart shall never enter.' God Allmighty cover You & Yours, Madam, with his wings in this
Life, & give You wings of your own in the Next.

I am wth respect & Gratitudes
Madam Yr Graces much
Obligd & Obedt Sevt
EYoung.

Wellwyn Jan 13 1742.
I beg Madam my
Humble Duty to my Ld
Duke &c:

129. [Welwyn, Herts.]. F. [?18 March 1742/3]. Philip
Yorke.[1]

Address: To / The Honble Philip Yorke / in St. James's Square / London.
Postmark: [obliterated, but not the London mark].
British Museum Add. MSS. 35350, f. 1.—Shelley, p. 159.

Friday Morning
Sir,
In the poem[2] which I took the freedom to address to you
the other day, my inclination would have led me to say more
of you, but my just sense of your modesty restrained me:
especially when I considered the repulse which I was informed by a good hand, you gave to the very excellent writer
of the Life of Cicero on a similar occasion.[3] My friend Mr

[1] Philip Yorke (1720–90), oldest son of the Lord Chancellor Hardwicke whom
he was to succeed on the latter's death in 1764. At this time he was a Member of
Parliament but known rather for his production, in an extremely limited private
edition of 1741, in conjunction with his brother Charles, of the *Athenian Letters; or
The Epistolary Correspondence of an Agent of the King of Persia, residing at Athens
during the Peloponnesian War*.
[2] The fourth 'Night' of Young's *Complaint*, published 10 March, was 'humbly
inscribed to the Honourable Mr. York'.
[3] Conyers Middleton's *History of the Life of M. Tullius Cicero* (1741).

Newcomb too has regretted more than once to me, that you would not allow him the honour to prefix your Name to his collection of poems, or suffer yourself to be known to the world as the patron of them, any otherwise than by Asterisks, and the praises he has so justly bestowed upon you.[1] As in these instances, (and I dare say in many others, for ingenious men will be intruding their Labours upon you;) you carried that excessive modesty which I know you have espoused in Theory very strongly into practice, I durst not venture to ask Your permission of inscribing my Nightly Thoughts /[verso, 'inclosed Verses' transcribed below; conjugate leaf]/ to you, nor transgress beyond what I thought might be agreeable to you, in the manner of addressing you. But as the inclosed Verses contain a panegyric that is real not fictitious, and your extraordinary qualities did naturally pour them upon the thought of the Writer,[2] I cannot deny myself the satisfaction of expressing to you in private that esteem which would perhaps have offended you, when laid before the public View. I hope you will pardon a trouble that proceeds from the truest respect of your

Much indebted
humble servt
E. Young.

/[verso]/ To
The Hon[oura]ble Philip Yorke
in St James's Square
London.

O Thou, whom Athens Lady of the Main,
Empress of Elegance, amongst her Sons
May count, Her letter'd Sons; proud to exchange
For thine, in borrowed guise, with mi [torn off]
Wrought to such just perfection of de [torn off]
Such truth of falshood, ev'n her gen [torn off]
More Attic Thou in Taste, in dicti [torn off]
Than Atticism's self! One Hybla [torn off]

1 Thomas Newcomb's *Collection of Odes and Epigrams, Occasioned by the Success of the British and Confederate Arms in Germany* (1743).

2 The terms here repeat those used in the preface to the fourth 'Night': '... Real, not Fictitious.... The Facts mentioned did naturally pour these moral Reflections on the Thought of the Writer.'

or thy young brow with rich tiara crowned,
Soft persias manufacture, dost thou wear
The form of Mage, of Satrap, of immortal,
(Like *Sparta's King of old, without his guilt
Medising;) Well the great Atossa, famed
first Epistolograph, may boast the palm
T'invent, but must from all her Glory shrink,
When thy Cleander rears his beamy head,
Refulgent o'er the Letter-writing Tribe.

* pausanias.

130. [?Welwyn, Herts.]. [Su.] 20 March 1742/3.
[?Richard Mead].[1]

Not traced.

131. [Welwyn, Herts.]. [?April 1743]. Duchess of
Portland.

Longleat MSS. (40) 67.

Madam

About an Age agoe I had the Honour of hearing from Yr
Grace; I think it was as far back as Christmas. In yr Letter
I was commanded to direct my Next to Whitehall. I did so,
& writ ye very next Post. Ever since I have subsisted on
Expectation. On wh very Few grow fat.

To what, Madam, shall I impute this long Silence?—
I think I have hit it off; Your Grace probably considers yt
Persons of my Profession should abstain from all manner of
Delicacys in Lent. But whatever is ye Cause, what ought I,

---

[1] Evidence of this letter is its listing for sale by Sotheby's as lot No. 213 on 6 May
1858 and again as lot No. 1030 on 10 June 1869 with the excerpt: 'A singularly
written letter, beginning: "As Litterary Addresses, by the Courtesie of the World,
are allowed to pass for Respect, I took the Liberty of your Name." March 20th
1742/3. Complimentary letter to one of his patrons.' The patron was probably
Young's physician Richard Mead who was complimented in the fourth 'Night' of
The Complaint (iv. 132).

in modesty, to infer from it? Why, This; That I am doing myself too great an Honour in writing to Your Grace again without sufficient Encouragement. I confess ye Fault, & asks [*sic*] pardon for it. But an overbearing, Uncourtly Desire /[verso]/ of Knowing ye Wellfare of a Noble Family,[1] every Branch of wh is entitled to ye very best Wishes of my Heart, makes me hazard this Breach of Delicacy. And if yr Grace has more Humanity than Politeness You will Pardon

May it please Yr Grace
Yr Graces most Obedt
& Obligd Humble Sevt
EYoung.

Madam, I beg my
Humble Duty to my Ld Duke,
& Humble Service to Mr Achard.
And my Envy to ye Little Ones for
that Innocence, wh never saw
twenty years of age (one person excepted)
Since the Fall.

132. Welwyn, Herts. [Th.] 2 June 1743. Duchess of Portland.

Longleat MSS. (41) 68.—Bath, p. 275; Shelley, pp. 162–3.

Wellwy[n] June
ye 2d 1743

Madam
    After so long Silence Yr Grace's Letter gave me ye greatest Pleasure. Had I known, or guest ye melancholy reason[2] You assign for not writing, I shd not have denyd myself ye Honour of writing to You; but I was really afraid Your Grace had taken something ill.

a reflection

You are pleasd, Madam, to begin yr Letter wth
both on my Understanding & Gratitude. I do assure Your

---

[1] This was a trying spring for the Portlands. The *Daily Post* reported that the Duke was 'dangerously ill at his house in Privy-Garden, Whitehall' (5 January), that they had lost their infant daughter Lady Frances (28 February), and that the Duke was a pall-bearer at the funeral of the Duchess of Buckingham (9 April).

[2] The death of her daughter (see previous letter).

Grace that I do, & ever shall look on your Correspondence (as I ought) not onely as a great Honour, but real Entertainment too. What You are pleasd to say about Miss Lee, is exstremely Kind, & if I wish Her well, I must obey Yr Graces commands in it.

As I take it, Madam, I am directly in yr way to Nottinghamshire;[1] & why shd You put yourselves to an Inconveniency to avoid me? /[verso blank, conjugate leaf]/ I do assure You I will neither hurt You nor Myself, I will receive You, as I ought to Entertain, not as Your Grace ought to be entertaind. I heartily rejoyce wth Mrs Montague,[2] whose truly polite merits I know & admire; & whose Virtues, with the World for my rival, I shall ever honour.

As for ye Advice Yr Grace gives me about Preferment, I take it with all my Heart.[3] What God Allmighty is pleasd to give, I shall receive with ye greatest Gratitude; nor shall I repine at what He is pleasd to deny; if His mercy is pleasd to continue to me his Grace, & my Understanding.

Your Grace pays me a high Complement in desiring a
long Letter; nothing but good sense can make such a ^{one} Agreeable to your Grace. And to say the Truth, at present I have no Sense to spare. Madam I have been confind to my bed for five weeks wth ye most Acute Distemper & all ye Severitys, those Butchers, /[verso]/ Surgeons are able to inflict, I have gone thro; Twenty Nights I had not twenty Hours Sleep; nor am I yet at all come to my Rest, or Strength; tho (I bless Allmy God) they tell me Im past all Danger.

This Discipline has ^{so} beaten down my Spirits, & Understanding, that had I not a strong Inclination to write to your Grace (after so long a time) I shd not have been able to do it. Pardon therefore Madam the Nothingness of what I write; please to accept my Duty & Goodwill *now*, & please to give me credit a little longer for my long Arrear of common

---

[1] Welwyn, being on the Great North Road, was on the way to Welbeck Abbey, northern seat of the Portlands, which they visited this summer.
[2] On the birth of a son, her little 'Punch', who lived only two years.
[3] That the Duchess had by this time written on Young's behalf to her cousin, the Duke of Newcastle, may be assumed from her letter to Newcastle of 14 May 1744.

Understanding. God Allmighty have You, Madam, & Yours in his ever favourable Protection, & please to number among Your real friends, & admirers of ye Excellencies Madam

Yr Graces most Devoted
& Humble Sevt   EYoung.

133. Gubbins, Herts.¹ Su. [?11 June 1743]. Duchess of Portland.

Longleat MSS. (45) 74.—Bath, pp. 276–7; Shelley, pp. 165–6.

Gubbins
In
Hertfordshire.
Sunday.

Madam

I think it my Duty to ask your Grace pardon for not waiting on You as I promisd. Madam I received a Visit that prevented it; I mean ye Visit of a violent Cold, wh stays with me longer than tis wellcome: I was forced by it to leave the Town for clearer air; I thank God I am better since I came to this place, but not well.

The Day after I saw your Grace I waited on ye ArchBp, who told me that my Ld D of Portland was very much my Friend. But that nothing was to be done without ye D. of Newcastle or Ld Carteret.² And presented me with His own

---

¹ The seat of Sir Jeremiah Sambroke (d. 1754), near North Mimms, about six miles south of Welwyn. A visitor in September 1736 made the following entry in his diary: 'Tuesday 15. We dined with Mr. Sambroke at Gubbins.... Very elegantly entertained. A Batchelor. His sister keeps house. A very understanding lady and skilled in the Mathematicks. Fine walks in the woods 2 miles about, laid out in a very elegant Tast. A round Wood the prettiest I believe in England. He has lost 1 eye and is almost blind of another and yet very chearful' (*The Diaries of Thomas Wilson D.D. 1731–37 and 1750*, ed. C. L. S. Linnell, 1964, p. 172). At the time of Young's visit Sambroke was operated on unsuccessfully by the oculist John Taylor who later published an account of his attempt to restore his vision (see Young's letter of 25 August).

² Once again, as in the 1720s, Young's hopes of preferment were dependent on Carteret, now Secretary of State for the Northern Province, and one of the Lords Justices, but the death of Wilmington on 2 July was to precipitate a struggle for power with the new Prime Minister, Henry Pelham, to whom Young had dedicated his sixth 'Night' in March 1744.

good Wishes in the /[verso]/ Handsomest manner; for which I humbly thank my Lord Duke, & your Grace. I realy beleive ye ArchBp is my Friend; but Your Grace knows tis Dangerous trusting the Clergy.

If, Madam, I have the Honour of hearing from You at this place (where I design continuing some time with my Friend Sr Jeremy Sambrooke) I desire to know how my Lord Titchfield does, who was ill when I saw your Grace. Perhaps You expect some entertainment, but Madam I am neither in a merry, nor in a Philosophical mood. Water gruel spoils my myrth, & an eternal Cough /[conjugate leaf]/ interrupts my Philosophy.

This minute I have the comfort of hearing that Preferment is come very near me. That is, Madam, that my next Neighbour, ye Minister of Hatfield, is made Canon of Windsor.[1] I left, Madam, Miss Lee in town; but I do not design Her the Honour of waiting on your Grace till I return to introduce her. I beg my Humble Duty to my Lord Duke, & hope your Grace will pardon this Nothing from an Invalid. I was blooded this Day, & tomorrow begin runing ye Gaun[t]let thro all ye Rods of an Apothecarys Shop. /[verso]/ You see, Madam, how dear we pay for Life. One would think there was something very Valueable in it yet ninety nine in a Hundred find it otherwise Nor can it be truly Valueable to any but Those who have something still more valueable in their principal point of view. You will pardon This if You consider yt I write on a Sunday.

I am Madam
Yr Graces most Obligd
& most Obedt Humble Sevt.
EYoung.

[1] Samuel Haynes (d. 1752), Rector of Hatfield (five miles south of Welwyn) from 1737 to his death. He was made Prebend of St. George's Chapel in Windsor Castle on the death of Andrew Snape (b. 1675), 30 December 1742. The appointment was reported in the March 1743 issue of *The Gentleman's Magazine.*

134. Welwyn, Herts. [Su.] 10 July [1743]. Duchess of Portland.

Longleat MSS. (42) 70.

Madam

Yr Grace is exstremely Kind both in your concern for my Health & your Invitation to Bullstrode, which I shall with great Pleasure accept off, if it is in my Powr.—The Letter wh I am about to transcribe for Yr Graces perusal, I receivd last Post from a Friend in town; And as we have All a natural Curiosity about the Last Behaviour, & Words of All yt leave this world before ^{us}, perhaps It may not be Unwellcome to your Grace. Besides probably You know the Writer of it, Dr Rundall late Bp of Londonderry.[1] It is written to Dr Sayer.[2]

Dublin. March 22
1743.

Dear Sr

Adieu for ever. Perhaps I may be Alive /[verso]/ when this Letter comes to your Hands. More probably not. But in either Condition your sincere Wellwisher. Beleive me, my Friend, there is no Comfort in this world, but a Life of Virtue & Piety: And no Death supportable, but One comforted by Christianity, And by its real, & rational Hope. The *First* I doubt not You experience dayly. May it be long before You want the *Second*. I have livd to be *Conviva Satur*; I have past thro Evel report, & good Report: I have not be[en] Injurd more than *Outwardly* by ye *Last*: & I have been solidly Benefitted by the *First*. May all who love the Truth in Jesus Christ, & sincerely obey ye Gospell be Happy. For They deserve to be so. Who ἀληθευεῖν ἐν ἀγάπῃ, seek the Truth in ye spirit of Love. Adieu.—I have no more /[conjugate leaf]/ strength—My Affectionate last Adieu to your Lady.   T. D.[3]

---

[1] Thomas Rundle (?1688–1743), Bishop of Derry, who died on 14 April, had been at Oxford during the time of Young's residence.

[2] George Sayer (1696–1761), D.D. (Oxford, 1735), Vicar of Witham, Essex (1722–61), Archdeacon of Durham (1730–61), and Rector of Bocking, Essex (1741–61).

[3] i.e. T[homas Rundle, Bishop of] D[erry]. His letter, with slight variations and addressed: 'To Archdeacon S——', was published in the memoir (1. clxvii–clxix)

A Letter of this Nature, suggests thoughts of good Effect on the mind. For ye Knowledge of what those Thoughts are, I refer Your Grace to your own bosom. Which I shd be very willing to transcribe, but not to yourself. I beg, Madam, my humble Duty to my Lady Oxford, & my Lord Duke, & my Humble Service to Mr Ashard. I am just come from Town, where I saw your Friend Mrs Donaland,[1] but our Interview was shorter than I desird. I yesterday marryd a young Lady of fivety, to an Old Gentleman of twenty five.[2] I fear they will never forgive me. I am with ye truest Respect & Gratitude

     Madam
     Yr Graces most Obedt H[umble] S[erven]t EYoung
July 10th Wellwyn.

135. [London]. [W.] 20 July [1743]. Duchess of Portland.

Longleat MSS. (70) 120.

Madam

I was chaind like a Monkey in a Corner of ye Court of Chancerry[3] from Eight in the Morning till near four in the Afternoon; the same will be my Fate Tomorrow; but ye first moment I am Unbewitchd I will have the Honour of waiting on Yr Grace & my Lord Duke to whom my humble Duty. I am with full sense of yr favours

                Madam

July. 20th   Yr Graces most Obligd
                   & Litigeous Humble Sevt
                     EdYoung.

accompanying *Letters of the Late Thomas Rundle, L.L.D., Lord Bishop of Ireland, to Mrs. Barbara Sandys*, ed. James Dallaway, Gloucester, 1789, 2 vols.

[1] i.e. Anne Donnellan.

[2] Record of the marriage, which probably took place in London, has not been found.

[3] His suit against the Wharton estate was being heard at this time.

136. Welwyn, Herts. [Th.] 25 August 1743. Duchess of Portland.

Longleat MSS. (44) 72.—Bath, pp. 275–6; Shelley, pp. 163–4.

Madam

I beg my humble Duty to my Lord Duke, & a thousand Thanks for all his Favours; particularly for his Last.[1] How much I am obligd to You Both? I hope Madam, the cause of those low spirits Your Grace complain of when I had the Honour of yr Last Letter, no longer Subsists. Your Grace is so kind as to invite me to Bullstrode; If any Friend of mine,
                                                    He
& of my Standing, shd acquaint me that   was going to make One in such a gay Assembly, I should smile at Him, in my Sleeve, for a Fool, who knew not his time of Day, & forgot that his Holydays were over. But your Graces Desires are Commands, & your Commands are Sacred. I propose to myself the Honour of waiting on yr Grace the latter end of next Month. If that is Agreeable /[verso]/ to You.
                                     or
I have made a Short Excursion,   I shd sooner have acknowledgd Those Favours wh lay me under so great an Obligation; But I met with no such Pleasing & Surprizing Pictures of Art & Nature as your Grace sets before me in your two last Letters: One would wonder how barren Rock shd furnish Nutriment to Support those large flourishing Trees of wh your Grace takes notice. These are strange Sights; But not so strange as to see a Rich overgrown Miser, who could purchase half a Country, where Nature shows us these rarities, It is not, I say, Madam, so strange to see
                                        see
Groves feeding on Rocks, as to   that Miser dining on a Flintstone; wh is a sight I have been lately honourd with in my Travels; & the worst part of the story is, I was obligd to dine with him, or to starve. /[conjugate leaf]/ Perhaps, Your Grace may desire to know the Difference between These two; As ye Question is Difficult, I must defer the Resolution of it, till I have the Honour of seeing You.—All

---

[1] The Duke's application to the Archbishop of Canterbury?

the News I can tell yr Grace, is, yt Ive lately convert wth a most exstraord[i]nary Person, Dr Taylor the famous Oculist.[1] He is member of every University in Europe but his own; He talks all Languages but his own, & has an exstreme Volubility of Tongue; but it is like ye Volubility of the ye [*sic*] Machine with wh they winnow Corn (I have forgot its name) & is excellent at throwing Dust in our eyes. In a word his Tongue is as well qualifd to blind Understandings, as his Hand is to put out our Sight. My near Neighbour, & valueable Friend Sr Jemy Sambroke, who has been blind twenty years, is now under his operations, but with such ill success that we are willing to Compound for his Life, wh was once thought /[verso]/ in Danger. Madam, may the gracious wing of Providence be ever stretchd out over Bullstrode, & may I find all as safe when I have the Honour of waiting on You, as I Now wish You, or, wh is ye Same thing, as I wish myself.

I am Madam
Yr Graces most Obligd
& most Obedt Humble Sevt
EYoung.

Wellwyn Aug 25th
1743.
My humble service to Mr Achard.

[1] Dr. John Taylor (1703–72), appointed oculist to George II in 1736, of whom the account in the *Dictionary of National Biography* says that he 'possessed considerable skill as an operator, but his methods of advertising were those of a charlatan'. One of his unnoticed works was *The Case of Sir Jeremy Sambrooke, Baronet, Fairly and Impartially Stated. Containing a full and exact account of the singular Disorder in the Eye of this Gentleman. With a faithful Relation of the great Variety of uncommon Circumstances attending his Cure and a clear Demonstration of the highest Probability of his Perfect Recovery. Humbly Inscrib'd to Himself.* 'By J. Taylor, Doctor of Physick; Oculist to his Majesty: and Member of several of the Colleges of Physicians in Foreign Parts.' It states that Sir Jeremy had been operated on early in June and that complications had delayed his recovery. The *Daily Advertiser* of 14 September carried an announcement by Taylor that his patient was 'now recover'd'. The dedication of the tract is dated 1 October 1743. It is apparent from the text of the tract that Taylor had been removed from the case on the advice of consultants. Although Sir Jeremy lived until 1754 there is nothing to indicate that his sight was restored.

137. Welwyn, Herts. [W.] 14 September 1743.
Duchess of Portland.

Longleat MSS. (46) 76–8.¹

[top portion of sheet cut away] Wells.

I humbly submit this to your Graces consideration.
~~Unless~~ And as humbly hope your Graces kind Assistance,
if there is room for it; & /[verso]/

Your Grace sees what a Fool I am; Your intimate Friend
Seneca calld me so two thousand years agoe. Omnes (says
He) male habet Ignorantia Veri Tanquam ad Bona feruntur,
/[new sheet]/ Decepti rumoribus. Deinde Mala esse, aut
Inania, aut Minora quam speraverint, Adepti, & multa
Passi vident. Major pars Hominum miratur ex Intervallo
fallentia.²

This your Grace perfectly well understands. These
Thoughts Seneca stole from You; & when I met them in
that old Fellow I admird his Judgment for stealing them
from such an Authority, but pityd his want of Ability to
give his Theft yt Lustre & Grace which It originally wore
on your Graces Lip, from wh I have heard ye Same sentiments more than once. I beg my humble Duty to my Ld
Duke, my Compliments to All wth You, & particularly to
Those yt will succeed You in your Fortunes & Virtues
when You are better provided for

I am Madam Yr Graces most Dutifull
Humble Sevt   EYoung.

/[verso]/ Wellwyn Sepr 14th
            1743.

[item 77 of the manuscript is a slip of paper with a translation into English of the Latin, written in another hand]/ All
men suffer by the ignorance of Truth. Deceivd by reports

---

¹ The first part of this letter has been cut away to the word 'Wells'. It is described
in the manuscript index to the Longleat correspondence as 'On the Duke of Newcastle' and clearly had something to do with the Duchess's efforts to have Young
given a Church preferment.
² Seneca, *Ad Lucilium Epistulae Morales*, cxviii. 7.

they are carried after things as if they were good; which after much trouble having attaind they find to be either bad or vain or inferiour to their hopes. Most men admire things which deceive them by reason of their distance. /[verso blank]

138. [?Welwyn, Herts.]. [?M. 25 September 1743]. Duchess of Portland.

Longleat MSS. (47) 79.—Bath, pp. 277–8; Shelley, pp. 166–7.

Madam

[The opening paragraph has been stricken out but has been deciphered to read: What you & my Lord Duke think to be the best method to be taken with the Duke of New-castle I know to be so But whom shall I get to present such a Promise (viz) the next vacancy Westminster Christchurch or Canterbury? I know no one but my Lord Duke, & him I am afraid to ask.][1]

But I think myself entitled to ask it of your Grace, since You condescend in your last Letter to ask me for a Transla-tion.[2] Pray, Madam, to what Bishoprick? I do not hear that his Grace of Canterbury is Ill.[3]

Madam I should have had the Honour of waiting [on]

---

[1] In this regard it is interesting to read the applications of Arthur Onslow (1691–1768), Speaker of the House of Commons, to the Duke of Newcastle for recognition of the Chaplains to the House of Commons. In one he wrote: 'Your Grace knows that the chaplains of the House of Commons have always been provided for in the Churches of Westminster and Windsor' (British Museum, Add. MSS. 32699, f. 130). Again: 'There being a vacancy in the Church of Canterbury of a prebend in the gift of the crown, and one very lately become so in the Church of Windsor, will you permit me to put you in mind of . . . the chaplain of the House of Commons' (British Museum, Add. MSS. 32728, f. 3). Further: 'In the course of promotions upon the death of the Arch-Bishop, if a vacancy in any of the Churches of West-minster, Windsor and Canterbury should happen I hope your Grace will not forget . . . the Chaplain of the House of Commons' (British Museum, Add. MSS. 32878, f. 312). Considering Young's compliments to Onslow in the dedication to his sermon: *An Apology for Princes* (1729) and the dedication of his first 'Night' (1742) to Onslow it is remarkable that there is no similar request for Young's promotion; one of Onslow's applications refers to a Chaplain of the House of Commons as 'my relation'.

[2] The pun on 'translation' arose from the passage in Latin in his letter of the 14th.

[3] While Young is obviously jesting, the Archbishop was reported, 7 November as continuing 'in a bad state of Health' on his return from Bath (*Daily Advertiser*).

You before now, had not a very melancholy Accident happend to prevent me.[1] The Plague rages in foreign Nations,
& there ye Sword is drawn, while we sit smiling under our
Vines & Figtrees. Yet some Calamities come on board our
little Isleland. There is a Young /[verso]/ man to whom I
wish exstremely ^{well}, nor ^{is} He altogether undeserving in
Himself, nor, I think, quite a stranger to your Grace. He is
going to be marryd, & my hands are chosen to be embrued
in the blood of his pretious Peace. The Nuptials are to be
the Latter end of this Week, at Putney. As soon as they are
over, & I recoverd from the formidable Duty I propose
seting out for Bullstrode, so Famous for Nightingales.

On reviewing Your Graces Letter, I find You mean a
Translation from Rome to Britain. Madam, was I not fully
satisfid that the Former is by far the better See of ye two, &
that Your Grace is absolute Mistriss of it, I shd comply with
your Request. There dwells Infallabi[li]ty, how then can
Your Grace be deceivd. I dare say if Lucifer himself was
to write in darkest characters to any Protestant King in
Christendom, the Roman Chair would undertake to
decypher it.

/[new partial sheet]/

However if Your Grace onely means to enquire whither
I understand Seneca as well as yourself, I will venture to expose myself to You, by leting You know yt I take his meaning to be—That He is a Fool that is seeking Preferment at
my ^{time} of day, & that success (should I have it) would onely
convince me that It deserved not so much Trouble in the
Pursuit.

/[in margin]/ Miss Lee gi [remainder cut away].

---

¹ A facetious reference to arrangements for the marriage of his stepson, Charles
Henry Lee, to Martha D'Aranda of Putney, Surrey, a marriage which Young
performed on the 29th.

139. London. [Sa.] 29 October 1743. Duchess of
Portland.

Longleat MSS. (48) 81.—Bath, pp. 278–9; Shelley, p. 62.

> Mr Tassells.
> Temple Bar.
> Oct 29.
> 1743.

May it please your Grace.

This day, by your Friend Mr Murrays Assistance I
carryd just one Half of my Point; the Other is referd to
Prince Posterity.[1] Mr Murray has certainly learnt your
Graces Art;[2] for He helpt me to the wing without cutting
off ye Leg. For the Matter Stood *thus*; I had two Annuitys
of Different dates;[3] that of the second Date He sliced off
for me with infinite Address & Dexterity, & left that of ye
First Date, Still sticking to the Dukes Estate. Tho I must do
Him this Justice, that if any man alive could have cut off ye
Legg too, He had certainly done ^it^ ; for there is no Tongue
/[verso]/ carrys a better Edge.

Your Grace's allways shines, & I Suppose can cut upon
an Occasion. But It is something reservd; And as your Grace
was pleasd to sheath it in Silence, as to One Particular, of
which I was in hope to hear You speak; I think it my Duty
to be silent too on that Matter.

On Teusday, Madam, I go to Wellwyn for some Writings
necessary to ye final Conclusion of this matter; For the
Chancellours Decree is not yet more than minuted,[4] & some

---

[1] Young refers to his suit in Chancery against the Wharton estate, entitled: 'Stiles
versus the Attorney General'.

[2] i.e. the art of 'dissection'; see the letter of 4 December 1740.

[3] Each was for £100: The first was by deed-poll of 24 March 1719/20, and the
second by indenture of 10 July 1722.

[4] The Chancellor's decree, issued 14 March 1740/1 (John Tracy Atkyns, *Reports
of Cases* [etc.], 1794, pp. 152–4, case No. 136), ordered both annuities paid but
disallowed a claim for expenses Young incurred in standing for Parliament at
Cirencester in 1722 (Charles Henry Parry, *A Memoir of the Revd Joshua Parry*,
1872, pp. 122–3) in support of Wharton. The Chancellor could not 'consider this
as a valuable consideration, for Doctor Young cannot be supposed to be a candidate
for a seat in the House of Commons upon any other view but serving his country,
and the part the Duke of Wharton took in the affair can be considered no otherwise
than as a desire or request at most'.

Trouble is to follow its being perfected, before a poor Creature embarkt in Law for 24 years, can come safe to land.

If Affairs permit me the Honour of seeing Bullstrode again this Season,[1] I /[conjugate leaf]/ will bring with me Mrs Donolans Paquet, as a Charm against any Misadventures in my Journey. I will not say, as the Religious carry Relicks; for That is making a Saint of Her; whereas I really think, Her onely ye very Best of Sinners. If she is not Content with that Character I am sorry for it; for it is ye Tiptop of what our Church admits.

This afternoon I waited on Mr Virtue,[2] He showd me a thousand things that pleasd me much; but nothing Half So pleasing as the Simplicity of his own Manners, & ye Integrity of his Heart. He has engraved Himself in my Memory & Esteem, for ever.

Captain Cole[3] was with Him Yesterday; but He was not very well. Miss Cole is in my /[verso]/ Head, perhaps when I see Her, see [she?] may change her Apartment. I have not yet embracd my Friend at your Graces Gate, but I sent him an Apology, & He says, that for the Sake of the Blessed Family He will forgive me. If yr Grace would knit the Friendship Stronger between me & Josiah,[4] (that I think is his name,) I humbly beg You to send Him, Bp Gastrells work I borrowd,[5] for I can not get it in Town, & I much

---

[1] Young had been at Bulstrode with Lady Peterborough on 21 October (Climenson, 1906, i. 169).

[2] George Vertue (1684–1756), engraver, whose patron, the Duchess's father, had died in 1741, and who was now being patronized by the Duchess. Young visited Vertue to arrange for an illustration that accompanied his fifth 'Night', published 16 December.

[3] Captain John Meric Cole (d. 1745), with his wife and daughter, lived at No. 4 Queen's Road West (now Royal Hospital Road), Chelsea from 1735 to 1741 (Walter H. Godfrey, *The Parish of Chelsea, Survey of London*, vol. ii). The family was patronized by the Countess of Oxford and their mentally deranged daughter Grace was especially the concern both of the Countess and of the Duchess as will appear later.

[4] On 28 November 1742 Elizabeth Montagu wrote to the Duchess: 'I hear your Grace's porter says you will not leave Welbeck these two months, and Elias is no lying man' (Montagu, 1810, ii. 227).

[5] Francis Gastrell (1662–1725), Bishop of Chester, had been appointed Chaplain to the House of Commons and later Canon of Christ Church by the Duchess's grandfather, Robert Harley (1661–1724), the first Earl of Oxford. The book Young speaks of was his *Moral Proof of the Certainty of a Future State*, 1725. Young's dependence on it for the later 'Nights' of *The Complaint* is discussed by Isabel St.

want to consult it once more on a particular Exigence. I will call on Josiah for it; & consult him about the Immorality [*sic*] of ye Soul, & I will return the Book safe & sound with his Comment when I have ye Honour to see your Grace. I beg the Duty of my Heart to my Ld Duke, & my best Compliments to ye Ladys. May Heaven have You & Yours in its peculiar Protection. I am Madam Yr Graces Most Obligd & most Obedt H[umble] S[ervant]

EYoung.

140. [London].[1] [Su.] 20 November 1743. Duchess of Portland.

Longleat MSS. (49) 83.—Bath, p. 279; Shelley, pp. 168–9.

Madam
   Such, & so frequent are the Calamities of human Life, that be our Conduct never so correct, our Station never so high, they one day or another will infallably Hook us in. Oh Madam! The Hook! ye Hook!—[2]Why was It not Advertisd? Why not a Reward proposd? Why not ye Germanick Empire that Reward? But alas! in its present Situation It would never have brought it, unless the Finder had been as Honest as ye Lady in C——t street.[3]
   Madam, I have diligently sought it High & Low; but in vain. I lookt for /[verso]/ it in the Presents of Inferiors; in the Nolo Episcopari of Bishops; In Speeches from the Throne; in the Self-condemnations of Fine Ladys; but in Vain. I found in all of them a Hook, but a Hook yt was by no means a Mysterie.
   Your Grace's Hook is All-mysterious. I therefore diligently sought it in every Page of the Relations. But not one Page could tell any Tale or Tydings of It.

John Bliss ('Young's "Night Thoughts" in Relation to Christian Apologetics', *PMLA*, xlix, March 1934, 37–70).
   [1] Young was still in London on the 24th when he negotiated the sale of the first five parts of the *Night-Thoughts* with Robert Dodsley (see Appendix A).
   [2] the 'hook' was the subject of humour in the Duchess's circle. 'Don't forget the needles', Mary Pendarves wrote to her sister, 'the hook for the D[uke?] is to be baited with an eel; I hope we shall catch a fine dish of gudgeons' (Llanover, 1861, ii. 182).   [3] Unidentified.

Yet Madam do not Despair. I hear the Daemon of Bull-strode Gallery, yt old Friend of mine, whisper in my Ear—'It shall be Found'—And Lo! Here it is

ᘚ.

/[conjugate leaf]/ I heartily congratulate your Grace on this most Happy, & Surprizg Recovery of your dear Hook, & beg my Heartyst Congratulations to ye two Ladys who doubtless have long wept ye Supposd Loss.

I beseech Yr Grace to be more carefull for the Future, & not to
        throw ye World into so terrible a Pannick for any more.

I beg my humble Duty to my Ld Duke, & my very best Compliments to ye Ladies &c:

I am Madam Yr Graces
Most Obedt & Obligd
Humble Sevt
EYoung.

Nov 20th
    1743.

141. Welwyn, Herts. [Sa.] 10 December 1743. Duchess of Portland.

Longleat MSS. (50) 85.—Bath, pp. 279–80; Shelley, pp. 169–70.

Wellwyn
Decem: 10th
1743.

Madam.

Such is ye Dangerous excellency of your Graces under-standing, that a man proves Himself quite a Hero who dares to converse with You. What will become of my poor unarmd naked Simplicity in So unequall a Combat? Why am I thrown in Pannicks when there is no Danger near me? Why am I told of impending Tempests? Why am I told of Ladys in Displeasure when I am Satisfid their Opinions are at Peace with me?

As for Mrs Donellan, I am not onely not afraid of her Anger; but I am confident of her Goodwill; for is it possible her Discernment can stop Short of ye real Meaning of my Heart? I therefore defie your Graces Pair of Bellows, /[verso]/ they may puff ye Coal of Enmity betwe[e]n us, till they burst. Tis all in vain. Mrs Donellan allways thinks justly; & Therefore I am Safe.

As for Lady Peterborow I have a high Sense of ye favour of her good Wishes. But how came I by them? Her great Goodness gave them to me purely as a Human Creature in Distress, so that tho they did me a great Honour, yet did they a much Greater to Herself.

As for Mrs Delany, she is very Kind in giving me a Place in her Remembrance; & please, Madam, to let her know (for she is a great stranger to ye secret) let her know therefore, that as long as ye prime Virtues, Decencys, & Elegancies, & Arts of Life preserve their due Estimation in ye World /[conjugate leaf]/ by No One who ever had once the Happiness of Knowing her, will she ever be Forgot.

As to ye Last part of your Graces Letter I perfectly understand it. And am exstremely Obligd by it. But if Yr Grace differs till the Great World is settled, I shall wear a Mitre in ye Millenium. The D. of Newcastle is our Pope. Ecclesiasticals are under his Thumb. And He is as Fixt as St Pauls, by his own Weight; in Spight of all ye Revolutions of the Little-court buildings round about Him. God be praisd for my Ld Dukes better Health.[1] I beg my Humble Duty to Him, & best Service to Mr Achard. The Ladies divide me, I hope they will give the crumbs to ye Little Ones. I am Madam, Yr Graces most Obedt & most Obligd H[umble] S[erven]t   EYoung

/[verso]/ Miss Lee gives her Duty to yr Grace. Her Brother is dying wth ye Smallpox.[2]

[1] The Duke had broken his arm in a fall from his horse while hunting.

[2] The London *Daily Post and General Advertiser* for 5 January 1743/4 reported: 'Cornet Lee, Nephew to the late Earl of Litchfield, Gentleman Usher to her Royal Highness the Princess Amelia, and Master of the Revels, lies dangerously ill of the Small Pox, at his house in St. James's Street.'

142. Welwyn, Herts. [Tu.] 17 January 1743/4.
Duchess of Portland.

Longleat MSS. (51) 87.—Bath, pp. 280–1; Shelley, p. 172.

Madam

Your Grace is pleasd to Complain in your Last, that I call You an Incendiary. I would prove You such in more senses than One. But You expect I shd retract; I will; & to make you full Amends, please accept of ye Title of an Extinguisher. What can quench honest Ambition more,
than robing it ^{of} Emulation, & hiding Laudable Example from its Sight. Has Dr Delany[1] been with Your Grace a Month, & does your Grace mention him, & *mention* him *onely*? Why did You mention Him at all? Had You not, You then might have robd me, & I known nothing of the Felony. But now I am robd, & murderd: /[verso]/ murderd my Strong & just Desire of receiving the Character of so Distinguisht a Person from so distinguisht a Pen. But Your Grace can set this right in your next; & I humbly hope You will.

As for Mrs Delany I greive for her Indisposition, what Pity tis yt One who cant but give Pleasure, shd ever suffer Pain. As for Lady Peterborow, I shd endeavour to cultivate my better acquaintance with her, was I not Apprehensive of too powerfull a Rival in the Pope; & who would be a Pretender in vain? As for Mrs Donallan, I suppose Your Grace was afraid to commit ye very Bright things she was pleasd to say, to yr own Bright style, lest Both together shd set the Paper on fire. Madam I rejoyce at Heart /[conjugate leaf]/ for my Ld Dukes recovery. My humble Duty to Him. Caroline gives her Duty to your Grace. Next to his poor Wife, she is the greatest sufferer, an Onely Sister, & most Belovd.[2] Thus You see, Madam, tho we begin gayly we end otherwise. Death steals into ye Latter end of my Letter, tho

---

[1] Patrick Delany, then Chancellor of St. Patrick's in Dublin and newly married (9 June 1743) to Mary Pendarves. The Delanys had come to Bulstrode in late November.

[2] Charles Henry Lee had died on 8 January.

He has hitherto spard the Latter end of my Life; nor can so bright an Assembly of Ladies, tho they hate him, quite fright him away. Had their meanest Admirers no Other Rival, they wd certainly carry their Point. Wth ye greatest Respect & Truth I am Madam

Yr Graces much Obligd & most Obedt
Humble Sevt EYoung.

Madam I hear that there are Prebendarys & Deanerys vacant,[1] either of which would mend my Stockings.

My Compliments if Yr Grace pleases
to Mr Achard &c &c:

Wellwyn
  Jany 17
  1743

143. [London]. [March 1743/4]. Duchess of Portland.

Longleat MSS. (39) 66.

Madam

    I had waited on your Grace instead of writing, had it been in my Powr; But *Business* onely brought me to Town, & like an old ugly Mistriss as she is, She torments me in it.

    Poor Mr Lees Affairs,[2] wh are perplext, oblige me to go tomorrow to his Widow at Putney for 2 or 3 days; the moment I return Ill have the Honour of waiting on Your Grace.

I am, Madam, in a very particular manner

Yr Graces most Obedt
& most Humble Sevt
EYoung.

[1] One deanery was that of Down in Ireland for which Mrs. Delany successfully petitioned for her husband (Llanover, 1861, ii. 234).

[2] Young was soon to be involved, as the guardian of Caroline Lee, in a lawsuit with the D'Arandas (see H. Pettit, 'Edward Young and the Case of Lee vs D'Aranda', *Proceedings of the American Philosophical Society*, 1963, cvii. 145–59).

I thank yr Grace for finding out ye Needle in a Bottle of Hay.[1] But I know yr Sagacity.

I beg my humble Duty to my Ld

I am very sorry for Yr Graces Cold, & hope I shall find [it] gone & forgot.

144. Richmond, Surrey.[2] [M.] 19 March 1743/4. George North.[3]

Address: To / The Revd Mr North / at Codicot in / Hertfordshire. *Postmark*: RG.
Reading (Collins) MSS.

Dear Sr

    Things so happen, that I must be be [*sic*] unavoidably absent till ye middle of next month. What shall I do? Can You take care of Easter Week, & ye Ninth of April?—I shall be uneasie till I hear from You.—If possible let   have   *me* ye satisfaction of knowing my Church will not be neglected, in these 2 material Points. I am

Dear Sr

Yr faithfull Humble Sevt

EYoung

Mr Newcombs
  at Kew
March 19th
  174$\frac{3}{4}$

  [1] A proverbial expression on which Young was probably punning on the name of the Duchess's cousin, the Hon. John Hay.

  [2] Young is visiting his old friend, Thomas Newcomb, chaplain to Charles Lennox (1701–50), Duke of Richmond.

  [3] George North (1710–72), Curate and Vicar (from 1743) of the church in Codicote, a village two miles north of Welwyn, frequently helped Young in the conduct of his church.

145. [Richmond, Surrey]. [March 1743/4]. Duchess of Portland.

Longleat MSS. (54) 92–3.

Madam

I am Here[1] fore some Days how many I can not tell. Which may be applyd to Life as well as my present Situation. And if This may be applyd to your Graces Life, how much more to mine? [remainder of sheet cut away][2]

[bottom half of letter sheet, top cut away]

Being obligd to be near my gentle Friends of Putney, till Affairs are settled between us; I have taken a Lodging on this Delicious Spot. And if your Grace has a mind to breath better air; & converse with purer Hearts than Whitehall can afford, You will be exstremely wellcome to ye most elegant Villa of

Madam

Yr Graces most Obedt

& much Obligd Humble Sevt

EYoung

Madam I beg humble Duty
to my Ld Duke &c:

Duchess of Portland to the Duke of Newcastle. [M.] 14 May 1744.

Address: For / His Grace / The Duke of Newcastle.
British Museum Add. MSS. 32703, f. 44.

May 14th 1744

My Lord,

Your Grace is no Stranger to the desire I have long had of serving Doctor Young, as I have taken the Liberty before

---

[1] i.e. at the seat of the Duke of Richmond. Mrs. Elizabeth D'Aranda, mother of Charles Henry Lee's widow, Martha, occupied a historic mansion known as 'The Palace', near the Putney–Fulham bridge on the south bank of the Thames.

[2] According to the manuscript index to the Longleat papers this letter was 'On his preferment'.

of applying to you in his favour by my Lord; his Character
is so universally Honourd & so well known to your Grace
that it is unecessary for me to say any thing on that head, &
you are a much better judge of his abillities than I can pretend to be: I know him to be a most worthy man, & have
long had a sincere esteem for him, & shall take it as a particular Obligation to my self if your Grace will obtain for him
the first Prebend that shall become Vacant in Westminster
Windsor or Christ Church.

I am my Lord
Your Graces
most Obedient Humble
Servant
M: Cavendishe Portland.

146. [Tu.] 29 May 1744. Duchess of Portland.

Longleat MSS (58) 98.—Bath, pp. 282-3; Shelley, pp. 178-9.

Madam
  It is with great Feeling of Heart that I look back on my
Lord Duke's & your Grace's late uncommon Goodness to
me.[1] On Saturday I waited on my Lady Oxford to thank her
for bringing You into the world. I could not get out of Town
till Saturday Evening. The town is a great Net, where Honest
men are caught like Flies, & know not how to disentangle
their Integrity; & where Knaves sit, like Spiders, spending
their Vitals in spining out Snares of Iniquity; These Spiders
are of various Kinds.[2] Some onely poyson the Principles of
Those they catch; These Spiders nest in the *Grecian*, &
at *White's*. Others are sure to suck the /[verso]/ Blood
of Those they get into their Clutches. One of ye First Sort
I saw crawling on Mrs Mon——gue's fair bosom. I would

---

  [1] On 17 April Young had dined at the Portland home in Whitehall (Llanover,
1861, ii. 295), but the reference is probably to a more recent entertainment as well
as to the renewal of the Portland effort to get him preferment.
  [2] The allusion is to lawyers and politicians with whom Young was having to
deal and who frequented the coffee-houses. The Grecian coffee-house was in the
Strand in Devereux Court near the Temple. White's Chocolate House was in St.
James's Street near the Royal Palace.

fain have brusht it off; but astonishing to say it! I found She
was fond of ye Monster. And It has workt its way quite into
her breast, & is quite Visible in that fair & Sweet Repository,
like a Spider enclosd in Amber. But give me leave to Say,
that Amber ye most illustrious, so poysond, will soon, wth
all ye better part of ye World, quite lose its powr of Attrac-
tion.[1]

As to the Second Sort of Spiders, the Blood-suckers, they
nest cheifly in ye Inns of Court; & Westminster Hall;[2] Two
or Three of These lately seizd on me at once, & playd their
parts so well, yt it is allmost Incredible /[conjugate leaf]/ to
think how much I am reduced.

But it is some Comfort to me to consider that your Grace
may be a Gainer by Both these Calamities. Yr Grace has a
Collection of Philosophical Rarities. Clap Mr M———[3] into
one Corner of yr Cabinet, as a Spider inclosd in Amber; &
hang me up in some old Clock-case, for a Skeliton, then
laugh at *Sloane*.[4]

And now, Madam, is it not a most melancholy Consideration, that I must soon be Re-entangled in this horrid Cob-
web of the Town? I will live There like a Tortoise, in a
Box; but it shall be a Box of Ierish Oak, that Spiders may
not come near me. My humble Duty to my Ld Duke I
am Madam

Yr Graces most Obligd & most
Obedt Humble Sevt   EYoung

May 29 1744.

---

[1] The pun depends on acquaintance with the magnetic characteristics of amber.
[2] The Inns of Court were residence halls of lawyers; Westminster Hall was the
seat of the principal Law Courts.
[3] i.e. William Murray.
[4] Sir Hans Sloane (1660–1753), 'the foremost toyman of his time' as Young had
earlier characterized him in *Love of Fame* (iv. 114), was an avid collector of various
rarities which subsequently formed the nucleus of the collections in the British
Museum. He had recently retired to Chelsea.

147. Welwyn, Herts. [F.] 1 June [1744]. Duchess of Portland.

Longleat MSS. (65) 110–11.—Bath, pp. 285–6.

Wellwyn
June. 1st

May it please yr Grace

I am truly Sorry for Mr Grosmiths Misfortune; but of Misfortunes it was one of ye best; for if a Mans bones are to be broken, Tis a Happy way so to break them as to stand in Need of a Man of Skill to let us into ye Secret. If Such a Little Innocent as Ld Edward[1] must be acquainted with Pain, let Those advancd in Years & Iniquities take heed that Their Complaints under it are not too violent. His Lordships Teeth have, it seems, got ye Start of his Tongue; I wish him Such Length of Days that his Tongue may Survive them, & make up the Difference. I am heartily glad that my Ld Duke has escaped the Gout; if his Grace feels no Pain, till He gives it to others /[verso]/ I dare ensure him from ye Gout for more than this Winter. Our Friends at Chelsea![2] —Alas! Madam, how many melancholy Scenes are there in the World, when we meet them so often within ye narrow Circle of our familiar Friends? What a comfortable Reflection is it to consider that there is a World, where they that give us Joy, will be under no Necessity of giving us Sorrow too; wh in our present One is inevitable. Mrs Montague Seems to be for picking a Hole in my Philosophical Surtout:[3] I give her Joy; It shows her present Situation stands in no need of Philosophy; when It does, she will speak with more

[1] The Portland son, Edward Charles, had been born on 31 March.

[2] i.e. the family of Captain John Meric Cole.

[3] The sixth 'Night' had been published on 30 March with the sub-title: 'The Infidel Reclaim'd ... Containing the Nature, Proof, and Importance of Immortality ... Where, among other things, Glory, and Riches, are particularly consider'd.' In December 1742, when asked by the Duchess for an opinion of *Night-Thoughts*, Elizabeth Montagu had replied, mistaking the authorship of the poem: 'At your Grace's desire I have read Mr. Hervey; I think he has some very good thoughts; but there is, in my opinion, a great deal of absurdity with now and then apparent nonsense. He says some pretty things on friendship, but the subject is worthy the tongue of angels, or angel-like mortals; there must be a mind of more steadiness and harmony than his to comprehend it' (Montagu, 1810, ii. 249).

Reverence of yt, wh will rock her Pains into Patience more effectually than a /[conjugate leaf]/ Coach & Six. When Wit laughs at Wisdom Ravens should pull out its Eyes, & young Eagles shd eat them. The surest Symtom of a Sound Understanding, is, neither to fear, nor value, Wit. Lady Wallingford[1] (to whom I beg my best Thanks & Respects) Surprizes me with her Goodness; The Mode of ye World is to be exstremely Civil, but safely, too; to shine away in Promises, provided they have Evasions in their Poket; but to remember that those forget themselves, & Sollicit for Trouble, This is a Character yt would make Saints in modern Rome, & would have made Goddesses in that of old. I know but one Lady on Earth yt rivals her in this most amiable Character. But Providence wh inspires Such Thoughts & considers ye Will as the Deed, has savd /[verso]/ Lady Wallingford any farther Trouble. Mr Leigh has relented, & my Neighbour[2] is returnd to his own House in Peace. I hope this Discipline has had its proper Effect, & given him a Heart fit for his grey Hairs. Ecclesiasticus, with me a most favourite Author, says *Much Experience is ye Crown of old men, & ye Fear of ye Lord is their Glory.*[3] If Mrs Leigh has given him this Crown, & He will wear it, tis ye most valueable Present He ever receivd in his Life. And I thank Mrs Leigh, by Lady Wallingford, for giving my Friend a better Ornament for his Head than ye most rosy Beaver he can possibly put on. Wth ye truest Sense of yr late Hospitality, & yr thousand repeated Indulgencies, I am, Madam

Yr Graces most Obedient
& most Humble Sevt
EYoung.

I rejoyce All are well, &
beg my humble Duty to
my Ld D. & humble ser to Mr A.
Caroline, Madam, sends her Duty.

[1] Mary Katharine Law, daughter of the economist, John Law (1671–1729) married (1734) her first cousin, Charles Knollys (1662–1740), known as 'Viscount Wallingford'. She was with the Portlands frequently at this time.

[2] Sir Samuel Garrard (d. 1761), of Lamer in Wheathampstead, Herts. His cousin, Martha (*née* Benet of Wiltshire), was married to Peter Legh of Lyme, Chester. She is mentioned in Sir Samuel's will (Somerset House, P.C.C. Cheslyn 431) and by the will of his brother Benet Garrard (Somerset House, P.C.C. Legard 265, probated 21 July 1767) was left £2,000 not to be touched by her husband.   [3] 25:6.

148. [?Welwyn, Herts.]. [W.] 20 June 1744. Samuel Richardson.[1]

Not traced.—Barbauld, ii. 4–6; *Monthly Magazine*, xxxvi (1 December 1813), 418.

Dear Sir,

Does Lovelace[2] more than a proud, bold, graceless heart, long indulged in vice, would naturally do? No. Is it contrary to the common method of Providence to permit the best to suffer most? No. When the best so suffer, does it not most deeply affect the human heart? Yes. And is it not your business to affect the human heart as deeply as you can? Yes.

Your critics, on seeing the first two or three acts of Venice Preserved, the Orphan, and Theodosius, would have advised the innocent and amiable Belvidera, Monimia, and Athenais, should be made happy; and thus would have utterly ruined our three best plays.[3]

But you ask, How came they then to give this advice?

From ignorance, or envy, or affectation of a delicate concern and high zeal for virtue; or from such a degree of infidelity as suffers not their thoughts to accompany Clarissa any farther than her grave. Did they look farther, the pain they complain of would be removed; they would find her to be an object of envy as well as pity; and the *distressed* would be more than balanced by the *triumphant* Clarissa. And thus would they be reconciled to a story, at which their short-sighted tenderness for virtue pretends to take offence.

---

[1] Young's acquaintance with Richardson apparently began at this time. It was during this summer that Young changed publishers for the *Night-Thoughts* and Richardson took over the printing. The last part done by the previous printer, 'Night the Sixth', had been published on 30 March. The preface to Richardson's printing of 'Night the Seventh' is dated '7 July 1744'. For discussion of this change in publishers and printers, see William M. Sale, Jr., *Samuel Richardson: Master Printer* (1950) and Pettit (1954, pp. 31–3).

[2] Character in *The History of Clarissa Harlowe* (1747–8) on which Richardson was at work.

[3] Thomas Otway's *Venice Preserved* (1682) and *The Orphan* (1680) were staples of the English stage; Nathaniel Lee's *Theodosius* (1680) had been revived at Covent Garden 9 April 1743.

Believe me, Christians of taste will applaud your plan; and they who themselves would act Lovelace's part, will find the greatest fault with it,

Your affectionate humble servant,

E. Young.

June 20, 1744.

149. [London]. W. [?27 June 1744]. Duchess of Portland.

Longleat MSS. (52) 89.

May it please Yr Grace

on Yr Grace

It greives me I cant have the Honour of waiting   ; Im going a Mile or 2 in ye Country. I have not slept since Ive been in Town: I had allmost as willingly have my Head stuck upon Temple Bar, as upon a Pillow under it, I have had no sleep since I came to Town, except a Half Hour Nap in ye Pulpit this Morning.[1] Pray my humble Duty to my Ld Duke. God preserve You All

I am Madam

Yr Graces most Obligd

Obedt Humble Sevt

EYoung.

Wensday

150. Welwyn, Herts. [M.] 9 July 1744. Samuel Richardson.

Not traced.—*Monthly Magazine*, xxxvi (1 December 1813), 419.

Wellwyn, July 9, 1744.

Dear Sir,

I am very sensible of the friendship you show me in your kind attention to my little affair; I am no farther concerned

---

[1] Young's duties as Chaplain in Ordinary to the King regularly brought him to London during the latter half of June.

about it. I shall let Sir John Stanley[1] know my opinion soon; at present I am pretty much engaged. I thank God I am well, and pretty much engaged in the *Last Night*,[2] and hope you are no less so in your undertaking.[3] It will have many more readers than I can expect. And he that writes popularly and well does most good, and he that does most good is the best author. What author to be compared with the author of his supreme happiness? God bless, preserve, and prosper you. I am, dear sir,

Your faithful and affectionate
humble servant,
E. Young.

151. Welwyn, Herts. [M.] 23 July 1744. Duchess of Portland.

Longleat MSS. (59) 100.—Bath, pp. 283–4; Shelley, pp. 180–1.

Wellwyn
July the
23d 1744

May it please Yr Grace
I am but just returnd to this Place from a long Absence,[4] or I shd have had the Honour of writing to your Grace sooner, to return the Sincerest Thanks for your & my Ld Dukes late great Goodness to me.

But tho, Madam, I have not written *to* your Grace, I have written *for* your Grace, & orderd a Copy of it to your House in Town a week agoe.[5] For if I have not written for your

---

[1] From letters between Young and Richardson just after Stanley's death in November of this year it is clear that Young's opinion had been sought about a work by Pierre Cuppé which had been Englished in 1743 as *Heaven open to all Men; or, a Theological treatise in which . . . is solidly prov'd by Scripture and reason that men shall be saved*, etc.

[2] This was probably the eighth 'Night' published the next spring, 7 March, rather than the ninth, which became the 'last', and was not published until January 1745/6.

[3] i.e. *Clarissa*.

[4] The contradiction of this statement with the place and date of the letter to Richardson of the 9th is not clear, suggesting a misdating of the letter (July for August?).

[5] i.e. 'Night the Seventh', which is without dedication.

Grace, for whom have I written? Not for Ten more in the Kingdom: At least not so many as there shd be. I mean not Madam, as to ye Composition, but as to the Subject, which is the most Delightfull, or the most Disagreeable in the World. And which of these it shall be, the Conduct of / [verso]/ ye Differently-disposd Readers is to determine.

Your Graces Turn I well know; & am sure of at least a Candid Reader in You. If this World was Eternal, & we were eternally to live in it; & that in perpetual Youth, & with the Conveniencies, nay the Glories of Life about us; Tho This to most would seem, at first view, a Desireable Situation; yet I am persuaded yt on farther Consideration we shd alter our Opinion: For, as *now* that we know we shall die, the Terror of it, flings all our Attention on what is *Agreeable* in this world, wth which we are, therefore, most unwilling to part; So, if we knew we were to live Here for ever, Then our Attention (so perverse is man) would be busie to find out all that was /[conjugate leaf]/ Disagreeable in it; That would most engage his Observation; & a Mind, whose Observation was so engagd, would be inclind to change This Scene for Another.

For my own part, Madam, I have good Reason to consider
it
myself, as on ye Verge of that Other Scene. And ~~into Ours~~ is a Situation yt is apt to give us serious Thoughts. ~~into Ours.~~ And the more serious any persons are, the more Gratefull
have
must they necessarily be to those, from [whom] they receivd Incontestable Proofs of Goodwill. I am, therefore, with the most sincere Esteem & Respect
Madam
Yr Graces most Obedt
& most Humble Sevt
EYoung

Pray Madam my humble
Duty to my Ld Duke
&c:

152. [Welwyn, Herts.]. [Su.] 29 July 1744. Samuel
Richardson.

Not traced.—*Monthly Magazine*, xxxvi (1 December 1813), 418–19.

July 29, 1744.
Dear Sir,
Mr. Cave[1] sent me last week a specimen of a spurious
copy of the Seventh Night, which, as to letter and ornaments,
mimics your's.—I understand not these things; I shou'd
therefore take it as a great favour if you cou'd inform me
what the meaning of this is; and, if it is a pirated edition,
what measures are proper to be taken. How glad shou'd I
be to see you here? I have felt some of your disorders since
I came home; I hope it was taken out of your stock, and
that you have the less for it. God prosper you in all things.
I am, with most hearty esteem,

Dear Sir.
Your affectionate humble Servant,
E. Young.

If, sir, any advertisement is proper, I beg you to order
Mr. Hawkins's[2] man to put it in the papers.

153. Fulham, Mdx. [Tu.] 30 July [1744]. Duchess
of Portland.

Longleat MSS. (60) 102.

Northend
July. 30th
May it please Yr Grace
I come this Moment from Cn Coles. I went to dine there
not knowing of his Illness. The first Person I met was Miss

---

[1] Edward Cave (1691–1754), publisher of *The Gentleman's Magazine*. Copies of
the seventh 'Night' printed on different papers presumably led to the suspicion of
piracy.
[2] i.e. the publisher, George Hawkins (d. 1780). Advertisements for the seventh
'Night' appeared in the *Daily Gazetteer* of 23 July and *Old England* of 11 August.

Parsons,[1] pale as Death. Who told me ye Occasion wh Yr Grace has by this Post from Miss Cole: Being pressed I dind with them; I thought I never saw so much Merit, & so much Misery together; there can not be a worse Match. But before I left them, either Miss Cole is an excellent Hypocrite, or her Heart was a little more at Ease. This I thought it my Duty to tell yr Grace, as I know it will give you some Consolation. /[verso]/

I have rarely seen a Family that seemed to me better entitled to escape Affliction, or of Hearts more tender to feel it, or of Understandings better qualifid to to [*sic*] support it. God Allmighty comfort them them [*sic*] under ye Worst; or if tis His good Pleasure, happily disapoint their present Apprehensions. That Such Tryals, by far ye most severe in Life, may be far distant from Yr Grace is ye hearty Prayr of Madam

Yr Graces most Obedient
& most Obligd Humble Sevt
EYoung.

Madam I beg
my humble Duty to
my Ld Duke, & Ly Oxford
&c: I set out for Tunbridge
God willing on Saturday next.

---

[1] Grace Parsons (1723–77), daughter of Sir William Parsons of Nottingham, and a niece of the Duchess of Northumberland at whose death (27 August 1738) she was left to the care of the Coles. In November 1738 Lady Mary Wortley Montagu wrote in a letter to a friend: 'The Duchess of Northumberland's will raises a great bustle among those branches of the royal blood. She has left a young niece, very pretty, lively enough, just fifteen, to the care of Captain Cole, who was director of Lady Bernard. The girl has 300 *l.* per annum allowed for her maintenance, but is never to touch her fortune till she marries, which she is not to do without his consent; and if she dies without issue, her twenty thousand pounds to be divided between the children of the Duchess of St. Albans and Lord Litchfield. The heirs-at-law contest the fantastical will, and the present tittle tattle of visits turns upon the subject' (Halsband, 1966, ii. 130–1).

154. Welwyn, Herts. [Su.] 16 September 1744.
Duchess of Portland.

Longleat MSS. (61) 103-4.—Bath, p. 284.

May it please your Grace
    I humbly thank yr Grace for your obliging Invitation, &
about ye Begining of next Month I design myself the
Honour of waiting on You.
    I am very Sorry for Ly Peterboroughs Indisposition;
                                                        wh
Which, by ye way, puts me in mind of my own,   I had
really forgot. But now I remember it my Head akes mightily,
& from eating a Load of unripe Fruit, I have been for a whole
Week in a good deal of Pain. And now having dischargd my
Conscience by doing Justice to myself; let me enter on a
more generous Province, & do Justice to my Cousin,[1]—
I grant that my Cousin, as /[verso]/ Your Grace rightly ob-
serves, is very Fit to make a Prince of ye Empire; nor would
Dutchland have disownd Him, had his Fortune dropt Him
There: But is This any Reason why yr Grace should dis-
affect his conversation? Wherein, thinks your Grace, lies ye
Blessing of Conversation? Is it in giving us an Opportunity
of admiring the Parts of Others, or of Displaying our Own?
If the First was all it presented us with, I know thousands
yt would renounce Conversation for ever! I know a young
Lady yt would turn Nun, tho she hates ye Pope: & I know
a Bishop yt would turn Hermit, tho It forfeited all hopes of
a Translation.—
    Reconcile yourself, Madam, to ye Blessings yt befall You:
Visit my dear Cousin, & be Happy, /[conjugate leaf]/ look
on Him & see what Sort of a Man it was yt inspird a Homer,

---

[1] Identified in the manuscript index to the Longleat letters as 'Genl. Colombine',
i.e. General Francis Columbine (1680–1746) of Hillingdon, near Bulstrode. Young
refers to him as an 'intrepid General' in his letter of 25 November. Columbine's
father, Brigadier-General Ventris Columbine (d. 1703), a native of Holland, had
served as page to Sir William Temple in Holland and had accompanied the Prince
of Orange to England in 1688. He had commanded in Holland at the time of
Young's father's service there as chaplain to Thomas Butler (1634–80), Earl of
Ossory. One of two possibilities would explain the relationship: (1) Columbine's
mother might have been a sister of Young's mother, or (2) Young's mother might
herself have been a Columbine.

& a Virgil; Such were their Heroes, & Such Heroes made them Wits; & does your Grace prefer a Wits, before that Important Being that can make them? By this time, no doubt, your Grace is convinct of my Cousin's Merit, & your own Mistake.

I beg, Madam, my Humble Duty to my Ld Duke, & best Compliments to Mr Hay. I am much obligd to Dr Tillotson for his Blessing.[1] But now I think of it, I can bless too, I blest Mr Stephen Duck yesterday with a Third Wife they were pleasd to come to Wellwyn for yt Benediction.[2] How long they may think fit to repute Such is Uncertain. Wth the greatest Respect & Gratitude I am Madam yr Graces most Obedt

& most Humble Sevt
EYoung

Wellwyn. Sepr. 16 1744.

155. Welwyn, Herts. [Su.] 18 November 1744. Duchess of Portland.

Longleat MSS. (62) 105–6.

Madam

I was in hope of getting the Better of my Disorder soon enough to have waited on Your Grace, but my Pains still persecute me, tho my Physitian tells me I 'am very well, that my Fever is quite gone, and as for a little Pain, that is Nothing, that every Body has more or less in this Reumatic weather:' This is ye Comforter Job has sent me under Pains half of which would make Him mad.

---

[1] By 'Tillotson' Young refers to John Tillotson (1630–94), Archbishop of Canterbury, in a whimsical allusion to the Duchess's infant son, regularly thereafter called the 'Archbishop'.

[2] Stephen Duck (1705–56), the 'thresher' poet and since 1735 Keeper of the Queen's Library at Richmond, had married Elizabeth Nevinson (1694–?1749) (cf. J. L. Nevinson, 'Stephen Duck at Kew', *The Surrey Archaeological Collections*, lviii, 1961, 104–7). Duck later took orders in the Church: 'On Sunday there was a great concourse of People at Audley Street Chapel, to hear Mr. Stephen Duck, the Poet, preach, who lately enter'd into Holy Orders' (*The Penny London Post* of 11 February 1746/7).

I should, Madam, have answerd Your Graces very Kind letter much sooner, had I not been in Hopes every day of finding myself able to take the Journey; but my Pains continuing, & my being necessarily obligd to return home /[verso]/ again a Week before Christmas, which now approaches, I humbly hope your Grace will excuse me; For why should I carry Complaints to Bullstrode, & make a Hospital of the House of Joy? I have heard nothing since your Graces letter of my old Friend Mr Percival,[1] & therefore hope your Apprehensions were false, & that Mrs Donalan is returnd with better News. I desire, Madam, my humble Duty to my Lord Duke, & Compliments to All; God preserve your Grace from Pain, both of Body & Mind. I am, Madam,

> Your Graces most Obligd
> & most Obedient Humble Sevt
> EYoung.

Wellwyn
Nov: 18.
1744

[in margin of conjugate leaf]/ Poor Dutchess of Leeds![2]
I hope in God all the Little Ones are well.

156. Welwyn, Herts. [Su.] 25 November 1744. Duchess of Portland.

Longleat MSS. (63) 107.

May it please your Grace
I find by your Letter that You writ in the Cold; I write in worse, I write in Pain: Notwithstanding, I propose waiting on your Grace some day this week (if I can) out of pure spight, to give your Grace ocular Demonstration how Unreasonable a Being You are. If ye Queen of Hungary had your Graces Powr, She would [not] want Soldiers, She would raise the dead to serve her, as your Grace has me.

---

1 The Hon. Philip Perceval (d. 1748), Anne Donnellan's stepfather.
2 Mary Godolphin, wife of Thomas Osborne (d. 1776), the fourth Duke of Leeds. A daughter, born on the 14th, had lived only two days (*Daily Advertiser*, 14 and 16 November 1744).

I little thought, Madam, when I was laughing in my last Letter, at my Physitian for thinking Pain no Evil, little did I think I was exposing myself to One of His Party. My Cousin the Intrepid General yr Neighbour,[1] tho He defies Death, yet is afraid of Pain: And my good Ld Duke (for whose /[verso]/ Recovery I bless God) considering the Condition He has been in, will (I fancy) be on our Side. The Gout is one of the best Antidotes against Stoical Opinions. But if Your Grace continues obstinate in that Persuasion, I know no better Revenge that my ~~Rentment~~ Resentment can take on You, than to wish (as I heartily do) that Pain which your Grace seems so fond off, may never come nigh You. I am, Madam, your Graces

Most Obedient

& most Obligd Humble Sevt

EYoung.

Madam
I beg my Humble Duty
& Congratulation to my
Lord Duke. &c.
 Wellwyn. Nov: 25
  1744

157. Bulstrode, Bucks. [Sa.] 8 December 1744. Samuel Richardson.

Not traced.—*Monthly Magazine*, xxxvi (1 December 1813), 419.

Dear Sir,

Dec. 8, 1744.

Our good friend Sir John!!²—The book³ you put into my hand, at his request, I read; but my opinion of it would have

---

¹ See the letter of 16 September.
² Stanley died 30 November at the age of 85.
³ *Heaven open to all Men: or, A Theological Treatise, in which, without unsettling the Practice of Religion, is solidly prov'd by Scripture and Reason, that all Men shall be saved or made finally happy*, the English version of a work in French by Pierre Cuppé, published in London in 1743. A third English edition appeared in 1751 and produced at least two responses: (1) *A Candid Examination of that celebrated Piece of Sophistry, entitled Heaven open to all men*, 1752, and (2) *A Short Answer to a Treatise entitled Heaven open to all Men*, 1753.

been no comfort to Sir John, or any that expected any consolation that they found not obviously presented to them in
the gospel. However, as things have fallen out, it troubles
me that I did not write; the reason was, I designed seeing
him at my return from this place; and subjects of that nature
are much better talked than written.

I hope, dear sir, you have made great progress in your
book, I long to enjoy it; for I value the heart much from
which it comes.—I desire, you know, at the first leisure,
what number of *my Impression*[1] are sold; if it sticks at this full
season, it should be re-advertised; I shall write to my bookseller[2] on receipt of yours.—I have been much out of order,
and a good deal in your way. My nerves were so tender, that
a door clapt, or a dog running by me on a sudden, gave me a
shock, which, I thank God, I did not understand before; but
by *His* mercy I am much better; and with a chearful heart
wish you much happiness, for I love the man who loves my
best benefactor.

God preserve you and your's.

I am, dear Sir,

Your affectionate humble servant,

E. Young.

Duke of Portland's,
at Bulstrode.

Richardson to Young. [London. *c.* W. 12 December
1744].

Not traced.—*Monthly Magazine*, xxxvi (1 December 1813), 419–20.

Rev. Sir,

As you propose to write to your bookseller, he will give
you that account of the sale of your excellent piece, which
I cannot, but by inquiry of him. This, to be sure, is the right
time for advertising it afresh, till near the holidays, and then

---

[1] i.e. 'Night the Seventh' of *The Complaint*.
[2] The seventh 'Night' was 'printed for G[eorge] Hawkins' and 'sold by M[ary]
Cooper', but judging from Young's letter of 29 July 1744 his reference would be to
Hawkins rather than to Cooper.

stop, and re-advertise when they are over. Every body I hear talk of it longs for the succeeding part, and to see the work altogether at a view. I am extremely concerned that you have been so much out of order in my way, as you call it; one of the most affecting ways in the world. I hope, on your recovery, (upon which I most sincerely congratulate you) the lost time, if any be lost by your past malady, will be retrieved with that chearfulness to yourself which you seem to have obtained.

Poor Sir John asked me several times after your opinion of 'Heaven opened to all Men'. He was much taken with the book; because he would have it that there was nothing in it contrary to the gospel. I think he was a very good man, and good christian; and his liking proceeded from that humanity and benevolence, which to me appeared to shine out in him with great distinction; rather than from the *extraordinary* occasion he thought himself under (human frailty allowed for) to recur to such a subterfuge. He was very serious with me, once or twice, because I had not read it. I told him (which was the truth) that I had but little time to read anything that I thought controversial, or shocking to fundamentals. On this occasion it was he told me, That he did not apprehend this to be such a piece; but that many texts were reconciled by it that he knew not otherwise how to reconcile; and that if he thought it a heterodox piece he would reject it. We both held ourselves suspended till your opinion of it came. Then Sir John was to reconsider it: I was to read it—But why say I this now?

You do me great honour in remembering what takes up the leisure time of such a scribbler as I am. I have been so much engaged in the Journals of the House of Commons, and in my other business, having not an overseer, that I have not gone so far as I thought to have done by this time.— Then the unexpected success that attended the other thing, instead of encouraging me, has made me so diffident!—And I have run into such a length!—And am such a sorry pruner, though greatly luxuriant, that I am apt to add three pages for one I take away! Altogether I am frequently out of conceit with it. Then I have nobody that I can presume to advise with on such a subject.—But last week, indeed, I took the liberty to send the beginning of it to my indulgent friend, Mr. Hill, whose sincerity I cannot doubt; but whose favour to me makes him so partial, that, if he approve, I shall not be without my diffidences. But if he prunes it, as I have requested he will, without mercy, then perhaps shall I have the courage to proceed with more alacrity: for though I remember your kind hint, that a folio may be short, and a duodecimo long, yet cannot I have the vanity to take comfort from the first, without I had such a judge as I have in my eye, to put me into heart, by pointing out to me where it may be best contracted. But this it would be a great presumption and vanity to hope for.

May a constant stock of health and flow of spirits attend you! The public is concerned in the wish! But were it not, the veneration, (the affectionate veneration!) I have for good Dr. Young, would be a sufficient motive for me to wish it, for his own sake, with that zeal, wherewith I am, and shall ever be,

Rev. Sir,
Your most faithful well-wisher,
and servant,
S. Richardson.

158. Bulstrode, Bucks. M. [?17] December 1744. Samuel Richardson.

Not traced.—*Monthly Magazine*, xxxvi (1 December 1813), 420.

Dec. 1744.

Dear Sir,

I thank you for your very affectionate letter. I propose, God willing, to be in town soon after Christmas, to print the *Eighth Night*,[1] for my indisposition has been such as rather to promote, than hinder, thinking;—I should be glad to show it you; neither your modesty nor my vanity must deprive me of the benefit which I know I may receive from your real sentiments about it. Are not you in the same way of thinking? Are not virtue and religion your point of view?

---

[1] Published 7 March.

Who therefore can be supposed to feel wrong and right, in things of this nature, more naturally than yourself? If I can return the favour in kind, I shall do it with pleasure and sincerity. But then you must read the composition to me,[1] for my eyes are weak. May the lesser felicities of this life, joined to those of your good heart, ever give you cause to rejoice! There is self-interest in this wish, for I shall partake in your satisfaction, and always continue,

Dear sir,
Your affectionate humble servant,
E. Young.

Monday, Bulstrode.

I leave this place, if please God, on Thursday, for Wellwyn.

159. [Watford, Herts.]. [? December 1744]. Duchess of Portland.

Longleat MSS. (64) 108–9.—Bath, p. 284.

May it please your Grace

You took notice (I remember) that my Servant lookt like an Antient Briton, I then dissented, & am now come entirely into Your Graces Opinion; for if He had been a Modern Briton, He could not possibly have lead me Such a Dance; but must necessarily have known more of his Native Land.

In a word, I set out from Bullstrode about *Ten*, rid four Hours, & my mans Horse Stumbling at *Two*, Tom wakd, & told me He fancyd we had mistook the way, & Seemd to take it ill of me that I had Sufferd Him /[verso]/ to be my Master so long; & told me if I would readmitt him into my Service, He would act in yt Character the first man we met, & ask him where we were. Which He did accordingly, & receivd in answer, That we were as far from Rickmansworth, exactly, as we were from Gerrards Cross:[2] On This, as I

---

[1] i.e. *Clarissa*.

[2] Bulstrode is at Gerrards Cross about seven miles from Rickmansworth. Watford, where Young stopped for the night, is another three miles. Welwyn is 17 miles beyond Watford.

designd to ride but gently, I desird him to go to sleep again,
which He did accordingly, & after some very dirty Dreams
that He could not possibly be Mistaken a Second time,
                                                  an
I brought him Safe into   Inn at Watford, about Sunset.

But I ask your Graces pardon, & beg Leave that I may
now wait on You into /[conjugate leaf]/ Better Company:
Beleive, Madam a Clergy-man for once, I do assure You
nothing could give me greater Pleasure than hearing of his
Graces Amendment. As for ye Ladies, they I suppose give
more Pain, than They feel, & therefore my Concern
naturally devolves on the Gentlemen. As for ye Little Ones,
I left my good Ld ArchBp[1] a little out of Order: I hope it is
                                       neither
over; for tho He ~~not~~ probably   Knows, or Designs it,
I assure yr Grace, the Arch Bishop gives me his Blessing
every Time I see him Smile. Caroline gives her Humble
Duty to yr Grace, I beg mine to my Ld Duke: &c: & am,
Madam, wth all Gratitude & Esteem

Yr Graces most Obedt
& most Humble Sevt. EYoung.

160. Welwyn, Herts. [Th.] 3 January 1744/5. Robert Dodsley.

Not traced.[2]

[1] i.e. the little 'Tillotson' of Young's letter of 16 September, the Portland infant son.

[2] Evidence of this letter is Sotheby's auction catalogue of 10 June 1869, where Lot No. 1031 is described: 'A. L. s. 1 Page 4° to Mr. Dodsley. In the matter of the purchase of a portion of Night Thoughts. Wellwyn, Jan. 3, 1744.' Accompanying the letter in the sale were 'Two Receipts, signed for six parts of the N. T.' The receipt turning over the sixth part of the *Night-Thoughts* to Dodsley was signed by Young on 26 January of this year (see Appendix A).

161. Welwyn, Herts. [Th.] 17 January 1744/5.
Duchess of Portland.

Longleat MSS. (66) 112–13.—Bath, p. 286; Shelley, pp. 185–6.

Wellwyn
Jan 17
1744.

Madam

I find by your Graces Letter that the Country, & so sweet
a Country, as your Graces is, is capable of having a Rival;
and that Rival, a perfect Dowdy: I must needs own, that if
the Country gives Ladys the Spleen, Town is their proper
Remedy, that Region of Assa Fœtida. But your Grace will
say It has its Aromaticks too; It has; but Some of them are
rather too Strong; & All of them are ~~affect~~ apt to affect the
Head to its Disadvantage; & to lead Weak ones by ye Nose.

But to ballance all this, & ten times as much more, Your
Grace says, It gives You the /[verso]/ Convers~~ion~~^ation of your
Friends; If it does, I grant Elysium could not give You
more. Your Grace mentions but Two in your Letter, &, if
a Maxim I read in your Graces Book at Bullstrode be True,
I am very near hating them Both; For That says,—'The
more a man loves any of your Sex, the nearer He is to hating
Them.' As for what Mrs Donallan says, There is so much
Gallantry in it, that in pure Decency I must consider it as
rank Rallery; but I do not like it the Worse for That; To be
rallyd by a young Lady at my Time of Day, is a Favour not
to be Despisd. And as for Lady Andover, pray Madam, my
best Respects; & tell her Ladyship, that by ye Quotation Yr
Grace /[conjugate leaf] takes from her Letter; I think she
resembles ye very Beautifull Youth (mentiond, as I remember, by Herodotus[1]) who perceiving his Person had kindled
a Passion in a Person very unfit for Thoughts of that Nature,
thought proper to disfigure Himself, to prevent a Consequence he so much Disapprovd.

And now, Madam, since we are at This Play, pray What
is your Grace Like?—Tis very Odd; yet It is very True;

---

[1] Although there are somewhat similar descriptions in Herodotus, nothing seems
to correspond closely enough to support Young's reference.

brought

You are like—the De[s]truction of Sodom; You have
an antient Gentleman & his two Daughters[1] together, made
Him Drunk with Vanity—& were not They Better, & He
Older than Somebody else, how could Your Graces Goodness be responsable for the Consequence? And now, Madam,
what am I Like?—Why I am like,—no I am not *Like*, but
actually *am* a Fool, & if Your Grace does /[verso]/ not burn
this Letter, I will not, I can not forgive You.

I beg my Humble Duty to my Ld Duke & hearty Congratulation on his Graces better Health, my tenderest
Regard to ye Little Ones, & humble service to Mr Achard

I am Madam
with respect & gratitude
Yr Graces
most Obedt & Obligd
Humble Sevt
EYoung.

162. [London]. Su. [?3 March 1744/5]. Duchess of
Portland.

Longleat MSS. (69) 118–19.

Madam
been
I should have glad of the Honour of waiting on Yr
Grace & my Lord Duke on Teusday. But I'm obligd to go
into ye Country tomorrow, or Teusday morning: I therefore
beg You Both to accept my best Thanks & Respects; & to
beleive me to be most truly

Madam
Yr Graces Obligd & ever
Dutifull Humble Sevt
EYoung.

Sunday.

[separate leaf] Your Grace is exstremely Good in writting
twice: I & Caroline were to wait on yr Grace, I think on

¹ i.e. Caroline Lee and Martha D'Aranda Lee.

Moonday last; I have been ill ever Since, nor was I well
Then. I ride every Day to pick up, but I visit no body being
as yet Nobody myself: I think I shall go home on Moonday,
I know yr Grace will be so good as to excuse my not wating
on You & my Lord Duke; why shd I terrifie ye Living wth
a Visit from ye Dead. I bless God I am in a mending way,
& propose waiting on You ye week after Easter.[1] Till then
I pray God Allmighty to be very gracious to those who have
been so very Kind to me. I beg my humble Duty to my Lord
Duke, & all those other respect wh I greatly owe, & cordially
pay to all yt are so Happy as to be under Yr Graces Eye.
I am Madam Yr most Obligd
> & most Obdt Humble Sevt
> EY.

163. [London]. Su. [?14 April 1745].[2] Duchess of Portland.

Longleat MSS. (71) 121.

Madam
If yr Grace dines at home tomorrow, & have not all ye
World with You I will have the Honour of waiting on You.
I came to town but last night; I ask pardon for being detained
so long by a Fever, when I was Preengagd to yr Grace; But
my Fault (as is ye Case with most Faults) has been abun-
dantly its own Punishment. I beg my best respects to my
Ld Duke & ye Ladyies; & my Loves to ye Groupe of Those
little Angels, whose Innocence defends their *Parents*, while
in ye mistaken eye of ye World They receive all their own
Protection from *Them*. With ye truest Esteem & Gratitude
I am
> Madam, Yr Graces
> most Obedient & Obligd
> Humble Sevt
> EYoung.

Sunday.

[1] Easter fell on 14 April this year. Young dined with the Portlands in their
Whitehall home on 16 April (Llanover, 1861, ii. 295).
[2] The date is conjectural, see note to the letter of 3 March.

164. Welwyn, Herts. [Th.] 2 May 1745. Samuel Richardson.

Not traced.—*Monthly Magazine*, xxxvi (1 December 1813), 421.

Wellwyn, May 2, 1745.

Dear Sir,

My house is full of friends, that congratulate my return to life; till now I knew not that report had buried me. But I cannot but steal from them to let you know, (this first post) how truly sensible I am of your late goodness.

I came home but last night, so can say nothing yet to the purpose about Mrs. Liston; all I see promises satisfaction on that point. Caroline is pleased with her; but not so much as with some one,[1] who has doubled his favours on her at the first interview, and made her apprehensible of the consequences of so warm an attack.

I know not if I did not leave a steel seal on your marble table in the parlour, where I sealed a letter the morning I left you; if it comes to hand, you'll lay it by.

Mrs. Liston is very well after her journey, and desires her duty to you and Mrs. Richardson. Caroline and I, by no means forget the respects we owe in Salisbury court;[2] yet must I particularly insist, that when you go to N. End,[3] you let Cleopatra and Octavia know, that by their favour I was so happy, that in their company, and so sweet a retirement, I thought with Antony—the world well lost.

I bless God I am pretty well. God preserve your health, and prosper your undertakings. My humble service to all friends, but particularly to Mrs. Richardson and Miss. I am, dear Sir,

Your much obliged
and affectionate humble servant,
E. Young.

Caroline gives her humble service to you and your's.

[1] An allusion to William Haviland (1718–84), whom Caroline is later to marry. Mrs. Liston, recommended to him by Richardson, apparently served as Young's housekeeper for the summer. See his letter of ?14 September 1745.

[2] Location of Richardson's city home as well as of his printing establishment from the 1730s.

[3] North-End Road, Fulham, site of Richardson's country home from 1738 to 1754.

Duchess of Portland to the Duke of Newcastle. Westminster. [F.] 17 May 1745.

British Museum, Add. MSS. 32704, f. 274.

Whitehall May 17 1745

My Lord
    As it is so long since I did my self the Honour to write to
your Grace I take the Liberty to put you in mind of a request
I made last year in favour of Doctor Young to be Prebendary
in Westminster, Christ Church, or Windsor, which shoud
first become vacant, & as your Grace was so obliging to
assure me in the most friendly manner you woud do all that
lay in your Power to serve Doctor Young; I hope your
inclinations are still the same to oblige
                                       Your Graces
                                       Most Obedient Humble
                                       Servant
                                       M: Cavendishe Portland

165. [Welwyn, Herts.]. [Su.] 19 May [1745]. Duchess
of Portland.

Longleat MSS. (57) 96-7.—Bath, p. 282; Shelley, pp. 177-8.

May 19th

Madam
    I rejoyce yt your Graces found Bullstrode so delightfull,
at ye worst it is a Beautie. To be pleasd with one's Own is ye
greatest Wisdom of human Life; & to have Reason to be so
                                       to
is the greatest Happiness of it. But   ballance this Pleasure
Yr Grace has lost your Friend, to whom You give the
Epithet of Amiable; Amiable is ye Softest word in our
Language & therefore by far the most proper for Ly
Andover.
    Yr Grace enquires wth great Goodness after my Health;
Thanks to Mr Achard (to whom my very humble Service)
I am well; Blest /[verso]/ with So much Indisposition only,

as is, I hope, Sufficient to keep me out [of] ye Danger of thinking myself Immortal.—What your Grace says of ye Battle,[1] carys in it so much Humanity, that it is quite worthy of a Dutchess; Or rather Such Sentiments make Dutchesses, without Coronets, of every Lady by whom they are entertained.

Another Instance of yr Graces great Goodness is thinking of poor Caroline; I beleive ye Thing is past Retreive; by my Direction She has written to Ld Litchfield to acquaint Him with it. She has not yet receivd his Ldps Answer, when She does, your Grace shall know it.[2]

Yr Grace shd not have been at ye trouble /[conjugate leaf]/ of transcribing yr Letter to your Cousin;[3] Tho Seeing is Beleiving, yet Faith is beleiving too, but yr Grace takes me for an Infidell. I wish the M——y[4] did, & then I might have a better Chance.

Your Graces Letter to ye Duke lays me under ye greatest Obligations; Nothing can be Kinder to me, or more to ye Purpose: when Your Correspondent can write half so well, I will certainly have ye Honour of waiting on Him. What a lucky thing it would have been if I like my Ld Edward had been born a Bishop? Poor Little Soul! I wish Your Grace does not find it has an Ill Effect on his Manners. However I am very Glad to hear yt He, & his little Lay-Relations are all /[verso]/ well, & I beg my humble Duty to their ~~Worthy~~ most Worthy, & (as yet) most Happy Father; But I beg Your Grace when You are next in the Way of Wives, yt you would forbear looking toward ye Bench tho his Grace of Canterbury is really a comely Person, for indeed, Madam, to have a second Child markt with a Miter might occasion Suspicion; & cause Mischeif without ye Assistance of an Iago to promote it. Caroline gives her humble Duty; & looks like a Fool, as she ought to do. If she performs as well every Part of her Duty in a Marryd state, she will make ye best of wt, I fear, is but a Bargain.

---

[1] French forces had defeated the English and their allies at Fontenoy with severe losses on both sides. The battle took place on the English date of 30 April (11 May N.S.).

[2] Young speaks of the Earl's letter to Caroline in his own letter to the Duchess of 21 August 1745.

[3] i.e. the Duke of Newcastle.   [4] i.e. Ministry.

Wth ye truest Sence of yr great Indulgence I am Madm Yr
Graces most Dutifull

                              Humble Sevt   EYoung.

Duchess of Portland to the Duke of Newcastle. Westminster. [Early] June 1745.

British Museum, Add. MSS. 32704, f. 440.

                                   Whitehall June 1745.
My Lord
    As it is more than a fortnight since I did my self the
Honour to write to your Grace in regard to Dr Young's
having the first Prebendary vacant in Christ Church, Westminster, or Windsor, I am apt to believe you did not receive
my Letter, by my not having heard from your Grace since,
but if you did; the merit of the Person I interest my self for
will I dont doubt excuse my giving your Grace this second
trouble.

                    I am my Lord
                    Your Obedient
                        Humble Servant
                        M: Cavendishe Portland

166. [Welwyn, Herts.] [Tu.] 11 June 1745. Samuel Richardson.

Not traced.—*Monthly Magazine*, xxxvi (1 December 1813), 422.

                                   June 11, 1745.
Dear Sir,
    I have a favour to request, but you must not grant anything but what is quite right; that is, quite convenient and
agreeable to you. My want of modesty in asking what is
wrong, will by no means excuse your want of fortitude in
granting it.—I propose (God willing) being in town on
Tuesday next, being then in waiting[1] till the end of the

                    ¹ i.e. as Chaplain in Ordinary to the King.

month. I am scarce well enough to lie in town, and should
be very glad of a bed at N. End, if absolutely, and in every
view, agreeable to you, not otherwise. Be frank, as you love
my peace; and I will thank you as much for your frankness
as otherwise I should have done for your hospitality. All
here salute you and your's.

I am, dear Sir,
Your faithful humble servant,
E. Young.

William Murray to the Duchess of Portland. [Tu.] 18 June 1745.

Longleat Miscellaneous MSS., vol. xiv, f. 92.—Bath, i. 364.

1745, June 18.—Few things can give me so much real
pleasure as an opportunity of doing what is in any respect
agreeable to your Grace, and therefore, if the case you
recommend should exist, I shall think myself very happy in
an occasion of contributing the utmost of my power to what
you wish. I think you conclude too hastily from the D[uke]
of N[ewcastle]'s silence. Nothing is now open, and he might
be afraid of taking the thing wholly upon himself beforehand, under the present incertainty of his being able to make
such an undertaking good without much difficulty. If I was
the Doctor, under your protection I would not despair of
Windsor, at least not in prose, whatever I did in verse when
the night inspired melancholy thoughts. I return the enclosed with many thanks. I never saw the spirit and diction
and simplicity of an original better kept up in a translation.
I wish your Grace a good journey and an agreeable summer.

167. Fulham, Mdx. [Tu.] 9 July [1745]. Duchess of Portland.

Address: To His Grace / The Duke of Portland / at Wellbeck near Mans-
field / Notting[h]amshire.
Postmark: 9/IY. Peny Post Payd [in triangle surrounding] TU.
Longleat MSS. (56) 94–5.

May it please yr Grace
I receivd the Honour of your Grace's Letter but this
moment, & tis so late that, by this Post, I have only time to
inclose ye Duke's Letter;[1] but very soon I will answer all the
Questions in your Graces Letter; but One thing is not to be
deferd, I mean, Madam, my endeavouring to express my
deep sense of Your Graces zealous Application in my Behalf,
for which I return my most humble Thanks, & with ye
greatest Pleasure shall embrace all Occasions of showing
myself truly Sensible of it. I beg my humble Duty to my Ld
Duke, & to my Lady Oxford & humble service to Mr
Achard &c: I am, Madam, in a very particular Manner Yr
Graces most
          Devoted & most Obligd Humble Sevt EYoung

[in margin] July ye Ninth: Northend.

168. Fulham, Mdx. [W.] 10 July 1745. Duchess of Portland.

Longleat MSS. 135.[2]

trouble your Grace with it, Whose Sincerity I most acknowledge, & admire; & whose Example in it is an Advantage
greater than any that Preferment is able to give.
    Madam, I sincerely rejoyce that God Allmy bestows so
much Health on a Family, where I think it is so much
deservd: I bless His Mercy mine is tolerable, & that is

---

[1] This refers to a letter from Newcastle to the Duchess to which she replied on
15 July. It has since disappeared along with parts of Young's letters to the Duchess
dealing with it.
[2] The top of this letter has been cut away. It was probably devoted to Young's
answer to the Duchess's questions mentioned in Young's letter of the day before.

pretty well for me. I beg my humble Duty to my Ld Duke, & Lady Oxford, my best Wishes, Service, & Affection to Mr Achard, & ye little Group of Innocence & Beautie around him. Wth ye highest Respect. Madam Yr Grace's most Obligd Obedt Sevt.
[in left margin][Nort]hend July 10. 1745   EYoung.

[verso blank]

Duchess of Portland to the Duke of Newcastle. Welbeck, Notts. [M.] 15 July 1745.

British Museum, Add. MSS. 32704, f. 504.

                                        Welbeck July 15th 1745
My Lord
    I return your Grace thanks for the favour of your Letter, I don't doubt there are many Solicitations for those those [*sic*] Preferments; but give me leave my Lord to say, that Doctor Young's is a peculiar Case having been a Chaplain to this King full thirty years without having received the smallest Preferment, & whose worth & abillities undoubtedly deserved a much earlier notice; but as your Grace has been so good to acknowledge his merit I don't question but as soon as it is in your Power you will give Doctor Young a proof of it which will be esteem'd as a favour by
                                        My Lord
                                        /[verso]/ Your Graces
                                        Most Obedient
                                        Humble Servant
                                        M: Cavendishe Portland

169. [London]. Su. [?18 August 1745]. Duchess of Portland.

Longleat MSS. (67) 114-15.

Madam
    Being seriously engaged in many Trifles, I have not been yet able to disengage from ye Bryars of this Town. But with

a few Slight Scratches, I am now got entirely free, & set out for Tunbridge early tomorrow.

If, Madam, my Ld Duke has heard from the Arch-Bishop,[1] I shd be glad to know ye result; that I may the better fashion my mind as to future expectations; & not sow Hopes, when the Harvest (like this last One) will not answer.

Half ye Evil of life is nothing but an illjugd expectation of Good; & really at my time of Life I know not wh is most Eligible, a late Success, or an early Despair. But there is one Success wh Fate cannot rob me of; wh is a Consciousness of your Graces & my Ld Duke's sincere endeavour to befriend me. This, Madam, I shall allways enjoy, & consider Wellwyn as my Bishoprick when I think upon it. With ye warmest gratitude & Duty to You Both

I am, Madam, Yr Graces
most Obligd & most Obedt
Humble Sevt   EYoung

Sunday morng.

/[verso in right margin]/ Madam I beg your Grace to give my humble Service & & [*sic*] many thanks to Mr Hay for ye favour of his Chambers.

170. Tunbridge Wells, Kent. [W.] 21 August [1745]. Duchess of Portland.

Longleat MSS. (72) 122-3.—Bath, pp. 287-8.

Tunbridge Wells
Aug 21

May it please your Grace
     had
I   the Honour but this very Post, of 2 Letters from yr Grace One of July 22. One of Aug: 20th. As for ye Comedians Yr Grace met in Notinghamshire I have no cause to envy You, for we have, at least as good a Pack at this Place. We have Men of Seventy that represent Boys of Eighteen; & Boys of Eighteen that represent Changelings, & many

---

[1] The Archbishop of Canterbury at this time was John Potter.

of your own sex yt represent Witches in the Morning, &
Angells in ye Afternoon, & Women at Night. The Subject
of ye Book You mention can never be too often reviewd, for
Faith, like *Virtue*, is never at a Stand; it is ever in Advance,
or Decline. And in one View it is more material than our
Speculations on Virtue, for it is the Root of it; And as for
all my *merely Morall* Friends, I shall be Sure to trust them,
when I am sure it is not their own Interest to cut my Throat.
Im truly much concernd at ye bad News from /[verso]/ from
[*sic*] Chellsea; God Allmighty alter things for ye Better!

But now comes a Severe Calamity of another Kind.—
Why did Your Grace let me know You was at Wellwyn?[1]—
Indeed it grieves me. But I have ever been in ye wrong Box.
As to poor Caroline, I fear the Affair proceeds: I made her
write to my Ld Litchfield, & she receivd a Letter from Him
that became the Prudence of his Character, & ye Nearness
of his Relation. But I fear it had too little Effect. All I can
bringe her to, is, that she will not marry him[2] in his present
Circumstances & in that I am persuaded I may rely on her.
She is at Wellwyn. As ^for^ yr Graces enquiries about her I
take ^it^ infinitely Kind; for what but your own good Heart
could put them into your Graces Head?—The D. of N;
receivd me wth great Complisance; ministerially kind, took
me by ye Thumb as cordially as if He designd it Should go
for Payment in full. /[conjugate leaf]/ In a Word, Madam,
with great Civility (for wh I thank Yr Grace) He told me
the King had made some Promises, & that He (the Duke
I mean) had his own Preengagements, but that ^He^ would
certainly do what He could. So that if Nothing is done, He
has kindly prepard me for it.

As for Mr Roberts;[3] He is Here; He returns his humble
Respects for the Honour Yr Grace does him in Supposing
Him of Consequence, & says—That He heard Mr Pelham

---

[1] The Portlands had passed through Welwyn, during Young's absence, on their
return from the north.

[2] i.e. Haviland.

[3] John Roberts (?1712–72) was secretary to the Prime Minister Henry Pelham.
Unfortunately for Young's chances Pelham's authority was limited by the greater
influence of his older brother, the Duke of Newcastle.

say—'*That besides my own good Title, ye Dutchess of Portland was a Person, & Character, wh it was very Proper for both Him & his Brother very much to regard*'—And Mr Roberts added from Himself, that if Yr Grace would^{be so kind as} to persist in yr kind pressing in my favour, it must necessarily Succeed; That yr Graces kind Importunity, would be the Dukes full Excuse to Competitors; that Application shd be made whatever fell, or was likely to fall; That a Deanery was as Easie to be got, as a Prebend, as Things Stand; That He would be sure to be my Remembrancer with Mr Pelham.

The Copy of Yr Graces Reply to ye Duke, wh You are so Indulgent as to favour me withall, /[verso]/ is Such an Instance of your Graces indefatigable Favour, that—I know not what to say: I have been so little usd to Such Treatment, that I am at a Loss how to behave under it. To return my humble Thanks falls very Short of my real Meaning.

Lady Oxford did me great Honour by having me in her Remembrance. I saunter, like your Grace, from Oak to Oak, but ~~my~~ I miss many Oaks I was formerly acquainted with in this Place. I enquird after them for ye Neighbours who tell me they are gone to Sea; but that meeting foul Weather in their Passage, they threw ye Ballance of Europe overboard, wh was pickt up by a French man of War. I rejoyce that ye Little Ones are well. I beg my humble Duty to my Ld Duke & humble Service to Mr Ashard & am Madam Yr Graces most Obligd & Dutifull Humble Sevt EY.

171. [Tunbridge Wells, Kent]. Sa. [?14 September 1745]. Samuel Richardson.

Not traced.—*Monthly Magazine*, xxxvii (1 March 1814), 142.

Saturday.

Dear Sir,

I bless God I am much better, and am sorry you are not at leisure to be well by coming to these waters. Our disorders are of the same kind. My friends at Chelsea are most obliging and good people.[1] My best wishes and respects

¹ The Coles.

when you see them. I heartily wish Mrs. Liston well; and thank you for my little acquaintance with her. I long to see you, and to talk over Clarissa, and Cibber, but design staying during the fair weather. When you send the next proof, pray send the two sheets *now* to b,[1] wrought off. My best service to Mrs. Richardson and her little family; and I shake the hands of my Shakespearian friends.[2] As 'tis a time of year in which nothing can be published, the world has no cause as yet to *complain*. ——My next paper finishes. God preserve your health, and indulgence to, dear sir,

Your truly affectionate servant,
E. Young.

172. Tunbridge Wells, Kent. [Tu.] 17 September 1745. Duchess of Portland.

Longleat MSS. (73) 124–5.—Bath, p. 288; Shelley, pp. 190–1.

Madam

Yr Grace flatters me, I pretend not to Instruct by my Letters, but to Obey; & to stand Candidate for yr good Opinion, by shewing my Sentiments close with yr own.— As for poor Colly,[3] his Impudence diverts me, & his Morals

---

[1] The reference is to Young's 'Night the Ninth and Last: The Consolation' which has appended to it 'Some Thoughts, occasioned by the Present Juncture Humbly Inscribed to His Grace the Duke of Newcastle', dated at the end 'October, 1745', although publication was held up until January 1746. The text of the principal poem begins on sheet B, with only one leaf, the title-page, preceding it. Presumably, Young withdrew 'the two sheets, *now* to b', which probably included a brief preface, and added the forty-seven pages of 'Thoughts' in October at the end of the last Night.

[2] See letter of 2 May 1745.

[3] Elizabeth Montagu had written to the Duchess on 27 August, ostensibly scandalized at the *camaraderie* of Young and Colley Cibber: 'I have great joy in Dr. Young. . . . I told him your Grace desired he would write longer letters. . . . He has made a friendship with one person here, whom I believe you would not imagine to have been made for his bosom friend. . . . You would not guess that this associate of the Doctor was old Cibber! Certainly in their religious, moral and civil character there is no relation, but in their Dramatic capacity there is some. But why the Reverend Divine and serious author of the melancholy "Night Thoughts" should desire to appear as a persona dramatis here, I cannot imagine. The waters have raised his spirits to fine pitch. . . .' (Montagu, 1810, iii. 9–10). It was at this time too that Mrs. Montagu told of being on a jaunt with Young and Mrs. Rolt, whose name turns up again in Young's letter to the Duchess of 12 June 1746.

shall not hurt me; tho, by the Way, He is more Fool than Knave; & like other Fools, is a Wit. He has a little Wit, a little Humour, & a little Knowledge; & will lose none o'nt. Pray to how many better Companions can Yr Grace help me, within ye Bills of Mortality? It was Prudery in Mrs M. to tell tales, & tis yr Graces Compliment to her Prudery, to take notice of it. I honour Mrs. M. for what is truly value-able in her, wh is much: Yet have I writ a Satyr on her in my

Heart; but Racks shall not extort it from _{me}. Ly Murray[1] I have have [*sic*] long known something of, & love her. But your Dutchess deserves not so much of your Esteem. I propose, Madam, staying Here, as long as the Weather will permit, /[verso]/ and then after a Few Days spent in London, waiting on your Grace. Your kind concern for poor Caroline is an Obligation to me, who am anxious for her Wellfare. I am heartily glad to hear so good News from Chellsea; there seems to be much *real Worth* in that Family, & its scarcity should make it pretious. Mrs M:s Many People, & Little Company, is prettily, & truly Sayd; but let her not com-plain, she shines ye more, she has often held me by ye Ear, till all about her were annihilated, &, in a numerous Assem-bly, there was neither Company, nor Person, but herself. There have been two or Three Ladys more here, whose Sence is not amiss.—Mr Roberts, Madam, is gone. Your Grace will hear soon from Mrs M: /[conjugate leaf]/ She is much better for the Waters. I know more of her than ever I did before; she has an excellent, & uncommon Capacity, which Ambition a little precipitates, & Prejudice sometimes misleads, but Time & Experience may make her a finisht Character, for I think her Heart is sound. As for yr Friend Mrs K——[2] I esteem her, as I do ye Portias, & Lucretias, her Fame rowls down to me thro Days of old. You see Madam, I lay myself entirely as [*sic*] yr Graces Mercy. You may quite ruin me if You please with a Lady, in whose

---

[1] Lady Elizabeth Finch (d. 1784), wife of William Murray (later Earl of Mans-field).

[2] Mrs. Henrietta Knight (d. 1756), now better known as the Lady Luxborough of William Shenstone's acquaintance. She was the daughter of Henry Viscount St. John and half-sister of the Earl of Bolingbroke. In 1727, she had married Robert Knight, created Baron Luxborough of Shannon in 1746.

Opinion, I have an Ambition of standing fair. I beg Madam my humble Duty to my Lord Duke &c: & am with ye greatest Sense of your Goodness

Madam, Yr Graces

most Obligd & Obedt Humble

Sevt   EYoung.

Tunbridge Wells
Sepr 17, 1745.

173. [Tunbridge Wells, Kent]. Tu. 17 September 1745. Samuel Richardson.

Not traced.—*Monthly Magazine*, xxxvi (1 December 1813), 422.

Tuesday, Sept. 17, 1745.

Dear Sir,

This day's rains have thrown down my imagination of staying long here, which was built on the sand. I go hence to Bulstrode; but if your house at N. End is open, I would halt there a night or two, and see my Chelsea friends, which are dear at Bulstrode. Be quite honest, nor let me put you to any shifts, for it is the same thing to me to be a day or two in town. I set out (God willing) on Monday next, and shall be one night on the road.—If you can send the papers before Monday, let me have them here.—And unless I can see you at N. End, I had rather be in town. For I find I thirst after you, on which account I have the better opinion of, Dear Sir,

Your affectionate and obliged

Humble servant,

E. Young.

174. Fulham, Mdx. [F.] 25 October 1745. Duchess of Portland.

Longleat MSS. (76) 129–30.—Bath, pp. 290–1; Shelley, pp. 194–5.

NorthEnd
Octr 2 5
1745.

Madam

Since, I find, your Grace is in the Secret,[1] give me leave to observe, That Writers, like other Sinners, when they have once given Way to ye first Temptation, are caryd

                     they are—

farther than they designd, & Sin on till—   What, Madam? You can guess, tis a bad Word, & I will not Shock yr Grace with it.

Ly Andover does me Honour in remembring that I exist.

                           not

Yet tis all Compliment, there is no Sincerity, or She had disapointed my Assignation with her. Why go to Town? Dishonourable Creature! She is gone only with her Husband.

But yr Grace, who are infinitely /[verso]/ kind to your Friends in Such Exstremitys, has taken Care that the Disapointment shall not prove fatal. Another Mistriss is the only Cure. And O the Charms, & ~~of a W~~ those Charms in my Bedchamber; O the Charms of a Wicker Chair. My Lady Dutchess! if You love Ly Andover, & I think You do, & I think she is well enough for a Womans Love; If You love her, I say, let her not know of this Rival, a Rival so

                            us

irresistable, & that opens her ~~white~~ Arms, to take wholly in, & hold us fast for Hours, (perhaps, fast asleep) It must make her despair; It must break—(& let it) her unfaithfull Heart.

Madam, ye Fit is going off. I am /[conjugate leaf]/ coming to Myself.—I have often seen our Friends at Chellsea, they are pretty well, & very Good: & therefore will certainly be

---

[1] Evidently the Duchess had learned of Young's work on 'Night the Ninth and Last'. When it was published in January of the next year, it was accompanied by a commentary in blank verse dated 'October 1745, Thoughts occasioned by the Present Juncture: Humbly Inscribed to his Grace the Duke of Newcastle.'

quite well in Time. I am glad with regard to Yr Grace, &
indeed, (as in Duty bound) with regard to the Church, that
what is most Episcopal in your Family is so well recoverd.
Tho ye publick Papers inform us, that ye Kirk is lately
Behavd very well.[1] I begin to relapse; Nonsence is a Distemper the Bark[2] will not cure, tho It may have Its Intermissions, those Intermissions are but short. I know but One
Instance to ye Contrary, & an Ambition to converse with
that Instance will hasten me to Bullstrode, Soon as possible.
I am Madam,

> Yr Graces most Obligd
> & Dutifull H[umble] S[erven]t
> EYoung

Pray my humble Duty to my Ld D.
& Congratulation to ye Little Ones on
such a Mother.

175. [?Fulham, Mdx.]. [Early November 1745].
Duchess of Portland.

Longleat MSS. (74) 126.

Madam
    Yr Graces Goodness is Insupportable; It gives me Pain;
I deserve not Such frequent Invitation; It honours, & re-
proaches me at ye same time. But indeed Madam I deserve
not ye Reproach as much as Your Grace, may (not unreason-
ably) imagine. I have a little Business in Town; but I veryly
think it will permit me to wait on Your Grace at Bullstrode,
by ye twenty first of This Month. My Respects to Lady
                        & please to tell Her
Andover,   that I desire her to hide herself,

---

[1] The *London Evening Post* for 17 October carried the following account under
the dateline: Edinburgh, 8 October: 'The Ministers of the West Church (being
under the Protection of the Guns of the Castle) continue to preach and pray as usual,
but we have no Sermons here, or in the Suburbs nor in several Places of the Country
near us.'
[2] i.e. quinine, used for relief of fever.

in ye Shades of Bullstrode for a Season, from Human Eye;
　　　　　　　　　　　　　　　　　　　　　　　would think
for shd ye Pretender[1] see her, I am persuaded, that He
England so much worth his /[verso]/ Acceptance, that tho I
am raising a Troop of Horse,[2] I fear both I & his Grace of
York[3] may call for our Cassocks again, when the young Hero
stings his Courser on Us, with two Spurs, beyond those
of *Rippon*, Ambition on One Side, & Love on ye Other.
I have much enjoyd our Friends at Chelsea; & yet it is
with Concern I see Mrs Grace Cole. I fear she is not well.[4]
I suppose I may have ye Honour of waiting on your Grace
Thursday next at Whitehall. Pleasd with that Thought,
& being ambitious of being abusd by Yr Grace for my late
Misbe[h]aviour, I subscribe myself with ye Greatest Duty
& Gratitude

　　　　　　　　Yr Graces most Obedt & Humble Sevt
　　　　　　　　　　　　　　　　EYoung

I beg, Madam, my
Humble Duty to my
Ld Duke &c:

　[1] On 12 September the *London Evening Post* had reported: 'The Rebels have had
the Assurance to come down to Perth, where they have proclaimed the Pretender
[James Stuart (1688–1766)] at the Market Cross. His eldest Son [Charles Edward
Stuart (1720–88)], who is there, has been join'd by several disaffected Persons.'
　[2] Young had subscribed £50 towards a voluntary defence association. Others of
his neighbours who contributed were Sir Jeremy Sambrooke, Elizabeth Cathcart,
and James West, each of whom subscribed £200, and John Shotbolt, who subscribed 10 guineas (William LeHardy, *Hertford County Records: Calendar to the
Sessions Books . . . 1700 to 1757*, 1931, vii. 583).
　[3] Thomas Herring (1693–1757), Archbishop of York from 1743, was active in
arousing the country to the dangers of the invasion. On 1 January 1745/6, the
General Advertiser announced publication of his *Sermon, preach'd at the Cathedral
Church of York, Sept. 22, 1745; On Occasion of the present Rebellion in Scotland.*
At the death of Potter in 1747, Herring became Archbishop of Canterbury.
　[4] Mrs. Cole died the next year.

176. [?Fulham Mdx.]. [*c*. W. 20 November 1745].
Duchess of Portland.

Longleat MSS. (75) 127–8.

Madam

The melancholy Cast of yr Graces Letter[1] inclines me to observe That the World is our School; Much Discipline & few Playdays, belongs to ye Nature of it. We have notwithstanding Pleasures allowd us here; but they are *moderate* Pleasures; & if we aim at *more*, we shall lose even Those; that is, we shall be whipt for it. And yet not to aim at more, is somewhat Difficult. For as we have a glorious Holiday before us in ye other World, where there are Large Delights, we are endowd with Appetites & Desires proportiond to them; wh Desires we are very apt to let lose here, among Objects too little to satisfie them; whence Unhappiness necessarily follows. For Unhappiness is nothing but Disapointment of our Desires; & Happiness is ye Contrary.

It is plain then, Madam, that Moderation of Desire is ye Single Receipt for Happiness on Earth. And our most gracious Governor wd have /[verso]/ [us] tolerably Happy even Here: But how shall He bring it about? If He leaves us to ourselves, our Desires grow exorbitant; our Minds take no Measure of ye Things about us; but gape as wide as if we were allready in ye Land of Immortality; & consequently they must famish on All ye World can give.

This, Madam, accounts for what seems very Surprizing, tho tis very Common. How often see we Persons possest of all yt Earth affords, as truly wretched, as if they were destitute of every Blessing in Life? How comes this to pass when their Accomodations are so large? Because their Desires are Larger; Because they let lose yt Proportion of Desire after Temporals, wh was designed only for Eternals; In a Word, because they can not bring down their highest Palates to ye Relish of a *moderate* Repast. The cheif Cause of human

[1] On 16 November Mrs. Delany spoke of having had a letter from the Duchess of Portland, and of finding her spirits 'very low' (Llanover, 1861, ii. 398). The latter part of Young's letter, as well as his next letter to Richardson, show that she was depressed by the political and military situation and its possible effects on the northern Portland holdings.

Misery is This, That men are Hot in eternal Pursuit of that
which—does not exist.

/[conjugate leaf]/ Since Such is our Folly, what shall we
do? Shall we be left to ye fatal Effects of it, & so be quite
Miserable? No; God-Allmy is too Good to Suffer it. His
Wisdom interposes where our Prudence fails. He has a
divine Art of reducing us to ye Relish of *moderate* Goods;
Since on Earth there are no other; When we will not chuse
ye Means of Happiness, He will force them on Us. He
kindly sends Fears & Afflictions, & when they once show
their ugly Faces, then bare Releif is Happiness, Escape is
Triumph, & moderate Enjoyments rise to high Delights.
When a Highlanders broad Sword is wav'd oer ye Head of
a fine Lady, her radiant Eyes are opend, she sees yt to be
True, wh before appeard Incredible; If He will suffer that
fair Neck & Shoulders to continue their Acquaintance a
little longer, she finds it possible to make a Shift to spend
one Evening, with some tolerable Degree of Content, without Opera, Ball, Assembly or Gallant. /[verso]/

But I hear Yr Grace say, Is ye Man mad? Is this his
Apology?—Madam, a Volume would not hold it, &, (if it
please God,) before the Week now begun is expird, I will
have the Honour of looking like a Fool before You for my
repeated Transgressions. My Ld Duke Ly Andover & Mr
Ashard do me great Honour, I will very shortly (I will not
say) Pay, but Compound, ye Debt. If, I mean, their Goodness will accept of a poor Twopence in the Pound. With ye
Greatest Truth, Respect, & Gratitude I am

Madam
Yr Graces most Obedt
& most Humble Sevt
EYoung.

177. Bulstrode, Bucks. Tu. 26 November 1745.
Samuel Richardson.

Not traced.—*Monthly Magazine*, xxxvi (1 December 1813), 422; Shelley, p. 195.

Bulstrode, Nov. 26, 1745.

My valued Friend,

After a very wet journey above and below, I arrived at this family, to arrive at which one would be glad to go through some difficulties. Virtue, prudence, peace, industry, ingenuity, and amiableness, dwell here. You will say I keep very good company; but you must know that anxiety has lately intruded without the least invitation from folly or vice. The duke has a considerable estate in and about Carlisle, which must have suffered much; nor can they yet see to the end of the mischief; so that the common calamity makes more than a common impression here. God Almighty send us good news, and good hearts.

What a heart have you to draw in *Clarissa's* final determination! The more I think of that occasion, the more am I smitten with it; and therefore wait with some impatience, the performance of your kind promise. There is a conveyance every Wednesday and Friday, from the Duke's in Privy Garden. I beg you would share with Mrs. Richardson and your little ones, the sincere regard and very best wishes of,

Dear Sir,
Your much obliged and
faithful humble servant,
E. Young.

Tuesday.

Richardson to Young. London. [Tu.] 3 December 1745.

Not traced.—*Monthly Magazine*, xxxvi (1 December 1813), 422.

London, Dec. 3, 1745

Rev. Sir,

I am greatly obliged to you for your admirable additions to the letter I sent you; but believe I shall insert them rather nearer the hour of her death, because in this letter, I do not make her so fully able to die in charity with Lovelace, as she hopes she shall do. Such noble, such exalted sentiments and expressions, will adorn her last hours, when above the world, and above the resentments she acknowledges in this piece. And only they are too exalted for the rest of the work, or they are entirely comfortable to the frame I have designed she shall then be in.—Most heartily again, therefore, I thank you for them, as I should for any other emendations, elevations, or intimations.

I cannot say I am so much pleased with Mr. Cibber's; because, the injury having been received above a month, I mean her to act, and to reason, coolly and deliberately; to touch with *warmth* the subject, but not with *passion*, that her determination may be the result of deliberation; since passion will admit of abatement, and when it subsides may be thought to alter. In a future letter to one of Lovelace's relations, who presses her for all their sakes to marry him, I give some further strength to her arguments and resolutions; since only to repeat the same, with which they hoped she might be led to dispense, after they had seen them, would have been not so well.

You will infinitely oblige me by a winter month at N. End, at your leisure and opportunity: I had thought, when you suffered Mr. Tasswell[1] to cheat me of you, as my business would not let me go so often as I wished to North-end, to have had you to myself in Salisbury-court every evening. Then how much should I have tired you!

God give you increase of happiness, and bless the noble family you so justly, I dare say, praise, for your sake, and you for theirs, prays

Your obliged and faithful servant,
S. Richardson.

[1] i.e. Tassel.

178. Welwyn, Herts. Su. [8 December 1745].[1]
Duchess of Portland.

Longleat MSS. (77) 131–2.—Bath, pp. 291–2.

Wellwyn.
Sunday.

May it please Yr Grace

I can not thank You too soon, or too much for ye late great Favours receivd at Bullstrode: a Place where a Person can not receive Civilitys but He must receive Honours at the same time. Nor can He return his Humble Acknowledgements, without being Proud under his Humility. But I assure your Grace I am as Sincere, as I am Proud, while I return ~~you~~ my Gratitude for your great Goodness to me.

I rid very Hard, & got Home by Three of ye Clock, wh You know Madam, is Dinner time. My Maid told me   ^{she} was glad I came so oppertunely, for by /[verso]/ that means she thought verily that She could provide me a Dinner against the next Day. I Suppose ye Wench had heard yt I eat Six times a Day at Bullstrode, & was for ballancing The Account. Nor was This ye Sole Felicity of my Journey. My Man was ill of a Fever; therefore when we came to St Albans, He desird I would Stop a Minute, that He might take something being ~~be~~ ill, & as He Sayd He thought his Blood was much inflamd. I stopt, & left him ye Liberty of having what He pleasd; on wh He drank half a Pint of hot Brandy; Then we put on apace, & by the time we had rid four Miles, his /[conjugate leaf]/ Horse Stumbled, tho twas the Rider drank ye Brandy. On ye Jolt, Tom wakt, & cryd Sr I have dropt the Bagg. I was in a Passion at his Negligence, & told him I should then have nothing for Dinner.—No Sr Says He with great Joy the Veneson is here; I only have dropt your leather Baggs.—Now, Madam, in those Bags was notg but my Shirts, Wigs, Shoes, Razors, &c: in short my whole travelling Estate. On being a little disgusted even at that Loss; He told me, to be sure Somebody must pick it up, & no Doubt would bring it after us: & then trotted on with

[1] The date of this letter is established by the next letter to Richardson.

great Tranquillity of Mind. Whilst I was considering how I shd best manage ye Handle of my Whip to knock him off his Horse, & leave him to be pickt up by ye next comer, with my Bags; /[verso]/ a Servant from my, & yr Grace's, honest Landlord at ye red Lyon,[1] overtook me with what was lost; wh was left on a Horse block[2] in his Inn-yard. Now judge, Madam, if I stand in need of Highlanders in Order to be undone. How long it may be before They strip me of my Shirt, wh I so happily recoverd, Heaven only knows.

Beware of Jesuits. 'O no, Says Yr Grace, He appears to be ye honestest Man yt ever livd. nor only to me, but to every Body, even Bishops take him to their Bosom'—True, Madam; & What does that amount too? It is no more than saying thus—'I kant but think him an Honest Man, *because* He plays ye Knave to Perfection.' My Ld Duke, Ly Wallingford, Mr Achard, & ye little Angels without Wings— but my Paper is rude, nor gives me leave to say more than yt I am ever wth Sincere Gratitude & Respect Yr Graces most Obligd &c:

179. Welwyn, Herts. [Tu.] 10 December 1745. Samuel Richardson.

Not traced.—*Monthly Magazine*, xxxvi (1 December 1813), 422.

Wellwyn, Dec. 10, 1745.

Dear Sir,

I received the favour of your's at Bulstrode, and came home on Saturday last. As Clarissa gives me particular pleasure, and as I know it will be of public benefit, you have a title to my best endeavours, in every shape, to render her most amiable in the eyes of the world. And if (but I hope *ifs* are out of the case) you and Mr. Grover[3] (to whom my

---

[1] The Red Lion Inn at St. Albans dates from the sixteenth century (W. Branch Johnson, *Hertfordshire Inns*, 1963, ii. 94).

[2] i.e. a stand for mounting a horse.

[3] John Grover (d. 1749), a clerk of the House of Commons who had charge of printing the transactions of Parliament. The *Monthly Magazine* has 'Mrs. Groom' and Barbauld (1804, ii. 14), which includes a portion of the letter of 10 December, has 'Mr. Groves'. Between the two it is obvious that the name was not written clearly.

humble service) are as good as your word this Christmas, and will bring some of your papers with you, I shall convince you of my sincerity. Mrs. R. and the little ones are entitled to my best wishes and services on their own account; and their being your's only doubles their claims from,

Dear Sir,

Your affectionate humble servant,

E. Young.

Fear is a passion of great use, and I hope this juncture will habituate our countrymen to such thoughts as will mingle kindly with those of God Almighty and of death.

180. Welwyn, Herts. [Th.] 19 December 1745. Samuel Richardson.

Not traced.—*Monthly Magazine*, xxxvi (1 December 1813), 423.

Wellwyn. Dec. 19, 1745.

Dear Sir,

I find you and Mr. Grover[1] (to whom my humble service) are two eels that are not to be caught; whereas you find me a perfect gudgeon. Whenever I swim with the stream of my own inclinations you are sure of me. However, I thank you for your superfluous care of throwing out the bait of your kind invitation. If Caroline has not waited on you she'll be less welcome to me; for she is not yet here. I bless God I am well: may that wonderful and gracious Being prosper all your wishes and undertakings! I am, dear sir,

Your affectionate, obliged

humble servant,

E. Young

The *times* and the weather will mend. A patient continuance in welldoing, and a perfect sense (from the multitude of evils flying round our ears, and the demerits of the best) that being out of great distress, is a great mercy; this, dear Sir, I think the cure for the spleen.

[1] Text reads 'Mrs. Groom', but see note to preceding letter.

181. Welwyn, Herts. [Su.] 2 February 1745/6.
Duchess of Portland.

Longleat MSS. (68) 116–17.—Bath, p. 287.

Madam

Yr Graces Goodness outruns me in all my selfish Designs, & while my Dullness is preparing my Petitions, shows me, that my Gratitude Should be paying my Thanks. I am as much surprizd, as Obligd, by Mr ———¹ kind zeal to serve One of whom He knows so little. It wd appear quite unaccountable to me, did I not conclude from this Instance, yt Yr Grace is not only my Friend, but my Friend-maker; Had you found ye Philosophers Stone & cd turn all to Gold; it wd not enable You to make so noble a present. At ye Name of ye two Ladies Yr Grace mentions, my mind is necessarily

struck wth those   two   brightest of Ideas, that of Beautie, & that of Wit. Those 2 brightest Shafts in the Female Quiver, how Dangerous /[verso]/ to our Sex?—But still more dangerous to Themselves; unless Heaven confers ye Shield of Discretion, at ye same time; as it has Done, abundantly, in these Instances; otherwise I shd have wanted Courage to give ym Joy of either of those Accomplishment[s], so courted, envyd, & admird, in ye World.

I sincerely greive at yr Graces Article from our Friends at ChelSea. Suffering Merit is ye most affecting Object of consideration upon Earth; If we are good, it threatens Us; If we are Bad, it threatens us still more; & our Concern for Others it may then be supposed to be very real & Sincere,

when it   is   accompanyd with an Apprehension for ourselves. I beg my best Wishes, & Respects when Yr Grace sees them again. And please to let them know yt I desire they wd take care of their Health, for they /[conjugate leaf]/ can not Suffer in it without puting Others out of Order.

¹ Evidently, from the allusion below to the 'Philosophers Stone', Andrew Stone (1703–73), under-secretary to the Duke of Newcastle.

Caroline gives her humble Duty to yr Grace. Her Lover is in Sterling Castle,[1] so yt she has a Chance of being a Widow before She is a Wife.

I shall religiously observe Yr Graces Injunction in yr PS. nor ever dedicate any thing to yt Gentleman,[2] but my humble Service & Thanks when You see him next, & my Gratitude forever. I rejoyce yt ye little Family are well; beging my humble Duty to my Lord Duke & humble Service to Mr Ashard. I am

	Madam
	Yr Graces most Obligd
Wellwyn	& most Obedt
Feb. ye 2d	Humble Sevt
1745.	EYoung.

182. Welwyn, Herts. [Tu.] 18 February 1745/6. Samuel Richardson.

Not traced.—*Monthly Magazine*, xxxvi (1 December 1813), 420.

Wellwyn, Feb. 18, 1745.

Dear Sir,

I have been under some pain ever since I received the favour of your last, or so kind a letter should not have been so long without a reply. But pain I have been acquainted with before, and have endeavoured not to be dejected under it. An even mind, undejected by ill, unelated by good, is an advice the wise heathens inculcated as much, if not more, than any other. Nor has scripture shewn it less regard. No single piece of wisdom seems to me so strongly guarded there as this equanimity. Two noble barriers are erected against our deviation on either hand. One in the history of Solomon, who, to suppress elevation, assures us the best is vain. One in the history of Job, who tells us the worst is supportable.

---

[1] Stirling Castle, near Edinburgh, held by the Hanoverian forces, was under siege in January by the army of Charles Edward Stuart, but by the date of this letter, it had been relieved by forces under the command of the Duke of Cumberland.

[2] The last of the *Night-Thoughts* had just appeared with a political appendix 'Inscribed' to the Duke of Newcastle. The 'Gentleman' to whom Young alludes must be Stone.

Which truth is the present I return to the good woman who favoured me with an ornament to my watch. There is a time when we should not only number our days but our hours. Her present may stand my friend in this view. A measurer of time is naturally an instrument of wisdom. But much more so is the good example of a valuable and valued friend. By which, above all other your repeated favours, I would have you judge how great obligation I lie under to be ever, dear sir,

Most sincerely your's,
E. Young.

Caroline joins my best regards to you and your's.

183. [Welwyn, Herts.]. [?February 1745/6]. Samuel Richardson.

Not traced.—*Monthly Magazine,* xxxvi (1 December 1813), 423.

Dear Sir,

I ask your pardon for stealing one of your books. On turning over my cargo, I find Dr. Cheyne[1] among my other books. On the 12th of March I am to do duty in town, and then shall have the pleasure of seeing you, and of hearing new pages in Clarissa. Caroline gives her humble service to you and Mrs. Richardson; and her excuse for not waiting on you is, that her sister Cox,[2] when she designed it, was taken dangerously ill, and she could not leave her; and another time, when the day was fixed, the footman she borrowed (for she has none of her own) disappointed, &c. which apology she shall supply herself when next in town. Which she will do with great pleasure: for I assure you she was your admirer before she saw you, and is more so since. She has just now read you over in your new and splendid

[1] Dr. George Cheyne (1671–1743) of Bath, author of *The English Malady* (1733) and more recently (1742) of *The Natural Method of Cureing the Diseases of the Body, and the Disorders of the Mind depending on the Body,* both printed by Richardson.

[2] Charles Henry Lee's widow, Martha D'Aranda, was now the wife of Dr. William Coxe (d. 1760).

suit,[1] (with which you was so kind as to present her;) and she is too much a woman not to like you still better for being so well dressed. But my thoughts run all on Pamela's younger sister, Clarissa; and I promise myself no small satisfaction from conversing with her in March. With the sincerest good wishes and service to all your's,

I am, dear sir,
Your affectionate and obliged
humble servant,
E. Young.

How fare our friends at Chelsea?[2]

184. [Welwyn, Herts.]. [?Tu. 4 March 1745/6]. Mrs. Grace Cole.

Not traced.[3]

185. Welwyn, Herts. [Tu.] 4 March 1745/6. Samuel Richardson.

Not traced.—*Monthly Magazine*, xxxvi (1 December 1813), 420–1.

Wellwyn, March 4, 1745.

Dear Sir,

We have lost our friend[4] for a season; but I hope we shall find him again. My acquaintance with him was not of long

---

[1] A sixth edition of *Pamela*.

[2] One of the people he was to meet in Chelsea during the second week of March was the new curate and aspiring poet, Joseph Warton (1722–1800), who wrote to his brother Thomas at Oxford on the 18th of his meeting Young and Joseph Spence: 'I am more & more every day convinced that Hutcheson's "Moral Sense" is Utopian & Imaginary and to this purpose must tell you what Dr *Young* said to me, (with whom I breakfasted the other morning)—"Proper Distrust of All Mankind is one of the most prudential Maxims". I spent two or three [hours] very agreeably & in Conversation he is a very . . . [hole in paper] & sensible & entertaining man. I have [rene]wed my acquaintance with Mr Spense. . . . I gave him & Dr Young subscription papers' (British Museum, Add. MSS. 42560, f. 9).

[3] Evidence of this letter is Young's remark in the next letter, to Richardson: 'I have written to that house of sorrow.'

[4] Captain John Meric Cole was buried 1 March, according to an entry in the Chelsea parish register.

standing; but from the high esteem he was in with persons I value, and from all that I know of him myself, I have a great opinion of his integrity, and his amiable qualities were obvious to all. I hope to read a paragraph of your's to his memory. I have written to that house of sorrow.

You show a kind concern for my little disorders. The piles I have suffered extremely, from a few years ago. They returned, but not to that degree. Surrounded with the reports of far greater calamities on every hand, I bless God for his great mercies. This moment I hear the knell of a young gentleman and neighbour cut off in his bloom, by the small-pox.[1] It is very near us. I am afraid for Caroline, to whose family it has been very fatal. She gives her best wishes, and humble service.

I am, dear Sir,
Your affectionate humble servant,
E. Young.

As I was going to fold my letter, I heard a second knell. Asking whose it was, it proved my next neighbour's. What has man to do but to know the vanity and avoid the vexation of human life? Evils fly so near and so thick about us, that I am half persuaded, my dear friend, that we should aim at little more than negative good here, and positive in another scene: escape here and enjoyment hereafter.

186. [Welwyn, Herts.]. [W.] 19 March 1745/6. Samuel Richardson.

Not traced.—*Monthly Magazine*, xxxvi (1 December 1813), 423.

March 19, 1745–6.

Dear Sir,

On my coming home (for I halted by the way) I found the very kind letter you mentioned when I saw you. You need not have put your name to it; the nature of the letter would have told me from whom it came. Who is there besides so

---

[1] The bells of several neighbouring churches could have been heard in Welwyn. Searches of parish registers by W. Branch Johnson, Hertfordshire historian, have failed to disclose either this burial or the one alluded to in the postscript.

capable of making other's concerns his own? Caroline was greatly struck with the Richardsonian generosity of it. And Caroline begs her best respects to Mrs. Richardson and yourself; and many thanks for this, and the present I brought her from you. She is far from well, but no symptoms of the disease we would particularly guard against; the disorder hangs chiefly on her spirits; and she told me, after she had dipt into your book, that she fancied flowers and tombs were (though seeming so remote) as near in nature, as in that author's composition.[1] May Almighty Providence spread its tender wing over you and your's. With true affection, esteem, and gratitude, I am   Dear Sir,

Sincerely your's,
E. Young.

187. Welwyn, Herts. [Su.] 6 April 1746. Duchess of Portland.

Longleat MSS (83) 136–7.—Bath, p. 292; Shelley, p. 200.

Wellwyn
Ap ye 6th
1746.

Madam

I had not omitted my Duty in returning your Grace my early sincere Acknowledgments for your particular Favours when I was in Town, but as soon as I returnd I was taken ill of a Fever, nor can I yet get clear of it. I heartily condole with every branch of your little Family for what they sufferd in their late Illness, & bless God for their recovery.

Your Graces kind regard to my little Interests is exstremely Good in You; Whatever shall be ye Event of these casual things, your Grace can never lose ye Satisfaction of having endeavourd to Befriend One, whose cheif Title to yr favour is his /[verso]/ being deeply Sensible of it.

Your Grace gives me great Satisfaction, by yr Account of your Friend Mrs. G. Coles better Health; & I shall ever set

---

[1] James Hervey's *Meditations among the Tombs* and *Reflections on a Flower-Garden*, printed at Richardson's press, were announced for publication in February.

a high value on whatever favours she is pleasd to confer on me.

Yesterday, Madam, the famous Mr Whiston calld on me, who prophesid severe things to this poor Nation,[1] he pretended to support himself by Scripture Authority; how just his pretence I can not absolutely Say, but I think there are so many publick Symtoms on ye Side of his Prophesie, as to hinder it from being quite ridiculous.

I wish, Madam, I could at all contribute to your amusement; but Sickness, is but a bad Correspondent; however tis better to have it for /[conjugate leaf]/ a Correspondent than a Companion. May your Grace ever keep it at a Distance; yet not out of Sight; For, as I take it, ye Sight or Thought of Sickness is ye Enjoyment of Health; & half ye World are unhappy under ye greatest Blessing Heaven can bestow, purely from forgeting that it may be taken from them.

I beg, Madam, my humble Duty to my Lord Duke, best Wishes & humble Service to all beside. Whether Whiston
             be
prophesie   wrong or right, in Tumults, & in Peace, in Sickness & in Health

     I am Madam Yr Graces most Obligd
      & most devoted Humble Sevt
       EYoung.

Madam Miss Lee gives her
Humble Duty.

188. Welwyn, Herts. [Su.] 20 April 1746. Samuel Richardson.

Not traced.—*Monthly Magazine*, xxxvi (1 December 1813), 423.

        Wellwyn, April 20, 1746.
My dear Friend,
 Your's of the 15th I received not till this day. I love and honour you for your humanity. I bless God I am much

---

[1] It was during this year at Tunbridge Wells that Whiston proclaimed the coming of the millenium in 21 years.

better, but not well. A great laziness and lowness hangs on
me. I have several years been much out of order about this
time, nor knew (till I read your's) that the æquinox had any
thing to do with it.[1] But I believe it has. I am heartily sorry
that you bear so strong testimony on that side of the question.
Of Miss Lee I will say nothing. She will, I believe, appear
before you to answer for herself.—You seem to intimate a
sort of quarrel with your pen.—I know no one that has less
reason to quarrel with his pen than yourself. Pray give my
best wishes, love, respects, to your fire-side. I am from my
heart, dear sir,

Your truly affectionate
and obliged humble servant,
E. Young.

189. Welwyn, Herts. Su. [?4] May 1746. Samuel Richardson.

Not traced.—*Monthly Magazine*, xxxvii (1 March 1814), 138.

Wellwyn, Sunday, May 1746.

Dear Sir,

I have lately received a very melancholy account of our
friend Mrs. Grace Cole; you would rejoice me greatly if you
could send me better news of so valuable a person.

Miss Lee is now in town, ill of the small-pox by inocula-
tion, but, I hear, in a very fair way of recovery.

Dr. Webster[2] was here this week, who told me you was
in perfect health, of which I give you joy. I hope all your
fireside is in the same happy way, to whom my best wishes
and services. I take for granted, Clarissa is putting on her

---

[1] Richardson's belief that the equinox had an ill effect on health has no more
support than the similar widespread belief that the equinoxes produce storms.

[2] William Webster (1689–1758), Vicar of Ware and Thundridge, Hertfordshire
villages about eight miles east of Welwyn. On 24 April *The London Evening Post*
had announced publication of his sermon: *A Seasonable Antidote against Popery*. The
sermon is not recorded as having been printed by Richardson. For other works that
were and for Richardson's high regard for Webster, see William M. Sale, Jr., *Samuel
Richardson: Master Printer*, 1950, pp. 68–70.

last attire, and that we shall soon see her in public. That
success may second all your undertakings is the sincere wish
of,

Dear Sir,
Your very affectionate and obliged,
E. Young.

190. Welwyn, Herts. Su. [?1 June 1746]. Duchess of Portland.

Longleat MSS. (80) 133.

Wellwyn
Sunday.

May it please yr Grace

   I receivd not ye favour of your Grace's Letter till very late
this morning, & being obligd to Officiate twice this Day, &
our Post going out soon after Service is over, I have but just
time to thank you for yr particular Goodness to me, & to let
yr Grace know yt as I have been very ill, & am now by Dr
Meads order drinking a Chalibeate[1] in this neighbourhood
for ye recovery of my Strength, wh is much impaird, I can
not wait on yr Grace till ye 17th But certainly will then if it
please God; & if You are still in Town. /[verso]/

   Your Graces Letter to Mr M———[2] is exstremely Kind;
& if, as You propose, You speak to ye Persons of Powr,
It will put an End to my Suspence, & fully convince me yt
I may be quite at rest one way, or Other.

   Madam I am much concernd & indeed surprizd at ye
Account yr Grace gives of Mrs G. Cole; I had lately much
better news from another Hand wh I consulted about her
Health. Yr Graces Letter shall be burnd, as You Desire.

---

[1] The chalybeate springs of Welwyn had been known for some years but Young
is credited with having rediscovered a spring in the garden of the old rectory, in use
before he had taken a more imposing residence on coming to Welwyn. He was later
to build Assembly Rooms opposite the spring with a bowling green adjacent as a
popular rendezvous 'for balls, routs, cards and gossip' (W. Branch Johnson, *Welwyn,
Briefly*, 1960, pp. 50–1).

[2] The Portland lawyer, William Murray, was becoming a parliamentarian of
considerable stature and was now engaged in prosecuting the rebel lords of the
Jacobite uprising.

I beg my humble Duty to my Ld Duke, & humble Service to
Mr Achard. And I am Madam
                                    Your Graces greatly Obligd
                                        & most Obedt
                                    Humble Sevt   EYoung.

191. [Welwyn, Herts.]. [Th.] 12 June [1746].
Duchess of Portland.

Longleat MSS. (85) 138–9.—Bath, pp. 292–3; Shelley, p. 201.

May it please your Grace
    I have been so thrown back in my hopd Recovery by a
severe cold that I can not keep my Word, in being in Town
on ye 17th; my Phisitian tells me he can not set me up for
Such a Journey under Ten Days, & I take for granted your
Grace by that time will be out of Town. I have a Brother
Chaplain[1] in waiting that will do my Duty at Court, till my
Health permits me to come to his Releif.
                                    been
    I should have   exstremely glad to have payd my Duty
to yr Grace; But as to ye Other Point, (viz) of having my
Curiousity Satisfid by being let into ye Particulars mentiond
in your Last; yt is of no moment. Yr Grace I am satisfid will
do what you can; & if I have the Honour of hearing from
You /[verso]/ it would ad to ye favour if yr Grace wd let me
know how fares our good Friend of Chellsea, for whom you
greivd me with so melancholy an Account in yr Last.
    Madam, I beseech you to take care of your Health, I have
a very particular sense of ye value of it at present, not only
from my own Want of it, but from ye Disorders & & [*sic*]
Indispositions of many of my Friends & Acquaintances. One
of them I find has the Honour of being known to yr Grace,
I mean Mrs Rolt,[2] from whom I receivd last Post a most

    [1] Unidentified.
    [2] Mrs. Thomas Rolt (*née* Anne Calvert), of Sacombe, Herts. It was in this year
that articles of agreement were drawn up with her husband's creditors for £3,000
(Hertford County Records Office: A. 5. 1769) and in 1747 that an Act of Parliament was drafted vesting his property in trustees (H.C.R.O.: 1771).

melancholy Letter, her sole Hope, it seems is in Bristol
Waters to wh she is going, & if she Shd fail, her Children
will fall into their Father's hands; wh is a most Surprizing
way (one would think) of falling into Ruin. In antient Story
it is Sayd of one Saturn, yt He eat up /[conjugate leaf]/ his
Children. As for my Cousin Rolt[1] I fear He will drink up
his. He has allready drank up one Half of an ample Estate;
& seems to be exceeding dry Still. So high runs his Fever,
caught by perpetually basking in ye too Sultry beams of yt
Sex, wh Seems designd by Providence for ye Comfort of wise
men, & ye Ruin of Fools. I am Madam

Yr Graces much Obligd &
most Obedt Humble Sevt
EYoung.

Madam I beg my humble Duty to my Ld Duke, & humble
Service to Mr Ashard, & (if yr Grace pleases) to Mr M——.[2]
When I last saw his Grace of N—— He told me He
had two or three to provide for before me. Three
are just now preferd[3] But perhaps His 2 or 3, like

Falstafs men in Buck'rum, m̲y̲ grow to 9 or X.[4] For
wh Fictions in ye Exstravagance of Poesy can exceed
ye wonderfull Realitys in human Life?—Yr Grace
will please to answer this puzzleing Question in
your Next.

June 12th

[1] As a Calvert, Mrs. Rolt would have been a cousin of Young's wife. That she
was of the related Calvert lineage is made evident by the record of her marriage:
'1731 May 8. Thos. Rolt and Ann Calvert Ba[chelor] and spinster, Gent. of St.
Gile's Camp's. She of St. Andrew's, Holborn; nobody to see it. Wm. Toone Father.
an old gentleman gave £1. 1s. and a Gent. from my Lord Baltimore £2 2s. he had
cert: 20 days' (Fleet Registers by J. S. Burne, p. 57).

[2] William Murray.

[3] Young is probably referring to the appointments to prebendaries of Frederick
Cornwallis (1713–83), Joseph Browne (1700–67), and Arthur Young (1693–1759).
Cornwallis went to St. George's Chapel, Windsor, and in 1768 was consecrated
Archbishop of Canterbury. Browne went to Hereford and in 1756 was elected
Provost of Queen's College, Oxford. Arthur Young, chaplain to Speaker Onslow,
went to Canterbury. The June issue of the *Gentleman's Magazine* also announced
the forthcoming appointment (11 July) of John Taylor (1704–66), a Carteret
protégé, to St. Peter's, Westminster.

[4] Shakespeare's *1 Henry IV*, II. iv.

192. [F.] 4 July 1746. Duke of Newcastle.

British Museum, Add. MSS. 32707, f. 394.—Thomas, pp. 594–5; Shelley, pp. 201–2.

July ye 4th
1746.

May it please your Grace.

If the multiplicity of yr Graces high Affairs could permit Your Grace to reflect—How severe it is for One of very long service, & known Attachment to his Majesty, after Promises from Those that hold them most sacred, & after all methods taken to recommend himself to yr Graces Patronage, ye Intercession of Friends, & his own Attempts in Letters which boast yr constant Favour; & at ye very Latter end of Life, when distant Expectations are no Expectations— Could, (I say,) yr Grace one moment reflect how severe it is, *Then*, to be thrown far backward in my Hopes, I am confident from your Graces known Equity & Humanity, You would much compassionate ye Case of

May it please yr Grace
Yr Graces most Obedient
& humbly devoted sevt
Ed Young.

My Lord, Both ye
Arch Bishops¹ are ready
to bear Testimony
to your Grace in
my Favour.

193. [Welwyn, Herts.]. [Th.] 17 July 1746. Duchess of Portland.

Longleat MSS (86) 140–1.—Bath, pp. 293–4.

Wellwyn
July 17.
1746.

May it please your Grace

Your Graces particular regard for Miss Parsons,² confirms me, in yt ⁱⁿ which I need no confirmation, your just

---

¹ i.e. Potter of Canterbury and Herring of York.
² Grace Parsons (see Young's letter to the Duchess of 1 June 1747).

Discernment, for most certainly her excellent Disposition is Indisputable. God forbid it should fall into bad Hands. Your Graces Apprehensions about her are such as every true friend of hers must entertain. For she seems left absolutely naked of Defence, but her own Prudence; & in so young a Creature, & beset by Such a World, how precarious a
Defence is That? I pressed her therefore, (after I heard ~~her~~ your Graces kind Invitation) to ye /[verso]/ utmost of my Powr to be frequently at Bullstrode, & with yr Graces Friends in Town; for I can not but have for her a very Sincere regard & affection.

Business, Madam, detaind me near ye Town till this Week. I was to wait on Mr M.[1] but He was not at his Chambers. I humbly thank yr Grace for his kind Intentions towards me. —I am very glad, but not surprizd, that He thinks with me, with regard to &c: Madam, tis Impossible, tis Impossible; tho I confess ye Devil has sufficient Footing in ye World, & never fails of a good Place at court.—Poor Mr Ashard, I am very Sorry for him, but from many late Instances of ye like nature in our /[conjugate leaf]/ own neighbourhood I have great reason to hope He will do well. For my own Part who lately crept out of ye same Condition He is now in, I am far from being reestablishd in my Health; as I have often in like condition found great Benefits from Tunbridge, I have good Hope from Drinking these Waters a due time, & when it shall please God that I am well, I know I shall be Better by waiting on your Grace; which I had much rather do now, if it was in my powr.—Lady Bute[2] I have formerly seen, but before she was Lady Bute; From what I then saw, I very easily beleive what I now hear of her Ladyps excellent accomplishments & Character; I am glad your Grace /[verso]/ has ye Happiness of her Conversation; I should be pleasd & proud to partake of such a Feast; but my Ambition has lately met with more Rebukes than One. Which should,

---

[1] William Murray.

[2] Mary Montagu (1718–94), only daughter of Lady Mary Wortley and Edward Montagu. Young's acquaintance with her before her marriage in 1736 to John Stuart (1713–92), third Earl of Bute, would have been through his friendship with her mother.

& I hope, will make me Wiser than to aim at anything more than humble Content for ye Future; which is Prudence at all Ages, but doubly Prudence at mine. With an infinite Sense of yr Graces very Singular Goodness to me, wth humble Duty to my Ld Duke, & ardent wishes for ye continud Wellfare of ye Little Family, I am

Madam

Yr Graces most Humble
& Devoted Sevt
EYoung

Pray Madam, my
best wishes & humble
Service to Mr Ashard.

194. Welwyn, Herts. [Th.] 17 July 1746. Samuel Richardson.

Not traced.—*Monthly Magazine*, xxxvii (1 March 1814), 138.

Wellwyn, July 17, 1746.

My dear Sir,

After long absence, long I mean to my feeling, I yesterday returned home, as to a pillow, which gives me that joy in rest of which you will not be able to entertain any idea these twenty years.

I received the *True Estimate*,[1] and shall, at my leisure, look it over, and return it.

You gave me great pleasure in what you read to me at N. End, I mean that part that was new to me; and I wish you would lessen your apprehensions of length. If all fixes, and satisfies attention, the longer the better.[2]

On his travels a very old man dines with me this day, the Rev. Mr. Watly,[3] whose character may be briefly given by

[1] Young's 1727 sermon, *A Vindication of Providence; or A True Estimate of Human Life* was reprinted at this time by Richardson for Henry Lintot (1705–58).

[2] This paragraph and the preceding one were omitted from the Barbauld edition of Richardson's correspondence and their place taken by the portion of a letter which follows next after this letter.

[3] Probably the 'Mr. Whatley, minister of Toft-in-Lindsey [Lincolnshire]' mentioned in the *Diary* (v. 39) of William Stukeley as paying him a visit on 29 October 1741.

comparing him to a frosty night. There are many thoughts in him that glitter through the dominion of darkness. Tho' it is night, it is a star-light night, and if you (as you have promised) should succeed him in our little hemisphere, I should welcome a Richardson as returning day. In a word, I love you, and delight in your conversation, which permits me to think of something more than what I see; a favour which the conversation of very few others will indulge to

Dear Sir,

Your affectionate and obliged

humble servant,

E. Young.

Pray my love and best wishes to your amiable fireside.

195. [?Welwyn, Herts.]. [?July–August 1746]. Samuel Richardson.

Not traced.[1]—Barbauld, ii. 15–16.

You convince me, every day, more and more, of the singularity of your character; your heart is, I find, set on doing good offices, and to those who are least capable of returning them. If there is any such thing as virtue, it consists in such a conduct; and if there is any such thing as wisdom, it consists in virtue! What else can furnish either joy or peace? For when a man has had years, reflexion and experience enough to take off the mask from men and things, it is impossible for him to propose to himself any true peace, but peace of conscience; or any real joy, but joy in the Holy Ghost. This, another might call preaching; but you, Sir, must either condemn the whole tenor of your life, or allow it to be common sense.

---

[1] This paragraph, from an otherwise unidentified letter, was substituted by Mrs. Barbauld for the second and third paragraphs of the preceding letter to Richardson. See H. Pettit, 'The Text of Edward Young's Letters to Samuel Richardson', *Modern Language Notes*, lvii (December 1942), 668–70, where the matter of Mrs. Barbauld's original mélanges of Young's letters to Richardson is compared with the text in the *Monthly Magazine*.

196. Welwyn, Herts. [Su.] 10 August 1746. Duchess of Portland.

Longleat MSS. (87) 142–3.

Wellwyn
Aug. the 10th
1746.

Madam

I have little Pleasure in ye Conversation of any that are any way inconvenienced by the favour they show me in their Friendship. Therefore without Judging of your Graces Judgment I absolutely acquiesce in it. Before this time I once flatterd myself with ye Happiness of paying my Duty at Bullstrode, but unforeseen Accident confines me longer Here. My Curate[1] had the good Luck to gain Preferment before me his Master, & yt in a most delicious Spot Wormly in Essex the Incumbent being just Dead, And till I can get another Curate I am tied by /[verso]/ the Legg. I am looking out sharp for another Subaltern, but have allready met with one Disapointment in it. I gave ye Refusal of it to my very next Neighbour Colonel Maguire.[2] But by his Ladie's persuasion He declines, it; who is of Opinion, yt however well qualified He may be, yet ye World would not well relish in a Protestant Pulpit so recent a convert from the Church of Rome. I suggested to her Ladyship that the Colonel could hardly surprize ye World more than, by what He had done allready. Her Ladyp said—That ye Colonel had indeed, (considering how young a man He was,) acted to ye surprize /[conjugate leaf]/ & astonishment of ye Oldest Commanders, in the *Empresse's Service.* I replyd, yt her

---

[1] Entries of burials in the Welwyn parish registers between May 1745 and March 1745/6 are signed by George North (1710–72), Vicar of nearby Codicote, Herts. It is likely that North may have served the Wormley parish for a short period. Wormley is now in Hertfordshire, on the border of Essex. Entries in the Wormley parish register between June 1746 and 17 September 1747 (when Sherlock Willis [1722–83] became the vicar) are unsigned.

[2] Lieutenant-Colonel Hugh Maguire (d. 1789) on 18 May 1745 had become the fourth husband of Elizabeth Malyn, widow of Charles Baron Cathcart (d. 1740), and hence was Young's neighbour in Tewin, Herts. The Empress under whom he would have served was Maria Theresa (1717–80), from 1740 ruler of Bohemia and Hungary.

Ladysp's modesty forgot *her own*. On wh she orderd her Coach to ye Door & with Half a Curtisie took her Leave.

To be serious, Madam, I will wait on yr Grace as soon as I can, being very desireous to pay my Respects where most due, whilst Heaven continues to me Life, & strength to make such Excursions; being very sensible yt most at my time of Day are confind at home by more melancholy, & irremoveable distresses than that I complain of. That Heavens Blessings & Graces may make your Lives happy & long, is the cordial Wish, & Prayr of Madam, Your Graces, & my Ld Dukes much Obligd & most Obedient humble Sevt

EYoung.

197. Welwyn, Herts. [Su.] 17 August 1746. Samuel Richardson.

Not traced.—*Monthly Magazine*, xxxvii (1 March 1814), 138–9.

Wellwyn, Aug. 17, 1746.

Dear Sir,

I was a little struck at my first reading your list of evils in your last letter. Evils they are, but surmountable ones, and not only so, but actually by you surmounted, not more to the admiration than the comfort of all that know you. But granting them worse than they are, there is great difference between *middle* and *old age*. Hope is quartered on the middle of life, and fear on the latter end of it; and hope is ever inspiring pleasant dreams, and fear hideous ones. And if any good arises beyond our hope, we have such a diffidence of its stay, that apprehension of losing destroys the pleasure of possessing it. It adds to our fears rather than encreases our joys. What shall we do in this case? Help me to an expedient; there is but one that I know of: which is,—that since the things of this life, from their mixture, repetition, defectiveness, and, in age, short duration, are unable to satisfy, we must aid their *natural* by a *moral* pleasure, we must season them with a spice of religion to make them more palateable: we must consider that 'tis God's will that we should be content and pleased with them: and thus the *thinness* of the *natural* pleasure, by our sense of joining an *obedience to heaven* to it, will become much more *substantial* and satisfactory. We shall find great account in considering content, not only as a prudence, but as a *duty* too.

Religion is all, and (happy for us!) it is all-sufficient too in our last extremities: a full proof of which I will steal from yourself. So all-sufficient is religion, that you could not draw in Clarissa the strongest object of pity without giving us in it (thanks to her religion) an object of envy too.

Pray my love and service to all, and to Mr. Grover among the rest, who has lately much obliged,   Dear Sir,

Your truly affectionate
humble servant, and
Clarissa's admirer,
E. Young.

198. [Welwyn, Herts.]. [Tu.] 23 September 1746. Duchess of Portland.

Longleat MSS. (88) 144–5.—Bath, pp. 294–5.

Sepr ye 2 3.
1746.

May it please your Grace
I am too well acquainted with ye Pains & Infirmities of human nature, not to compassionate those that in any Degree labour under them. But I greatly hope that in this there is less Occasion for my Compassion at Bullstrode, than when your Grace writ.

I have not yet got a Curate, but hope sometime next month to get some neighbouring Clergyman to officiate for me One Sunday, & That will give a Fortnights Absence, wh I propose to dedicate to my paying my Duty at Bullstrode if nothing interveens to prevent it.

Yr Grace delights in Curiositys I therefore inclose One[1] to you, wh is worth ye best Cockle shell in your Museum. A snails shell it must /[verso]/ not be, for mine is all Expedi-

---

[1] Apparently a letter from, or at least concerning, his neighbour, Lady Cathcart, now the wife of Colonel Hugh Maguire, and at this time *en route* to her husband's home in Ireland.

tion; If yr Grace had such a Thing as a Flash of Lightning in ye Corner of your Cubbard it would be ye most proper Return you could make for my Present. It was indeed a Clap of Thunder to Ly C——t who is now panting in the Irish Seas under ye Consequences of it.

Yr Grace's mentioning ye Dutchess of ——[1] in your Last, put me in mind of this Letter. I receivd it ye next Day after Date. I desire you to keep it by You till I have the Honour of waiting on You. If ye Dutchess plays her Cards no better than my Lady, she will be in Danger in a little time of being calld *Hussy* instead of *Her Grace*. I send it for yr private Amusement only, & beg it may be a Secret /[conjugate leaf]/ for I would not appear as a Confidant in such an Affair; much less as ye Betrayer of the Betrayer.

How One false Step naturally betrays us into another? Had her Ladyp never marryd her Grandson,[2] she had never been a Lyar; & if she had never been a Lyar, she had never been Transported; which, in this Case, is, I think, a severer Fate than that of being Hangd.

I beg, Madam, my humble Duty to my Ld Duke, my Service to Mr Achard & best Wishes to All, especially to Ly Harriot. When I am at a Loss for a Curate I can not forget his Grace ye little Archbishop. What if He made his first Ecclesiastical Campaign in ye Fields of Wellwyn? His Innocence wd recommend his Doctrine to my Parishioners exceedingly & it wd be an infinite Honour to, Madam,

Yr Graces most Obedt & Obligd
Humble Sevt   EYoung

/[verso]/ PS. This moment I receive Advice that the Happy Couple are soon to return from Ireland in perfect Peace. Since there are no Spiders in Ireland, I wonder how so many Webs are spun there to catch English Butterflys. Her Ladyp is still I beleive but a fair Penitent, as well as yr Grace's Dutchess; I wish they were both as ready to repent of their *Sins*, as they are of Their *Follys*; But that is ye case of but Few; & ye Reason I take to be this, (viz) That *Folly's* Hell is in this World, but ye Hell of *Sin*, in ye Next.——But not

---

[1] Unidentified.
[2] Lady Cathcart was now 55 years of age and her new husband at most in his 30s.

many let their Minds go a Woolgathering to ye next World. And yet without it, there is no Prudence, Safety, Reputation, or Peace in this. And they that seek them without it, not only *do*, but *must* fail. Because it is contrary to ye Allmighty's fixt, & Original Plan, & Law; which no human Effort, or Wisdom, we are sure (if sure of any thing) can possibly Repeal.

[in left margin of second leaf]
I am deeply concernd for poor Miss Cole, & beg my hearty Service to Miss Parsons when yr Grace sees Her.

199. [Welwyn, Herts.]. [? October 1746]. John Grover.

Not traced.[1]

200. [?Welwyn, Herts.]. [Th.] 16 October 1746. Duchess of Portland.

Longleat MSS. (89) 146–7.—Bath, pp. 295–7.

Octr 16. 1746.

May it please yr Grace

Compassion is not only a Duty, but a Blessing; It is attended wth a Pleasure, not only in common wth all other Virtues, from a consciousness of doing right, but with a Pleasure of its own peculiar growth, wh the Uncompasionate can never enjoy: The more Sensible we are of Others Calamities, ye more Sensible we must be of our own Escape, as we lament ye former, we bless God for ye Latter; the First gives us Pain, ye Second, Delight: Hence arises that *mixt* Sensation wh an honest Heart feels at ye Objects of Pity; wh to many is a Riddle, & wh while they feel, they do not Understand.

---

[1] Young's letter to Richardson of 11 November 1746 refers to 'one of my letters' to Grover, apparently of recent date.

What an Object of Compassion[1] did yr Grace lay before
me in yr Last? A human Creature, & One of ye tenderest
Sex, & One of ye most deserving in it, & an old Acquaintance, & a Friend, & a Friend yt has so much contributed to
ye Happiness of Others, to be thus Afflicted! If This was
All, the Account would be very melancholy; but This is far
from being All. It strikes me in a Light still more affecting.

For consider, Madam, a Person depriv'd of Reason ~~from~~ ^{by} any
Cause, by Pride, Malice, or Impetuous Desire, is one of ye
most melancholy Objects under Heaven; And if it touches us
so much even when ye Cause is *criminal*, how much must we
be affected when *Virtue* is ye Occasion of it? How much more
affected Still, when a Virtue so *Rare* as that of /[verso]/ filial
Affection is ye Occasion of it? I call it a *Rare* Virtue, because
Family-Affection naturally *descends*; It descends by *Instinct*;
& when it *ascends*, it is pure Virtue yt turns ye stream.

How Virtuous, *there*fore, as well as Unfortunate must our
dear Friend be? And *Unfortunate Virtue* calls for all the Compassion & Concern wh ye most tender Heart can yeild. But
then we shd consider on this Occasion that Virtue itself may
be guilty of Excess; that we may stretch it into a Fault; &
(what you, Madam, will hardly beleive) that we may love a
Parent too well; Which we actually do, when we give Him
our *whole* Heart. There's Another who claimes ye Supreme
Seat in it. Had our poor Friend consider'd yt her Father is
still Alive, yt He can never die, yt He is about her Path, &
about her Bed; That Father, I mean, which gave her that

[1] Alluding to the distress of Miss Grace Cole, who had lost her father in March
and whose mother was dying at the time of the Duchess's letter to Young. An
entry in the Chelsea parish register records the burial of Mrs. Grace Cole on 17
October. The following 29 January Mrs. Delany wrote of Miss Cole: 'Poor Mrs.
C. is to be boarded in the country and . . . the Duchess of Portland wanted some
trusty person to attend her. . . . Mrs. C. is never outrageous; it may rather be called
a total loss of memory than madness, though she is as incapable of doing anything
for herself, as if she was in the strongest frenzy' (Llanover, 1861, ii. 454). In her will
made 9 June 1754 the Countess of Oxford left 'to my Daughter Margaret Dutchess
of Portland the yearly sum of fifty pounds to be by her applied for the use of Mrs
Grace Cole a lunatick during the life of the said Mrs Grace Cole' (Somerset House,
P.C.C. Glazier 824, pr. 11 August 1756). The Duchess in turn making her will
9 October 1771 desired 'my dear daughters will be so good to take care that Mrs
Grace Cole may have every thing that will make life easy and comfortable & I give
for that purpose thirty pounds a year in addition to the fifty pounds a year left by
mother' (Somerset House, P.C.C. Ducarel 436, pr. 4 August 1785).

Father whom she mourns; That Father who, tho He has Angels for his Children, not only permits, but *invites*, nay *commands* her to call Him by that *tender Name*; & promises yt if she does so, that He will give her his *Blessing*; Such a Blessing as no Parent on Earth can give; that He *will never leave her, or forsake her*, (as her Other Parent has done;) but stretch His wing over her, with ye utmost Tenderness, both in this Life, & ye next—Had, I say Madam, our poor Friend *fully* considerd This; It wd have been such a Cordial to her Heart, as wd have made her laugh at /[conjugate leaf]/ Monroe;[1] *This* Consideration wd have done what Medicine can not do, It ^{wd} have softend her Affliction, & have prevented the Calamity.

A Calamity, I mean, to Us; for what it ^{is} to her, God only knows. We know no more of her, than of ye state of the Dead. She is actually dead to our Manner of Life, nor know we at all what her present Condition is as to Happiness or Misery. That, doubtless, depends on ye Nature of the Ideas that pass thro her Mind; & that we know no more of, than of ye Dreams of those yt sleep. The Beggar in his Dream may be ^a King; & she, under this melancholy Appearance, may be Happy for ought we know to ye Contrary. For *now* Madam, she exists in a *Separate State*. We exist under ye Reign of *Reason*; She is in the Kingdom of wild Imaginations only.

Let this Consideration, Madam, comfort us; let us hope ye Best of Her; as we do of Friends departed in *Another* way. Let us look on her, as a *Living* Monument of ye *realy* Deceasd; & then, like other Monuments, it will naturally put us in mind of ye Vanity of human Life. And it will do yt Kind, & Needfull Office in a Manner as much more Effectual than Other monuments, as it is more Uncommon & Surprizing than They. Thus her *reputed* Calamity will be our *real* Benefit; & such, past Dispute God Allmighty designs it to be. For all his *Dispensations* to particular Persons are *Instructions* /[verso]/ to Mankind in General. His good Providence designs One person to be, as it were a Glass to Another; & to show us our *possible* Misfortunes by ye

---

[1] James Monro (1680–1752), prominent London physician to Bethlehem Hospital for lunatics.

actual Misfortunes of Those about us. Since then these melancholy, but most Usefull Glasses are around us without number; Since we may see ourselves in them in every Hour of ye Day, methinks our Souls shd be better Dresd than generally they are. But these are Glasses in wh *Birthday* Suits make but a poor Appearance, & therefore we turn from them. How many Heads are now full of Birthday Suits? How little do they think of that Hour, when ye gayest Tulip-bed of St James's on ye 28 instant[1] will look as despicable in their Sight as ye Wardrobe of Longlane?[2] A fine *Deathbed Suit* we
most glorious
shd purchase at any rate. It is by far ye [~~finest~~ (?)] Apparel we can put on.—But pray, Madam, dont tell them So, for they will certainly think you mad.

Madam Im still under Difficultys about my waiting no You; my Schemes have been disapointed; & at present tis not in my powr to fix ye Time. Miss Lee gives her Duty to your Grace. I beg mine, & humble Service, & Best Wishes to my Ld Duke, Lady Wallingford, Mr Achard, & those beautifull Flowrs of Innocence yt smile about yr Table, & might make a Nosegay for an Archangel; but I hope twill be very late before He gathers them. I am Madam, wth Respect yr Graces

most Obedt & Obligd Humble Sevt   EY.

201. Welwyn, Herts. [Tu.] 28 October 1746. Duchess of Portland.

Longleat MSS. (90) 148–9.—Bath, pp. 297–8; Shelley, pp. 204–5.

Wellwyn
Octr 28th
1746

May it please yr Grace

I have got myself a Curate,[3] & was preparing to set out for Bullstrode, but an unforeseen Accident denys me ye

---

[1] When the King's birthday would be celebrated.

[2] Site of the Smithfield Market, London stockyards.

[3] Young's letter of 5 December 1746 makes evident that his curate is once again George North of Codicote.

Pleasure & Honour of waiting on You. And what is still worse is, that it is a Publick Misfortune wh includes my own. The Murrain¹ among ye Cattle is got within four miles of us, to a Place calld Wotton,² & I am obligd with another Justice to hold a Sessions once or twice a Week, to put ye Act of Parliamt in Execution for preventing its spreading further; & to pay ye poor sufferers what they are entitled to, by yt Act, provided they perform ye Conditions of it.

I have, Madam, endeavourd to get a Curate in *this* Capacity allso, but I find it is Impossible, so that I am absolutely confind, & for /[verso]/ how long is quite Uncertain.

One particular Fact I must tell Yr Grace, which will show very particular Care is necessary. A Farmer had half a dozen Cows drop at once, by Act of Parliament He is obligd to dig a Hole, & bury them. He was willing to spare that pains, & finding an old Calk-pit [*sic*], He tumbled them in, & threw Earth over them. But it happend that this Pit was so near ye Road, that in a few Days, the Road became offensive to Passengers, & if it gives them nothing more than Offence, Happy are they.

The following pretty Tale for a Tragedy may perhaps be new to Yr Grace.—Ly C—— at 59 is smitten with ye gay Feathers of 33, & after short ceremoniny [*sic*] of Billing,
her
& Pruning, takes him into   Nest.³ 33 finds it very well featherd, & had a great mind to pluck some /[conjugate leaf]/ Plumes of it for his private Use. This made Dame Partlet
At This the Cocks-comb rose & could not bear ~~this~~ it.
bristle against him   It came
to a little Sparing; War was declard, & 33 must show all his generalship on this Occasion. To this End he thought it prudent to strengthen himself by Allies. And it happend very fortunately for him, that there was a young Princess in ye Family of 18,⁴ whom 59 took from ye Dunghill, &

---

¹ A serious epidemic among cattle between the years 1747 and 1751 is discussed by William Le Hardy in the *Calendar to the* [Hertfordshire] *Sessions Books,* 1931, vii. 368–9. Le Hardy also reports Young's appointment as a Justice of the Peace about this time (p. 379).

² Now known as Watton-at-Stone.

³ Further, about Lady Cathcart and Colonel Maguire.

⁴ Unidentified.

~~tossed~~ tossed her into a Tub of Soapsuds, out of wh, she soon rose, like Venus out of ye sea, the Delight of her Ladysp's Eyes, & ye Confident of her Heart. This Venus fell in love with Mars, wh was very happy for him, for she returned ye favours she receivd from him with ye Key of her Ladyps
made him run
Scritore, where He found ye Will, wh has   mad. In his Distraction He snatches both away to Ireland, where the young Princess personates her Ladyp, who is kept out of Eyesight, for fear of telling Tales. And as she before discoverd ye Undutifullness of her Husband, /[verso]/ so very lately are her eyes open as to ye Treachery of her bosom-Friend. And yet none but these two are ever sufferd to come near her. Can your Grace easily feign a greater Picture of Distress? I own I can not. And yet for this terrible Sore, she neither has, nor is like to have, any other Plaister than Potatoes & Milk.[1]

How dearly do we often pay for ye Gratification of an idle Desire! If such Tales as these were *Fiction*,[2] they would be of Use; but when they are *Real*, methinks they might make any one tremble yt is within ye Possibility of ye like Misfortune.—Pray, Madam, make this a Secret or conceal its Author.—I beg my humble Duty to my Lord Duke, my humble Service to my Ly Wallingford, Mr Achard, & ye little Family. I heartily wish yr Grace & them better Health than we enjoy in this nighbourhd allmost every One is out of order. Miss Lee gives her humble Duty. I am, Madam, Yr Graces most Obedt

& Obligd Humble Sevt EY.

[1] On the death of her husband, about 1766, the widow returned once more to her Hertfordshire home where she lived until her death in 1789. In 1786, when she was in her 90s, Horace Walpole wrote: 'I was told t'other night that Lady Cathcart, who is still living, danced at Hertford to show her vigour at fourscore . . . She would risk another incarceration—it is woful to have a colt's tooth when other folk have none left.'

[2] The bizarre story of Lady Cathcart's Irish experience was made the basis of Maria Edgeworth's novel, *Castle Rackrent* (1800).

202. Welwyn, Herts. [Tu.] 11 November 1746.
Samuel Richardson.

Not traced.—*Monthly Magazine*, xxxvii (1 March 1814), 139–40.

Wellwyn, Nov. 11, 1746.

Dear Sir,

I thank you for enabling me, at my time of day, to think with great pleasure of living another year. A summer bearing such fruit as you kindly give me cause to expect, may excuse me for wishing to see longer days than we at present enjoy. I consider Clarissa as my last amour; I am as tender of her welfare as I am sensible of her charms.[1] This amour differs from all other in one respect,—I should rejoice to have all the world my rivals in it.

The waters here are not new things,[2] they were in great vogue fifty years ago; but an eminent physician of this place dying, by degrees they were forgot. We have a physician now near us who drinks them himself all this winter. And a lady comes seven miles every morning for the same purpose. They are the same as Tunbridge, and I myself have found from them just the same effect.

As to the melancholy part of your letter, our Chelsea friend,[3] poor soul! But God is good. And we know not what we pity. She is dead to us; she is in another state of existence; we are in the world of reason; she is in the kingdom of imagination; nor can we more judge of her happiness or misery, than we can judge of the joy or sorrow of a person that is asleep. The persons that sleep are (for the time) in the

---

[1] Richardson had written to Aaron Hill on 29 October of *Clarissa*: 'Old Mr. Cibber has had the patience to read it thro'; and is for taking away whole Branches; Some of which, however, he dislikes not: But these very Branches Dr. Young would not have parted with' (Victoria and Albert Museum, Forster Collection 458 vol. xiii, f. 63).

[2] Annotating this passage, W. Branch Johnson (*Welwyn, By and Large*, 1967, p. 16), wrote: 'They are first mentioned in the pages of the antiquary, William Camden, at the end of the sixteenth century, as "a chalybeate spring in the corner of the rector's garden". A hundred years later there lived at Holly Hall a physician, Luke Eeles, who died in 1707; it was presumably he to whom Young referred as bringing them into vogue. Twenty years later Nathaniel Salmon, author of a *History of Hertfordshire* in 1728, mentioned "a mineral spring of the Tunbridge [Wells] sort".'

[3] Grace Cole.

kingdom of imagination too; and she, as they, suffers, or enjoys, according to the nature of the dreams that prevail.

I heartily rejoice, that at length you find benefit from your tar-water; tar by winter, and steel by summer, are the two champions sent forth by Providence to encounter and subdue the spleen.

Miss Lee joins me in the kindest regard and humble service to Mrs. Richardson and her amiable fireside. She gratefully acknowledges the receipt of your many favours, and hopes you'll put it in her power to shew her sensibility of them by her care of you at Wellwyn. And, she says, you'll still oblige her more if you bring a female Richardson along with you.

I bless God I am well; and I am composing, but it is in wood and stone, for I am building a steeple to my church;[1] and as a wise man is every thing, I expect from you, as an architect, a critic upon it.

When you see Mr. Speaker,[2] I beg my best respects and grateful acknowledgements for his enquiring after me.

I had almost forgot to tell you, that an Irishman has run away with one of my neighbours, and that with such circumstances of intrigue and distress, that its truth alone hinders it from being an excellent romance: just as fiction alone hinders your's from being an excellent history.[3]

If you see good Miss Parsons, tell her she has the best wishes of my heart.

I humbly thank you for the kind offer of something you have printed. I hope soon to be in town, and to prevent your designed trouble. I am, with true regard, and sincere affection, dear Sir,

> Your most humble servant,
> E. Young.

---

[1] 'From his window at Guessens Young looked over to the church, still without its tower after the collapse seventy or eighty years previously—sufficient funds had never been obtained to rebuild it. It is commonly said that he gave at his own cost the bell turret, with clock and two bells, that was to do service at its west end until 1834; but the Vestry minutes show that at least part of the cost was met, at the authorization of the Vestry, by the sale of the fallen bells and, when the proceeds proved insufficient, a payment of £5 from the rates' (W. Branch Johnson, *Welwyn Briefly*, 1960, p. 50).

[2] Arthur Onslow.　　　　　　　　　　　　[3] See previous letter.

Pray my service to Mr Lintot. I thought of making some additions to that piece;[1] but, on second thoughts, I let it alone; so that it may go to the press as it is.

Pray my humble service to Mr. Grover; and tell him the poverty I mentioned in one of my letters to him, is now fallen on me.

You say, my dear friend, that I can't but think true; but to live as one ought requires constant, if not intense, thinking. The shortness and uncertainty of life is so evident, that all take it for granted; it wants no proof. And what follows? Why this, because we can't deny it, therefore we forget it; because it wants no proof, therefore we give it no attention. That is, we think not of it at all, for a very odd reason, viz. because we should think of nothing else. This is too strictly expressed, but very near the truth. Ask Cibber if he's of my opinion.

203. Welwyn, Herts. [Su.] 16 November 1746. Samuel Richardson.

Not traced.—*Monthly Magazine*, xxxvii (1 March 1814), 139–40.

Wellwyn, Nov. 16, 1746.

Dear Sir,

On your telling me you drank tar-water, I borrowed Mr. Prior's Narrative,[2] where I find such an account of it, that I design to drink it myself, and to give it to any neighbour that will pledge me. But that author cautions us about frauds in tar which will defeat our expectations from it. He says it must be *Norway* tar, of a deep brown, and pretty thin, (page 170.) Since you drink it, 'tis your interest to know where the best is to be had, and if you do know, and are at leisure to procure me six gallons of it, 'twill much oblige,

Dear Sir,

Your truly affectionate and

obliged humble servant,

E. Young.

---

1 *A Vindication of Providence.* See Young's letter to Richardson of 17 July 1746.
2 *An Authentic Narrative of the Success of Tar-water in Curing a great number and variety of Distempers* (1746), by Thomas Prior (?1682–1751).

There's a Wellwyn carrier at the Windmill in St. John street, Smithfield, who comes out of town, Mondays and Thursdays, every week.[1]

I have now but an inch of life left, and am for setting it up on a save-all[2] of your providing. Miss L. joins me in hearty good wishes and service to your fireside.

Pray how fares Clarissa?

204. Welwyn, Herts. [Su.] 23 November 1746. Duchess of Portland

Longleat MSS. (91) 150–1.—Bath, pp. 298–9.

> Wellwyn
> Nov: 23.
> 1746.

Madam

It greives me that I can not wait on You, but ye Occasion that subsisted when I wrote last, still continues; & what is worse, encreases. Nor are ye poor Cattle ye only Sufferers. A Pluretick Fever is epidemical in this Nighbourhood; Few escape it, & many Die. And yet ye Survivors are as Gay as ever, & as free from Apprehensions of Death, as if they were Immortal. This is so strange & yet so True that it naturally excites mere worldly Curiosity to enquire into ye Cause of it.

Can You conceive, Madam, ye Cause of so astonishing a Truth? I take it to be This. The shortness, & Casualty of Life, & ye Certainty of Death, are such obvious, & quite Indisputable Points, yt it seems nonsense to talk about them. And from not Talking, they come to not Thinking, about them too. Those Points want no Proof, & therefore they give them no Attention. That is, They think not /[verso]/ of them at all, for ye odest Reason in ye World, (viz) Because ye Points are so very Certain, that they shd think of little else.

[1] From 1741 Kershaw's coach, plying between Hitchin and London, came through Welwyn. One of the carriers about this time was a Thomas Watson (cf. R. L. Hine, *History of Hitchin*, i. 1927, 306).

[2] 'A contrivance to hold a candle-end in a candlestick while burning so that it may burn to the end' (*Oxford English Dictionary*).

By this time, I hear your Grace say—'Tis pity this Gentleman had not continud in his Pulpit; He preaches very well; I suppose his Parishioners will have ye Favour of my Letter next Sunday'—Why truly, Madam, This is naturally enough sayd. But how comes it to be Natural? This, I conceive, is the Reason; (viz) That on any serious Subject a man can't talk common Sense, but it will fall in with Something we have heard from ye Pulpit, & hence we naturally enough call it *Preaching*. But this is not so much to ye Discredit of wt is sayd, as to ye Credit of ye Pulpit; showing evidently, that Religion & Good-understanding are ye Same Thing. And if, Madam, you call wt I have sayd *Preaching*, I will present you

wth many Profligates, that by ye Same Rule, Yr Grace must call *Divines*. Yr Grace little thinks therefore yt while

You accuse me of Preaching, that you are puting Sr—— into Orders; & presenting Ministers of State wth Lawn Sleeves. /[conjugate leaf]/ For even These, in Conversation, will take ye side of Virtue; not out of Conscience, but out of Pride; not to save their Souls, but to preserve their Characters as men of Sense.

But I am out all this while, I have been talking to yr Grace as a *Divine*, whereas I find You are a Physitian; I had one of yr Grace's Patients wth me this morning, Mr Terrick;[1] from whom yr Grace need desire no other Fee, than that of being one of his Audience, by wh (if I know Yr Graces Tast). you will think yrself richly payd. How comes it to pass, Madam, that I have so many Rivals in yr Graces Favour? How comes it to pass, that at every Turn, I hear of yr Graces Goodness? Is This like a Dutchess? Is not this

---

[1] Richard Terrick (1710–77) was highly regarded for his preaching. In the spring of 1742, he had been recommended to the Duke of Newcastle by Arthur Onslow, Speaker of the House of Commons, on the illness of Alured Clarke, first (31 March) as a Prebend of Westminster and later (25 May) as a Canon of Windsor. He was granted the latter post on 26 May just before the death of Clarke (British Museum, Add. MSS. 32699, ff. 130, 258, 262). In the fall of 1745 Terrick had been active in arousing the country to the dangers from the Jacobites. The *General Advertiser* of 1 January 1745/6 announced publication of *A Sermon preach'd before the Right Hon. the Lord-Mayor . . . December 18, 1745, being the Day appointed for a General Fast, upon Occasion of the present Rebellion*. In 1757, Terrick became Bishop of Peterborough and in 1764 Bishop of London.

being a little out of Character? If You continue this extraordinary Practise, I shall return ye *Preacher* upon You; for
be assurd One good Example, & in such a Station, outpreaches
/[verso]/ all ye Pulpits in Christendom.

I therefore thank yr Grace for yr excellent Sermon, & I
hope I shall be much ye better for it. For what can be Such
a Spur to Age, as to have Youth get ye start of it, in what is
Right? Nay, if it does not get ye start of Age, but only treads
on its Heels, even that is a great Reproach; & men never
bid fairer for Virtue, than when they fly from Shame as well
as Guilt, But take it not ill if I call even You an old Lady, for
tis sayd—'Wisdom is grey Hairs, & an unspotted Life is
old Age.'[1]

The good Company yr Grace has with You, makes me
still more regret my Confinement at this Place. To Them
& Mr Achard I beg my humble Service, & my humble
Duty to my Ld Duke. With ye Sincerest Wishes Best for ye
that can happen to You, & Yours, I am

May it please yr Grace
Yr Graces most Obedt
& much Obligd Humble Sevt
EYoung.

205. Welwyn, Herts. [Tu.] 2 December 1746. Samuel Richardson.

Not traced.—*Monthly Magazine*, xxxvii (1 March 1814), 140.

Wellwyn, December 2, 1746.

Dear Sir,

I thank you for my tar; I will be out of your debt for that
as soon as I get to town, but never out of your debt of many
more material favours. I shall brew it soon, and then I'll
drink your health in it to give myself a better title to my own.
You said in your last that you was somewhat better for tar-
water. In long chronical cases perseverance is the point. And

---

[1] The Wisdom of Solomon (*Apocrypha*), 4:9.

so it is in the greatest point of all. No man is so profligate but he is good for moments; perseverance only is wanting to make him a saint. As you persevere in the great point, persevere in this; to a good heart add a good constitution, and then you are only not an angel, as happy as mortality can admit. That you may be so is the prayer of, dear sir,

> Your affectionate and obliged
> humble servant,
> E. Young.

206. Welwyn, Herts. [F.] 5 December 1746. Duchess of Portland.

Longleat MSS. (92) 152–3.—Bath, pp. 299–300; Shelley, pp. 207–8.

> Wellwyn
> Decemr 5
> 1746.

May it please your Grace

I once saw a poor Deserter shot in Hyde Park. Six Musqeteers were employd in this melancholy Office. The Three first stooping shot at his Breast; & then ye Other Three shot over them, at his Head, & killd him after he was Dead.[1] Such, Madam, is your Request supported by Mrs Delanys; either of them would have struck dead the stoutest Resolution I could possibly have taken to disobey your

---

[1] A similar account appears in a letter of 23 March 1752 written by a contemporary of Young's: 'Will your Ladyship give me Leave, to transmit in Writing, what I heard in Conversation? An Event that lately happend; and told by a Person, who was Eye-Witness to the Whole. A Soldier was condemned to be executed for Desertion. A young Man, in the Prime of Life, with the Bloom of Health in his Countenance. Being come to the Place of Execution, He prepared Himself for Death, without any apparent Emotion of Fear; opened his Breast, without any Change of Countenance; and drew the Cap over his Eyes, without the least Trepidation in his Limbs. Six of his Comrades were draughted out, and ordered to advance softly forwards. Being come within four Yards of the Criminal, they received the Signal to fire; and shot each his Ball quite through the Body. After this, the Corpse, with the Face uncovered, and the Wounds bleeding, was extended on the Ground; and the whole Regiment, to make the Terror more impressive, marched over its Legs. The Sight was so awful, that one of the Soldiers fainted away, as He passed by the dismal Spectacle; and the Account so affecting, that I observed the Tears stealing down the Cheeks of a Lady, where it was related' (*Letters by James Hervey*, 1797, iii. 258–9).

Commands. But, Madam, my Resolution was quite ye Contrary; & tho I am in fact a Deserter, yet am I an Innocent One; Or rather I am not a Deserter, but taken Prisoner by ye Enimie; & detaind in Chains, wh I am willing to break; but ye Links of it are too Strong, & too Many. For first, Madam, next Weeks Fast insists on my Stay 2ly [secondly] Yr Friend Mr West[1] who is Patron to my Curate, calls him to Town. And lastly, my Little House is full of London Guests, /[verso]/ with whom I am on ye foot of some Form, & therefore can neither dislodge nor abandon them. This Frosty Weather thaws human Hearts; & as they sit round a good fire their kind Affections flow in such Abundance, that I find my Friends disposed to oblige for some time.

I would therefore, Madam, have You & Mrs Delany reflect, That if You had a Person with You, whose Company You desired, yet if his Inclinations were elsewhere, You would consider him as Absent still; so on the other hand, as I assure you You have my Inclinations, consider me as Present, & treat me as kindly as You possibly can. When a man is personally Present, Form may Supply ye place of Goodwill, & make handsome Treatment consistent with real Disregard; But kindly to treat ye Distant in place, this is pure Virtue; This is ye Treat which Angells give us, & therefore, not absurdly to be hopd from Those who who [*sic*] bring them most into our Thoughts.

/[conjugate leaf]/ However, Madam, give me leave to own, that I have my Objections to You. Some few Marks of mere Mortality are still upon You. Your Grace is guilty of a Fault, & of a Fault wh Few would be guilty of; You Oppress with yr Condescension & Civilitys; I am realy out of Countenance at yr yr [*sic*] repeated kind Invitations; &, Particularly, when Yr Grace thinks proper to distrust your own Powrs, & call in Allies to assist your unreasonable Indulgence towards me. My Ld Duke, the Dean,[2] & Mrs. Delany! With such Allies as These a less powrfull Potentate than yr Grace might certainly make a most Succesfull Campaign. Suppose the Empress-Queen had a mind to prevail

---

[1] James West (?1704–72), Member of Parliament for St. Albans, Herts., from 1741 to 1768, George North's patron and fellow antiquarian.
[2] Patrick Delany, since May 1744, Dean of Derry.

wth ye Prince of Monaco to accept of a Million, & distrusting her own Powr shd engage ye King of France, & ye Pope, & ye CZarina to Succour her Endeavour, & ensure her Success;[1] Would not this be very exstraordinary? Make a very small Alteration, put Parson for Prince, & yr Grace may make ye Application. Wth my Duty to ye Allies & cordial good Wishes to All. I am Madam, Yr Graces

most obligd & Obedt Sevt   EY.

Miss Lee sends her humble Duty.

207. [London]. [W.] 17 December 1746. Duchess of Portland.

Longleat MSS. (93) 154.—Bath, pp. 300–1; Shelley, p. 209.

Decemr 17
1746

May it please yr Grace

I am now in Town, & passing by Whitehall I made my Bow to your Graces House & was sorry to find it empty. To how many Houses in this great Town might I bow, in which I have formerly enjoyd agreeable Conversation, but shall enjoy it no more? Whose Inhabitants have taken a far longer Journey from them, than to Bullstrode? Such Thoughts, Madam,
                                                          Talkative,
will occur to People in Years, & as Age is naturally
it will
          teise other folks with them. How like a perfect Dream seems All yt is past? And a Dream it realy is: All is absolutely vanishd, All our Plans, our Labours, even our most Innocent Amusements, & Delights; All is as if It had never been; except Virtue & Vice, These tho past are still with us; The First is Immortal & can not die; the Second will be Immortal too, unless it is put to Death by Repentance. Now since as an Arabian Proverb says, 'The Remembrance

---

1 Young's fancy is playing with the European heads of state, at this time involved in the War of the Austrian Succession (1740–8).

                                                                    same
of past Joys is a Sigh'[1] /[verso]/ And since by the   way of
Speaking, the Infirmities of Age may be calld a Groan; what
fine Musick must a Veteran make in so Delightful a Concert
as is now at Bullstrode? Besides, conversing with ye Blossoms
                              to
of human Life is apt   betray persons in years into a Supposi-
tion that They are Beings of ye Same Nature, & in ye same
                                                        what
State of Existence; wh is an absolute Mistake. For   is
Wisdom in ye Young is Folly in the Old; & so, on ye Re-
                        Reason
verse. For which   I once resolvd to renounce Yr Graces
Acquaintance; till I considerd that the Mischeif of Yr
Graces age was ballanced by ye Benefit of your Example.

    Your Grace wonders what all This means, & what gives
Occasion to such random stuff. Why, Madam, to tell you
ye very Truth, I am now in a Coffee-House waiting for a
Rascally Attorney,[2] who having robd me allready of all my
Money, would now rob me of my Time, & rather than do
nothing, (which is very Tedious) I was determind to write
Nothing to Yr Grace For which Affront I humbly ask par-
don, & am, Madam,

                              Your Graces most Obedt
                              & Obligd & Humble Sevt
                                        EYoung

(For ye Attorney is come)
I send no compliments because [*sic*]

---

[1] The source of the proverb has not been found. A variant of it had appeared in
Robert Blair's *The Grave* (1743):

                        Of joys departed
            Not to return, how painful the remembrance!

                                                    (ll. 108–9).

[2] Unidentified.

Richardson to Young. [London]. [W.] 24 December 1746.

Not traced.—*Monthly Magazine*, xxxvii (1 March 1814), 140–1.

Dec. 24, 1746.
Rev. Sir,

I am in great and unusual arrear with you; but I beg of you to believe, that it is not owing to the want of a true and sincere respect for you, and of a due regard for your favours. But you gave me hope of seeing you in town, when I thought to thank you, and to desire you to thank good Miss Lee, for both your kind invitations: I am sorry your stay in town was so short, as not to permit you to give me this hoped for pleasure.

You tell me, Sir, in one of your favours, that you are composing, but that it is in wood and stone. A worthy work! But, Sir, I expect, the world will still expect more durable works from Dr. Young than wood and stone can furnish.

Then, having given your orders, the workmen acquit you of any further cares than those that require your purse and your weekly inspection. But they cannot employ your nightly meditations; your writing studies; a whole creation ever opened and opening before you, with new and improving beauties. And can Dr. Young say, that he has sung the God of that creation enough, while he affords him faculties undecayed, and a judgment still improving?

The important, the solemn subject you mention, may be best, (I humbly suppose) cultivated by meditations intended for the public eye. Can you better prepare to meet the last solemn hour, than by preparing others to meet it too? The good man is in a daily course; which, like a taper once lighted, pursues its way to a bright extinction, illuminating, till that awful period, all around it. Every hour makes the next happier and easier, till the fear of death is subdued; and then chearful thoughts must intervene, and the soul will be at leisure to expand itself. Think not then, good Sir, to let the solemn so very much engross you, as to excuse you from the serene and the chearful; but let us see, that what you have conquered, humanly speaking, conquered, the less considerate must not still think terrible. But I know, Sir, you must, you cannot help thinking in such a way, as will instruct the world to think; and will here rest the point, in the hope at least, that it cannot be otherwise.

I hope, sir, you find benefit by your tar-water. I exceeded your quantity, for the sake of filling the cask, for the better carriage. I promised myself some benefit from it; but am afraid my nerves are too much unbraced ever to be greatly bettered by human medicines. I have, however, been much worse, and so must sit down, and pray for patience and resignation; thanking God it is no worse.

A happy season to you, and many happy seasons; with my wife's and little girl's likewise, to you, and to Miss Lee, are the wishes of,

Rev. Sir,

Your most obliged and

faithful servant,

S. Richardson.

208. Welwyn, Herts. [Su.] 28 December 1746. Duchess of Portland.

Longleat MSS. (94) 155–6.—Bath, pp. 301–2; Shelley, pp. 210–11.

May it please yr Grace

I am sorry I could not have the Honour & Pleasure of waiting on yr Grace after so many very kind Invitations. But Yr Grace is in ye midst of very agreeable ^company^ , wh wants not that Inspiration You are so well able to give. So surrounded what Madam, can You possibly want? If you call for ye Delicacys of Art or Imagination, Miss Parsons & Mrs Delany have them at their Fingers Ends. If to qualify these Sweatmeats You call for ye Substantial Bread of Reason & Argument, you have One with You who with that Bread has strengthened mans Heart against ye Insults of Infidelity. Would your Grace like Drake,[1] travel round the World in

---

[1] Sir Francis Drake (?1540–96) had been the subject of two recent biographies. Samuel Johnson's had begun in the *Gentleman's Magazine* in 1741 and in 1742 appeared John Campbell's more authoritative life in his *Lives of the Admirals and other Eminent British Seamen*.

search of Curiositys? Madam, You may spare yrself that Pains [*sic*], the Mighty S——,[1] like Atlas, on his broad Shoulders will bring ye World, like a Rareshow, to your own Door; He can present You with all the Wonders /[verso]/ of Ægypt, pour ye sevenfold Nile into ye Basin at Bullstrode; & luckily (at this Season) give your Grace a Pyramid, as a Modell for a Xtmas Pie.

But think me not, Madam, So Stupid or Profligate as to depretiate his learned & excellent Works; tis as Usefull, as it is entertaining; tis an entertaining Comment on ye Scriptures, & a noble Pillar to Support our Faith. What can so strengthen our Beleif, as to have set before our eyes still extant Monuments of antient miraculous Facts? By this means Faith is allmost lost in Knowledge; & ridiculous Infidels grow still more Ridiculous in our Sight. Most of our Travellers go abroad to damage their Religion, Few to mend it, therefore This Work[2] is still ye more commendable.

I am truly glad, Madam, that Miss Parsons is at Bullstrode, of whose Accomplishmts & Virtues I have a great Opinion; & I consider it as a Providential part of Reward to her Virtue that she is near yr Grace. Tis obvious to conceive that it many ways must be of great advantage to her at this critical period of Life. Who knows but ye whole future Happiness of it, may depend on this Visit? On very minute Causes depend ye greatest Events of our Lives. And when on Retrospect we observe /[conjugate leaf]/ them, We are apt to cry, 'A lucky Accident!' & so rob Providence of its just Glory; & ourselves of ye best Instruction. When we read ye various Manners & Fates of Nations, we do Justice to Providence, & acknowledge without Hesitation ye full Evidence of ye Divine Hand over them. Providence is no less Present to (wt we are pleasd to call) every Accident of

our Lives. But its Interposition seems to be written there in a smaller Characters; in such as we can not or will not read.

---

[1] Dr. Thomas Shaw (1694–1751), author of *Travels or Observations relating to several Parts of Barbary and the Levant* (1738).

[2] The accuracy of Shaw's observations had been attacked by Richard Pococke (1704–45) in his own *Description of the East* of 1745, and had been answered in 1746 by Shaw's *Supplement*, which is possibly the work to which Young alludes.

                                                                     if
But   our Eyes are bad, as to this Point, it is worth our while
to put on our Spectacles; For I am persuaded that every
Person at all advancd in Life, may wth due attention, read
                                                in their own Lives
as Usefull, & probably, more affecting Lessons,
as they can in their Bibles. And This I presume among
Others, was One Important Reason, wh gave the saying—
'*Know Thy Self*'—So much fame for Wisdom among ye
Antients.

But yr Grace will say, I know not myself when I write thus
to You. But pray, Madam, why not? May I not have ye
liberty to repeat to You yr own Thoughts /[verso]/ when I
can furnish nothing better? And these are yr own Thoughts,
as far as I can collect them from yr Conduct. And if That
imposes on me, wh of Us, Madam, is most to blame?

The Infection among ye Cattle does not spread; & the
Pleuretick Fever is more mercifull than at first. I bless God
I escaped it; & I rejoyce at Miss Parson's Recovery. She
has happily got rid of one Pain in her Side; but she is at a
time of Life very liable to Another. If the shaft shd come
                                                              it
from a wrong Quiver Yr Grace will gently extract   & apply
a Medicinal Balm more pretious than that of Gilead. For
what Tree drops Wisdom? But tho You are an excellent
Surgeon in these delicate Cases, yet pardon me if I advise
You (Strange Advice to a Dutchess!) to be a Tinker. Mend
one Hole, by making Another. It is ye surest Method if I
have any knowledge of ye female Heart. And if I know my
own, I am with ye greatest Respect
                         Madam
                              Yr Graces most Obedt
                                 & Obligd Humble Sevt
                                    EYoung.

Madam Miss Lee gives her humble
Duty, & I desire mine to my Ld Duke
& best Respects to all near & Dear
to your Grace. Wellwyn. Decmr 28. 1746

209. Welwyn, Herts. [Su.] 11 January 1746/7.
Samuel Richardson.

Not traced.—*Monthly Magazine*, xxxvii (1 March 1814), 141.

Wellwyn, Jan. 11, 1746–7.
Dear Sir,
   I always suspected the world to be a little foolish, but on
further thought I find it not only foolish, but folly itself,
folly in the extreme.
        Non vitiosus homo es, Zoile, sed vitium.[1]
A full and strong conviction of the vanity of the present, and
of the importance of the future, is, I think, the most complete
notion of human wisdom. Now the very reverse of this seems
to be the almost universal maxim of mankind. But it is
something, you'll say, to be wise for the present. But in that
too they as notoriously fail. For what is being wise for the
present, but taking care of one's self? And what is one's self
but body and soul? But they neglect the first as much as the
last; or rather they neglect the first by neglecting the last; for
a wise Providence has so ordered it, (to make our happiness,
though divided by different states and periods, yet still, as it
were, of a-piece) that virtue is the best physician. And what
is virtue, but obedience to reason? And reason, I think, strict
reason, as virtue's apothecary, provides for us, at this time,
tar water. I have found from it surprising good effects; and
I am verily persuaded, that if you can but be obstinate in
your perseverance, you will do the same. Despair often
imposes itself upon us under the specious, but false character, of modesty and resignation. But those soft and amiable
virtues must be quite consistent with the full prerogatives
of courage and resolution, or they are cheats; they are not
what they pretend to be. It is with the human virtues, as with
the divine attributes, they are allies, not rivals. As much as we
take from their consistency, so much we take from their very
being. Despair not, my dear friend, but proceed and prosper;
and let us, when we meet in the summer, jointly praise and
adore that indulgent Providence which has sent so very noble

   [1] Martial, xi. 92: 'You are not a wicked man, Zoilus, but wickedness itself.'

a remedy in our days; and, I am sorry to say, in our necessities.

You make an apology for not writing: I write, because I'm at leisure; you forbear, because you are not; and both these are equally right: so that your apology wants an apology. If I'm apprehensive that I lay a tax on your time (which I know is so precious with you) by my writing, I shall be forced to forbear. Clarissa is my rival, and such a rival I can bear: she'll pay me what you owe me, tho' you shou'd owe the correspondence of an age. To the children, not of your pen, and to Mrs. Richardson, Caroline joins in the best wishes and respects.

I am, dear Sir,
Your affectionate and
obliged humble servant,
E. Young.

They who have experienced the wonderful effects of tar-water, (of which I am one) reveal its excellencies to others; I say reveal, because they are beyond what any can conceive by reason, or natural light. But others disbelieve them, tho' the revelation is attested past all scruple, because to them such strange excellencies are incomprehensible. Now give me leave to say, that this infidelity may possibly be as fatal to morbid bodies, as other infidelity to morbid souls. I say this in honest zeal for your welfare. I am confident, if you persist, you'll be greatly benefited by it. In old obstinate, chronical complaints, it probably will not show its virtue under three months; tho' secretly, it is doing good all the time. I will pay my tar bill in Hilary term. Adieu.

210. Welwyn, Herts. [Su.] 11 January 1746/7. Duke of Newcastle.

British Museum, Add. MSS. 33710, f. 41.[1]—Thomas, p. 595; Shelley, p. 200.

> Wellwyn
> Hertfordshire
> Jan 11th
> 1746.

May it please your Grace.

Will your Grace pardon me, if, conscious of your high Engagements, and timerous of interrupting, I presume only just to subscribe mself, with ye most profound Respect, and humble Hope of your graciously promisd Favour,

> May it please your Grace
> Your Grace's
> most Obedient &
> Dutifull Humble Sevt
> Edward Young.

PS.

I have been, my Ld Duke,
twenty four years on Duty.[2]
My Children,[3] both as to Age,
& service, wear Mitres.
And ye Dutchess of Portland
has told me (what I hope
is true) That your Grace
will be Kind.

---

[1] Young sent this letter under cover of his letter of 17 January to the Duchess for her approval.

[2] Young must be alluding to his having stood unsuccessfully for Parliament in the contested election at Cirencester in March 1722.

[3] i.e. clergy younger than he.

211. [Sa. 17 January 1746/7].¹ Duchess of Portland.

Longleat MSS. (96) 159–60.—Bath, pp. 303–4.

May it please yr Grace
    As You are my Oracle, I have obeyd ẏour Commands.²
But I consider my Letter only as a Carriage for yr Graces
Artillery: Tis yr Influence must do all ye Execution. But
whatever Success attends yr Engineering I shall thank You,
if not for Success, yet for yr Good Example. Few will do so
much for their Friends: Wt then will become of they [*sic*]
Foes? And yet they are recommended to their Goodwill. But
in this, as in some other Debts, ye Verge of ye Court is a
Sanctuary. Virtue has great Advantages, Its *cheif* Advantage
is out of Dispute; but ^if^ it was out of ye Case too, methinks
its present Advantages shd recommend it to our Favour. Wt
Reputation does it gain? Wt Esteem & Affection Secure?
Men are so fond of Reputation, yt by Letters, & Arms &c:
they will take infinite Pains to procure it. Virtue wd bring
it at a cheaper rate. But yt Study they think harder /[verso]/
than Algebra, & had rather lose a Limb than another mans
Wife. I beleive the Reason why men prefer Vice to Virtue, is,
because, it must be ownd, that Virtue is more like a Wife,
than a Mistriss; Virtue has equall (not to say far Superior)
Joys; but then ye Joys of Virtue have ye Misfortune of being
Unprohibited Goods. If they want more Pleasures than
Virtue can afford, why do They not seek them, where your
Grace, & Mrs Delany have so happily found them, in ye
curious & elegant Arts? These, tho not Morall, are Intellectual Pleasures, wh is next door to ye Former; & Both are true
Marks of ye Human race; Such as are Incommunicable to
ye Creatures beneath us; & Such, as may one Day, (if we
please) set us on a Level with Those glorious Beings, wh are
at present infinitely above us; wh are now now [*sic*] our
Directors & Guardians, but will be (if we are Wise) our dear

¹ The date of this letter is determined from the following letter.
² The death of Nicholas Clagett, Bishop of Exeter, on 8 December had moved the
Duchess to renew her interests in Young's advancement. Clagett was succeeded on
8 February 1746/7 by George Lavington (1684–1762) who is said to have had the
unsolicited support of Hardwicke and Newcastle.

Companions, & familiar Friends. /[conjugate leaf]/ This is a
triumphant Consideration, & allmost makes it an Astonishment, yt good People shd be (wh notwithstanding they are)
afraid of Death. Now, Madam, since to converse with Those
who have wisely chosen to gather their Flowrs of Pleasure
out of ye two Upper Beds of human Happiness, ye *Morall* &
Intellectual, & have left ye Leeks & Onions of *Sensuality* to
those inferior Beings whose Poverty of Nature affords them
no better Repast, & to those Ægyptian Constitutions of our
own Species, wh have no Passion for ye Promisd Land;
Since, I say, to converse with Such is ye greatest Happiness,
& Improvement in this Scene, & ye fairest Promise of a
Better, Your Grace will easily apprehend that it was with no
small concern that I found myself debard ye Possibility of
waiting on You at Bullstrode, as I proposd to do. I am
Madam yr Graces

most Obedt & Obligd
Humble Sevt   EYoung

Miss Lee gives her Humble Duty
to yr Grace.
[in left margin of front of second leaf]
I beg Madam my humble Duty to my Ld Duke, my humble
service to Mr Achard, & my Non-episcopal Blessing & best
Wishes to ye Little Ones.

212. Welwyn, Herts. [Tu.] 20 January 1746/7. Duchess of Portland.

Longleat MSS. (95) 157–8.—Bath, pp. 302–3; Shelley, pp. 211–12.

Wellwyn
Jany 20.
1746/7

May it please Your Grace
    On Saturday I sent Your Grace a Letter by a Courrier,
like other Princes, wh I hope came to hand. That for ye D.
of N——[1] I sent open, hoping You would be so good to

---

[1] The letter to Newcastle of 11 January.

Seal it, after Perusal. How Affairs may goe, by yr Graces favour, I can not tell; but at present to me they are very Mysterious. On yr Graces Saying in a Letter, about 6 Weeks, or more agoe,—That a Friend of yours wd be considerd, if any Removals beneath were occasiond by Bp Clagets Death, thro ye Dominion of Selflove, I construed Myself to be ye Man meant; & employd my thoughts in Sumptuous Plans for ye Consumption of my future Abundance; Taking it for granted that Your Grace had receivd some Intimation of ministerial good Intention towards me. From this golden Dream I was awakd /[verso]/ by ye Thunder of Mr Robert's Letter;[1] wh indeed, did not Kill me, but filld me with great Astonishment, as being utterly at a Loss how to reconcile His Storm, & Yr Grace's Sunshine together. This Astonishment was Scarce over, when Your Grace filld me with New, by taking a Dead Cause in Hand, for Dead in all Appearance it Seemd to me. Now ye Question is, Whether Your Grace will please to Explain, or to keep me in ye Dark, as they do Nightinggales, that they may Sing the Better. The First will be ye Kinder Office, tho ye Latter will be ye better Jest. But I acquiesce in This, That Yr Grace will certainly do what is most Proper to be done.

Madam, I write this Letter, least my Courrier should have ~~an~~ got Drunk, & given my Letter directed to ye Duke (to whom my humble Duty) to some Dutchess of his own. She will be surprizd to find herself in your Graces Company, with two or /[conjugate leaf]/ Three Ministers of State about her. And who knows but that I might find my Account in her Acquaintance; *Tis certain Nell Gwin made Dr Ken a Bishop.*[2]

When Mrs Delany calls for Inspiration, the Sun shd call for Light. I long to see, but not to Judge, her Performance; & I think I make a prudent Choice; For if People have not

---

[1] Not extant.

[2] When Thomas Ken (1637–1711) was chaplain to Charles II he had refused to open his home to Nell Gwyn (1650–87), saying that 'a woman of ill-repute ought not to be endured in the house of a clergyman, and especially the King's chaplain' (William Hawkins, *Short Account of T. Ken, D.D.*, 1713, p. 9). When the see of Bath and Wells fell vacant in 1684, the King said it should go to 'the good little man that refused his lodging to poor Nell' (J. L. Anderson, *The Life of a Layman*, 1851, p. 142). It was Young's father who preached the sermon at Ken's consecration to the bishopric on 25 January 1684/5.

more Vanity than sense, it will ever be less Pleasurable to criticise than to Enjoy. I beg my humble Service to Her & Mr Achard, & am

> Madam
> Yr Graces
> most Obligd & Dutifull
> Humble Sevt
> EYoung

Miss Lee Sends her
Humble Duty to yr Grace.

213. Welwyn, Herts. [Tu.] 3 February 1746/7.
Duchess of Portland.

Longleat MSS. (97) 161–2.—Bath, pp. 304–5.

> Feby 3d
> 174$\frac{6}{7}$.

May it please your Grace

I return my most cordial Thanks for the Pains You have been pleasd to take in my Favour; If that will not do, Nothing will, & I resign my chimericall Expectations, which it is a Shame I shd have retained so long. I consider it as a sort of a Curse on the Clergy, that ye Nature of their Provision in *this* Life keeps them generally gaping after Preferment so long, that they forget ye Next.

Business, Madam, calls me to Town in about three Weeks, when I shall not fail to pay my Duty at Whitehall. I receivd a Letter last Post, requesting Miss Lees consent to petition ye Parliament for the sale of Frogmore; I know nothing at /[verso]/ all about it. I suppose Miss Parsons may have talkd with your Grace concerning it.[1]

---

[1] The lease of Great Frogmore House, Windsor, being part of the estate of Mary Dutton, Duchess of Northumberland, who had died 27 August 1738, had been bequeathed to Grace Parsons with the stipulation that if she married without the consent of her guardian, or if she were to die without issue, the estate was to be divided among the heirs of the Duchess of St. Albans and of the Earl of Litchfield (Somerset House, P.C.C. Brodrepp 220). As maintenance of the house was proving unsatisfactory, the trustees of the Northumberland estate were attempting to dispose

Madam, I must let you know that I have a new Nighbour[1] at ye House that was my Lady Cathcarts; she is an Irish Lady, & This is ye scheme (viz) she is to have possession of this English Villa in lieu of an old Castle in ye utmost North of Ireland, frowning over ye Sea, in which Lady Cathcart is to be Imprisond, till some generous Knighterrant shall come to her Releif & rescue her immaculate Virginity from the merciless Tyranny of ye Gyant Maguire.

My Law-business is occasiond by Disputes arising from ye Death of poor Mr Lee.[2] Mr Murray is my Council; & allways shall be so, for He gave me excellent advice when He bid me expect Nothing. And your Grace was an excellent Prophetess, /[conjugate leaf]/ when You sayd we should not obtain a Positive Answer. None ever receivd Other than an Ambiguous Answer from ye antient Oracles, And your Grace knows who was the Author of them. And yet Mr. Roberts & your Grace is for having me go to Delphos. I will when I am in Town if Yr Grace continues of ye same Opinion, being in This, & all Things.

Madam
Yr Graces most Obedt
& most Humble Sevt
EYoung.

As I must soon Resign in much more material Points, I bless God I am Resignd in This. I humbly thank yr Grace for your kind Wishes & Endeavours, & shall call off my Thoughts from so dead a scent to Other Game: I shall send them to take a Turn /[verso]/ not among the stalls, but among the Tombs, of Westminster Abby; There Ambition will go out, as a Taper in a damp Vault: I will no longer set my Thoughts on ye Pinnacle of the Temple, to take a View

of the lease. Caroline Lee's consent, with that of the other residuary legatees, was necessary before sale could be effected. The lease was finally sold in August 1748. (For a full account of Great Frogmore House, see T. Eustace Harwood's privately printed *Windsor Old and New*, 1929.)

[1] Unidentified.

[2] For a full account of this suit, entitled: 'Caroline Lee and Frederick Young, infants, by Dr. Edward Young their next friend, plaintiffs, *versus* Elizabeth D'Aranda, widow, and William Coxe, doctor of physick, and Martha his wife, defendants', see H. Pettit, 'Edward Young and The Case of "Lee vs D'Aranda" ', *Proceedings of the American Philosophical Society*, cvii (15 April 1963), 145–59.

of ye Glories of the World, least I fall down & worship Him to whom they belong. Nor do I, Madam, take this Resolution alltogether out of ye regard to That Motive which *ought* to determine me, to it; but out allso of mere Human, secular Prudence; for I find that Expectation, in a Point of this Nature, hurts me much more than Despair.

I beg Madam my humble Duty to my Lord Duke &c. Pray let Ld Edward know he need not any longer be jealous of me as to His Palace at Lambeth.—Were all Bishops as Innocent wt a glorious Bench shd we have in ye House of Lds?

214. [February 1746/7].[1] Duke of Newcastle.

British Museum, Add. MSS. 32710, f. 250.—Thomas, p. 596; Shelley, pp. 212–13.

May it please Your Grace.

Permit ^{me} humbly to state my Case. I have been Chaplain to his Majesty, (Prince, & King) for more than five & twenty years.[2] Some years agoe, by ye Dutchess of Portland, I obtaind yr Graces Promise of Favour after Two or Three were preferd. After more were preferd, I presumd to wait on Your Grace,[3] & You was pleasd to renew my Hopes. Since that Vacancys have been made, But how far I may still flatter myself with Hopes of Your Grace's Favour, I can not tell.

But This I know, that I have sought all ye means in my my [*sic*] Powr, to show that great Respect I owe to Your Grace. Not yt I pretend to ye least Title to your Graces Protronage [*sic*], but most humbly hope Your Regard so far only, as the Nature & Reason for Things, to the generous & equitable mind, even of a Stranger, would speak in ye Favour of One who has servd so long, without any Reward but the Honour of it.

---

1 The date is that of the endorsement on the back of the letter.
2 Since Young had been in clerical orders only since 1724, he may be counting earlier years in political service or it is possible that the letter was dated inaccurately.
3 See Young's letter to the Duchess of 21 August [1745].

Pardon me, my Lord Duke, ye Liberty I take in writing This & permit me, in most humble Hope of learning Your Graces good Pleasure, to subscribe myself.

May it please your Grace
Your Graces most Obedient
& Dutifull Humble Sevt
EYoung.

215. [London]. [?M. 23 February 1746/7]. Duchess of Portland.

Longleat MSS. (100) 165.—Bath, p. 305.

Madam

My Long service to his Majesty; my Court to the 2 Brothers,[1] & yr Graces Recommendation, These Three found a *very just Title* to Favour. The Dukes absolute Promise to me myself, yt after 2 or 3 were provided for, I shd be preferd; This *heightens* yt Just Title; Yr Graces last so signal Interposition in my Favour, makes yr Just Title *still Higher*. After This to sue, wd be Mean in any that wanted not Bread: It wd be Mean at any time of Life; but Monstrous, at Mine. I am therefore fully resolvd to stir no farther, wh is only taking Pains to be Despisd.

But I long to thank yr Grace for yr Zeal to befriend me, & therefore will wait on You punctually by Ten Tomorrow morning; being obligd to be at Lincolns Inn before Twelve.

I am Madam
Yr Graces Dutifull
Humble Sevt
EYoung.

[1] i.e. Henry and Thomas Pelham (Duke of Newcastle).

216. [London]. F. [?27 February 1746/7]. Duchess of Portland.

Longleat MSS. (99) 164.

Madam

If ye Duke would have done anything for me, He wd have made a merit of it to yr Grace. Your hearing nothing from Mr Stone is a decisive Answer. I will expose myself no more.

I am sorry I could not pay my Duty to your Grace sooner; but if You are at home between six & seven on Sunday Evening I will have ye Honour of waiting on You.

Yr Graces much Obligd
& most Obedt Humble Sevt
EYoung

Friday morning.

217. [London]. [Tu.] 3 March 1746/7. Duke of Newcastle.

British Museum, Add. MSS. 32710, f. 297.—Thomas, pp. 596–7; Shelley, pp. 214–15.

March ye 3d 1746.
7

May it please yr Grace.

The Dutchess of Portland lately sent to Mr Stone, & expressing her sollicitude for my success, transmitted, thro his hands my Letter to yr Grace. But she not having heard any thing from Mr Stone since, her Grace fears the worst, & I am persuaded the multiplicity of higher Affairs has prevented Yr Grace from considering the *full state* of my Case; how *singular* it is, & how very *Distinct* from all Others that apply for yr Graces Favour.

I am, my Ld Duke the *only Person* living that has served above twenty years for Nothing; The *only Person* who served his Majesty when Prince, that was not preferd; And, I beleive, ye *only Person* that is in a worse situation with Yr Grace, than He was four years agoe. Then, yr Grace was pleasd to promise to provide for me after 2 or 3; but *now*, I have nothing of an *express*, & *certain* nature to rely on.

This, may it please yr Grace, seems somewhat Hard: But This is not the Worst: I am confident yr Grace does not consider, that not only my Fortune & Family, but my Character too, feels ye stroke of my being thus overlookd. It is not only my *Loss*, but my Reproach & Infamy. For what must the World think of me, who by so professd & eminent a Patron of Worth & Learning, am thrown aside? And that too, when all possible Efforts of various Kinds have been made to procure his Favour; & When Both ye Arch Bishops & Mr Pelham are ready to second the D[utches]s of Portland's Intercession with yr Grace? And when Yr Grace yourself (I flatter myself,) would be prevaild on to recommend me, if the Disposal of Preferment, was in Other hands? There's not only something Uncommon, but something strange, therefore, in my Case; Especially, if it be considerd, that confering Favour on me /[verso]/ will, in Effect, be prefering *Two*; since my Term must be short in it; For I have many years been asking Blessing of my Juniors on ye Bench,

& can not reasonably hope much of Life ‸to come.

For These Reasons I am not my Ld Duke more sorry, than *Ashamd*, of a Repulse. That yr Grace would not brand me, is, in Effect, ye favour I presume to ask. And therefore I most humbly hope Yr Grace will reconsider my Case. For why should I of all men be made a Contradiction to yr Grace's generall Conduct? Why should I be made ye *single* Drawback, from yr illustrious Character of encouraging Letters; & of succouring such t̶h̶a̶t̶ ‸as eminently suffer in their Equitable Pretentions, & can plead so just a Title to his Majestys Favour?

With ye most profound Respect I beg leave to subscribe myself,

> May it please your Grace
> Your Grace's most Obedient
> & most Dutifull Humble Sevt
> Edward Young

218. Welwyn, Herts. [Th.] 9 April 1747. Samue
Richardson.

Not traced.—*Monthly Magazine*, xxxvii (1 March 1814), 141–2.

                                        Wellwyn, April 9th, 1747
Dear Sir,
    The delightful weather we have had brings forward ou
season for the steel-water, and consequently of my enjoying
you at this place, for your health, and my great pleasure
I do assure you, from the authority of the best physicians, and
from experience, which is a better physician than the colleg
can afford, that this spring has every virtue of Tunbridg
in it.
    I have corrected the *Eighth Night*,[1] you will let me know
when you have occasion for it. I forgot to tell you that thi
place will be as salutary to Clarissa as to yourself; for amic
your multiplicity of affairs, how you can sufficiently attend
to her charms is to me astonishing. Though we are told tha
Venus rose from the sea, yet I do not remember that it wa
from the sea in a storm; which seems to me no unapt resem
blance of your London life. My best love and service to yoι
and your's. I am,
                        Dear Sir,
                        With true affection and esteem,
                            Your faithful humble servant,
                                        E. Young.

219. Welwyn, Herts. [Th.] 16 April 1747. Duchess o
Portland.

Longleat MSS. (101) 166–7.—Bath, pp. 305–6; Shelley, pp. 216–17.

                                                Wellwyɪ
                                                Ap: 16
                                                1747.
Madam
    Amid so many dear Domestick Engagements of Heart, &
so many loud Calls from ye Gay & Great around You, is i

---

[1] This formed part of a volume of the *Night-Thoughts* containing the last thre
'Nights', printed by Richardson, but not published until 30 January 1747/8
For the delay, see Pettit (1954, pp. 36–7).

possible Your Grace can think of One so much out of ye way,
of such an Invisible being as yr humble servant? I beleive
not; I must therefore let Yr Grace know yt You commanded
me to write; & that This comes therefore from ye Pen of
Obedience, not of Presumption. But as I have no Business,
& but little Invention what shall I say? I will [illegible word]
tell You a melancholy, but true, Tale, of too late a Date.

A young Woman (now about twenty one) of good Birth &
better Principles was some years in my Family. About two
years agoe her much older sister,[1] who had long been governess of my Family & me, marryd, settled in town, & carryd
her younger sister with her. A young Apothecary in good
Business & Circumstances /[verso]/ courted her, won her
Affections: mutual Vows of Marriage were passd. Things
standing thus, she came down for a month or two   to me   ye
latter end of last Autumn. The thing was kept warm by
Letters every Post; I invited, nay pressd him to come down
to her, knowing ye Pain of absent Lovers. But Business, He
sayd, hinderd him. She returned to Town in high Expectations, just before I was last there. The spark visited Her;
but his Behaviour was cold; she burst into Tears: On which
He sayd. 'My Dearest I understand those Tears; They
upbraid me. And so far they agree with my own sentiments;
I upbraid myself. You feel, I see, the Force of Love, &
therefore will ye more easily pardon ye same Weakness in
Another. I feel it to Distraction, but ask ten thousand Pardons, tis for Another Person. I courted Her some years agoe,
but she absolutely /[conjugate leaf]/ refusd me; which
occasiond the fatal step I have taken with You. But since
You have been in ye Country, I have receivd intimations
that she has thought better of it. The Temptation is irresistable, & therefore we must part.'—And so He took his
Leave: A Duke cd have done no more.

The Heathen Deities were sayd to laugh at ye Perjuries
of Lovers; & if yr Grace is as much a Heathen as You are a

---

[1] Mrs. Letitia Ward (1695–1761), second wife of Alexander Ward (d. 1750) of
Charles Street, Westminster. She was the second daughter of William (d. 1729) and
Letitia (1669–1700) Battell of Digswell, Herts., adjacent to Welwyn on the south.
Her father had been Rector of Digswell from 1687 to his death. Her younger sister
was probably Isabella, daughter of her father's second wife, Margaret (d. 1737).

Goddess, You perhaps may laugh with them. But I can not.
If she lives a thousand years she'll never feel greater Pain.
And a good Heart in Pain is the most melancholy sight in
the World. The sole Consolation is, That a good Heart in
pain, by pain will be made still Better. But what young Lady
of yr Grace's Acquaintance would better her Heart on terms
like These? With Respect & Gratitude I am

> Madam
> Yr Graces most Obedt
> & most Humble Sevt
> EYoung.

My humble Duty to my Ld Duke,
My humble service to Mr Achard,
And may Providence extend its
wing over ye beautifull Blossom
of yr Graces Blood, & preserve ym
from every Blast.

220. Welwyn, Herts. [Su.] 3 May 1747. Samuel Richardson.

Not traced.—*Monthly Magazine*, xxxvii (1 March 1814), 142.

Wellwyn, May 3, 1747.

Dear Sir,

Mr. Grover, in a late letter, told me he designed to come
with you to Wellwyn, but that the loss of his mother prevented it. This made me take it for granted you designed to
come. Miss Lee, who has talked with Mrs. Richardson,
intimates the contrary. Mr. Grover's concern wants amusement. Your quitting tar-water demands steel in its room;
since Wellwyn has steel, and is a new place to Mr. Grover,
Wellwyn is a perfect refuge to you both, putting me quite
out of the case. Mr. Grover told me in his letter that you was
exceeding good; not designing it, I suppose, as an article of
news. But the best have their faults, and the wisest their
errors; if therefore you favour me not with your company,
or give satisfactory reason for the contrary, I shall charge
you with both. I hope in God, you do not continue to com-

plain as you did in your last. Dispense my love and service
to Mrs. Richardson, and her little ones. I am,

Dear Sir,

Most truly your affectionate

humble servant,

E. Young.

In a fortnight's time the Chalybeate season begins.[1]
My humble service to Mr. Grover.
P.S. Since I writ my letter, a poor lady with a cancerous
breast called on me. Some time ago (having seen prior,[2]
several of that kind that had been relieved, and some cured
by tar water,) I advised her to drink it; she has drank it nine
weeks, and is now frightened out of her wits, because it has
occasioned a bloody discharge. But I hope, on the contrary,
that it is a good sympton; for how should a load of peccant
matter be carried off without a discharge? I beg you to tell
the case to your neighbour, and my fellow-critic on Clarissa,
Mr. ———,[3] the surgeon, and desire to know his opinion in
the matter. As he is a surgeon of great repute, and has drank
tar water himself, he must be a competent judge in the case.
Please to give my humble service to him, and let him know
he'll greatly oblige me, if he will speak out in this very
compassionate case.

221. [Welwyn, Herts.]. [? Mid-May 1747]. Duchess of Portland.

Longleat MSS. (98) 163.[4]

Your Graces most Obedient

& most Humble Sevt

EYoung.

Miss Lee gives her Duty to yr Grace. I beg mine to my Ld
Duke, humble Service to Mr Ashard, & best Wishes to our

---

[1] i.e. when the spring water in Welwyn, rich in iron, would be drunk for its
possible medicinal properties.

[2] Thus the printed text, a mistake for 'in Prior', referring to the work on tar-
water by Thomas Prior.

[3] Mr. John Freke (1688–1756), Richardson's physician identified in Young's
letter of 17 May.   [4] The body of this letter is missing.

little Examples, without Resemblance to whom, we are told, none shall enter into Heaven.

I had the Honour of writing to yr Grace near a month agoe.

222. Welwyn, Herts. [Su.] 17 May 1747. Samuel Richardson.

Not traced.—*Monthly Magazine*, xxxvii (1 March 1814), 142.

Wellwyn, May 17th, 1747.

Dear Sir,

I thank you for the hopes of seeing you here; and if you consider how few are the joys of age, you will not think I flatter you when I say, I greatly rejoice at it. Nor am I very sorry for the multiplicity of business of which you seem to complain; it is profit, credit, and health. As for the request you are pleased to make me, about Clarissa, if I am better qualified for it than yourself, you may command my utmost in it. Nor is this a present, but a debt; I ask a much greater favour of you, in correcting the press for me as to the octavo edition.[1] With true solicitude for your better health, and ardent wishes for your welfare in every shape,

I am, dear Sir,
very affectionately,
your humble servant,
E. Young.

Miss Lee joins my best wishes and service to you and yours. I beg my very hearty respects to Mr. Freke, and a thousand thanks for his kind advice, which is followed.

1 i.e. of the second volume of the *Night-Thoughts*.

223. Welwyn, Herts. [M.] 1 June 1747. Duchess of Portland.

Longleat MSS. (102) 168–70.—Bath, pp. 306–7; Shelley, pp. 218–19.

Wellwyn
June ye 1st
1747.

May it please yr Grace.

I am glad yr Grace has had so pleasant a Ramble, & that you stopd short of Ireland, which is fond of an English Dutchess, & cares not to let them fly home again, when once in her Net. Cor[n]bury,¹ Your Grace says, is a charming Place
, & fit for such a Master. My Lord I know not, but from Mr Pope,² & yr Grace; Now Pope was a Poet, & might therefore fib; my Ld Cornbury must therefore thahk [*sic*] yr Grace for ye good Opinion I have of him.

The Dutchess of Queensberry³ is, Yr Grace says, very entertaining, & so are all Oddities; Peevishness /[verso]/ & Pride are in their own Nature the most Ridiculous things in ye World, & therefore must be exstremely entertaining to such as only see, not suffer from them. If Mr Foot⁴ would take her Grace well off, You would find her much more entertaining still.

I congratulate yr Grace on ye Nuptials of Miss Parsons;⁵ That must, I think, be a very happy Couple if it is not *his* Fault; but a good Wife sometimes makes a bad Husband; as great Prosperity corrupts good Manners.

¹ Cornbury Park, the seat of Henry Hyde (1710–53), Viscount Cornbury, an inveterate Jacobite, whose house guest at this time was the Viscount Bolingbroke. Although the *Dictionary of National Biography* says he never married, the *Complete Peerage* cites the *Political State of Great Britain* for November 1737 as authority for his marriage to 'the Hon. Miss Lee, da[ughter] of the Earl of Litchfield', i.e. Anne (1686–1743), sister of Lady Elizabeth Young.

² Pope and Cornbury had been close friends and Pope had publicly complimented him in 1738 in *The Sixth Epistle of the First Book of Horace Imitated* (ll. 60–3).

³ Cornbury's sister, Catherine (d. 1777), wife of the third Duke of Queensberry, celebrated for her beauty and eccentricities, such as dressing in the fashions of her youth.

⁴ Samuel Foote (1720–77), who had just come into fame as a satiric mimic.

⁵ Grace Parsons had been married 28 May 1747 to Thomas Lambard (1705–70) of Sevenoaks, Kent ('Pedigree of Lambard compiled by T. Streatfeild from the Lambard MSS.', *Halsted's History of Kent*, ed. Henry H. Drake, 1886, i. 52).

Your Grace has sent Ld Titchfield to Westmin[s]ter; no doubt It gave your Grace some care & Concern, & so will every thing in life yt is Valueable, & worth our Wishes. It is greatly for my Lords advantage, & therefore will be greatly for /[new sheet]/ your Graces Happiness. Whatever Advantages a Private Education may have, two very great ones it certainly wants, Emulation, & early Experience in ye Tempers & Talents of Others; the First is ye greatest spur to Diligence; & ye Last is an absolutely necessary Qualification for making any Figure in publick Life. And why, Madam, should we despair of seeing his Grandfather revive in Him? When Ld Titchfield is prime Minister I will apply again for Preferment, & not before. And I think myself happy that your Graces Wishes concur with my Resolution of neither Visiting nor writeing any more.

If your Grace continues your Resolution of leaving the Town in three weeks from ye Date [of] /[verso]/ your Letter, I shall not have the Honour of waiting on Your Grace the latter end of this month, when I am obligd to be on Duty at Kensington. If, I mean, the Gout will give me leave.

Your Grace is jealous either of my bad Head or bad Heart without cause; For I do assure your Grace, that I have not ye least suspicion of Insincerity in your Graces favour to me; but with true Gratitude of Heart remember & acknowledge the manifold Instances of your Partiality to One, who has no title to it, but his true sense of Your Grace's Prudence, Virtues, & Accomplishments, so rarely seen in so eminent a situation, & so conspicuous a Point of Light. /[conjugate leaf]/ Your Grace is so kind as to invite me to Bullstrode; I have ye Assureance to invite You Madam, & my Lord Duke, & Mrs Mountague &c: to Wellwyn I am but four Hours from You, & it may be some amusement to You to laugh at a Country Parson. Madam I shall be proud of that Disrespect & am with ye greatest Truth Madam

Your Graces most Obedient
& Obligd Humble Sevt
EYoung.

Madam, I beg my humble Duty to my Ld Duke, humble service to Mr Achard, & Reverence to ye Innocents.

224. [? June 1747]. Sir William Bunbury.

Not traced.¹

225. Welwyn, Herts. [Su.] 5 July 1747. Sir William Bunbury.

Not traced.—*Correspondence of Sir Thomas Hanmer*, 1838, pp. 347–8.

Wellwyn, July ye 5th, 1747.

Sir,

In answer to ye favour of your letter about ye Play,² I wrote you word, that if you would do me ye honour of a visit for a day or two wth Mr. Garrick,³ we would read ye Play together &c: I continue to wish the same favour being but four hours from town. But as I fear you have now left town, & as I am uncertain where this may find you, I only desire to know if ye Letter I mention came to your hand, and if you have any commands for,

Sir

Yr most Obedient & Humble Sir,

E. Young.

226. Welwyn, Herts. [Su.] 19 July 1747. Duchess of Portland.

Longleat MSS. (103) 171–2.

May it please yr Grace

My schemes are quite broken, I can not go to Tunbridge tho a ten years Habit, & my Health require it. Miss Lee is gone to Ditchley, & has left my Family on my Hands, which I can not leave without Detrement. And tho I bless God my Circumstances are enough both for my Purposes, & Ambitions, yet they can not suffer any Diminution without being

---

¹ Evidence of this letter is found in the letter of 5 July.
² Young was reviving his tragedy, *The Brothers*, written in the 1720s but not produced until 1753.
³ David Garrick (1717–79), since April a partner in Drury Lane Theatre.

felt. The Reason why I accepted not of ye Honour Yr Grace
offerd me in Town was, That I was obliged to be at Wellwyn
on Wensday, & it was but on Moonday Yr Grace made me
yt very kind Offer.

/[verso]/ Madam, I beg I may not be misunderstood, I do
assure You, I am exstremely sensible of ye distinguished
Honour done me, by Yr Graces so particular Countenance,
& ye very first moment that I can with any tolerable convenience I will wait on You & my Ld Duke (to whom I beg
my humble Duty & Thanks) at Bullstrode.

Bees & silkworms are very improving society, & cd we
imitate as much as we admire them, we shd be more excuse-
able for piquing ourselves on our Parts, than we are at
present. I shall be allways proud to ad one Insect more to yr
Graces Family. In ye mean time I beg Yr Grace to give more
into Compassion, than Resentment; nor let my Misfortune
be longer considered as my Fault.

/[conjugate leaf]/ I accept, Madam, my Ld Archbishops
Blessing with great Gratitude; but not to wrong ye Rest of
yr Little Family, I must observe, that there is none of them
but what gives a Blessing to Those with whom they converse. That your Grace may long enjoy yt Natural, High,
Sincere, & Virtuous, Happiness, which such a Fireside was
designd by Heaven to give is ye cordial Wish-es & sincere
Prayr of

> Madam
> Yr Graces most Obedt
> & Obligd Humble Sevt
> EYoung

I beg my humble service
to Mr Achard
Wellwyn July 19. 1747.

227. [Welwyn, Herts.]. [W.] 5 August 1747. Samuel Richardson.

Not traced.—*Barbauld*, ii. 23.

August 5, 1747.

Dear Sir,

If I do not see you now, I shall despair of ever seeing you at Wellwyn. The season of the year, the fineness of the weather, the vacation from business, the smallness of the distance, the benefit to your health, the gratification to your friend, the regard to your promise, and, perhaps, the company of Mr. Cibber, (to whom my humble service) may possibly incline you to confer this much desired favour on,

Dear Sir,
your truly affectionate
humble servant,
E. Young.

My love and service to Mrs. Richardson and the little ones.

It will be no interruption to your amour with Clarissa. She may travel with you, and be assured of a hearty welcome.

228. [Welwyn, Herts.]. [? August 1747]. Duchess of Portland.

Longleat MSS. 208–9.

Madam

According to yr Graces commission to me, I have made enquiry into ye Conveniences at my Neighbours at ye Swan Inn.[1] There are ten or more good Beds, & two good Chambers with two beds Each. This is ye state of ye Swan Inn. But why shd not your Grace do me ye Pleasure & Honour of taking a Bed with me? In some views it may possibly be more convenient to You. Your Grace will favour me with a

---

[1] The Swan, now the Wellington, two doors from Guessens, 'may well date from the 13th century' (W. Branch Johnson, *Hertfordshire Inns*, 1962, i. 103).

Line to let me know your time, & yr Intentions. I beg my
humble Duty to my Lady Oxford, & my Lord Duke. That
a good Providence may guard yr Wellfare, & succeed yr
Designs is the Prayr of

Madam Yr Graces
much Obligd & Obedt Humble Sevt
EYoung.

/[verso blank; conjugate leaf, recto blank; verso]/

PS.

  Your Grace sees that I have finishd my no Letter; & out
of pure modesty I forbore mentioning in it what I have
most at Heart; & what therefore I hope you will permit me
to whisper in a Postscript. I mean Madam, that I wish Yr
Grace would so manage matters as to spend a Day at Wellwyn. It will be a proper Rest in so long a Journey; & I will
have the Honour of endeavouring to render that Day as
agreeable to You & my Lord Duke as possibly I can.

**229. Welwyn, Herts. [Th.] 10 September 1747.
Duchess of Portland.**

Longleat MSS. (104) 173–4.—Bath, p. 307.

Wellwyn
Sepr ye
10th
1747.

May it please Yr Grace

  The Honour of yr Graces Letter of ye 5th I receivd not
till yesterday. And rejoyce that all is well. My Lady Oxford
(to whom I beg my humble Duty) does me great Honour in
remembering me, nor could I have a greater Pleasure than
an Oppertunity of waiting on her, for I *know* her Ladysps
worth so that surveying the Magnificence of ye Place would
be ye least part of my satisfaction at Wellbeck.[1]

---

[1] Young was never to visit Welbeck.

I am concernd for Mrs Delanys Loss, but hope her Apprehensions for Mrs Dews will happily be disapointed.[1] If we did not suffer as much (perhaps more,) from what we Fear, /[verso]/ than from what we feel, the world would be much Happier than it is.

His Grace the little Archbishop will not catch a Fever in his Return, the Weather is now very moderate, & I beg Him to be my Guest in his Return. Your Grace is so good as to think of taking me up in your Journey, but before Miss Lee returns it [is] not in my Powr to be from home, & Her I expect not till ye begining of next Month, at which my Ld Litchfield comes to Town to wellcome his Unckle Fitzroy[2] to England; & then will bring Miss Lee along with him. As my present Fate necessarily fixes me here, your Grace will be sure to find me on my Post whenever you return, & I shall for ye future consider my Post, as a Post of Honour since it gives me an Oppertunity of paying my Duty to yr Grace in your Wellbeck Expeditions.

/[conjugate leaf]/ I dind yesterday at Stevenage[3] in order to prevent the Infection of ye Cattle from being spread among us, wh has allready begun from that Place. Your Graces Friend at ye Swan (for he pretends great Intimaccy wth yr Graces Family) is very sollicitous for your Health, ye Return; the Latter of wh may I suppose, make him so tender of ye Former. With all due & hearty Respects to my Ld Duke ye Little ones, & Mr Achard I am

Madam

Yr Graces most Obedt

& Obligd Humble Sevt

EYoung.

[1] Mary Delany had lost her mother in August and was concerned for her sister's health (Anne, Mrs. John D'Ewes).

[2] Fitzroy Henry Lee (1699–1750), Commodore and Commander-in-Chief of the Leeward Islands Naval station, was welcomed to England from aboard the *Suffolk* in November by promotion to Rear-Admiral. In his will (Somerset House, P.C.C. Greenly 120), made 21 September 1744, he left £100 to his niece Caroline. He is said to have been the source of Smollett's Commodore Trunnion in *Peregrine Pickle* (1751).

[3] A village about three miles north of Welwyn.

230. Welwyn, Herts. [Th.] 8 October 1747. Duchess
of Portland.

Longleat MSS. (105) 175.

Wellwyn Oct ye 8
1747.

May it please Yr Grace
   The day after I left You at St Albans¹ I was seizd with a
sore throat, which was severe on me for some Days, & then
ended in a Fever, of which I have not yet got ye better. Many
of my Neighbours are in ye same Condition, & those that
are not befriended more by Nature than by ye Physitian,
die. It cheifly affects my Head, which makes writing very
Uneasie to me & therefor I humbly hope Your Grace will
pardon this short Advertisement from
                              Madam
                       Yr Graces most Obedt
                          & Obligd Humble Sevt
                                 EYoung.

   I humbly beg
My service, Love, &
Humble Duty where
most Due.

231. Welwyn, Herts. [F.] 16 October [1747]. Robert
Dodsley.

Address: To Mr. Dodsley at / Tullys Head in Pall Mall / London. *Postmark*:
Wellin 17/OC.
Colorado MSS. (Pettit); See reproduction opposite.—Pettit, 1954, p. 37.

Wellwyn
Oct. 16
Sr
   I am sorry Illness prevented your calling on me. I have
been near Death my self, but I bless God am better.—If you

---

   ¹ Young had apparently accompanied the Portlands from Welwyn to St. Albans
on their return from Welbeck to Bulstrode.

Welwyn
Oct: 16

Sr I am sorry I shall never have your
calling on me. I have been over Dr Young
.1749. but I beg you an answer — If you
will give a hundred Guineas you shall have
the whole Copy. If you will not I beg you
to call on Mr Hawkins, & will direct as to y
usual Discou. I am Sr yr humble St

EYoung.

will give a hundred Guineas you shall have the Whole Copy.[1]
                                                          He
If you will not I beg You to call on Mr Hawkins, &   will
direct as to ye small Edition. I am Sr   ∧
                              Yr Humble Sevt
                              EYoung.

**232. [Welwyn, Herts.]. [Su.] 25 October [1747].
Duchess of Portland.**

Longleat MSS. (106) 176–7.

                                                    Oct 25.
May it please yr Grace
   I ask your Pardon for not writing sooner, & what is more
I ask your Pardon for not writing now. For I can say nothing
to ye Purpose. Pain admits of no Rival it entirely engrosses
our Attention. I am free but very few hours in the twenty
four from ye severest twinges of ye Rheumatism; & my
cheifest comfort is, that at my time of day it is not worse.
   I congratulate you on ye good Health, which your Grace
is so good to let me know is now enjoyd at Bullstrode; may
it continue, as it is natural it should, it is ye Portion of Youth;
smiles are as naturally ye growth of early Days, as Flowrs are
of ye spring; The most yt Age can pretend to is to complain
but a Little.
   However yr Graces kind Invitation is not thrown away
on me, I enjoy it, & find it a better Cordial than any my
Doctor has yet prescribd.
   /[verso]/ I should have been very glad to have met Mr
Murray,[2] I know he has parts, Your Grace knows if He has
anything else. I think Mr Terrick a valueable man, & I
believe He will rise apace; there are severall Openings for
him at present. Your Grace is fitting up your Dairy, &
making alterations in yr Garden. The first Princesses were

---

   [1] i.e. to the last three 'Nights'. Hawkins announced them as 'Vol. II' on 30
January 1747/8 and later (7 April 1749) bought them of Young for 60 guineas
(see Appendix A).
   [2] Apparently not William Murray with whom Young was already well acquainted, but possibly a nephew, David Murray (1727–96), now a student at Christ
Church, Oxford.

Dairy maids; & Paradise was nothing but a Garden yt wanted no Alterations.

I heard yesterday from Miss Lee, she is still at Ditchley, her Lover, who has been two years at Inverness, Is coming to Town to meet her, but so long an Absence has given her time to reflect, & she seems to me disinclind to give him ye meeting, unless it can be on terms wh Prudence can justifie, & I much question if such Terms are to be had, tho General B[l]akeney[1] professes for him ye greatest Friendship, & has promisd to recommend Him to Mr Pelham /[conjugate leaf]/ & the King. She is a young Creature of a sweet Temper & good sense, & as I cordially wish her Happiness I should rejoyce if I cd flatter myself, that Your Grace, as Occasion offers, would give her ye Credit & Advantage of your Countenance in life. I beg, Madam, my humble Duty to my Ld Duke, & best Respects to ye Ladys & Mr Achard. I am

Madam
Yr Graces most Obedt
& Obligd Humble Sevt
EYoung.

Madam one particular in your Graces Letter I forgot, Which is, that Bullstrode air is wholsome & fit for an Invalid. I know it to be so, & think it would be my cure; but like ye Invalid at /[verso]/ at [sic] ye Pool of Buthesda,[2] I am such a Crip[p]le I know not how to get into it. Even ye very Hand I write with is a Cripple, & my Head is but little better.

Duchess of Portland to Young. Bulstrode, Bucks. [W.] 4 November 1747.

British Museum, Add. MSS. 32713, f. 384.[3]

Bullstrode Novr 4th 1747

I am very sorry to find by your Letter that your health is still so indifferent that you Cannot yet fix a time when we

---

[1] William Blakeney (1672–1761), Major-General in the army and Lieutenant-Governor of Stirling Castle.   [2] John 5:2–9.

[3] This is the only letter of the Duchess to Young that has survived. It reached Newcastle through his secretary Roberts and is among the Newcastle papers.

may have the pleasure of seeing you. I have been so often Disappointed in the great desire I have of serving you that I shoud almost Dispair that any thing woud be done were there not so great a number of Vacancys[1] but as I am determined not to be made a fool of any longer in that point I will not write any more but shoud be glad you woud acquaint Mr Roberts that if they have a mind to *Please me* they must either make you Dean of Winchester or Residentiary of St Pauls nothing less will I accept or I must insist upon your sending this Letter to Mr Roberts as my Unalterable Determination.

My Lords Comps attends you & best wishes mine attends miss Lee.

I am your
Sincere & Faithfull
Humble Servant
M: Cavendishe Portland

233. Welwyn, Herts. [Su.] 8 November 1747. Duchess of Portland.

Longleat MSS. (107) 178.

Wellwyn
Nov: 8
1747.

May it please yr Grace

It is my Duty by ye first Post to return your Grace my humble Thanks for your very kind Letter, wh I have conveyd to Mr Roberts.[2] And whatever is ye Result, I shall ever love yr Grace for yr Goodness to me, & honour & admire such a bright Example in an Age of Clouds & thick Darkness.

The Papers say that ye Suffolk is come in, Commodore Lee is on board her, & my Ld Litchfield will come to Town to meet his Unckle, & bring up Miss Lee with him, Which I am very glad of, for I am impatient for ye Honour of

---

[1] The death of John Potter, Archbishop of Canterbury, on 10 October, and the reported refusals of the office by two bishops had stirred the clerical community.

[2] i.e. the letter just preceding this.

waiting on yr Grace; & tho my Pains are still frequent, & pretty severe, /[verso]/ yet if I can get a Post-chaise across ye Country, (for I am afraid of ye weather) as soon as Miss Lee comes home, I will set out for Bullstrode, provided my Pains do not encrease. I drink Tar Water for them; & should be glad to know if any such thing is to be had in yr Graces Nighbourhd.

I heard yesterday a high Character of Mrs Lambert[1] from some Ladies her Nighbours, which pleasd me, but by no means surprizd me, as I must consider her as a lovely Vine planted in Kent by your happy hand; & I question not but she will bring forth Fruit in due season.[2] I beg my humble Duty to my Ld Duke &c. And am with all Truth Gratitude & Respect

> Madam
> Yr Graces most Obligd
> & most Obedt Humble Sevt
> EYoung.

Samuel Richardson to Young. London. [Th.] 19 November 1747.

Not traced.—*Monthly Magazine*, xxxvii (1 May 1814), 326–7.

Nov. 19, 1747.

It was an infelicity to me that I was not able to wait on you at your Wellwyn. One part of the time I could have made the excursion, then I must needs wait for other people. I have a very great fault in being will-less. But I will begin, however, late, to be will-full, and to snatch my opportunities as they offer. What contentions, what disputes, have I involved myself in with my poor Clarissa, through my own diffidence, and for want of a will! I wish I had never consulted any body but Dr. Young, who so kindly vouchsafed me his ear, and sometimes his opinion. Two volumes will attend your commands, whenever you please to give me your direction for sending them. I think I shall publish in about a fortnight.

---

[1] Mrs. Lambard, the former Grace Parsons. See the letter of 1 June 1747.
[2] Seven children were born to the couple in the first ten years of their marriage.

Miss Lee may venture (if you and she have patience) to read these two to you. But Lovelace afterwards is so vile a fellow, that if I publish any more I don't know (so much have some hypercritics put me out of conceit with my work) whether she, of whose delicacy I have the highest opinion, can see it as from you or me.—And yet I hope, at worst, there will be nothing either in the language or sentiments that may be so very censurable, as may be found in the works of some very high names, who have, uncalled for by their subjects, given us specimens of their wit, at the expence of their modesty, and even of common decency. Nay, sometimes to the dishonour of human nature.

234. Welwyn, Herts. [Su.] 22 November 1747. Duchess of Portland.

Longleat MSS. (108) 179–80.—Bath, p. 308.

May it please yr Grace

Since my Last I have been in a very bad state; my Days more than ever Painfull, my Nights allmost Insupportable. What I have felt is, I hope, to Yr Grace quite inconceiveable, for so, I am sure, it must be if you was never afflicted with ye Rheumatism yourself. But I bless God I am much, very much better, yet still can not go abroad without suffering by it. As soon as I can I shall attempt waiting on your Grace for Miss Lee is with me now, & sends her humble Duty.

Tho your Grace is so kind to offer it, there is no need of any other Tar-water than that /[verso]/ you mention; its proportions are exactly right. And it is ye only Medicine from wh I receive any manner of Releif.

I do not yet hear anything of ye Result of your Grace's Letter. Tis this day a Fortnight since I had Mr Gore's[1] Promise to put it in Mr Robert's Hand, who I suppose had it ye next Day. And I desird it might be returnd, which is not yet done.

I humbly thank your Grace for ye Offer of your Chaise, I may possibly ask ye favour of having it meet me at

---

1 Charles Gore (? d. 1754) represented Hertfordshire in Parliament at this time.

Ricksmansworth; but as yet I am all Uncertainty &
Complaint.

A second Work[1] by ye Author of Pamela, will be publishd
in a Fortnight, & I fancy your Grace will find amusement
in it; If I mean your Tast is for a melancholy Tale.
/[conjugate leaf]/ I have heard it formerly, & not without
a Tear. But, as I remember, your Grace laughs at Fiction;
If so I must visit others to see them weep. Fictitious Tears
are Detestable, Tears from Fiction are not so. May your
Grace never have Occasion for any other.

I am Madam

Yr Graces most Obligd

& most Obedt Humble

Sevt

EYoung.

Madam I beg my
humble Duty to my Ld Duke &c.
Wellwin, Nov: 22, 1747.

235. Welwyn, Herts. [Tu.] 24 November 1747. Samuel Richardson.

Not traced.—*Monthly Magazine*, xxxvii (1 May 1814), 327.

Wellwyn, Nov. 24, 1747.

Dear Sir,

Many thanks for your kind present! My impatience sends
for it by the bearer. Your humble servant Miss Lee is in
haste to read it, and I am all ear. Be not concerned about
Lovelace. 'Tis the likness, not the morality of a character we
call for. A sign-post angel can by no means come into competition with the devils of Michael Angelo.[2] Wishing you
as much health as fame, I am,

Dear Sir,

Your faithful humble servant,

E. Young.

[1] The first two volumes of Richardson's *Clarissa: or, The History of a Young
Lady* were published on 1 December (Sale, 1936, p. 48).
[2] One of Young's early poems was 'On Michael Angelo's Famous Piece of the
Crucifixion; Who is said to have stabbed a person, that he might draw it more
naturally'.

236. Welwyn, Herts. [Su.] 29 November 1747. Duchess of Portland.

Longleat MSS. (109) 181–2.

May it please yr Grace.

I receivd ye Letter you mention & returnd a full answer[1] to it, in wh I proposd accepting ye favour of yr Grace's Chaise as far as Ricksmansworth, which was then my Plan of waiting on You. But my Pains on ye least cold return with violence, & tho I passionately desire to pay my Duty to your Grace, as yet I want both strength & Courage for ye Attempt. I have not heard one syllable from Mr Roberts, but receivd ye Inclosd[2] last Post from another Hand, wh puts an End to ye Affair. Indeed, Madam, I am ever your Grace's both in sickness & in Health, & I find this /[verso]/ Comfort in my Disapointmt, that it makes my sincere Gratitude to yr Grace, appear to me less mercinary than otherwise it might have done.— Miss Lee gives her humble Duty, & has a full sense of yr Grace's Indulgence to her Insignificancy. As for ye Ladies now with yr Grace I would send them my best Compliments, but that I fear, It would only make them regret that they do not come from a younger Hand. I heartily hope my Ld Duke by this time is perfectly recoverd, for I never in my whole Life was half so well Qualifid, as at present, to pity those that are in Pain. Gout is the Brother-Disease to mine; but I realy beleive it mild as Abel in comparison; Mine is ye Murtherer, mine is Cain.

/[conjugate leaf]/ As I have heard nothing at all from Mr R——,[3] I take it for granted that by this time You, Madam, have; If not, it will ad a great Mystery, to my little Disapointment. That You may ever succeed when your

---

[1] Young's letter of 22 November 1747.

[2] This letter, apparently crucial to any hope of Young's preferment, has not been found. Presumably its implications, without further explanation, were that George II would never assent to Young's advancement.

[3] John Roberts.

Wishes are not set on so unlucky a Card, is ye sincere
Prayr of

Madam

Yr Graces

ever Devoted

Humble Sevt.

EYoung.

Wellwyn
Nov: 29
1747

237. Welwyn, Herts. [Su.] 6 December 1747. Duchess
of Portland.

Longleat MSS. (110) 183–4.

Wellwyn
Decem 6
1747.

May it please your Grace

I accept yr kind Offer of ye Powders with ye greatest
gratitude; for I can not but catch at anything wh promises
me ye least Releif. Nor is yr Grace's Kind, & I am satisfid,
very Judicious, Advice, less wellcome than yr Powders, &
I will inviolably observe it. To reconcile that profound
Taciturnity of a month old to common Politeness, must, I
think, require more than common Address.

If your Grace can conveniently send the Powders to Mrs
Wards[1] in Charles- /[verso]/ street Westminster, she will
convey them to me. Miss Lee gives her humble Duty to
your Grace: I have from Her whom I dare beleive, a very
amiable Account of Domestic Happiness at Ditchley; wth
which I am ye more pleased, because I have receivd rumours
to ye Contrary; and because I think *Him*[2] in a particular
manner entitled to that Happiness which He is so Able, &
so Willing, to give to all He converses with.

[1] Letitia Ward.

[2] George Henry Lee, the third Earl of Litchfield. His marriage to Diana Frankland, daughter of Sir Thomas Frankland, Bart., of Thirkleby, Yorkshire, brought
together two persons fourth in descent from Charles II and Oliver Cromwell. There
were no children of what the Lee family historian called 'this interesting union'
(Elsie Corbett, *A History of Spelsbury*, 1962, p. 205).

Your Grace says You write in such Hast that you fear I can not read your Letter; Madam, I can read it, & understand it, /[conjugate leaf]/ I wish I could deserve it too; but that I never can. However set ye same Indulgence which inspird that kind Letter, set it down as some little degree of merit, that I own a Debt, which I shall never be able to pay. My Humble Duty & Best Wishes to my Ld Duke & All, & beleive me to be

Madam
Yr Graces most
Devoted & Obedt
Humble Sevt
EYoung.

238. Welwyn, Herts. [Su.] 27 December 1747. Duchess of Portland.

Longleat MSS. (111) 185–6.

Wellwyn
Decemr 27.
1747

May it please yr Grace

I begin to flatter myself that I shall find some permanent good Effects from your Grace's kind Present, for, these many years on Colds or other Accidents I have been subject to Rheumatic Pains, but as they were never before so severe or obstinate I never made any Provision against their Return.

Mr & Mrs Terrick were here this last week, & Mrs Terrick told me that my Lady Wallingford had been confind by ye

Gout. I beg my best Respects to   her   Ladysp & warmest Wishes for her Recovery from those Pains of /[verso]/ which I so well know ye Cruelty, & to wh her sex has so little Title.

Some time since I desired that Mr R——[1] at his most convenient Leisure would return to me your Graces Letter. I had in Answer, that He for my service had put it into ye Hands of Mr St——,[2] & that as soon as it was returnd to

---

[1] John Roberts.   [2] Andrew Stone.

him He would return it to me. This three Weeks agoe & I have heard no more of it.

Your Grace told me in a late Letter, that You imagind I had some Friends which I did little suspect, which ^is^ some ballance to My having sometimes suspected Persons to be my Friends, which provd otherwise. /[conjugate leaf]/ If I have such unsuspected Friends, the greater is their generosity of soul, & the more like are they to that Great & only Friend on whom we can ultimately rely; a sure Friend, but Invisible to All, as These are to me.

Let ye transient Pleasure of Lady Andovers short stay be amply made up to your Grace in the Enjoyment of that little stranger Lord Titchfield. And I hope in God my Lord Dukes Complaint will be so far abated, as not too much to interrupt the Delight your Grace must necessarily find in such a Child. I beg Madam, my humble Duty, best Respects Love & Service, Respectively, & am ever

> Yr Graces most Obligd
> & Devoted Humble Sevt
> EYoung

Miss Lee desires her
Duty to yr Grace.

239. [Welwyn, Herts.] [? January 1747/8]. Samuel Richardson.

Not traced.—*Monthly Magazine*, xxxvii (1 May 1814), 327.

Dear Sir,

I have read or heard Clarissa thrice, and the last kiss was the sweetest. I will venture to say that they who read it but once will like it least. From the lazy therefore, however well qualified to judge, you must not expect your due.

No novelist before you ever aimed so much at instruction, and your execution is as happy as your aim is good. It will be owing to the folly or guilt of their parents if all the female youth of our age go not to school to Clariss[a]. Miss Lee is entered already, and hopes, from your kind partiality, that you will place her in the middle class. She pays you her sincere thanks and best wishes. Go on and prosper, and enjoy, and, as generous as your heart is, be not content to make every body happy but yourself, particularly,

Dear Sir,

Your affectionate humble servant

and admirer,

E. Young.

My love and service to your Clarissa'd fire-side. May they all live to be fair comments on their father's work!

Please to accept one of the bound volumes of Night Thoughts from Mr Hawkins.[1]

240. London. [W.] 27 January [1747/8]. Duchess of Portland.

Longleat MSS. (112) 187.

Charles Street

Jan: 27.

May it please Yr Grace

Last night Business drew me to Town, & engages me very closely till it is over. The very first moment I can I will pay my Duty to your Grace, in the mean time I beg you to accept it by letter, & to favour me with the satisfaction of knowing that All under your Roof is well. I return many Thanks for ye Powders, I am, I bless God, better, but not quite free from Pain; & hardly expect to be so, till I am Powder myself. I am

Madam

Yr Graces

most Obedient

& most Obligd

Humble Sevt

EYoung.

I beg Madam
My humble Duty
to my Ld Duke
&c:

[1] 'Nights' VII–IX, published 30 January 1747/8, printed at Richardson's press.

241. [Welwyn, Herts.]. [March 1747/8]. Duchess of Portland.

Longleat MSS. (114) 190–1.—Bath, pp. 309–10; Shelley, pp. 57–8.

May it please yr Grace

Except Betterton,[1] I never knew a Player yt was a good Tragedian; & I never knew a Dancing Master that was a genteel man. And ye Cause is ye same, They both overshoot ye Mark; This is a Fault not to be feard in yr Grace's Band. And ye Reason is plain. For when Persons of low Education undertake Characters of Dignity, they can only *guess* at what it is, & so mistake; but when Persons in high Life do ye same, they *know* what true Dignity is; They, for ye time, only change their *Habits* & *Names*; whereas ye Former must change their *Manners*, & *Nature*; wh is a much Harder Task.

Besides, Madam, who so likely to act a Part well, that is to Pretend to be, wt they are not, as Persons of a Court Education? Dissimulation, wh is puting off ourselves, & Simulation, wh is puting on Anothers Character, I take to be ye whole Science of a Courtier. Nor do I speak this to their Dishonour, but ye Contrary: For, thro ye Depravity of our Nature there is so much in ye Human Heart that ought to be conceald, that I can not but lay it down for a Maxim that 'They who know not how to Dissemble, know not how to Please.' If This startles yr Graces Delicacy, consider, Madam, wt is Virtue, & Religion itself? It is little more than curbing ye naturall Tendencys of our perverse Hearts. If therefore Courtiers instead of curbing, or altering their Passions (wh they can do to Admiration) on secular Motives, they did ye same, on nobler Views, Courtiers would be the

---

[1] Thomas Betterton (?1635–1710), a universally admired actor of his time. The subject of this letter is Young's response to a private performance of his tragedy, *The Revenge*, of which the Countess of Bute wrote to her mother, Lady Mary Wortley Montagu. Lady Mary's response, 10 May 1748, follows: 'I give you thanks (Dear Child) for your entertaining account of your present Diversions. . . . I remember very well the play of The Revenge, having been once acquainted with a party that intended to represent it (not one of which is now alive). I wish you had told me who acted the principal parts. I suppose Lord Bute was Alonzo by the magnificence of his Dress. I think they have mended their choice in The Orphan [by Thomas Otway]' (Halsband, 1966, ii. 400–1).

best Christians in the World. Yr Grace may, therefore, /[verso]/ congratulate some of yr Friends on being so near That, wh I dare say, they very little suspected.

For ye Reason given above, I beleive wth yr Grace, that ye Play will be acted to great Perfection. And there is no Entertainment yt cd give me greater Pleasure. But then I like not ye Reason You give for my being present at it. '*Since you are to Preach so soon &c:*'[1] says yr Grace. I perceive; Madam, ye satyr that is couched in this Argument. You mean 'Since you are to Preach you cant do wiser than to come to ye best School for Acting a Part.'—I grant, Madam, no Preacher can come up to his Precepts; but then He thinks it his Duty so to do; Whereas many a Taylor has acted Alexander ye Great, who never thought it his Duty to demollish ye Persian Empire. This is the Difference (wh yr Grace wd artfully sink) between a Roscius[2] & a St Paul.

However yr Graces Tartness should not rob me of an Entertainment that would give me so great Delight, had I not many real Tragedys, at this severe season, acting round abt me at home; in several Familys Distresses, Disorders, & Death. And why has Providence orderd that melancholy Tales shd give us Pleasure, but to habituate our Hearts to tenderness, that they may not grow Callous, when Oppertunitys offer, wh ^{may} render our Tenderness of some real Use?

I fear Madam, I can not be in Town soon enough. But if ^{not} I am ^{not} utterly at a loss for some Consolation under ye Disapointmt of my Desire to wait on You /[conjugate leaf]/ But ^{For} my Comfort is, that even at this Distance my Pride will be highly gratifid, tho my poor famishd Eyes & Ears do not share in ye Entertainment. For, as it is sayd, that Pygmalions statue grew warm under his Embraces, & of stone became Flesh;[3] so, I am persuaded, how dull &

---

[1] 'This Day the Rev Dr Young is appointed to preach before his Majesty at the Chapel Royal' (*General Advertiser*, 23 March 1747/8).

[2] The celebrated comic actor of Rome in the first century B.C.

[3] Young alludes to the legend that Pygmalion fell in love with his statue of Galatea and was rewarded by having her brought to life by Aphrodite to become his wife. It was in this same year that Jean-Philippe Rameau based an opera on the legend.

Inanimate a Figure soever *The Revenge* may make on ye
common stage, its Condition will be very much alterd under
Such Hands; Their Approbation (not to mention their Performance) will give it Life.

I beg my best Compliments for ye great Honour done
me; & am, (very Untheatrically speaking)

May it please Yr Grace

Yr most Obedt

& most Obligd

Humble Sevt

EYoung.

Madam
Pray my humble
Duty to my Ld Duke
&c:

242. Welwyn, Herts. [Tu.] 12 April 1748. Duchess of Portland.

Longleat MSS. (115) 192.—Bath, p. 310.

Wellwyn

Ap 12

1748.

May it please Your Grace

Miss Lee joyns me in my best Thanks for the favours we
lately receivd in Town; I left it Ill, & tho I bless God I am
better, yet have I no reason as yet to boast.

This minute I receivd ye Rumour of a great Victory in
Flanders,[1] I wish tomorrows Papers do not blast our Laurels.
—I should have waited again on your Grace before I left
Town (as Miss Lee told me You desired) but I was in pain,
& unwilling to make wry faces in Company. Miss Lee has
acquainted Ld Litchfield & her Unckle ye Admiral of her
                                                    is
determanition to marry, so yt matter ~~being~~ past Retreive,
tho /[verso]/ against ye pressing Advice of us All. I wish

---

[1] Young had heard an early report of peace negotiations at Aix-la-Chapelle by
which, according to *The Westminster Journal* of 16 April, France was to 'return all
Flanders' to the allies of Britain.

Count Sax[1] found our officers as irresistable, as they are found to be at Home: This irresistable Hero[2] is at Portsmouth taking his leave of his Friend General Blakeney, who there sets sail for Minorca. I expect him Here at his Return He is purchasing a Majority, ye Bargain is agreed between ye Parties, & ye Dukes leave is waited for, & expected very soon. The man seems to me to be ^a Plain & Honest man, & I can see not much she could fall in love with unless it is his Integrity. Which methinks shd have more Charms for an old Philosopher than for a young Lady. I must give your Grace Joy of Dr Drummonds Mitre.[3] I hope all is well at Whitehall. My humble Duty to my Lord Duke &c: I am Madam

> Your Graces most Obligd
> & most Obedt Humble Sevt
> EYoung.

243. [Welwyn, Herts.]. [Sa.] 30 April 1748. Samuel Richardson.

Not traced.—*Monthly Magazine*, xxxvii (1 May 1814), 327.

April 30, 1748.

Dear Sir,

I received the favour of your books,[4] for which I thank you much. I have not yet read them. When I have you shall hear further from, dear sir,

> Your affectionate humble servant,
> E. Young.

My love and service to all yours.

P.S. Since I writ the above I have read your two volumes through; and am much pleased, nor less surprized, at the many alterations you have made for the better. Clarissa has put Pamela's nose out of joint. I am almost out of heart as

---

1 Count Maurice de Saxe (1696–1750), Marshal General of the French forces.
2 William Haviland.
3 Robert Hay Drummond (1711–76) became Bishop of St. Asaph in Kensington Church on 24 April and later (1761) Archbishop of York.
4 Volumes 3 and 4 of *Clarissa*, which had been published on the 28th (Sale, 1936, p. 48).

to my hopes of seeing you at Wellwyn. If you let this summer slip, I shall be quite so. But the same regard that makes me wish you here makes me cautious of pressing. We need not press but for what is against inclination. And to see you here with your inclinations is what must give the satisfaction I desire. If you should find yourself in the humour for Hertfordshire air, I flatter myself Mr. Grover would bear you company, to whom my love and service.

244. Welwyn, Herts. [Sa.] 4 June 1748. Duchess of Portland.

Longleat MSS. (108) 193–4.—Bath, p. 311.

May it please yr Grace

I much thank you for your very kind Letter, which has set my Heart at rest from ye uneasiness of foolish Expectation & Suspence. Your Graces Endeavours were not ye less Kind for being Unsuccessfull; & to the Kindness of a Friend our Gratitude is due, & not to his success.

I should think myself Happy to see Bullstrode in its Glory, but I fear it will not be in my Powr; The Bride & Bridegroom &c:[1] are with me, & how long their stay, & what Expedition Lawyrs will make in their Concerns with them, (in which I am concernd) is as yet Uncertain, for there is a suit still /[verso]/ depending about her Brother Lees Will which we must attend, till it is finishd.[2]

whom

A Young Gentleman[3] was with me last week, with Your Grace lately made an Assignation. He has but four

---

[1] The marriage of Caroline Lee and William Haviland, now a major in the army, was to take place in Welwyn on 13 July. The *General Advertiser* for 18 July reported: 'On Wednesday last Major Hevland [*sic*] was married by the Rev. Dr. Young, at Welling in Hertfordshire to Miss Lee, Daughter of the late Lady Elizabeth Young: a Lady of great Beauty and considerable Fortune.'

[2] The suit against the D'Arandas was actively pursued during June of this year (H. Pettit, 'Edward Young and the Case of Lee vs D'Aranda', *Proceedings of the American Philosophical Society*, April 1963, cvii. 145–59) but was still unsettled in the following year (8 May 1749, Public Record Office, C12/1450/69).

[3] This may possibly have been Sir William Bunbury who is mentioned in the *Gentleman's Magazine* for May of this year (xviii. 237) as being made 'vicar of Mouldon Hall, Suffolk, besides rector of Reed, Hertfordshire'.

thousand pounds a year, & He came into my Nighbourhood to take Possession of a Parsonage of one Hundred & twenty pounds per an:, but it seems, it is for ye Benefit of a Minor.

I give yr Grace Joy of a glorious piece of News, which probably You may live to see accomplishd, I shall not. Mr Whiston was with me this Morning, & has assurd me that eighteen years hence the Jews will be converted, & that twenty years hence the Millennium will begin; & next Week He begins a Course of Lectures in Town to /[conjugate leaf]/ satisfie ye World in that Particular. Lady Wallingford will probably have a Curiosity to see ye New buildings at Jerusalem for that City is to be rebuilt. Till that Happy scene arrives yr Grace may look with satisfaction on ye Beauties of Bullstrode, but afterwards it will be of no manner of note. If Mr Achard will travell so far, He would probably see that the Mathematicks are as yet but in their Minority. I beg my humble Duty to my Lord Duke & best Wishes & Respects to All. I am

Madam
Yr Graces much Obligd
& most Obedt
Humble Sevt
EYoung

Miss Lee gives
her Duty to
yr Grace.
Wellwyn, June ye 4th 1748.

245. Welwyn, Herts. [Su.] 25 September 1748. Duchess of Portland.

Longleat MSS. (109) 195–6.—Bath, pp. 311–12.

Madam
    I ask Ly Primrose's[1] pardon & your Grace's, that I did not wait on her sooner & oftener, but it was a pretty while

---

[1] The daughter of Peter Drelincourt (1644–1722), Dean of Armagh, and wife (1739) of Hugh, third Viscount Primrose.

after she was In these parts, before I knew of it, & afterwards, I was prevented from that honour exstremely agst my Inclination. Tho I know not what I had lost by it till after my Visit, when she gave me much occasion to think well of her understanding, besides her professing her just & great Opinion of your Grace.

Madam, I accept your very kind Invitation, & his Grace's, to Bullstrode with great Gratitude, & Pride; but whether I shall be so happy as to take ye Advantage of it, as yet I can not say. Mrs Haveland is now in town puting her Goods on board for ye North, but she returns to me next week for some (as yet) uncertain time; I suppose, it depends on ye Majors being commanded to his Post. All that I, therefore, can at present say is that when ever Health & Circumstances admit, I shall be happy in paying my Duty to You.

I am exstremely [glad] to hear so comfortable an account of ye /[verso]/ matrimonial Harmony between Mrs & Mr L——d;[1] & indeed ye more so, because I had lately heard quite ye Contrary; & with this particular circumstance, that tho ye Fact was true, yet Mrs L——d to all her Acquaintances declard ye Contrary. Which I accounted for in my own mind for yt uncommon sweetness of Temper, & Prudence, of wh I think her Mistriss. And tho much urgd (as the Persons knew me to be no stranger to Mrs L——d) all I sayd, or could say, was, That if ye Report was true, I thought myself confident that Mrs L——d was not ye occasion of it.—Or if she is, no Appearances in your sex are ever to be trusted.

Your Grace mentions not a word of my Lady Oxford, tho I writ in hopes of paying my Duty to her on her Journey. Which puts me in mind of Yr Graces going by my Door last year Yourself, as if it had been a strangers. Madam, unextinguished Ambition will put such Things in ones head, tho I who am so often receiving fresh Honours from your Grace, have, I confess, ye less reason to complain.

If, Madam, Mrs L——d is still with you, I beg my best /[conjugate leaf]/ Compliments, & let her know that her Friend Mr Richardson left me but on Saturday last, & that

[1] Lambard.

she may expect to see before Christmas part of her own amiable Picture in ye Remaining part of Clarissa.

I know your Grace has no great Esteem of this Author, therefore in a Letter to You I shall suppress my admiration of him, & will only, instead of Panegyrist, turn Prophet, & let your Grace know that your greatgrandchildren will read, & not without tears, ye sheets which are now in ye Press.[1] They will pay their Grand Mamma's debt to this poor Injurd man; & injurd in a Point wh would touch him most nearly, if He knew your Grace, & knew yr Opinion of him. I beg my humble Duty to my Lord Duke, & best Regards to all; And the present Health you enjoy may continue, & as much Happiness never fail to descend on Bullstrode, as is consistent with ye Prospect of Better Things. I am

Madam
Yr Grace's much Obligd
& most Obedient
Humble Sevt
EYoung.

Wellwyn Sepr 25
1748.

246. Welwyn, Herts. [Su.] 30 October 1748. Duchess of Portland.

Longleat MSS. (110) 197.

Madam

I humbly thank your Grace for your kind Enquiry after my Health, & your Kinder Invitation to Bullstrode, which I should accept with great Pleasure, if it was in my Powr. But your Grace can easily imagine what a state He must be In, who ten Days agoe was at ye Point Death, & escapd by ye loss of a vast Quantity of Blood, at ye Tongue, Neck, & both Arms, four Blisters &c: My Case was somewhat singular, for in about fourteen hours time, I was well, & given

---

[1] The last three volumes (5, 6, and 7) of *Clarissa* were published on 6 December (Sale, 1936, p. 48).

over by my Physitians. By their Directions I am now under a Course, which is Impracticable /[verso]/ but at Home. And indeed Madam I am tird with writing these few Lines, (which I thought it my Duty to do) & therefore beg You to excuse

Madam
Yr Graces most Obedt
& Obligd Humble Sevt
EYoung

Wellwyn Oct 30
 1748.

I beg my humble Duty to my Ld Duke, humble service to Mr Ashard & best Wishes & Respects to the Little Ones.

247. Welwyn, Herts. [Th.] 3 November 1748. Caroline Lee Haviland.

Address: To Major Haviland / at Dundee / In / Scotland. [superscribed: 'At Glasgow.'[1]] *Postmark*: 4/NO.
Reading MSS. (Collins).

Wellwyn
Nov: 3rd
1748

Dearest Child
 I thank you for your kind Letters, & I thank God for the happy Contents of them, that He has protected you from Accidents in your long Journey, & I hope ere this brought you safe to ye End of it. May He make a little comfortable Nest for You in Dundee, & feather it soft with all ye Blessings of This life, and with that which you will find ye sofest [*sic*] Down of all, ye Hopes of his favour in the Next.
 The Papers say that there are but three Regements to continue in Scotland, & General Blakneys is not One of them; and that /[verso]/ the Rest are soon to go for Ireland. Wherever Providence disposes of You remember that you

---

[1] The forwarding address shows that the Havilands had moved on with the regiment to Glasgow preparatory to shipping to Ireland.

have a Friend at Wellwyn, & come to him as soon as You can; where you shall find a most hearty Wellcome. Mrs Ward & July[1] are still here, & to them I leave the news of our Neighbourhood; and with my Love & humble Service to the Major shall only assure you that [I] am

> Dearest Child
> Yr very Affectionate
> Humble Sevt
> EYoung.

248. [? November 1748]. Caroline Lee Haviland.

Not traced.[2]

249. Westminster, Mdx. [Tu.][3] 22 November 1748. Duchess of Portland.

Longleat MSS. (111) 198–9.—Bath, pp. 312–13.

> Charles Street
> Westminster.

Madam

I am greatly obligd to your Grace for your enquiry after my Health. It is, I bless God much better, but my yesterdays Journey to this place has much fateagud me. I am very sorry for Mr Hay, but hope a Lisbon sun may do much, when there are no Physitians to hinder its Operation. Tho I think there is something both in Mr Hay's Manners, & Appearance, that looks as if He was more fit to make an Angel, than a Man; as ye World goes.

---

[1] It has not been possible to identify Caroline's friend July.

[2] Evidence of this letter is the Sotheby catalogue for an auction of 18 January 1877 in which lot no. 164 is described as follows: 'Another long and interesting A. L. s. to the same [Mrs. Haviland] commencing "Dear Child," &c. 3 pages 4to addressed to Major Haviland, of Gen. Blakeney's Regiment, at Glasgo', &c franked by W. Hutchenson (before dating) with seal and portrait, n.d. 3/31-Waller.'

[3] Young is staying at the London home of his neighbour, Mrs. Ward.

This moment I receivd a Letter out of Scotland, & find by it that Mrs Haveland /[verso]/ will soon have it in her Powr (& I dare say in her Inclination) to wait on Lady Bell Monk[1] in Ireland. Thus are we tossd about on the face of the Earth till we are gatherd to our Fathers.

I rejoyce that all is so well at Bullstrode, The Health of those we esteem is our best Cordial under ye want of our Own.

A Friend of your Graces not long since deceasd in Hertfordshire,[2] has I hear many Claimants to what he left behind him, but I hope no one will claim his bad Example of dying Intestate, which occasions all this trouble. I hear his Curiosities will come into ye Hands of your Friend Mr West.

/[conjugate leaf]/ Now I am in Town I shall talk with Mr Richardson on the Point mentiond in your Graces last Letter but One; & if I find him guilty either of Impertinence or Illnature, I shall have a Less Opinion of mankind than I had before; for I own I conceivd him to be as incapable of either as any man on Earth. But we are all very frail, & He that answers for another in allmost any thing, only shows that his Knowledge of human Nature is not equall to his Zeal for his Friend: I beg my humble Duty to my Ld Duke; & my best Compliments to Lady Wallinford & Mr Aschard. I am

Madam
Yr Graces most Obedt
& much Obligd
Humble Sevt EYoung.

Nov 22
1748.

---

[1] Lady Isabella Bentinck Monck, sister of the Duke of Portland, married (31 October 1739) to Henry Monck.

[2] James Bisse (1668–1748), a physician of Codicote, a village adjacent to Welwyn on the north.

250. Welwyn, Herts. [Su.] 18 December 1748.
Duchess of Portland.

Longleat MSS. 202–3.—Bath, p. 314.

> Wellwyn
> Decemr 18
> 1748.

Madam

Not being at home when your Graces Letter came,
This can not come to you till Thursday; & on Thursday
sennight that is St Thomas's Day I am obligd to be at
home again, if I have the Honour of waiting on You; &
that time is so short, that I had rather chuse some other
Oppertunity.

When I was in Town I talkd wth ye Author of Clarissa,
He & ^yr Grace I find from ye begining were of different
sentiments,[1] tho I dare say of equall good Intention; You
for, He against ye Match; He against it, from ye great
/[verso]/ Inequality of Age; Yr Grace for it, from (I suppose)
such an Opinion of ye young Ladys Temper & Prudence, as
renderd ye Objection of no Weight: You profesid Good, &
He, Ill; & now You are both for verifying your several
Prophesies, which is all that I can make, on my best enquiry,
of this Matter.

Mr L—— being often in ye Tunbridge season at ye
Wells, & she, never, tho much enquird after, gave I find
some ground for suspision; but whether a just ground or not,
they themselves alone can tell.

I have got Mr Monk to write to Ireland to procure Mrs
Haviland, who will soon be there, the Honour of Lady Bell's
Countenance at her Arrival in a strange Land. /[conjugate
leaf]/

May This, Madam, find your Grace happy; Happy in
yourself, & in all You hold Dear. This I ardently wish,
because whenever I have ye satisfaction of hearing Good

---

[1] i.e. about the marriage of Grace Parsons.

News from Bullstrode, I shall be truly capable of enjoying
it, tho I am not in ye Place. I beg my humble Duty to my
Ld Duke, & my humble service to Mr Achard, & am

Madam
Your Graces
most Obedient—
much Obligd
Humble Sevt
EYoung.

251. Welwyn, Herts. [Su.] 8 January 1748/9. Caroline Lee Haviland.

Historical Society of Pennsylvania MSS.

Wellwyn
Jany ye 8th
1748.

I assure Dearest Mrs Haviland that she much Obliges me
by her kind Correspondence & that I have more than Entertainment. I have ~~have~~ a great Comfort in her Letters, in
which I discover a Heart that is quite rightset, & a Discernment beyond her years. For Gods sake, Child, continue on
what you justly call ye *safest side*. But that is a Modest
Expression, for it is certainly a Glorious side, as well as a
safe one.

You ᴬ safely & Properly communicate with any
Protestant Congregation, tho in some Forms they may
differ from ours. God Allmighty will regard nothing as to
You, in the Performance of that /[verso]/ blessed, &
sublime Duty, but ye Disposition of your own Heart. And
if that is duely prepard tho thro want of Oppertunity, the
Performance of ye Outward Act, is denyd to your Wishes,
rest assurd that in ye sight of an Allgracious God your
Duty is done; & you will be considerd by Him as an Actual
Communicant.

                                                              such
As ye Duke[1] is arrivd, I hope to hear in your next that ye
Majority is settled. I am obligd to you for talking with ∧
a Relish of Wellwyn, but shall set you down for a little
Hypocrite if you do not see it as soon as possibly You can.
Our Friends at Stagnoe[2] are well & much Yours; the Sea-
Officer is with Them. My best Love & service to ye Major;
tell him I have not supd on Him a great while. Tom tells me
/[conjugate leaf]/ the Fish will not be good till some time
hence. Tell him however that ye net wears apace, if therefore
I do not see him pretty soon He may possibly be worse than
his word. Our poor Friend Mrs Wingate[3] is certainly Worse,
but God wonderfully supports her spirits; & it was but
                        she told me
yesterday morning that ∧   she was very Happy. You
see what it is to have an Allmighty Friend. I like Mrs
Hollows[4] very well. She desires her humble service to You.
Your Friend shall be very wellcome, & I will treat him ye

[1] Charles Lennox (1701–50), 2nd Duke of Richmond, general of the regiment to
which Haviland was attached.
[2] Stagenhoe, the home of the family of Giles Thornton Heysham (d. 1767), in
St. Paul's Walden, Herts., a village five miles north of Welwyn.
[3] Dinah Wingate of Welwyn. She lived until the spring of 1752 when her burial
on 20 May is recorded in the parish register (Hertford County Record Office,
Bishop's Transcripts).
[4] Mary Hallows (1710–90), daughter of Daniel Hallows (1670–1741), Vicar of
All Saints, Hertford, was to be with Young as his housekeeper and companion for
the rest of his life. She had been left £50 outright and shared with two brothers and
two sisters in a £30 annuity by her father's will (Somerset House, P.C.C. Spurway
267, pr. 27 October 1741). She never married. In 1774 when Elizabeth Montagu
wrote to the Duchess of Portland about a female companion for James Beattie
(1735–1803) in the event of his wife's death, she described her memory of what could
only have been Mary Hallows, as 'some matron cloathed in grey, who sat at the head
of [Young's] table in decent sort, helped the guests, took care that the Doctor should
not forget he was at dinner; and when the tablecloth was taken away, the sober
gentlewoman shrunk back into her muslin hood, and with composed serenity of
countenance listened to the conversation of the company. With the same affability
and discretion she poured out the coffee and made the tea, and such was her temper
and deportment she was fit to have been the High Priestess in the temple of the Great
Apollo, if he had wanted a domestic establishment. Never did I see her disturbed in
any of her great offices of carving, helping to sauce, or sweetening the coffee, by any
of the sublime or witty things Dr. Young uttered. Often have I dropped the bit of
chicken off my fork, by a sudden start at something new and ingenious said by our
friend, while she, with a steady hand and sober mind, divided the leg of the goose
from the side, and other things that equally required an undivided attention' (Bath,
1904, i. 340).

better, because he brings me a Letter. Gods Providence take
you Both under its wing.

Most affectionately Yrs
EYoung.

PS.
Mrs. Lambert is brought
to bed of a son.[1]

252. Welwyn, Herts. [Su.] 29 January 1748/9.
Duchess of Portland.

Longleat MSS. 200–1.—Bath, p. 313.

May it please yr Grace

I rejoyce that Mrs Lambert has made her spouse so
agreeable a Present.[2] Such Presents are great Peacemakers,
where Peace is wanted; & pour fresh Oyl into ye Lamp of
Love, where it burns ye brightest. I heartily hope my Friend
R———n[3] was a false Prophet. Prophets of old had two
Provinces, One was to Foretell; ye Other was to Instruct.
Tho He may have faild in ye First, yet He has not in ye Last.
Has your Grace read his Clarissa? What a beautifull Brat of
ye Brain is there? I ~~would~~ wish your Grace would stand God-
mother, & give it its Name;—*Clarissa ye Divine.* /[verso]/
That Romance will probably do more good than a Body of
Divinity. If all Printers could turn such Authors, I would
turn Printer in order to be In[s]trumental in promoting such
Benefit to Mankind.

And yet, Madam, this excellent Offspring of ye Imagination was in danger of having been stifled in its Birth; of, at
least, of having been made a Changeling. I think your Grace
knows Mr Littleton; He, Mr Fielding, Cibber,[4] &c; All

---

[1] Christened Thomas, he was born 13 December 1748, only to die in infancy.

[2] See note to Young's letter of 8 January 1748/9 to Caroline Haviland.

[3] Richardson's observations on the Lambard marriage are of extensive concern
later on. See Young's letter to Richardson of 10 September and others following.

[4] George Lyttelton (1709–73), later (1751) Baron Lyttelton, Henry Fielding, and
Colley Cibber were only a few of the more memorable of Richardson's acquaintances
who offered advice on *Clarissa*.

of them pressed the Author very importunately to make his story end Happily. But does not yr Grace think that it is infinitely better as it is? It does end Happyly, most happily for Clarissa in ye sense of all who do not terminate their /[conjugate leaf]/ notions of Happiness at ye Grave. The Reader that has most Faith & Virtue, will be most pleasd with this Composition. I look on it therefore as a sort of Touchstone for ye Readers of this Virtuous Age, who while they think they are only passing their Judgment on Anothers Ingenuity, will make a Discovery of their own Hearts.

Yr Grace is so good as to desire to see me in Town; when in Town I shall have ye Honour of waiting on You; but I have no thoughts of being there soon. Tho some of my Neighbours seem to have an irresistable Call to ye Green Park.[1] The cold Weather, I suppose, makes them fond of Fire. Instead of Squibbs, & Crackers, I shall humbly content myself with Sun, Moon, & Stars. These glorious Fireworks of that Great King who in ye noblest sense is ye *Author of Peace*; & *Lover of Concord*. /[verso]/

To His blessed Protection, Madam, & Guidance I recommend You, & Yours, & am

> Yr Graces most Obedient
> & obligd Humble Sevt
> E Young

I beg humble Duty to my Ld Duke
& humble service to Mr Achard.

Wellwyn
Jany 29
1748.

---

[1] The peace brought about by the treaty of Aix-la-Chapelle was to be celebrated in Green Park on 27 April when it is likely that Young was present. Preparations had begun in October when on the 22nd the *General Evening Post* announced: 'The Green-Park (between St. James's and Hide-Park Corner) is fix'd upon for playing off the Fire-Works on the Proclamation of the Peace. . . .' It was for this occasion that Handel composed his Fireworks Music. There is in the British Museum a full contemporary account of the festival, including two issues of *A Description of the Machine for the Fireworks* [etc.], 1749, published by Bowyer and Dodsley (1889b10/5).

253. [Welwyn, Herts.]. [Th.] 9 February 1748/9.
Samuel Richardson.

Not traced.—*Monthly Magazine*, xxxvii (1 May 1814), 328.

                                        Feb. 9, 1748–9.
Dear Sir,
    The inclosed is for Mrs. Delany; but she lets me not know
in her letter where she lives.[1] I believe you know, and therefore I beg the favour of you to seal and direct it. You, I
remember, desired me to write to you my opinion of Clarissa.
Therefore I leave the inclosed open, and there you may read
it. And if my heart lay open before you, you would find that
letter a true transcript of it. Pray my love and service to Mrs.
Richardson, and her little Clarissas. I am,
                        Dear Sir,
                Your truly affectionate and obliged
                        humble servant,
                            E. Young.

254. Welwyn, Herts. [Th.] 9 February 1748/9. Mary
Delany.

Address: To Mrs Delany.
Yale University Library (Osborn Collection).

Madam.
    You carry your Complisance too far when You make an
Apology for conferring a Favour. For such is your Letter;
but your Request I do not well understand. If your meaning
is
    only to learn the real Value of Clarissa, it is too high a
Compliment to desire my Opinion, when Dr. Delany is so
near You. However I will give you my Opinion most sincerely. I know no Work that discovers more excellence of

---

[1] See following letter, to Mrs. Delany. The Delanys lived near Dublin in a house
called Delville.

both Head & Heart together, in ye Writer, than This. What Entertainment? What Instruction? It might perhaps sound odly, if I should say, that ye Bench of Bishops might go to school to ye Writer of a Romance; & yet, I think there are but Few, who might not be both ye Wiser & Better for reading it. But tho All may find their Advantage in it, yet they that have Daughters will find themselves, more particularly, indebted to Mr Richardson. For, I conceive, that *Clarissa*, may not improperly be /[verso]/ be [*sic*] calld—*The Whole Duty of WOMAN*.[1] To point out all I would particularly commend, were Endless; I shall therefore only just touch a single Particular in the First, & in the Last Volum. In the First, how inexpressibly Tender & Affecting are ye scenes between Clarissa & her Mother? Tell me not, Madam, of any of yr Friends, that have read those exquisite scenes with dry eyes, least, tho they are Mrs Delanys Friends, I shd entertain but an indifferent Opinion of them. In the last Volum, my Friend (pardon ye Vanity) my *Friend* Mr Richardson has performd the Difficult Task of making a Deathbed an object of Envy, I think more effectually than Any that have gone before him. In a word I look on it as a Work of true, & uncommon Genius; & like all such the more it is read, the more it will be likd, so yt as yet its Reputation, tho great, is as yet but in its Minority. And I verily beleive it will be read with Profit & Admiration, as long as ye mutable Language in which it is written, is able to convey its pretious Contents to our Posterity. /[conjugate leaf]/

And now, Madam, having complyd with your Request, give me leave to make one to You, in my Turn. Miss Lee, who livd with me, is marryd to one Major Haviland of Gen[era]l Blakneys Regiment, & by this time I beleive they are arrivd in Ireland. If she falls in yr way I beg You to countenance the stranger, & to give her ye Comfort, Credit, & Instruction of Mrs Delanys Acquaintance. She is a good Girl, tho no Clarissa; but by this Request, I think I take ye fairest way to make her so. I beg my best Regards to Dr Delany, & let him know, that the first hour I hear he has set

---

[1] The allusion is to the popular book of religious conduct: *The Whole Duty of Man* (1659), ascribed to Richard Allestree (1619–81), and frequently reprinted. In 1753, William Kenrick (1725?–79) was to publish *The Whole Duty of Woman*.

his foot on English Ground I shall endeavour to find him
out. With my best Wishes to You Both, I am
　　　　　　　　　　　　　Madam
　　　　　　　　　　　　　Yr Obedient
　　　　　　　　　　　　　Humble Sevt
　　　　　　　　　　　　　EYoung.
Wellwyn, Hertfordshire
　　Feb. 9
　　　1748.

255. Welwyn, Herts. [M.] 20 February 1748/9.
Duchess of Portland.

Longleat MSS. (113) 188–9.—Bath, pp. 308–9; Shelley, pp. 221–2.

　　　　　　　　　　　　　Feb ye 20th
　　　　　　　　　　　　　　1748
　　　　　　　　　　　　　　　9
　　　　　　　　　　　　　Wellwyn
May it please yr Grace
　　As I opend my Chamber Window this morning pretty
early, I was struck with ye most beautiful Landskip I ever
saw. Houses, Trees, Woods, Fields, all was coverd with
one entire sheet of snow, not a single Footstep to be seen,
not ye least violation of its immaculate Virginity. What an
amiable Emblem of universal Innocence was This? But
since as I conceive Our Innocence is not yet quite Universal,
　　　　　　　　　　　　　in
I was obligd to think of it　　another View, & imagine our
whole polluted species doing Pennance in a White Sheet (as
ye Custom still prevails in Scotland)[1] for their secret sins.
　　/[verso]/ Now please, Madam, to observe that I send All
this to your Grace purely as an Article of News. You in
Town are in another World, & know nothing of what passes
in the Natural scene of Things. In your Hotbed Climate
Frost is Warm, & in your Seacoal Situation snow is Black;
In all things you are unlike Us Innocents in ye Country;

---

　　[1] Penance for incontinence included the ordeal of standing in church robed in a
white sheet (Ebenezer C. Brewer, *Dictionary of Phrase and Fable*, 1963, p. 953).

with You Honesty is not ye best Policy, nor is ye Worthy ye
most Honourable man at Court.

But your Grace long ere This censures me for my Triviality. The Weather you say is a common Topic of Discourse,
yt indeed you have often met with it in Conversation, but
that you never saw it signd & seald in the solemnity of an
Epistle before. Madam, I acknowledge ye Indictment, I
plead Guilty, I own my Letter is a kind of /[conjugate leaf]/
Frost Piece, & far fitter to make a page among ye winter
Months of an Allmanack, than ^in^ any other Composition.
But I assure your Grace that that [*sic*] the Frost has only
nipd my Fingers, it is got no farther; my Heart lies ten Degrees at least southward of my Hand, & if Yr Grace could
look into it, You would see with what intense Warmth, &
perfect Respect I am

Madam
Yr Graces most Obligd
& Dutifull
Humble Sevt
EYoung.

Madam
  That my Ld Duke may
before this be on a better
than a Chineese foot,[1] & yt
ye Little ^ones^ may long trip it
with ye foot of Fairies
on Mrs Delanys—*Light phantastick Toe*
~~is ye hear~~ before they know wt Pain means
is ye hearty Prayr of their humble sevt
& Admirer.
  My humble service to my Physitian
    Mr Achard.

[1] i.e. bound up on account of the gout from which the Duke suffered.

256. [Welwyn, Herts.] [Su.] 26 February [1748/9]. Caroline Lee Haviland.

Address: To Mrs Haviland.
New Jersey MSS. (Hyde).

Dearest Mrs Haviland I can not but write by Mr Christie,[1] who seems to be a very agreeable & sensible young Gentleman. Poor Mrs Wingate declines, I was with her Yesterday; she told me yt Mrs Read[2] enquird sollicitously about your Voyage & Welfare. Mr Christie says you will be in Dublin in ye Winter. There I suppose Mrs Delany will pay her Compliments to You. Im very glad yr Passage is so short; & yt you have escapd being slowd up with a Military Throng. God send you a safe Arrival. My hearty Love & Service to ye Major. I expect some Bulls[3] in your next.

Yr truly Affectionate
EYoung

Feb. 26

257. Westminster, Mdx. [March 1748/9]. Sir William Bunbury.

New York MSS. (Houghton).—*Correspondence of Sir Thomas Hanmer*, ed. Sir Henry Bunbury, 1838, p. 348.

Charles Street
Westminster

Sr

I hear a Report that, by your permission, my Play is destind to ye Stage.[4] Sr I do not, I can not believe it. It was on

Other Conditions ye Play was entrusted with Sr T: Hanmer, & afterwards (at your Request) with You. I had full Promise from Both of You, that it should go no farther

---

[1] Unidentified.   [2] Unidentified.
[3] i.e. Irish 'bulls', ludicrous misuse of words.
[4] Since Young is in London the 'report' about *The Brothers*, of which nothing has been found in print, must have been by word of mouth.

without my Consent. The very Report has allready done me
Hurt, (& that Substantial Hurt) in more Points than One;
what then, Sr, think You must ye Execution do? I therefore
Entreat you by Justice, Honour, Friendship, & even Com-
passion to One whose Confidence in You has layd Him at yr
Mercy, to put me out of Pain from Apprehension of future
Contingencys, by Restoring the Trifle to

Sr

Yr most Obedient

& most Humble Sevt

EYoung.

Sr I had waited on You
but I am not very well.

258. [Westminster, Mdx.].[1] [Sa.] 25 March 1748/9.
Sir William Bunbury.

Not traced.—*The Correspondence of Sir Thomas Hanmer*, ed. Sir Henry
Bunbury, 1838, p. 349.

March 25, 1748.

Sir,
     I thank you for ye favour of yours, wch gives me full
satisfaction. The eagerness of my Letter was owing to my
surprize at ye report and ye violence of ye asseverations whch
accompanyd it; And I hope you will not construe it as a
meditated distrust of your honour; For, I assure you that I
am with true esteem and gratitude,

Sr,

Yr most Obedient

& most Humble Sert,

E. Young.

     [1] Young was still in London, as on 7 April he executed the assignment of the last
three parts of the *Night-Thoughts* and *A Paraphrase on Part of the Book of Job* to
Andrew Millar (see Appendix A).

259. Welwyn, Herts. [Su.] 9 April 1749. Caroline
Lee Haviland.

Not traced.[1]

260. [Welwyn, Herts.]. [?Sa. 6] May 1749. Samuel
Richardson.

Not traced.—Barbauld, ii. 25–7.

Recd. May 8, 1749.

Dear Sir,
When I was in town, I ask'd you if you had read Dr.
Hartley's book.[2] You told me you had not.[3] I was sorry for
it; for I had a curiosity to know your opinion of it. I have
since read it a second time, and with great satisfaction. It is
certainly a work of distinction; by men of distinction therefore it ought to be read. It is calculated for men of sense.
I make no doubt but that it has its gainsayers; but therefore
it is a proper subject for your discussion and discernment.
So few books have any thing new in them, that those which
have are entitled to our particular regard. All I will venture
to say about it, is, that there is no man who seriously considers himself as immortal, but will find his pleasure, if not
his profit, in it. And if you are not one of those men, give
me leave to say, you have greatly imposed on
Dear Sir,
Your very affectionate and
most humble Servant,
E. Young.

[1] Evidence of this letter is the Sotheby catalogue for an auction of 18 January
1877, where a letter to Mrs. Haviland is described as follows: 'Another, to the same,
and alludes to Mrs. Delany at a place not two miles out of Dublin, &c. directed to
Major Haviland, at Drogheda, in Ireland, 2 pages 4to. Wellwyn, Apr. 9, 1749.'
Drogheda, pronounced Dro'heda, is a municipal borough town in County Louth,
thirty-two miles north of Dublin. Haviland's regiment was stationed there.

[2] David Hartley (1705–57); *Observations on Man, His Frame, His Duty, and His
Expectations*, had been published in February by Charles Hitch (d. 1764).

[3] It had, however, been printed at Richardson's press, according to William B.
Sale, jr. (*Samuel Richardson: Master Printer*, 1950, p. 244).

P.S. I have not been very well since my return home, or you had heard sooner from me. I hope all are well, especially the *little sufferer*, of whom I heard such ill news when I was in town.—It is evident that Dr. Hartley has thought for himself; a character, without which, no writer can be of any considerable value. And thus far the author I recommended to your perusal resembles yourself, which is a sort of bribe to you in his favour.

261. Welwyn, Herts. [Su.] 7 May 1749. Duchess of Portland.

Longleat MSS. (114) 204–5.—Bath, p. 314.

May it please yr Grace

About three months agoe I had ye Honour of a Letter from your Friend Mrs Delany. As its Contents were of ye greatest Importance, I immediately wrote an Answer; and
that Duty done, took ye Liberty to close my Letter with an humble request for a Favour at her hands with regard to poor Mrs Haviland now in ye Barrack at Drogeda, & in ye insuing Winter proposing to be at Dublin, where I thought I could not do better for her, either with regard to her Happiness, or Reputation, than to recommend her to the Countenance of Mrs Delany. /[verso]/
But I have had no Letter from Mrs Delany since.[1] Which, considering Mrs Delanys Goodness & Complaisance, makes me suspect that my Letter never came to her Hand. I remember at that time I doubted if my Direction was right. And therefore I humbly beg the favour of your Grace, to let me know How I am to direct to her. Tho I should have thought that a Letter directed to Mrs Delany in Ireland, could not have miscarryd. She shines not only with her own

---

[1] The Delanys were in Ireland at this time and about to come to England. In a letter to the Duchess of Portland of 14 February 1748/9, Mrs. Delany wrote: 'We cannot set forward till the latter end of May' (Llanover, 1861, ii. 505).

Light, but with that of her spouse, & how with such a Lustre
to lead it, could a Letter lose its Way?

I hope, Madam, your Graces little Family are all well.
I beg my humble Duty to my Lord Duke, my humble
service to Mr Achard & am

Madam
with all Respect Your Graces
Most Obedient
& most Humble Sevt
EYoung

Wellwyn May 7th
1749.

262. [Welwyn, Herts.]. [W.] 24 May 1749. Samuel Richardson.

Not traced.—*Monthly Magazine*, xxxvii (1 May 1814), 328–9.

May 24, 1749.

My dear Sir,

Most modern writers are mere *remembrancers*; they give
you no new lights, only kindly put you in mind of what you
knew before. Some may be considered as *news writers*, they
amuse you (if not instruct) by their novelty; and the degree
of credit you will afford them is at your own discretion, In
this last view I recommend my friend Dr. Hartley. I neither
approve, nor indeed understand, the whole, but there are
parts I am fond of; particularly his proofs of the truth of
Christianity; and the reasons he gives for the probably
approaching ruin of these western kingdoms. But this by
the by.

I heartily wish the diet drink may succeed to your expectation. I bless God I am well; and am very sorry to hear of
your nervous symptoms increased: too great application
hurts you. I wish you could bear being idle; but that I fear
would be a harder task to you than your table of contents,
which I long to see. Next month I hope to have the pleasure
of seeing you at N. End; for I am covetous of a demand on

you for your company at Wellwyn; where you will find a lover of your virtues, and an admirer of your talents, in,

> Dear Sir,
> Your truly affectionate
> humble servant,
> E. Young.

263. [Welwyn, Herts.] [Su.] 9 July 1749. Samuel Richardson.

Not traced.—*Monthly Magazine*, xxxvii (1 May 1814), 329.

July 9, 1749.

Dear Sir,

I have more reason to be sensible of the flight of time than you; however you cannot but be sensible that summers last not for ever. I should think myself happy in an opportunity of conversing with you, for serious minds are but rare. When you will give me that opportunity I cannot tell; but the sooner the kinder. Make the performance of your promise as agreeable to your own humour as you can. Let me know the time, and I will meet you with a post-chaise at Barnet, and snatch you to this place. I have just read a book published by Mr. Millar, *Deism revealed*,[1] which I think excellent. Perhaps Mr. Millar might not be unwilling to come down with you; I should be very glad to see him, or any other friend of yours. Peace be within your walls, and Paradise within your breast. I am,

> Dear Sir,
> Your obliged and truly affectionate
> humble servant,
> E. Young.

My love and service to all that is dear to you.

---

1 Richardson had printed *Ophiomaches; or, Deism Revealed*, by Philip Skelton (1707–87), published in March by Andrew Millar (1707–68). Millar had published the last three parts of Young's *Night-Thoughts* and on 7 April of this year had purchased the copyright of the three for £63 (see Appendix A).

264. Welwyn, Herts. [M.] 10 July 1749. Caroline Lee Haviland.

New York MSS. (Houghton).

> Wellwyn
> July ye 10th
> 1749.

My dear Child. It is long since I writ to You, but I made Apology by Miss July, being not willing to write till I had seen ye Lawyers, & talkd with Mr Monk.[1] Who after all ye Lawyrs demand of Powrs sent over by ye Major to enable them to proceed, tells me that nothing more than ye Knowledge of ye Majors Christian Name is necessary, which I have given them, & now they assure me ye Affair will be finishd in a Month. So much for *That*.

And now let me enquire how you do, & when we may flatter ourselves with any tolerable Hopes of seeing You at Wellin. I hear you are got /[verso]/ to Dublin, I am sorry Mrs Delany is not there, nor likely to be there all this summer. I saw her & ye Dean at ye Dutchess of Portlands last week, & found they were taking a House in Town, so that their stay will not be short.—This is our Assembly Day, but we are exstremely thin from its falling in with ye Assizes at Hertford. Poor Mrs Wingate allways enquires after You, but it is greatly to be supposd she can not enquire long. The Miss Heyshams[2] were much mortified last Assembly from being ecclipsed by a Sister of Lady Marchmont,[3] by all very greatly, & very justly admird. My Love & Service to ye Major. Let me hear from you as soon as conveniently you can; for considering yr present Condition no Friend but must have some sollicitude about You. God Preserve You. Most truly yours

> EYoung.

[1] Monk was apparently a representative of the Earl of Litchfield. Young's own marriage settlement included £3,000 in trust with 'Litchfield and William Monck', according to later entries in Young's account with the Gosling Bank.

[2] Elizabeth, Anne, and Jane, daughters of Giles Thornton Heysham. Elizabeth (d. 1774) was to become the wife of Young's son Frederick in 1765.

[3] i.e. a sister of Elizabeth Crompton, second wife (1748) of Hugh Hume (1708–94), 3rd Earl of Marchmont. She was to marry Edward Barker of Hatton Garden (Holborn), London, on 20 October 1750.

265. Welwyn, Herts. [Tu.] 3 August 1749. Duchess
of Portland.

Longleat MSS. (115) 206-7.—Bath, pp. 314-15.

May it please yr Grace

You desire me to tell you how yr Heart shall get clear of
forming ineffectual Wishes. It is, I grant, a sad Distemper,
yet tho yr Grace does me ye Honour of making me yr
Physitian in ordinary, yet can I not in Conscience wish You
quite free from this Disease, because I verily think there is
no such thing as a Perfect Cure of it, but Death. However
there are some Palliatives that may soften ye Pain it is apt to
give us.

First, Madam, I can administer to yr Grace a malicious
kind of Consolation from the great number of your Fellow
sufferers, for no Disease is so Epidemic. But This is, I know,
a Medicine that will go against your stomach. /[verso]/

I had rather therefore observe, That frequent Blows of
Disapointment deaden ye sensibility of the Heart; And thus
this Distemper, at long Run, like ye scorpion, cures the
Wound it gives.[1]

But the cheif Recipe I would prescribe, may be calld ye
Ballance. I mean, Madam, that your Grace should not permit
a Disapointed Wish to give you more Pain, than a sucesfull
one gives You Joy: and then I am persuaded You would find
ye Violence of your Distemper, in a great Measure, abated.
But to play ye Mountebank no longer, I descend from my
stage into a perfect Patient myself; & must own that I am
as much, if not more Distemperd, in spight of all my Quakery,
than your Grace. For I severely feel ye Disapointment of my
sincere Desire of seeing Bullstrode, which /[conjugate leaf]/
Pleasure is denyd me by Friends that are to be with me for
ye summer. I humbly beg that my not waiting on Your Grace
may not be misunderstood. For I am ashamd of having been
honourd with so many kind Invitations: & should be still

---

[1] 'The scorpion . . .', a proverbial expression (Morris Palmer Tilley, *A Dictionary
of the Proverbs in England in the Sixteenth and Seventeenth Centuries*, 1950, p. 588).

more ashamd of not enjoying the Advantage of Them, if ye
Occasion of it was not most Real, & Unavoidable. With ye
truest sense of your many, & great Indulgences I am
                              Madam
                         Yr Graces most Obedient
                              & Dutifull
                                   Humble Sevt
                                   EYoung.

I beg, Madam, my humble
Duty to my Ld Duke, humble
Service to Ly Wallingford &
Mr Achard, best Wishes
& Respects to ye Little Ones.

Wellwyn, Aug the 3d
    1749.

266. [Welwyn, Herts.]. Tu. [?22 August 1749].
Duchess of Portland.

Longleat MSS. (117) 210.

Madam
    I am realy greatly distressed by your Graces Goodness to
me in permitting me the Honour of waiting on You at
Stevenage;[1] because tho I most seriously desire it, it is not
in my Powr. I had two Persons[2] come to me last night from
Town, after a long-promisd Visit, & who leave me tomorrow
morning. So yt I cant possibly leave them.
    On yr Graces Return, if You put it not in my Powr to
enjoy ye Pleasure, I am now denyd, I shall take it for granted
                                                    You
that yr Grace takes this ill at my hands; wh I beg   not to
do, ~~but~~ for I solemnly assure you that I am much paind wth

---

[1] i.e. to see the Portlands on their way to their northern estate. On 25 August,
Mrs. Delany reported their safe arrival at Welbeck (Llanover, 1861, ii. 513).
[2] The visit of Richardson and Grover to Welwyn is mentioned in Richardson's
letter to Young of 9 September.

my present Disapointment. With all Duty & Respect to yr
Graces Fellow travellers, I am

Madam
Yr Graces much Obligd
& ever Obedt Humble Sevt
EYoung.

Teusday Noon.

Richardson to Young. [London.] [Sa.] 9 September 1749.

Not traced.—*Monthly Magazine*, xxxvii (1 May 1814), 329.

September 9, 1749.

Rev. and Dear Sir,

On reprinting your Night Thoughts, in 1 vol. 12 mo.
which I am desirous to put to press myself, in hopes that it
will not be the less correct for it, I find that the preface to
the fourth night is temporary. I imagine you will make some
little alteration in the latter part of it, as it leaves the reader
doubtful whether you will proceed with the excellent work,
when the whole is before him complete.

Be pleased to give me your orders on this head.

Poor Mr. Grover![1]—You have doubtless read in the paper
that poor Mr. Grover is no more; a violent, a malignant
fever, brought on by an obliging over-heating walk to Ember
Court, and to carelessness of himself when hot and fatigued,
the occasion. He will be greatly missed by a whole House of
Commons. It was not easy to find out so much as one half
of his merits. I knew not of his illness till he was in danger.
I have all his very greatly disordered affairs likely to be
upon me. He was the support of a maiden sister, as he had
been of a decayed father, mother, and family. I have got her
(a worthy creature) to N. End to my good wife. He was too
much regardless of money to leave her very happy in that
particular. I am endeavouring to get those who valued him
to be kind to her.

[1] John Grover, who as Clerk of the ingrossments for the House of Commons,
worked closely with Richardson in the printing of Parliamentary transactions.

Have you with you yet your dear friend,[1] whom you mentioned to me in the chariot, as we went to Sir Jeremy's?[2]— Let me be intitled to your joint prayers, if so. If not, forget me not in yours.

Be pleased, with my cordial respects, to thank good Mrs. Hallowes for her kind acceptance of my poor Clarissa.[3] Mine also to Mrs. Ward, if with you; and to Mrs. Heysham, and your bachelor friend at next door.[4]

The hospitable reception I and my departed friend met with (for your sake) at Sir Jeremy's, deserves my grateful acknowledgments to the two ladies, and the good baronet. I am,

Dear and Rev. Sir,
Your faithful and obliged servant,
S. Richardson

Pray, sir, forget not, if you have opportunity, to put me right with her grace of Portland. I should despise myself were I capable of the behaviour with respect to Mrs. Lambert, that I have been accused of. I would not lie under such an imputation (as, unknown to myself, for a long time I lay under), if I could help it, from the Duchess of Portland, above all the persons in the world; and this I say respecting rather the good woman than the duchess. The true friendship that all mine, as well as myself, bore to Miss Parsons, would have required, if she had had any favour for us, equal to the love we disinterestedly bore her, and still bear her, that she should have given me an opportunity to clear myself, and not left me to wonder at, and my wife to regret the loss of her friendship. My heart is too big, obscure man as I am, to expostulate on this occasion with a lady whom I looked upon as one of my own children. It would not be so big did I not know that it was incapable of deserving either her anger or her long silence. Could I know the asperser,

---

[1] i.e. Thomas Colborn (1682–1761), Vicar of Walpole St. Peter, Norfolk, who had been at Oxford (Corpus Christi College) during Young's residence.

[2] Sir Jeremy Sambroke.

[3] Richardson had brought out a second edition of *Clarissa*, in four volumes, 15 June.

[4] John Shotbolt (d. 1760), a Welwyn tanner who lived next to Guessens in a house known as Ivy Cottage.

327

I would keep the secret, if made one; only guard against the man in future.

Pray, sir, inform me of the situation of poor Miss Cole. I loved her as cordially as I loved Miss Parsons. If I could add to her happiness in any way it would increase my own. The good duchess will be able to inform you of all that relates to her, I dare say. You see, sir, that I presume you have not seen her grace yet, on her return from Walbeck.

267. [Welwyn, Herts.] [Su.] 10 September 1749. Samuel Richardson.

Not traced.—*Monthly Magazine*, xxxvii (1 May 1814), 329-30.

September 10, 1749.

My Dear Sir,

Accept my various thanks for your late company, for Gideon,[1] for Clarissa, (to Mrs. H.) and for the hopes Shotbolt gives me of seeing you again before I die. Did you know how much pleasure it would give me, I should see you soon. But not with our late friend. How was I struck at the news! If the vigour of life falls, why am I still alive? Neither you nor Solomon can tell. Pray let me know how your poor little sufferer does. I feel for her, and for you. How do you do yourself? Let me know. The pains we feel for others is the price we pay for those pleasures, the bare prospect of which supported so gloriously poor Clarissa in her last extremes. My love and service to all, dear sir, most yours,

E. Young.

P.S. Since the above was written, I received the favour of your's. I thank your kind care for the next edition of Night Thoughts; the preface you mention may be entirely omitted. I'm sorry for poor Grover's sister; accept the five guineas I

---

[1] The printed version has 'Gidson', a mistake for 'Gideon', an epic poem by Aaron Hill, the first two books of which had been published about 1716, and to which three had now been added and the whole retitled: *Gideon, or, the Patriot*, dedicated to Bolingbroke and printed by Richardson. On 18 May of this year Hill acknowledged receipt of twelve copies of the book from Richardson (Victoria and Albert Museum, Forster Collection 458, vol. xiii, f. 117).

Joseph Highmore's portrait of Edward Young, aged 71 years
(see Samuel Richardson's letter to Young of 17 December 1754, p. 414)

An engraving by Joseph Brown of Christian Friedrich Zincke's enamel portrait of the Duchess of Portland, aged 25 years (see p. 142 n. 2)

Joseph Highmore's portrait of Samuel Richardson, aged 61 years

Avenue of Chestnut trees in the garden formerly belonging to the Revd. Dr. Edward Young. at Welwyn. Herts

'Avenue of Chesnut trees in the garden [of Guessens] formerly belonging to the Revd. Dr. Edward Young at Welwyn, Herts.' From a series of pen and wash drawings of Welwyn in the Hertfordshire County Record Office, made by J. C. Buckler (1794–1894) in

sent by Shotbolt. My dear Ely friend is not yet come.[1] Let us, dear Sir, mutually exchange our prayers. Mrs. Heysham, Ward, and Hallowes, (all three) acknowlege your favour, and are much yours.—When I go to Gubbins, I will do your grateful heart full justice there. The duchess is not yet returned; I will talk with her at large. And then you shall hear from me again. In the mean time be not so very anxious about it; leave such disturbance to the guilty.

268. Welwyn, Herts. [Su.] 17 September 1749. Duchess of Portland.

Longleat MSS. 212.—Bath, p. 315.

May it please yr Grace

It grieves me that I can not wait on You at St Albans, as I designd, but am necessarily prevented. Your Grace will perceive by ye Inclosd,[2] that I must have had great Inclination to talk with You. My Friend Mr Richardson, yr Grace will perceive, is very Uneasie, & I am confident is very

me

Honest; if therefore on ye Perusal You can furnish (at yr Grace's leisure) with any thing of Consolation to Him, I shall rejoyce.

I am Madam exstremely sensible of ye many & undeservd Honours I receive at yr Hands. Wt wd I not give to wait on You & my Ld Duke at Wellwyn? I wish yr Grace wd change ye Conditions for any other on earth; for such is my state of Health, that so late in ye Year I dare not be from Home.

Madam, ye Bar to my Design & Promise of waiting on yr Grace at St Albans, was a Coach full of Ladies who came to dine with me.

The latter part of ye Inclosd, is ye only part yt desires ye favour of yr Perusal, & such answer to it as your /[verso]/ Graces Benevolence shall think proper; for I know poor

---

[1] i.e. Thomas Colborn.
[2] Young had apparently sent the Duchess Richardson's letter to him of 9 September 1749.

Richardsons great Delicacy is quite in Pain about it. And ye
Blessing of a Peacemaker is what, on this Occasion is
ardently coveted by

> Madam
> Yr Graces most Obligd
> & most Obedient
> Humble Sevt
> E Young.

Wellwyn Sepr 1 7
 1749:
Madam I beg my humble Duty
to my Ld Duke &c:

269. Welwyn, Herts. Th. [21 September 1749]. Duchess of Portland.

Longleat MSS. 213.

> Thursday
> Wellwyn

Madam
   Your Grace, & my Lord Duke (to whom I beg my sincerest thanks) do me ye greatest Pleasure & Honour[.] I
shall look on Friday as ye longest Day of my Life, & Sunday
as ye shortest, if yr Grace is determind to leave me on
Moonday.[1]
   As for poor Richardson, I rejoyce that Yr Grace indulges
me in an Oppertunity of speaking more largely on it. For I
am fully Confident, that on a clearing up, it will not be in yr
Graces powr not to have a Value for Him. With ye warmest
sense of yr promisd Favour. I am Madam
>   Yr Graces most Dutifull
>   & most Obligd Humble Sevt EYoung.

   [1] It appears from this and the following letter that the Portlands' stay in Welwyn
was from Friday evening, 29 September, to Monday morning, 2 October.

270. Welwyn, Herts. [Su.] 8 October 1749. Duchess of Portland.

Longleat MSS. 214–15.—Bath, p. 316.

> Wellwyn
> Octr ye 8th
> 1749.

Madam

Accept my most cordial Thanks for ye Honour Your Grace & my Ld Duke so lately did me at this Place. Had You continued but four Hours longer ~~longer~~, You would have seen the Ladies you talkd of ye night before, Mrs Montague & my Lady Sandwitch.[1] They dind at ye Inn, & drank Tea with me; & I breakfasted with them the next Day, after which they went to Town, Both their Husbands, as I understand, being there. As far as I can look into   Her at present I like Lady Sandwitch very well. Her Manner is very unlike that of her Friend. They came from Hinchingbrook, where Mrs Montague has spent /[verso]/ some time with her Ladyship. I askd her if she had any commands to Bullstrode; for that I should write soon; she answerd, that   can she should write herself on Teusday night. Your Grace tell whether her Veracity is inviolable, or not.

I hope your Grace had a Pleasant Journey, a safe Arrival, & ye Happy Wellcome of finding all Well. My hopes are ye more lively on this Occasion at present, being awakend by a sad Fire which happend in our Nighbourhood ye Night after yr Grace left us, which has reduced three poor Families to great Distress. It was occasiond by a careless Disposal of their Lime.

I defer writing to poor Richardson till by your Graces favour I hear wt Mrs Lambart /[conjugate leaf]/ says to his Letter. If He was to blame, it is evident He repents; and it is ye Interest of us all to wish that much Powr may be afforded to Repentance. But I presume no farther; Your

---

[1] Elizabeth Montagu and Lady Sandwich (Judith Fane, wife of John Montagu, fourth Earl of Sandwich) had been at Hinchingbroke, near Huntington, seat of the Earl of Sandwich, for the election of a mayor and a grand ball.

Grace knows what is fit & Right to be done in ye Case, and I am confident will be for no other Measures in it.

    With ye truest Respect & Gratitude

I am Madam

Yr Graces most Obedt

& most Obligd

Humble Sevt

EYoung.

/[verso]/ PS.

Since I writ ye former Part of my Letter North[1] Mr Wests Friend came to make me a Visit, & in ye course of our Conversation (without ye least Provocation or Hint from me) told me that ye Rise of his Friend was owing to some secret He had to communicate to Persons in Powr.[2] I sayd I Questiond it. On wh He told me that He had it from Mr Wests Agent at St Albans, who stood in such Nearness to him, that his Information could not be questiond.

271. Welwyn, Herts. [Su.] 15 October 1749. Samuel Richardson.

Not traced.—*Monthly Magazine*, xxxviii (1 December 1814), 429.

Wellwyn, Oct. 15, 1749.

Dear Sir,

    I trouble you with this, out of the pure kindness of my heart, which feels a pain lest you should suspect me to have neglected the commission you gave me with regard to the Duchess of Portland and Mrs. Lambard. The duchess passed by me on her return without stopping, desiring me to dine with her at St. Alban's, which I could not do. But the next week after, the duke and duchess came from Bullstrode, and made a three-days' visit, in which I had full time to talk over your affair. But she was a little on the reserve, and told me she would write to me fully when she had heard from Mrs. L.

---

[1] George North, Vicar of Codicote, Herts.

[2] James West was patronized by the Duke of Newcastle who later (1762) got him a pension of £2,000 a year.

to whom she would write as soon as she got home, which is now near ten days, but I have not yet had the expected letter; as soon as I have, you shall hear farther from,

Dear Sir,

Your obliged and truly affectionate

humble servant,

E. Young.

My love and service to all your's.

272. Welwyn, Herts. Tu. [?24 October 1749]. Duchess of Portland.

Longleat MSS. 216–17.—Bath, pp. 316–17.

Madam

Yr Grace is exstremely obliging, & your Present very Acceptable. I have now a [*sic*] another Flock[1] besides that of my Parishioners, & I fear much the more Innocent of ye two.

I receivd ye Honour of yr Graces first Letter, but it was after mine to [your] Grace was written, or I shd have made my Acknowledgments for it. Mrs Hallows knows not how to express her sense of your Graces so great Favour; & Mrs Ward is not with me. I am sorry to hear that I have seen ye best of Lady S——h;[2] & as for her Companion I found her out before Yr Grace did, which occasiond ye Disregard I showd her at Tunbridge, of wh I know she complaind to your Grace.[3] The paragraph You favour me with, Madam, relating to Mrs Lambart gives me real Pleasure, /[verso]/ for poor Richardson is a lowspirited man, & not only deserves, but wants satisfactions.

I return, Madam, my particular Thanks for ye Receipts & Medicine, & for that especially that encounters a sorethroat, my greatest Enemie to which I am most subject; but I shall stand less in dread of it for ye Future.

Lady Primrose & a Friend of hers, were some time since, about taking a House in Oxfordshire, but ye Bargain went

---

[1] The gift was a flock of sheep, referred to later in his letter of 20 January 1750/1.
[2] Lady Sandwich (see letter of 8 October).
[3] Young had apparently been in Tunbridge Wells in June, when Elizabeth Montagu was there for three weeks.

off, & they cd not get it. Some time after Ly Prim[r]ose met her Friend, & was regreting that they misd that pretty Place. No, says her Friend I have taken it. How so, says Ly Primrose, with great Joy. Why says her Friend I have marryd ye Landlord of it. Wh is very true. It is one Captain Hervey,[1] with whom I am well acquainted.

Your Grace asks, on a very proper Occasion, 'Is it Possible for a man to glory in his Villainys?' /[conjugate leaf]/ Yes, Madam, so very Possible that some have committed Villainys purely to Glory in them. But ye Gentleman in question fixd his prudent choice on something more substantial, & we may suppose in pure Gayety of Heart from his Exstraordaniry success, let ye secret inadvert ently drop from Him. For that it did come from Him in Conversation, & that with a Person of low Rank, I have indisputable Conviction. That yr Grace may long enjoy the Inestimable Fruits of Virtue, & have no secrets to communicate, but what yr Foes, without any Danger to your Reputation may hear, is ye hearty Prayr of

Madam
Yr Graces most Obligd
& most Dutifull
Humble Sevt
EYoung.

To my Lord Duke, ye
Little Ones, Miss Granville,[2]
& Mr Achard, ye very
best Regards of their
most humble sevt.
Wellwyn. Teusday night.
/[verso]/ Madam

As for ye little ArchBishop who is so good as to remember me, I thank him for it, & please to let Him know yt if I ever ask blessing of a Bishop again, it shall certainly be of Him.

---

1 Henry Harvey of the King's Regiment of Horse was commissioned a cornet 11 March 1726/7 and captain 21 December 1738 (Public Record Office, *A List of the Colonels*, etc., *of His Majesty's Forces*, 1740). Probably this is the Henry Hervey of Ipsden who died in 1764 and is buried at South Stoke, Oxfordshire.

2 One of the daughters (? Anne) of George Granville, Lord Lansdowne.

273. Welwyn, Herts. [Sa.] 28 October 1749. Samuel Richardson.

Not traced.—*Monthly Magazine*, xxxviii (1 December 1814), 429–30.

Wellwyn, October 28, 1749.
Dear Sir,

I inclose to you part of the Duchess of Portland's letter, just now received, which, though very short, I hope may give you some satisfaction.[1] If you have any further commands for me in that or any other affair, they will give real pleasure to,

Dear Sir,
Your truly affectionate
humble servant,
E. Young.

I beg my love and service to Mrs. Richardson, and the little ones. Accept of Mrs. Hallows' humble service and best wishes.

I have had a letter from Mrs. Lambard that may make Mr. Richardson perfectly easy; nor has he been neglected as he imagined; for the only time she has been in town since she married, which was but a very little while, she went to his house in town.

Richardson to Young. London. [?Tu. 31] October [1749].

Not traced.—*Monthly Magazine*, xxxviii (1 December 1814), 430.

London, October.
Rev. Sir,

Most heartily do I thank you for the trouble you have given yourself in relation to the report made to my disadvantage concerning Mrs. Lambard and her husband. Had I been capable of deserving such a report I should have hated myself more than I should almost any other person.

---

[1] See Richardson's letter to Young, following.

I had besides so true, so pure a respect for the lady. The most that ever I said, when I was told that the marriage proved not happy, was (for I knew not the gentleman so much as by fame or character,) that I was sure, if so, it must be the husband's fault, for that I knew not the woman who was more capable of making herself and the man she married happy, than she; and that as well from principle as sweetness of temper.

I will make myself easy upon it. And yet, sir, you will observe that what her Grace writes, and which you have been so kind to send me, is very different from what she was pleased to write, or tell you, on this very matter, since, but for what you kindly mentioned to me of the duchess's charge, I had not known that there was, or could have been, such a surmise. Be it as it will, it is strange, methinks, that my wife, who was so greatly obliged to Miss Parsons for her declared value for her, should never be favoured with one line, or the least notice, from Mrs. Lambard. This made the resentment, when I heard of it, look like a rooted one. Yet, it seems, she was so good as to call at my house in town. My people below stairs there very often neglect to acquaint me with persons calling upon me. My wife, as well as myself, had so much esteem for this lady, that on her account I hold them more inexcusable than ever. But thus far must I excuse them, that, had Mrs. Lambard left a card, I am sure I should have had it.

I am expecting down the last proof of the new edition, in one volume, of your noble work.[1] A noble work it is indeed! I never before read it in series: the first numbers only when they came out; the second part, as I printed it, under your inspection; and the second edition of that second as I re-printed it, another printer doing Mr. Dodsley's part. But, now printing the whole, it is not possible for me to express my admiration of it. You must not, sir, shut up your next to divine labours here. You will not. Do you consider that this work stands alone, absolutely alone? A monument of God's

---

[1] Richardson is printing the *Night-Thoughts*, for publication by Millar and Dodsley, for the first time in one volume. It was announced as published 30 January 1750/1 (*General Advertiser*). Richardson had originally printed 'Nights' 7–9 for Millar alone.

goodness to you, in such gifts, such talents, as must exalt human nature, and amend it at the same time.

You have received, I presume, a volume of Dr. Foster's[1] Discourses, in part of your subscription of a guinea. The other is not printed yet. Also, from the author's, through Mr. Millar's hands, the book intituled, 'Free and Candid Disquisitions,' &c.[2] If you, or Mrs. Hallows, (to whom, I beg, my sincere respects,) have any commission to give either to my wife or self, you will greatly oblige us both. I am, dear and rev. sir,

> Your most obliged and faithful
> humble servant,
> S. Richardson.

My wife and her's desire their cordial respects.

Be pleased to make my compliments to your next door neighbour.—Not married yet, I doubt! Poor man![3]

274. Welwyn, Herts. [Su.] 5 November 1749. Samuel Richardson.

Not traced.—Barbauld, ii. 27–8.

Wellwyn, Nov. 5, 1749.
Dear Sir,

I have read Miss Fielding with great pleasure.[4] Your Clarissa is, I find, the Virgin-mother of several pieces; which, like beautiful suckers, rise from her immortal root. I rejoice at it; for the noblest compositions need such aids, as the multitude is swayed more by others' judgments than their

---

[1] The printed version has the misreading 'Tosser's'. The first volume of *Discourses on all the Principal Branches of Natural Religion and Social Virtue*, by James Foster (1697–1753), popular dissenting preacher, had just appeared (*Gentleman's Magazine* for October, xix. 480), having attracted 2,000 subscribers. The second volume was published in 1752.

[2] An anthology of extracts from churchmen by John Jones (1700–70), who was to become Young's curate in 1757.

[3] John Shotbolt.

[4] A novel by Sarah Fielding (1710–68), advertised in January as *The Governess; or, Female Academy: being the History of Mrs Teachum and Her Nine Girls* by the author of *David Simple* (*Gentleman's Magazine*, xix. 48). It was printed by Richardson and presumably the copy sent to Young was of a second edition.

own. How long was *Paradise Lost* an obscure book? Authors give works their merit; but others give them their fame; and it is their merit becoming famous, which gives them that salutary influence, which every worthy writer proposes, on mankind.—Suppose, in the title-page of the *Night Thoughts*, you should say—*published by the author of Clarissa*. This is a trick to put it into more hands; I know it would have that effect. I have disposed of Miss Fielding into five very proper hands. I am very much obliged to the authors of the *Candid Disquisitions*; and, if I knew how, should be glad to return my thanks in a more particular manner, both for their favour to me, and their noble (and I hope useful) zeal for Christianity. In the mean time I beg Mr. Millar to return them my best respects and heartiest wishes for their success. The old bachelor is very much your's. Please to let me know when the *Night Thoughts* are finished; for I have a few presents to make. Heaven spread its wing over you and your's; to whom best wishes and service.

I am, dear Sir, your's,
E. Young.

275. Welwyn, Herts. [Th.] 16 November 1749. Duchess of Portland.

Longleat MSS. 218.

May it please yr Grace

I was exstremely struck with a Paragraph which I saw yesterday in the publick Papers.[1] And tho every thing at

[1] The 'paragraph' has not been located. It presumably reported the illness of Lord Tichfield. Young was himself to have a severe shock this month whenever it was that word reached him of the death of Caroline Haviland. Caroline's burial in Drogheda, 13 November 1749, is recorded in the Dublin Public Record Office: 'Mrs Haviland Wife of Major Haviland of Lieut Genl Blakeneys Regiment' (Parish [of St. Peter's] Register of Drogheda, Dio[cese] of Armagh Baptisms, Marriages & Burials 1747–1772 [transcribed by Sir William Bethan, Ulster King of Arms] Dublin P.R.O. M 5127). On 26 November 1749 Mrs. Delany was to write to her sister from Bulstrode: 'Poor Dr. Young is in great trouble; his daughter-in-law, Mrs. Haviland, (the lady recommended to me in his letter [9 February 1748/9]), is dead, it is said she died suddenly in her coach between Drogheda and Dublin' (Llanover, 1861, ii. 522).

this Juncture must be foreign to your Grace which contributes not to the Recovery of One so very Near, & so justly Dear to your Grace, yet cd I not forbear to write a single Line, to assure You that it is (as it ought to be) my most fervent Prayr to Heaven to restore my Lord Titchfield to his Health, & your Grace to your Peace. With great Concern & ye truest Respect I am

Madam Yr Graces most Dutifull
& Obligd Humble Sevt
EYoung.

Pray my humble Duty
to my Ld Duke &c:
Wellwyn. Nov 16 1749

276. Welwyn, Herts. [Tu.] 12 December 1749. Samuel Richardson.

Not traced.—*Monthly Magazine*, xxxviii (1 December 1814), 430.

Welwyn, December 12, 1749.

Dear Sir,

Some time ago you let me know that the Night Thoughts were near printed off. I return my most cordial thanks for the great trouble your friendship has taken for me in correcting the press.

I beg Mr. Millar to have a dozen of my Night Thoughts, the new edition, bound for me after the best manner. One of which I beg you, sir, to accept, and I shall give orders about the rest.

I wish you and your's all the happiness, [that] the comforts of earth, and prospects of eternity can inspire. But, instead of wishes, I think I should send my congratulations. How happy is the man whose head has secured him one immortality, and whose heart entitles to the other! God grant me the capacity of conversing with you a thousand years hence; where our sentiments will be published without the help of the press, and our intercourse be kept up without

the expedient of epistles, and where it will be needless for
me to tell you, as now, that I am,

> Dear Sir,
> Most truly your's,
> E. Young.

Mrs. Hallows sends her best regards.

277. Welwyn, Herts. [Tu.] 26 December 1749. Duchess of Portland.

Longleat MSS. 219.—Bath, p. 317.

May it please yr Grace

My Eye is just as it was, I can not make use of it without
Uneasiness; but it would be Greater Uneasiness to me, not
to thank yr Grace in a few Words for yr most kind Enquiry.[1]
I rejoyce, in ye Wellfare of yr amiable fireside, & hope ye
little Exception to it in ye Archbishop, will soon cease. I do
not hope, but Prophesie that my Ld Titchfield will advance
in all things to yr own Hearts Desire. It is Natural to Mrs
Delany to leave Marks of great Ingenuity behind her whereever she goes. And still more Natural to leave them there,
where she knows they will be Relishd by an exquisite Tast,
& be Acknowledgd bye a Heart in which it is her Glory to
have so large a share. To Her & ye Dean I beg my best
Compliments, my humble Duty to my Ld Duke. With ye
most cordial Good Wishes & Respects to You & Yours I am

> Madam
> Yr Graces most Obedient
> & most Obligd
> Humble Sevt
> EYoung.

Mrs Hallows desires Yr Grace
to accept of her Duty.

I propose to myself the
Honour of waiting on yr
Grace in ye Spring
    Wellwyn Decemr 26, 1749.

[1] It seems likely that Young suffered damage to one of his eyes as a result of
shock at word of Caroline's sudden and wholly unexpected death.

Richardson to Young. London. [M.] 1 January 1749/50.

Not traced.—*Monthly Magazine*, xxxvii (1 May 1814), 327–8.

London, Jan. 1, 1750.

Accept, Reverend and dear sir, with the wishes of many happy new years, the accompanying little piece.[1] It is strictly true that I had no intention of printing it. But reading it to a little assembly of female friends one Sunday night, one of whom was labouring under some distresses of mind, they were all so earnest with me to print it, that person in particular who is my wife's sister, that I could not resist their entreaties; and, as they were all great admirers of Clarissa, I thought I could not do better than, by historical connexion to the piece, point the use of them in a distress so great as my heroine's is represented to be.

I have printed but a small number. Your approbation, or the contrary, will give me courage to diffuse it, or to confine it to the few hands for which it was designed; notwithstanding the booksellers' names in the title page.

Mrs. Hallowes will accept of that in which I have written her name, to whom I wish all happiness; in which I am sure is included yours. I am, Sir,

> Your affectionate and faithful
> humble servant
> S. Richardson.

Mr. Millar has your orders about the new edition of the Night Thoughts. He withholds publication, I believe, because the octavo edition is not all sold.

[1] *Meditations Collected from the Sacred Books; and Adapted to the Different Stages of a Deep Distress; Gloriously surmounted by Patience, Piety, and Resignation being Those Mentioned in the History of Clarissa as drawn up for her own Use.* It had probably been sent to Young especially as a consolation of his grief at the death of Caroline. Richardson's bibliographer says of it: 'Printed, but apparently not published' (William M. Sale, jr., *Samuel Richardson: Master Printer*, 1950, p. 198).

278. Welwyn, Herts. [Su.] 7 January 1749/50. Samuel Richardson.

Not traced.—Monthly Magazine, xxxvii (1 May 1814), 328.

Wellwyn, Jan. 7, 1749.

Dear Sir,

I thank you much for your very valuable present, and advise, desire, and press you to publish it, for the sake of all the afflicted, to whom it will be the richest cordial; and also for the sake of the profane, to whom it may be the greatest charity; for many may be tempted to read the glorious word of God when thus taken out of their Bible, who are fools enough never to read it, in it; and thus, in time, by your pious stratagem, may become proselytes to common sense and their own welfare.

Nor do I only press you to publish it, but also to insert it in your next edition of Clarissa; for now her character is established, your reason for not inserting it at first ceases. And it will much add to the verisimilitude, and pathos, and sublimity of the work; the first of which is the chief point in all fictitious composition, and the two last are the chief excellence of almost all composition whatever. With the most cordial prayer for the welfare of you and yours, I am,

Dear Sir,
Your affectionate admirer,
E. Young.

279. [Welwyn, Herts.]. [Tu.] 27 February 1749/50. Duchess of Portland.

Longleat MSS. 211.

May it please yr Grace

My Complaint continues, & it is some Uneasiness to me to write; but it wd be a greater not to let you know by my own Hand the great sense I have of yr Graces Goodness in enquiring after me. They that think of things out of the World, give us the best Proof of their being Virtuous in it.

But tho I am so much out of ye World, I have still One Eye, & One Heart at your Grace's service. The First occasions a short Letter, the Other a lasting Esteem & Gratitude in

Madam

Yr Graces

Much Obligd

& most Dutifull

Humble Sevt

EYoung.

I rejoyce that all is so
near well, & beg humble
Duty to my Ld Duke, &c:

Feby 27
1749.

280. [Welwyn, Herts.]. [Tu.] 10 April 1750. Samuel Richardson.

Not traced.—*Monthly Magazine,* xxxviii (1 December 1814), 431.

April 10, 1750.[1]

Dear Sir,

I thank you for the Universal History,[2] and your very kind present; Mr. Stevens,[3] at the Temple Gate, will soon have money of mine in his hands, if he has not already, and he will pay you for the History. Mine and Mrs. Hallows' love and service to you and your's. My eye makes writing

---

[1] Printed text has '1780'.

[2] Richardson had printed *An Universal History,* which was advertised in the *London Evening-Post* of 29 March as 'This Day . . . publish'd' in 20 volumes. The same paper carried another advertisement for *Additions,* in seven volumes, to the *Universal History.*

[3] 'My friend Mr Henry Stevens Hatter at the Temple Gate' was left a mourning ring and 20 guineas in Young's will, made 25 April 1760. From the beginning of Young's account with the Gosling bank in 1751 to November 1762, Stevens made deposits, averaging £235 annually, to the account. No mention of Stevens has been found in the city directories of that period, nor has it been possible to identify him further. In 1753 he witnessed the will of Benjamin Tassel (Somerset House, P.C.C. Hutton 3/4), Young's 'townlandlord' when he was courting Judith Reynolds.

troublesome to me; pardon therefore the shortness of my letter. I am, dear sir,

Very affectionately your's,

E. Young.

281. Welwyn, Herts. [F.] 20 April 1750. Duchess of Portland.

Longleat MSS. 221.—Bath, pp. 317–18.

May it please yr Grace

I was lately in conversation with a certain Gentleman who pressd me much to bring my old Tragedy[1] on the stage; & He told me that your Grace had promisd to second him in that request. I should be very glad to know at yr Graces leisure if this be True; for I have certain inferences to make from ye Veracity, or the Contrary of this Reporter. I beg Yr Grace to pardon my Liberty, & my Brevety, for I am still under my late complaint as to my Eye. When ye sun is highest ye Shadow is least. I can not say that ye shortness of my Letter proceeds from ye Height of my Regard; but I can truly say that it is absolutely consistent with it. For I am with the most real Respect & Gratitude

Madam

Yr Graces most Dutifull

& Obedt Sevt

EYoung

I beg my humble Duty
to my Ld Duke &c:
   Wellwyn
   Ap 20 1750.

---

[1] By 'old tragedy' Young may be referring either to *The Revenge*, which was produced at Drury Lane in October 1751, or *The Brothers*, which he had withdrawn from production in 1724 and which Garrick was to produce in 1753. The identity of the 'certain Gentleman' is not known.

282. [Welwyn, Herts.]. [Su. 8 July 1750]. Arthur Onslow.

Not traced.¹

283. [Welwyn, Herts.]. [Su.] 8 July 1750. Samuel Richardson.

Not traced.—*Monthly Magazine*, xxxviii (1 December 1814), 431–2.

July 8, 1750.
Dear Sir,

In the inclosed I press the Speaker to give in to your proposal.² As you are so kind as to deliver it to him, I beg you to second my request. If you find it difficult to prevail, I will put you in a way that is sure of success. Tell him that you will bear him company. Do this, and so double and treble your obligations on,

Dear Sir,
Your truly affectionate and much
indebted humble servant,
E. Young.

Shew the Speaker this letter. It will do far more to carry my point than the inclosed. For I bribe high (if a Speaker of the House can be bribed): I bribe with fifty miles of his conversation, with whom posterity will converse with pleasure.

284. [Spring or Summer 1750]. Edward Cave.

Not traced.³

¹ Evidence of this letter is in Young's letter to Richardson of this date.
² It appears from this and later letters that Richardson had proposed to Onslow that they visit Young at Welwyn. Onslow did not visit Welwyn until October.
³ Evidence of this letter is in a letter from Cave to Richardson of 23 August 1750 (Barbauld, i. 166–70). Cave was replying to a letter of Richardson's of 9 August, praising what he had read of *The Rambler*. Johnson's *Rambler* had been appearing

Richardson to Mary Hallows. London [W.] 5 September 1750.

Not traced.—*Monthly Magazine*, xxxviii (1 December 1814), 431.

London, September 5, 1750.

Dear Madam,

My wife, with her kindest respects, desired me to acquaint you that she is sorry that you should think you wanted any mediation to engage her in any commissions that you should think proper to employ her. She has bought the things at the best hand, by means of a brother of mine, an upholsterer. I hope they will please, and encourage you to employ her again in any other service.

As I knew the good doctor's just regards for Mrs. Hallows, and her's for him, I take this opportunity by her to mention to him that, in reprinting in small his Night Thoughts, I think that part of the first preface, if he approves of it, should stand to all future editions, which is not temporary. In the last edition there is no preface at all. I had taken notice to the doctor that the latter part of it was proper only to the work as published in parts before the whole was completed. Upon which the doctor directed the whole to be omitted; and, I thought, intended to give a new preface. But, not reminding him of it, it passed without any. And, if the doctor has no objection, I would put to the small new edition the following first part of what he had at first prefixed. Which I transcribe, lest he should not have it by him.

'PREFACE

'As the occasion of this poem was *real*, not *fictitious*, so the method pursued in it was rather *imposed* by what spontaneously arose in the author's mind on that occasion, than *meditated* or *designed*. Which will appear very probable from the nature of it. For it differs from the common mode of

twice weekly, beginning 20 March. Cave wrote, in part: 'I have had letters of approbation from Dr. Young, Dr. Hartley, Dr. Sharpe, Miss C——, &c. &c. Most of them, like you, setting them in a rank equal, and some superior, to the Spectators ... but, notwithstanding such recommendation, whether the price of *two-pence*, or the unfavorable season of their publication, hinders the demand, no boast can be made of it.'

poetry, which is from long narrations to draw short morals. Here, on the contrary, the narrative is short, and the morality arising from it makes the bulk of the poem. The reason of it is, that the facts mentioned did naturally pour these moral reflexions on the thought of the writer.'[1]

The doctor will give me his commands on this head. My best respects and those of all mine to him; together with my wife's to you. Conclude me, dear Mrs. Hallows,

Your affectionate and faithful servant,
S. Richardson.

285. [Welwyn, Herts.] [Su.] 16 September 1750. Samuel Richardson.

Not traced.—*Monthly Magazine*, xxxviii (1 December 1814), 432.

Sept. 16, 1750.

Dear Sir,

I came home two days ago[2] and found your kind letter to Mrs. Hallows, but go out again soon for some little time. On my return I shall write to the Speaker, who has promised to be here next month, and I hope and take for granted that you will bear him company. I thank you for the direction about the Preface and absolutely consent to it. Mine and Mrs. Hallows's love and service to good Mrs. Richardson, and many thanks for the late favour she did us. I have hurt my eye, which makes writing uneasy to me, for which reason I so soon subscribe myself,

Dear Sir,
Your affectionate and much obliged
humble servant,
E. Young.

[1] The one-volume edition of the *Night-Thoughts* published in April 1751 carries this paragraph as the preface to the whole poem, and it was regularly used thereafter.
[2] Young's letter to the Duchess of Portland of 21 October shows that he had been at Winchester helping with his son's admission to Oxford.

286. [Early October 1750]. Arthur Onslow.

Not traced.[1]

287. Welwyn, Herts. [Tu.] 16 October 1750. Samuel Richardson.

Not traced.—*Monthly Magazine*, xxxviii (1 December 1814), 432.

Welwyn, October 16, 1750.
Dear Sir,
The beginning of this month I writ to the Speaker, who had fixed on this month for the honour he had designed Welwyn, to let him know that October was come, and that you was ready to shorten his journey by your company. To speak in the language of sacred poesy—Why is he so long in coming? Why tarry the wheels of his chariot?[2]—If you can answer these questions, I beg it as a favour at your hands. My letter for the Speaker was directed to Leicester-Fields. My love and service and thanks to Mrs. Richardson for the last favour. Mrs. Hallows joins in her respects and best wishes to you, sir, and your lovely fire-side. I am,
Dear Sir,
Your affectionate and obliged
humble servant,
E. Young.

288. Welwyn, Herts. [Su.] 21 October 1750. Duchess of Portland.

Longleat MSS. 222.—Bath, p. 318; Shelley, pp. 227–8.

May it please Yr Grace
The many & great favours I have receivd at yr Hands makes it my Duty to comply wth yr Requests; Your high Rank makes it my Ambition, & your Graces amiable Accomplishment makes it my Pleasure, & ye Honour You did

---

[1] Evidence of this letter is in Young's letter to Richardson of 16 October.
[2] Judges 5 : 28.

Wellwyn last year, makes it an absolute Debt in me to wait on You. Now it may seem somewhat odd that a man can not comply with his Duty, & his own earnest Desires.

But indeed, Madam, the Case realy stands thus.—Soon after I had the Honour of your Graces Last Letter, I was obligd to go to Winchester where I had a son[1] at the Then Election, standing for a Fellowship of a College in Oxford; Applications to ye Electors &c: detaind me there till ye latter end of September. Then Business /[verso]/ carryd me into Surrey[2] where I continued some time determining on my Return to Wellwin to set out for Bullstrode. But on coming Home, I found a letter from the speaker proposing to meet his son from Cambridge at my House.[3] This I know not

how well to decline, & hoping their Meeting would be soon, I still proposd waiting on yr Grace afterward. But ye speaker put it off from time to time, & now at last He has let

me know that He will be with me Tomorrow, & probably He may stay till ye End of ye Week. This pushes me too far into ye Winter to venture a Journey, for ye least Cold flings me into Pains of which my Ld Duke may have some Idea, but yr Grace can have none at all. With my humble Duty to my Ld Duke, humble service to Mr Achard, & best Wishes falling thick as Autumn Leaves on yr Little Family, I am

     Madam Yr Graces most Obedt
      & Obligd Humble Sevt
       EYoung.

Wellwyn: Octr 21 1750.

[1] Frederick, who had been at Winchester since 1742, and was now in his 18th year, was admitted to Balliol College a year later, 4 November 1751 (Thomas, p. 182).

[2] Perhaps it was at this time that Young arranged for a plaque commemorating his mother in the church at Chiddingfold with lines 473–4 of the third 'Night':

> Here lyeth the Body of Judith widow of
> the Revd Edward Younge, late Dean of
> Sarum, dyed December ye 8th in the
> 69th year of her age, anno Domini 1714.
> Life's a debtor to the Grave,
> Dark Lattice letting in Eternal Day.

[3] The son George Onslow (1731–1814) became the first Earl of Onslow in 1801. His father (Arthur) was accompanied to Welwyn by Richardson.

289. Welwyn, Herts. [Su.] 4 November 1750.
Duchess of Portland.

Longleat MSS. 223–4.—Bath, pp. 318–19; Shelley, pp. 228–9.

May it please yr Grace

Notwithstanding my Truant behaviour this Summer, I am not alltogether absent from Bullstrode. I am as much there, as a Person at this Distance can possibly be. I run over most of your Alterations in my Fancy, & am exceedingly pleasd with them; nor am I at all surprizd at it, considering whose Tast & Genius presides over that Scene so very capable of shining; & I am persuaded that your Grace can change most things for the Better, but yourself. This, Madam, I think is Courtly, & on ye Credit of it, I beg leave to slip into your Flower-Garden of which you are so fond, Why truly it is a /[verso]/ most Gorgeous Apartment of your Paradise. What Shapes! What Colours! What Combinations of them! What Varietys! What inimitable Patterns for Human Art to copy after! Even a Dutchesses Fingers are fardistancd by them, Poor Solomon! what a beggarly Appearance dost Thou make in all thy Glory compard with These? But I am apt to beleive Madam, that if Solomon was with us, & sufficiently disengagd from ye Infatuations of his Seraglio, He wd be likely to say something to this Purpose 'If those things so delight us, if ye Glories of ye Vegetable World, so much claim our Admiration; how much more so, the Glories, the Flowers of ye Morall World; where there are so many deformd & poysonous Weeds to set off, as so many Foils, their Amiability? Where there are ten thousand Mackleans[1] to one Dke of Portland? /[conjugate leaf]/ These are Flowrs indeed worth rearing; Flowrs that engage ye Care, & Cultivation, & Superintendence, & Affection of Superior Beings, fill their Invisible Paths amongst us with Fragrancy, & ever shine in their Sight. Pardon ye boldness if I say yt the Archangels Michael & Gabriel &c: are Florist with regard to These; They gaze on them, & protect them for a Season, & then so make their Fate

---

[1] The trial (13 September) and execution (3 October) of the highwayman, James Maclaine (or Maclean) (1724–50), had gained wide notoriety.

are bright
as Happy as their Beauties   They will gather them
one Day in glorious Clusters, & present them to ye Supreme
to whose Great Protection, I who am but grass, most cordially
recommend your Grace & the little Flowrs of yr Family, &
Subscribe myself with great Truth

> Madam Yr Graces
> Most Dutifull
> Much Obligd
> Humble Sevt
> EYoung.

I beg my Duty to my Ld:
humble service to Miss
Granville, Dr Carleton[1]
& Mr Achard, whose Cold
I am too well qualifid
to compassionate by
one of my own
          Wellwyn
          Nov: 4th 1750

/[verso]/ Mrs Ward & Mrs Hallows beg the favour of Yr
Grace to accept their Humble Duty.

290. [Welwyn, Herts.]. [M.] 10 December 1750.
Samuel Richardson.

Not traced.—*Monthly Magazine*, xxxviii (1 December 1814), 432.

Welwyn, December 10, 1750.
Dear Sir,
    When you and the Speaker last made me happy, he told
me he received yearly, as a present to the chair, the sacred
volume, and that he would give the next to my altar. My
altar is now finished, and I want to know at what time of the
year that present is made to him, for to that hour I would
stay; but, when that time is elapsed, if I should find that kind
promise is forgot (and yet I by no means would have the

---

[1] Unidentified. A Dr. Carleton died 1 December 1757 at Bedford House.

least hint given to him about it,) I would furnish myself elsewhere.[1] Mrs. Ward and Mrs. Hallows join me in love and humble service to you and your's.

E. Young.

This is very bad weather for the nervous. Pray let us know how you do. We have all had our complaints, which makes it extremely natural for us to enquire after the health of our friends.

291. Welwyn, Herts. [Th.] 13 December 1750. Samuel Richardson.

Not traced.—*Monthly Magazine*, xxxviii (1 December 1814), 432.

Welwyn, December 13, 1750.

Dear Sir,

Dr. Cox, physician in Cork-street, wishes me to beg your vote for him as physician to Westminster Hospital.[2] He says, he is sure I have an influence with you. That opinion is such a bribe to me to make my application in his favour

---

[1] Young willed a folio Bible to his church, presumably the one he was soliciting at this time. From Richardson's letter of 2 January it appears that the binding was done by [Thomas] Baskett.

[2] William Coxe (d. 1760), a Fellow of the Royal College of Physicians from 1748, had married Martha D'Aranda, widow of Young's stepson, Charles Henry Lee. The election of Coxe was reported in *The Penny London Post, or Morning Advertiser* for 24 December as follows: 'On Friday [the 21st] a general Board was held at the Blue-Coat School in Westminster, for the Election of a Physician to the Westminster Infirmary, in the room of Dr. Hawley who has resigned. The candidates were Dr. William Cox, and Dr. John Pringle; upon casting up the Ballot the Numbers were as follow. For Dr. Coxe 196 Dr. Pringle 128 Majority 68.' A more intimate account of the election appears in a contemporary diary with the following entry for December 1750: '21. The Ballot for a Physitian at the Infirmary in James Street. Dr Cox carried it against Pringle by a majority of 58. The greatest contest for a thing of this nature I have heard of. Duke of Newcastle, Mr Pelham, Princess Amelia for Dr. Cox and Duke of Cumberland, Bedford etc. for Pringle who was Physitian to the Army. People threatened for not voting on one side that they should lose the Duke of C's business. Strange way of treating mankind. Our Church and dependants all voted I believe for Dr. Cox who is a man of good sense and religion' (*The Diaries of Thomas Wilson D.D. 1731–37 and 1750*, ed. C. L. S. Linnell, 1964, p. 259).

that I do it most heartily, being persuaded that he is a skilful and honest man. Pardon this liberty and trouble from

Dear Sir,
Most truly your's,
E. Young.

Richardson to Young. London. [W.] 2 January 1750/1.

Not traced.—*Monthly Magazine*, xxxviii (1 December 1814), 432–3.

London Jan. 2, 1750–51.

Dear and Rev. Sir,

I had been half, and more than half, engaged to vote for Dr. Pringle, if I voted at all, for a physician in the Westminster Infirmary, before your recommendation of Dr. Cox came to hand. All I could therefore do to serve the latter gentleman, was by not voting at all. And I forbare accordingly. I congratulate you on his election.

Monday was se'nnight I attended the Speaker at Ember Court, with Mr. Edwards,[1] author of the Canons of Criticism; and staid there four days. The Speaker wished for you often. So did Mr. Edwards, who is a worthy man. So did I, you may be sure.

And it fell from him, that he would send you the Bible for your altar, as soon as it came to his hand, which generally was, he said, soon after the sitting down of the parliament. He spoke of his intention with the same warmth and delight, that he mentioned it to me in our passage from Welwyn to London; and that was with a great deal.

I am acquainted with Mr. Baskett, and, unknown to the Speaker, desired him, as a friendship to me, to hasten the ornamenting and binding of it, for that the Speaker had intended it as a present to a worthy divine for his church. And a noble present, said Basket, it will be, for it will soon be scarce, and probably, on that imperial size, never reprinted. He promised to give it extraordinary dispatch.

---

[1] Thomas Edwards (1699–1757).

I told the Speaker your altar was finished: and it shall not long want, said he, its noblest piece of furniture.

He always with delight mentions his excursion to Welwyn, and your kind treatment of him there. What then must I say for myself. Most heartily I thank you for it, my rev. and dear Sir. And that is all I can say. Excuse the lateness of the acknowledgment.

Your friends (and they are numerous, as you know) are continually enquiring whether you don't think of coming to town; and when: as if I knew your motions. It is true, when I have a mind to give myself reputation, and consequence, I talk of being acquainted with Dr. Young. But, that I may not be thought too vain, I tell them, that you do not acquaint me either with what you are doing, or with what you design to do. I was pressed by a lady, said I, to ask the Doctor who his best characters (his worst, his Lorenzo, it would not have been reasonable to have asked him) in his Night Thoughts were: and he would not satisfy the lady (one of his greatest admirers) through me, but gave me such an answer, as being reported to the lady, she called him a great courtier, and I cannot tell what. Though she still admires him, and cannot help it. Had I given myself high airs of intimacy with the Doctor, added I, I should have been a good deal mortified; since we little folks can hope for no notice but as we attach and pin ourselves to the skirts of the great and the good.

My respects to the good ladies. As Mr. Ward[1] is now removed from town, I hope Dr. Young, whenever he comes to town, will give me and my wife (who, with all ours, is his great admirer) his company. We have a spare bed in Salisbury-court, as well as at N. End.

Be so good as to tell Mr. Shotbolt, that I was greatly concerned that I lost his company in Aldersgate-street. I was kept, where I was indispensably obliged to dine, till after seven at night. Then I judged, at his Temple-Bar friends had taken hold of him; and so attempted not to call on his friend. Be pleased also to tell him, that the Speaker mentioned him of his own accord with honour; and I will

---

[1] This is probably a misreading for 'Mrs. Ward'. At the death of her husband, in 1750, Mrs. Ward went to live in Welwyn.

accompany him on a visit to Leicester-Fields, which is expected of him, at a proper time. As this will give your next neighbour pleasure, I know you would be displeased with me, should I apologize to you for this freedom of,

Rev. Sir,

Your most affectionate humble servant,

S. Richardson.

Many happy seasons attend you, and all you love, and all who love you. I need not mention Mrs. Ward and Mrs. Hallows: to whose goodness I owe obligation.

292. Welwyn, Herts. [Su.] 6 January 1750/1. Duchess of Portland.

Longleat MSS. 220.

Wellwyn
Jany ye 6
1750.

May it please yr Grace

I receivd not the Letter You mentiond; it is no more
it is in ye
in my powr to leave a letter of Yours unanswerd, than
Powr
    of a shadow, not to fall from an interposing Body, when the sun, like your Grace's Genius, shines upon it. And my not having receivd yr Grace's former Letter, leaves me much in the Dark as to yr Last. The Transcript You honour me with is dated from ye Westminster Journal;[1] why then not refer me to That, & avoid the Trouble of transcribing it?— I rejoyce, but am by no means surprizd, to hear so good an account of my Ld Titchfield; that fine Youth promises yr Grace a Pleasure of some Duration; a Pleasure that will shine like a summers sun, to ye last Hour of yr Life; & not like ye short, & dim gleams of our late gloomy /[verso]/ Days; which is the common Case with Human Pleasures. I bless God, excepting now & then, pretty severe Rheumatick

---

[1] No copies of the *Westminster Journal* for December or January have been located.

Pains, I have had very good Health, tho amongst a Nighbourhood which has sufferd much by a frequently relapsing
Fever; which plays with mankind, as a Cat does with a
Mouse; it lets them go for a little while, for ye cruel sport
of catching them again.

That You, & Yours, Madam, may escape this Grimalkin;
that your   ^{years} may be multiplyd, & rise above each other in
Happiness, Till they end in the Greatest, is the hearty
prayr of

Madam
Yr Graces most Obedient
& most Obligd
Humble Sevt
EYoung.

I much thank yr Grace for
ye Transcript & humble hope
ye Sequell.
Pray, my humble Duty
to my Ld Duke
   Mrs Hallows gives
her humble Duty to yr Grace.

293. [Welwyn, Herts.]. January 1750/1. Samuel
Richardson.

Not traced.—*Monthly Magazine*, xxxviii (1 December 1814), 433.

Jan. 1750–51.

Dear Sir,
   Your acquaintance is pretty large, and your taste is pretty
universal; now the question is, if, from these two together,
you can give me any light how to provide myself with a pair
of handsome gilt candlesticks for my altar; for very handsome
they must be to suit the rest. Should any such knowledge fall
in your way, favour me with a hint about it. You have not
been long enough in the world to be in haste. I, as one going
down hill, am for having all my purposes go fast, least I
myself should outrun them, and leave my designs behind me.

Mrs. Ward and Mrs. Hallows join my best wishes and humble service to you and yours. As the public stands in need of good advice, I wish you success in your study; as you, I fear, stand in some need of health; I wish you out of it as often as you can break that powerful enchantress—imagination's chain.

I am, dear Sir, ever your's,

E. Young.

294. Welwyn, Herts. [Su.] 20 January 1750/1. Duchess of Portland.

Longleat MSS. 248–9.—Bath, p. 322.

Wellwyn
Jany 20th
1750.[1]

May it please yr Grace.

Your last Letter is an Emblem of the World, full of Misfortunes & Death.[2] What reason have they to bless Heaven who escape so many Chances against them? Yet how Few are there who can find out in the Calamities of Others God Almightys Admonition to Themselves?—My Ld Bolingbrookes Letter[3] is written is [in] a Masterly manner: ~~For~~ What

pitty it is yt fine Talents, & Integrity should ever be parted? While together they make an Angell; & their separation gives us the precise & compleat Character of Lucifer. And yet from the begining of the world thus has it been more or less. It is very Observable, that all curious Arts were found out by the Descendants of Cain. Who by the /[verso]/ way, fled his Native Country; & had a Mark of Infamy fixd upon Him.[4]—I rejoyce at Mrs Murrays

---

[1] This letter was misdated 1756 by the Historical Manuscripts Commission (Bath, p. 322).

[2] Among the deaths the Duchess may have mentioned are those of the Right Honourable Thomas Thynne, Lord Viscount Weymouth, and the Revd. Dr. Anstey of Trumpington, both on the twelfth of this month.

[3] Bolingbroke's *Letter on the Spirit of Patriotism* had appeared in 1749.

[4] While Bolingbroke had fled England after the death of Queen Anne, the Duchess's grandfather, Robert Harley, Earl of Oxford, had remained to face imprisonment on charges of treason and eventual acquittal.

recovery, & when I have a sore Throat your Grace shall certainly be my Physitian.—I knew not that Mrs Belenden was dead.[1] Does your Grace converse with my Lady Cowper?[2] She is come into my Nighbourhood, & claims old acquaintance with me. I think there is something agreeable in her Manner, for as yet I know her no farther. I have no thoughts at present of seeing the Town soon, but I shall see it the sooner because your Grace is in it. I wish there were a few more such scatterd up & down in it, to sweeten its corrupted Mass, & reprieve it for another Century. I hope that Wellwyn will, this summer, lye in the Way of your Graces Travels; if so I will show You what /[conjugate leaf]/ a fine Colony of sheep yr Grace has transplanted from yr own Arcadia into a foreign land.[3] I wish I could prevail with my Flock to imitate their Innocence. But They, like their Betters, make Innocence their Prey; for they have stolen two of my Lambs.—

I am, madam, exstremely concerned for ye young Lady You mention; for her Acquaintance with yr Grace obliges me to conclude that she deserves a much better Fate.[4]—With a thorough sense of the Obligation I lie under for your good Wishes, & ye frequent kind Offices, & Honours you do me; I am

> May it please yr Grace
> Yr Graces most Obedient
> & most Humble Sevt
> EYoung.

Mrs. Hallows with all Duty
acknowledges ye Honour of yr Graces Notice.
I beg my humble Duty to my Ld Duke
& let ye Little ones take my Heart, & divide
it amongst them.

[1] Margaret Bellenden of Beaconsfield, Bucks., two miles west of the Portland home of Bulstrode.

[2] Lady Sarah Cowper (d. 1758), a daughter of William, Earl Cowper (d. 1723). She had taken a house near Cole Green, Herts., about six miles west of Welwyn, in the summer of 1750 (Llanover, 1861, ii. 584).

[3] The 'flock' mentioned in Young's letter of 24 October 1749.

[4] This was probably Elizabeth Montagu's sister, Sarah Robinson (1723–95), about to marry against her family's wishes, but with support from the Duchess (Climenson, 1906, i. 280).

295. Welwyn, Herts. [Su.] 27 January 1750/1. Vincenz Bernhard Tscharner.[1]

Burgerbibliothek Bern, MSS. Hist. Helv. xii. 91.—Thomas, p. 598.

Wellwyn Jan: 27
1750.

Revd Sr

Being from _{Home} on the arrival of your Letter, this is the first Post I could return my Acknowledgments for it. Private Lodgings there are none to be had near me; but there is a Publick House of very good Repute, & all convenient Accommodations just by me. This Week I am engagd, but the next Week I shall rejoyce in the Favour of yr Company. I beg my best Compliments to your Noble & Learned Friend.—I desire You to bring with You that Edition of ye *Night Thoughts* which you mention, & I shall with great Pleasure answer your Questions concerning it. I have Sr, at present, & expect more Company at my own House, or else that should be at your Service.

I am Sr
Yr most Humble Sevt
EYoung.

The Publick House,
I mean, is the Swan Inn
in Wellwyn, but two Doors
from my Own, by which means I shall enjoy _{you} the more

---

[1] Tscharner (1728–78), a native of Bern, Switzerland, accompanied by a Count Sternberg, a Mr. Frisching, and 'other companions', was visiting England at this time. Early in March he wrote to the Swiss scientist and author Albrecht von Haller (1708–77) of a four-day visit to Young in Welwyn. Reporting on the visit with emphasis on his inquiries about the *Night-Thoughts*, he wrote in part: 'Voici ce que Mr Young lui-même nous a apris: Lucia fut son Epouse et Mère de Narcisse: elle étoit Soeur du Comte de Litchfield auquel le cinquième Livre des Pensées est adressé, et petit-fille du roi Charles II par sa Mère. Narcisse avant sa Mort ayant été mariée à Philandre, fils de Milord Palmerston, C'est par cette famille et par celle de Lucia que le Dr Young se trouve allié à quelques Maisons des plus distinguées dans le royaume. Philandre et Narcisse moururent tous les deux dans un Voyage qu'ils avoient entrepris en France pour rétablir leur Santé et dans lequel leur digne Père les accompagna. Leurs morts se suivirent avec un très court intervalle. Young lui-même profondément affligé par cette double perte prit encore au passage de Calais à Douvre une fièvre qui le mit au bord du Tombeau. Ces tristes accidents furent l'Ocasion et le Sujet des Pensées nocturnes qu'il composa effectivement dans le Silence de ces Nuits que l'affliction et les insommies lui rendirent encore plus noires' (Thomas, pp. 599–600).

**296. [Welwyn, Herts.]. [Su.] 10 March 1750/1.
Samuel Richardson.**

Not traced.—*Monthly Magazine*, xxxviii (1 December 1814), 431.

March 10, 1750.
Dear Sir,
Many thanks for your many favours, particularly your last enquiry. Those gentlemen have been with me, and I find them, according to your report, persons of reputation.[1]
My friend Mr. Shotbolt has kindly promised to do me a service in town, with regard to which your advice and experience may be of use, if not necessary; I shall be obliged to you, therefore, if you'll permit him to consult you about it. Nor will you forget to introduce him to the Speaker.
Mrs. Hallows and Mrs. Ward join in best wishes and humble service to you and your's, with,

Dear Sir,
Your truly affectionate
and much obliged,
E. Young.

**297. Welwyn, Herts. [Tu.] 19 March 1750/1. Samuel
Richardson.**

Not traced.—*Monthly Magazine*, xxxviii (1 December 1814), 431.

Welwyn, March 19, 1750.
Dear Sir,
I am distressed in a point which I am almost ashamed to own. I have some excellent landscapes, which I ordered to be cleaned, and they have, in my absence, varnished them, which will spoil my pictures. When you see your friend Mr. Heymore,[2] I beg you to ask if any art can take off the varnish,

---

[1] Tscharner and Count Sternberg (see preceding letter), who had also made the acquaintance of Richardson.

[2] Joseph Highmore (1692–1780), who had painted a series of twelve illustrations for *Pamela* in 1744. (These paintings are now divided among three galleries: the Tate in London, the Fitzwilliam in Cambridge, and the National in Canberra, Australia.) Highmore was later to do the portrait of Young now in All Souls College, Oxford.

and rescue my pictures from ruin. Of, if it can't be got off, if any thing can prevent the mischief of its cracking the paint.

Having thus christened my own child first, let me thank you for your's,[1] which I received by Shotbolt. It was (if I may so speak) born a christian, there's not only innocence but virtue in it. May it answer the good end of which it was conceived; and, by reforming one half of our species, make both happy. If it does not, 'twill be the fault of the patients, not the medicine; which, as the bishop says of his panacea, has great vitality in it. My best wishes and service to all your's. I am, dear sir,

> Your affectionate and much obliged
> humble servant,
> E. Young.

298. [Welwyn, Herts.]. [Th.] 26 March 1751. Samuel Richardson.

Not traced.—*Monthly Magazine*, xxxviii (1 December 1814), 433–4.

March 26, 1751.

Dear Sir,

Many thanks for Mr. Highmore's information; and your kind promise. Our Clarissas are neatly bound in dark-coloured calf-skin. But what you send will be most welcome in any dress.

Mr. Cibbers' is a surprising letter,[2] and, like many more extraordinary's, rather to be admired than commended, and we love to be admired, though it is sure that *superior beings* only commend. They that fear death least, are least inclined to jest with him; they reverence the sender in the sent; and 'tis certain that death is the Almighty's messenger, and sent

---

[1] Richardson's 'child' was apparently a sermon 'concerning the pernicious and excessive use of SPIRITUOUS LIQUORS' by Isaac Maddox (1697–1759), Bishop of Worcester, perhaps in the edition announced in the *Daily Advertiser* of 12 March.

[2] Apparently a private letter, perhaps one that Richardson had sent on for Young's advice, rather than one of his earlier (1742, 1744) published letters addressed to Pope. It may have had to do with what Richardson once referred to as his 'contention' with Cibber 'about the character of a good man' (cf. Richardson's letter to Lady Braidshaigh, *Selected Letters of Samuel Richardson*, ed. John Carroll, 1964, p. 171).

with such insignia as are designed to make serious the human heart; and serious our friend's heart perhaps may be; if so, there is no harm in the letter; for a comedian may be allowed to wear the mask to the last.

Such levities more gain men's affection than their esteem. But their esteem is most worth of the two. For affection may be withdrawn, but their esteem cannot. The last of these truths I now feel, and the first you, dear Sir, need never fear from

Your much obliged and obedient,
E. Young.

Mr[s] Hallows is much yours. My love to your beloved. My respects to the Speaker when you see him.

299. [Welwyn, Herts.]. [Tu.] 9 April 1751. Samuel Richardson.

Wellesley College Library MSS.—*Modern Language Notes*, xxxvii (1922), 314–16.

Dear Sr

I gratefully accept ye Kind offer you made me of being under yr Roof for some days while I transact an Affair in Town.[1] I shall be with you on Moonday next, God willing. That God willing, who this moment sets a thousand Agents at work for my sake, of wh I know nothing, tho they are all within me; & shd any one of ym cease to work it wd prove my instant Death: I mean ye Animal Functions. Yet how merry shd I make ye World, shd they hear me say, 'If it please God, I will rise from my seat, ['] or, 'I will open my

---

[1] Young opened an account with the banker Francis Gosling on 17 April with a deposit of £520. On the 18th he added another £50 and bought a £500 Bank Annuity of the 2nd Subscription (1746). At the same time he gave Gosling power of attorney to receive interest on several investments which show up in the books in August as follows: £3,000 in three per cent bonds of 1731 in trust with Lord Litchfield and William Monck; £2,000 in three per cent bonds of 1726; £1,900 in Bank Annuities of 1746; £400 in New South Sea Annuities; and £500 in South Sea Stock, for a total investment of £9,800 at face value (access to the bank ledgers was through the courtesy of F. M. Cattell, Esq., Manager of the Gosling Branch of Barclays Bank, 19 Fleet Street, where the accounts were copied in 1966).

Mouth['] or, 'if it please God I will set Pen to paper.[']&c:
so Ignorant are our Wise ones both of God & Man. And
now, Sr, wh is ye most respectable Being, a Monarch on his
Throne, or a Beggar's Brat at ye breast, whose Ignorance
is not its Crime?

You see I treat You very familiarly, by permitting every
thought yt rises in my mind to run thro my Pen, to ye Interruption of those Thoughts of yrs, for wh I hope yr World
will soon be ye Better. Mrs. Hallows salutes You & Yrs.
I am Dear Sr

> Yr much Obligd
> Humble Sevt
> EYoung

Ap. 9. 1751.

300. [Welwyn, Herts.]. [Late] April 1751. Samuel
Richardson.

Not traced.—*Monthly Magazine*, xxxviii (1 December 1814), 434.

> April — 1751.

Dear Sir,

I cannot too soon return my hearty thanks for your last
favours I received. How few are they in whose conversation
I can find any account? The fewer they are, the more to be
valued. Enter into my meaning, and I shall have the better
hope of waiting on you at Welwyn, when business permits.
I shall say no more, for I should blush to be too plain in so
selfish an invitation. I am, dear Sir,

> Most your's,
> E. Young.

*To the Bricklayer.**

My friend! concluding miracles were ceased,
Your pride I blamed, and thought your pains misplaced;
But *now*, applaud, what I pretend to blame,
After Clarissa, you shall rise to fame.

Mrs. Hallow's is most obliged. We must see Mrs.
Richardson, or you disoblige us both.

*To Sir Charles.*¹
What hast thou done? I'm ravish'd at the scene,
A sword *undrawn*, makes mighty Caesar *mean*.
*Alluding to an expression of my father's.

301. Welwyn, Herts. [Sa.] [20 April 1751]. Vincenz Bernhard Tscharner.

Burgerbibliothek Bern, MSS. Hist. Helv. xii. 92 (31).—Thomas, p. 598.

Worthy Sr
   I am much obliged to You for your Letter. Mine to You, was to remind You of your Kind Promise to let me wait on you at Wellwyn on yr Return from ye Bath, which is a Favour I much desire, & shall allways acknowledge. I beg my best Respects to Count Sternberg, & please to assure him, that I am

Sr
His, & your
most Obedient
& Humble Sevt
EYoung.

Wellwyn
Ap [Paper torn away]
[In another hand] (20. April. 1751)

302. Welwyn, Herts. [F.] 26 July 1751. Duchess of Portland.

Longleat MSS. 225–6.—Bath, p. 319.

May it please your Grace
   A Lady of my Acquaintance² who has a good Hand at Matchmaking, and who has lately brought together the Proprietor of Pensilvania,³ & a Daughter of ye Lord Pom-

¹ Sir Charles Grandison, protagonist of Richardson's next novel (1754).
² Unidentified.
³ Thomas Penn (1702–75), second son of William Penn (1644–1718), founder of Pennsylvania, and Lady Juliana Fermor, daughter of Thomas Fermor (d. 1753), first Earl of Pomfret, were married in London on 22 August (*London Evening Post* of 24 August).

fret is now with them at my Lords seat in Northamptonshire,
& is to spend some Days with [me] at her Return, I expect
ye latter end of this Week; Which unavoidable Accident
denys me that Honour, & Pleasure; which ^{yr Grace} so very
obligingly offers me. But I most humbly request, that at
going into ye North, or at your Return, or Both, You would
refresh my spirit, by resting yourself under my Roof.

I rejoyce in the Restoration of your Graces Health; And
I hope I may congratulate my most worthy Lord Duke on
the same Account. There has been /[verso]/ nothing but
Death about me. Mr West calld on me not long agoe, and
gave me the Pleasure of hearing You was well, & of carrying,
or forgeting to carry my Respects to your Grace, with ^{whom}
He was to dine that Week. He came into these parts in order
to purchase for his sister a considerable Estate of One Lady
Cotton.[1] Our Neighbour Lady Caroline Cowper[2] is gone to
Bristol for her Health.

Your Grace perceives I pump hard for News; and therefore I will give it over; and content myself with assuring
You, that Words can not express the satisfaction it will give
me to wait on Your Grace at Wellwyn; And to thank You
for your numberless most Kind Invitations; And to make ye
best Apology in my Powr, for suffering them to be thrown
away, on

> Madam
> Your Graces
> Most Devoted
> & ever Gratefull
> Humble Sevt
> EYoung.

I rejoyce Madam
yt ye Little Ones are
well & beg my Humble
Duty to my Lord
    Wellwyn
July 26. 1751.

[conjugate leaf, verso]
Mrs Hallows's humble Duty to yr Grace.

---

¹ Unidentified.
² Lady Georgiana Caroline Carteret (d. 1780), second wife (1750) of William,
second Earl of Cowper.

303. [Welwyn, Herts.]. [Tu.] 30 July 1751. Samuel Richardson.

Not traced.—*Monthly Magazine,* xxxix (1 April 1815), 230.

July 30, 1751.

Dear Sir,

Have you leisure or appetite to read so long a prayer?[1] If you have, what think you of it? How fares my friend Sir Charles? I long to see him and you at Wellwyn. The summer wastes. You promised me,—must you lose your credit, and I despair. Befriend both, and come. Heaven bless you and yours. My love and service. Mrs. Hallowes salutes you. Most truly your's,

E. Young.

Richardson to Young. [London]. [Th.] 1 August 1751.

Not traced.—*Monthly Magazine,* xxxix (1 April 1815), 230-1.

Aug. 1, 1751.

Can I have appetite to read such a prayer as that you have sent me? How can my good Dr. Young ask me such a question?

What do I think of it?—Why, I think of it as a piece of inspiration.

But let me ask you, sir, What did you intend I should do with it?

I have a character, Dr. Bartlett, whom my Sir Charles reveres for his piety, good sense, grey hairs, sweetness of

---

[1] Although Young was to ask Richardson to burn this prayer in another week its successor was undoubtedly to become 'Devout Thoughts of the Retired Penitent' in 'Letter IV' of *The Centaur not Fabulous* of 1754. Interestingly, the exploit which was to give title and substance to Young's work had already taken place in April of this year, although it had certainly not yet taken its place in the consciousness of Young. The event was an April fool's hoax reported in *The Gentleman's Magazine* (xx. 153-4) of 'An authentick Account of the surprising CENTAUR, the greatest wonder produced by Nature these 3000 years, lately proposed to be exhibited to public View, &c.'

manners; who might be desired by Sir Charles, on the very occasion, to compose such a prayer for him. And how would it illustrate the character of that sound divine; whom I am afraid to make write, for fear I should not keep up the character given him! And how would it adorn and exalt my work!

But see what an impenetrable heart I discover, that such a next-to divine prayer cannot properly affect it! That such a prayer against self cannot banish selfishness from it!

If you have an intention to publish it, as sometimes I think and hope you have, from the title you have affixed to it, it may do more good; and there will end my solicitude (even with a preference against my above request) for self.

You are extremely good in reminding me of a journey to Wellwyn. My wife spoke of it three days ago with pleasure, and a wish, that I hope may be yet answered—at least, that we may go down one day, and come up next.

Our respects to Mrs. Hallowes. And to yourself, sir, all manner of felicity in this world, and the reward of your pious labours in that to come! I am,

Reverend Sir,
Your most affectionate and obliged
humble servant,
S. Richardson.

304. [Welwyn, Herts.]. [W.] 7 August 1751. Samuel Richardson.

Yale University Library, Tinker MSS.—*Monthly Magazine*, xxxix (1 April 1815), 231.

Aug. 7, 1751.

Dear Sir,

I beg you to burn the prayer I sent you; I showed it but to few, and repent that I showed it to them: for what I now send you is better. I would print it; if you would be so good to determine the manner, letter, &c.

As for Sir Charles, if I mistake not, he is not enough a profligate to make this prayer in character for him.

But the same pen is ready to do Dr. Bartlett what service you please,[1] provided I see him and Mrs. Richardson soon at Wellwyn. Mrs. Hallows joins in the request, and respects to you both.

On second thoughts I will not print it, unless you and some one of your friends, most judicious in these matters, are sincerely of opinion that it will do good; and do not see any objection, of other kind, against it; and unless you give proof of your sincerity by some correction in it.

I shall, dear sir, look on your manner of lettering stopping, &c. as half the composition; for I know it will have half the good effect, at least on the many. As to those arcana of your art, my copy is scarce any direction. It is written by Mrs. Hallowes, and partly her composition (for she is really a good divine), and you know how to correct ladies—but men too. And I beg, sir, in the most serious manner, your honest critique on what I send. For I write to the heart, and you are master of the heart; and therefore properest judge in England on this occasion. Pray let me be the better pastor for being acquainted with you; I fear I am not enough popularly plain. Pray speak out, and do oblige, dear sir, your most affectionate humble servant,

E. Young.

One thing I would have unmentioned as a test of your integrity; but I must mention it; I am too long. Tell me where to shorten.

I know your foible, you love to commend. But just rectitude is better than benevolence itself.

A prayer for Sir Charles must have less of severe self-condemnation, and more of gratitude in it. This is not a prayer for a good man; if it was it would not suit my design, which in effect is a satire on the present age.

[1] The character of the clergyman in Richardson's *Sir Charles Grandison*, Dr. Ambrose Bartlett, offers a very brief prayer at one point in the novel.

305. [Welwyn, Herts.]. [Tu.] 3 September 1751.
Duchess of Portland.

Longleat MSS. 227.—Bath, pp. 319–20.

May it please yr Grace

Your Commands are sacred, and therefore I write. But my
Eye incommodes me, and therefore I write shorter than I
ought. But I will make some amends for the Brevity of my
Letter, by ye Importance of it. For I shall speak of your
Grace's Friends. Mrs Donoland is seting out for Ireland to
take Possession of Wealth on her Mothers Death. Mrs
Delany in a Letter, & that a very Ingenious one, to a Friend
of mine, says, among other Things that—There is but One
Dutchess of of [*sic*] Portland. In which she speaks ye sense
of the Nation. And give me leave to ad, that I beleive there
is but One Lady Oxford. To whom & my Lord Duke, I beg
my humble Duty.

I desire, Madam, my humble service to Mr /[verso]/
Achare, & please to let him know, that I should take it as a
Favour, if He could let me know, how I can direct a Letter
to Mr Stapfer.[1] I beg my best Respects to my Lord Titchfield, & his Relations, & am

Madam
Yr Grace's
much Obligd
& most Obedient
Humble Sevt
EYoung.

Mrs Hallows desires yr Grace
to accept her humble Duty.
    Sepr ye 3rd
        1751.

---

[1] Johann Friedrich Stapfer (d. 1775), theologian of Bern, Switzerland, of whom
Young would have learned from Tscharner on his visit to Welwyn in March. Young
naturally turned to the Swiss John Achard for help in addressing a letter which, if
Young indeed wrote it, is now unknown.

306. [Welwyn, Herts.] Th. [12 September 1751].
Duchess of Portland.

Longleat MSS. 294.

May it please yr Grace

I promisd to write to You at Wellbeck, & I was as good as my Word. I writ about a Week agoe, And begd a Favour in my Letter. I should with great Pleasure wait on you both at Stevenage, & St Albans; But I am confind by a sore Throat. It is Better than it was, but not well. My Letter to your Grace gave You some Account of your Friends Mrs Donoland, & Mrs Delany, & I hope by this time it may be come to your Hand. I desired to know if Mr Ashare could let me know how to direct to Mr Stapfer. I heartily wish yr Grace a safe Arrival at Bullstrode; And with my respective Dutys to All, am

Madam
Yr Graces much Obligd
& most Obedient Humble Sevt
EYoung

Thursday

307. [London]. [Su.] 29 September 1751. Duchess of
Portland.

Longleat MSS. 228.—Bath, p. 320.

May it please yr Grace

In order to give the Reason for not waiting on yr Grace, according to your, & my Ld Dukes very kind Desire, I find myself obligd to let you into a secret, which I desire You not to communicate. I am, Madam, printing a Piece of Prose,[1] and am obligd to correct the Press myself; which forces me to be in Town, till that Affair, is over. And if I can so hasten it, as to have it done in Time, the Piece, & its Author shall wait on You together. If not I shall send your Grace the Piece, as soon as finishd. I shall send it to no One else, not

1 Untraced, but see Young's letter to Richardson of 30 July preceding.

puting my Name to it; & for some Reasons desiring /[verso]/ the Writer may be conceald. Which Reasons, your Grace may possibly guess at, if You do the Thing ye Honour of a Perusal. As for the Performance, let that be as it will, I am sure ye subject is such as will meet with your Approbation. To show your [Grace] that my Good wishes (as in Duty bound) run very, very high for You, & Yours, I wish You All more Happiness than You deserve. My humble Duty to my Lord Duke, my humble service to Mr Ashard. And as for ye Young, I wish them ye greatest Blessing; First, that they may long enjoy the Example of such Parents, & then, that they may set their Children ye same.

 I am, Madam, Yr Graces

Most Dutifull
& Humble Sevt
EYoung

Sepr 29
1751.

308. [?London]. Th. [?October 1751].[1] Duchess of Portland.

Longleat MSS. 296.

May it please yr Grace
 You do me great Honour, & if you will be so good as to pardon me for appearing before You in my Book, as I ride every Day for Health, I will wait on You tomorrow morning
    w
between T elve & One. I am

Madam
Yr Graces most Dutifull
& Obligd Humble Sevt
EYoung

Thursday
Pray my humble Duty to his
Grace &c.

---

 [1] Because of the cryptic and doubtless whimsical character of this letter, there can be no certainty even of the year in which it was written.

309. [?Welwyn, Herts.]. [?M. 11 November 1751].
Theophilus Leigh.

Not traced.[1]

310. [Welwyn, Herts.]. [Sa.] 23 November 1751.
Samuel Richardson.

Not traced.—*Monthly Magazine*, xxxix (1 April 1815), 231.

Nov. 23, 1751.
Dear Sir,
   I designed, and sent you word that I would be with you
on Tuesday next, as supposing that day of the week most
convenient to you. But I since find that I must be in town on
Monday, and beg the favour of a bed that night, without in
the least otherwise altering your own purposes. You see what
liberty I take, and I hope it will provoke you to the like with
me; though to provoke a person to confer a favour is, I
confess, on second thoughts, a very odd way of speaking.
                                     I am, dear sir,
                                       Most your's,
                                         E. Young.

   [1] Evidences of this letter are the catalogues of the Anderson Auction Co. of New
York, of 8 January 1914 (Lot No. 385) and of the Walpole Galleries of New York, of
11 August 1922 (Lot No. 251). It is described as inserted in 'The Complaint, 18mo.
old vellum gilt edge London 1751' and Young is said to have mentioned that aside
from sending him his son he 'sends by the same Hand Exiguum Pignus which I
beg you to accept'. Leigh (1694–1785) was then Master of Balliol College, Oxford,
in which Frederick Young matriculated 12 November 1751. The little gift accompanying the letter was undoubtedly the copy of the *Night-Thoughts* in which the
letter is now preserved.

311. [Welwyn, Herts.]. [Su.] 1 December 1751.
Duchess of Portland.

Longleat MSS. 229.

[In the hand of Mrs. Hallows]
May it please Your Grace
   I am extreamly obliged to you for giving me the great
sattisfaction of knowing Heaven has so tenderly treated my
Lord Titchfield in so terrible a distemper:[1] All the world
would have so Amiable a Youth tenderly treated.
   If all the World was as grateful as your Grace justly
expresses yourself on this Occation; they woud be Happier
than they are: Heaven pours down the Materials of happiness
upon us, and expects we shd work'em up to that degree of
Felicity of which they are capable and which Heaven
designed for us by our own wisdom. And Gratitude is the
chief Artist in this Supream Manufacture.
   I impatiently long to receive farther good news with
regard to my Lord Titchfield, and assure your Grace, that
his perfect Recovery will make me a very great sharer in your
Graces own happiness on That Account.
   Pray my humble Duty to my Lord &c.
                           I am Madam
                     Your Graces much Obliged
                   And Dutiful Humble Servant
                           EYoung.
Decr 1 1751
I beg your Graces pardon
for writing by a borrowed
hand; but I have hurt one
of my Eyes; And this is
written by Mrs Hallows, who
desires her Humble Duty
to Your Grace.

      [1] The Duchess's son was recovering from smallpox.

312. [Welwyn, Herts.]. [Su.] 8 December 1751.
Duchess of Portland.

Longleat MSS. 230–1.

[In the hand of Mrs. Hallows]

May it please Your Grace

I most heartily congratulate You on the recovery of my
Lord Titchfield: And might congratulate my Country on
the same account, for bright Example in High Station is the
greatest blessing it can receive. I have not seen Lord Orrery's
book,[1] I have sent for it: I hear a great character of it. If he
has used excellent Talents to a bad purpose he himself is
another Dr Swift,[2] & the Dirt, his Wit has thrown on the
good Doctor, will probably be pick'd up by the world to be
return'd on his Lordship. Thus what he design'd as simple
Murder on anothers Character, will turn out Suicide in the
End: Nor is this an Uncommon Case: To check the spleen
of a /[verso blank; conjugate leaf]/ malicious world, a wise
Providence has so order'd it that few can discharge their Ill
will on others without hurting themselves. Nothing [is] so
Natural as the In-Cog visit you made in Dover Street & the
pleasing sight You stole there. Your Grace sees that stolen
goods are sweet. But your Graces Theft puts me in mind of
an old Thief in Martial who to keep his hand in, when he
coud find no other game stole his own shoes.[3] Wishing the
continuence of all Blessings on your Grace & Family

I am Madam Your Graces
Most Dutiful
And Obliged Humble Servant
EYoung.

My humble Duty to My
Lord Duke, Lord Titchfield &c.
Mrs Hallows desires
her Humble Duty to Your Grace
8th Decr 1751.

---

[1] *Remarks on the Life and Writings of Jonathan Swift* (1751) by John Boyle
(1707–62), 5th Earl of Orrery.

[2] In *Conjectures on Original Composition* (1759), Young elaborated this attack on
Swift and identified it specifically with his objections to the fourth book of *Gulliver's
Travels*.   [3] Martial, *Epigrams*, viii. 59: 'On a One-eyed Thief'.

313. [Welwyn, Herts.]. [Tu.] 10 December 1751.
Samuel Richardson.

Not traced.—*Monthly Magazine*, xxxix (1 April 1815), 231–2.

Dec. 10, 1751.

My dear Sir,
   Is it quite impossible for you and Mr. Millar to favour
me with your company at Wellwyn? If so, is it impossible
for you to give me an evening at Barnet?[1] If it is not, I beg
you to do it. For, in the first place, I have been ill, and cannot
possibly go to town; and, in the next place, I cannot close
what I have under my hand without consulting you on a
remarkable particular in it. If you and Mr. Millar can swallow these ten miles, be so good as to let me know it, and to
chuse your own day and hour, and I and Shotbolt will wait
upon you at the Mitre[2] there. I ask this great favour with as
great tenderness, and if it is in the least disagreeable to you
I retract my request. Wishing you and your's all health and
peace,

I am, dear sir,
Your most affectionate and obliged
humble servant,
E. Young.

   Mrs. Hallows begs her humble service to yourself and
Mrs. Richardson. She tells me that you never was treated
civilly at this house, particularly with regard to a bed; and
that she is in pain for an opportunity of making one for whom
she has so great an esteem, some little amends.
   Pray my service to Mr. Millar and his.

[1] About midway on the road from London to Welwyn.
[2] According to W. Branch Johnson (*Hertfordshire Inns*, 1962, i. 37), the Mitre
dates from 1633.

314. [Welwyn, Herts.]. [Su.] 15 December 1751. Samuel Richardson.

Not traced.—*Monthly Magazine*, xxxix (1 April 1815), 232.

Dec. 15, 1751.

Dear Sir,

Mr. Shotbolt and I dined at Barnet yesterday; I was surprized and most ashamed at reading your letter; the most inexcusable blunder was occasioned by my misunderstanding Mr. Millar's. You came out of love, and with some inconvenience; I shall dare see your face no more. But, though you cannot pardon me yourself, intercede for me with the ladies, and Mr. Millar.

Your most obliged
and most unpardonable
humble servant,
E. Young.

Mrs. Hallows' humble service waits on Mrs. Richardson and the rest of the good family, with the compliments of the season near at hand.

Richardson to Young. London. [W.] 18 December 1751.

Not traced.—*Monthly Magazine*, xxxix (1 April 1815), 232.

London, Dec. 18, 1751.

Mr. and Mrs. Millar, Miss Johnson, and myself, most heartily rejoice, that it was not owing to ill health, or sad accident, that we were deprived of the very great pleasure we had all proposed to ourselves, of a richer evening and morning than we could have given ourselves, had not expectation made us look out of our own company for a delight we were very, very loth, as long as hope could continue, to despair of.

The notice of meeting was certainly too short. We did all we could to suppose the mistake owing to the letter. But our loss—you cannot, sir, be just to yourself, if you do not suppose it an heavy one.

It was indeed inconvenient for me to go: yet, to have deferred the meeting was more so to Mr. Millar, as he was preparing the publication of a new piece of Mr. Fielding: so that we were bound down to that day, or to a very distant one.

Dear and Reverend Sir, cannot you with convenience favour me either in Salisbury-court, or at N. End?—If not, cannot you write your commands?—If neither, you may, at the beginning of the next month, command at any place the attendance of one whose love of Dr. Young no disappointment can abate.

Mr. Shotbolt is the very sixth person, for whose company we could have wished, in order to complete the felicity of the proposed evening and morning. The bachelor would have been pleased to have been admitted to a conversation tête-à-tête with two ladies; an honour which his own tan-yard has not given him, although one hundred of them at a time have been obliged to him for a floor to bound upon, and a roof to cover them, especially when he was secure of the rest of his company; and that, though one of them was a maiden lady, no plot was laid against him.

Those ladies, and the two men, most cordially desire you, Sir, Mrs. Hallowes, and Mr. Shotbolt, to accept of their best respects, and of their wishes of the season. And they say, that you can make them rich amends whenever you please.

Your friend, the Speaker, has been greatly distressed by the illness of one of the most promising little girls (the child of his advanced years) that parent ever boasted. It was the worst sort of small-pox. But, contrary to all expectation, the distemper has taken a favourable turn.

I am, dear, reverend, and good Sir,
Your ever obliged, affectionate,
And faithful humble servant,
S. Richardson.

315. [Welwyn, Herts.]. [Tu.] 24 December 1751.
Samuel Richardson.

Not traced.—*Monthly Magazine*, xxxix (1 April 1815), 232–3.

Dec. 24, 1751.

O, dear Sir,

What a paragraph in the last Newspaper![1] Add this paragraph to balance it:—Heaven has one more angel than it had last week. When you see the Speaker, my duty and love to him.

I thank you for your last very kind letter. How glad shall I be to see our Barnet party at Wellwyn; chuse your own time; to me it is entirely indifferent. When you see Mr. Millar, let him know I received his kind present, and am enjoying them. Mrs. Hallows joins with me in wishes of happiness to both the good families.

I am, dear Sir, your very
Affectionate humble servant,
E. Young.

Dec. 24, 1751.

316. [Welwyn, Herts.] [Th.] 9 January 1752. Samuel Richardson.

Not traced.—*Monthly Magazine*, xxxix (1 April 1815), 233.

Jan. 9, 1752.

Dear Sir,

My hopes of consulting you, on what I had written,[2] are over, as to the present: for, from a cold, I have such an indisposition in my eyes, I cant read without pain. Notwithstanding, if you and my good company of Barnet can take it into your hearts, to think an airing this way to be as much for your health and amusement, as it will most certainly be for my pleasure, you will not drop your kind thoughts for seeing Wellwyn as soon as you can, with Sir Charles in your pocket.

I am, dear Sir, truly your's,
E. Young.

[1] Anne, only daughter of Speaker Arthur Onslow, had died on 20 December.
[2] Presumably an early version of *The Centaur not Fabulous*.

---

317. Welwyn, Herts. [Su.] 19 January 1752. Archibald MacAulay.[1]

Not traced.—Charles Howe, *Devout Meditations*, 2nd ed., 1752 [1753] *Gentleman's Magazine*, lxiv (August 1794), 700; Nichols–Doran, *Works*, 1854, I. cv.

Kind and Worthy Sir,

How shall I sufficiently thank you for the favour and honour of your very valuable present.

The Book of Meditations I have read, and more than once; and I shall never lay it far out of my reach: for a greater demonstration of a sound head, and sincere heart, I never saw. . . .

Dear Sir, I cannot but return to my favourite Meditations; for, in truth, I am fond of them. I think you was a lucky man in meeting with the manuscript; and I know you was a worthy one, by bringing it to the press. The world is your debtor for it. My part of the debt I will pay, as far as hearty thanks will go towards it: and I wish I could do more.[2] But I am surprised that the author's name is suppressed:[3] for I know no name to which that work would not do an additional credit: and, why a man's modesty should rob him of his just honour, when, by that honour, his modesty can be no more offended, I know not. I wish you would consider this, with regard to future editions. I desire you, Sir, to insert me in the list of your friends, for such I am, and such I am obliged to be by your unexpected and unmerited favour. I am,

Your's, &c.
E. Young.

Wellwyn, 19th January, 1752.

1 MacAulay was promoting a book he had published the year before, *Devout Meditations*, by Charles Howe (1661–1742). He was presumably related to George MacAulay who married Howe's granddaughter.

2 Young's letter was included in the second edition of the work, announced in the *Public Advertiser* of 28 April 1753 as published: 'This Day with a Recommendatory Letter by the Rev. Dr. Edward Young'.

3 Howe's name appears in the second and later editions.

318. Welwyn, Herts. [Tu.] 26 May 1752. Duchess of Portland.

Longleat MSS. 232.

May it please yr Grace

I was somewhat alarmd at your long silence, for fear I should find ye Cause of it in my self. But your Graces Letter has turned my Fear into Concern for your late Indisposition. I am but too well qualified to compassionate that Distemper. For I am now a close Prisoner to it myself; After many Remedies tryd in vain, I am now going to venture on ye Iron Peartree water,[1] of which the Papers tell such Wonders. I am now Madam so swelld in my Hands that I can scarce write. And have been long a Prisoner to this Disease; as soon as I can break my Chain, I shall /[verso]/ fly to Bullstrode, loaded with ye most gratefull Acknowledgments for your Graces most Kind, & repeated Invitations to

Madam

Yr Graces most Ogligd

& ever Dutifull

Humble Sevt

EYoung.

I beg, Madam, my
Humble Duty to my Ld Duke,
& best Wishes to All beneath
your Roof.

    Mrs Hallows desires yr Graces
Acceptance of her humble Duty.
    Wellwyn May 26.
      1752.

---

[1] Iron Peartree water was a trade name for water from a 'Well, near Godstone in Surrey' publicized in a half-page article in the *London Evening Post* of 12 October 1751, as having cured gout, rheumatism, gravel and stone, green sickness, and distress resulting from heavy drinking. It was offered for sale at the well or 'at the Green and Gold Lamp in Parliament-Street, Westminster, and no where else in England'.

Richardson to Mary Hallows. London. [Su.] 21 June
1752.

Not traced.—*Monthly Magazine*, xxxix (1 April 1815), 233.

Dear Madam,

My wife's thanks and mine attend the good doctor and
you, for your kind invitation. Mr. Shotbolt and we talked of
a very agreeable scheme: but we are the worst people in
England to put in practice. We have no present prospect of
managing such an excursion. It is, however, really a great
self-denial to us both. I am fraid I shall not be able to see
Peterborough this summer. If I can, assure yourself of
troublesome guests for a night or two.

The Doctor was so kind as to say, he would oblige me
with a little part of a manuscript, and I promised to return
it, if I made not use of it to his liking. Methinks I would
rather he would publish it as he once intended. But, if not,
shall be greatly obliged to him for it on the above condition.

My wife desires her cordial respects to the Doctor and
you. She always mentions your civilities to her with great
gratitude and esteem. She often says, How happy is the
Doctor in Mrs. Hallowes! How happy is Mrs. Hallowes,
at the feet of such a Gamaliel![1] While I shake my head and
whisper, 'It is owing to such good women as these, Bett,
that so many of your sex are unprovided for, and that there
are so many widowers and bachelors.'

Be pleased to tell Mr. Shotbolt, that, if he had been half
as much in earnest to persuade any woman to have him, as
he was to prevail on my wife to take the talked-of excursion,
he had one good woman every day in the week to have
quieted his conscience and his cares, instead of an hundred
indifferent onces collected through the country, every
Summer-Thursday, hopping about in his shed.

The snuff-box is a nothing. The snuff is however good.

My girls would have great pleasure in being acquainted
with Mrs. Hallowes. They desire their compliments to you
and the Doctor.

---

[1] Paul was 'brought up . . . at the feet of Gamaliel' (Acts 22:3).

I most heartily, Madam, thank him for his kind reception of me;[1] and you for your kind care of,
Your most obliged and obedit servant,

                          S. Richardson.
London,
June 21, 1752.

My respects to good Mrs. Ward. I thought to have made her one short visit when I was down, but was in too much hurry.

319. Welwyn, Herts. [Tu.] 23 June 1752. Sir William Bunbury.

Historical Society of Pennsylvania MSS.—*Correspondence of Sir Thomas Hanmer*, 1838, pp. 349–50.

Dear Sr

By his Majestys Letter to ye Archbishop &c: You see how ye most Noble of Charitys is at present distressed.[2]

I beg ye favour by yr means to know, if Mr Garrick is willing to act ye Tr
a
gedy[3] in your hands, early next Winter

---

[1] Richardson and Francis Gosling had called on Young, Saturday 13 June, and stayed the night in Welwyn (Victoria and Albert Museum, Forster Collection 458, vol. xiv, f. 78).

[2] The Society for the Propagation of the Gospel in Foreign Parts, founded in 1701, apparently had the support of George II, though the letter to which Young refers has not been located.

[3] i.e. *The Brothers*, which Garrick produced the next year, 3–17 March. Although it then ran only eight nights, Young's account with the Gosling bank shows that on 12 March 1753 Young gave the society £1,000 in 3 per cent bonds of the year 1726 for which Young paid £928. 2s. 6d. Cash deposits in the account, 22 March, presumably his share of proceeds of the play, came to £392. 15s. 1d. (including 16s. 7d. received for 'a bad moidore', an old gold piece, probably contributed to the receipts for the author's night). Young thus increased his gift to the society by adding the considerable sum of £535. 7s. 5d. to his profits from the play to make up the £1,000 given to the society. Commenting on Young's benefaction, Richardson wrote to Lady Braidshaigh: 'I had some talk with him on this great action. "I always, said he, intended to do something handsome by this society. Had I deferred it to my demise, I should have given away my son's money; all the world are inclined to pleasure; I myself love pleasure as much as any man; could I have given myself a greater by disposing of the same sum to a different use, I should have done it"' (Barbauld, 1804, vi. 246–7, in a letter possibly misdated: 'Feb. 24, 1753').

for the Benefit of yt Charity; if so ye Profits arising from it
shall be given to ye Propagation of ye Gospell in foreign
Parts. I am, Dear Sr

Yr Affectionate
& Obedient Humble Sevt
EYoung.

I beg, Sr, my best Compliments to my Lady
Wellwyn June 23
　1752.

320. Welwyn, Herts. [M.] 29 June 1752. Duchess of
Portland.

Longleat MSS. 233.

May it please yr Grace
　I am exstremely sensible of ye great Honour I receive
in your so frequent kind Invitation to Bullstrode. But my
Returns of Pain are so frequent, & severe, that two Days
together quite Free, is an Exstraordinary with me. Whenever I am able to promise myself that I can be a Guest, &
not a Burthen to your Grace, I will most certainly pay my
Duty to you; or rathe[r] indulge my own Inclination, &
Pleasure under Pretence of doing so. For to live in ye world
without Pretences is great singularity. /[verso]/
　Madam my Heart writes on to ye End of my Paper, but
my Hand as bigg as two can not follow it. Pardon me therefore, if with my humble Duty to his Grace, & very best
Wishes to all You hold dear, I subscribe mself

Madam
Yr most Obligd
& most Obedient
Humble Sevt
EYoung.

Wellwyn
June 29
1752.

Mary Hallows to Samuel Richardson. Welwyn, Herts. [Tu.] 2 July 1752.

Not traced.—*Monthly Magazine*, xl (1 September 1815), 134.

July 2, 1752.

Good Sir,

Our summer Thursdays are fleeting to the years before the flood; and, as I find, have no charms for the lady of your affection; but the best doctor says, if you will give Mrs. Richardson and a Miss Richardson to our wishes, he will give them a syllabub, on the bench under a tree, where the deception is;[1] and says, if it would be agreeable to Mrs. Richardson, she would have time for some walks, &c. were she and Miss to come first, sir, in order for you to fetch them, but not till it was impossible for you to subsist without them, to quiet your cares and fatigues in administering to the public weal.

Our near and good neighbour Mr. Shotbolt received your message with undaunted courage; but for all that methought looked rather conscious; but begged his humble service to a gentleman that he respected and honoured; and, as that was a point we all agreed in, parted very good friends. The doctor will send you the manuscripts you desire next time Mr. Shotbolt comes to town, which I think I said in my hurry on Sunday night. Mrs. Ward, sir, is much obliged by your favourable regard, and begs her humble service, as does the good doctor, and your honoured and unworthy correspondent, to yourself, Mrs. Richardson, and the Misses, from, sir,

> Your most obedient and obliged
> humble servant,
> Mary Hallows.

Wellwyn.

---

[1] In Young's garden stood the façade only of a summer house with the inscriptions: 'Splendide Mendax' under a window and 'Invisibilia non Decipiunt' over the door (see Appendix B).

321. Welwyn, Herts. [Su.] 19 July 1752. Duchess of Portland.

Longleat MSS. 234.

[In the hand of Mrs. Hallows]

May it please Your Grace

I have taken the Drops but two Days, & think I already receive benefit from them. And as I am sattisfyd that as long as I live, I shall have more or less of this complaint, & some of my friends are likewise subject to it: I beg the favour of Your Grace, to let me know where these drops are to be sold; for to me, it is a very agreeable Medicine, & I think I shall make Use of it as long as I live: How very kind then was your Grace for thinking of me in my Distress! The health which you bid fair to restore (at least in some degree) shall ever be devoted to Your service, by

Madam

Your Graces hopeful Patient

And most Obedient Humble Servant

EYoung.

Wellwyn 19 July
  1752

Post S. As my right hand is
Affected pardon me for borrowing Mrs Hallows's, who gives her her [*sic*] humble Duty to Your Grace, as I mine to my Lord Duke &c

322. [Welwyn, Herts.]. [?Su. 26 July 1752]. David Garrick.

Not traced.[1]

---

[1] Evidence of this letter is Garrick's letter to Sir William Bunbury of 28 July in which he spoke of having had a note from Young 'this morning' (*The Letters of David Garrick*, ed. David M. Little and George M. Kahrl, 1963, i. 182). In the same letter Garrick expressed himself as somewhat indignant 'that the Doctor did not care to intrust me wth the Play wch I could have return'd to him next Monday

323. Welwyn, Herts. [Th.] 6 August 1752. Duchess of Portland.

Longleat MSS. 235–6.—Bath, p. 320.

May it please yr Grace

I this day receivd ye Drops, & with them a Demonstration of your great *Kindness* to me. As for yr Graces *want of Capacity* mentiond in your last, I am not in ye least concernd about it. For I bless God I have more than I want, wh is more than most Princes can say.

Madam, I should never more have mentiond to You anything about Preferment, but since yr Grace glances at it in yr last, pardon me, if out of pure Curiosity I ask, wt yr Crony ye Archbishop of Canty[1] meant, by a Letter to me 2 or 3 years agoe, in wh He says—'That he wd say nothing to me, but that He had acquainted my Friend ye Dutchess of Portland wth wt concernd my Interest.'—I suppose his Grace meant to say something yt was Agreeable, Unconcernd for anything more. For I have neither heard from, nor writ to Him since.

Yr Grace, if You please, may at yr leisure Unriddle This: if not, I am quite contented to continue still in ye Dark. For, I am with most chearfull resignation to ye Will of Heaven, & a most thankfull Heart for /[verso]/ its numberless

or Tuesday at Wellwyn, as I am going that Way . . . in ye road to Yorkshire—however delicate ye Dr may be with regard to his Play. . . . I have taken some pains to be at Liberty to act the Doctor's Play the Ensuing Season. . . . I intend to wait upon Dr Young the beginning of next Week & then I hope to be satisfy'd of his Intentions. . . .' In a letter of 17 August, Garrick wrote: 'Dr. Young's play will do —greatly. It is much the best modern play we have, and written with great tragic force. I do not imagine that Millar is connected with him; however I shall know that at my return; for I am to spend half a day with him at Wellwyn. The Doctor seemed desirous to wash his hands of the play, and to give it up to my care and direction' (*Letters*, op. cit. i. 172; the editors have assigned the letter tentatively to the year 1751, but it is almost certainly of the year 1752). Garrick's letters to his brother George (op. cit. i. 186–7) make clear that he spent a night in Welwyn at the White Swan, probably Friday, 15 September, on his return from Yorkshire.

[1] i.e. Thomas Herring, Archbishop of Canterbury. There are no letters among his extant relics in Lambeth Palace. The Duchess's acquaintance with him would have dated at least from the 1740s, as he served as Archbishop of York (1743–7) and was especially active for the Hanoverian cause during the Jacobite rebellion, in which the Portlands were deeply concerned for their northern holdings.

Mercys, & Blessings, & among the last particularly, for
yr Graces Favour,

> I am, Madam,
> Yr most Obligd
> & Dutifull
> Humble Sevt
> EYoung

I beg my humble Duty
to my Ld Duke; & may
Heaven continue to bless
all You hold dear.

Wellwyn
Aug ye 6th
1752.

324. [Welwyn, Herts.]. [Early August 1752]. Duchess of Portland.

Longleat MSS. 237.

[In an unidentified hand]

May it please your Grace
   I am extreamly obliged to you, for the very kind enquiery
you make:[1] And shall be proud to be permitted to communicate to your Grace what my own intentions are, when I know
more of that matter; having yet heard nothing at all of it. Nor
thought any thing about it; but I soon shall have an opportunity, which I will make use of, for my farther information.
   I frequently make use of your Graces Guacum,[2] with good
effect; and as, I thank God, I am pretty well, I have not yet
enter'd on the powders.

   [1] It is highly probable that the Duchess has asked about the possibility of Young's
having his play, *The Brothers*, produced and that the opportunity of which he
speaks alludes to the coming visit to Welwyn of David Garrick.
   [2] Gum guaiacum, from a West Indian tree, was prescribed as a 'sudorifick [i.e.
sweat-producing], vulnerary [i.e. for wounds], and anodyne, taken inwardly from
a Scruple to a Dram, mixed with an equal weight of sugar-candy . . . [and] also good
in Difficulty of Breathing, and in Asthmas; in which Cases it is common to add to
it an equal Quantity of washed Sulphur . . . [mixed] together into a Balm with Syrup
of Coltsfoot' (*A Complete History of Drugs*, by P. Pomet, translated into English
with large additions [by John Hill], 1748, p. 196).

Madam, I have heard that from the condition of the Duke of Whartons Lead Mines, that there will be more than enough to pay all Debts: and a considerable over plus to the Family.[1] If your Grace knows any thing certainly concerning this matter, I sho'd be greatly obliged to You, to be inform'd of it, as soon as your Grace conveniently can: For it will be of consequence to me on the whole, and particularly on the very point Your Grace mentions. /[verso]/

Madam I beg my humble Duty to my Lord Duke &[c]

And am

With great Gratitud[e]

Your Graces Most Oblige[d]

And Most Obedient

Humble Servant

EYoung

Mrs Hallows
presents her humble Duty.

325. [Welwyn, Herts.]. [Tu.] 14 November 1752. Samuel Richardson.

Historical Society of Pennsylvania MSS.—*Monthly Magazine*, xl (1 September 1815), 134.

Dear Sr

I have a Tragedy[2] wh I am desireous of reading to You. For, (on this Occasion) it is your Misfortune that you can Think & Feel; wh few men can. And I shd be inexcusable to let it come abroad without that advantage I hope from your hearing it, if I can obtain it.

The time to me is Indifferent, when   you   are most at leisure, & most willing to communicate your sincere Judgment to me, favour me with a Line; & I will be your Guest for a

[1] Profit on lead mining in the Swaledale, Cumberland, holdings of the Wharton estate went from £814 in the second half of 1751 to £5,937 in the first half of 1752, according to the report of the Master in Chancery (Public Record Office, C101/Unknown 145).
[2] *The Brothers*.

Night. My best Wishes & service to good Mrs Richardson,
& ye Tender branches around yr Table.

I am, Dear Sr, very truly Yrs

EYoung

Please to say nothing of it.[1]

Nov: 14

1752.

I hope, Dear Sr, you suffer not much by yr late frightfull
Accident.[2] Mrs Hallows desires you to accept her best
Respects.

326. [?December 1752]. William Webster.[3]

Not traced.—William Webster, *Two Discourses*, 1753.

Dear Sir,

I have read over your discourses with appetite; and find
in them much piety, perspecuity, eloquence, and usefulness.
God grant them all the success they deserve, you wish, and
the world wants.! Most assuredly, Devotion is the balm of
life; and no man can go unwounded to the grave.

I am yours affectionately,

Ed. Young.

[1] Garrick similarly asked his correspondents to say nothing of his visit to Young,
and apparently had advised Young to keep the visit secret in order not to publicize
his plans for the theatre.

[2] Richardson's shop had caught fire and narrowly escaped complete destruction.
He described the incident at length in a letter of 20 December to Lady Braidshaigh
(Barbauld, 1804, vi. 217 ff.).

[3] William Webster (1689–1758) was Vicar of Ware and Thundridge, Hertfordshire villages about nine miles east of Welwyn. A regular author of theological books,
he published *Two Discourses*: I. *On Prayer* . . . [and] II. *On the Sacrament*, to which
Young's letter was prefaced, in January 1753.

327. Welwyn, Herts. [Tu.] 2 January 1753. Duchess of Portland.

Longleat MSS. 236–7.

[In the hand of Mrs. Hallows]

May it please Your Grace.

I find that I am very much in favour with the Faries: I have receiv'd another present from them: and I know not but by conjecture where to pay my thanks; but I will venture to send them to your Grace, You being a Person more liable to suspision than anyone I know on such occasions as these. I bless God I am pretty well; and have not spent half of what your Grace was so good to send me last:[1] so that I am richly provided for futurities. I hope your Grace, who sends so much Health abroad, keeps a sufficient stock at Home.

That Heavens blessing may rest on You and Yours, is my hearty prayer. I beg my humble duty to my Lord Duke, and best Wishes and respects to all you Love.

> I am Madam
> > Your Graces much Obliged
> > > And Obedient, Humble Servant
> > > > EYoung

Wellwyn 2d Janry 1752/3
Mrs Hallows desires her humble Duty.

328. Welwyn, Herts. [W.] 8 August [1753]. Duchess of Portland.

Address: To the Dutchess of / Portland at Bullstrode / Bucks.
Postmark: 8/AV welwyn.
Longleat MSS. 238–9.

May it please yr Grace

I heartily rejoyce at my Lord Titchfields Escape, & at every other Felicity, that falls to your Graces lot. I bless

---

[1] i.e. more of the Duchess's elixir of guaiacum.

God my Pains are much abated; nor must I at ye same time forget Your great Goodness for furnishing me with such effectual arms against my greatest Enimie.

I am Glad that Your Grace is pleasd to Naturalize Foreigners,[1] & heartily rejoyce that they are not Wolves.

I had with me this day an Irish Dean, who represented Dr Delany to me, with whom he has lately been, as a Person in high Spirits, which makes me hope things turnout better than was apprehended.[2]

I thank yr Grace for the Verses,[3] they are much better than I left them. If every thing improves Thus under your Graces hand, You will lay me under great Temptation to give You farther Trouble. /[verso]/

Whenever I receive the Honour of your Commands, I shall, God willing, pay my Duty to You at St Albans. With great Gratitude, & Respect I am

Madam
Yr Graces most Obedient
& most Humble Sevt
EYoung.

I beg my humble Duty
to my Lord Duke, &
all ye rest of yr Family
command my best Wishes,
& Esteem.

---

[1] In November Mrs. Delany wrote from Bulstrode to another correspondent of having seen 'such beauties of foreign birds as gave me great pleasure' (Llanover, 1861, iii. 241).

[2] Delany had been sued by the relatives of his first wife, Margaret Tenison (d. 1741), and the case was pending. In December it was decided against him but the finding was reversed in 1758.

[3] Perhaps Young's *Sea-Piece* (1755), some stanzas of which were revisions of stanzas in his *Foreign Address* of 1735.

329. [Welwyn, Herts.]. [Th.] 20 September 1753.
Samuel Richardson.

Not traced.—*Monthly Magazine*, xl (1 September 1815), 134.

Sept. 20, 1753.

Dear Sir,

I have read your kind and valuable present;[1] yet it hurts
me. You keep me in awe by your good sense: I dare therefore
to say but little. Yet must I say what is extraordinary to be
said, the wisest man in England may be wiser for reading
a romance.

My kindest love and services to those that love you, and
to those you love.

I am, dear Sir,
Your truly affectionate
and much obliged,
humble servant,
E. Young.

What ambition I have I am willing to conceal, and therefore will not ask to see you here; though Mrs. Hallows (most
yours) is most importunate with me so to do.

If you see the Speaker—but, who dares put words in your
mouth?

My best compliments and thanks to Sig. Barretti,[2] for
his ingenious present, if you meet with him.

330. [Welwyn, Herts.]. [Th.] 22 November 1753.
Samuel Richardson.

Not traced.—*Monthly Magazine*, xl (1 September 1815), 134–5.

Nov. 22, 1753.

My dear Sir,

We want proper help here in the country. I am not very
well. I have been for two or three weeks under a painful

---

[1] The first four volumes of Richardson's *Sir Charles Grandison* were published
on 13 November. Richardson had evidently sent an advance copy.

[2] Guiseppi Marc' Antonio Baretti (1719–89)'. His present was probably *La Voix
de la discorde, ou la bataille des violons*, which he had published this year in two
versions, French and English.

lowness of spirits. I have often a sort of moving pain on my left side, and near my heart; and am pretty much troubled with wind and frequent indigestions.

Pardon the great liberty I take in requesting you to give, in my name, two guineas to Dr. Heberden,[1] and to desire his advice. Mr. Gosling,[2] on sight of this letter, will repay the doctor's fee: but who will repay your kindness?

I know how precious your time is; it grieves me to trouble you; and I beg that it may be at your utmost leisure that you confer this piece of real friendship on,

dear Sir,
Your much obliged
and truly affectionate
humble servant,
E. Young.

As I am scarce known to the doctor myself, I am almost forced to give you this trouble.

Richardson to Young. [London]. [M.] 26 November 1753.

Not traced.—*Monthly Magazine*, xl (1 September 1815), 135.

Nov. 26, 1753.

My dear Dr. Young,

You will before now have heard from Dr. Heberden; God give success to his advice! I sent to him your letter the moment it came to my hand; with two guineas inclosed, as you directed. Last night he sent me back your letter, with a few lines, signifying he had written, and with them inclosed the returned fee. He is a fine-*spirited* man, as I have found on too many occasions for the quiet of mine.

From your symptoms, as in your letter, I have no apprehensions of unwished consequences; for they are symptoms

---

[1] William Heberden (1710–1801), popular London physician.
[2] Francis Gosling (1720–68), Young's banker.

that I have been taught, by much worse of my own, not to be alarmed at in myself; yet *as a stitch in time* holds equally in respect to health as to raiment, let me beg of you, in order to be near assistance, to give us your company in town. Tell Mrs. Hallows that she may depend upon our care of you. I was concerned that you made so bad an excuse (as the affair you was last in town being troublesome,) for not obliging us. Where should a man go, in such a case, but to his friend? Surely I may hope for the honour of being thought such. Warmth and welcome, in this season, I can engage for you; I need not say in my wife's name as well as my own. Due respects to Mrs. Hallows, and your next door neighbour; and repeated wishes to have you in Salisbury-court; conclude me,

> Reverend and dear Sir,
> ever your's,
> S. Richardson.

331. [Welwyn, Herts.]. [Tu.] 11 December 1753. Samuel Richardson.

Not traced.—*Monthly Magazine*, xl (1 September 1815), 135.

> December 11, 1753.

My dearest Friend,

Whose hospitable arms received the sick,[1] I bless God I am better; and by no means despair, through his mercy and blessing, on my good friend Dr. Heberden's assistance, of a perfect cure. You rejoyce in the good of all, much more of those that love you; you will therefore pardon this intrusion into the multiplicity of engagements,—heaven prosper them all; and may you and your's for ever rest in peace and safety under the feathers of the Almighty. Mrs.

---

[1] Mrs. Delany wrote on 9 December: 'Dr. Young is, I believe, in London; I sent my compliments to him by Mr. Richardson, with whom I suppose he is' (Llanover, 1861, iii. 253).

Hallows, with me, most cordially salutes you and good
Mrs. Richardson.

I am, dear Sir, most your's,

E. Young.

332. Welwyn, Herts. [Su.] 16 December 1753. Duchess of Portland.

Address: To Her Grace / The Dutchess of Portland / at Bullstrode / Bucks.
Postmark: 17/DE.
Longleat MSS. 240–1.—Bath, pp. 320–1.

May it please yr Grace
    I receivd with Joy your kind Remembrance of me; but
far otherwise at ye same time Your Graces black Catalogue
of Calamities. You say Mrs Donallan has been in Danger;[1]
we see therefore that a good Understanding is no Security.
You say Mrs Montague is in Danger,[2] therefore it is certain
that Wit can make nothing more than a poor Name Immortal. You Say, Madam, that Mrs Delany is Better;[3]
therefore she to my sorrow, has been Ill. Long may she live,
not only to give a Lustre to your /[verso]/ Graces Grotto,
but an Ornament to your sex.
    When such as These suffer, what Impudence is it in me
to complain? Tho You Madam, have had more than your
share, yet have you not engrosd all Colds to yourself. I have
been much out of Order, but am, I bless God, much better;
& rear my head once more to see most of my old Acquaintance & Friends drop before me. My Ld Thanet[4] was with

[1] She had just recovered from a serious fever.
[2] She suffered a chronic lung ailment.
[3] The Delanys had reached Bulstrode by 16 November and were with the Portlands there and in London until the middle of January when they took a house in
London. On 2 December Mrs. Delany had written to her sister Anne D'Ewes:
'. . . I have had great entertainment too from Dr. Young's letters to the Duchess,
which she has been settling, and read me above three score: they are I think the best
collection of *men's* letters I ever read: strong sense, fine sentiments, exalted piety; they
are written with as much ease and freedom as politeness can admit of to a great lady,
and the compliments are delicate, without the least flattery; so far from it, that it is
plain he takes every opportunity of shewing that he is above it, and by that how
well he knows the persons he addresses, and for wit, and lively and uncommon
imagination he is most excellent' (Llanover, 1861, iii. 247).
[4] Thomas Tufton, 6th Earl of Thanet (d. 1775).

me not long agoe, & now I am at a loss how to return his
Visit. That a good Providence may take You & Yrs into its
kind Protection, is, & ever shall be ye Prayr of

> Madam
>> Yr Graces most Obedient
>> & most Humble Sevt
>> EYoung.

I beg my humble Duty to
his Grace, & best Complimts
to Mrs Delany with
a long &c: Dec 16 1753
/[conjugate leaf]/

PS.

Mrs Delany's *Humiliation* (wh yr Grace speaks of) & yr
own *Presumption*, is to me Mysteriou[s] & Unfathomable.
Uncommon Excellence is a sure Charm against Humiliation.
And ye Presumption of conferin[g] Favours is a new Figure
of speech which few Uninspird by Bullstrodes clear air would
be able to Decypher. But I suppose You two Ladies influenced by this Season of Town-entertainmts are pleasd to
put your merry Meaning in Masquerade, to make a Country
Parson stare, & your own polite Circle smile. Nor can I take
it ill. Jokes at Christmas want no Excuse. However since I
have detected You, I beleive You Ladies will be more sparing of your Rallery in your Next. But since Rallery is a
symtom of Health, may it continue, may it encrease, for I
assure You, on that Consideration, the more You two Invalids are pleasd to laugh at your humble servant, the more
abundantly will he Rejoyce.

333. [?Welwyn, Herts.]. [Tu.] 18 December 1753. Samuel Richardson.

Not traced.—*Monthly Magazine*, xl (1 September 1815), 135.

Dec. 18, 1753.
Whatever congratulations you may have received, I
believe, dear sir, that not one half of your revenue of fame is

yet come in.[1] For I am reading Sir Charles the second time, and like it much more than before. And I am persuaded that apologies will be made you for the defective applause which you have hitherto received.

E. Young.

334. [?Welwyn, Herts.]. [F.] 21 December 1753. Joseph Warton.

Not traced.—J. Wooll, *Biographical Memoirs of ... Revd. Joseph Warton*, 1806, p. 218; Thomas, pp. 601–2.

Dec. 21, 1753

Dear Sir,

I am deeply concerned that I cannot serve you; it would give me much more than common delight to have been any way instrumental to your happiness, for I know and love your amiable worth, but indeed my connection with Mr. ———[2] is very slender. I have not seen him these six years; I hope therefore you will excuse me; and do not suppose me to be 'Dissimulator opis propriae, mihi commodus uni',[3] for it is not the case. You have indeed the very best wishes of my heart; but as I am your truly sincere, so am I your sadly impotent friend, and, dear Sir,

oblig'd humble servant,
Ed. Young

My hearty love and best service to your good Mother.[4]

[1] Volumes i–iv of *The History of Sir Charles Grandison* had been published on 13 November and vols. v–vi on 11 December (Sale, 1936, p. 76).

[2] This is almost certainly John Roberts, secretary to Henry Pelham, to whom Warton would have been directed in seeking preferment. Young's last reference to Roberts was in 1747. Warton was to get a church in 1754 but despairing of advancement became a schoolmaster.

[3] Horace, *Epistles*, ix. 9.

'. . . a mean dissembler . . .
To make a property of your esteem.'
(Philip Francis).

[4] Warton's father had died in 1745. His mother, *née* Elizabeth Richardson, was of a Surrey family.

397

James Elphinston[1] to Young. Brompton, Mdx. [M.] 24 December 1753.

Not traced.[2]—*Forty Years' Correspondence between Geniusses ov boath sexes and J. E.*, 1791, i. 38–9.

Sir,

The cause of the boldness which presents you this Poem, ought possibly to have prevented it. The original is too well known abroad to be new to you, Sir; yet will you not wonder, that a piece so titled is still so new in England. If so, what chance has a version? Only this, that many of those with whom Religion needs not the aid of novelty, and most, with whom she does, being strangers to the beauties of French Poetry; both may find in their native tongue such happy entertainment, that those may be delighted with the reason of their faith, and these may be sung out of infidelity.

Two or three peculiar compliments, more expected perhaps where the poem was written, than designed by its generous Author (who pleads equally the cause of all Christians), have been easily omitted in the translation, become so much still more truly Catholic.

Your distinguished benevolence, and your friend Mr Richardson, make me hope, Sir, for a pardon I would prefer to most praise; and eager to deserve a patronage, which would yield me a solid pride. Of this in any event I must find some, in being with a veneration unalterable as unborrowed,

Sir,

Your most humble
and most obedient servant,
James Elphinston

Brompton,
Dec. 24, 1753.

---

[1] Elphinston (1721–1809), who conducted a private school in Brompton, now part of London, had translated from French into English verse a contemporary work by Louis Racine (1692–1763), entitled: *Religion*. His version was announced for publication on 17 December 1753 (*Public Advertiser*).

[2] The text of this letter, and of the two following, has been reconstructed from the version in Elphinston's *Correspondence*, where it appears in an eccentric system of phonetic spelling promoted unsuccessfully by Elphinston.

335. [Welwyn, Herts.]. [Tu.] 1 January 1754. James
Elphinston.

Not traced.—*Forty Years' Correspondence*, etc., 1791, i. 41.

Sir,
    I much thank you for the favour of your useful and excel-
lent book. I think it is well translated: but were it worse
done, it would be of service to Religion; which I am persuaded is your principal view. God Almighty prosper your
commendable efforts in it!
                     I am, Sir,
                         Your sincere wellwisher
                             and Faithful humble servant,
                                 E. Young.

Jan. 1, 1754.

James Elphinston to Young. Brompton, Mdx. [M.]
7 January 1754.

Not traced.—*Forty Years' Correspondence*, etc., 1791, i. 40–1.

Sir,
    The honour of your letter, and still more that of your
approbation, have animated me to hope that your goodness
will not deny me a consequential favour, which may not a
little promote that usefulness you are pleased to think may
flow from my translation, and lend *Religion* the aid of a name,
which has placed its glory in adorning.
    Rousseau's[1] recommendation could irradiate only the
original, if the name of Racine needed additional lustre; but
could promise little for a version made after his death; and
which, appearing quite anonymous, affords too good a plea
to those who desire one, for leaving dormant in the shops a
performance that might as much alarm as entertain. May I

---

[1] i.e. the poet Jean-Baptiste Rousseau (1671–1741).

not crave, therefore, Sir, the permission of publishing part
of your Letter as may seem necessary; or your approbation
in any form you judge more conducive to answer your
benevolent wishes? But, as none tastes more strongly the joy
or generosity, unless perhaps he who confers it; so none can
more abhor its abuse, than he who must rejoice as much in
being,

Sir,
Your most obedient
as your most obliged servant,
James Elphinston

Brompton,
Jan. 7, 1754.

336. [Th.] 14 March 1754. Samuel Richardson.

The Pierpont Morgan Library MSS. MA1024.[1]—Barbauld, ii. 32–3;
Monthly Magazine, xli (1 April 1816), 230–1; Nichols–Doran, 1854, i.
xciv–xcv; Shelley, pp. 232–3.

March 14. 1754.

Joy to you dr Sr, & Joy to the World; you have done
great things for it. And I will venture to affirm That no one
shall read you without either Benefit, or—Guilt.[2] Pray ask
Mr. Cibber from me, where now are the *fine Gentlemen* of
the Stage? Sir Charles has enter'd a Caveat against their
wanted Applause; and Mr. Cibber signs it, or incurrs the
mentioned Guilt.

You have, my dear Friend, made a long & Successful
Campaign. God grant you may live long to reap ye Fruits
[of] it; & continuing by yr Conduct to vindicate yr

---

[1] The holograph of this letter is part of a Richardson manuscript and is said to
have been transcribed by 'a Kinsman' of Richardson. It accompanies Richardson's
letter of 27 September 1754 to his 'adopted sister, my dear Mrs. Watts' (cf. Richardson's letter to Susanne Highmore, *Gentleman's Magazine*, June 1816, lxxxvi. 506–8).

[2] Young was reading the seventh (and last) volume of *The History of Sir Charles
Grandison*, just published.

Pen[1] convince ye Hypercriticks, that Sir Ch. is by no means drawn beyond ye Life!

Shall I tell you what I think. You would not let me if you knew what I was about to Say. When the Pulpit fails, other Expedients are necessary. I look on you, as a peculiar Instrument of Providence adjusted to the peculiar Exigence of the Times; in which all would be *Fine Gentlemen*, and only are at a Loss to know what that means. While they read, perhaps, from pure Vanity, they do not read in vain; and are betrayed into Benefit, while mere Amusement is their Pursuit. I speak not this at a Venture; I am so happy as already to have had Proofs of what I say.

And as I look on ˄you as an Instrument of Providence, I likewise look on you as a sure Heir of a double Immortality; when our Language fails, one indeed, may cease; but the Failure of the Heaven and the Earth will put no Period to the other. These are great Words, but your Modesty must bear what your Worth imposes, and permit your Friends to let loose the real Sentiments of their Hearts.

Tully says, that if Virtue could be seen, all the World would stand in Admiration of her Charms. You have rendered her visible; & that in the most striking Colour. Therefore Tully's no Prophet, or you are much more.

To call these Compliments, would be Affectation in you; or to think them so, would be a Mistake. You are capable of neither; and therefore I'll go on. But on second thoughts to censure, not to Praise.

It is a little vain in you, dr Sr, to observe, that the Female World is much obliged to Mr. Addison. What if Alexander, after his Return from Babylon, should have talked of the Martial Merits (tho' great) of his Father Philip? Would not all have said, it was to throw the Thoughts of the Hearers, on his own? What greatly strikes me, & evidences as much as any thing, your Intimacy with the Human Heart, is the Scene where little Emily comes to Confession. But of what? rather of her Virtue, than her Crime. It is, I think, in the highest Degree, natural, tender, exquisite, and original—

---

[1] Barbauld (and Doran) read 'sex', and as the Richardson holograph is clearly 'Pen', the obvious misreading must come from the original manuscript no longer extant.

I am got no farther in the Volume: But could not forbear returning my own, and Neighbour's Thanks the first Post, for a Favour so delightful to, dear Sr,

Your very affectionate,

And much obliged Humble Servant

E. Young.

For our Sakes repent not of assuming the Pen; but be sure, for our and your own sake, to pay your self the Arrear of your Care for the future.

Benjamin Fletcher to Charles Reynolds, Chancellor of Lincoln. Welwyn, Herts. [F.] 19 April 1754.

Address: To / The Revd Dr Reynolds[1] / Chancellor at St Marys Church / Lincoln. *Postmark*: 24 AP.
Dr. Williams's Library, Jones papers B 17 [2] (3).

Sir

I am desired by Dr Young of Wellwyn to write to you (as Chancellor of this Diocese) to know if you have got or can tell whether there is in your custody a Terrier[2] or particular of the living of this Parish of which the Eldest Fellow of All Souls College Oxford is intituled to on any Vacancy. I have applied to the Warden of the College of All Souls for this Purpose, but they have not any such particular; but inform'd me that it was likely for the Chancellor of this Diocese to have such an Account in their custody. To which Dr Young desires the favour of yr Answer hereto on this account directed to him or me.[3] Dr. Young presents his compliments to you, who am Sir

Yr most Obedt Servt

B: Fletcher

Wellwyn in Hertfordshire 19th April 1754

[1] Charles Reynolds (1702–66), son of the Bishop of Lincoln, Richard Reynolds (1674–1743), was Chancellor of Lincoln from 1728 to his death.
[2] A survey of landed property.
[3] The letter is endorsed: '2d May 1754 A Copy of this Terrar sent per post 13s. 8d.' There is among the Jones papers in Dr. Williams's Library a receipt: 'Oct 18th 1759[?4] Recd of the Revd Mr Jones the Sum of 8s 9d for an Attested Copy of Wellwyn Terrier p H. Watson' (B 17 [2] (21)).

337. [Welwyn, Herts.]. [Tu.] 25 June 1754. Duchess of Portland.

Longleat MSS. 242.—Bath, p. 321.

May it please yr Grace

Thro a long absence from home,[1] I have but just now receivd the Honour of your last Letter. I heartily rejoyce with you on my Lady Oxfords good state of health; & am sorry to hear that yr Grace has had reason to complain. You cure every body but yr self. I thank your Grace I have found great benefit from yr medicine. I should have been very glad to have waited on you at St Albans,[2] had ye Fates permitted. I receivd a present of his late publishd sermon[s][3] from Dr Delany; & as bound in gratitude, as well as charity, much rejoyce in the turn his Law-affair has taken in his favour.

/[verso]/ I am glad, Madam, that my friend Mr Richardson has had ye happiness to recover Your Grace's good opinion. I am confident he deserves it. As for ye Fountain from wh ye mischeif sprang, I am sure it is a foul one; & therefore desire not to be better acquainted with it.

I direct this to Bullstrode, taking it for granted, that ere this time you must be There. Whereever You are may Heavens blessings attend You, & Yours, to whom I humbly

---

[1] On 29 June Richardson was to write to Mrs. Delany: '. . . Dr. Young . . . had been in town, somewhere behind the Royal Exchange, for three weeks, without letting me know a syllable of the matter till the very day that, ready booted, (Friday, last week) he called in Salisbury-court, leaving word (I was out) that he was very desirous of seeing me at Welwyn. I wish that he is not concerned in some plot, by his privacy from his sincerest friends. He is an absent man, you know, Madam, and if he be in a plot, it will not long be a secret. Of this we may be sure, it will not be against the state' (Barbauld, iv. 89–90).

[2] The Duchess had gone to Welbeck late in May on the illness of her mother.

[3] The word has been cut short on the right-hand margin but almost certainly was originally in the plural and in that event referred to *Sixteen Discourses upon Doctrine and Duties, more peculiarly Christian: And against the reigning vanities of the age*, a collection of Delany's sermons published this year from Richardson's press (cf. W. M. Sale, jr., *Samuel Richardson: Master Printer*, 1950, p. 166).

&

offer my most sincere Respects   Dutys, & am wth due
sense of yr repeated favours,

                              Madam
                                  Yr most Obedient
                                  & most Humble Sevt
                                  EYoung.

June 25
1754.

338. [Welwyn, Herts.]. [Su.] 14 July 1754. Samuel
Richardson.

Not traced.—*Monthly Magazine*, xl (1 September 1815), 135.

                                          July 14, 1754.
My dear Sir,
   I have a thing I would send immediately to the press; its
about the length of five sermons; and, as I am distant from
town, it can go on but slowly.[1] I would fain show it you
before I put it out of my hands; I put it in my pocket for that
purpose, when I called at your door.
   Mr. Shotbolt tells me you resent, &c.; it was not in my
power to see you before, which shall be explained when we
meet. There are so many catching at you, and you are so
unwilling to be caught, that I fear Wellwyn stands a bad
chance. Heaven prosper you and your's, to whom my best
wishes and humble service; Mrs. Hallows joins me in both.
I am, dear Sir,
                              Your most obliged and affectionate
                                  humble servant,
                                  E. Young.

   I print myself, because I cannot stay to talk with booksellers, and they are not at hand.

                    [1] *The Centaur Not Fabulous.*

339. [Welwyn, Herts.]. [Su.] 21 July 1754. Samuel
Richardson.

Not traced.—*Monthly Magazine*, xl (1 September 1815), 135–6.

July 21, 1754.
Dear Sir,
　Blot, add, alter, as you please; and, if then you approve it,
print it; if not, lay it by.

To the Speaker.[1]

Immortal Milton! first of British names! Each hair of
such an head an honour claims. And sure he pays its utmost
honour due, Who thinks t'attain a present worthy you.

> 　　　　　　I am, dear Sir,
> 　　　　　Your truly affectionate
> 　　　　　　and most obliged
> 　　　　　　humble servant,
> 　　　　　　　E. Young.

My respects to the ladies, and Mrs. Hallows' to you.

Richardson to Young. [London]. [W.] 24 July 1754.

Not traced.—*Monthly Magazine*, xl (1 September 1815), 136.

July 24, 1754.
　I see nothing, dear and reverend sir, to alter in your
dedication. Print it, you say; but in what size, page, type,
&c.? Do you intend the piece to be in the nature of a pamph-
let, or bound book? Cheap, or to bear a price? As Dr.
Delany's sermons, or those of the Bishop of London? Or
still closer?
　Your lines to the speaker are very apropos. Do you design
a letter to him besides, giving him the history of the precious
locket; and your opinion of the hair being a proof, as to

---

[1] These verses were to accompany Young's gift to Onslow of a locket containing
a lock of Milton's hair. See next letter from Richardson.

colour,[1] of the genuineness of his picture of that admirable bard, when a young man? I hope you do.

Accept of my best thanks for your goodness to me at Wellwyn, and for your most agreeable company to, and at, Barnet.[2]

Mrs. Hallows will be so good as to accept likewise my acknowledgments for her civilities. My wife desires her best respects and thanks to her for her kind care of me.

To you, sir, she desires to be most cordially remembered.

Be so good as to make her and my compliments to your worthy neighbour, with thanks for his friendly offices to me.

I am, Sir,

Your greatly obliged

and affectionate

humble servant,

S. Richardson.

340. [Welwyn, Herts.]. [?Su. 28 July 1754]. Arthur Onslow.

Not traced.[3]

341. [Welwyn, Herts.]. [Su.] 28 July 1754. Samuel Richardson.

Not traced.—*Monthly Magazine*, xl (1 September 1815), 136.

July 28, 1754.

My dear Sir,

What I propose is, after the thing is printed, to let some bookseller have it. The length of it will be that of five or six

---

[1] There is no description of the colour in any of Young's extant letters. According to the artist George Vertue, in a letter of 12 August 1721, Milton had 'light brown lanck hair' (*Monthly Magazine* of 1 May 1814, xxxvii. 330).

[2] In a letter of 23 July 1754 to another correspondent Richardson wrote: 'I went last Wednesday [17 July] to Dr. Young's, at Wellwyn, at his Request. A Friend [perhaps Speaker Onslow] carried me down by the Barnet Road. . . . Ye Dr. accompanied me back to Barnet, and dined with me there; at his own motion' (Victoria and Albert Museum, Forster Collection 458, vol. xiv, f. 132).

[3] Evidence of this letter is in Young's letter to Richardson of this date.

sermons. And I beg the favour of you to determine the manner of printing it; in which I shall thankfully acquiesce, for I understand nothing at all of it.

The reason I print it myself is because I have not had an opportunity of talking, satisfactorily, with any bookseller about it.

In the dedication, instead of—*your centaurs into men*— I would (if you approve it) have it—*your monsters into men*.[1]

I propose not sending you all the copy at once, but letter after letter, being four in all.[2]

I have sent the locket in a letter to the Speaker; but forgot mentioning the colour of the hair: when you see him please to supply that defect.

Another reason for my printing myself is, if I like it not when done I can suppress it.

I much like the book you gave me, 'Observations on Lord Orrery;'[3] it has manners, wit, and spirit.

You, sir, and Mrs. Richardson, are very good, and shall ever have a demand on the best wishes and services of,

Dear Sir,
Your much obliged
and obedient servant,
E. Young.

Mrs. Hallows and friend Shotbolt are much your's.

342. [Welwyn, Herts.]. [Th.] 1 August 1754. Samuel Richardson.

Not traced.—*Monthly Magazine*, xl (1 September 1815), 136.

Aug. 1, 1754.

Print, dear sir, in the way you propose. The number one thousand. You will have the first letter on Monday morning.

---

[1] This change was adopted.

[2] There were five letters in the first edition, six in subsequent editions, and a conclusion and postscript in both forms.

[3] i.e. Patrick Delany's *Observations upon Lord Orrery's Remarks upon the Life and Writings of Dr. Jonathan Swift*, announced in the *Gentleman's Magazine* as published in May 1754 (xxiv. 247).

I wish *Italics* and *Pointings*, &c. were as in Sir Charles Grandison; my copy no direction for those things.

I ask pardon for sending so slovenly a copy; but my eyes are bad; and I had rather compose two letters than write one.

Have you had an invitation from your friend in the Isle of Ely?[1] If you should have a mind to see that part of the world I will carry you, and thank you too.

Mrs. Hallows joins my best wishes and services to you and my friend Mrs. Richardson. I am, dear Sir,

Truly your's,
E. Young.

If you see any thing wrong in the letter, please to dele it, or let me know it.

Richardson to Young. [London]. [M.] 5 August 1754.

Not traced.—*Monthly Magazine*, xl (1 September 1815), 137.

Aug. 5, 1754.

Rev. Sir,

I have no objection to a separate publication, as you say you are fond of it, whatever booksellers might have, who have hopes of a concern in it. I will put it directly in hand.

I have had an invitation from the lady in the Isle of Ely.[2] She tells me that she was to invite you, sir, as well as me, in her father's name, as well as in her own, on account of his indisposition not permitting him to attend you. Methinks I could wish you would pay them a visit which she says would be so very consolatory to her good father; and I thank you for your kind offer of accompanying me thither; but I cannot, as I have written to the lady, with any conveniency go this summer. All my spare time will be taken up in fitting up a house at Parsons Green, which I have taken, on being obliged to quit that at North-End.

I presume you would not have the separate letters sell under twelve-pence each? And be put into a publisher's

---

[1] Thomas Colborn's daughter was one of Richardson's correspondents.

[2] The first name of Thomas Colborn's daughter is not known. The death of her mother, Mary, in 1753 accounts for the 'indisposition' of her father (Edward J. Howman, 'Extracts from Parish Registers', *East Anglian*, 1869, iii. 90).

hands? Have you a wish for a particular publisher? Roberts or Owen, I think, would either of them do it justice. Yet Dodsley generally deals with Cooper, against whom there can be no objection.[1]

Though you put not your name, or by the author of, &c. suppose you give leave to have it not denied that it is your's? Or whispered by the publisher by way of confidence. It will spread, by that means, to the credit of the piece, and you will not be obliged to give a sanction to the report or whisper.

Every body will guess to whom the dedication is made, by Lady T——.[2] Would you be careless on that head, should the piece be guessed to be your's? Mr. Winnington once told me, that Lady T—— was vindictive, and jealous of being in print.

I will attend, as you desire, to the copy; though, I dare say, it will be needless. You shall see every proof; so will be more secure of the printing.

On casting-off your copy, I find it will make too much for six-pence, done in the manner I proposed; and not enough for a shilling, were it to be printed on the large type through-out, that the preface to the Observations on Lord Orrery is printed on. As you design it for the good of the public, sup-pose you sell each for six-pence to gentlemen? The dedication included, this first will make but five half-sheets; four would do. It ought to make eight for a shilling; and will not make seven, I doubt, print it as loosely as we can. Do your three succeeding letters make more or less than the first, *dedication included*. If they make less they cannot be more than six-pence each.

Your determination is necessary before we begin the letter itself. I will send you a proof of the dedication as soon

---

[1] Copyright to *The Centaur* was assigned to Dodsley on 19 February 1755 for £200 to be paid Young in six months (see Appendix A). When *The Centaur* was published, probably in February 1755, it bore the imprint of A. Millar and R. and J. Dodsley. Records of Gosling's bank show deposits to Young's account of £100 each from Robt. Dodsley and Andrew Millar on 29 August 1755.

[2] Ethelreda (or Audrey) Harrison (d. 1788), estranged wife of Charles Towns-hend (1700–64), third Viscount Townshend. She shared with the politician Thomas Winnington (1696–1746) a reputation for gallantries, eccentricities, and wit. Following Richardson's caution, Young dedicated *The Centaur* 'To the Lady ******', dropping the inital 'T'.

as possible. That will the better enable you perhaps to resolve.

With respects to good Mrs. Hallows,

> I remain, sir,
> Your faithful and affectionate
> humble servant,
> S. Richardson.

I need not say I received safely this morning your first letter.

343. [?Welwyn, Herts.]. [M.] 5 August 1754. Samuel Richardson.

Not traced.—*Monthly Magazine*, xl (1 September 1815), 136–7.

> Aug. 5, 1754.

Dear Sir,

On second thoughts, considering the length of the letters, I am for publishing them letter after letter; and the first as soon as it is printed off, notwithstanding the time of the year; if you see no cause to the contrary.

I know, sir, your discernment; and, if any thing occurs that will mend the letter, by your own pen, or a hint to me, deny not the favour to one that will much thank you for it.

I have read your extract;[1] pray proceed. It will do much good; and put your works in more and the best hands.

Though this publishing the letters separately is a sudden thought, yet, for many reasons, I am fond of it; unless you have one that can knock them all in the head.

> Dear Sir,
> most your's,
> E. Young.

---

[1] This may have been Richardson's *Copy of a Letter to a Lady*, printed this year for private circulation only.

344. [?Welwyn, Herts.]. Su. [11 August 1754].
Samuel Richardson.

Harvard University (Houghton MSS.), by permission of the Harvard College Library.—Barbauld (facsimile), 1804, vol. vi; Nichols–Doran (facsimile), 1854, ii. 416 (facing); Ralph Straus, *Robert Dodsley*, 1910, p. 354; Shelley, pp. 235–6.

       [In another hand] August 12[1]—1754
Dear Sr

If you knew any proper Artist in yt way, I wish You wd show him ye Grotesque Picture of a Centaur in my Dedication. If I cd have a Cut of it, I wd prefix it to ye Letters. It wd (I think) have two good Effects.

1st It wd carry ye Reader wth more appetite thro ye Dedication, as leting him into ye meaning of ye odd Picture before him.

2ly It wd look as if there was more Occasion for ye Dedication (wh is pretty long) than there seems to be at present.

This seems to me a Trick to cheat ye Publick. The Question is if you'll be an Accomplice in it.

A man of ~~of~~ Tast in sculpture may improve on my sketch. And reconcile anything in it, yt is wrong, to ye sculptor's art, or reject it. I wish I knew Hogarth,[2] or yr Friend Mr Hyman.[3]

You, Dear Sir, will be so good to correct me in this suddain thought; as you have kindly done in others relating to this Affair.

      Yr affectionate, & much Obligd
        EYoung
Sunday.

---

[1] The date is that on which Richardson received the letter.

[2] William Hogarth (1697–1764) had been illustrating books since 1723.

[3] Whether Young wrote 'Hyman' or 'Hymore' is not clear as the name crowds the right edge of the paper. He may have confused the spelling between the names of Francis Hayman (1708–76), an illustrator already well established (cf. Iolo A. Williams, 'English Book-Illustration, 1700–1775', *The Library*, 1936, xvii. 1–21), and Joseph Highmore (1692–1780), the painter and close friend of Richardson.

Richardson to Young. London. [W.] 14 August 1754.

Harvard University (Houghton MSS.), by permission of the Harvard College Library.—Ralph Straus, *Robert Dodsley*, 1910, p. 355.

Dear and Revd Sr,

I will endeavour to find out a proper Person for a Copper Plate. Your Reasons for me, are unanswerable. The Trick is an innocent one; even a charitable one, to cheat People into their own Good. Heartily am I an Accomplice in it. But it is not in my Power to mend it. Your Directions are extremely picturesque, and well adapted. I hope this fine Weather will induce you to visit your excellent Friend, and his worthy Daughter, near Wisbech.[1] My best Wishes attend them.

My Wife thanks Mrs. Hallowes and You, Sr, for your Pigeons. Our best Respects attend her.

Ever, Sir
Yours most Affectionately
S. Richardson

London, Aug. 14 1754.

345. [Welwyn, Herts.]. [Su.] 3 November 1754. Duchess of Portland.

Longleat MSS. 243–4.

[In the hand of Mrs. Hallows]

May it please your Grace

I am very sorry for your Graces complaint concerning your eyes; it is what I have suffered many years, & suffer still. I have read poor Mrs Hallows almost blind, she has worn Spectacles almost this seven years. I bless God I enjoy more health than I deserve; there has been a mighty fall of people around me this year; The death of Sir Jeremy Sambrok[e][2] is a great loss to the living, but a most happ[y] release to Himself. I think your Graces pity is most rightly

---

[1] i.e. The Colborns.   [2] 4 October.

bestowed upon the Queensberry family.¹ When I read the paragraph in the New[s] I was astonished & coud not believe it. My Lor[d] Duke, & your Grace do me the greatest honou[r] in your kind invitation, but my situation at presant is such that it is not in my power to accep[t] of it; When you come to Town for the Winter, I ma[y] /[verso blank; conjugate leaf]/ possibly be so fortunate as to pay my Duty to You. To my Lord Duke, to the Young Lady's & Mr Achard, I beg my best respects and with the sincerest Wishes for Heavens blessing on You All, I am

Madam
Your Graces much Obliged
And most Obedient
And most Humble Servant
E Young

3 Nov 1754
Mrs Hallows gives
her humble Duty to Your Grace.

346. [?Welwyn, Herts.]. [?November 1754]. [?Charles Douglas].²

Not traced.—Llanover, 1862, 2nd Series, i. 42–3; Thomas, p. 611.

My Dear Dear Sir,

Your pain is your glory; it is not from weakness, but virtue. What a monster is man without a tender and feeling heart! how unlike his most dear and blessed Redeemer! over his dead friend Jesus wept!

Nor is this stroke of heart more a misfortune than a mercy to you. From Endowments of nature and fortune what strong temptations have you to be fond of this world, and how could divine paternal tenderness more powerfully caution you against it than by what has happened.

¹ Henry Douglas (b. 1723), Earl of Drumlanrig, son of Charles Douglas, third Duke of Queensberry, had been killed by accidental discharge of his pistol while on a trip to Scotland with his parents, his brother, and the wife whom he had married in July, the Lady Elizabeth Hope. The bereaved family had stopped at Bulstrode on their return to London.

² This undated letter, said to have been a copy in the hand of Mrs. Delany, was almost certainly directed to Charles Douglas (1726–56), younger and only brother of Henry Douglas, whose death is reported in the notes to the preceding letter.

As for the deceased, what Christian does not admire his behaviour in his last hour and piously envy his release! In one word, God is love, and does nothing but to bring our hearts to himself, and I am of opinion that there *never* was any human heart entirely his which has been *un*wounded by *some* distress! this considered (and with the additional weight which your own excellent thoughts must naturally give it) will inspire resignation, and real resignation must forever be accompanied with a degree of joy, considering what a friend it makes for us in lieu of the dearest we can possibly lose.

That this joy may fill your and your very worthy parents hearts is the warmest wish and earnest prayer of, dear Sir, your and their

Truly affectionate and obedient
Humble servant.

Richardson to Young. London. [Tu.] 17 December 1754.

Not traced.—*Monthly Magazine*, xl (1 September 1815), 137.

London, Dec. 17, 1754.

What, dear and reverend sir, have you done?[1] Could I have thought you, or any of my friends, would have been able to make me an ungrateful man; yet you have done it. For, can I thank you for a present, that your sitting alone would have made invaluable to me? you have put a price upon a favour that has no price; and Mr. Highmore—but I say no more, only to ask, was it right, dear sir, to do as you have done in this particular, by

Your before too much obliged
and faithful humble servant,
S. Richardson.

[1] Young's account with Gosling's bank shows a payment of 10 guineas to the portrait painter, Joseph Highmore, on 1 December, thus paying for a portrait of himself which had been commissioned by Richardson. The portrait hangs in All Souls College, Oxford, and was reproduced in the front of the Nichols–Doran edition of Young's *Works*, 1854.

I could not forbear complaining to our friend Mr. Shotbolt on this occasion. He will state the fact between us to
Mrs. Hallows; she is prepared to think all you do is right,
but in this instance will, I hope, think it possible that Dr.
Young can be once wrong.

347. [?Welwyn, Herts.]. [M.] 30 December 1754.
Duchess of Portland.

Longleat MSS. 245.

May it please yr
    Grace

I should have had the Honour of waiting on You in
Whitehall, had not Indisposition obligd me immediately
to quit
       London for Hackney,[1] where at inconvenient distance,
I was forcd to do with difficulty the little Business yt calld
me to Town.

I knew not, Madam, yt Lord Titchfield had ye smallpox;
I hear[t]ily give you Joy of his Recovery. As for ye little
Archbishop, I shall look on it as his giving me his Blessing,
when I hear that he is quite safe.[2]

That all ye Branches of your noble Family /[verso]/ may
ever flourish, & ye roots very, very late, decay, is my earnest
Prayr. And more particularly I am inclind at present to wish
all my good Friends well: for I never had such a Fall of all
about me as this year. The last seven years swept not away so
many. And but moonday last I had a worthy Friend struck
wth ye dead Pallsy.[3] This is a melancholy Account, I wish
you could ballance it with ye contrary from your side of ye

---

[1] Now a part of metropolitan London, Hackney was then a village about five
miles north-east of the City, on the river Lea. The full meaning of Young's
explanation is not clear.

[2] Edward, and his sisters, Elizabeth and Harriet, all had recovered early in the
new year.

[3] The 'dead palsy' was paralysis, often the result of a stroke. The identity of the
friend is not known.

World. I beg my humble Duty to my Lord Duke, & best respects to all You love.

I am Madam
Yr Graces
Most Obedient
& Obligd
Humble Sevt
EYoung

Dec 30
1754.

Richardson to Young. London. [Tu.] 21 January 1755.

Not traced.—*Monthly Magazine*, xli (1 April 1816), 231–2.

London; Jan. 21, 1755.

Will my dear and good Dr. Young excuse the liberty I have presumed to take with his dedication, particularly now I have seen the whole together, and am delighted with the noble things contained in the book?[1] I am apt to think that the reader is not sufficiently prepared in that dedication for the solemn and elevated subjects of the following letters, and that a few pages cancelled will answer a good end, after some such manner as I have presumed to offer in a waste sheet of the print; which I enclose.

In *another* edition I would humbly propose, in the 16th line of p. 24, instead of the word *incredible*, to add these, *incomprehensible to our finite reason*.

Page 31, 32.—What, sir, do the words, *High Court of Justice*, &c. allude to?

Page 92.—For *corpse* read *corps*.

Page 125, last line but two, for *Centaur* read *Centaurs*.

Page 131.—Is there not some omission in the first line?

Page 158, line 3, *Heaven is on my side already*—Query?

In another impression methinks it were to be wished that all from, *If this is a man of pleasure*, p. 161, to, *from a higher*

---

[1] i.e. *The Centaur Not Fabulous*, which has been in process since August.

hand, p. 163, were omitted, as it interrupts, by ludicrous images, emotions that were nobly excited.

For the same reason, suppose, in p. 163, were omitted the words, *Fain would I bury* &c. to the end of the paragraph, *real men*, p. 164?

Page 172, line 18, after *cedar*, put a parenthesis.

Page 173.—Papal infallibility pretends not to *foresee*.

Page 207, lines 18, 19, suppose they run thus in another impression—*Oh! spare thy paternal tenderness*, &c.

Page 225.—Need five points so important be crowded into one letter?

Page 252.—Suppose the words, *may be Gods*, be changed into these, *may recover that likeness*?

Page 291.—Suppose the words, *Thou Joseph, thou Jacob of Heaven*, were omitted in another impression?

Page 296, line 10, suppose it be read, *nature of my design*, and, I am willing to hope, *the truth of history*, &c.?

Page 307, line 11, *bodies*, plural, *its*, singular.

Page 314.—Bolingbroke Castle was not exposed to public view till since the new style began.

Page 325, line 4, for *leaves* read *leave*.

There are some other things that, in another edition, if I may be forgiven the above, I would take the liberty to suggest. Fired with the noble sentiments that abound in this admirable piece, how could an attentive reader forbear interesting himself in it, and to wish it all of a piece, lest the serious mind should be sorry for some condescending levities and images, and lest the lighter minds should take hold of such to evade the force of the diviner parts; and so less good should follow from the excellent performance than the pious author hoped for.

Once more, my dear and good Dr. Young, forgive (however presumptuous in this instance) the *humblest*, but one of the most sincere, of your admirers,

S. Richardson.

Many happy years attend you, and also your good Mrs. Hallowes; not forgetting your worthy neighbour.

348. [Welwyn, Herts.]. W. [?22 January 1755].
Samuel Richardson.

Not traced.—*Monthly Magazine*, xli (1 April 1816), 232.

Wednesday.

My dear Sir,

All your remarks are most just. I find that I am safer in your hands than my own; I beg you, therefore, to blot, add, alter, as you think good; and let not *delay* or *expence* be any objection to any thing *now* practicable, and you kindly wish to be done.

And, particularly, I beg the favour of your eye and pen on the close[1] now sent.

Page 131, line 1st, should be, 'lower *for their* height.'

N.B. *For their* is omitted, and I will pay some person for inserting it, through the whole edition.[2]

You say, sir, you have other remarks to make, do not forget them, for that is forgetting the interest of

Dear Sir,

Your most obliged

humble servant,

E. Young.

As another edition[3] is precarious, I would make in this all amendments I possibly can. Pray forget not your suggestions you can give me.

I desire this last sheet again before worked off.

349. [Welwyn, Herts.]. Su. [?26 January 1755].
Samuel Richardson.

Bodleian Library, Montagu MSS. d. 18.—*Monthly Magazine*, xli (1 April 1816), 232.

Infinitely am I indebted to my dear ^& most worthy friend, who ^has taken such trouble for me; & most particularly for

---

[1] A 'Conclusion' is dated 'Nov. 29. 1754', but to that is added a 'Postscript' to which Young apparently now refers.

[2] Copies of the first edition have this handwritten correction uniformly made.

[3] Three editions appeared in 1755.

ye Dedication part; I reinclose it lest you shd have no Copy
of it; & beg yt so much may [be] cancelld, & destroyd as
both yr very kind, & most judicious Insertions require; &
that they may instantly be put in ye Press.

Tomorrow I expect ye last Sheet, & when I return yt, I
shall I shall [*sic*] consult with you if the d[eletion]s p. 161[1]
&c: can be made in this Edition. Expence, if yt is all shall
not hinder it.

Wth ye Sincerest Gratitude,

Dear Sr
most truly Yrs
EYoung.

Mrs. Hallows joyns me
in best wishes, & respects
to You and Yrs.
Sunday
in hast.

350. [Welwyn, Herts.]. [W.] 5 February 1755. Mary
Delany.

Not traced.—Llanover, 1861, iii. 326–7; Thomas, p. 602; Shelley,
pp. 239–40.

Madam,

I humbly thank her Grace for conveying to me so very
good news[2] by so worthy and elegant a hand; and I congratulate you, Madam, and the world on the Divine mercy to that
noble and virtuous house in the day of fear and affliction.

The day of affliction is the day of glory to the Christian!
What you say of the Duchess claims indeed my admiration,
but by no means gives me any surprise. Her former conduct
so prepared me for it, that all surprise at aught commendable
in her Grace is over.

I accept the Dean's good wishes with great gratitude,
nor is it the only favour I am obliged to him for. I have lately
read his excellent sermons: they are well-timed, the world
wanted them, and they prescribe well for the present

---

[1] Pages 161–4 (2 leaves) were substituted for the originals in the first edition.
[2] i.e. of the recovery of the Portland children from smallpox.

distempers. But I fear Dr. Hays[1] has the advantage of him; as physicians (generally speaking) are more successful in their attack on diseases than divines.

I bless God I am very well in health; but my hurt eye is still a check on my pen. I beg, therefore, that you, Madam, and they who so justly enjoy your love and esteem, will not by the shortness of my letter measure the most sincere respect and duty of their and your

Most obedient and obliged humble servant,
E. Young.

Feb. 5, 1755.

351. [Welwyn, Herts.]. Th. [?13 February 1755].[2] Samuel Richardson.

Not traced.—*Monthly Magazine*, xli (1 April 1816), 232.

Thursday.

Dear Sir,

Your's dated Friday I received not till yesterday. I will send a correct copy of the first letter on Sunday, which is the first opportunity.

I hope Mr. Galloni will soon have the success with you which he has had with me; I find myself much the better for him.

As you have been so very kind to the dedication, I beg leave to rely on your inspection for that, and the letters shall follow faster than the press can work.

I am, dear Sir,
Most your's,
E. Young.

Remember that in your former letter[3] to me are these words, viz. 'There are some other things which, in another

---

[1] A physician of Windsor who with Dr. Heberden had attended the children.

[2] The date is estimated from the reference to the London dentist, 'Mr. Galloni', and from a letter of Richardson's of 21 February speaking of his correspondent's having 'visited Dr. Young on Tuesday morning last [18 February] at my own house, when I was under a slight operation' (Barbauld, v. 133). The 'operation' was presumably on Richardson's teeth. The correspondent who visited Young was Mark Hildesley (1698–1772), a clergyman about to be made bishop of Sodor and Man, who would have been known to Young at least from the early 1730s when he was serving as Vicar of Hitchin, nine miles north of Welwyn.

[3] Richardson's letter of 21 January.

edition, I would take the liberty to suggest,' and favour me
with them.

When you see Lady Bradshaw, pay my humble service.

352. [Welwyn, Herts.]. [Th.] 6 March 1755. Samuel
Richardson.

Not traced.—*Monthly Magazine*, xli (1 April 1816), 232–3.

March 6, 1755.

I hope, my dear sir, that you will soon be richly paid by
your skilful tormentor for your time, pain, and peace.

On Sunday, which is the first return, I will send another
letter, and the rest as fast as ever I can. If you chance to hear
any material criticisms, oblige me with them; I shall make
use of most of your's. You will send me one of the books,
for I have no compleat copy.

Have you heard any thing of Mr. Hervey's last performance?[1] Either I mistake, on a cursory view, or it is, or may
be, of pernicious influence. I thank you for Leland,[2] it is a
sound and useful book.

Accept the best wishes and respects of Shotbolt, Hallows,
and

E. Young.

I am glad your *Sentiments*, &c. are published.[3] It will be
a touchstone, and tell you, by its reception, or rejection, who
read for amusement, and who to be wiser than they were
before.

[1] James Hervey's *Dialogue between Theron and Aspasia* was announced in *The
London Evening Post* of 11 February for publication 'on Tuesday the 18th' and in
the same paper of the 18th as 'this day . . . published'. As a fictionalized defence of
the Calvinist doctrine of imputed righteousness it was attacked by John Wesley and
others and *A Defense of Theron and Aspasia* was published after Hervey's death (cf.
London Chronicle of 6 March 1760). At the first publication of Young's *Centaur*
(4 March), the *London Magazine* printed an excerpt from 'Letter II On Pleasure'
and followed it with the 14th Dialogue of Hervey's work as 'beautifully opposed'.

[2] John Leland (1691–1766), author of *A View of the Principal Deistical Writers
in England during the last and present Century* (February 1754).

[3] Richardson had just published his *Collection of the Moral and Instructive Sentiments*, in three volumes.

353. [Welwyn, Herts.]. [Su.] 23 March [1755].
Samuel Richardson.

Not traced.—*Monthly Magazine*, xli (1 April 1816), 233.

March 23.

Dear Sir,
    Till I looked over the copy you sent me I knew not how much I was obliged to you; accept my sincere thanks for your many excellent alterations.
    But p. 227, I think it should be—'Their erudition will not *permit them* to be at a loss to know what I mean.'
    I should be glad, at your leisure, to know how many are printed in this revised edition.
    Most affectionately your's,

E. Young.

Did you send one to the Bishop of Durham?[1] If you have not, please not to send one till the new edition.

354. [Welwyn, Herts.]. [Su.] 30 March 1755. Samuel Richardson.

National Library of Scotland MS. 585, No. 1069.—*Monthly Magazine*, xli (1 April 1816), 233.

My dear Sr
    If You have heard no Objection made to 227, it may pass unnoted as an Error. The 2d Edition I suppose near finishd. I must beg yr Conveyance of three of them. One to ye Bp of Durham, One to Dr Heberden. One to myself.
    I am much greivd yt You are still under Those cruel hands; but I greatly hope, & am much persuaded, that when ye Operation is over you will not repent of what's passd, but rejoyce in having chosen of Two Evils ye least.
                                        I am Dr Sr
                                            most Affectionately
                                            Yrs   EYoung.

    [1] Richard Trevor (1707–71), Bishop of Durham from 9 November 1752.

I am proud of ye Deans[1] approbation.
March 30
1755.
[In the hand of Mrs. Hallows.] My Most Humble service
waits on You Sir, & good
Mrs Richardson, &c
Mary Hallows

355. Welwyn, Herts. [Su.] 6 July 1755. Bennet Langton.[2]

Address: To Mr. Benet Langton / near Spilsby in / Lincolnshire. Postmark 7/IV.
Yale University MS. C3162 (quoted with permission of Yale University and McGraw-Hill Book Company, Inc.).

My dear Sr
  You greatly oblige me by your kind Present, & your kinder Letter. They are Both ye peculiar Natives of Lincolnshire. Both of exquisite Tast. Proceed, Dear Sr, in yr litterary Pursuits; Heaven bless you in them. And if your Progress is equall to yr setting out, I will venture to prophecy that ye Name of a Langton will be frequent in the mouth of late Posterity.
  It is therefore with Ambition, as well as with great sinserity, & ye truest Affection that I subscribe myself
Dear, & Uncommon Sr
Yr most Obedient
& humble sevt
EYoung.
Pray my best Respect to yr Father,
Mother, Unckle, Mr & Mrs Battel[3]
  July 6
  1755.

[1] The Delanys were now in London, having taken a house in New Street, Spring Gardens.
[2] Langton (1737–1801) was courting acquaintance of literary men at this time, having written twice in the spring to Dr. Johnson about his *Dictionary*. What 'present' the young man sent to Young is not known.
[3] Langton's father was Bennet Langton (1696–1769); his mother, *née* Diana Turnor (1712–93); his uncle, Peregrine (1703–66); Mr. Battel was the Revd. Ralph Battell (1697–1780), Rector of Somerby and Bag Enderby, Lincolnshire, brother of Young's Welwyn friend Mrs. Ward (Letitia Battell) (cf. will of William Battell, Somerset House, P.C.C. Brook 280 of 28 April 1726, pr. 9 October 1728).

356. [Welwyn, Herts.]. [Su. 10 August] 1755.
Samuel Richardson.

Not traced.[1]

357. Welwyn, Herts. [Su.] 10 August 1755. Robert
Dodsley.

Address: To Mr Dodsley / at Tully's Head / Pall-Mall / London. *Postmark*:
Welwyn 11/AV.
University of Colorado MS.

Sr
    My heart fails me now at what I have designd. My Addi-
tions, wh are large, will only Disgust former Purchasers;
& lengthen wt for its general Use is too long allready.[2]
I am therefore determind entirely to drop that Design of

Sr
Yr Humble Sevt
EYoung

Aug: 10
1755.

358. [Welwyn, Herts.]. [Su.] 7 September 1755.
Duchess of Portland.

Address: To her Grace The Dutchess / of Portland at Bullstrode / Bucks.
Postmark: 8/[SE].
Longleat MSS. 246.—Bath, pp. 321–2.

May it please yr Grace.
    I have publick Duty allways three Days in the Week, &
often much more; and at present I have no Curate; nor can I

    [1] Evidence of this letter is the auction catalogue of Puttick & Simpson, 25 Jan-
uary 1853, Lot 698: 'A. L. s. 1 page 4to 1755, Returning portion of a manuscript
transmitted by Richardson for his perusal, begs the conveyance to Dodsley, of a
parcel, it is for another, smaller edition, of his Night Thoughts.' See letter to
Dodsley, following.
    Dodsley was preparing a new edition of *Night-Thoughts*, which Young had
apparently thought of augmenting. The 'additions' were probably the 'parcel' sent
to Dodsley under cover of the untraced letter to Richardson, just above. The new
edition in, duodecimo, was published 14 October.

get any. It is therefore utterly out of my powr to accept your Grace's Kind, & most obliging Invitation; which otherwise, I should have accepted with ye utmost satisfaction; & shall ever remember with the greatest Gratitude.

I congratulate You, Madam, and ye Publick on Lord Titchfields Recovery; the Publick is your Rival; nor will you be sorry for such a Rival in your Love.

With what a Relish You speak of your most amiable Friend? Your Grace has an excellent Pencill; I never saw a more lovely Family Piece, except at Bullstrode.

They, Madam, that are Happy in their Friends, /[verso]/ and near Relations, enjoy more than any other Circumstances of life can give. And that this for ever may be your Case is ye Prayr of one who has missd Friends where they were most to be expected; & found them, Thanks to your Grace, where they were least deservd, by no means an uncommon Case. I am

Madam

Yr most Obligd

& Dutifull Humble Sevt

EYoung.

I receivd lately a Compliment
from yr Friend Lady Primrose,
as she passd by with Ld Westmoreland.[1]

My best Wishes & Respects to All, my humble Duty to his Grace; & Mrs Hallows, begs You wd accept of Hers.
Sepr 7
1755.

359. [Welwyn, Herts.]. [Sa.] 20 September 1755. Samuel Richardson.

Not traced.—*Monthly Magazine*, xli (1 April 1816), 233.

Sept. 20, 1755.

I received yesterday, dear sir, a letter from Mr. Millar, which says, that he saw you the night before in health and

---

[1] John Fane (?1682–1762), seventh Earl of Westmorland, recently appointed Lord High Steward of Oxford University and later (1759) to become Chancellor of the University.

good spirits. God preserve them, for, either wanting, life is
little worth. To support my own spirits, I have been singing
a song,[1] which I send you, and I wish it may be at all to your
taste.

My benefactress, good Mrs. Richardson, has it greatly
in her power to rejoice Mrs. Hallows, by making Wellwyn
as agreeable as she can to her and you.

I am, dear sir,
Your most obliged humble servant,
E. Young.

The Sailor's Song To The South;
Occasioned by the Rumour of a War.

Peace! heavenly Peace! what loud alarms!
Why gleams the *South* with brandish'd arms?
War, bath'd in blood, from curst Ambition springs:
   Ambition mean! ignoble Pride!
   Perhaps, her ardors may subside;
When weigh'd the Wonders *Britain's* sailor sings.

Hear, and revere—at *Britain's* nod,
From each enchanted grove and wood,
Hastes the huge oak, and shadeless forests leaves;
   The mountain *pines* assume new forms,
   Spread canvas-wings, and fly thro' storms,
And ride o'er rocks, and dance on foaming waves.

She *nods* again: the labouring earth
Discloses a tremendous birth;
In smoaking rivers runs her molten ore;
   Thence, monsters of enormous size,
   And hideous aspect, threatning, rise;
Flame from the deck; from trembling bastions roar.

---

[1] The verses appended to this letter are revisions of a portion of Young's poem:
The Foreign Address: or, the Best Argument for Peace (1735). They were advertised
as 'The Sailor's Song to the South' and announced as published 'this day' in *The
Public Advertiser* of 3 October. They were incorporated as part of *A Sea-Piece*,
announced as published 'this day' in *The Public Advertiser* of 26 November.

These ministers of fate fulfil
  On empires wide an *island's* will,
When Justice wakes, her vengeance know, ye powr's!
  In sudden night, and ponderous balls,
  And floods of flame, the tempest falls,
When brav'd *Britannia's* awful senate low'rs.

She gladly sheaths her courage keen,
  And spares her nit'rous magazine,
Her cannon slumber till the proud aspire
  On lawless plunder; then they blaze!
  They thunder from resounding seas!
Touch'd by their injur'd master's soul of fire.

Then ruin runs! the battle raves!
  And rends the skies! and warms the waves!
And calls a tempest from the peaceful deep;
  In spite of Nature, spite of *Jove*,
  While all serene and hush'd above,
Tumultuous winds in azure chambers sleep.

A thousand deaths the mighty bomb
  Hurls from her disembowel'd womb!
Chain'd, glowing bolts, in dread alliance joyn'd
  Redwing'd by strong sulphureous blasts,
  Sweep, in black whirlwinds, men and masts,
And leave singed, naked, blood-drown'd decks
                                  [behind.

Dwarf laurels rise in tented fields,
  The wreath immortal *Ocean* yields;
There war's whole sting is shot, whole fire is spent,
  Whole glory blooms! How pale, how tame,
  How lambent is *Bellona's* flame,
How her storms languish on the Continent?

From the dread front of ancient war
  Less terror frown'd; her scythed car,
And castled elephant, and battering beam,
  Stoop to those engines, which deny
  Superior terrors to the sky,
And boast their clouds, their thunder, and their flame.

The flame, the thunder, and the cloud,
The night by day, the sea of blood,
Hosts whirl'd in air, the yell of sinking throngs,
The graveless dead, an *Ocean* warm'd,
A *Firmament* by mortals storm'd,
To patient *Britain's* angry brow belongs.

Or do I dream? Or do I rave?
Or see I *Vulcan's* sooty cave,
Where *Jove's* red bolts the giant brothers frame?
The swarthy gods of *toil* and *heat*,
Loud peals on mountain anvils beat,
And panting tempests rouze the roaring flame.

Ye sons of *Ætna*! hear my call;
Let those unfinish'd bawbles fall,
That shield of *Mars*, *Minerva's* helmet blue:
Your strokes suspend, ye brawny throng
Charm'd by the magic of my song;
Drop your feign'd thunder, and attempt the true.

Begin: and, first, rapid *flight*,
Fierce *flame*, and clouds of thickest *night*,
And ghastly *terror* paler than the dead;
Then borrow the *North* his *roar*,
Mix groans and deaths; one viol pour
Of wrong'd *Britannia's* wrath; and it is made.

360. [Welwyn, Herts.]. [Su.] 9 November 1755. Joseph Warton.

Not traced.—John Wooll, *Biographical Memoirs . . . of Revd Joseph Warton*, 1806, pp. 215–16.

Nov. 9, 1755.

Dear Sir,

You do me an honour.[1] I shall not fail to keep your secret.[2] I heartily wish you success in this and all things.

[1] Warton dedicated to Young his *Essay on the Genius and Writings of Pope* (1756).
[2] i.e. authorship of the *Essay*. Warton wrote to his brother Thomas: 'I have a letter from Dr. Young to tell me he will keep the thing a Secret & to thank me'

If this or any other occasion calls you to town,[1] I am but four hours from you; and you will be most welcome to,

Dear Sir,

Your oblig'd humble servant,

Ed. Young

Richardson to Young. London. [F.] 23 April 1756.

Not traced.—*Monthly Magazine*, xlii (1 August 1816), 39–40.

London, April 23, 1756.

Dear and Rev Sir,

The daughter of your much esteemed friend, Mr. Colborn, and her father, have a very valuable young clergyman, Mr. Forester, for whom they have great regard.[2] Miss Colborn wishes me to write a line to her papa's dear Dr. Young, in both their names, requesting his interest with some of his good and great friends, to procure for the said young gentleman a chaplainship of a regiment, either in England or Ireland. I could not refuse writing to you, sir, on this subject, and hope you'll excuse the trouble. I wish it were in my power to serve Mr. Forester, for the sake of his character, and for the sakes of his recommenders.

(British Museum, Add. MS. 42560, f. 49). A letter (in the same collection) from Robert Dodsley on 11 March [1756] expresses pleasure that 'the book is at last finisht' (it was printed in Oxford) and asks Warton to send copies to him and to the bookseller Mary Cooper. On 8 April Dodsley wrote again: 'Your Essay is publish'd, the price 5 s. bound. I gave Mrs. Cooper directions about advertising, and have sent to her this afternoon, to desire she will look after its being inserted in the evening papers. . . . You have surely not kept your secret: Johnson mention'd it to Mr. Hitch as yours Dr. Birch mention'd it to Garrick as yours and Dr Akenside mention'd it as yours to me—and many whom I cannot now think on have ask'd for it as yours or your brother's' (John Wooll, *Biographical Memoirs . . . of Revd Joseph Warton*, 1806, p. 237).

¹ Warton had just taken a position in Winchester as Usher, or Second Master.

² On 21 February Richardson had replied to an appeal from Miss Colborn on behalf of Richard Forester (1727–67), in part as follows: 'I am sorry that Mr Forester, as your friend, has met with any disappointment in his secular affairs. Pity that true love for a worthy object should have been the occasion of it. I am much concerned at the heavy indisposition that your good papa laboured under at the time of your writing, which hindered him from writing to his friend Dr. Young, on the subject of the resignation. I am of opinion that the doctor could do much in it, by his intimacy with the Duke and Duchess of Portland' (*Monthly Magazine*, 1816, xlii. 39). It was in this year that Forester became Vicar of Ashwell, Herts.

How do you, my dear sir? How does Mrs. Hallows? And pray, sir, how are your teeth? Mine are leaving me apace. O this Galeni?[1] Yet time of life was against him and me. How much did I suffer; and at what expence of time as well as money: but regulars seldom recommend quacks. It was our good friend Mr. Watson[2] that drew me in—with a good intention I am sure. But why do these same regulars of the different tribes of physic, leave to empirics our teeth and our eyes? as if such essentials to mortal felicity were beneath the attention of these solemn and superb prescribers? But may not this be owing to their own moderation? Content with the mischiefs each of the branches may do in his particular way, they leave to an under-set of operators to pull out our teeth and put out our eyes.

You, I hope, can give a more favourable account of the success of the operation you underwent in Salisbury-court.

I am removed; but be pleased to remember, that we have equal conveniences to those we had before for the accomodating a dear friend on his coming to town. My wife and girls most cordially join prayers and wishes for your health, and in respects to Mrs. Hallows, with, sir,

Your affectionate and
faithful servant,
S Richardson.

361. [Welwyn, Herts.]. [Tu.] 27 April 1756. Samuel Richardson.

Not traced.—*Monthly Magazine*, xlii (1 November 1816), 331.

April 27, 1756.

My dear and very kind friend,

I rejoice to hear from you, and I shall rejoice more to see you; and, therefore, when in my power, shall gratefully

---

[1] The dentist, mentioned in Richardson's letter tentatively dated 27 February 1755, where it is spelled 'Galloni'.

[2] William Watson (1715–87), who was knighted in 1786, had begun a distinguished career in medicine as apprentice to an apothecary named Richardson. In 1763, he was named as an executor of John Shotbolt's will (Somerset House, P.C.C. Tyndall 468).

accept your invitation, and think myself happy under your new roof, which I hope you find as convenient as your former.

Miss Colborn may rely on my self-love for doing for the young gentleman all that is in power; for nothing could give me greater pleasure than do ought that would be welcome to her most worthy father.

As Juvenal says of a boxing-match, I think it is a blessing, *paucis cum Dentibus*,[1] to escape out of the hands of Galleni; mine have been distempered ever since, and rather worse than before. I am very, very sorry, for the bad account you give of your's. And your saying that your friend Watson innocently betrayed you into it, makes me think that, what Solomon says of enemies and friends, may be applied to fools and the wise—'Separate thyself from fools, and take heed of the wise.'[2] Though integrity is but scarce, yet is there more integrity than infallibility in the world.

I beg Mrs. Richardson and your whole fire-side would accept my and Mrs. Hallow's most affectionate good wishes and respects. We are both in debt at Salisbury-court, but more particularly, my dear Sir,

Your much obliged humble servant,
E. Young.

April 27, 1756.

362. [?Welwyn, Herts.]. [Tu.] 27 April 1756. Duchess of Portland.

Longleat MSS. 250.

May it please your Grace

I know not how to write;[3] nor know I how to forbear.— When I am going to say something, which I might possibly

---

[1] *Satire* iii. 300–1:

This is a poor man's liberty in Rome.
You beg his pardon; happy to retreat
With some remaining teeth, to chew your meat.
(Dryden)

[2] Ecclesiasticus 6 : 13: 'Separate thyself from thine enemies, and take heed of thy friends.'

[3] Lady Margaret, the Portland daughter of 16 years of age, had died on 23 April.

say to Another on a like Occasion, I am checkd by my sense
of your own good Understandings; & when I would drop
my Pen, there seems something Unnatural & Undutifull
in it. What then can I do? I can only repeat your own
Thoughts, by saying, That all things shall work together
for Good to those yt love God.

                        short as it is, & ought to be,
        But saying even This   may possibly
want an Apology at this Time; & all ye Apology I can
make is, That nothing which nearly affects yr Grace can be
thought on without Concern by

                    Madam, Yr Grace's
                        most Obedient, & Obligd
                            Humble Sevt
                                EYoung.
Madam
I beg my humble Duty
to my Ld Duke, & best
Respects to All yt is
Dear to You   Ap 27. 1756.

363. [Welwyn, Herts.]. [Su.] 2 May 1756. Mary
Delany.

Not traced.—Llanover, 1861, iii. 425; Thomas, p. 603; Shelley, pp. 241–2.

Madam,
    What very ill news you send me! I knew not that her
Grace's misfortune spread so wide: I knew not that so many
of those nearest her heart had been ill.[1] God restore them
to their perfect health, and so give double comfort to her
Grace in the possession of her endangered felicities!
    If, Madam, I see London before you leave it, I shall think
my journey very happily timed, but as at present I have no
curate and pretty much duty, I fear I shall not be able to wait

    [1] Mrs. Delany wrote to her sister on 24 April of the death of Lady Margaret and
the illness of both the Portland boys. On 3 June she reported the death, 'hastened
by hearing of the death of Lady Margaret', of their former governess, Elizabeth
Elstob (Llanover, 1861, iii. 431).

on you and the Dean (to whom my best wishes and respects) unless your stay is longer in town.

I beg my humble duty to my Lord Duke and her Grace. Though, Madam, I share with you in a tender sense of all that pains her, yet I cannot but congratulate her at the same time on having the very best cordials under any distress—*a good head, a good heart,* and *a good friend*; and that friend of such a character that it is with pride as well as pleasure that I subscribe myself

Madam,

Her most obedient and humble servant,

E. Young.

May 2nd, 1756.

364. [Welwyn, Herts.]. [Tu.] 6 July 1756. Samuel Richardson.

Not traced.—*Monthly Magazine,* xlii (1 August 1816), 40.

July 6, 1756.

My dear Sir,

Pardon my ambition, fain would I see under my roof together, two persons whose virtues I honour. A man of high moral merit no pen can better draw than your's, and such, perhaps, you have rarely seen. If I mistake not, I can shew you one in my friend Colborn. Such a sight, in such a world, how much to be desired! Especially by one who is supposed to have drawn human excellence beyond the life. Come and see in him a justification of your pen.

Mr. Shotbolt told me you had some such thoughts; dear sir, do not drop them, but continue that indulgence to one who, under the due sense of your many, many indulgencies, is,

Your truly affectionate,

and very much obliged,

humble servant,

E. Young.

If you brought good Mrs. Richardson with you, how truly welcome to Mrs. Hallows and to me.

365. Welwyn, Herts. [Su.] 11 July 1756. Samuel
Richardson.

Not traced.—*Monthly Magazine*, xlii (1 August 1816), 40.

Wellwyn, July 11, 1756.

Being blooded in my right arm last night, I am obliged,
dear sir, to borrow Mrs. Hallows' hand to let you know, that
my friend Colborn is not yet with me; as soon as he is you
shall know it; and my hopes of your good company is a
cordial to me under my present small indisposition. That
all indispositions may keep at a distance from your door,
is the cordial wish of,

Your truly affectionate debtor,
and humble servant,
E. Young.

Mrs. Hallows begs her best compliments may be acceptable to Mr. Richardson, Mrs. Richardson, and the young
ladies.

366. [Welwyn, Herts.]. [Th.] 29 July 1756. Duchess
of Portland.

Address: To Her Grace / The Dutchess of Portland / at Bullstrode / In Bucks.
Longleat MSS. 251.—Bath, pp. 322–3; Thomas, p. 242.

May it please yr Grace.

Heaven reestablish your Health, and restore your spirits,
without either of which the Living have Little to boast above
the Dead. Last Week Ly Cowper gave me an Account of
Mrs Delany, but mentiond not her Indisposition, of which
I suppose she was Ignorant, for she professes a great Value
for her; For ye sake of All that know her, as well as her own
I heartily hope her perfect Recovery.

But to come still nearer to yr Grace's Heart; I congratulate You on Ly Harriots Health; nor less on Ld Titchfields
late gaind Reputation. May He one Day be the Pride of the

Nation, as He is now of ye University.[1] And then the Publick will thank your Grace for giving it an Ornament which
posterity shall not forget. /[verso]/

Poor Ld Andover![2] But as I know not his Character, I can
not tell if his Death is to be deplord, or Envyd. Nothing is
more to be Envyd than ye Death of ye Good. Last Night I
buryd a most Valueable Woman, and her Profligate Husband, now on his Deathbed I shall bury very soon.[3] He was
her Death by his Unkindness, & his own, by his Debauchery. The Difference of their last Hours, to which I have been
privy, carrys in it an Instruction, which no Words can
express.

Your Grace is so kind as to enquire after my Health;
I have had a very dangerous Fever, which was not easily
subdud. But God Allmighty is pleasd to continue me Here
longer at my Peril. I say, Madam, at my Peril; for [?], if we
do not truly Repent, longer Life will prove, in ye Event, a
Curse; and if we Do, Death, which we so much dread, is the
greatest Blessing. /[conjugate leaf]/

I beg my humble Duty to my Ld Duke; and hope all the
the [sic] Rest of your Good, and amiable Family will accept
the best Wishes, and Respects of

Madam
Yr Graces most Obedient
& Obligd Humble Sevt
EYoung.

Mrs Hallows gives her humble Duty.

July 29
  1756.

[1] 'We hear from Oxford that there was the greatest Appearance of polite Company
this Week at the Commemoration of the Benefactors to that University, ever known
on any Occasion. On Tuesday Mr. Warton, Professor of Poetry, spoke in the Theatre,
his Inauguration Speech in Latin. Afterwards Verses were spoken by the Marquis
of Titchfield in English [and a succession of other students]. . . . The Names of the
Nobility, Ladies, &c were so large, that an exact Account is not yet known' (*The
Public Advertiser*, 12 July 1756).

[2] William, 'Lord Andover died suddenly by a Fall from his Chaise, in Oxfordshire' on 19 July (*The Whitehall Evening Post*, 20 July 1756).

[3] Ann, wife of Benjamin Fletcher, Welwyn attorney, was buried on 27 July.
Her husband was buried on 5 August. Young's curate, Jones, left a memorandum,
now among the Bishop's transcripts of the Welwyn church in the Hertford County
Record Office, to the effect that the old parish registers 'fell into the hands of a
wicked and unconscionable Attorney (B. F.) who did great mischief'.

367. [Welwyn, Herts.]. [Tu.] 17 August 1756.
Duchess of Portland.

Address: To her Grace The Dutchess of Portland at Wellbeck / In Nottinghamshire. *Postmark*: 18/AV.
Longleat MSS. 253.

May it please yr Grace,
    I hope that after a pleasant Journey You are safely arrivd
at Wellbeck. And your spirits are such as to receive all the
Enjoyment so fine a Place may naturally inspire. As your
Grace did me great Honour & Pleasure in your Passage
thither, I humbly hope the same Indulgence at your Return.
    For indeed, Madam, it is great Joy to me to see so noble
a Family in all its Branches doing such Credit to their high
Station in Life. Especially in an Age which affords us so
many Instances, most melancholy Instances of the Contrary.
    Some such your Grace mentiond; and my Fortune has
thrown me into Two noble Familys /[verso]/ most notoriously ignorant in what real Nobility consists.[1] That your
Grace's House may have many Rivals, but no superior in
the Path it has chosen, is the Prayr of
                            Madam
                with ye greatest Respect
                    Your Graces
                        Most Obedient
                        & most Humble Sevt
                            EYoung.

Madam, Mrs Hallows joyns me in desiring that our
humble Dutys, & best Respects may be accepted by Those
so worthy of them.
Aug 17
    1756

    [1] One of these would have been the Wharton family; the second was probably the
Lee family.

368. [Welwyn, Herts.]. [Su.] 12 September 1756.
Samuel Richardson.

Not traced.—*Monthly Magazine*, xlii (1 August 1816), 40.

Sept. 12, 1756.

I cannot, my dear sir, invite you to see my dear friend
Colborn, for I grieve to say that sickness detains him from
me: but can invite you to see one who longs to see you as
much as Greenland longs to see the sun. It has been above
a half year's night with me.[1]

My love, service, and best wishes, to all under your wing,
and may your wing be long extended over them; late, very
late, may you take your flight. A late illness has put such
thoughts in my head: but I bless God I am now very well.
But you may make me better whenever you please. I am,
dear sir,

Your most obliged,
and truly affectionate,
humble servant,

I must add, and admirer, for Sir Charles
Grandison[2] is on my table,
E. Young.

Mrs. Hallows is most your's.

Robert Dodsley to Young. [London]. [Th.] 7 October
1756.

Birmingham Public Library, Dodsley's Letter Books, 149158, vol. 2.

Sir,
I have sent you by the Welwyn Carrier my audacious
attempt at writing a Tragedy,[3] but am afraid, that next to

---

[1] The duet 'Over the hills and far away' in Gay's *The Beggar's Opera* (1728)
begins: 'Were I laid on Greenland's coast . . . too soon the half year's night would
pass.'

[2] The seventh volume was reprinted this year.

[3] Dodsley's *Cleone* was produced at Drury Lane in December 1758 and ran for
sixteen nights.

my presumption in making such an attempt, my temerity in venturing it under your inspection, will subject me to the imputation of much self confidence. As I would not willingly give the least shadow of reason for such an accusation, I will confess, that if it had not already receiv'd ye approbation of some very judicious friends (too partial perhaps in this instance) I durst not have hazarded its appearance at the Bar of so hallowed and experienc'd a Judge: nor can I yet resign it to its fate without strongly solliciting that Tenderness which a first fault may hope to find, & that Candor, which the first attempt of an Author unassisted by Learning may justly claim. I shall be extremely obligd to you for your opinion of it and also for any remarks you will please to favour me with; only as ye Copy is fair & I want to shew it to a friend as soon as you can return it you will be so good as to put your observations on a separate Paper. I am &c.

369. [Welwyn, Herts.]. [Th.] 14 October 1756. Robert Dodsley.

Not traced.[1]

Richardson to Young. [London]. [Th.] 4 November 1756.

Not traced.—*Monthly Magazine*, xlii (1 August 1816), 40.

November 4, 1756.
Rev. and dear Sir,
    I deferred rendering you my sincere thanks and those of my wife, as I now do, for your kind entertainment of us last week, till I could acquaint you with my having ordered to the carrier the books of which I desired your's and Mrs. Hallows' acceptance. You will be so good as to allow the

---

[1] Evidence of this letter is the catalogue of Puttick & Simpson of 19 March 1850, Lot 419: 'A. L. s. 1 page 4to, to Dodsley, Oct. 14, 1756: Promising to return a play, and making some remarks upon it.' This letter would have been Young's answer to Dodsley's letter of the 7th, just preceding.

larger set a place in some obscure corner of your library. The pocket volumes, perhaps, will be more acceptable to the lady.

I send also, as I promised, Mr. Sheridan's Treatise on Education[1] (of which, when perused, I desire the return), and with it a copy of the translation of the German verses you wished to have.[2]

I am, sir, with equal gratitude and respect, and kindest compliments to Mrs. Hallows, my wife's to both included,
Your most faithful and affectionate
humble servant,
S. Richardson.

370. [Welwyn, Herts.]. [Tu.] 9 November 1756. Samuel Richardson.

Not traced.—*Monthly Magazine*, xlii (1 August 1816), 40–1.

November 9, 1756.

I could not be at peace, dearest sir, till I had sat down to thank you for your monstrous present. Is it not enough to oblige us with your goodness, but must you fright us too? I love, honor, and envy you, and would do more if I could; and, perhaps, I do more, to your satisfaction, by assuring you, that I shall ever greatly enjoy what you have sent me. I borrow another hand for this, my own being out of order; but it is written with my own heart, which is, as it ought to be, dear sir,
Truly your's,
E. Young.

Good Sir,
I am vastly surprised, and infinitely thankful.
Mary Hallows.

Our love and best service to Mrs. Richardson, and our heartiest good wishes to those whom you both hold most dear.

---

[1] *British Education, or the Source of the Disorders of Great Britain* (1756), by the elocutionist Thomas Sheridan (1719–88).

[2] 'Ode on the Death of Clarissa', a translation of 'Die todte Clarissa' by Friedrich Klopstock (1724–1803), which had been brought to England by Bernhard von Hohorst who is to visit Young in January.

371. [Welwyn, Herts.]. [Tu.] 21 December 1756.
Samuel Richardson.

Not traced.—*Monthly Magazine*, xlii (1 August 1816), 41.

Dec. 21, 1756.

My dear Sir,
    I know not the merit or demerit of what I send; if it has
merit I beg you give it more.[1] How much does the *Centaur*
owe to you? If it has no merit, keep the secret, and all is well.
    I have no copy but what I send; I wish it was fairer, but
writing pains me, therefore pardon this copy. When you
have read it favour me with a line.
    You know how much we both are obliged to you, think
then with what sincere love and esteem we are,
                              Dear Sir,
                    Your affectionate humble servants,
                                        E. Young.

    I have read Sheridan with improvement and pleasure, and
thank you for him.
    Our humble service and best wishes to Mrs. Richardson.

Richardson to Young. [London]. [Late December
1756].

Not traced.—*Monthly Magazine*, xlii (1 August 1816), 41.

Rev. and dear Sir,
    What honour do you do me! How shall I bear it? Yet, have
been able, from an hurry of appointments which are beginning to take place, to glance only on the first page, and to
read your kind letter; what a sweet repast for the retired part
of this evening will your subject be! Your servant gives me
not so favourable an account of your health as I wish for. It
is a bad season of the year, I find it so at Parson's Green, to

    [1] From Richardson's letter of 14 January 1757 it is apparent that Young is now
sending the first draft of what is to become his *Conjectures on Original Composition in
a Letter to the Author of Sir Charles Grandison* (1759).

which place my females are confined at present (later than usual in the season) by rheumatic complaints; and the dangerous indisposition of two valuable friends, who are with us as guests; one a Salisbury-court neighbour, (Miss Dutton;)[1] the other, good Mr. Edwards,[2] author of the Canons of Criticism. May all your complaints, good and dear Sir, speedily vanish; they will, I doubt not, on better weather, and with the free exercise you are accustomed to take. Mrs. Hallows' tender care must be efficacious to the recovery of a friend so invaluable. My best wishes and respects, and all happiness of the approaching season attend you both.

I am, dear Sir,
Your most affectionate and
obliged humble servant,
S. Richardson.

372. Su. [2 January 1757]. Samuel Richardson.

Not traced.—*Monthly Magazine*, xlii (1 August 1816), 41.

Dear Sir,

I hope in God that this will find you and your's, especially the invalids mentioned in your last, in good health.

I have added to the letter I send you, if you have perused it, I will send for it on to-morrow sen'night; not before, in hopes that, in the mean time, you may favour it with some strokes of your pen.

Under great sense of gratitude for the many friendships, I am,

Dear Sir,
Your most affectionate
and humble servant,
E. Young.

Sunday.

[1] Margaret Dutton, daughter of Thomas Dutton (d. 1741) and lifetime friend of the Richardson's.

[2] Thomas Edwards (1699–1757), critic, whose *Canons of Criticism* was first so called in a third edition of 1748.

P. S. On second thoughts, you possibly have not had leisure to look over it as you would. I will not, therefore, send for it till I have the favour of a line from you.

Many, many years to you all; and as happy as earth admits.

Richardson to Young. London. [F.] 7 January 1757.

Not traced.—*Monthly Magazine*, xlii (1 November 1816), 332.

Allow me, rev. and good Sir, to gratify the wishes of Major Hohorst, captain of the Grenadier Guards in the service of the King of Denmark, a worthy and pious man, before he quits this kingdom, to be personally acquainted with the author of the Night Thoughts, the Centaur, &c. &c. whom he, and his countrymen of taste and seriousness, very greatly admire for his works. He sets out for Welwyn on purpose, and will return in a day or two, after he has given himself this very great satisfaction; that he may have the pleasure of saying, when he is abroad, that he has seen and conversed with Dr. Young.

The loss I have sustained of two dear friends,[1] and the illness in my own family, have obliged me to take more time than it was otherwise necessary for me to do, with regard to the favour you intrusted me with: a favour indeed! I will soon have it ready for your commands; and am, with fervent wishes for the return of many happy seasons, and my respects to good Mrs. Hallows, dear and rev. Sir,

Your greatly obliged and faithful
humble servant,
S. Richardson.

London; Jan. 7, 1757.

All mine join their best and kindest respects, &c.

---

[1] On 17 January, Richardson wrote to another friend: 'We lost poor Miss Dutton; and in about a fortnight after, Jan. 3d, good Mr. Edwards' (Barbauld, 1804, ii. 106). Both the young lady and the critic Edwards were visiting Richardson at the time of their deaths.

373. Welwyn, Herts. [Su.] 9 January 1757. Duchess of Portland.

Address: To her Grace the Dutchess of Portland at White Hall / London.[1]
Postmark: 10/1A (for January) WELWYN.
Longleat MSS. 255.

May it please yr Grace

To Obligations on obligations before heapd on me Your Goodness infinitely adds by your very kind Inquiry after my Health. I have been confind above a month with violent pains in my Ear, Teeth, Face, & Head; which confine me still, or I had long since acknowledgd the Honour of your Letter, and the great Benefit of yr Powders, wh Mr[s] Hallows (who desires yr Grace to accept her humble Duty) has taken to great Releif of Rheumatic complaints, as well as I.

That your Complaints, Madam, may be soon, & entirely removd, and that You yourself may not be the only person which You can /[verso]/ not cure, is, & shall be, the fervent Prayr of one who has receivd great releif in Pains of ten years continuance from ye Powders.

All Gratitude & Duty, & Respects, & best Wishes, I humbly hope will be accepted at Whitehall from

Madam
Yr Graces
most Obligd &
most Obedient
Patient & humble Sevt
E Young

Jany

As for Mr West, his Fortune must be a Mystery, till his superlative Merit ceases to be so.
/[in margin of conjugate leaf]/ I shd greatly rejoyce in a Letter wh assurd me that yr Grace was perfectly well.— Death has of late been so busie in my Neighbourhood, yt I hope he has had no leisure to come into yours. Within two

---

[1] The Portland town house was in Privy Garden, Whitehall.

years last past he has swept allmost every Gentleman of my acquaintance into better Company.

Jany 9

  1757.

374. [Welwyn, Herts.]. [Th.] 13 January 1757. Samuel Richardson.

Not traced.—*Monthly Magazine*, xlii (1 November 1816), 332.

January 13, 1757.

How am I struck, dear sir, with the sad, sad news you send me? What are we? How close our affections cling to this earth, which will so soon return the fond embrace, and take us into its cold bosom. I am by no means in haste with regard to what you mention; the longer the papers are in your hands the kinder and the better.

I am obliged to you for bringing me acquainted with Major Hohorst; he is a very agreeable, and, I believe, a very valuable man; he has promised to send me news from abroad, which I am to communicate to you.

That all the complaints in your family may entirely cease, and the new year bring you new blessings and comforts, is the warmest wish of,

Dear sir,

Your most affectionate and obliged

humble servant,

E. Young.

Mrs. Hallows desires all the good family to accept her very best wishes, and regards, and respects.

I will write to my friend Colbourn very soon.

Richardson to Young. [London]. [F.] 14 January 1757.

Not traced.—*Monthly Magazine*, xlii (1 November 1816), 332–5.

January 14, 1757.

My dear and good Dr. Young, I am sure, will forgive me the following humble suggestions, with regard to the admirable piece he has entrusted me with.[1]

'What favours have I received at your hands?' At the hands of the author of Sir Charles Grandison! Dear sir, has not the account been more than balanced? Surely, this is beyond the merit of this author, and, as well here as in many other passages, you do him too much honour.

'An antient of the greatest antiquity.' Would you not choose to name him at the bottom of the page?

'O my friends! there is no such thing under Heaven;' as what, dear sir? Mean you not, as a friend—as a true friend? In which addition, suppose instead of 'O my friends,' to avoid the repetition of the word, it were, 'O sirs!'

'It is become a common prostitute, often enjoyed by those that are unworthy of that sacred name.' The idea of a *prostitute*, and the word *enjoyed*, joined to the words *sacred name*, are they connectible? Suppose, after 'the word is too common,' it were thus—'*It is often assumed by those who are unworthy of that sacred name.*'

Suppose the word *always* were inserted as marked in the margin?

For '*abridgement* of the press,' suppose it were *restraint*?

'If legal authority stands centinel,' &c. Alas, sir! that it does not, and the press groans beneath infidelity, indecency, libel, faction, nonsense; suppose this small alteration—'*If legal authority were to stand centinel at the press, and admit none,*' &c. And suppose to the word *restraint*, as the subject is a very tender one, were added the words, *licentiousness of the press.*

---

[1] This letter, and those that follow having to do with the *Conjectures*, have been discussed by Alan D. McKillop in 'Richardson, Young, and the *Conjectures*', *Modern Philology*, xxi (May 1925), 391–404.

As you do the writer of the history of Sir Charles Grandison the honour of directing to him your two letters, and give him other honours, which modesty will not allow him to claim, will it not look to some that his request to you to write on the two subjects, *Original* and *Moral*, was made to you in hopes of receiving some kind compliments from your friendly partiality; could not, therefore, some powerful and deserving friend be substituted, as knowing I have the honour of corresponding with his valued Dr. Young, to put me upon requesting you to touch upon these two subjects? And will not the requester be of more proper importance to engage such a pen? I conceive that the alteration may be easily made; suppose like this—'Your worthy patron, our common friend, by putting you on the request you make me, both flatters and distresses me. How can I comply! Is it not late—He thinks the press overcharged, &c. ['] as above.

Page 3.—Would you choose, good sir, to illustrate the merits of authors by an allusion to so sadly solemn a truth, as the fall of our first parent? Especially as it hath too often been sported with by those whose intentions were totally different from yours?

Was not Icarus the person who fell by soaring too high?

Page 4.—Suppose, sir, the Scripture allusion [King of Salem] omitted? And the passage to run thus:—'Excellence which seem to common readers as dropped,' &c.

As I presume that Lucretius need not be set up for an example, however original, would it not be enough to quote his words without his name? Thus—*a sequestered path*: —————— Nullius ante Trita pede—————— or here, if you please, to insert *Lucr.*?

Will you, sir, be pleased to reconsider the passage hooked in relating to the *weakly brats*? Or, if it be continued, suppose the whole paragraph be made to run thus—'As for translations and imitations, those echoes of another's voice; shadows of another's worth; those weakly brats dropt by the fame of ancient authors at almost every door, and by childless moderns fathered as their own;' the great originals, in whose right we pretend to inherit, are still themselves in actual possession, and by the art of printing, secured in it from Goths and flames, and the mouldering hand of Time; and, like Saturn, 'who was said to have devoured his own children, swallow up the fame of their progeny in the blaze of their own superior glory.'

Page 5.—*Of* strength . . . *of* exertion, that *makes* imitations, &c.

And 'extinguish our own,' instead of '*putting an extinguisher on our own,*' suppose?

Page 6.—'Might be reversed.' What, sir, and the dwarf sink under the weight of the giant? Is not that rather the case when modern giants stunt their own growth by holding up the mighty ancient to view, on the shoulders of a feeble translation or imitation?

Page 7.—'Of those heathen authors', *historical writers excepted,* 'who had shone,' &c.

'Attentively read,' *the lovers of improvement* 'will have a school to go to,' *whose principal form stands as high as that on which Homer is enthroned.*

Would you choose, sir, to join Adam and Pallas together? Has not Milton too often mingled the Christian and Pagan theologies?

'Infantine genius hath its infancy.' Suppose thus, 'The former, *like other infants, must be nurtured,*' &c. omitting the words, 'has its infancy.'

Page 8.— '*Tête-à-tête,*' suppose this were put '*hand in hand.*'

Page 9.—Suppose, dear sir, I should offer the following long passage to your consideration, after the words, 'And, in this sense, some are born wise.' But here, my friend, let me digress into a caution against the automathers, the self-taught philosophers, of the age, who set up genius above, not human learning, but divine truth. I have called genius wisdom, but let it be remembered, that in the most refined ages of heathen genius, when the world by wisdom knew not God, it pleased God, by the *foolishness of preaching, to save those that believed.* In the fairy land of fancy, genius wanders wild; it hath there almost a creative power, and may reign over its empire of chimeras. The wide field of nature is also before it, and there, as far as visible nature extends, it may freely extend its discoveries. But can the noblest original painter give us the portrait of a seraph? No: he can give but what he sees, though what he sees he can infinitely compound and embellish. But can genius, human genius, strike out divine truth unrevealed? Be the statuary ever so excellent, he can never produce a diamond statue out of a marble block.

This digression is long. I was frightened, I was shocked, at the thought, that some unballasted mind, warm in the confidence of youth, might possibly be misled by this unguarded pen into the most fatal of all errors. Return we now to warn them against such suppressions of genius, as debase it to the level of dullness.

Some, I have said (and in what sense I have said it will not now be mistaken) 'are born wise; but as they,' &c.

Page 10.—'Has its share in the charge.'

Page 12.—'Joy. The joyous.' Suppose the word *joy* changed to the word *delight*?

'As ethics, a real immortality.' Suppose it be said, 'as ethics *christianized*, a real immortality?' In condescension to well-meaning slight objectors?

'Let Homer,' &c. Would you not choose, sir, to cite the author who tells this of Homer?

'Not damp our spirits, like a knell, *nor* incline us *only* to borrow,' &c.

Page 18.—'To be the follower of ancient authors.'

'The writer's own genius,' &c. Is not that which follows these words rather too bold? Might not the paragraph end at the word *worshipped*?

For 'the god of song,' suppose Apollo, as the patron of poetry; as, afterwards, Phoebus as the owner of the chariot?

P. 19.—Pope's, sir, I venture to say, was not the genius *to lift our souls to Heaven*, had it soared ever so freely, since it soared not in the Christian beam; but there is an eagle, whose eyes pierce through the shades of midnight, that does indeed *transport* us, and the apotheosis is your's. Whether this may suggest any softening, or any improvement to the passage, must be submitted to you; but, surely, an *heroic* poem ought not to be mentioned in these terms, which so exactly belong to a *divine* one? The author of one wishes to have his name swim down the stream of time on the wreck of Bolingbroke; the other dedicates his early muse to *Him* who gave him voice, and consequently *his work is remote from all imitation*. Should there not be here some distinction of *imitators of other authors*, and imitation of nature, in which respect poetry is called one of the imitative arts? The tame imitator of other poets is a copier of portraits, the true genius a noble painter of originals, to whom nature delights to sit in every variety of attitude.

Indeed sir, I cannot imagine that Pope would have shone in blank verse; and do you really think he had invention enough to make him a great poet? Did he not want the assistance of rhyme, of jingle? What originality is there in the works for which he is most famed? Shall I say, that I wish you would be pleased to reconsider all you say of the creative power of Pope? There is a hasty scratch through some of the lines in this page; excuse it, sir, and let me beg of you to alter, particularly, the same paragraphs, lest you should be thought to degrade, by a too minute allusion, the awful wonders of creation. Suppose, sir, when you ask, What does the name of poet mean? you answer after some such manner as this— '*It means a maker*, and, consequently, *his work is something original, quite his own*. It is not the laboured improvement of a modern cultivator bestowed on a soil already fertile, and refining on a plan already formed; but the touch of Armida's wand, that calls forth blooming spring out of the shapeless waste, and presents in a moment objects new and various, which his genius only could have formed in that peculiar manner, and his taste only arranged with that peculiar grace. These two enchanting gifts of taste and genius were *possessed by Shakespeare in a surprising degree, in both dramas*,' &c.

Page 21.—'An infallible receipt against disturbing our passions.'

Considering how very licentious and wretched in every view most of Dryden's comedies are, can it be said he writ them for eternity? Suppose it be thus altered, 'He writ tragedy for subsistence, and his other compositions for fame; *and if he had had no other wing to reach* even eternal fame *but his incomparable ode*,' &c.

'Tully's assassin found him reading,' &c. Should not the authority for this be quoted?

Page 23.—'Shakespeare, Bacon, Newton,' are great originals. Forgive me for omitting *great men*, because, strictly speaking, Bacon—*The wisest, brightest, meanest, of mankind*, was not therefore, strictly speaking, a *great man*; and, though Shakspeare as an *author* was so far *greater* than Addison, as more an *original*, yet was he inferior to him as a man; because, in his best writings, *less useful*—for *man* to *man* is only *great* with respect to his fulfilling the important purposes for which man was made. But are not the three originals I have named men of detached excellence, *bordering*, &c.

Pray, sir, may it not be hinted, as a piece of justice, that Addison was sometimes *original*; and, in his Sir Roger, as much so as Shakspeare.

Page 24.—If, sir, you disapprove of the above criticism on originals, may not what is placed between hooks be omitted?

And may not also what is said of Cain be dispensed with; the passage running thus—'become ancients ourselves; and old Time, that sure weigher of merit,' &c.

Page 24, 25—How noble, how admirable, is your conclusion! I am inspired by it to offer the following to your forgiving consideration.

Are not love of vain fame, and forgetfulness of certain death, both to be accounted for from human abuse of divine goodness? On a second review, you will possibly approve the small additions proposed in this view.

Suppose, after the words, 'I find it in the marvellous goodness of God,' *abused by the marvellous perverseness of man*? In this point, &c.

Page 26.—'In absolute oblivion of a fall.' This, *as the former case, proceeds from man's folly and vice*, perverting to his destruction *the wisdom and goodness of God*. The all gracious Creator *designed that he should have a certain task*, &c.

'In the next.' But the task of life would be overlooked, and its enjoyments tasteless, *if that terrible proportion*.

After the words *draw its sting*, suppose the following?

Some merit it hath, but, like all human merit, *nothing whereof to glory*. Though our hearts are in mercy hardened against continual fear, they are, in equal mercy, alarmed by calls frequent and loud enough to awaken so much as is needful. Though unconcerned we see the *many* fall around us, when the dart strikes a *friend* it strikes home to ourselves. The *private* fates are overlooked with an unheeding eye, the judgment of nations makes individuals tremble. Though we feel not for others, pain preaches to our hearts, and the languors of decaying nature force upon us leisure and attention. There are who *deafen* themselves to all these calls with the rattle of amusement; but their fearlessness is wilful. There *are* (would they were more!) who *need* them not; but, wakeful in their duty, are never alarmed, because always prepared. These make a due use of both the impelling and restraining mercy, the desire of immortality, and unaffectedness with hourly mementos of death. The gentle slumber indulged to support our frail nature is from Providence, and, as such, they gratefully and temperately enjoy its blessing. The fatal lethargy into which it is so often perverted is the work of man, combined against himself with his worst foe; and, as such, the wise break from it by urging to its utmost the pursuit of *real* immortality. A larcae, that whoever suffers to sleep in his bosom, or to delude him by chiming the false jingle of mortal fame, will find, too late, was placed there for the most important purpose.

Thus you see, &c.

The *two supreme*; were it not better, for obvious reasons, to say, *for writing two great articles of our creed,* &c. The soul's immortality, and the being of a God, are the two supreme of a Mahometan creed, because they only believe in it.

I submit, as I ought, all the above to your better judgment.

I thank you for gratifying the curiosity of Major Hohorst. He is full of gratitude for your kind reception of him; speaks of you with love, reverence, and admiration, as he before did of your works.

I am, sir, with the most respectful affection,

Your obliged and faithful servant,
S. Richardson.

All mine desire be your's and Mrs. Hallows'.

375. [Welwyn, Herts.]. [Th.] 20 January 1757.
Samuel Richardson.

Not traced.—*Monthly Magazine*, xlii (1 November 1816), 335.

January 20, 1757.
Dear, dear sir,

What pains have you taken? What masterly assistance have you given? What thanks are your due. I think I shall profit by your every remark; and I am sure I shall ever acknowledge a friendship which, in kind and proportion, I shall never be able to return.

We embrace all your good family with the tenderest regard, and pay them our best wishes, which, on many accounts, are so greatly due.

I am, dear sir,
Most affectionately your's,
E. Young.

For the admirable addition to my last poetry all thanks are due.[1]

376. [Welwyn, Herts.]. [Th.] 24 February 1757.
Samuel Richardson.

Not traced.—*Monthly Magazine*, xliii (1 May 1817), 327.

February 24, 1757.
My dear sir,

If not inconvenient to you, I will lodge with you on Monday night next; I am under a necessity of returning the next day. I must borrow one hour of you to hear me read the letter,[2] as now, by your assistance, amended; for it is so

---

[1] Richardson had written to a correspondent on 15 December that Young was 'about to give the world a collection of his works, at the entreaty of the booksellers, who have a property in them, in four twelves [duodecimo] volumes' (Barbauld, 1804, iv. 112). The edition was announced for publication on 21 May in the *London Evening Post.*

[2] Perhaps it was on this occasion that Samuel Johnson heard Young read the *Conjectures* (cf. James Boswell, *The Journal of a Tour to the Hebrides*, in *Boswell's Life of Johnson*, ed. G. B. Hill, rev. L. F. Powell, 1950, v. 269).

transcribed, that, without some hints to you, it will be unintelligible.

My very best wishes and service to all.

I am, dear sir,
Your truly affectionate and much
obliged humble servant,
E. Young.

Mrs. Hallows is much your's.

377. [Welwyn, Herts.]. [Sa.] 26 March 1757. Samuel Richardson.

Not traced.—*Monthly Magazine*, xliii (1 May 1817), 327.

March 26, 1757

My dear sir,

I am summoned to attest a point in Chancery on Tuesday next, and am under a necessity of returning the Wednesday morning.

I would, with your kind leave, lodge with you on Tuesday night, but indeed, indeed, [*sic*] I shall rest very ill if I am not permitted to lie where I am fully satisfied no one is dislodged for me; an evil conscience will be my bedfellow if I lodge not in a garret. Mrs. Hallows joins in this my request; and in best wishes, and best respects, with,

Dear sir,
Your most obliged and most
affectionate humble servant,
E. Young.

Richardson to Young. London. [Tu.] 10 May 1757.

Not traced.—*Monthly Magazine*, xliii (1 May 1817), 327.

London; May 10, 1757.

Rev. and dear Sir,

I was in hope of an opportunity, by Mr. Shotbolt, the last time he was in town, to have transmitted safely to you your

453

excellent and charmingly spirited manuscript; but he called not upon me, as usual. Put me in the way to send it safely to you. Two or three small observations I have taken the liberty to make, and pasted on so lightly, as that they may be taken off without deforming the manuscript. In the margin also I have, here and there, made this mark ✕, where I have intended a reference to you on re-perusal, chiefly from mistakes of the transcriber. In one place you ascribe the cartoon to Michael Angelo—I believe justly; but had a doubt in favour of Raphael.[1]

I am sorry I was so much indisposed last time you were in town as to give you pain; I am much obliged to your kind concern for me. I am in Mr. Watson's hands still, but better; yet these unsteady nerves! I hope you are in good health; God continue to you, dear and rev. sir, that blessing for many happy years!

How proceed you in your second letter?[2] Hurt not yourself, good sir, by your kind partiality to a man happy in your good opinion; and then how shall I rejoice to read in print such noble instances of the doctrine you advance in favour of the moderns! Surely, sir, this piece is the most spirited and original of all your truly spirited and original works! What memory, what recollection, does it display. With all the experience of years, it has all the fire and (corrected) imagination of youth.

Believe me to be, dear sir, with the greatest sincerity and affection,

Your greatest obliged and faithful
humble servant,
S. Richardson.

All our kindest respects to good Mrs. Hallows.

1 In the published version there is no reference to either artist.
2 The *Conjectures* concludes with the postscript 'How far Addison is an original you will see in my next . . .' It was never published.

378. [Welwyn, Herts.] [Th.] 12 May 1757. Samuel
Richardson.

Not traced.—*Monthly Magazine*, xliii (1 May 1817), 327–8.

May 12, 1757.

My dear and most valued friend,
  I am glad at heart that you are better; I learnt it before
from Mr. Watson—God continue his success.
  Mr. Shotbolt next week will be in town, and bring me the
papers. I am sorry, very sorry, your observations are few and
small; I know how to value what drops from your pen—let
me have all it can afford.
  I have written a second letter but it by no means pleases
me—the subject is too common, and I cannot keep out of
the footsteps of my predecessors.
  For the lasting and endless welfare of you and your's, Mrs.
Hallows joins the warmest prayers of, dear sir,
                    Your truly affectionate
                        and greatly obliged,
                            humble servant,
                                E. Young.

379. [Welwyn, Herts.] [Su.] 15 May 1757. Samuel
Richardson.

Not traced.—*Monthly Magazine*, xliii (1 May 1817), 328.

May 15, 1757.
Dear sir,
  Mr. Marriot¹ does me the honour of desiring me to
recommend him to your valuable acquaintance; and the credit
of being supposed to have some interest in you, and my
opinion of Mr. Marriot's polite manners and integrity,

  ¹ James Marriott (?1730–1803), who was to be made Vice-Chancellor of Cambridge University in 1764, had at this time, 25 March, received the degree LL.D.,
from the University. What his connection with Young may have been is unknown,
but as his widowed mother is said to have married 'a Mr. Sayer', it may have been
through the Sayer family that the acquaintance was made (cf. Young's letter to the
Duchess of Portland of 10 July 1743).

incline me to comply. Nor am I under the least apprehension
but that, on farther knowledge of him, you will see ample
cause to excuse the liberty now taken by,

Dear sir,

Your truly affectionate and very much
obliged humble servant,

E. Young.

380. [Welwyn, Herts.]. [Su.] 22 May 1757. Samuel Richardson.

Not traced.—*Monthly Magazine*, xliii (1 May 1817), 328.

May 22, 1757.

My dear sir,

A thought is come into my head which should have been
there long before. You have many fair daughters;[1] variety
to youth is pleasant; Mrs. Hallows is a good, and not unlettered, woman; she would think herself extremely happy in
making this place as agreeable as possible to any of your's,
which you should be so good to favour us withall.

If, in a word, you will spare us one out of your abundance,
she shall be as welcome as if there was not another on
earth; and Mrs. Hallows shall wait on her with a conveyance
to, dear sir,

Your most obliged and ever affectionate
humble servant,

E. Young.

One of your daughters has had ill-health[2]—change of air
and new amusement may possibly be of service; and, if a
physician should be wanted, I have a good one within call.
Look not on this as a compliment, I should truly rejoice in
your compliance with my request. Besides, I have a very

---

[1] Mary, or 'Polly' (1734–83), Martha, or 'Patty' (b. 1736), Anne, or 'Nancy'
(1737–1803), and Sarah (b. 1740).

[2] 'Nancy's' decline accompanied a disappointment in love; she never married.

good chalybeate,[1] which sometimes is a great friend to the
sex.

I hope in God your own health continues to mend. My
love and service to all.

381. [Welwyn, Herts.] [Su.] 29 May 1757. Samuel
Richardson.

Not traced.—*Monthly Magazine*, xliii (1 May 1817), 328.

May 29, 1757.

Dear sir,

How much your kind letter rejoiced and obliged me, I
shall not, and I hope I need not, say. All I shall say at
present is, that (God willing) Mrs. Hallows will breakfast
with Miss Nancy in Salisbury-court on Tuesday se'nnight;
and that I hope they both will sup with, dear sir,

Your affectionate
and humble servant,
E. Young.

Suppose you should ask Dr. Heberden if the steel-water[2]
might not be of service to my fair guest; and, if so, in what
quantity, &c.

Miss Polly and Miss Patty have laid me under much
obligation to them, for the pleasing hope of seeing them one
day (if it shall so please God,) in this part of the world. To
good and kind Mrs. Richardson, Mrs. Hallows's and my
best service and thanks.

1 'Wellwyn deserves to be mentioned for its spaw, newly revived by the Reverend
and Learned Dr. Young. . . . The Waters have the same qualities as those of Tunbridge; and were so reputed to have 50 years ago; but an eminent Physician at the
time, who was a great Patron of them, dying, they were neglected, till within these
six Years, that they were revived by the great Genius I have mentioned; who, in his
own Case, has found them to have the same Effects as those of Tunbridge used to
have' (*A Tour through Great Britain*, By a Gentleman, 1753).
2 i.e. the Welwyn chalybeate spring water.

Richardson to Young. London. [Tu.] 19 July 1757.

Not traced.—*Monthly Magazine*, xliii (1 May 1817), 328.

London; July 19, 1757.

Is it not time, my reverend and dear sir, to release you and good Mrs. Hallows from the trouble and care my good girl has so long given you? It is; and I will contrive in the beginning of next week, if that will not be too long a trespass, to ease you of her, and to have her accompanied to us by a proper person, if I cannot myself be him; as I am afraid I cannot, because of these unhappy tremors, which a more than usual exercise encreases. A million of thanks, dear sir, for your goodness to her, and to Mrs. Hallows for her's.

I have given up myself for this fortnight past wholly (as to medicinal helps) to tar-water, and those about me think I am already the better for it. My spirits, I think, are a little mended, and that is a great article.

How proceed you, sir, with your second letter? I long to see it; the perusal of it, as you favoured me with that of your other incomparable one, would give me high pleasure. May I soon hope to be so favoured?

Your next neighbours, I hope, are well, and will be long happy in each other. Be pleased to make my kindest compliments to them both.

I am, dear and reverend sir, with the most grateful respects of all mine,

Your ever-obliged and most faithful
humble servant,
S. Richardson.

I am glad to hear you like Dr. Smollet's History of England.[1]

---

[1] Tobias Smollett's *A Compleat History of England, deduced from the Descent of Julius Caesar to the Treaty of Aix-la-Chapelle, 1748*, in 4 vols., was announced as published in *The Gentleman's Magazine* for April (xxvii. 191).

382. [Welwyn, Herts.]. [Th.] 21 July 1757. Samuel
Richardson.

Not traced.—*Monthly Magazine*, xliii (1 May 1817), 329.

My dear sir,   July 21, 1757.
    What you call our trouble is, indeed, our very great
pleasure; Miss Nancy is a very agreeable and sensible companion; and my best fruits, which I from the first proposed
as her chief entertainment, are not yet ripe—you must not
rob her of them, nor us of her. Trouble not yourself about
her conveyance; I myself will deliver her (God willing) safe
into your hands, when the hour is come, which, I trust, is
yet at a considerable distance; for indeed, indeed, [*sic*] she is
as welcome to me as if she was my own. Besides, dear sir,
consider—either Miss Richardson flatters us, or her health
is rather bettered by this air, which is good, and I persuade
her to take it on horseback as often as it is agreeable to her.
    I truly rejoice that my old friend tarwater is of service;
God encrease its good effects on you, and then it will give
spirits to us all. I am, dear sir,
                        Your greatly obliged and truly
                            affectionate humble servant,
                                    E. Young.

Accept your dear daughter's duty, and Mrs. Hallows' best
respects.
P.S. I have read Clarissa thrice, and the last kiss was the
sweetest.

Richardson to Young. [London]. [Tu.] 26 July
1757.

Not traced.—*Monthly Magazine*, xliii (1 May 1817), 329.

                                        July 26, 1757.
    How good are you, reverend and dear sir, to my girl—
how good to me. These are the days she will, as long as she

lives, distinguish as the happiest of her life—ever an admirer as she was of Dr. Young and his works. But let her not encroach; let her not in the least inconvenience you and good Mrs. Hallows.

What is the fruit, sir, that she must wait its ripening? The apricot, a very pretty fruit, and generally grateful to the female palate, begins to ripen already with us; with you, perhaps, it will be a fortnight later.

I should rejoice to see you at Parsons-green; I shall not like the place quite so well as I shall do after you have seen it. Perhaps you have business that will call you soon to town.

'Dear Mrs. Hallows, we will take the utmost care of our kind friend, at both houses, if he will favour us; and of you too, if you can be spared.'

'Nancy, my dear, be sure—but I have great confidence in your discretion.'

May I, sir, repeat my enquiry after your second letter?

I rejoice in the good account Dr. Webster, two or three days ago, gave me of your good health. God long continue to you that invaluable blessing. All mine join in this prayer with,

Reverend and dear sir,
Your affectionate and obliged servant,
S. Richardson.

Respects to your next-door neighbours.

383. [Welwyn, Herts.]. [Sa.] 30 July 1757. Samuel Richardson.

Not traced.—*Monthly Magazine*, xliv (1 November 1817), 327.

July 30, 1757.

Many, many thanks, to my dear friend, for his so cordial invitation to Parson's-green.

I will gladly accept it as soon as it is in my power: but very soon it cannot be. And, till then, I earnestly beg the

favour, you will permit me to enjoy the great pleasure your
indulgence has put into the hands of, dear sir,

Ever your's,
E. Young.

All here join me in the best wishes and respects to you all.

I shall speak of the second letter when I have the pleasure
of seeing you. I have great avocations, and cannot succeed
to my wish.

**384. [Su.] 11 September 1757. William Slade of
Deptford.**[1]

Not traced.—Nichols–Doran, *Works*, 1854, I. cv–cvi.

September 11th, 1757.

Dear Sir,

The scripture can only give us light as to our final acceptance with God. Our own *fancied impulses* may deceive us.
No man can have a full *assurance* of salvation, for this plain
reason, namely, 'Because the end can never be certain, when
the means of attaining that end are uncertain.' Now, though
for the time past a man may have lived well, yet he is not sure
that he shall do so for the future. And the scripture has
cautioned us against flattering ourselves with full assurance
of salvation, when it says, 'Let him that standeth take heed
lest he fall.'

That this short and plain consideration may restore your
peace of mind, is the hearty prayer of,

Your affectionate humble servant,
E. Young.

[1] This letter, known only from Nichols-Doran, appears to be in answer to a casual
inquiry by a person not otherwise connected with Young.

385. Welwyn, Herts. [Tu.] 27 September 1757.
Samuel Richardson.

Address: [part missing] [Sa]lisbury Court Fleet Street / London.
Yale University Library (Osborn Collection).

Wellwyn 27. 1757.
September

[In the hand of Mrs. Hallows]

My Dearest of Friends

    My Neighbour being in hast, I have but just time to tell
You, that Your infinitely kind Letter[1] can never be forgotten, by

Your mos[t] obliged
And most Affectionate
EYoung

What use I shall be able to make of Your goodness I cannot
yet tell My health being in a state of variation & great
uncertainty. Thursday Morning. Mrs. Hallow's humble
Service attends Mr. Richardson & his truly valuable House
/[conjugate leaf]/ That Amiable Young Man, poor Hohurst
is Dead![2] From two bloody pitched Battells, & many warm
Skirmishes, he escaped unhurt: But when the enemy had
turnd his back, a violent Fever gave him no quarter—and,
am I, still alive? I pity the dying, & envy [the] Dead.

386. [Su.] 23 October 1757. Samuel Richardson.

Not traced.[3]—Barbauld, ii. 40; Shelley, p. 244.

October 23d, 1757.

Dear Sir,

    O my dear friend! little do you think how you oppress me
by your great goodness to me: and more still by the uneasi-

---

    [1] Not extant.

    [2] Young had learned of the death of Hohorst from Klopstock (see his letter to
Klopstock of 27 October).

    [3] The manuscript of this letter was offered for sale by Southgate on 26 April 1827
as part of item No. 130, property of Captain Markham Sherwill.

ness you yourself are under. My spirits fail me; I am very low; and am designing for the bath as my last resource.

However, considering my time of day, I bless God that it is not still worse with me. What I suffer, I look on as *necessary* discipline; and humbly hope it may be some small expiation of great offences; and I am bound in reason to consider it as a blessing, if God grants me the grace of patience and resignation under it.

To the divine mercy and favour I recommend you and your's, with a heart full of gratitude and sincere affection.

E. Young.

Richardson to Young. [London]. [M.] 24 October 1757.

Not traced.—Barbauld, ii. 41–2.

October 24th, 1757.

Rev. and Dear Sir,

How much am I grieved for your continued lowness of spirits! I am glad that you are going to Bath. Change of air, of place, of scene, will, I hope, restore them. I have heretofore tried the Bath waters, and that more than once. I have more hopes in your case. Your nerves are good, your constitution is sound, and your muscular flesh is firm.

Suppose, dear and good Sir, you favour us for a few days in your way thither? Mrs. Hallowes can, perhaps, attend you while here. I have pleasure in thinking that I have a daughter[1] there, who loves and honours you, as all mine do; and indeed every one does who has the pleasure of knowing you. Mr. Ditcher, her husband, will rejoice to have it in his power to serve you. Mr. Leake[2] and his agreeable family will do all they can to make the place (and the situation in it which you shall choose) convenient. Come to me, dearest Sir; we will write to my daughter and her husband to provide for you the conveniencies you shall choose. So that from

---

[1] Richardson's daughter Mary had recently been married to Philip Ditcher, a surgeon.

[2] James Leake (d. 1764), Mrs. Richardson's brother, a bookseller.

Salisbury-court to Bath, shall be all the way a preconcerted journey; and you shall immediately enter there on the well-aired lodgings, that my daughter will cause to be ready for you.

Dr. Oliver[1] is the most eminent physician there, and so deemed for many years past. Favour me with giving him my sincere compliments. I will answer for his care, his skill, and his love.

God Almighty bless and preserve you, and continue for many happy years to come a life so useful to the world; and give you health to make it agreeable to yourself, prays with ardour,

Dear Sir, your most affectionate and
obliged humble Servant,
S. Richardson.

387. Welwyn, Herts. [Th.] 27 October 1757. Friedrich Gottlieb Klopstock.[2]

Not traced.—*Auswahl aus Klopstocks Nachlass*, 1821, 237; Thomas, pp. 603–4.

Dear Sir,

What obligations do I lie under to you for your so kind repeated and undeserv'd regards to a stranger? a stranger to your person, but not to your fame and merit. Poor Hohorst made me acquainted with that.

If by your means he layd hold on the rock of ages, what overflowing thanks is he now paying to his friend on Earth, amidst the joys of Heaven?—His enemies flew before him; but their ally, the fever would give no quarter. He seem'd possess'd of most amiable qualities; and is he gone in the flower of youth? and am I still alive?—Humanity obliges me to say, that *I pity the Dying*; and my age and infirmities obliges me to say, that *I envy the Dead*. Sir, I received no letter from you before this, and I shall esteem it as an honour to my name, and a cordial to my Decays, to receive any future Instance of your favour.

---

[1] William Oliver (1695–1764).

[2] The German poet Klopstock (1724–1803) was an enthusiastic admirer of Young's *Night-Thoughts*.

God Almighty prosper your pious and celebrated endeavours for promoting his glory, and then crown you with
blessings, that will make you look with contempt on all the
applauses of the world.

My letter had been longer, if my health had been better.
Favour therefore with your pardon, and your prayers.
Worthy Sir,

Your much obliged,
obedient and affectionate
humble servant
E. Young.

Octr. 27. 1757
Wellwyn in
Hertfordshire.

P.S. You are so kind as to desire my friendship; Dear Sir,
you have my heart, and it would be one of the greatest
blessings of my age, if I could embrace you before I die.

Not being willing, to quit so kind a correspondent, I am
obliged to borrow anothers hand, to go on, which makes it
natural for me, to date my letter from the verge of Eternity;
how long it may be before the great master of Eternity and
Time, shall bid me launch, is uncertain; but be it sooner or
later, as in Heaven so in Earth, his blessed will be done. I
rejoice in being able to write to one (how rarely to be found)
who can relish thoughts unseasoned by the domineering
interests of the world, that is, who can relish things, a true
taste of which, renders empire and even Genius, tho' equal
to your own, insipid and of little worth. Adieu, worthy Sir,—
Adieu.—

388. [Welwyn, Herts.]. [Tu.] 1 November 1757.
Samuel Richardson.

Not traced.—*Monthly Magazine*, xliv (1 November 1817), 327.

Nov. 1, 1757.
My dear sir,

On Thursday (God willing,) I set out for the Bath;
where all related to you will be dear to me. I lodge at Mrs.

Bowden's,[1] in Wade's-passage: she was partly a parishioner of mine. If I can be anyways serviceable to you, your kind commands will rejoice the heart of

Dearest sir,

Your ever obliged and affectionate
humble servant,

E. Young.

Mr. Shotbolt says, you are better: God be praised.

389. Bath, Somerset. [F.] 30 December 1757. Friedrich Gottlieb Klopstock.

Not traced.—*Auswahl aus Klopstocks Nachlass*, 1821, p. 239; Thomas, pp. 604–5.

Dear, Dear Sir,

I most cordially salute you, and your other amiable Self.[2] Your most obliging Letters found me at the Bath; with a multitude of others, seeking our better Health; and, till all gracious Heaven shall please to restore it to me, I am much incapable of answering your so affectionate Letters, as I wish, and as I ought to do: Till then, therefore, favour me with your pardon. And please to accept the most sincere wishes of my Heart, and my fervent prayers to Heaven for your full comfort on this side the Grave, and your perfect Happiness in a far better and Eternal Scene; and measure not my Respect, but my Infirmity by the shortness of my Letter, and be most assured, that I am and ever shall be, my dearest, and as far as your Celebrated Name will permit, unknown Friend,

Your most affectionately
Devoted Humble Servant

E. Young.

Bath in
Sommersetshire,
30. Dec. 1757.

1 Mrs. John Bowden (*née* Dorothy Wingate) was a cousin of Jane (bur. 20 March 1747/8) and Dinah (d. June 1752) Wingate of Welwyn and is mentioned in both their wills (Somerset House, P.C.C. Strahan 134; Bettesworth 174).

2 Klopstock's wife, Meta, whom he had married in 1754. On 22 December Richardson had written to Meta Klopstock saying, 'I have transmitted to [Young] the letter you inclosed in that you favoured me with' (Barbauld, 1804, iii. 141–4).

390. [Bath, Somerset]. [Tu.] 3 January 1758. Samuel Richardson.

Not traced.—*Monthly Magazine*, xliv (1 November 1817), 327.

Jan. 3, 1758.

My dearest friend,

Numberless are your favours: Mr. and Mrs. Ditcher are to me extremely kind. I bless God I at last find benefit from the waters—as to appetite, rest, and spirits. I have now, for three nights, had pretty good rest; after two sleepless months: and I believe that persevering in the waters is the point; at least, in my complaint.

But, at my time of day, how dare I to complain of small things, on the brink of the grave, and at the door of eternity! What a mercy that I am still here! What a fall have I seen around me! I was here twenty years ago,[1] and scarce find one of that generation alive.

I rejoice, I greatly rejoice, to hear that you are better. Might not Bath be as much your friend as mine? In some points our cases are similar. I think you told me in a letter that you once found benefit from it: if you would try again, I would attend you to your last hour.

But, say you, are you idle all this time? No—I am on a great work. How great a work is it? To learn to die with safety and comfort. This is, as should be, my business: Unless I think it too much to spend my superannuated hours on that which ought to have been the business of my whole life.

I called this morning on Mr. and Mrs. Ditcher, to know if they had any commands; but have none, but to acquaint you with their health and duty. Mrs. Hallows joins my very particular good wishes and respects to Mrs. Richardson and all, especially our dear friend Miss Nancy, to whom Mrs. Hallows, at present a little out of order, will write very soon.

May the new year, dear sir, make you a present of health, spirits, and peace; and, as for a good prospect beyond the reach of new years, that I know you give yourself.

Most affectionately your's,

E. Young.

[1] There is no other record of this visit to Bath, which, if it was in 1737 or 1738, would have included Young's wife, Lady Elizabeth.

Richardson to Young. [London]. January 1758.

Not traced.—*Monthly Magazine*, xliv (1 November 1817), 327–8.

January, 1758.

Rev. and ever dear sir,

I congratulate you, with my whole heart, on the good effect the waters have at last had on your health. I hope that the God of all mercies will soon enable you to rejoice all your friends with the desirable news of your perfect recovery.

What may we not promise ourselves from so sound and good a constitution; from your regularity and temperance; from the exercise you are enabled to take; and from the powers of such a mind invigorating the whole. A mind which can enjoy, and even enlarge itself, by that very sleeplessness, which tears in pieces the health of others.

'Our cases in some points similar!' Ah, my dear and good sir—but that exercise, that journeying, which will contribute to your cure, I am unable to take. What a motive do you give me to make you a Bath visit, were I able: but I hope, on your return, I shall not be deprived of the blessing of your company, and the favour of Mrs. Hallows's—as was my request by my daughter Ditcher. I have been often at Bath; but remember not that I received benefit from the waters: the late worthy Dr. Hartley[1] once whispered me, that I need not expect any.

'You are about a great work—to learn to die with safety and comfort.' My dear sir, you, that have been so admirable a *teacher* of this very doctrine in your excellent *Night Thoughts*, must be more than a *learner*. You have not left too *superannuated hours* (which I hope, if ever they come, are far, very far *distant*) that great work. How comfortably therefore may you enjoy life, as well as contemplate the closing scene.

Thanks to you, dear and reverend sir, for your good wishes of the season. Health attend you for many happy one's, prays

Your ever-affectionate and obliged
humble servant,
S. Richardson.

[1] The philosopher David Hartley had settled in Bath in 1742 and practised medicine there until his death, 28 August 1757.

I congratulate you, my good Mrs. Hallows, on the happy success of your prayers and cares: all mine love you for both.

P.S. I am sorry that sleeplessness is your complaint: but when you sleep you are awake to noble purpose,—I to none at all; my days are nothing but hours of dozings, for want of nightly rest, and through an impatience that I am ashamed of—because I cannot subdue it.

391. [Bath, Somerset.]. [? January 1758]. John Jones.

Not traced.[1]

392. [Welwyn, Herts.]. [Su.] 30 April 1758. Samuel Richardson.

Not traced.—*Monthly Magazine*, xliv (1 November 1817), 328.

April 30, 1758.

With the utmost freedom of a true friend to truth, and to me, favour me with your full opinion of the *Dedication*:[2] for I am, my dear sir, somewhat uneasy till I can determine myself about it; and my own judgment is at a loss.

Is there any thing *mean* in what I say *of myself and my long service at court?*

Is there *impropriety, or too great length in what follows about the army?*

---

[1] Evidence of this letter occurs in Jones's petition of 2 April 1760, seeking to improve conditions of his employment as Young's curate. He said in part: 'I have always retained a very grateful remembrance of his [Young's] encouraging declaration to me from Bath, "That whether he should live or die, I should find him my friend"' (Dr. Williams's Library, Jones papers B. 17[3](2)).

[2] i.e. 'To the King', the dedicatory introduction to *An Argument drawn from the Circumstances of Christ's Death for the Truth of His Religion, A Sermon preached before His Majesty at Kensington, June, 1758.*

Pray let me know your real sentiments: or shall I take your silence as a tender way of your letting me know that you disapprove?

Dear sir,
Your truly affectionate
humble servant,
E. Young.

Mrs. Shotbolt has presented my neighbour with a girl.[1]
P.S. If you have been so good as to read the Sermon, please to let me also know your thoughts of that.

Richardson to Young. [London]. [Tu.] 2 May 1758.

Not traced.—*Monthly Magazine*, xliv (1 November 1817), 328–9.

May 2, 1758.

Dear and reverend sir,

Had I not been forced to wait for the power of holding a pen, from my grievous nervous disorders, I would before now have congratulated you with my whole heart, on your happy recovery, and safe arrival at your Wellwyn: which I now do.

I send you inclosed proofs of your Sermon. Should you not call it a Sermon, or Discourse; and say where preached in the title, and by whom? And your booksellers' names? and to whom dedicated?

On reading cursorily the discourse, I thought there were two or three places (which I cannot, on reperusal, find again,) that were not quite so clear to my clouded understanding as the rest of the excellent piece—all new and original as it is, like your other writings.

As to the Dedication, I am far from thinking your mentioning length of service *mean*: will it not rather be thought, or misunderstood, to carry with it something of complaint, or even of reproach; and as if your neglecting your month

---

[1] Elizabeth, named for her mother, was baptized on 21 June (Welwyn parish register). Both the mother and the daughter, as well as a son Thomas, are mentioned in John Shotbolt's will, made 11 June 1763, and proved 15 December 1766 (Somerset House, P.C.C. Tyndall 468).

for some years past were owing to resentment? I humbly think this part cannot be too delicately mentioned: especially, as you have touched upon it with great feeling in more places than one, in your 'Night Thoughts,' so long ago— *My master knows me not*, &c.:[1] and nothing resulted from the just sensibility. Some of your great admirers in that divine work thought you descended too much for the superiority you appeared in to them. Suppose, sir, you stop at your well-known seniority in the present chaplainship, without carrying the hint to Leicester-house; leaving it upon them to recollect, that you could have gone further with justice, had preferment been your sole view. It is right, however, not to be quite silent on the subject.

Might not, sir, the manner of introducing what relates to the army be less violent, if I may so express myself, and the connexion be made more easy? Might not a word be said first, as to the influence of faith upon the present welfare of society, as well as upon the future happiness of individuals; and so applied briefly to men's civil character in society; and then, more at large, to their military character?

I would not let this post slip: and therefore will neither apologize for my freedom, nor enlarge, nor yet lose the opportunity my staggering fingers have, more kindly than for some time past, afforded me. Only, when your strength commences, be pleased to remember that Parson's-green is very conveniently situated near Kensington; as well the good Mrs. Hallows, as our dear Dr. Young and You have not seen Parson's-green yet.

Nancy thanks you, sir, for your kind remembrance of her. My wife and all mine join their best wishes and respects with those of,

Rev. and dear sir,
Your ever-faithful, obliged,
and humble servant,
S. Richardson.

I send not your copy, because of being within compass of a frank.

---

[1] 'My very master knows me not' (*Night-Thoughts*, iv. 55).

393. [Su.] 14 May 1758. Samuel Richardson.

Not traced.—*Monthly Magazine*, xliv (1 November 1817), 329.

May 14, 1758.

A thousand thanks, my truest friend, for restoring me to common sense. I shall follow your advice in the Dedication; and now, on reflection, think it monstrous that I stood in need of it. I now see how weak myself, and what a friend is worth. I could not forbear writing to you by this post; being pained with the thought of your thinking me a fool any longer. This day se'nnight I propose sending the Dedication as it shall stand.

The Advertisement[1] on a blank page after the Dedication; would that be wrong? If so, put it a postscript. In this I shall be entirely determined by you. I shall cordially embrace you the first moment it is in my power.

Your's,   E. Young.

Our very best wishes to all.

394. [Welwyn, Herts.]. Su. 28 [May 1758]. Samuel Richardson.

Not traced.—*Monthly Magazine*, xliv (1 November 1817), 329.

My very kind and dear sir,

I cannot sufficiently thank you for your most judicious remarks and additions. You see what use I have made of them; but, whether well or ill, I earnestly desire you to judge; and, with utmost freedom, to *add*, *erase*, or *alter*, and *finally fix* the whole for the press: for indeed, and indeed, I rely more on your judgment than my own.

I bless God that I see, by your handwriting, that your nerves are better.

---

[1] The 'Advertisement', which appeared on the verso of the title-page, consists of one sentence: 'The writer, not knowing that this argument had been made use of by others, thought it excusable to send it to the press; as it endeavours to show, that the *death* of Christ, as well as his resurrection, gives evidence to the truth of his religion.'

I shall not *wait* till the last fortnight of June.—When the *Dedication* is printed, I shall be glad of a copy of it for a friend. Truly your's,

E. Young.

Sunday, 28*th*.

395. [Welwyn, Herts.]. [Su.] 4 June 1758. Samuel Richardson.

Folger Shakespeare Library MS.—*Monthly Magazine*, xliv (1 November 1817), 329.

Dear Sr

Page 20. Line 8. *Depended*, shd be, *depending*. This [is] easily mended by ye Pen. All else is very right. And ye Dedication-book[1] may be prepard.

If you give me leave, ye Thirteenth instant, I will take a bed with You.[2] With all Love & Respect to You & yours I am

Dear Sr
Yr most Obligd
EYoung

June ye 4th
1758.

396. [?1–7 July 1758]. Thomas Secker, Archbishop of Canterbury.[3]

Not traced.[4]

[1] A copy of *An Argument* printed on large paper and bound in a gold-stamped cover is among the books in the British Museum which came from the Royal Library.

[2] On 23 June Richardson wrote to Mme Klopstock, who had heard of a Young made a Bishop: 'Dr. Young . . . is now in *Waiting*, as we call it, in the Duty of King's Chaplain, at Kensington Palace, near London. He obliged me with three Days before he went into waiting. Edward is his Christian Name. Phillip is that of the new-made Bishop [in March Philip Yonge (1709–83) had been made Bishop of Bristol]. We who are his Friends, think he has not had Justice done to his merits. He would have been a Credit to the Bench of Bishops.'

[3] Thomas Secker (1693–1768) had been confirmed as Archbishop of Canterbury on 21 April of this year.

[4] The evidence of this letter is Secker's answer which follows next.

Thomas Secker, Archbishop of Canterbury, to Young.
London. [Sa.] 8 July 1758.

Not traced.—Croft, 1781, iv. 420; Shelley, pp. 247–8.

Deanry of St. Paul's, July 8, 1758.

Good Dr Young,

I have long wondered, that more suitable notice of your great merit hath not been taken by persons in power. But how to remedy the omission, I see not. No encouragement hath ever been given to me to mention things of this nature to his Majesty. And therefore, in all likelihood, the only consequence of doing it would be weakening the little influence which else I may possibly have on some other occasions. Your fortune and your reputation set you above the need of advancement; and your sentiments, above that concern for it, on your own account, which, on that of the Public, is sincerely felt by

Your loving Brother
Thos. Cant.

397. [Welwyn, Herts.]. [Su.] 9 July 1758. Duchess of Portland.

Longleat MSS. 257.—Bath, pp. 323–4.

May it please your Grace.

I am very sorry that, when You did me ye Honour of calling at Mr Richardson's, I was not there. But much more sorry for your Grace's Indisposition: God in his Mercy remove it for ye sake of many; & particularly of two such sons for whose Wellfare ye Publick Concern will rival your Own.

Was I not at present confind for want of an Assistant I should rejoyce to add to ye number of your *Animals*, or rather of your *Plants*, for at present I have no Locomotive Faculty.

I hope with your Grace that my Lord Anson's News[1] may be Good. And now pardon me, Madam, if I presume to enquire after some News from Your Grace!

I have lately by a *Dedication* taken on me /[verso]/ to put his Majesty in mind of my long service, but, I take for granted, without any manner of Effect. I perceive by your Grace that all Hopes are over; but tho Hopes are over, my Curiosity is not; that is rather encreasd. For ^as I was Chaplain to his Majesty, even at Leicester House; & as all other Chaplains, There, were soon preferd after his Majestys Accession, but myself; & as many, many Years agoe ye D. of Newcastle promisd me (thro ye D. of Portlands kindly presenting me to Him) Preferment after Two then to be provided for by Him before me; & as there is no Instance to be found of any Other so long in service under total Neglect; there must be some particular Reason for my very Particular Fate, which Reason, as I can not possibly guess at ^it I most ardently long to know.

Your Graces Interest with Persons in Powr is at least so great, as to be able to gratifie my /[conjugate leaf]/ my [*sic*] very Natural, & very strong Curiosity a little in ^this Point.

And if You, Madam, will do so, as it is a Thing I greatly desire, I shall look on your kind Information as my Piece of Preferment, & ever acknowledge it as a strong, & lasting Obligation on

Madam
Yr Graces
most Dutifull
& Obligd Humble Sevt
EYoung

To my Lord Duke, yr Grace,
& all You love, & value
ye greatest Respects
of Mrs Hallows, & EY.

[1] George Anson (1697–1762), Lord Anson, First Lord of the Admiralty, was at the moment in command of a fleet of war vessels covering operations against the coast of France. His fleet put in at Plymouth just a week after Young's letter to the Duchess.

PS. This may seem to yr Grace an extraordinary request; but please, Madam, to consider, here has a Thing happend, wh never happend before, & wh very probably will never happen again; how Natural then for Any, especially
~~from~~ _{for} him who is most concernd in it, to wish (if possible) to know ye Cause of it; for I'm not conscious of the least Cause I have given for it.

July 9th
1758

398. Welwyn, Herts. [W.] 12 July 1758. Duke of Newcastle.

British Museum, Add. MSS. 32881, f. 293.—Thomas, p. 606.

May it please your Grace.

I should not presume to trouble You with this Letter,[1] if I was not confident that on reading it, your Grace will forgive me.

I was Chaplain to his Majesty even at Leicester House. All his other Chaplains were preferd soon after his Majestys Accession. About ten years agoe the Duke of Portland recommended me to your Grace. Your Grace was so Good as to promise me your Favour after Two were preferd who stood before me.

Soon after your Grace bid me not wait You, saying, You would send for me, when Proper. Ever since I have been

---

[1] This is the last known of Young's applications for preferment. When Richard Terrick (1710–77) was made Bishop of Peterborough in 1757 there was a report in a private letter that 'His Grace of Newcastle would fain have promoted Dr. Young to Peterboro', but at that moment the D[uke] of C[umberland] was all powerfull in Church as well as in State' (Charles Lyttelton to William Lyttleton, 6 June 1757 in Maud Wyndham's *Chronicles of the Eighteenth Century*, 1924, ii. 254). 'Dr. Young', however, could have been either Edward or Arthur (1693–1759) of Canterbury.

hoping for that Honour. I lately presented a small performance to his Majesty in hopes that it might bring to his mind
my long service; but I know that without your Graces favour
I have no Hopes; nor dare I presume to ask yt Favour,
having been denyd it so long. How I came to lose it I can
not so much as conjecture. My Lord Duke! as I hope *for
Divine Mercy*, I am not conscious of the least Misbehaviour:
I am not conscious of any Word, or Deed, that could give
ye least shadow [of] Offence; and if I have given none, my
Fate is as unaccountable, as it is Singular.

/[verso]/ And it is so very Singular, that on closest Enquiry, I can not learn that ye Like ever happend before; &
probably, never may again. I therefore hope Pardon for this
most humble Representation of it to your Grace, from One,
who tho, by some means to him quite Inconceivable, he has
forfited his Title to your Graces Kind Promise, & so lost
all his Hopes, yet still retains entire his real Respect, &
Duty; & begs leave to subscribe himself with all Acquiescence, & submission to Your good Pleasure, & his own bad
Fortune,

May it please your Grace
Your Graces
Most Dutifull, &
Most Humble Sevt
Edward Young

Wellwyn in Hertfordshire.
July 12
1758

Can not, my Honourd Lord Duke! a most gracious
Promise of Ten years old, & Royall Service of above Thirty,
in some measure, stand my friends?

399. [Th.] 7 September 1758. Duchess of Portland.

Longleat MSS. 259.—Bath, i. 324; Shelley, p. 249.

May it please your Grace
   I am greatly concernd for my good Lord Duke, & hope
                      be
in God that He may   soon restord to his perfect strength.

Your Grace is exstremely Kind in ye noble Offer You
are pleasd to make me; whither it is Teneble with Wellwyn,
or not, I can not tell; But be it so, or not, your Graces Goodness lays me under an eternal Obligation.

If it should not be Teneble with Wellwyn, will Your
Grace pardon me, if [I] ask a bold Question? Can your great
Indulgence go so far as to give it to my son? As That would
greatly encrease my great Obligation; That would much
more /[verso]/ than double the Favour of giving it to myself.

My son, Madam, is a student at Balliol College in Oxford;
He is between twenty five, & twenty six years of Age; I left
ye choice of his way of Life to himself; He chose Divinity;
his Tutor writes me word, that he makes a laudable Progress
in it, and he will take Orders very soon.[1]

I thought it my Duty to let your Grace know something
of the Person in whose behalf I presume to ask so very great
a Favour. I beg my humble Duty to my Ld Duke, my best
Respects to ye rest of your Graces Family; & my Compliments to Mr Achard.

I am, Madam
with great Gratitude, & profound Respect
Your Grace's most Dutifull
& most Humble Sevt
EYoung

Sepr 7
1758.
/[conjugate leaf]/

PS
If, Madam, I can obtain that Request I now presume to
make, I shall look on all former Disappointments as Advantages, when ending in what I so very much desire.

---

[1] Frederick did not, however, take orders. He had been absent from College
during his third year (1753-4) and apparently had been a problem to his father. On
8 March 1755 Elizabeth Montagu had written to her sister, Sarah Scott, of the
affair: 'I have just got Dr Youngs new work call'd the Centaur, I have not yet
lookd into it, but I expect to find two species in the book as well as the title, for
the Doctors pegasus is half horse half ass. I remember you had heard some things to
the disadvantage of Dr Youngs character in regard to his behaviour towards
his son, I believe if you enquire farther you will find that the young man is a worth-
less irreclaimable profligate Mr Richardson (the author) has been concernd in their
affairs, & he acquits the Father of any blame & charges the son very heavily' (MS.
letter in the library of Edward T. Collins of Reading, Berks.).

400. [Su.] 8 October 1758. Samuel Richardson.

Not traced.—*Monthly Magazine*, xliv (1 November 1817), 330.

Oct. 8, 1758.

Dear sir,
   I shall be happy if you can read what I send:[1] much happier if you would correct as you read; at least, be so good to mark what should be corrected or omitted by me.
   I beg my leave and service to all; particularly to Miss Nancy: am I not to see her this season? When you give me leave, with the greatest pleasure I will convey her to this place; which would much rejoice in the sight of another, whom I shall not name.

I am, dear sir,
Your truly affectionate
and most obliged
E. Young.

Mrs. Hallows is most your's.
   I have added some things, in which I cannot acquiesce without your judgment on them. I have added, as you desired, Mr. Addison's death; and particularly request your kind assistance with regard to that.

Richardson to Young. London. [W.] 11 October 1758.

Not traced.—*Monthly Magazine*, xliv (1 November 1817), 330.

London; Oct 11, 1758.

Rev. and dear sir,
   Mr. Shotbolt delivered to me your precious parcel on Monday night; and I could not do any thing else till I had run through it. *Run through it* I may well say—for my reading was rapid; and, when I came to the end of it, I thirsted

---

[1] A new version of the *Conjectures on Original Composition*. On 11 September Richardson had written to Mrs. Delany: 'Dr. Young is finely recovered, and, if *I guess* right, will one day oblige the world with a small piece on Original Writing and Writers . . .' (Barbauld, 1804, iv. 118).

for more. Do I not miss many very fine strokes? Have you not much reduced it? I am charmed with what you have added of Mr. Addison: what memory, what judgment, what force of writing, what unabated vigor of mind. Surely, sir, this spirited piece is the most spirited of all your spirited works.

You will allow me to keep it for a more deliberate reading, after I have cleared my hands of some infinitely less delightful subjects. Mean time, may I not hope that you will proceed with the other part of your excellent design?

I am greatly obliged to you, sir, for your kind question about, and invitation of, my Nancy: her honest heart is entirely with you. Her mother begins to think of home; her daughter being safely delivered of a daughter; but is not yet returned. And Patty, who is with her mother, and Nancy, who is with me, are necessary correspondents: and the winter comes on very fast.

My kindest respects to good Mrs. Hallows. I am, sir,
Your greatly obliged and affectionate
humble servant,
S. Richardson.

401. [Welwyn, Herts.]. [W.] 6 December 1758. Samuel Richardson.

Not traced.—*Monthly Magazine*, xliv (1 November 1817), 330.

Dec. 6, 1758.

My dear sir,

I fear, I much fear, you are not so well as I wish; Mr. Jones[1] gave me but an indifferent account: when it is much in your power and inclination, pray let me know how you do. I received the paper and the books, and thank you for them, and particularly for the reduced price: if you are determined

---

[1] John Jones (1700–70), Young's curate from Michaelmas 1757. Jones was named an executor of Young's will and was left £200 'for his pious assistance in my Parish'. In April 1767 he was made Vicar of Shephall, Hertfordshire. His papers in Dr. Williams's Library, London, contain much information about Young's last years.

to be obliging as long as you live, you are sure all the world will wish for your life.

I believe by this time all your family is with you—pray my love and service to them all; and tell Miss Nancy that she owes me a summer: Mrs. Hallows joins in best wishes and respects, and says Miss Nancy owes her a letter.

I am, dear sir,

Your truly affectionate and much

obliged humble servant,

E. Young.

402. [Welwyn, Herts.]. Su. [?17 December 1758]. Samuel Richardson.

Not traced.—*Monthly Magazine*, xliv (1 November 1817), 330.

My dear sir,

The leisure you have given me has occasioned me greatly to alter my scheme—which makes the review of my papers necessary. With what kind corrections you have afforded them, please to let me have them by my servant: I propose returning them very soon.

I hope in God this will find you recovered from the ill-effects of that alarming accident dear Miss Nancy's letter acquainted us withal.[1] To her, good Mrs. Richardson, and all, our most hearty love and respect: Mrs. Hallows will be

---

[1] An account of the 'alarming accident' appeared in *The Public Advertiser* of 30 November 1758: 'Tuesday Evening last [28 November] as Mr Richardson, of Fleet-street, an Attorney at Law, was talking with a Gentleman at Charing-cross, a Dray which stood near him was drove into the Pathway by another Carriage going carelessly by with such force, that Mr. Richardson received a violent Blow in his Breast and was killed on the Spot.' That Samuel Richardson was the 'Gentleman' with whom the victim of this accident was talking appears from his letter to Young of 24 May 1759 in which he speaks of 'my poor friend and namesake, who was killed by my side some months ago'. Richardson's namesake was almost certainly the 'John Richardson of the Inner Temple London Gentleman' mentioned in Chancery proceedings of 13 December 1735 (Public Record Office, C31. 98 pt. 1, f. 947). He was also probably the lawyer alluded to in Johnson's *Rambler* No. 188 of January 1752 as an acquaintance of fifteen years and identified by Mrs. Piozzi as 'one Richardson, an attorney' (*Anecdotes of the Late Dr. Samuel Johnson*, ed. S. C. Roberts, 1925, p. 35).

soon out of Miss Nancy's debt. Health and peace, and the Giver of both, be with you. I am, dear sir,

Your most obliged and truly
affectionate humble servant,
E. Young.

Sunday.

Richardson to Young. [?London]. [M.] 18 December 1758.

Not traced.—*Monthly Magazine*, xlvi (1 August 1818), 44–5.

Dec. 18, 1758.

Rev. sir,

I am very sorry for my delays, but I could not avoid them, from infirmity and avocations, equally unavoidable. Could not hold a pen very often. The dreadful accident Nancy told you of, has unhinged me. In obedience to your commands, I thought I had some little matters humbly to suggest; but my few observations cannot be read, I am afraid, not even by myself. Transcription cannot be attempted by me till I can get steadier fingers. I never could dictate. But, as you have changed your scheme, I think my observations will be quite needless, till I have the favour you make me hope for, in a return of the manuscripts, with your last hand. One thing, however, I take the liberty to mention—That, when in the former part you say so many glorious things in behalf of original writing, and to discourage imitations; so justly extol the great men of antiquity, as well as among the moderns; yet in the last part, make such mere nothings of all human attainments and genius; I could not but wish that the piece was made two distinct pieces, or subjects: for they are both laudable in a high degree; one for the delight of learned men; the other, and, doubtless, the most eligible, for the sake of true piety and our everlasting welfare. My head is confused, and I do not express myself, perhaps, to be understood.

Let me ask, however great and noble what you say of Mr. Addison's death is, whether it may not bear shortening? Will it not be thought laboured? And when, from the different nature of diseases, some of them utterly incapacitating, and deliriums happening often, it is not, or may not be, discouraging to surviving friends, to find wanting in the dying those tokens of resignation and true Christian piety, which Mr. Addison was graciously enabled to express so exemplarily to Lord W.[1] Sir J. S.[2] was a good man; yet I have heard you mention his hard and painful death with no small concern. Forgive my freedom; but I know you will.

And now, Sir, let me say, that your message to me by man and horse, riding all night, affrighted me till I opened your letter; I thank God, nothing unwished for happened to add to my apprehensions and my sad feelings, for I had lain awake from two this morning: wicked sleeplessness!

I am, dear and Rev. Sir,

Your's ever,

S. Richardson.

403. [Welwyn, Herts.]. [?W. 20 December 1758]. Samuel Richardson.

Not traced.—*Monthly Magazine*, xlv (1 April 1818), 328.

Dear sir,

What I send, I would have now printed; the rest shall follow. I would have but a small number printed; you be so kind as to determine the number for me.

I see some marks of your's in the sheets I send, but I do not understand them: however, let me not lose the advantage of them; but correct as you please,—the more you do so, the kinder.

I shall take the advice in your last, and separate the heterogeneous parts. The joys of the season, and the blessings of Heaven, be on you all.

My dear sir,

Most affectionately your's,

E. Young.

Wicked sleeplessness is my complaint also; pray let me know how you do.

---

[1] Edward Henry Rich (d. 1721), 7th Earl of Warwick, Addison's stepson.
[2] Jeremy Sambroke.

Richardson to Young. [?London]. [F.] 22 December
1758.

Not traced.—*Monthly Magazine*, xlvi (1 August 1818), 45.

Dec. 22, 1758.

Rev. and dear sir,

I presume you design the same type and manner as the
Centaur?

I am sorry that sleeplessness is your complaint. But, when
you sleep not, you are awake to noble purpose: I to none at
all; my days are nothing but hours of dozings, for want of
nightly rest; and through an impatience, that I am ashamed
of, because I cannot subdue it. Continue, dear Sir, your
prayers and blessings, to

> Your most faithful
> and affectionate servant,
> S. Richardson.

Due respects to good Mrs. Hallowes. All mine are most
cordially your's! Many happy seasons!

Why, Sir, but a small number?—Shall it be 500, 750, or
1000?

Thank you, Sir, for your kind acceptance of my humble
advice. As I am able, I will look after the marks you mention.

Richardson to Young. [?London]. [Tu.] 26 December
1758.

Not traced.—*Monthly Magazine*, xlvi (1 April 1818), 238–9.

Dec. 26, 1758.

Forgive, dear and reverend sir, the following humble
suggestions, in obedience to your condescending call upon
me.

Page 1.—*And perhaps not over-important in its end*—[yet,
dear sir, afterwards the introduction of that noble anecdote
is mentioned as its end, and an important one. Allow me to
ask, Is not expectation here too greatly raised? Suppose some

such change as this]—*in its end*; rewarding myself, however, with digressing into subjects more important, and from which my thoughts ought not, at this season of life, to make too long excursion. A serious thought, standing single among many of a lighter kind, will sometimes strike the careless wanderer, who roamed only for amusement, with useful awe: as monumental marble, scattered in a wide pleasure-garden, (and such there are,) will call to recollection those who would never have gone to seek it in a church-yard walk of mournful yews.—To one such moment I may conduct you, within which the sepulchral lamp still burns; but, unlike those of old, will not be extinguished, but made illustrious, by being produced after so long a time, in open day.—Consider, then, the lighter parts of my work as irregular walks, which the superannuated gardener hath not strength [and yet, sir, I am afraid the comparison, without your assistance, will not hold; since the *superannuated gardener*, preserving his *judgment*, though not his *strength*, might *direct* his *under-gardener*, or *journeyman*, to *trim up*, &c.] to trim up very nicely; but which yet he makes as pleasant as he can, because every one leads to some wholesome spot, or useful point of view.

You remember, that your worthy patron, &c.

Ibid.—*Proper authority stood centinel of the press*, &c.] Will not this phrase give offence to the liberty-mad? Suppose it were therefore omitted, and the whole to run thus:—Overcharged it could never be, if none were admitted but such as, &c.

Page 2.—*These advantages composition*, whether we write ourselves, or, in humbler leisure, peruse the works of others, *affords us. While we bustle through the thronged walks of public life*, it gives us a respite at least from care, a pause of refreshing recollection. *If this country*, &c.

Ibid.—*Smiles cannot prevent or cure.*] Among these are the languors of old age. If those are held honourable who, in an hand benumbed by Time, have grasped the just sword in defence of their country; shall they be less esteemed whose unsteady pen still vibrates to the last in the cause of religion, of virtue, of learning? Both are happy in this, that, by fixing their attention on objects most important, they escape numberless little anxieties, and that *taedium vitae*, which hangs often so heavy on its evening hours. Why not this intimate some apology for my spilling ink, and spoiling paper, so late in life?

Ibid.—*The mind of a man of genius is a fertile,* &c.

Page 3.—*Encreasing the* mere drug of books, while all that makes them valuable,—*light, knowledge, and genius,* &c.

Page 4.—*Imitator's undertaking*; but the river and the imitation creep humbly along the vale.

Page 5.—*Equality which he denies.*]

After all, the first ancients had no merit in being *originals*; they could not be *imitators*. Modern writers have a *choice* to make: they may soar in the regions of *Liberty*, or move in the soft and shining fetters of *fair Imitation*; and she has as many plausible reasons to urge, as *Pleasure* had to offer to *Hercules*. Hercules made the choice of an hero; and, as such, is ennobled.

Yet think not, ye asserters of classic excellence, that I deny the tribute it so well deserves. *He that admires not,* &c.

Page 6.—*Learning, destitute of* this superior aid, *is fond,* &c.

Ibid.—*Famed examples.* As beauties less perfect, who owe half their charms to cautious art, she inveighs against natural unstudied graces, and harmless indecorums; and sets rigid bounds to that liberty to which genius, &c.

Page 9.—Would you, sir, let go the word *licentiously* in this place?

Ibid.—*Beggar'd at last, and lose their reputations, as,* &c. Two good similes: but *younger brothers* are not usually *persons born rich.*

Page 10.—Is not *thirdly* too sermon-like? Suppose,—The *third* fault I find with a spirit of imitation, is, &c.

Page 12.—Should not the address,—*Thou, thyself; you, yourself*; in the same paragraph, be uniform?

Ibid.—*Self-worship* is a spirited expression: but is it not a dangerous one?

Import from abroad; suppose,—*import* from classic land? This will except that assistance from the light of revelation, which, perhaps, ought to be excepted.

The man who thus reverences himself will soon find the world's, &c.

Page 13.—For tingling, tinkling: altered in original.

Once more, good sir, excuse these freedoms, and those in my former letter; and allow of my daughter Patty's transcription, instead of mine. My first runnings, as I may call them, are not legible; and my vibrating fingers will not suffer me to transcribe without pain, and, perhaps, after many attempts. Always your's, dear sir. Many happy revolving seasons.

S. Richardson.

404. [Welwyn, Herts.]. [Su.] 7 January 1759. Samuel Richardson.

Not traced.—*Monthly Magazine*, xlv (1 April 1818), 239.

Jan. 7, 1759.

Dear sir,

Your *dele* of my parade at the beginning is most just and judicious.

Your *monumental marbles*, most beautiful, and the happiest thought in the world for my purpose.

I would have the part I now send put to the press as soon as you please; and the remaining part of the *first letter* shall be sent you soon.

Mr. Spence[1] is with me, who sends, with mine and Mrs. Hallows's, his best wishes and respects.

Heaven's blessings be with you all! so prays,

Your most obliged
E. Young.

[1] Joseph Spence (1699–1768) was collecting anecdotes of literary personages. His *Anecdotes*, eventually published in 1820 after his death, included a number ascribed to Young. Another visitor about this time was John Newton (1725–1807), later friend and collaborator of the poet William Cowper (1731–1800), who wrote to his wife on 6 January of this year: 'I put up at Welling [Welwyn], sent a note to Dr. Young, and received for answer that he would be glad to see me, & spent an hour with him. His conversation was agreeable, and much answerable to what I expected from the author of the "Night Thoughts". He seemed likewise pleased with me. It would have surprised you to hear how I let my tongue run before this great man. He approved my design of entering the ministry, and said many encouraging things upon the subject, and when he dismissed me, desired that I would never pass near his house without calling upon him' (*Night Thoughts*, ed. James Robert Boyd, 1854, pp. 34–5).

405. [Welwyn, Herts.]. [Th.] 11 January 1759.
Samuel Richardson.

Not traced.—*Monthly Magazine*, xlv (1 April 1818), 239.

Jan. 11, 1759.

Dear sir,

I so soon send you the last part of my first letter, in hopes that it may receive the same favour from you as did the former part,—which was very great.

I conclude with Mr. Addison; and that part more particularly entreats your kind correction.

Most part of what I now send I dictated to female hand,— the errors of which, in spelling, the composer will easily amend. My thanks to Miss Patty; her transcripts wanted no amendment. I read part of it to Mr. Spence, who seemed struck with its vivacity. I wish there is not still too great length. Be quite frank, and you will most oblige,

Dear sir,
Your most obliged,
E. Young.

Richardson to Young. [?London]. [W.] 24 January 1759.

Not traced.—*Monthly Magazine*, xlvi (1 August 1818), 43–4.

Jan. 24, 1759.

See, dear and reverend sir, the trouble you have brought upon yourself by your condescension: this one time more forgive me. My Patty my transcriber.

Page 2.—*Though, on the contrary*, being born amongst men, and of consequence piqued by many, and peevish at more, *he has blasphemed*, &c.

Might not the observation on nicety (page 2,) come in naturally in page 1, after *human face divine*; thus,— *If this author's definition of a nice man is just*, he was the nicest man alive: but at so nice a writer, how does the reader of any delicacy sicken. He has so satirized human nature, as to give a demonstration in himself, that it *deserves*, &c.

Then the *second* remark, in page 2, comes in its proper place, thus introduced,—*Though, on the contrary, being born,* (&c. as above)—he has blasphemed a nature little lower than that of angels, *and assumed by far higher than they,—surely the contempt of the world,* &c.

Page 2.—Do not the words, *For as,* begin a new paragraph oddly? Suppose thus,—I remember, as I and others, &c.

Page 3, line 2.—Is *repute* the word?

Page 3—Forgive, sir, the following free suggestions, line 11.—The general fault of imitators, who often, like Alexander's courtiers, copy the defect and infirmity of their hero along with, if not without, his excellencies. Imitation is struck with the loud report of former fame,—which damps the spirits, and, at best, calls out attendant laurel-bearers to follow in the funeral procession of dead renown. Emulation listens to it, as to a sprightly trumpet, inspiring redoubled ardor to be foremost in the field of Fame. *She exhorts us, instead,* &c.

Page 3, 4.—Which blessed him with all her charms. Alexander *would* have been more original if he *could,* since he wept for want of new worlds to conquer. Rather, therefore, he wept not like his namesake of Greece, for *new worlds* to conquer, but was contented to triumph in the *old.* His taste partook the error of his religion: it denied not worship to saints and angels; that is, to writers who, canonized for ages, have received their apotheosis from established and universal fame. True poesy, like true religion, abhors idolatry; and, though she honours the memory of the exemplary, and takes them willingly, yet cautiously, as guides in the way to glory,—she makes nothing less than excellence her aim, and looks for no inspiration less than divine. Though Pope's *noble Muse* may, &c.

Page 4.—*Instead of* one: perhaps it was granted; for *when I was,* &c. Is your information true here, sir? I have heard, that he did not more than *talk* of such a design that he once had. I believe, either Dr. Warburton or Mr. Mallet, or both, would have let us know this, had there been the least room for it.

By noble hands, *too noble*, &c.—you mean not Bolingbroke's, I presume?

Page 5.—*Not swept so clean*. Not swept so clean, did I say? To our stage in its present state (and yet its present state is much better than it hath been in some former times,) the stables of Augaeus were a place of safety and neatness. In those stables men were devoured by horses: in our licentious comedies, how often does the brute devour the nobler man; devour him body and soul too? What a mass of corruption? Were there an Hercules to extirpate the wild beast, who is often too rampant, even in our tragedies, the theatre might easily become again a temple sacred to virtue and improvement; but, till then, what do we more in bringing on now and then a play, be it ever so correct and blameless, than endeavour to sweeten a pestilential vault by pouring in, once a twelvemonth, a pint of rose-water?

Page 12.—*Would not be felt* by Addison.

Page 12.—*But was for softening tyranny* into the appearance, at least, of lawful monarchy; though, when provoked, his punishments were severe, and sometimes arbitrary. All dunces (and who of his friends and admirers did he deem such? Who that were not so did he deem otherwise?) he looked upon as criminals by nature, and dreaded them as Sparta the Helots. Addison, born to rightful sway, reigned mildly as a parent, and was best pleased to reign by the public voice.

——————— Volentes, &c.

Page 14.—*Had been immortal, though he had never writ*. Yes, surely, had he been the most unlettered good Christian, he had been immortal by the best title; even though he had died the most suddenly.

Page 14.—You know the value of his writings; you know, too, that his life was amiable, was exemplary: but you know not, I believe, that his death was triumphant. This is a glory granted to very few; nor is it of much consequence to the individual. That parental hand, which sometimes snatches home its children in a moment, is equally gracious in its various dispensations. Yet, where strength and opportunity are given for virtues to shine brightest at the point of death, the example is certainly meant for general good. Such was that of Addison: *for after*, &c.

Page 15.—Instead of, *in words penetrating as lightning, and almost as short*; suppose,—*in a very short sentence, but penetrating as lightning.* See in what peace, &c.

Page 15.—May I presume to offer to you, sir, the concluding of this fine paragraph at the word eternity; omitting what follows,—*How gloriously*, &c. to *greatness of heart?*

Page 15.—I think you will not doubt, but many a reader may, both the probability and truth of what I tell you.

Page 16.—Should there not, sir, be given some more particular proof of the truth of this story, (Lord W. and Mr. A. only present, and the former not a good young man.)— than an allusion to Tickell's Lives; and Mr. A. said, to expire as soon as he had spoken the admirable sentence? The particulars must have been had from some one: why not name from whom? You write the story now for the world.

Page 16.—*How came this* anecdote, so honourable to human nature, to lie so long unknown? Alas, my dear friend, the world thinks differently from us on points like these. He who falls in a duel is talked of as dying honourably. The despairing suicide attracts an honourable attention for a while: but, in general, the living scene occupies the talk of the day; and, in that too, the bad makes most noise, while the good is sunk in silence. Petty efforts in arts or arms are echoed far and near: they glitter of themselves in the world's eye. But that *faith which overcometh the world* will be little *regarded by it*: and such was Addison's. When his soul scarce animated his body, faith and charity animated it into a warm effort at saving more than his own.

[Is not the next full bold?]

Page 16.—*Indisputably true.* Here, sir, suppose you name the authority? Then, suppose you insert,—This story was hinted at, though very obscurely, in two finely pathetic lines by Mr. Tickell:—He taught us, &c.

Suppose, sir, you omit the rest of that p. 16, for *raising him an immortal monument* is not gathering a few sticks. It may suffice to leave out a *page immortal*, &c.

Page 17.—O! that the contrast of Lord B.'s death,[1] cursing and blaspheming, could be introduced: very dreadful I have heard it was.

I presume, (additional to my other presumptions,) that what follows might be shortened. Shall I dare to think that there are stiffnesses, not usual to Dr. Y.'s pen, here and there, in this latter part. But what affects me most of all is, that there may not be wanting some, who, from such very great things being said, and so much, of Mr. Addison's death, by so admired an author, and so good a Christian and divine, will be apt to think less of a still incomparably greater death, both in manner and fact, had both been mere men,— as well as in efficacy. In this latter, however, I am sure Dr. Y. will take care that Mr. A. appear but as an *imitator*; and a *very very* humble one,—though great as a *mortal* in that light.

Forgive me, sir, all my impertinencies, once more, I beg; and believe me ever

Your faithful and affectionate
humble servant,
S. Richardson.

406. [Welwyn, Herts.]. [W.] 7 February 1759. Friedrich Gottlieb Klopstock.

Not traced.—*Auswahl aus Klopstocks Nachlass*, 1821, i. 249; Thomas, p. 605.

Pardon, dear Sir, so long a silence after your so very kind Letter; Rheumatism robbed me of the use of my Pen, which I can but very ill hold now: therefore in answer to yours, I entreated a Friend to write the Inclosed.

However, I can not lay my Pen aside, without from my heart condoling your very, very great Loss.[2] I am too well qualified so to do, having not long ago, undergone the same Calamity.—I say, not long ago; for tho' it is many years since, yet was the wound so deep, that it seems even now

---

[1] Henry St. John, Viscount Bolingbroke, had died of cancer of the face on 12 December 1751.

[2] Klopstock's wife had died 28 November 1758.

recent, and often bleeds, as if it had been received but yesterday.

God Almighty in his great mercy comfort you with many, many other blessings—Fata contraria fata rependens. Virg.[1] This, dear Sir, is the fervent prayer of your obliged, affectionate

humble Servant
E. Young.

Feb. 7, 1759.

407. [Welwyn, Herts.]. [?April 1759]. Samuel Richardson.

Not traced.—*Monthly Magazine*, xliv (1 November 1817), 329–30.

Dear sir,

I am greatly obliged by your just remarks; and have profited much by them: but, as I have added much of my own, some of your's I have omitted.

Pray my love and thanks to Miss Patty, for her assistance in this great trouble given by, dear sir,

Truly your's,   E. Young.

I have hinted, (as you suggested) at Lord Bolingbroke.— Not he, but Lord Littleton, was meant as to Pope's Epic; but I have blotted it out.[2]

God preserve your health; mine is a little shaken by the damps. I am now in such a fog that I cannot see a yard before me.

You will still, sir, be my friend where you see occasion: I fear there is too much.

Where I have not taken you at length, I have often taken the hint, and made the best use of it that I could.

[1] *Aeneid*, i. 239 ('fates to fates I could oppose'—Dryden).
[2] In the *Conjectures*, Young had deplored Pope's imitation rather than emulation of Homer and implies that it was out of deference to contemporary authority. Bolingbroke was thought to have influenced Pope in his *Essay on Man*. George Lyttelton (1709–73), first Baron Lyttelton, had published *An Epistle to Mr. Pope from a Young Gentleman at Rome* in 1730.

408. [Welwyn, Herts.]. [Sa.] 14 April 1759. Duchess of Portland.

Longleat MSS. 261.

Ap 14
1759.

May it please yr Grace.

I return many thanks for the joy you have given   me   by the most agreeable contents of your kind letter.[1] I can easily conceive your Graces great sollicitude, during the dependences of a point of so very great moment to your own happiness, and the happiness of one so justly dear to You; but that sollicitude is greatly (thanks to Heaven) over-ballancd by your present satisfaction in having well accomplishd the most material transaction in human life.

Your Graces Relations are now encreasd; /[verso]/ and since they may now encrease yearly,[2] may every encrease make a new article in the list of your enjoyments, till You arrive at those Enjoyments, which will admit of no Encrease, or End. I beg Lady Weymouth to accept my most sincere congratulation; & my hearty Prayr for her as great happiness as that most happy state of life can confer on those who deserve it most, in the little number of whom, I beleive, her Ladyship justly claims a place.

May your Grace allways (as now) hear *from*, & *of*, Ld Titchfield to your perfect satisfaction; and may the next news I hear /[conjugate leaf]/ of my Ld Duke be more to my satisfaction than that which you can afford me now. Virtue is no security against the Accidents of human life; but it is a great security to our patience under them.

I bless God my complaints are few; and your Graces happy Letter would have betterd my health if it had stood in need

---

[1] It becomes apparent that the Duchess had written about the forthcoming marriage (22 May) of her daughter Elizabeth (1734–1825) with Thomas Thynne (1734–96, third Viscount Weymouth, later (1789) first Marquis of Bath. It was by this marriage that Young's letters to the Duchess of Portland eventually came to rest at Longleat.

[2] Ten daughters were born to the couple.

of it. And that I may never hear less wellcome news from the same Quarter, is ye Prayr of

Madam, wth all respect
Yr Graces most Dutifull
& obligd, humble sevt
EYoung.

Mrs Hallows desires
Yr Grace to accept her
humble Duty; & I beg
mine, wth my best wishes
for his health, to my Ld Duke;
& my best respects to All.

409. [?Welwyn, Herts.]. [Late] April 1759. Samuel Richardson.

Not traced.—*Monthly Magazine*, xlvi (1 August 1818), 45.

April 1759.

Dear sir,
    Dispose of as many copies[1] as you please: one to the Speaker, with my respects and duty.

Mr. Doddington,
Duchess of Portland,
Dr. Heberden,   One copy of each:
Mrs. Johnson,[2]   not saying by whom
The Hon. & Right Rev.   sent.
    Lord Bp. of Durham,[3]

I would sell the copy to the persons mentioned, but I know not the reasonable price for it: that I leave to your determination; or, if you like not that, to their honour.

---

[1] *The Public Advertiser* of 10 May announced the *Conjectures* as 'This Day' published.

[2] If 'Mrs.' is correct it would refer to the Miss Johnson who had accompanied Richardson and the Millars to Welwyn only to be disappointed in not finding Young there in December 1751. In view of Richardson's letter to Young of 24 May, however, it seems probable that it is a misreading of 'Mr.' (i.e. Samuel Johnson).

[3] Richard Trevor (1707-71).

I greatly grieve that you are doubly absent from me through your indisposition: God remove it! Accept my thanks for your kind and material assistance in this little attempt. Pray send me three or four copies for my friends here; and if, hearing objections, any thing material occurs, it would be well if I knew it, with regard to the second.

What can I send you but my best wishes? I wish much more was in the power of,

Dear Sir,
Most your's,
E. Young.

My love to all.

No apology for delay; I truly rejoice at the occasion of it.

410. [Welwyn, Herts.]. Su. [?Early May 1759]. Samuel Richardson.

Not traced.—*Monthly Magazine*, xlvii (1 March 1819), 134.

Sunday.

Dear sir,

If there should be any future impression,[1] please to let me know it, for I have something to alter and add.

Peace be with you all, Amen.

Most your's,
E. Young.

Hard, hard, this double exclusion; I can neither see your person nor your mind. However, in imagination, I embrace both, till some happier hour shall grant me more.

Pray send me four copies more.

---

[1] A second edition of the *Conjectures* was announced in *The Public Advertiser* of 18 June as 'This Day . . . published'.

411. [Welwyn, Herts.]. Tu. [22 May 1759]. Samuel
Richardson.

Not traced.—*Monthly Magazine*, xlvii (1 March 1819), 134–5.

Tuesday.

Dear sir,

I have seen my Letter advertised but twice;[1] this is not
allowing it fair play. I wish you could let me know, by your
nephew's[2] pen, why it is denied the assistance which is given
to other publications.

I received two large and valuable books, and am in pain
till I know how I can be out of debt for them.

Your friends were so good as to call on me yesterday; but
their stay was very short. The lady, who seemed to have been
of the first form in your school, I should have been glad to
have conversed with much longer. Shotbolt tells me, that
you flatter Wellwyn with some hopes of seeing you; if so,
I have a happy day to come. That you and your's may have
many, is the cordial prayer of, dear sir,

Your most obliged,
E. Young.

Richardson to Young. London. [Th.] 24 May 1759.

Not traced.—*Monthly Magazine*, xlvii (1 March 1819), 135–6.

London; May 24, 1759.

I have been very unhappily engaged, my dear and good
Dr. Young,—ever since some mislaid papers came to my
hands, relating to a most troublesome account of long standing, which I had put into the hands of my poor friend and
namesake, who was killed by my side some months ago,[3]—in
endeavouring to settle them in such a manner as may prevent
future trouble from base and designing parties to my family,

---

[1] 10 May (*Public Advertiser*) and 12 May (*The London Chronicle*).

[2] William Richardson (1733–88), a printer, son of Samuel's brother William
(1691–1755).

[3] John Richardson (see note to letter of ?17 December 1758).

when I am no more;—an account of sixteen years, which I only (now that poor man is gone,) could tolerably settle. How has this undelightful task affected me; and increased those disorders, which sleepless nights and painful reflexions on some ungrateful attacks aggravated.

I live in hopes of seeing my beloved and revered Dr. Young as my guest. Is not the season approaching that annually brings him to town? And then I will briefly account to him for the indispensableness of a task so hateful in the depth of my evil days; when an utter incapacity sometimes of putting pen to paper became a severely attendant evil. My Patty's illness has contributed its part to my affliction; and now the death of a worthy sister, who was interred on Sunday night, the 12th of this instant; and that of her husband, who on last Saturday dropped down dead, as he was looking out of his chamber-window. Dear sir, what awful Providences! In the past two years, (to go no farther back,) what have I not suffered! But I am sure of being entitled to your pity and prayers. Yet hard, hard, indeed, that disinclination to the pen should add to the incapacity I frequently had to resume it; though to my dear Dr. Young, who only in this life, by his pen, could give me consolation. But I will not dwell further on these melancholy subjects, after I have thanked you, sir, as I gratefully do, for your kind regrets on my silence.

I sent the books as you directed. The Speaker repeatedly thanks you; and bid me tell you, that he was highly pleased with the spirited performance. He read to me passages with which he was most struck; and bid me tell you that he was beginning to read it again, which he should do with an avidity equal to that which at first possessed him.

Mr. Johnson is much pleased with it: he made a few observations on some passages, which I encouraged him to commit to paper, and which he promised to do, and send to you.

Mr. Millar tells me that he has but very few left: so small a number as was printed, I wonder he has any. Mr. Dodsley's must surely be near gone. Be pleased, then, to send up your additions, &c. Dr. Warburton commends highly the spirit of the piece; and, with a few observations and explana-

tions, subscribes to the merit of the whole. That good man,
Mr. Allen, of Bath, is pleased with every line of it; and
warmly expressed to me, on a visit he made me at Parson's-
green, his approbation. Your promised succeeding Letter is
much wished for: is it, sir, in forwardness? I hope it is. Had
not your agreement with your booksellers best be postponed
till they, united, make a more formidable appearance as to
bulk?—no small consideration with booksellers, with regard
to the works of a favourite author.

Give me leave to say, that I miss, on reperusal, passages
which gave me great pleasure, in the classical part [shall I
call it] of the piece. But, nobly as the death-scene of Addison
is treated, I am not sorry, methinks, in what I have already
heard said, that it was somewhat shortened there.

I have put down, as you generously ordered me, two
guineas for the benefit of Mr. Hill,[1] of Buckingham: he will
have a pretty subscription made for him.

The books sent you down, that you expressed yourself
to my worthy Mrs. Bennet (who is full of your kind and
courteous behaviour to her,) as at a loss about, were brought
to me by Mr. Oram,[2] who had some difficulty to procure them
for you; as he said you were earnest for him to do. They cost
him a guinea: I told him there were accounts betwixt Dr.
Young and me, and obliged him to take it from me on your
account.

I have received from abroad the accompanying letters.

I can only answer the worthy Mr. Majes, of Hanover, as
to the request he makes for his friend, that the reverend
author of the Night Thoughts can best explain his own
works; and that I shall send the letters to you: be pleased to
return them when you have done them. In Germany, they
revere Dr. Young in his works more than they do those of
any other British genius.

[1] Robert Hill (1699–1777), known as a 'learned tailor', had been the prototype
and beneficiary of a character study by Joseph Spence, *A Parallel; In the manner of
Plutarch: between a most celebrated Man of Florence; And One, scarce ever heard of,
in England*, 'For the Benefit of Mr. Hill'. The book had originally been printed at
Walpole's Strawberry Hill press and published by Dodsley on 2 February 1759,
but its sale was such that it was reprinted in London at Richardson's press and
advertised in a second edition on 10 February.
[2] Unidentified.

God continue to you, dear sir, that health and those spirits which irradiate so happily the afternoon of your valuable life! I love your worthy Mrs. Hallowes for contributing her kind cares and solicitudes to so desirable and necessary a purpose. Ever, ever, sir,

> Your most affectionate
> and faithful servant,
> S. Richardson.

412. [Welwyn, Herts.]. [F.] 25 May 1759. Samuel Richardson.

Not traced.[1]—*Monthly Magazine*, xlvii (1 March 1819), 136.

May 25, 1759.

Dear sir,

What severe tryals! I feel them; I feel them deeply. But God is good; and, perhaps, his goodness is most shown in our afflictions: if so, we might partly rejoyce even in them. And, if we could (as we ought,) bless God for them, then might we find comfort in all parts of our lives. But who, alas! is wise enough to be so happy as the Divine Mercy has not only designed, but commanded, us to be?

I shall not send a copy till I have the pleasure of Mr. Johnson's letter on the points he spoke of to you; and please to let him know that I impatiently wait for it.

Pray be frank with me; do you not wish that on Addison was shorter still?

I return the letters, with great respect to the writers of them; but the questions are so many, and of so complicated a nature, that I know not well how by letter to return a full answer to them; though I should be most glad to do any thing to the satisfaction of the gentlemen from whom they came.

Pray my duty to the Speaker. What would I give for Dr. Warburton's remarks? They might be of great use.

[1] The manuscript of this letter was sold in Marburg, Germany, by the firm of J. A. Stargardt, 7 November 1957. Efforts to trace it have been fruitless.

How am I obliged to you for tiring yourself with so long, and delighting me with so short, a letter!—For short to me would be the longest you ever writ.

I have lately had a fever, in common with many of my neighbours, and am not quite recovered; which occasions me to be so short, at present, with regard to the foreign correspondents. Most of the conjectures at my obscure meaning are right: the adventure of Lysander and Aspasia is a true history.[1] This is all that at present I can say. If it shall please God to reinstate me, I shall be willing to give the enquirer farther satisfaction, and am much concerned that I cannot do it now.

I thank you for paying Mr. Oram[2] for me; and for your very kind invitation,—but, as yet, doubt if I shall be so happy as to accept of it. Nothing but inability shall deny me that pleasure.

May Heaven, which usually reserves its comforts till we need them most, cast on you and your's a most merciful eye. This is, and shall be, the cordial prayer of, dear, dear sir,

Most affectionately your's
E. Young.

Richardson to Young. [London]. [Tu.] 29 May 1759.

Not traced.—*Monthly Magazine*, xlvii (1 March 1819), 136–7.

May 29, 1759.

Thanks to my dear and good Dr. Young for his kind letter by Mr. Shotbolt.

I hope, sir, you are quite recovered of your feverish complaint.

I have written urgently to Mr. Johnson: but it would be pity to baulk the sale. Mr. Millar has ordered one thousand to be printed.

I was very desirous that the anecdote of Addison's death-scene should be inserted: yet, so many admirable things as there are in every page of the piece, was half sorry to have

---

[1] *Night-Thoughts*, v. 1033–58.
[2] See Richardson's letter to Young of 24 May, above.

that made the sole end of your writing it. Your subject of original composition is new, and nobly spirited. How much is your execution admired! But three good judges of my acquaintance, and good men too, wish, as I presumed formerly myself to propose, that the subject had been kept more separate and distinct. They think the next to divine vehemence (so one of them expressed himself,) with which original writing is recommended, suffers some cooling abatement; which it would not have done, had the solemn subject been left to the last,—when the critic, the scholar, the classic, might properly have given place to the Christian divine.[1]

One of Dr. Warburton's remarks was, that the character of an original writer is not confined to subject, but extends to manner: by this distinction, I presume, securing his friend Pope's originality. But he mentioned this with so much good humour, that I should have been glad to have heard you both in conference upon the subject.

This is not a favourable day to me. May every one, for many happy years, be more so to you, my dear Dr. Young, prays,

Your most affectionate
and faithful servant,
S. Richardson.

413. [Welwyn, Herts.]. [?Th. 31 May 1759]. Samuel Richardson.

British Museum, Add. MSS. 32352, f. 173.—*Monthly Magazine*, xliv (1 November 1817), 329; Scott and Samuel Davy, *A Guide to Two Collections of Historical Documents* (facsimile), 1881.

Dear sir,
I have made a few corrections and additions in this copy, which I desire may direct the press.

[1] At this point the *Monthly Magazine* text follows with the paragraph beginning 'Let me ask (however great . . .' from Richardson's letter to Young of 18 December 1758.

Peace and blessed hope be with you, which is the whole, and that, indeed, ample, portion of mortal man.

> Dear sir, most your's,
> E. Young.

It was very kind in you to send to Mr. Johnson's; and unfortunate to me that you sent in vain.

414. [Welwyn, Herts.]. [?Early June 1759]. Samuel Richardson.

Not traced.—*Monthly Magazine*, xliv (1 November 1817), 329.

Dear sir,

Since the press is in haste, all I can say is, that I would have as few capitals as possible: I blotted them out of the *latter part* of the first edition; but forgot it in the *former*—which I would have of a piece.

Page 14, line 11, dele *on*.

I bless God my fever is over; but (as natural) it has left a languor, which makes me good for nothing.

Pardon, therefore, if I spare myself and you the trouble of saying more.

> Indeed, dear sir,
> I am ever your's,
> E. Young.

Page 3, line 4, *them* should be *those*.

Manner (as Dr. W. says,) may be *original*; but a *manner* different from that of the ancients, with good judges, will run a great risque—a risque which new *subject* will escape.

415. Welwyn, Herts. [Th.] 21 June 1759. Samuel
Richardson.

Not traced.—*Monthly Magazine*, xl (1 September 1815), 134.

June 21, 1759.[1]
Dear Sir,
   Endless are the favours you confer. I owe you Mr. Hill's
subscription. I received with gratitude some acts of parliament;[2] there is one which I particularly want, viz. an act that
determines the fees of justices' clerks. If you have it, I should
be much obliged to you for it.
   Mrs. Hallows joins my respects and very best wishes to
you and all your's; and my hopes of seeing you and good
Mrs. Richardson at Wellwyn; though already more in debt
than I will ever be able to pay. I am, dear Sir,
                              Your very affectionate
                                    humble servant,
                                    E. Young.

416. [Welwyn, Herts.]. [Su.] 29 July 1759. Duchess
of Portland.

Longleat MSS. 263.

May it please yr Grace.
   I bless God I am well; and am sorry to hear your Grace
say only that you can *walk a little*:[3] May You soon receive
the full reestablishment of that Health, in which so many are
concernd as well as your self. May the good News of it soon
return that Joy to Longleat,[4] which you have so lately
receivd from thence. And may You deal in the rich Traffic

   [1] Although assigned to 1753 in the *Monthly Magazine*, the letter belongs to this
year as the reference to 'Mr. Hill's subscription', mentioned in Richardson's letter
of 24 May, makes clear.
   [2] Richardson had been printing proceedings of Parliament since 1753 (cf.
William M. Sale, jr., *Samuel Richardson: Master Printer*, 1950, pp. 76–85).
   [3] The Duchess had sprained her ankle in a fall.
   [4] Home of the Duchess's daughter, Elizabeth, now Lady Weymouth.

of Happiness for Happiness, till you arrive at that Happiness, which is final, & compleat. /[verso]/

But, Madam, not on Longleat only must I congratulate
your Grace. From Warsaw, and Turin You may receive
articles of much Joy: such is ye Character which I hear from
all hands of my Lord Titchfield,[1] that I am persuaded that
his Country will reap ye Fruits of his Travels; that he is
gathering Knowledge, & Experience, which will be layd out
on the publick Good; and that [illegible word stricken out]
he will
        pass from Climate to Climate, from Court to Court,
till he becomes ye Ornament of his Own.

That this, & every thing else which can contribute to your
reasonable, & lasting satisfaction, may be the Case is, and
shall /[conjugate leaf]/ be ye Prayr of

                              Madam
                         Yr Graces
                           most Dutifull
                           & most Obedient
                             Humble Sevt
                               EYoung

Pray my humble Duty
to my Lord Duke, &
Lady Harriet.
    Mrs Hallows begs leave
to present her humble
Duty to your Grace.

July 29
  1759.

**417. [Welwyn, Herts.]. [Sa.] 11 August 1759. Samuel
Richardson.**

Yale University Library (Tinker MSS.).—*Monthly Magazine*, xlvii (1 March
1819), 137; Frederick G. Netherclift, *A Hand-Book to Autographs* (facsimile),

---

        [1] Now on the grand tour of the Continent.

1862, p. 465; *Catalogue of the Collection of Autograph Letters and Historical Documents formed between 1865 and 1882 by Alfred Morrison*, 1892, vol. iv (facsimile).

Aug. 11, 1759.

Dear sir,

I have been grieved ever since I saw you[1] at the sad effect your kind journey had on you: I hope in God that it is entirely removed.

I have two favours to beg of you, viz. that I may receive, by the hands of my good neighbour Shotbolt, dear Miss Nancy; and my bill: I will pay it immediately by our friend Mr. Gosling.[2]

I and Mrs. Hallows greatly wish all happiness and health to Parson's-green; to her particularly, who, I fear, still wants it most. We have a better air than you can boast, and Miss Nancy shall have a safe horse on which to enjoy it. I preserve my green-gage plums for her arrival. I am, dear sir,

With truest affection,

Your most obliged humble servant,

E. Young.

I have good tar-water.

418. [?August 1759[3]]. Samuel Richardson.

Reading MSS. (Collins).

Dear Sr

If Miss Nancy will be so good as to be ready early on Saturday morning I will have ye Pleasure of carrying her to Wellwyn. I am Dear Sr

most affectionately Yrs

EYoung

[1] In a letter to Lady Bradshaigh of 2 August 1759, Richardson wrote: 'Wednesday last week [25 July] I made a Visit to Dr. Young at Wellwyn. Returned the next Day. But 25 Miles distant and a fine Road' (Victoria and Albert Museum, Forster Collection 458, vol. xi, f. 251).

[2] There is no record of a payment to Richardson from Young's account in the Gosling bank, however, until 24 May 1760, and then for only £10. 17s. 10d.

[3] The date of this note is wholly conjectural and assumes that Young went to London in place of his neighbour Shotbolt.

John Jones to J. Waller. Welwyn, Herts. [Tu.] 4 September 1759.

Address: To / Mr Waller, / Attorney at Law / in St Neots / Huntingdonshire
Dr. Williams's Library, Jones papers, 39 B. 19.[1]

Wellwyn, 4th Septr 1759
Sir,
Immediately upon my return, I acquainted Dr. Young with what you had told me relating to the necessity of alienating the legacy mentioned, during the life time of the donor, so as to be for a whole Twelvemonth out of his possession before his Decease.

The Doctor upon this representation is convinced, and is therefore solicitous to have the Deed of Gift executed & inrolled immediately in due form of law, considering his Age & the uncertainty of Life. And upon my mentioning your Character, known integrity & care about business committed to your Trust, he desires that you Sir will take upon you the whole management of this affair, so as to do it effectually & speedily, that a benefaction of such consequence to the poor of this place may not be lost, for want of safe & timely execution.

The next time you go this way to London, it may be advisable for you to pay your respects to Dr. Young, who will be glad to see you, & to transact all yt shall be necessary on His part.

I hope your cold is abating. Your friendly Hospitality will always be gratefully recognized by,
Dear Sir,
Your affectionate &
obliged humble Servant
John Jones

If you shall find it necessary to write about this affair, please send by Post to Dr. Young.

P. S. The Dr. approves very well of investing his Donation in a landed Estate; but since that cannot be done with

[1] This, the first of six letters between Young's curate and the Huntingdonshire attorney, has to do with Young's establishment of a charity school for boys.

sufficient expedition at present, he thinks it necessary in the meantime (till a proper purchase offers) to take the method of securing the matter mentioned in my letter.

J. Waller to John Jones. St. Neots, Hunts. [Th.] 20 September 1759.

Address: To / The Revd Mr. Jones / at Wellwyn.
Dr. Williams's Library, Jones papers., 39 B. 19.

Dr Sir

I receiv'd the favour of your Letter wth the instructions to draw Deed of Settlemt from Dr. Young for wch I am much obliged to You. I therefore now trouble You wth the parcel for the Dr. & shall take it as a particular favour if You'd take care to convey any Letter or parcel that may be necessary during this Transaction to be sent to me here wch may be done many ways from You. I am

Sir
Yrmsthble Servt
J. Waller

St Neots 20th Septr 1759

419. [Welwyn, Herts.]. [Su.] 28 October 1759. Duchess of Portland.

Longl   SS. 265.—Bath, p. 325; Shelley, pp. 254–5.

Octr 28
1759.

May it please yr Grace.

From my heart I rejoyce at the delightfull scene of your Graces family-happiness in all the noble, and lovely branches of it. For that is a happiness of all other under Heaven the most valueable, except that which is in the still narrower space of our own bosoms.

May the pleasure, and satisfaction, which you found at Longleat be but the begining of those joys, that shall arise from prudent, and fortunate disposal, of those you love, in the marriage-state; in which we throw the die for the highest stake in human life. /[verso]/

To make that hazardous Die turn up aright, nothing bids fairer than that similitude of tempers which ^{you} have discoverd in my Lord, and Lady Weymouth. It not only gives present happiness, but its promises of future are very great, because it is a private bisque in our sleeve, which caprices of out^{ward} fortune can never rob us of.[1]

As far as I can judge of Lady Harriets temper (I think I have observd it) it seems to me to be such, that it will be a difficulty on your Grace to find its fellow in our sex: May she find it, or (what will be more to her honour, and pleasure) *make* it, in the man she honours with her hand.

As for my Lord Titchfield, may You ever Madam receive accounts of him, & ~~fro~~ news /[conjugate leaf]/ from him, as agreeable, as was your last; that your heart, which, you say, is with him, and which, I say, is then in good, & sweet company, may for ever rejoyce in him, and in the prospect of his conveying his mother's and father's virtues into future times, to bless those, who, by his laudable conduct, will probably be put in mind of days past, & recollect to whom they owe such a son; & so be the less surprizd, tho not less pleasd, with what they love or admire in him.

I bless God my health is pretty well[.] With humble Duty to my Ld Duke, & Lady Harriet, I am with great gratitude

Madam

Yr Grace's most Dutifull

& most Obedient

Humble Sevt

EYoung

Mrs Hallows desires
yr Graces acceptance
of her humble Duty.

---

[1] Mrs. Delany reported having a letter from Longleat from the Duchess of Port-land: 'She likes the place *extremely*, but says she likes the master much more, whose *attention* and *tenderness* to Lady Weymouth, *and engaging behaviour to them all*, makes her quite happy; he seems now *devoted to a domestic life*, and I hope in God, that will fix him firm and sure' (Llanover, 1861, iii. 564). The Duchess's pleasure in finding her daughter's husband 'devoted to a domestic life' can be appreciated in view of Weymouth's reputation for drink and gambling.

420. Welwyn, Herts. [Th.] 20 December 1759.
Duchess of Portland.

Longleat MSS. 267.

May it please yr Grace

Mr Richardson, my old, & worthy friend, knowing yt I
had ye honour of being acquainted with your Grace, writ to
me yesterday to ye following effect. (viz)

'That he knew Mr Tho Poole, who has addressed the
Duke with regard to becoming his servant; that he has reason
to think exstremely well of him; but wishes not for any favour
in his behalf, but as it may suit his Graces good pleasure,
& convenience.'

Pardon, Madam, ye liberty I take in troubling you with
this particular, as I could but ill resist ye desire of my friend
Richardson, who requested ye favour of me.

That your Grace, & all your noble family /[verso]/ may
smile this happy season, nor less in the remaining part of
your year, and life, is the sincere prayr of him who is with
all gratitude, respect, & Duty

Madam
Yr Graces
most Obedient
& most Humble Sevt

I beg my humble Duty
to my Ld Duke,
Lady Harriet &c:
Decemr 20
1759.
Wellwyn

EdYoung

PS
I have lately buryd two near
neibours, Mrs Sabin;[1] & my
friend Mr Harrison of Balls, who
in his 80th year dyd without a
groan. He has left his Widow
20000 l. to dispose of as she
pleases.[2]

[1] Susanna Sabine of Tewin, Herts., about three miles east of Welwyn on the
river Mimram, as was Young's home of Guessens. Her will (Somerset House, P.C.C.
Arran 517) was proved 13 December 1759.

[2] The will (Somerset House, P.C.C. Arran 401) of George Harrison of Balls
Park, Hertfordshire, six miles east of Welwyn, mentions Young's neighbour John
Shotbolt as a kinsman. It was proved the day before this letter was written.

421. [Welwyn, Herts.]. [Th.] 10 January 1760.
Duchess of Portland.

Longleat MSS. 268.

May it please yr Grace.

The regard yt would have been vouchsafd to Mr.
Richardson's recommendation if my Ld Duke had ^{not} disposed of ye place before, must most thankfully be ackno^w-
legd by Mr Richardson, & myself. If his Grace has a more
proper servant, which possibly is ye case, we rejoyce in our
disapointment.

If your Grace had a value for Mrs Clayton,[1] and if her
character was such as you represent, I congratulate yr Grace
on her Death.

With death, Madam, I am too well acquainted by the loss
of an only Brother, & an only Niece, both within this last
month.[2] My Niece dyd of a cancer on her journey to Waters
that were prescribd as a perfect cure.

/[verso]/ It is sayd that we shall have the celebrated Lady
Townsend[3] for our neighbour at Balls; When her situation
in marriage is considerd, & that of many more, & of two
whom I have ye honour to know, Lady Mary Wortley, &
Lady Wallpole,[4] &c, &c, &c. How greatly must it heighten

[1] The death of the 'Wife of Wm Clayton, Esq; member for Bletchingley Surry'
on 2 January is reported in the *Gentleman's Magazine* (xxx. 46). She was Lady
Louisa Fermor, a daughter of Thomas Earl Pomfret, mentioned in Mrs. Delany's
correspondence (Llanover, 1861, iii. 348).

[2] i.e. Revd. John Harris, who had been married to Young's sister, Anne, and
Harris's daughter, Jane, wife of Revd. Walter Bigg. Harris died at Ash, Surrey,
9 December 1759. His will (Somerset House, P.C.C. Lynch 16), drawn 20 October
1759, proved 3 January 1760, has the clause: 'to my much esteemed Friend and
Brother, Dr. Edward Young I give Twenty Guineas to be laid out in a piece of
plate with my own and his sister's arms which I desire may always remain in his
family as a token of that love and friendship which I hope and desire will always
remain between his children and mine'.

[3] Lady Ethelreda ('Audrey') Townshend (d. 1788) was the wife of Charles
Townshend (1700–64), third Viscount Townshend, and the daughter of Edward
Harrison whose brother's death Young had mentioned in the preceding letter to the
Duchess. She was living apart from her husband at this time.

[4] Lady Mary Wortley Montagu (1689–1762) had been living abroad, separated
from her husband, since 1739; Sir Robert Walpole's maintenance of a mistress was
public scandal.

the Happiness of Haveing a Lord, & Lady Weymouth now under your roof to rejoyce your heart with the blessed Reverse.

That Madam, Your present happiness may long continue, & encrease with theirs; and that Lord Titchfield, & my Lady Harriet may draw equall prizes, in that most considerable, & most hazardous Lottery of life; in a word yt your Graces own peace, & happiness may grow on every other branch of your noble, & amiable family, till a far more happy scene than this /[conjugate leaf]/ shall consummate your Joy; is ye Prayr of

> Madam
> Yr Graces
>   most Dutifull
>   & Obligd humble Sevt
>   EYoung.

I beg Madam my
humble Duty to his
Grace, Lady Harriet &c:
  Mrs Hallows hopes
ye Grace will accept
her humble Duty.
Jany 10th
1760

422. [Welwyn, Herts.]. [?Feb.–Apr. 1760]. Samuel Richardson.

Not traced.—Barbauld, ii. 45 (end of letter dated 3 January 1758).[1]

I am now (as it is high time) 'setting my house in order,' and therefore desire you to send by the carrier the parcel of Sermons, (which were packed up when I was in town,) that I may commit them to the flames.

[1] This letter, which was put into that of 3 January 1758 by Mrs. Barbauld, very certainly belongs to the spring of 1760 when Young made his will and settled his account with Richardson. On 5 February Young wrote 'this my last Will with my own hand', directing 'that all my manuscript writings whether in books or papers Imediately on my decease may be burnt my book of accounts alone excepted'. He did not, however, sign the will until 25 April. With a later codicil the will was proved 30 April 1765 (see Appendix C).

And please to favour me with my full and long debt to you; for I am in pain to have it discharged.[1]

That the wing of an indulgent Providence may be ever stretched over you and yours, is the earnest prayer of, dear sir,

Most justly yours,
E. Young.

J. Waller to John Jones. St. Neots, Hunts. [Th.] 10 April 1760.

Address: To / The Revd Mr. Jones / at Wellwyn.
Dr. Williams's Library, Jones papers, 39 B. 19.

Dr Sir

I have but just now been able to get the Draft of Dr Youngs Deed from Mr Booth[2] wch he has approv'd, it shall be immediately Engross't and I hope for the pleasure of waiting on the Dr & You next Tuesday to get it executed. It has given me great uneasiness that the Affair has been so long delay'd but it has not been in my power to prevent it,

---

[1] On 24 May Young gave Richardson a cheque for £10. 17s. 10d. (Barclays Bank, 19 Fleet Street, London, Registers of Gosling's Bank.)

[2] Probably James Booth (d. 1778), whose conveyances were models of the legal profession. The transaction was recorded the following Tuesday (15 April 1760) and is extant in the Public Record Office (Close Roll 34, Geo. II, Pt. 7). By it Young transferred to eleven trustees for the purchase of premises 'in or near Wellwin' £1,500 in South Sea annuities, 'the income from which premises to be applied to the clothing and education of sixteen poor boys of the said parish of Wellwin, and ten shillings to be given to the rector from time to time for the preaching of a sermon before the trustees once a year in Wellwin church, in which sermon it is strictly forbidden that there should be any mention made of the said Edward Young.' The charity school thus established has since been incorporated into the state system. The trustees were Sir Samuel Garrard (d. 1761), of Lamer Wheathampstead, Herts., Thomas Shallcroft of Digswell, Herts., Gyles Thornton Heysham of Staggenhoe, St. Paul's Walden, Herts., Richard Serle of Lockleigh, Herts., Charles Jenner, D.D. (1707–70), Archdeacon of Huntingdon, Henry Yarborough, D.D. (1691–1774), Rector of Tewin, Herts., Nathaniel Freeman, D.D., Rector of Ayot St. Peters, Herts., William Willmott (1721–95), clerk, Rector of Digswell, Herts., Richard Wynne (1719–99), clerk, Rector of Ayot St. Lawrence, Herts., George North (1710–72), clerk, Vicar of Codicote, Herts., and Young's curate, John Jones, described as 'clerk, Rector of Bolnhurst, co. Bedford'.

and therefore I hope You'll excuse me to the Dr and make my Comts to him, and accept the same—Yourself from
>Dr Sir
>Yr most Obliged hble Set.
>J. Waller

St Neots 10 Apl 1760

J. Waller to John Jones. [St. Neots, Hunts.] [M. 14 April 1760.][1]

Dr. Williams's Library, Jones papers, 39 B. 19.

Dr Sir

I was very sorry to hear of your being so ill as not to be able to attend the Bps Visitation at Hatfield, but I hope you are now got well. I fully propos'd my self the pleasure of waiting upon Dr Young & you to morrow, but find myself under an absolute necessity to defer my Journey till after Bedford Q[uarter] Sessions & our Assizes which begin next Week. However I have sent the Deed of Settlemt to be inroll'd that no Inconveniency may happen for default thereof and as soon as I have it return'd whch I have desired may be wth all convenient speed I will get over to Wellwyn. I beg you'l present my most humble Duty to the Dr & accept my most hearty wishes for the recovery of Your health and the Increase of your prosperity and believe me to be wth great respect
>Sir
>Yr most Obliged hble Servt
>JWaller

[1] The date of this letter is clear from mention of Waller's proposed visit to Welwyn.

423. [Apr.–May 1760]. John Scott.[1]

Not traced.—John Hoole, 'An Account of the Life and Writings of John Scott, Esq', in *Critical Essays on Some of the Poems of Several English Poets, by John Scott*, 1785, p. xxx; Thomas, p. 199.

Sir, I thank you for your present;[2] I admire the poetry and piety of the author and shall do myself the credit to recommend it to all my friends.

424. [Welwyn, Herts.]. [Th.] 29 May 1760. George Keate.[3]

British Museum, Add. MS. 30992, f. 1.—Thomas, p. 612; Dapp, p. 28.

Sr

I much thank you [for] ye noble Present You made me.[4] I read it over & over to myself & others with great pleasure.

I am glad to hear that you think ye report of Voltaires death is groundless.[5] If you come to any certainty in yt point, the Knowledge of it, would oblige

Sr

Your obedient
& Humble Sevt
E Young

May 29
1760.

[1] John Scott (1730–83), a Quaker poet of Amwell, Herts., near Welwyn, between Ware and Hertford.

[2] A copy of his *Four Elegies, Descriptive and Moral*, announced as published 24 April 1760 (cf. R. Strauss, *Robert Dodsley*, 1910, p. 371).

[3] George Keate (1730–97) of the Inner Temple had visited the Continent in the years 1754–7 and had made the acquaintance of Voltaire.

[4] Keate's first publication, *Ancient and Modern Rome*, a poem in blank verse, which Keate had published anonymously on 11 March (*The London Chronicle* and the *Whitehall Evening Post*).

[5] *The Public Advertiser* of 7 June was to carry the following story: 'Paris, May 26. M. de Voltaire, who passed for dead throughout France last Month, without having had any Illness to give Rise to the Report, is in perfect Health; and will soon publish a new Opera, which is to be acted at his Seat at Tournay.'

J. Waller to John Jones. St. Neots, Hunts. [F.] 25
July 1760.

Address: To / The Revd Mr Jones / at Wellwyn / To be deliver'd at his
House on Friday July 25th 1760 / Carr[iage] p[ai]d.
Dr. Williams's Library, Jones papers, 39 B. 19.

Dr Sir
    I am sorry I can't do myself the pleasure to wait on Dr
Young this week, but I shall most certainly (God willing) be
at Wellwyn on Friday the 8th of August in my way to
Gunnersbury, and I'l then stay and hope to finish all that
remains to be done relating to the Charity. I have got the
Deed Inroll'd in Chancery and the Stock is transferr'd wch
is all that is requir'd on Dr Youngs part and therefore there
is no reason for him to be uneasy. If you come here as your
Letter intimates next Week I hope You'll make use of Your
old Lodging and if your Stay be not longer than the time of
my setting out, I shall be glad to accompany You back to
Wellwyn. My most humble Duty attends Dr Young wth
Compts to Your self & I am
                                    Dr Sir
                                    Yr most Obliged hble Servt
                                    JWaller

St Neots 25 July 1760

425. [Welwyn, Herts.]. [Th.] 7 August 1760. Duchess
of Portland.

Longleat MSS. 270.

                                                    Aug. 7, 1760.
May it please yr Grace.

    As good news from Turin[1] must ever be a Cordial at
Bullstrode, I rejoyce at it; but more particularly at yr Graces
article of News from Longleat. I heartily wellcome ye little

_____
1 Where Lord Titchfield is at this time.

stranger to this World:[1] If she carrys half yt Innocence out
of this world, wh she has brought into it, she will be a very
happy Being; & considering into wt hands she is fallen, we
have great reason to hope ye Best. Family-happiness is by
far ye greatest happiness yt Earth can afford; may yr Grace
see its yearly encrease, till it ends in far more than this scene
can pretend to.

I am very sorry his Grace is so lame; but his good Health
will support his spirits under it, and enable him to get rid of
it ye sooner. The most perfect Human happiness is ever a
little Lame; our Joy halts more, or less, on this side ye grave;
if it is not sick of any great Calamity we must be Content.
/[verso]/ What a terrible Calamity yr Grace mentions with
regard to ye family of ye Bishop of Cloyne?[2] Considering his
so valueable character, yr melancholy account must hurt us
ye more.

I never heard of ye Barkleyans before;[3] and it is too soon
to hear of them Now. I grant ye young men lay under some
temptation; for it is no small Glory to be ye Founder of a
New Sect; but ye Glory costs somewhat too dear, if we must
part with our Senses for it.

But I leave his Congregation to take a turn in yr Park, &
enjoy ye noble Improvements in it.[4] Yr Grace says—'Our
great Works are now allmost finishd; however we shall allways find something to do.'—This I am glad to hear on more
accounts than One. Lady Giffard, a sister of ye famous Sr
William Temple, & a supposd Partner in his Works, enjoyd
great Health in exstreme Old age. Being well acquainted
with her, I askd her, by what /[conjugate leaf]/ means she
carryd such perfect health into such a length of life. She told
me, yt her cheif Receipt for yt great Blessing was—'*To be
allways a Doing*'—In proof of wh, she assurd me yt she began

---

[1] A daughter, Louisa, born to Lord and Lady Weymouth in March.

[2] The widow of George Berkeley (1685–1753), born Anne Forster (1700–86),
was living with her daughter Julia in Oxford at this time. Her son George had taken
the degree M.A. (January 1759) and had recently become Vicar of Bray. What the
'terrible Calamity' may have been is not known.

[3] A sect denying physical reality (cf. Johnson's *Idler* for 17 June 1758 and
especially the Cambridge correspondent to the *London Magazine* for March 1760).

[4] The Portlands had just returned from a trip to Welbeck and had apparently
stopped for a few days at Bulstrode *en route* to their town house where they were
reported to have arrived on the 13th (*Public Advertiser*).

to learn Spanish, & made herself Mistress of it after Three-score.[1]

While yr Grace is beautifying yr Place, You are preserving yr Health; and the longer your Operations, ye longer, in all probability will be your Enjoyment of them. That long may be your enjoyment of them, & every other Blessing is ye Prayr of

Madam
Yr Graces most Dutifull
& most Obedient
Humble Sevt
EYoung

My humble Duty to
his Grace & Ly Harriot.

Mrs Hallows begs yr Grace's   PS. Rheumatic Pains
acceptance of her most   excepted, I bless God, I
humble Respects, & Duty.   am well.

426. [Welwyn, Herts.]. [M.] 11 August 1760. George Keate.

Postmark: 12/AU.
British Museum, Add. MS. 30992, f. 2.—Thomas, p. 612.

Dear Sr

I close with your Opinion, with Regard to what You was so Good as to send me of Mr Voltaire's; My opinion of some other of his Performances, You will learn from some sheets,[2] which I have orderd to be sent you from my Dear Friend Mr Richardsons Press; and wh I desire You to accept as a Mark of that Regard with wh I am

Dear Sr
Yr Faithfull, Obligd,
& Obedient Humble sevt
EYoung

Aug 11th
1760

[1] If Young is right about the time, Lady Giffard would have begun the study of Spanish after the death of her brother in 1699. She herself died in 1722 in her 83rd year.

[2] Unless the 'sheets' were an unbound copy of Young's *The Sea-Piece*, dedicated to Voltaire in 1757, the reference is not clear.

427. [Welwyn, Herts.]. [M.] 8 September 1760.
Samuel Richardson.

Yale University Library (Tinker MS.).—Barbauld, ii. 57–8; Shelley, pp. 259–60.

Sepr 8. 1760

Dear Sr

I have receivd ye Papers—And how greatly am I con-cernd, yt I can not take ye advantage of ye infinite pains you have taken for me? But every day puts it more, & more out of my powr—[1]

It is wth difficulty yt I can read wt yr Friend[shi]p, & Genius, & Virtue, has sent me: But still greater difficulty am I under sufficiently to thank you for it.—To write is Uneasie to me; must I despair of ever seeing you? Or have I yt pleasure in life still to come?—Success, & Peace, be ever with You!

Amen.

wh is ye natural Style of those yt have enterd the Intermediate state between this scene, & ye next: A dim Apartment it is, wh excludes Action, but favours Thought.
[Written vertically in the left margin] Heaven be favourable to Miss Pattys health!

[1] Following this paragraph the Barbauld version inserts two paragraphs, not in the original manuscript, but probably from a letter of about this time as they include another allusion to Young's difficulties with his eyes: 'Pray give my humble duty to the Speaker, and tell him that I greatly enjoy his so kind remembrance of me; and long to kiss his hand. I find little assistance from art; but my complaint itself, in one view, is an excellent glass, making things invisible more legible than they were before.'

On 11 November 1760 Bishop Hildesley was to write to Richardson at hearing 'the account you give me of Dr. Young's impending misfortune' (Barbauld, v. 142) and to get Richardson's answer, probably later in January; 'I have the great pleasure of congratulating you, on Dr. Young's good state of health and on his abated apprehensions of the calamity he feared' (ibid. 145; the 'Sept.' date of the letter is patently wrong).

J. Waller to John Jones. St. Neots, Hunts. [Th.] 11
September 1760.

Address: To / The Revd Mr Jones / at Wellwyn / Herts / Carr. pd.
Dr. Williams's Library, Jones papers, 39 B. 19.

Dr Sir

Be pleas'd to present my Dutiful respects to Dr. Young &
acquaint him that every thing relating to his Charity is com-
pleated, which gives me great pleasure.[1]

I have agreed for the Purchase wch You saw a Shaddow of
as we pass't thro' Eaton, but whether it be dear or cheap I am
not able to say. I ought, and do beg your pardon for being
so bad company on our last Journey to Wellwyn but I hope
the fatigue and being in the Night will plead my Excuse.
I wish I could see you often, for your company both delights
and instructs me. I am

Dr Sir
Yr very Obliged hble Servt
JWaller

St Neots 11th Setr 1760

---

1 Among the Jones papers in Dr. Williams's Library is the following record: 'Mr
Waller's Bill to Dr. Young: 1759, & 1760/1759 Oct. 1. Drawing draft of the Deed
Settlement of the School & fair Copy very long & spec'l. £2:2:0 / 6, Attending Dr.
Y. wherewith, to settle the uses —— /1760 Apr. 1 &c Pd. Mr. Booth to p[er]use &
settle the Draught £2:2:0 / His Clerk £0:2:6 / My agent for his several [?calls] on
Mr. Booth £0:10:0 / Fair copy of the Draught for Mr. Booth to keep by him
£0:7:6 / Carriage of the Draft to & from London £0:2:0 / Engrossing there of 2
skins £1:0:0. / Parchment & Duty £0:12:6 / 15. Journey to Wellwyn & attending
Dr. Y. to execute ye Deed & taking his acknowlt &c in order for the Inrollment
£1:1:0 / Paid for Inrollment £2:1:0 / Aug. 7: 12 & 13. Attendance three days, as
Not[ar]y Public to see the Trustees execute the Deed of Trust & a Letter of Attorney
for accepting 1500 £ Stock —— / Fair copy of the Deed for the Trustees £0:7:6 /
The Blanks were left for the Dr's Discretion And he made the Sum to be *Sixteen
Guineas* £16.16.0 / Which he paid me, May 1, 1762 & for which I gave him a
Receipt in the name & for the use of Mr. Waller. The sums expressly charged Come
in all, as on the other side to £10:8:0 / The Doctor acknowledged the whole to be a
very reasonable Bill, & spoke handsomely of Mr *Waller*, as he well deserves, taking
notice that he is the reverse of the generality of the profession &c.'

428. [Welwyn, Herts.]. [W.] 5 November 1760. The Trustees of the Welwyn Charity School.

Dr. Williams's Library, Jones papers, 39 B. 19.

A circular Letter humbly presented to the several Gentlemen whose Names are underwritten /[in the hand of John Jones].

Sir,
    As you have already favoured me with your hand as a Trustee with regard to my endowment of a little School at Wellwyn, I beg of you to double that favour by signing the inclosed order to impower me to receive the Interest of the Fifteen Hundred Pounds which by the deeds you have signed, are transferred to you. I am,

Sir,
Your most obedient
& much oblig'd
humble Servant   E. Y.

Wellwyn
    5 Novr 1760

Sir Samuel Garrard	The Reverend
Thomas Shallcross Esq.	Dr. Jenner
Gyles Thornton Heysham Esq.	Dr. Freeman
Richard Serle Esqr.	Dr. Yarborough
	Mr Wilmot
	Mr. Wynne
	Mr. North
	Mr. Jones

429. [Welwyn, Herts.]. [Th.] 20 November 1760. Duchess of Portland.

Longleat MSS. 272.—Bath, pp. 325–6.

May it please yr Grace.
    More than once, I have heard the famous Mr Addison say, That it was much his Wish (if it so pleasd God) to Die

in the summer, because then walking abroad he frequently contemplated ye works of God, which gave such a serious turn, & awfull Composure to ye mind as best qual[i]fied it to enter ye Divine presence.

Summer scatters us abroad into ye Fields to gather Wisdom there, if we please. The storms of Winter drive us back to shelter, & Contemplation gives place to Company. Happy they yt enjoy such as those wh[o] your Grace says are now with You. Musick is a delicious Entertainment; & the only one that I know of, which ^{Earth} enjoys in common with Heaven. Long may you enjoy those Pleasures Here, which bid /[verso]/ fairest to end in such as will never cease; *Lovers of Reading* & *Work* are most likely to make Those their Choice.

I was not at home when Your very Kind, & very Ample (for it is very fresh & good) Present arrivd; but I am now enjoying it, under a deep sense of the frequent, and much undeservd Honours conferd on

Madam
Yr Graces
Most Dutifull, &
Most Obedient
Humble Sevt
EYoung.

I beg, Madam, my humble Duty to his Grace & Ly Harriet.

Mrs Hallows begs yr Grace to accept of Hers. My best Compliments to Mr Achard.

Novr 20
1760.

430. [Welwyn, Herts.]. [Tu.] 20 January 1761.
Duchess of Portland.

Longleat MSS. 274.—Bath, p. 326; Shelley, p. 262.

[In an unidentified hand]

Jany 20
1761

May it please your Grace

I have taken some Hours to consider of the very kind offer
your Grace is so good to make me.¹ I am old, & I bless God
far from want; but as the Honour is great & the Duty small,
& such as need not take much from my Parish, and especially as your Grace seems desirous I should accept it; I do
accept it with great Gratitude for Your remembrance of one
who might easily & naturally be forgotten.

The Honour, indeed, is great, & in my sight, greater
still, as I succeed to so Great & Good a Man: Would to God
I could tread in all his other steps as well as this.

I am Madam
Yr Graces most Dutiful
& most Obliged
Humble servant
EYoung

431. [London.]. [February 1761]. Duchess of Portland.

Longleat MSS. 295.

[In an unidentified hand]

May it please Your Grace.

Great thanks for shelter under your Roof and, for so
peculiar indulgences There; Nor must elegant amusements

¹ 'Her Royal Highness the Princess Dowager of Wales [Amelia] has appointed
Dr. Edward Young (Chaplain to his late majesty) to succeed the late Stephen Hales
[1677–1761] as Clerk of the Closet to her Royal Highness. It is but Justice on this
Occasion to compliment her Royal Highness's Choice of Gentlemen of so much
Eminence in their Profession' (*The London Evening Post*, 7 February 1761). Hales
had died on 4 January.

be forgotten; Among the rest, those two pictures; without any pretence to skill, or sagacity, indeed, Madam, I discovered the murderer at the first glance, so strongly marked are their oposite tempers, in their aspects; that if an imaginary Cain, & Abel, was to be drawn, it coud hardly be better done.

This is my humble opinion. But how came I to emerge, out of my own Muddy element, into such curious enquieries, & polite converse, in Your land of Rarities? My collection is large but it lies chiefly in the Church-Yard; and a Death's head, is the Capital picture I can boast. I little thought, a month agoe, that I shod have been call'd out of my private path, so late in /[verso]/ Life: But Your Grace was pleased to call me out of it, in quest of Honours; now the road to Honours lies up hill, & indeed the steep assent has put me a little out of breath: The natural app[e]tite of Age, is for Rest, which I have fasted for at least a fortnight: This has sunk me a little, but otherways, I bless God, I am very well. Please to accept my repeated acknowledgments for various favours, nor think me an Arch Bp when I profess myself

Madam,
Your Graces most dutiful
And devoted Humble servant
EYoung.

My humble duty
to my Ld Duke & Lady Harriot, & L. Edward.
               Mr
My humble service to   Achard.

PS. If Ld Bute[1] falls in your way, please Madame, to let him know, that I was to pay my duty to him before I left Town.

---

[1] John Stuart (1713–92), third Earl of Bute, principal adviser to George III at this time and hence the authority to whom Young would pay his respects for his appointment as Clerk of the Closet to Princess Amelia.

432. Welwyn, Herts. [Su.] 22 February 1761. George Keate.

Postmark: 22/FE.
British Museum, Add. MS. 30992, f. 3.—Thomas, pp. 612–13; Shelley, p. 263.

                                    Wellwyn 22 Feb. 61.
Sir

I thank you for your congratulation on my succeeding the worthy Dr. Hale's. If I coud follow him in all his steps, I shod deserve your congratulation indeed. As for my welfare, which you so kindly enquire after, I bless God, I am pretty well, but not quite as well as I was forty year agoe. But I hope, thro' divine Mercy, forty years hence, to be better still. While I continue Here, I shall number those amongst my happy hours, which you shall please to enliven by Your agreeable conversation. This Year's spring will be doubly welcome to me if You make good your promise to, Sir,
                        Your Obedient humble servant
                                    EYoung.

433. Welwyn, Herts. [Su.] 15 March 1761. George Keate.

British Museum, Add. MS. 30992, f. 4.—Thomas, p. 613; Shelley, p. 263; Dapp, pp. 32–3.

Sir
    In the earlier part of my Life, I often designed, & much desired to visit Geneva: And tho' fate denied me that favour, it has granted me a greater; for now, Geneva has made me a visit to me,[1] in so clean & decent a Dress, that I am scarce more in love with her Wisdom, than with her Beauty.

But as you say, Sir, in your Dedication to Mr Voltaire, this is not designed to be your panegerick, but a grateful Acknowlegement of your Valuable present to, Sir,
                            Your Obliged
                        & Obedient humble servant
                                    EYoung.
Wellwyn 15 March 1761.

[1] Keate's *Short Account of the Ancient History, Present Government and Laws of the Republic of Geneva* had been published on the 11th of this month.

434. [Welwyn, Herts.]. [Th. 9 April 1761]. Elizabeth
Montagu.[1]

Not traced.—Climenson, ii. 236–7.

Dear Madam,

Your letter, etc., lay me under great obligations, but the
greatest lies in the kind promise you make me that I shall
kiss the hands of two fair Pilgrims at Wellwyn. I hope they
are too much Protestants to think there is anything sacred
in the shrine you speak of. I have too many sins beside, to
pretend that I am a Saint. Was I a Saint and could work
miracles I would reduce you two ladys to the common level
of your sex being jealous for the credit of my own; which has
hitherto presum'd to boast an usurp'd superiority in the
realms of genius and the letter'd world. For you, Madam, I
shall say nothing, for who can say enough? Miss Carter has
my high esteem for showing us in so masterly a manner that
Christianity has a foil in one of the brightest jewels of Pagan
Wisdom, a jewel which you will allow she has set in gold.
Might not such an honour from a fair hand, make even an
Epictetus proud without being blamed for it? Nor let Miss
Carter's[2] amiable modesty become blameable, by taking
offence at the truth, but stand the shock of applause, which

---

[1] On 19 September last Mrs. Montague had called on Young and later sent him
a powder for his rheumatism from Dr. Messenger Monsey (1693–1788). She
described her visit in September in a letter to her husband: 'I call'd on Dr. Young
at Welling and staid about two hours with him, he received me with great cordiality,
and I think appears in better health than ever I saw him. His house is happily
opposite to a church yard, which is to him a fine prospect; he has taught his
imagination to sport with skulls like the gravedigger in Hamlet. He invited me to
stay all night, and if my impatience to see you had not impell'd me on, I had been
tempted to it. His conversation has always something in it very delightful; in the
first place it is animated by the warmest benevolence, then his imagination soars
above the material world, some people would say his conversation is not natural.
I say it is natural of him to be unnatural, that is out of the ordinary course of things.
It would be easier for him to give you a catalogue of the Stars than an inventory of
the Household furniture he uses every day. The busy world may say what it pleases,
but some men were made for speculation, metaphysical men, like jars and flower pots,
make good furniture for a cabinet tho' useless in the kitchen, the pantry and the
Dairy' (Climenson, ii. 199–200).

[2] Elizabeth Carter (1717–1806), poet and miscellaneous writer, whose translation
and annotation of *All the Works of Epictetus which are now Extant* in 1758, published at the suggestion of Archbishop Thomas Secker, was a considerable success.

she has brought upon herself; for tho' it pains her, it does credit to the publick, and she should support it patiently, as her Stoical Hero did his broken leg. I rejoice that you are recovered; I too, Madam, have been very ill of late, and stand in no small need of a cordial: hasten therefore your favour,[1] which the sooner it is, will be the kinder to, dear Madam,

Your most obedient
and obliged, humble servant,
E. Young.

435. [Welwyn, Herts.]. [Su.] 12 April 1761. Friedrich Gottlieb Klopstock.

Not traced.—Elizabeth Smith, *Fragments in Prose and Verse: Memoirs of Frederick and Margaret Klopstock*, 1810, ii. 209–10.

April 12, 1761.

I Thank you for the melancholy, yet pleasing sight of your dear wife's monument. I read in it the Christian character of her husband.[2] Its last word was the common salutation of the primitive Christians, when they met each other,—*Resurrexit*. Should not our hearts burn within us at the blessed sound? That word carries in it all our hope and joy. We shall soon bury all our other hope and joy, never to rise again. And shall Beings that have no end, prize any thing that has? CHRIST is indeed the truth, and the world a lie. Infidels believe it, and are undone.

I love your faith and virtue, I admire your genius, I deplore your loss, I pity your distress, I pray for your prosperity, and shall be ever proud of your commands; being, most cordially,

My dear Sir,
Your most obedient and most humble servant,
E. Young.

[1] The visit was made about the end of April.
[2] i.e. the inscription on the tomb of Meta Klopstock.

436. Welwyn, Herts. [Su.] 12 April 1761. Count Christian Günther Stolberg.[1]

Not traced.—J. J. Eschenburg, ed., *Eberts Episteln*, Hamburg, 1795, ii. 86–7; Thomas, pp. 610–11.

My most honour'd Lord,

I am not more exalted by the great honour Your Lordship has done me, than I am surprized at it. And I am equally desirous and unable, to express my deep sense of Your goodness to me. To be sollicitous in quest of what is Right, and to dart an eagle's eye into distant lands, that You may discover the least appearance of Good; and then so nobly to countenance that which You fancy You have found, shews such an uncommon zeal for virtue, as the truly Virtuous only can possess, and from which the truly Vicious only can withhold their veneration and esteem.

But how, my most worthy Lord, shall I sufficiently pay my gratitude and devotion to Your admirable Lady? I regret my age on no account more, than that it robs me of the power of expressing myself with that warmth and energy which I wish to do. Who can enough value an honour so high, so peculiar and, I believe, so unprecedented an indulgence to me? Presume I stand Sponsor with such exalted names? Am I worthy to give my Blessing to the fortunate Infant already so bless'd? Blessed by such descent! Blessed by such examples! And if my most ardent prayers can ought avail, still further bless'd! As we read of the little ones in the Gospel, may our most adored Redeemer take up Your *Magnus Ernest Christian*[2] in his everlasting arms, and bless him! Bless him in Time! Bless him in Eternity! May he make this Wilderness an Eden to Him, and then make that Eden appear as a Wilderness, if compared with his Blessings in a far superior Scene!

---

[1] Count Stolberg (1714–65) of Holstein. His wife is said to have been influenced by religious pietism and their invitation to Young to sponsor their latest child came as a result of their acquaintance with the *Night-Thoughts* in Ebert's translation (see Ebert's letter to Young of June 1761).

[2] Nothing further is known of this child. Of the eleven Stolberg children, two, Christian (1748–1821) and Friedrich (1750–1819) are remembered as minor poets.

If, my Lord, I was not divided from You by seas and lands, and, what is still worse, by an insurmountable mountain of *near fourscore years*, I should be ambitious of kissing Your hands. But as things now stand, my heart only can travel so far; and that indeed, my good Lord, does its duty, which I hope You will condescend to accept from one who is with profound respect,

My most honoured Lord
Your's and Your most estimable Lady's
most obliged, and most dutiful, and thrice humble
and obedient Servant
E. Young.

Wellwyn, Hertfordshire,
April the 12th. 1761.

437. Welwyn, Herts. [Su.] 3 May 1761. Elizabeth Montagu.

Address: To Mrs Montagu / In Hill Street, near / Berkley Square / London.
Postmark: WELWYN.
Princeton University Library MS.

Dear Madam

You will be so Good as to burn what I sent before, & to recommend This to Mrs B. with ye warmest Good wishes of my Heart.[1]

Yr recommendation will enable this Trifle, perhaps, to make some impression on her; wh I send purely for an Amusement, which in her Case is of more Use than anything else.

---

[1] Young refers to verses he had written to console the widow of Admiral Edward Boscawen (1711–61) for the loss of her husband on 10 January 1761. These verses were an early draft of what he later published as *Resignation*. On 28 November of this year Elizabeth Montagu's sister, Sarah (Mrs. George Scott) wrote: 'Dr. Young has written a poem on "Resignation", and dedicated it to Mrs. Boscawen. I have not seen it, but have heard it much praised, and am told he wrote it at the desire of my sister Montagu and Miss Carter, who requested it in a visit they made him on their road to Tunbridge, where my sister spent the summer' (John Doran, *A Lady of the Last Century*, 1873, p. 98).

Thanks sincere, & many for the Honour, & Pleasure I so lately receivd.

> I am Dear Madam
> Yr most Obedient,
> & Obligd Humble Sevt
> EYoung.

Pray my humble service
to Mrs Carter, & my
Duty to ye Dutchess
May ye 3d 1761.

438. [Tu.] 26 May 1761. Elizabeth Montagu.

Not traced.[1]—Climenson, ii. 240–1.

Dear Madam,

I hope you will alow that a Curiosity is better than a good thing. I send you a Paper[2] which may be called a Curiosity, as it is printed, but not for ye Publick, only for yr ease in perusing it.

I much thank you for ye bright specimen of Genius you was so kind as to send me.[3] I admire it as much as you. I hope you are recover'd of the Indysposition you mention'd in your Last, and that you, the cloud remov'd, will continue to shine on,

> Dear Madam,
> Your most obedient
> and Humble Servt,
> E. Young.

May 26, 1761.

[1] Offered for sale in Maggs Bros. catalogue No. 445 of 1923 as item No. 3010, but not located.

[2] Extant copies of the privately printed *Resignation* (1761) carry a note on the death of Richardson, which did not come until 4th July. Young must here be talking of an intermediate version of the poem.

[3] This probably refers to a dialogue 'Berenice and Cleopatra', which Mrs. Montagu was circulating at the time and which is reprinted by Climenson (ii. 238–40).

439. [Tu.] 2 June 1761. Elizabeth Montagu.

Not traced.[1]

440. [Welwyn, Herts.]. [Su.] 7 June 1761. Johann Arnold Ebert.

Not traced.—J. J. Eschenburg, ed., *Eberts Episteln*, Hamburg, 1795, ii. 83; Thomas, p. 607.

Dear Sir,
    From age I have long been very weak, and have lately been, and am now, much indisposed. I am greatly oblig'd for Your very valuable and very learned present.[2] I wish I understood the Notes better than I do at present. If it shall please God to grant me more strength, and I so become a better Master of what You have written, You will excuse those defects which Age makes me guilty of; and that You may arrive at Age without its infirmities, is the cordial prayer of,
                    Dear Sir,
        Your most oblig'd and truly affectionate humble
                    Servant
                    E. Young.

Mr Richardson salutes You, and is much Yours
June 7, 1761.
    I received the book but last month.

    [1] Evidence of this letter is the entry under Young's name in Herbert H. Raphael's *Horace Walpole: A Descriptive Catalogue of the Artistic and Literary Illustrations . . . for the Extension of the Original Edition of Walpole's Letters into Eighteen Volumes* (Bristol, 1909): 'A. L. s. concerning a book by Dr. Hawksworth. To Mrs. Montagu. Date: June 2, 1761. Seal.' The book referred to would have been *Almoran and Hamet, an Oriental Tale* in 2 vols. by John Hawkesworth (?1715–73), which was announced for publication on the same date as this letter (*London Evening Post* of 28 May 1761). Attempts to locate the 18-volume extra-illustrated Walpole have been fruitless.
    [2] Ebert had sent Young a copy of a new edition of his German translation of his *Night-Thoughts* and other works. Young presented the book to his former patron, John Carteret, now first Earl Granville, with the following inscription: 'Doctor Young desires Lord Granville, to accept this Book, with his humble Duty. Wellwyn 12 Novr: 1761.'

Ebert to Young.[1] [June 1761].

Not traced.—J. J. Eschenburg, ed., *Eberts Episteln*, Hamburg, 1795, ii. 73–82.

Reverend Sir,

If the highest degree of esteem and veneration, pay'd to as high a degree of virtue and genius, may be a sufficient excuse for such a liberty, as I am now going to take, I am sure I want no further apology for this address to You. I cannot, must not suffer You to leave this world, or leave it myself, (which was very likely to have happen'd but a few years ago) without discharging at least some part of the debt of gratitude, I owe to You long since, and the whole sum of which I am not able to pay on this side heaven. As by the all-gracious providence of God You were chosen to be my guide to that happy place; so I hope I shall there be enabled to do justice to me as well as to You in pouring out all the grateful sentiments of my overflowing heart, in mixing my tears of joy with those of all the blessed souls, to whom Your excellent writings have been a means of salvation, and my applauses with those of the angels themselves. All I can do *here*, is to tell You for once by letter, what I have been telling You in my thoughts almost every day these fifteen years past: that I revere in You one of the chosen vessels of God, to bear his name before the gentiles of this age; one of the most valiant, powerful, and (I may add) fortunate heroes and champions sent from above for asserting the cause of religion and virtue; one of those writers, that applied the noblest talents to the noblest use, and may be said (as Your worthy friend and confederate in that glorious undertaking [Richardson], tho' armed with weapons of another kind, was justly said by You) with a genius as well *moral*, as *original*, to have cast out evil spirits, and made a convert to virtue of a species of composition (poetry, and satire in particular) once most its foe. I therefore bless that hour, when I first became acquainted with Your excellent writings, and at the same time with Your heart, which must appear to every attentive and

---

[1] This letter was apparently written about the same time as Young's to Ebert, of 7 June, the two letters obviously crossing one another.

feeling reader to have at least as great a share in them, as Your head. 'Tis to those, I owe (next to the sacred writings) the greatest improvement, with the purest and most heavenly delight of my mind, the best secret consciousness I ever had of doing some good to others, and that honest fame I have got among my countrymen, for helping them to a sense and relish of their beauties. In short, 'tis on account of these, that I am glad and proud to think myself as highly oblig'd to You, as any man can possibly be to another; and that I honour and respect You as my spiritual father, next to him who gave me life, and whom God Almighty, by his Infinite goodness, has preserved till now (as I hope he has You) to my inexpressible joy at an age of above fourscore years.

O! why cannot I pay my filial duty to You in person as well, as I did to him last summer at Hamborough? Why was I never allow'd to visit, as so many others were, that awful and delicious *retirement* of Yours, *the residence of virtue and literature?* or the *bower* and the *winding walks, where the muses twine the bay for virtuous Young?* to hear there the divine harmony of Your *life, symphonious to Your strain, (that noblest hymn to heaven!)* and to see You, with the close attention of Your genius, *practise o'er the angel in the man?* or to enjoy at least Your improving, inspiring conversation but for one evening?

As I always rejoice, whenever I meet only with Your name somewhere, how should I exult, if I could be so happy as to see Your dear self! Believe me, Sir, that alone would be a more than sufficient reason for me to take a journey to England, if I were not prevented by my circumstances from doing so; and I, upon my return, should think all my pains over-paid, and myself the happiest man alive, tho' I had seen nothing there, but You and Mr. *Richardson.* But the accomplishment of that, as of most other pious wishes, is reserv'd for heaven. 'Tis there I hope, by the infinite mercy of our God, to enjoy Your whole eternity, and hear and admire with listening and admiring seraphs a song, still more sublime than this You sung on earth, which was but 'a prelude to that;' tho' even this prelude may be now more highly and universally applauded by those poets of heaven, than it has been *here*.

'Angels that grandeur, men o'erlook, admire.'

I doubt not, but Your humanity will pardon those effus-
ions of my grateful heart, which broke out with the more
impetuosity for having been restrained so long. Were I so
happy as to be now in Your presence, I should not have
presumed to give them a vent. But this is perhaps the only
advantage a letter has of a conversation; the honest freedom,
I mean, allow'd to it, to express more plainly and fully either
the petitions of want, or the thanks of gratitude. *Literae non
erubescunt.*

You will by this time have receiv'd the first volume of my
new edition of Your Night-Thoughts. I began to translate
them about ten years ago after having studied them for four
years almost night and day. I chose to attempt it in prose
rather than in verse, that I might render Your thoughts, if
possible, in all their original energy, without the least allay,
with a scrupulous, tho' not anxious, exactness; which, by
the way, as I may assert without prejudice, no one modern
language is capable of performing, but the German, as it
bears such a near affinity to the English, not only with
regard to single words, but also to the strongest expressions
and boldest constructions. But in order to compensate in some
manner the want of versification, I endeavour'd to make my
prose as spirited, poetical and harmonious, as possible. If I
may trust to my sense of the beauties of the original and to
the uncommonly favourable reception, the translation has
met with, for the success of my labour, I have not failed in
my attempt. After several editions, there are now about 5000
copies of it, and together with them the glory of the immortal
poet, and the solid advantages rising from the poem, spread
over all Germany. Since that time I have translated also *The
Last Day, The Force of Religion, The true Estimate of human
Life, The Centaur* (tho' there was already publish'd another
translation, but a very indifferent one) and the two *Epistles to
Mr. Pope.* Your Tragedies have likewise been translated,
but by another hand.

The edition, the first volume of which I have now the
honour to present You with, and to which the Satires will be
annexed, is accompanied with the original text, and some
critical and explanatory notes, that may serve for a commen-

tary to it, pointing out the most eminent beauties, and the passages from ancient and modern writers You may have imitated or hinted at. But with respect to those of the latter sort, I have proceeded, I hope, with great caution, and taken care not to transgress the rules prescribed by good sense and Mr. *Hurd* in his Essay on Poetical Imitation. For I take not a similarity of one single thought or expression in two authors to be an infallible proof of their having imitated each other, where there are no other reasons to make it more probable. However, such quotations may have their use, either as illustrations, or as tending to show the superiority of the original, or as promoting a moral end, the more to inculcate an important truth on the mind of the reader,

> 'By repetition hammer'd on his ear.'

And such are the greater part of those contained in the remarks.

Among other German Poets You will find frequently mentioned Mr. *Bodmer*, Professor at Zurich in Switzerland, and Author of an epic poem, entitled *Noah*; and the lines quoted from it are imitations or translations of those in the Night-Thoughts referred to in my notes. This liberty, which in my opinion merits rather praise than censure, he has excused somewhere in that work, and at the same time publickly declar'd his esteem and gratitude to his benefactor. Besides these You will find other passages, which, tho' not close or purposely designed imitations, yet seemed to deserve a place even over-against such a work as Yours, as well on account of their likeness, as because the author more than once confess'd to me, that, during the course of his labour, he was often kindled and warmed by Your flame. The performance is, I dare say, one of the noblest and most original productions of human genius; and the Author so happy, as to be already known to You; I mean, Mr. *Klopstock*, our—*more* than *Milton*, our *Shakspeare* and *Milton* united.

I come now, Sir, to what chiefly engaged and encouraged me to write to You. I took last summer a journey to Copenhagen, to visit two of my dearest and most intimate friends, the more dear to me for being also in the same degree with me Your and Mr. *Richardson's* sincere admirers; Mr. *Klop-stock* and Mr. *Cramer*, German Chaplain to the King, and one of our best poets and orators. There I had the pleasure of seeing Your letters to the former of these gentlemen in Your own hand-writing, which I had long before communicated to me only by a copy. I became soon acquainted with several persons distinguished both by their rank and merit, to whose favour my translation of Your Works serv'd me instead of an introduction and recommendation. The most principal amongst these were Baron *Bernstorff*, a favourite Minister to the King, and Secretary of State in the department of foreign affairs, a *truly great man*, alike respectable for his sense, learning, taste, humanity and piety,—the *Pitt* of Denmark; a Lady *Pless*, born Countess of *Berkentin*, and widow of a Chambellan, and a Countess of *Stolberg*, born Countess of *Castell*, wife to the Count of *Stolberg*, who is, what they call Grand-Gouverneur to the Queen Dowager, and Knight of the Dannebrog; both of them in every respect the most sensible and amiable women I ever saw. The latter, who has got Your *Night-Thoughts* almost by heart, to show her high esteem for You, desir'd me to invite You to do her the honour of standing godfather to the child she then was big of; which afterwards I was prevented to do by various avocations. About three weeks ago I received a letter from her amiable daughter, acquainting me in her mother's name, that, the night before, after having read with her almost the whole day your 7th. Night, she was happily deliver'd of a son; that she had invited the Queen Dowager, Baron *Bernstorff* with his wife and sister, and You, Sir, to be his sponsors at the font; and that she desired me to acquaint You with that news, and to assure You, that she was proud of having chosen the two greatest and worthiest men in the world she knew, and should think herself happy, if You would accept her invitation. I think myself to be so too in having been charged with that agreeable and honourable commission.

Give me leave, Sir, before I conclude, to propose You some questions concerning a few passages of Your *Night-Thoughts*, the meaning of which I don't fully comprehend, and which You'll be so kind as to explain to me at Your leisure. I certainly should not apply to You for it, if I knew any other man that was able to do.

In an Advertissement prefix'd to the third Night I wanted to give some account of *Narcissa*, but could give no other but what I had by report. Whether it be just or not, You may judge. It runs thus: 'Under the name of *Narcissa*, the Author laments the death of his dearly belov'd daughter in law, born Countess of *Litchfield*, betroth'd to the son of Lord *Palmerston*, whom the Poet calls *Philander*, and of whose death-bed he makes such a noble and pathetical description in his first night. They both made a voyage to France, accompany'd by her father, in order to restore their health there; but they died both of 'em, on the way. This circumstance clears up what in the following Night is said concerning the interment of *Narcissa*. Dr. *Young*, on his going back, was himself seized with a violent fever, which is hinted at in the beginning of Night the IId. and VIth. Soon after died *Lucia* his Consort, whose death is but touch'd upon in Night the Vth at the end, but more particularly lamented at the beginning of Night the Sixth. She was, by her mother's side, granddaughter to King Charles II, born Countess of Litchfield, and sister to the Earl, the Vth. Night is inscribed to'— N.IVth, v. 355–57, I translated these lines as litterally as I could, but at the same time confess'd, that there must be a satire or allusion hid under the words: '*scenes* and *vacant* posts,' which appears also from their being printed in Italicks.—Who is (N.VIII.) that *H——* starting at his *Moor*? I remember indeed to have read, I know not where, a story of a gentleman, that imagin'd to have found his mistress at a masquerade, but embrac'd his Moor.—May I ask You, what is meant in the same Night by the Hermitage of *Calista*, which *Lorenzo* is threaten'd to be sent to with *L——*? Is it an allusion to that of the late Queen *Caroline*, where among other statues of philosophers was placed that of *Locke*?

I beg Your pardon for having troubled You so long with my scribble, and for the many faults of expression I must have committed, as I am writing in a language, which I learnt almost without any instruction or practice, tho' by an assiduous reading and study of the English Classicks I endeavour'd to attain to a perfect knowledge of its genius. But perhaps I should not be able in any language whatsoever to express all the sentiments of esteem and veneration, with which I shall always be living and dying,

Reverend Sir,
> Your
>> most humble, most obliged, and most devoted Servant,
>>> I. A. Ebert.

441. [Tu. 16 June 1761].¹ Andrew Millar.

Address: To Mr Millar in ye *strand*.
Bodleian Library, MS. Montagu d. 1 (facsimile).

Pray give the bearer Mr Thrimpton,² the *Night-thoughts*, on my account

> EYoung.

442. Welwyn, Herts. [M.] 29 June 1761. Johann Arnold Ebert.

Not traced.—J. J. Eschenburg, ed., *Eberts Episteln*, Hamburg, 1795, ii. 84–5; Thomas, pp. 607–8.

Dear Sir,
    You fill my heart with gratitude, and cover my cheeks with blushes. How pleasing to our vanity are applauses undeserved, tho' Conscience whispers much better advice! —But of that no more.

    This hour I receiv'd the favour of Your letter; and this hour, as in duty bound, and at heart inclined, I sit down (tho' much indisposed) to answer it. An immediate answer its most obliging contents demand; but my Age and Infirmities (tho' much against my will) confine me to a very short one, which is, as follows.

---

¹ The date is that recording receipt of the letter.
² Not identified.

Please to let the Countess *Stolberg* know, that the surprizing and very high honour, she is pleased to do me, shall be
written on my tomb, which is not far off; and when I rise
from it, I hope, I shall meet my little Godson, and his
excellent Mother, in a place where no lands and seas will
divide me from the blessed pleasure of conversing with
those, whose virtues I love, honour, and admire.

If my health mends, You, very soon, will hear farther from
me; if it does not, You will pardon one, who wants not the
heart, but the hand, to tell You, with how much gratitude
and esteem he is,

Dear Sir,

Your most obedient and obliged humble Servant,

Ed. Young.

P. S. For its compelled brevity, *mea litera erubescit.*—If
You see Mr. *Klopstock*, please to let him know, that I love
his heart, and admire his head, and wish the person, who
gives the world so much pleasure, the full, but late, enjoyment of a pleasure far beyond what the world can give. His
friend and mine, Mr Richardson,

vivit adhuc et vescitur aura aetherea;[1]

but that hand, which has so written, as to touch every heart,
now so trembles, that it can write no more. His years are
drawing to an end, like a tale that is told; a tale, which he can
tell so very well. But he cannot wholly leave us; his *honest
fame* defies the dart of Death.

Pray, Sir, give me leave to present my best respects to my
Coaeval, Your aged Father; and let him know, that I congratulate him on such a Son. A Son, who pays him for a
short life received, by giving life immortal to his Name. For
indeed, Sir, by Your stile I should take You for a native of
Britain; and for a Native of ancient Athens by the sense,
which that stile conveys.

Adieu, Dear Sir, Adieu.

Wellwyn,
June 29. 1761

---

[1] 'Mr. Richardson is living up to this moment and breathes the heavenly air.'
Young is adapting slightly a passage from Virgil's *Aeneid* (i. 546).

443. Welwyn, Herts. [Th.] 2 July 1761. Elizabeth Montagu.

Not traced.¹—Climenson, ii. 248.

Dear Madam,

You and I are playing blind man's buff; we both fancy we are catching something, and we are both mistaken. You say you have sent me two somethings, and I have not received so much as one, and you expected one from me, which is not yet come to your hand, which will kiss your hand this week, and if you are at the trouble of reading it over you will find a sufficient excuse for my delay. By what you say in your kind letter, you give me a very keen appetite for both the books which you promise. I have heard nothing yet of the time of my going to Kew:² when I am there I shall make it my endeavour to enjoy as much of you as I can. I have been in very great pain with my rheumatism for some time, but now, I bless God, I hope the worst is over. May health and peace keep company with that benevolence and genius which are already with you.

I am, dear Madam,
Your much obliged
and most obedient humble Servt
E. Young.

Mrs. Hallows sends her best respects.
Wellwyn, the 2nd July, '61.

¹ Offered for sale by the Rains Galleries of New York City, 27/8 January 1936, as coming from the Mortimer C. Merritt Library, and again by the City Book Auction of New York, 20 November 1943, and once again by Parke-Bernet Galleries of New York City, 18 October 1955. Its present whereabouts is not known.
² i.e. in connection with his new honour of Clerk of the Closet to the Princess Dowager of Wales.

444. [Welwyn, Herts.]. [Tu.] 21 July 1761. Elizabeth Montagu.

Not traced.—Climenson, ii. 251.

Dear Madam,
   On your very kind invitation[1] I have inquired if it is in my power to accept of it, but I am not yet satisfied in that point. Probabilities will not excuse me if her R. H. should go to Kew. I should be very happy to be with you. I have so much to say to you that at present I shall say nothing. You will hear further of me in a little while. I beg my humble service to Mrs. Carter. May the Waters continue to be as serviceable to you as I would be if it was in my power.
                         I am, dear Madam,
                              Your obliged
                    and most obedient humble Servt
                              E. Young.
July 21, 1761.

445. Welwyn, Herts. [Th.] 30 July 1761. Elizabeth Montagu.

Address: To Mrs Montagu / at Tunbridge Wells
Postmark: 31/IV WELWYN.
New Jersey MSS. (Hyde).

Dear Madam
   I am extremely sensible of your favour: I feel it, &, therefore I shall not forget it; but, I have a Friend with me whom I cannot leave; &, I have a Steel water near my own house. and her RH sent me word that she would send to me, when she wanted me; for These reasons I deny myself the great pleasure of waiting on You. I have orderd some stanza's to be sent You,[2] they are of a cooling nature, & may quallify

   [1] Richardson had died on 4 July, and apparently Mrs. Montagu had invited Young to Tunbridge Wells as a relief from depressed spirits.
   [2] On 30 August 1761, after leaving Tunbridge Wells, Mrs. Montagu wrote to Mrs. Carter: 'I found on my table a poem on "Resignation" by Dr. Young; he sent me a copy for you which I will send. . . . You will be pleased I think with what he says of Voltaire, you know we exhorted him to attack a character whose authority is so pernicious' (Climenson, ii. 257).

Your waters, which for some constitutions are too warm.
Mrs Hallows presents her respects to You [;] Mrs Carter
will accept of mine[.] /[verso]/
    I am,
        Dear Madam, with gratitude
and sincerity

                            Your Obligd & Obedient Servt
                                        EYoung.

30 July 1761.

446. [1761]. Frances, Lady Boscawen.

Not traced.—*Resignation*, privately printed; Thomas, pp. 624–5.

Madam
    Not to deceive you by the Title, I must let you know that
tho' Resignation is my chief point, yet I touch on other
Topics; Topics most tending to promote our Attainment of
that supreme Virtue, such as the Vanity of this Life and the
Value of the Next; Patience; Prayer; Death; the great
Goodness of the Deity, etc.
    The greatest part of what, in the following Pages, I have
written to you, I have written also to myself: They stand in
most Need of Resignation that are nearest to their End. God
assist us both in the full use of that Reason which He has
bestowed on us; and then we are sure of his farther favour;
through the Intercession of the Best of Friends; Who
brought us such very glad tidings as may well make the most
heavy News this World can bring to sit light on our hearts.
    What I send you is ill adapted to the present Taste, and I
am sorry to lay you under the Dilemma of being either
Singular, or Dissatisfied with it.
                            Madam
            Your most Obedient and most Humble Servant.

447. [W.] 2 September 1761. Elizabeth Montagu.

Not traced.—Climenson, ii. 257–8.

Dear Madam,

I was in too much haste and ordered a thing[1] to be sent to you (which I suppose you have received) before I had read it myself. On reading it, I find my distance from the Press has occasioned many errors; so that in some Parts I have had the impudence to present you with perfect nonsense.

Page 18, Stanza 2nd, should be thus (viz.)—
    'Earth, a cast Mistress, *then* disgusts, etc.'
Page 34: It should be thus (viz.)—
    'Receive the triple prize, etc.'
Pray pardon this trouble from, dear Madam,
                Your much obliged and most obedient
                      H. Servant,
                      E. Young.

P. S.—I know not how to direct the enclosed,[2] excuse my insolence in desiring you to do it for me.

448. [W.] 2 September 1761. [Unknown].

Victoria and Albert Museum MS.

My Dear & Most honour'd Sir,

I was in too much haste, & ordered a Thing to be sent to you (which I suppose You have receiv'd) before I had read it Myself. On reading it, I find my Distance from the Press has occasioned many Errors; so that in some Parts I have had the impudence to present you with perfect Nonsense.

Page 18 Stanza 2d shod be *thus*,
(viz) Earth, a cast Mistress, *then* disgusts, &c:

[1] *Resignation.*
[2] Possibly the 'enclosed' was Young's letter to Lady Boscawen, just preceding.

Page 34. It shod be *thus*,
(viz) *Receive* the triple Prize &c:

Sepr 2d, 1761.

Pray pardon this trouble from
Hon[oure]d Sir
Your most Obedient
And most Humble Servant
EYoung.

John Jones to Joseph Spence. [Welwyn, Herts.]. [Th.] 3 September 1761.

Not traced.—Joseph Spence, *Anecdotes* . . . , ed. Samuel Weller Singer, 1820, pp. 455–6.

Sep. 3, 1761.

Dear and Esteemd Sir,

I have many times wondered why you never called upon us again at Wellwyn. Dr. Young, I am sure, would have been *glad to have seen you*, and will still be so, every time you pass through this little Hamlet. He told me lately, that if he could see you, he would, or at least can, furnish you with ample materials, nor do I doubt but they will be pertinent, *relating to the life of his late friend Mr. Richardson, the poetical prose-writer.* He expected to have been called to Kew this summer, and if he had been summoned, I intended immediately to write to you. If her Royal Highness the Princess of Wales should *still go thither, you will soon know,* and may have an opportunity of conversing with him there. *He sends* his Respects to You.

I have on a slip of paper noted down what occurred to me since I saw you, about your *ancestor Neville*; and also, what fell in my way to corroborate the account given you by Mr. Pope, relating to the case of *old Noll, and the probability of* his being the Person who came to imspect [*sic*] the corpse of Charles I. at Whitehall, and uttered, *Cruel Necessity,* &c. I am upon the whole inclined to think, that He must have been the Man.

If I can recover those short minutes, you shall have them
on the opposite side; if not, when I shall have the pleasure of
seeing you. But God knows how long I shall continue at
Wellwyn; *For I have still many pressing* calls to return into
Bedfordshire. Please to tell me *privately in a Letter, if you
can* (upon *occasion*) recommend a proper Successor.—I would
have sent you this free postage, but am not sure that your
friend *Mr. Herbert is still in Parliament.*

Believe me to be, Dear Sir,
Your very respectful
and affectionate Servant,
J. JONES

Catherine Talbot[1] to Young. Southwark, Surrey.
[Th.] 3 September 1761.

Bodleian Library, MS. Eng. lett. c. 209, ff. 92–3.

The excellent Poem of an Author long rever'd was recd at
Lambeth some Days ago. The Person to whom it was sent,
little suspecting that she was known even by Name to Dr
Young, was not a little perplex'd to guess by what means
she came to be so greatly oblig'd: She now takes this earliest
Opportunity of returning her most grateful Thanks.

I believe this short Message is all I ought to write; but
alas! Sir, you have thrown so irresistible a Temptation in my
Way, that, however you may suffer by it, you must not
complain.

To talk of a Friend, with whom (during this short Interval
of Life) we can no longer converse, is a pleasing Indulgence
of such Feelings as are not inconsistent with the Resignation
you so admirably teach. Among the many engaging Subjects of Mr. Richardsons Discourse, when He favor'd us with
a Visit, his excellent Friend at Welwyn was always one; &
the last Time He was here he mention'd your being engag'd

---

[1] Catherine Talbot (1721–70) and her mother lived in the household of Thomas
Secker, Archbishop of Canterbury.

in the valuable Work that now lies upon my Table. Had his beneficent Life continued I knew I should have seen /[verso]/ it—but to receive this farther Obligation in a manner from *Him* now He is gone, & to receive it through your own Hands, has peculiarly affected, & delighted me.

Forgive me (if the Question be improper) for asking what is become of a Letter he once told me You intended (& of which He said so much that I was impatient to hear of its being sent) to Monsr Voltaire? Your Address to Him in this Poem must surely, if He has not laugh'd away all Feeling, make Him yet stop on the Verge of Eternity, to look around, & even to look *up*. If you can pursue this charitable Endeavour, & convince Him, or some of his too numerous Readers, that Murmur, & Ridicule are miserable Companions, & fatal Guides, how can even *Your* Moments be better employ'd?

To excuse the Freedom I have taken permit me to say that unknown as I am *You* are my very old Acquaintance, with whom I have past many of my most delightful Hours: You have cost me many a Tear, smooth'd for me many a Care, & imprest such Thoughts upon my Mind as I hope to thank you for a thousand Ages hence. In the mean Time allow me to cherish a Hope that if either /[conjugate leaf]/ the Care of the Press, or Attendance on your royal Mistress should call You awhile from your Retirement, You will sometime or other vouchsafe to bestow half an Hour on

Sir

Your most exceedingly oblig'd
obedient & humble Servt.

C. Talbot

Lambeth
   Sept. 3d 1761.

449. [Welwyn, Herts.] [Tu.] 6 October 1761. George Bubb Dodington, Lord Melcombe.

British Museum, Add. MS. 42560, f. 82ʳ¹.—Historical Manuscripts Commission, *Report on Various Collections: The MSS. of Miss Eyre Matcham*, 1909, p. 50; Shelley, p. 264.

Indeed; my good & honourd Ld! I have not been in Town since January last.—I probably may be mistaken in my fancy'd amendments; but in truth I have done my best; for I was pleas'd & proud of the Task. There is much Noble & Usefull sense in it, Which Will be more applauded than Obey'd.

> I am my Dear Ld!
> With great truth, & Affection
> Yr much Obliged
> & Most Obedient Servt
> EYoung

Octr 6th 1761

I know but little of Lord Bute, but admire his Uncle² as much as you my dear Lord! God preserve you, & prepare us both for the Urn you mention; Pollio³ will soon visit Us here on an equal Foot.

---

¹ The manuscript is a copy of the original by Thomas Warton, the Younger. The original manuscript of the letter has disappeared. It was offered for sale in 1913 by Maggs Bros. (Catalogue No. 303, Lot No. 783), with the following description: 'A. L. s. from Edward Young to Dodington, 1 page, 4to, 17th Oct., 1761. Also the original Autograph MS. of a Poetical Epistle from Dodington to the Earl of Bute, and entitled "Of Wisdom and Cunning and their Consequences", etc. Written on 16pp., folio, and consisting of nearly 300 lines. The Two £5. 5s. In the Letter, Young suggests to Dodington an alteration in the wording of the Epistle.

> Pollio! to thee, my Patron and my Friend
> The secret Councills of my soul I send
> Long since thy Godlike Unkle held me dear
> (Fate gave me, early to thy House's Care)
> He dy'd, and left me Unattach'd and Free,
> Left me, a Legacy from Him to Thee. Etc.'

² John Campbell (1678–1743), second Duke of Argyll, one of the politicians who brought about the fall of Walpole.
³ Bute.

450. [Welwyn, Herts.] [Sa.] 17 October 1761.
George Bubb Dodington, Lord Melcombe.

British Museum Add. MS. 42560, f. 81^{r1}.—Historical Manuscripts Commission, *Report on Various Collections: The MSS. of Miss Eyre Matcham*, 1909, p. 50.

What my Good Lord! if it ran *thus*
(viz)—If we can judge aright
        From a fair Morning of Meridian Light
    As to the Other place, the 2 verses you have reinstated
Sets all right. I am much obliged by the serious Ode you
sent me, as I think it introduces me to your Heart which I
find in good Health. The Ode is a beautifully finished piece.
We in the Country Stare, & Wonder, & look as Wise, and
as well satisfied as we can; & talk much because we know
not what to say. Your thinking some of my Notes not
Useless to you gives me pleasure for indeed, I am

> My dear & Hond: Lord
> Your affectionate
> & much Obliged
> & most Humble Servant
> EYoung

Octr: 17: 1761

    There is an ease & Simplicity in the above alterations
(which I think right Especially in an Epistle) & allmost the
Reverse of Flattery.

451. [Welwyn, Herts.]. [Su.] 18 October 1761.
Duchess of Portland.

Longleat MSS. 275.

May it please Yr Grace,
    You are obligd to your late Hurry for yr higher Relish of
Bullstrode; I am glad to hear your Grace speak of it so much

---

1 As with the preceding letter, this letter is taken from a transcript made by
Thomas Warton, the Younger.

in ye stile of a Lover; a Taste for Retirement is one of our surest Indications of a reasonable mind; & a Passion for ye Throng speaks as loudly ye quite contrary Character; what a Multitude do I abuse?

My Ld Duke, Lady Weymouth, Lady Harriot, & Ld Edward do me great Honour in their kind Remembrance; let them add to ye Favour by their Acceptance of my humble Duty for it.

I have not yet seen, but have sent for his Grace's sermon; & long for ye Pleasure, which I am fully persuaded I shall receive from it. I give You, Madam, & the Publick, Joy of his present Situation.

I receive very melancholy Letters from my poor /[verso]/ Patient Mrs Boscawen; by which I find that I mistook my Talent when I set up for a Physitian. As for Mrs Montagu I have not had ye Honour of seeing her since Aprill; But then her Letters; Your Grace well knows that they can make me ample Amends.

I seriously joyn yr Grace in lamenting ye D. & Dutchess of Leeds.[1] They are my Nighbours, & I honourd them as much, & Know them as well as any Persons whom I never see. Of ye Deceasd I hear a most amiable Character; and I am not at all Surprizd that ye Mother of a Lord Titchfield should severely feel their Loss. That You, Madam, may fully, & long enjoy the very great, & peculiar Blessings which Heaven has bestowd on You, & then change them for Greater, is ye hearty Prayr of

Madam

Yr Graces

Most Obligd

Most Dutifull

& ever Devoted Humble Sevt

EYoung

[In another hand]

Oct 18 1761

[conjugate leaf]

---

[1] They had lost a son of smallpox on 15 August, Thomas, Marquis of Carmarthen, who would have been 14 years of age on 5 October.

PS.

Madam I have an Unknown Correspondent in Worcester-shire, One Mrs Mary Wright, who writes in behalf of 2 excellent young Ladys who are sufferers by Mr Montague, Ly Butes Brother:[1] Tho I am somewhat surprizd at her supposing that my my [*sic*] Intimacy with his Majesty can secure these 2 distressd Ladys a comfortable Pension; Yet what surprizes me most, is, that I receive her Letters under Franks of ye Duke of Portland.

Mrs Hallows has ye Honour of sending her most humble Duty.

As to yt Health wh Yr Grace so kindly enquires after, I bless God it is pretty Good, & I have much more Cause to be greatly Thankfull than to Complain. And very thankfull I am to ye blessed God, & to Those whom He has made my Friends.

Madam it is an exstremely bad Day at Wellwyn. You have good Luck if Bullstrode escapes. /[verso]/

Madam

Since I writ my Letter I receivd what I take ye Liberty to inclose. Yr Grace may possibly understand it; tis Mysterious to me.

Baron Melcombe (Dodington) to Young. Hammer-smith, Mdx.[2] [Tu.] 27 October 1761.

Bodleian Library, MS. Malone 26, f. 161.—Croft, 1781, iv. 415; Joseph Spence, *Anecdotes* . . ., ed. Samuel Weller Singer, 1820, pp. 456–8; Nichols–Doran, *Works*, 1854, ii. 83.

La Trappe, Octr 27th 1761

Dear Dr

Ye seem'd to like the Ode I sent you for your Amusement, I now send it you as a Present.[3] If you please to accept of it,

---

[1] Edward Wortley Montagu (1713–76), Lady Mary's scapegrace son, who had come into his inheritance at the death of his father in January.

[2] Site of Dodington's country home 'La Trappe'.

[3] The letter was accompanied by two sets of verses, published in the Nichols–Doran edition of Young's *Works*.

and are willing our Friendship should be known when we are gone you will be pleas'd to leave this among those of your Papers, which may possibly see the Light by a posthumous Publication.[1] God send us Health while we stay /[verso]/ and an easy Journey

My dear Dr Young
Yours most cordially
Melcombe

452. [Th.] 29 October 1761. George Bubb Dodington, Lord Melcombe.

British Museum, Add. MS. 42560 f. 81ᵛ.[2]

My dear & Honourd Lord
The verses I sent you on Resignation were not designed for the Publick; but I find they are got into Hand's which will publish them when they dare; & I may not long keep them in awe: I will therefore publish it myself And to that End I have altered it Much the present Beginning of it is on the other side Now the question, My Lord is; if the Striking verses, you are so kind as to have written to me might not with sufficient propriety be Prefixd I think there *happens* to be a peculiar Propriety in it, considering the Similar Contents of Both. Your Judgement & pleasure on this Point is humbly desird My Dear Lord by

Yr most Devoted
& obedient Servt
E Young

Octr: 29 1761

Genius Soars, & virtue guides
Where Omnipotence resides
          Suppose it was *thus*
He who Parts & Virtue gave,
Bad thee Look beyond the Grave;

---

[1] Dodington died nine months later, on 28 July 1762.
[2] The manuscript is a transcription of the original by Thomas Warton, the Younger.

Genius Soars, & Virtue guides,
When the Love of God presides.
There's a Gulph twixt us, & God
Let the dreadfull Path be trod,
Why stand Shivring on the Shore? &c.[1]

453. [Welwyn, Herts.]. [Su.] 28 February 1762. George Keate.

Postmark: 1/MR.
British Museum, Add. MS. 30992, f. 5.—Thomas, p. 613; Dapp, p. 36.

Dear Sir
    I thank You for Your kind, and valuable, & luckily timed present.[2] I have long been ill of a Fever; & am but just creeping out; the pleasure your piece gave me, was of the cordial kind, & I think I am the better for it; the work you mention I have not yet seen, when I have my opinion shall be no secret from You. I wish you better health than is at present enjoyed by

Dear Sir
Your obedient and
faithful humble servant
EYoung.

28 Feby:
1762

454. [? Welwyn, Herts.]. [? Spring 1762]. George Keate.

Not traced.[3]

    [1] The verses are Young's suggestions for Dodington's verses that had accompanied his letter to Young of 27 October.
    [2] Probably a draft or early printed copy of Keate's *Epistle from Lady Jane Grey to Lord Guilford Dudley*, published later this year, and indebted to Young's treatment of the subject in *The Force of Religion, or Vanquished Love* (1714).
    [3] At this point in the collection of Keate letters to Young in the British Museum is a record of a sixth letter 'given to Mrs. T. Tyhe', otherwise unidentified (British Museum, Add. MS. 30992, f. 6).

455. [Welwyn, Herts.] [Su.] 14 March 1762. Duchess of Portland.

Longleat MSS. 278.

March 14
1762

May it please yr Grace
    The first Use I make of my longdisabled Hand is to pay my Duty where so greatly due; I have been long ill, & since I see such Numbers in this pretty severe season drop around me, a great Blessing is it yt I am still alive.
    I have made, Madam, a Winter's Campaign in my Chamber; fought a long Fever, wh drew much Blood from me; ye Physitian stood by, & saw ye Battle, & sometimes took Part with ye Disease, tho He had a Subsidy from me.
    I hope there has been no Bloodshed at Whitehall, that all there is in perfect Peace; tho there seems to be an allyd Army of Casualtys, & Distempers in ye Field. Fever & Rheumatism are to me as formidable as France, & Spain.
/[verso]/
    May you Madam, his Grace, Ld Titchfield, Lady Harriot, Ld Edward, enjoy all your Desires, accept my humble Duty, & best Wishes, rejoyce in each other, & in His continual Favour, & Protection, who can give Comfort in sickness, & Joy in Death; the First I have experienced, God grant the Last. Illness, and Age were designd to make us serious; Happy they that are so, without their Aid,

nor can I ever be more so
all
than when I subscribe myself with   possible Respect, and Gratitude

Madam,
Yr Graces Devoted
& most Obligd, & most Obedient
Humble Sevt
E Young.

456. [Welwyn, Herts.]. [Th.] 27 May 1762. Duchess of Portland.

Longleat MSS. 277.—Bath, p. 326; Shelley, p. 265.

May it please yr Grace.

Of all ye severe Dispensations,[1] with which a good God is pleasd [to] wean our Affections from those Objects, wh can never satisfie them, ye most severe, is ye Loss of those we love: And if by his Grace, & our own Prudence we can support our spirits under That, we may congratulate ourselves on a Magnanimity that is able to stand ye greatest Shock of this short scene; into wh we were brought with no other Intent, than by our Gratitude for its Comforts, and Acquiescence in its Discipline to make ourselves fit Candidates for that glorious scene, where Fears shall be wipd from every Eye. /[verso]/

Madam

May that Friend who will never leave, or forsake us, continue to speak Peace to your soul, by inspiring it with true Discernment of those Blessings, which are wrapd up in the melancholy Veil of our present Afflictions; & with ye most lively Hope of those Joys, which are free from all those unple^a sant, but wholesome Ingredients, wh ever imbitter ye highest Happiness of human Life: This is ye fervent Prayr of

Madam
Yr Graces
Most Dutifull
& most Devoted
Humble Sevt
EYoung

I beg my Duty & best
Wishes to his Grace,[2] Ly Harriet,
& Ld Edward.

May 27
1762

[1] The Duke of Portland died on 1 May in his 63rd year.
[2] Lord Tichfield has now become the third Duke of Portland.

John Jones to Young. [?Welwyn, Herts.] [Th.]
27 May 1762.

Dr. Williams's Library, Jones papers, B. 17 [3] (6).

27 May 1762

Reverend Sir,
    Pursuant to my late respectful intimations to you in
transient conversation upon the Subject of my present ill
health & the unpromising aspect of some of my affairs,
which disable me very much from doing you & your parish
all the service I could wish; I judge it to be a point of honour
& decency as well as prudence on my part, to give you this
timely notice in writing, That as my health & affairs now
stand I dare not take upon me the farther supply of your
charge at Wellwyn beyond Michaelmas /[verso]/ mas [*sic*]
next; when, if it be the will of Providence to permit it, I shall
have completed with you upon that charge (I hope without
discredit to you or to myself) the revolution of five years;
hoping then to resign my trust with the same probity & good
conscience with which I at first undertook it, & have ever
since endeavoured to execute it.
    I have been unsuccessful in both my late attempts to
provide for you a proper Successor in the cure. Nothing in
my little power hath been wanting to oblige & accommodate
you herein. And as I can do no more myself, nor have any
farther prospect of Success in this matter, I must & do
humbly refer it to your own better Success upon trial. [con-
jugate leaf]/
    I thank you, Sir, very heartily for all favours to me during
my stay with you; and desire you to continue a kind remembrance of me after I am gone from you.[1]
    If I can well be of service to you in my succeeding
Situation, you may command me.
    I flatter myself that my distance from you will not be so
great on this change, but that I may sometimes without much

---

[1] On 28 August, Jones wrote to Thomas Birch of his intention of staying on
with Young out of 'compassion and humanity' (John Nichols, *Literary Anecdotes*,
1812, i. 620–1).

inconvenience make a short excursion to see you; being,
with all due regard and deference,

> Reverend Sir,
> Your most obedient
> humble Servant
> J. Jones.

To the reverd
Dr Young

**457. [Welwyn, Herts.] [Tu.] 1 June 1762. Duchess
of Portland.**

Longleat MSS. 279.—Bath, pp. 226–7; Shelley, pp. 265–6.

May it please Yr Grace.

I read your Letter with uncommon Pleasure: No sight
is more delightfull, or more beneficial, than that of a rightly
disposd Mind: If Britain could show us more of them, it
would be an happier World than that in which we, now, live.
The whole Secret of being Happy ourselves, and making
those so, that are near us, Is, to preserve a a [*sic*] true Relish
of Life, unabated by any anxious Fear of Death. Providence
has provided for your Grace what may make Life most palatable; may it long continue to You, Madam. *Such* Children;
& to them *Such* Dispositions. It is not only a great, but a very
rare Blessing; and your Grace can scarce look anywhere out
of your own Family, without seeing great Cause for rejoycing
in it. And all Blessings are doubled by ye Peculiarity of them.

May, Madam, Bullstrode Air second your Prudence to ye
perfect Reestablishment of yr Health: /[verso]/ As for my
own, which wth that of Multitudes more, has suffered much
through ye Whole of ye late unwholesome season, it is but
indifferent: I have not, I bless God, much Pain, but much
Languor: If it was Less, I would certainly pay my humble
Duty to your Grace; if it should be much More with due

submission to ye divine Will I must pay my Duty to Heaven:
In either Case I shall equally, & most sincerely be,

Madam

Yr Graces

Most Obedient, &

Ever Dutifull

Humble Sevt

EYoung.

May his Grace, & Ly Harriot
accept my humble Duty;
And wth great Gratitude
for yr Grace's Notice
Mrs Hallows begs You
will accept of Hers.
June 1st
1762

458. Welwyn, Herts. [Tu.] 27 July 1762. Duchess of Portland.

Longleat MSS. 280.

[In an unidentified hand]

May it please Your Grace,

I have long flatter'd my self, with the pleasing, and Ambitious hopes, of paying my duty at Bullstrode; but I find
it is beyond my power: Many have complain'd of their Eyes,
in the late unwholsome season; Mine, which were never
good, have suffer'd greatly: God's blessed will be done, but
I fear the worst. I am forced to borrow a hand to write this.[1]

Therefore, Madam, I humbly beg your Grace, not to
misconster[2] my conduct into any disrespect, indeed, it is

[1] In a letter to Thomas Birch at this time, Jones had remarked on Young's
being 'in a pretty odd way of late, moping, dejected, self-willed, and as if surrounded with some perplexing circumstances' (John Nichols, *Literary Anecdotes*,
1812, i. 620). In this same letter Jones told of having 'at last obtained of Dr.
Young the two manuscripts in folio containing a collection of Mr. Doddington's
Letters during his residence at Venice, for a present to the British Museum'.
Again, on 28 January 1764, Jones reported receipt of a third volume of these
letters for the Museum (op. cit., p. 626).

[2] A variant of the modern 'misconstrue'.

infinitely far from it; for I am, with the most profound regard, sincere gratitude, and earnest prayer for Your welfare,
& the welfare of all whom you hold dear,

Madam /[verso]/

Your Grace's

Most obedient,

And devoted humble Servant

EYoung.

Wellwyn July 27,
     1762.

Madam
          I beg my duty to Lady Harriot,
and best service, to Mr Ashare.

459. Welwyn, Herts. [Tu.] 3 August 1762. Duchess of Portland.

Longleat MSS. 281.

[In an unidentified hand]

May it please your Grace
     Infinite thanks are due for your most kind, and most
indulgent Invitation, but by my Letter to your Grace, You
have seen how absolutely incapable I am of enjoying it.
                                                    not
     My sight is so much impar'd—But I must   complain;
at my Years many are worse; Heaven's Will be done; May
this misfortune Teach me, more clearly to see the things
that are Invisible; the blessed hope of Which, is the only
                                           ents
thing that can render Life's enjoym   truly sweet, or
alleviate those troubles which no soul shall escape: Those
hopes, will gradually remove whatever of Disagreeable
[nature] may now, Naturally hang on Your Graces Mind,
and restore the delightful Habitation of Bullstrode to its
former Lustre.
     /[verso]/ My Lord Duke did me the honour of Calling
Upon me but his stay was very short. I beg my Duty to Lady
Harriot and Lord Edward and my best Wishes to Mr

Arshard. May they all contribute their respective shares (as
I am perswaded they will) towards Your Graces happiness,
and so join the sincere Prayr of
                           Madam
                                Your Graces most Obliged
                                         devoted
                           And most   humble Servant
                                         EYoung.
Wellwyn
August 3d
    1762

Mrs Hallows begs her humble Duty to your Gra[ce]

460. [Welwyn, Herts.] [Tu.] 24 August 1762.
Duchess of Portland.

Address: To / Her Grace the Dutchess of Portland / at Bullstrode / Bucks.
Postmark: 25/AU.
Longleat MSS. 282–3.—Bath, p. 327; Shelley, pp. 266–7.

[In the hand of Mrs. Hallows]
                                    Wellwyn Aug 24, 1762
May it please Your Grace,
   I congratulate you, on Prudence and spirit to go abroad,
in quest of Rational Amusements & its sweet Companion
Health; Which may You ever find. I am sadly Confind, by
my sight greatly impaired; and other Complaints, which I
am unwilling to trouble Your Grace withall; My Case is
this; I have been troubled near Thirty years, with Rheumatic
Pains; they have been now long entirely ceased; and my
                                                        i
Physitians tell me, that Nature throws all that Misch ef on
my Eyes, & Head; which has undergone, & is still under-
going great discipline, & to very little purpose; This is bad,
but what greatly aggrevates it is, that it denies me the power,
which from my soul I ardently desire, of paying that Duty,
which I shall ever owe to your Grace. But notwithstanding
all I have said, and all I feel, Notwithstanding Dark Days, &
sleepless Nights, such is my Age that I must not complain.

Heaven's blessed Will be done; And may it not deny me the comfort of seeing those in Felicity, whose welfare, I am bound in gratitude to have most at Heart.

I pray, Madam, my Duty to Lady Harriot, & Lord Edward, & true regard to Mr Arshard. In sickness as well as in Health

I am

Madam Your Graces most Dutiful

And most devoted Humble Servant

EYoung.

Mrs Hallows begs
leave to profess
herself Your Graces
most Dutiful humble Servant.

461. Welwyn, Herts. [Tu.] 2 September 1762. George Keate.

British Museum, Add. MS. 30992, f. 7.—Thomas, p. 614; Shelley, p. 267.

Wellwyn Sepr 2d. 1762

Dear Sir

I much thank you for your kind enquiery after my Health; I wish I coud return such an answer as I know woud be most agreeable to you, but it is far otherways; I am, & have long been much out of order, my sight is so far gone that I am obl[i]ged to borrow a hand to write to you. Rheumatic pains of thirty years standing are entirely ceased, & have been so for half a Year: The fatal consequence of which is that the malignity is fallen on my Head & Eyes; for which I have long undergone, & still undergo severe discipline, & to very little purpose.

When I am capable of writing to you in a more agreeable manner You shall hear further from Dear Sir,

Your faithful & Obed: Servant

EYoung

Much thanks for
your kind Present.[1]

---

[1] The 'present' is not known. It may have been a copy of Lord Melcombe's lines addressed to Young and published in *The Public Advertiser* on 23 August. See Young's letter to the Duchess of 8 January 1763.

462. [Welwyn, Herts.] [?Autumn 1762]. Duchess of Portland.

Longleat MSS. 297.

[In the hand of Mrs. Hallows]

May it please your Grace

God grant that you may long enjoy those little Amiable Associates, which are now giving so great delight: Till you are so happy as to converse with Angels, Your Grace must despair of better Company. The pleasure of Heaven, as I conceive, consists chiefly, in the outflowings of kind affection, on Objects worthy of it.

I beg Lady Weymouth, Lady Harriot, & Lord Edward, to acept my humble duty. But what shall I say to Your Grace? Indeed I am at a loss; Your kind regard to my present distress, touches my Heart, & fills me with infinite gratitude for it: I shall make the best use, of the kind advice You are so /[verso]/ good, to give me: But my very Late time of day, forbids any sanguin hopes of much releif, but we must do our best; and patiently acquiesce in the divine Providence, for the result; how meloncholy so ever our own condition may happen to be; the happiness of our Best Friends, will shed no small comfort on it.[1] That your Graces may be Great, and Lasting, is the Prayer,

of Madam

Your Graces most devoted

And most Obliged hum^ble Serv^ent

EYoung.

Mrs Hallows
begs your Graces
Acceptance of
her humble duty.
Pray Madam, my best respects to Mr Arshard.

[1] Adding to Young's troublesome health and loss of sight at this time was a disturbing situation reported by Jones in a letter to Birch of 4 September: 'The loss of a very large sum of money, above 200*l.*, is talked of; whereof this vill[age] and neighbourhood is full. Some disbelieve; others say, "It is no wonder, where, about eighteen or more servants are sometimes taken and dismissed in the course of a year"' (John Nichols, *Literary Anecdotes*, 1812, i. 622). That there was something to the gossip appears from Young's account with Gosling's bank showing that he had been sent £500 in 24 bank notes on 2 September.

463. [Welwyn, Herts.] [? September 1762]. Mrs. Anne Brett.[1]

Not traced.—*The Literary Gazette and Journal of Belles Lettres, Arts, Sciences, &c.*, 29 April 1862, p. 266.[2]

Madam,—The second part of the thing you speak of, [3] I wrote at Lyons in France; where, by the carelessness of a servant, it was left behind, nor could I ever recover it. But why are you so inquisitive about these matters? It must be owing to your prudent concern for those good things which can never be lost; of which I give you great joy. May we ever think intensely of things inconceivable and eternal! then shall we become those happy glorious, and rare beings, which may be called Christians indeed: then shall we smile at the world's terror, and rejoice at the thoughts of death.

I am, Madam, your faithful humble servant.

E. Young.

Philander was the husband of Narcissa.[4]

464. Welwyn, Herts. [Su.] 19 September 1762. Mrs. Anne Brett.

Not traced.—*The Literary Gazette and Journal of Belles Lettres, Arts, Sciences, &c.*, 29 April 1862, p. 266.

Madam,—Philander was both my son-in-law and my friend.[5] Nothing but your regard for religion, could so much engage

---

[1] The identity of Mrs. Brett has not been established.

[2] Although this letter follows the next one in its original published form, the context suggests that it was Young's first, and evasive, attempt to answer Mrs. Brett's question about the identity of the prototype of 'Philander' in the *Night-Thoughts*.

[3] The allusion is almost certainly to a proposal made by Young in the last paragraph of *A Vindication of Providence* (1728) in which he promised to 'infer a true estimate of human life' in a second discourse. In 1754 there appeared *A New Estimate of Human Life* whose authorship has not been determined, although it was ascribed to a 'Dr. Hill' by the editor of the fifth volume of Young's *Works* (1773).

[4] In terms of Young's identification of 'Philander' in the next letter to Mrs. Brett, 'Narcissa' becomes his stepdaughter, Elizabeth Lee.

[5] i.e. Henry Temple.

your attention to that work. I congratulate you on your care
for the next world; our want of care for that, occasions all
our troubles in this. For what can trouble those who have an
eternity of joy in their power? Their troubles, if they have
any, well bourn, are the greatest good, as they, of all things,
most promote their salvation.

I am, Madam, your humble servant.
E. Young.

Wellwyn, Sept. 19, 1762.

465. Welwyn, Herts. [Th.] 25 November 1762. Thomas Newcomb.

Address: To the Rev. Mr. Thos. Newcomb at Hackney near London.
Not traced.—*The Gentleman's Magazine*, lxvii (February 1797), 91; John
Nichols, *Literary Anecdotes of the Eighteenth Century*, 1812, ii. 698; Nichols–
Doran, *Works*, 1854, i. cvi–cvii; Shelley, pp. 267–8.

Welwyn, Nov. 25, 1762.

My Dear Old Friend,
    And now, my only dear old Friend, for your namesake
Colburn[1] is dead; he died last winter of a cold, caught by
officiating on the Fast-day: he has left one daughter, I
believe in pretty good circumstances; for a friend of his,
some time ago, settled upon her twenty pounds a year; and
he, no doubt, has left her something considerable himself.
I am pleased with the stanzas you sent me;[2] there is nothing
in them of *eighty-seven*; and if you have been as young in
your attempt on the Death of Abel,[3] it will do you credit;
that work I have read, and think it deserves that reception
it has met withal. The Libel you mention, I have not seen;
but I have seen numberless papers which shew that our body
politic is far from being in perfect health: as for my own
health, I do not love to complain; but one particular I must
tell you, that my sight is so far gone, as to lay me under the

---

[1] i.e. Thomas Colburn.
[2] Possibly the stanzas were Newcomb's 'congratulatory ode' *On the Success of the
British Arms . . . addressed to His Majesty*, published in 1763.
[3] This 'sacred poem, written originally in the German language' is said to have
been published in 1763, but from the date of Young's letter would appear to have
been earlier.

necessity of borrowing a hand to write this. God grant me grace, under this darkness, to see more clearly things invisible and eternal; those great things which you and I must soon be acquainted with! And why not rejoice at it? There is not a day of my long life that I desire to repeat; and at fourscore it is all *labour and sorrow*. What then have we to do? But one thing remains, and in that one, blessed be God! by his assistance we are sure of success. Let nothing, therefore lie heavy on your heart; let us rely on Him who has done so great things for us; that lover of souls; that hearer of prayers, whenever they come from the heart; and sure rewarder of all those who love Him, and put their trust in his mercy. Let us not be discontented with this world: that is bad; but it is still worse to be satisfied with it, so satisfied, as not to be very anxious for something more.

My love and best wishes attend you both; and I am, my good old friend, sincerely yours,

E. Young.

P. S. I am persuaded that you are mistaken as to your age; you write yourself eighty-seven, which cannot be the case; for I always thought myself older than you, and I want considerably of that age. If it is worth your while, satisfy me as to this particular.

466. [Welwyn, Herts.] [Th.] 2 December 1762. George Keate.

British Museum, Add. MS. 30992, f. 8.—Thomas, pp. 614–15; Shelley, p. 269; Dapp, p. 37.

Dear Sir

I receive your repeated favours with gratitude; but also with consern: Forbare to oppress me with them. I shod see your Face at Wellwyn with more joy, if you ran my inability to return them, less in debt: All that is in my little power is at your service; my power allways little, but now less: The misfortune I mentioned to you in my last letter hangs heavy on me; Books, my wonted refuge are of no further use.

And, Wisdom at One entrance, quite shut out. But this is a Melancholy subject both to you & me: Pardon therefore this short Letter, nor measure my regard by it; for I am truly

Dear Sir

Your Affectionate & Obedt Servant

EYoung.

Decr 2d
1762.

Mrs Hallows gives her Compliment

467. Welwyn, Herts. [Su.] 2 January 1763. Duchess of Portland.

Longleat MSS. 228.

[written in the hand of Mrs. Hallows]

May it please your Grace

As a person of 83,[1] may be allowed to doubt, if he shall congratulate your Grace on another New Year, give me leave Madam, to wish You, & Yours, (to whom my humble duty) all that happiness, which this ever-changing (& to the Good only Comfortable) Scene will admit.

As my days of Writing, and even of Reading, are Over, excuse me, if I endeavour to give You, some small amusement, by a scrap of writing, from another Hand. The following Lines, were sent me by the Ld Melcombe, scarce a Month before his Death,[2] & may seem to be somewhat Ominous of it.

> Kind Companion of my Youth,
> Lov'd for Genius, Worth, and Truth!
> Take what Friendship can impart,
> Tribute of a feeling Heart,
> Take the Muse's latest Spark,
> E'er we drop into the Dark /[verso]/

[1] Young will be 80 in the summer; he was baptized 3 July 1683 in the parish of Upham, Hampshire.

[2] Lord Melcombe died 28 July 1762. The lines were published in *The Public Advertiser* of 23 August 1762 under the title: 'Lord Melcombe to Dr. Young, not long before his Lordship's Death.'

> He who Parts, and Virtue gave,
> Bad thee look beyond the Grave,
> Genius soars, and Virtue guides,
> Where the Love of God presides.
>   There's a Gulph, 'twixt Us, and God,
> Let the gloomy Path be trod
> Why stand shivering on the shore?
> Why not boldly venture o'er?
> Where unerring Virtue guides
> Let us brave the Winds and Tides,
> Safe thro Seas of Doubts, and Fears,
> Rides the Bark, which Virtue steers.

Thus, Madam, My good Friend took a short step thro the House of Lords, into that long Home where Lords & Commons, & all Us, their most Inferiors, are on a perfect Level; and who, from that Level, will rise highest God only knows. How greatly incumbent is it on us all to think on this, and to court our Utmost, for His Almighty Favour? /[conjugate leaf]/
I am, Madam,

> With most sincere & profound Respect
> Your Graces most indebted
> And dutiful humble Servant
>   EYoung.

Pray, Madam,
my service & best wishes to Mr. Ashard
Mrs Hallows desires her humble Duty to your Grace
Wellwyn Jan 2d 1763

468. Welwyn, Herts. [Tu.] 4 January 1763. George Keate.

British Museum, Add. MS. 30992, f. 9.—Thomas, p. 615; Shelley, p. 270.

Dear Sir
    I have the very great pleasure to let you know, that the very humble wish, which you make at the latter end of your Letter, is not made in vain.

As for the task you assign me; the feebleness of my sight, has given me an utter aversion to a pen & ink; & probably, it is very lucky that it has done so; for, there is some reason to fear, that I have not so many spirits to spare on any under-taking, as I had some years agoe; but, on this head, I shall speak further, when I have the pleasure of seeing you Here, which perhaps, may give me those spirits, which are now wanting, to

Dear Sir,
Your affectionate,
and obliged humble servant
EYoung.

Wellwyn,
Jany. 4th,
    1763.

469. Welwyn, Herts. [Th.] 13 January 1763. Duchess of Portland.

Longleat MSS. 230.

[In an unidentified hand]

May it please your Grace.

As you do not disapprove of my Lord Melcombs Lines; I beg leave to send You some more of the same serious Cast, & by the same Hand, which were sent to me by him, at the same time with the Former. And this I do the rather, because in the first Stanza, he seems to me, to prophesie our present political Animosities: And, so Congratulate himself, on his nicely-tim'd, & narrow escape from them———

An Ode.

I

Love thy Country, wish it well,
    Not with too intense a Care,
'Tis enough, that when it fell,
    I, its Ruin did not share. /[verso]

2

Envy's Censure, Flattery's Praise,
   With unmov'd Indifference, view;
Learn to tread Life's dangerous Maze
   With unerring Virtue's Clue.

3

Void of strong Desire and Fear,
   Lifes wide Ocean trust no more;
Strive thy little Bark to steer
   With the Tide, but near the Shore.

4

Thus prepar'd, thy, shortned Sail,
   Shal, when'er the Winds encrease,
Seizing each propitious Gale,
   Waft thee to the Port of Peace.

5

Keep thy Conscience from Offence,
   And, Tempestuous Passions free,
               /[conjugate leaf]/
So, when thou art call'd from Hence,
   Easy shall thy Passage be;

6

Easie shall thy Passage be,
   Cheerfull, thy alloted Stay;
Short th' Account 'twixt God, and Thee,
   Hope shall meet thee on the Way,

7

Truth shall lead thee to the Gate,
   Mercy's self shall let thee in;
Where, its never-changing State,
           Enjoyment
Full ~~Perfection~~ shall begin.

Madam

These Lines, tho' written I believe, in an embroider'd Coat, an Archbishop need not, as I take it, look on them, as beneath his Solemnity.

/[verso]/ I am sorry Mrs M has chosen Sunday evening; for, Religion has not met with greater enemies from any quarter, than from Philosophers, Politi[ci]ons, & Wits. Few Wits consider, that their brightest Abilities are nonsense, unless they teach them two very plain lessons; which are often beneath their Ambition, (viz) to lie down in Peace, & to Rise in Glory. I beg my humble Duty to Lady Harriot & Lord Edward, & my true regard to Mr Ashard

I am

Madam

Your Grace's most indebted

and most devoted humble servant

EYoung

Wellwyn 13nth Jany
1763

470. Welwyn, Herts. [Su.] 6 February 1763. Thomas Broughton.[1]

Yale University Library (Osborn Collection).

Revd Sir

Having often supply'd this Neighbourhood myself with Books of Piety, I have the more difficulty, & was forced to take the greater time, to dispose of those with which I was favour'd by the Society. Please to accept of the Note on the other Page, for the use of this Charity.[2]

from

Revd Sir

Your faithful humble sevt

EYoung

Wellwyn
Hertfordshire
     Feb: 6th
         1763

---

[1] Secretary of the Society for the Propagation of Christian Knowledge. He is identified by reference to the banknote in the second sentence. The letter has been endorsed: 'Herts Welwyn 6 Feby 1763 25272 Dr Young Recd 8 Feb 1763 Ansd 10 do T. B.'

[2] Young's cheque for five guineas made out to Thomas Broughton for the S.P.C.K. was paid at the Gosling bank on 18 February.

471. Welwyn, Herts. [Su.] 27 February 1763. James Elphinston.

Not traced.[1]—*Forty Years' Correspondence between Geniusses ov boath sexes and J. E.*, 1791, i. 107.

Sir,

I thank you much for your valuable present.[2] I think there is a spirit in your poetry, and a propriety in your plan; and that the world may be the better for them both. If I were better in health, I should be more particular. But as, from my age, I have small cause to presume, that that will mend; pray be so good as to excuse,

> Sir,
> your obliged,
> and most humble servant,
> E. Young.

Welwyn.
Feb. 27, 1763.

472. [?Welwyn, Herts.] [Spring 1763.] Earl of Bute.

Not traced.[3]

[1] The manuscript of this letter was offered for sale by Parke-Bernet Galleries of New York 17–18 October 1944 as from the Drexel Institute of Technology of Philadelphia; its present location is not known. The present text has been restored to contemporary spelling from the phonetic transliteration of its published form following the practice of Elphinston.

[2] i.e. verses entitled: *Education.*

[3] Evidence of this letter is Young's letter to the Duchess of Portland of 2 June 1763, in which he wrote: '. . . that letter I answered long since, with my fullest acknowledgments to my Lord Bute for his unmerited indulgence to me.'

---

473. Welwyn, Herts. [Th.] 24 March 1763. George Keate.

British Museum, Add. MS. 30992, f. 10.—Thomas, p. 615; Dapp, p. 49.

Dear Sir

I thank you much for the pleasure You have given me, in reading your poem;¹ & thank You still more, for the pleasure you promise me, in your good company: I am disengaged, and am

Dear Sir, your Affectionate
and faithful, & Obedient servant
EYoung

Wellwyn
24 March
    1763.

P.S. I like the Poem much in General for the Novelty of its Subject & Variety in its Composition.

---

474. Welwyn, Herts. [Th.] 14 April 1763. George Keate.

Address: To George Keate / At Archibalds / in Harley Street. *Postmark*: 15/ AP. British Museum, Add. MS. 30992, f. 11.—Thomas, p. 616.

Wellwyn April 14th 1763.

Dear Sir

What you say conserning the Term *Fancy* may, for ought I know, be very just; I therefore drop my opinion about it.

As for the Inscription, I am too vain to make any Objection to it; but not so very vain, as not to thank you for it.²

As to my health, I bless God I am pretty well but suspect myself to be a little older, than I was ~~forty years agoe~~; I wish Age & Wisdom were inseperable; but if they were, one Ounce of Wisdom in Youth, in the ballance of the sanctuary,

---

¹ Keate's blank verse poem *The Alps* was published on 25 April.
² Keate had dedicated *The Alps* to Young.

outweighs a pound in Grey hairs; I congratulate you therefore, on having much the Advantage of, Dear Sir,

Your very Affectionate, and
Obliged humble servant.
EYoung.

Mrs Hallows sends her Comp[liment]s.

**475. Welwyn, Herts. [Th.] 28 April 1763. Andrew
Millar.**

Address: To Mr Millar / Bookseller in the Strand / London. *Postmark*: 28/AP.
Victoria and Albert Museum, Forster 9709, 5, f. 31.

Dear Sir,

I remember that to the *Night* ~~ninth~~ inscribed to the Duke
of Newcastle, I prefix'd some verses, but I do not remember
that there was any thing of the *Rebellion* in them; but whatever they were, they are the Property of Mr. Dodsley to
whom that Night was sold,[1] I wish you success in Your
present proceeding, and am with Mrs Hallows's & my
Comps: to Mr Millar

Dear Sir
Your faithful humble Servant
EYoung

Wellwyn
April 28
1763

[1] It is 'Night the ninth' which Young had dedicated to the Duke of Newcastle
and to which he had appended 'Some Thoughts occasioned by the present Juncture',
namely, the conduct of the government in the Jacobite rebellion of 1745. It was sold,
however, to Millar and not to Dodsley (see Appendix A). On 3 June, following this
letter, Millar and James Dodsley were awarded an injunction against Robert Taylor
forbidding his 'printing publishing & vending' any more of 'a Book intitled The
Complaint or Night Thoughts on life, death & Immortality to w[hi]ch are added
some thoughts on the late Rebellion & a Paraphrase on part of the Book of Job
Edinburgh printed by A. Donaldson & T. Reid for Alexander Donaldson 1761
price 3s bound', a publication dubbed 'a pirated Edition' (Public Record Office,
C33 Part 2 420/307).

---

476. Welwyn, Herts. [Th.] 3 May 1763. George Keate.

British Museum, Add. MS. 30992, f. 12.—Thomas, p. 616; Dapp, p. 50.

Welwyn May 3d 1763

Dear Sir

I am glad you sent one of your Poems to Mrs Montagu,
I am glad of it for her sake, & your own, for her sake because
she knows how to relish your favour, & for your own because
it will give a begining to an acquaintance, wch will give
you no small pleasure, & perhaps some surprize, surpriz,
[*sic*] at finding a bright power in another sex, but rarely to
be found in your own.

As to my health, it is not so good as I coud wish but better
than I ought to expect, it is so good, as to demand my utmost
thanks to God that 'tis no worse, but not so good, as not to
want a cordial under it, and I know of none more powerful,
than that which refreshes us, from the face of a Friend. I am,
Dear Sir, Your faithful, Aaffectionate [*sic*] and Obliged
humble servant EYoung.

477. Welwyn, Herts. [W.] 1 June 1763. Johann Arnold Ebert.

Not traced.—J. J. Eschenburg, ed., *Eberts Episteln*, Hamburg, 1795, ii.
88–9; Thomas, pp. 608–9.

My dear Sir,

The late Earl of *Granville*, who was a perfect master of
Your language, having heard, that You had translated the
first part of the Night-Thoughts, desired it of me, and
highly approved of Your performance. The second part I
have not yet received. I am obliged to You for translating
the *Resignation*. I am sorry, I did not furnish You with
something more worthy such a Patronage.

I beg my profound respect to the Countess of *Stolberg*,
my very best wishes to Her, to Mylord, and my little

Godson, who, I hope, will resemble them in the features of his mind, that thus the benefit of their excellent examples may be a blessing to more than the present times. I will take care, that Abbé *Arnaud's* Character of my dear friend, Mr. *Richardson*, shall be prefix'd to his Works.[1] Mr *Warton's* second Part of *Pope* is in great readiness, and I believe, You may see it soon.[2] My sight is so bad, that I can examine nothing, and if it was not, so bad at present is my health, that I can attend to nothing. I should take the greatest pleasure in complying with Your request, and any other of Your commands which, will ever be most welcome to me, who am, with the most cordial good wishes, and highest esteem,

Dear Sir,
Your most obliged and most
humble Servant.
E. Young.

Wellwyn,
June 1st. 1763.

478. Welwyn, Herts. [Th.] 2 June 1763. Duchess of Portland.

Longleat MSS. 285.—Bath, pp. 327–8; Shelley, pp. 271–2.

[In the hand of Mrs. Hallows]

May it please Your Grace.

In yesterdays Newspaper, I read an article, with infinite sattisfaction; I beg leave to give Your Grace Joy, on that happy occation. May you Madam, & Lady Harriot,[3] I shod say Grey, (to whom my humble Duty) find your fullest sattisfaction in it. Parents deserve our Congratulation on nothing so much as on their final, & happy disposal of those whom they Love, & who deserve their Love, so well, as Lady Grey. The accomplishment of this important point, takes a

---

[1] François Arnaud (1721–84), member of the Académie des Inscriptions since 1762 and of the Académie française in 1771.

[2] It was not to appear, however, until 1782.

[3] The Portland daughter, Lady Henrietta, was married to George Henry Grey, Earl of Stamford, on 28 May.

great Load from the Tender Maternal heart, & promises
serene Days to the remainder of Life.

I hope your Grace is entirely free from the painful indisposition, of which You complained in your last, that Letter
I answer'd long since, with my fullest acknowlegments to
my Lord Bute, for his unmeritted indulgence to me: But
that indulgence, I am conscious, Must be owing to your
Graces favour, to whom therefore, on That Occation, my
principal, & most sincere acknowlegements, & thanks, are
Due. /[verso]/

Once more I give Your Grace Joy, of so happy a conclusion, in an affair, which must have had a just title, to your
most tender concern, & that it may yearly present you, with
new occations of Joy, till Your joy receives its full comple-
tion, where there is neither Marrying, nor giving in Marriage, is the Prayer of,

Madam, Your Graces
Most Obliged,
And most Dutiful humble servant
EYoung

I beg my humble Duty
to my Lord Duke; and humble service, to Mr Arshard.
Wellwyn, June 2d
  1763.

/[conjugate leaf]/

PS.

Madam, I have just now read, inserted in the publick
Papers, some Letters, of the Lady Mary Wortley, in which
are some things, to the Publication of which, I am sattisfied,
that in her last hours she woud not have given her consent.

It is a Malloncholy thing to consider that any thing which
hurts Virtue shod contribute to Fame.

479. Welwyn, Herts. June 1763. Trustees of the Welwyn Charity School.

Dr. Williams's Library, Jones MS. 39 B. 19.[1]

Gentlemen,

As you were so kind to consent to be Trustees for my little Charity School at Wellwyn, I take the liberty to apply to you for a small additional favour in the behalf of this School, being at this time not well enough myself to execute my wish herein. I am advised by persons who wish well to this design, & understand our Laws, that it will be prudent to provide in due time beforehand a large & well-bound paperbook of the folio-size, to enter therein a true & exact copy of the Deed enrolled in Chancery for ye establishment of the said School, the Rules & Orders thereof, & all subsequent transactions of the Trustees in the execution of their Trust relating to it, & for the good management of it.

Your seasonable act of friendship in providing such a Book, & procuring such Entries to be made, at my expence, will always be thankfully acknowledged by,

Gentlemen
Your affectionate
& obliged humble Servant

Wellwyn, June
  1763

[1] The draft of this letter, which was never sent out, has the following notes by Young's curate, J. Jones: 'To the Revd Dr Yarborough Rector of Tewing, Mr Wilmot Rector of Digswell, Mr Wynne Rector of Ayot St Laurence and ——* of Wellwyn Herts. *He desired also my name to be inserted. I promised to assist. Drawn up at ye request of Dr Y.= Read to him, & to be transcribed, that it might be signed by him, as he had a few days before proposed & promised.—The truth is, he had considered farther about the expence; wch he is willing enough to save, if he can, in his life-time.'

480. Tunbridge Wells, Kent. [Tu.] 19 July 1763.
Duchess of Portland,

Longleat MSS. 287.

[In the hand of Mrs. Hallows]

Tunbridge-Wells, July 19 1763.

May it please Your Grace

I had not the pleasure & Honour, of receiving Your
Graces Letter till this Morning; And I was not willing to
sleep till I had return'd my humble thanks, for your kind
offers, with regard to Buxton-Wells: But my want of Rest,
& Appetite, has forced me to this Place, where I propose,
God willing,   to continue   the remainder of the season, tho hitherto I have recd no benefit. W^e have Here much Rain, &
little Company, no person of Quality being upon the place
but Lady Abercorn.

As no one, Madam, has more reason to rejoice in Your
Happiness than myself; I thank you for the Character you
favour me with, of my Lord Grey, nor is any other Character
worthy of Lady Harriot.

I hope in God you will receive the benefit propos'd from
Buxton-Wells, & that no future pains, will lessen your relish
of those great blessings, which his Goodness has bestowed
on your Grace. /[verso]/

For my own part 'tis high time for me to be absolutely
resigned to His blessed Will, nor will I despair of the riches
of his Grace, to enable me so to be.

I am, Madam,
With all possible respect & Gratitude
Your Graces most Obliged
And most Devoted humble Servant
EYoung.

Mrs Hallows begs Your Grace to accept her humble Duty
And I beg my humble service to Mr Arshard.

481. [Welwyn, Herts.]. [Su.] 11 September 1763.
George Keate.

British Museum, Add. MS. 30992, f. 13.—Thomas, p. 617.

Dear Sir
   I truly rejoice on your recovery of your Health, for I
know its Value: As for my own, my, time of day, forbids me
to hope much or to complain. I bless God that what I now
suffer, his Mercy deffered so long: I have now all the infirmities of Age, & amongst others my sight is near gone,
which troubles me, I fear, more than it ought to do; but his
blessed will be done, in whom is all our hope. I thank you
for the curious transcript you sent me, Your company will
be heartily welcom[e] to, Dear Sir,
                              Your faithful, & Affectionate
                                   humble servant,
                                        EYoung.

Sepr 11th 1763.
   Mrs Hallows
sends her Comp[limen]ts

482. Welwyn, Herts. [M.] 7 November 1763. Earl
of Bute.

Cardiff Public Libraries, Cardiff MS. 3. 615, bundle 11, item 183.

My Honoured Lord
   How greatly am I concern'd? that the badness of my
sight, denies me, the justly, & earnestly desired honour, of
waiting on your Lordship, when so near;[1] but I conceive
some hope from your much experienced goodness, that it
will vouchsafe to accept my humblest duty, most cordially,

   [1] Bute had retired from Court at the end of September to his newly acquired
estate in Luton Hoo, Bedfordshire, about nine miles west of Welwyn.

tho' most imperfectly, in this manner, paid to Your Lordship, & my Lady Bute, by

My most honoured Lord,
Your Lordship's most obliged,
Most Obedient,
and ever devoted humble Servant,
Edward Young.

Welwyn, Hertfordshire
Novr 7th 1763.

483. Welwyn, Herts. [Th.] 29 December 1763.
Johann Arnold Ebert.

Address: To / The Rev. J. A. Ebert / Professor at / Brunswick. *Postmark*:
2/IA welwyn.
Bodleian Library, MS. Montague d. 18.—J. J. Eschenburg, ed., *Eberts
Episteln*, Hamburg, 1795, ii. 90–1; *A Select Collection of 300 Autograph
Letters of Celebrated Individuals of all Nations, engraved in Facsimile*,
Stuttgart, 1849; Thomas, pp. 609–10; Shelley, p. 273.

Dear Sir
Pray give my very best respects, to the Countess of
Stollberg, & let her know, that with the greatest sincerity,
& joy of heart, I congratulate her, on the happiness, &
virtues of those she holds most dear; & that I shall emplore
the Divine mercy, for the continuance of all blessings on
them, & her. Further let her know that I request in return,
her Prayers; hoping that tho' our Fortune has appointed us
to be strangers in this World, Yet yt we may be intimate in
that happy Country, where there is no such thing as Brittle
Friendships, & they that Love, will both love, & be loved,
for Ever!
I have not yet recd the 3rd Vol: of Your work, the late
Earl of Granville, a person of the very highest distinction,
who understood Your Language, desired me to lend him
your two former Volumes, which he read with the highest
approbation, & applause.
I thank you, dear Sir, for your kind wishes, but my great
Age, & ill health, disable me from being so large in my

respects to you, as I ought, & Wish to be. That God may encrease Your happiness, & succeed Your Learned, & Pious Labours, is the hearty Prayer
of, Dear Sir
Your Obliged, & Obedient Servant
EYoung.

Welwyn,
in Hartfordshire.
December 29th
  1763.

484. Welwyn, Herts. [Su.] 12 February 1764. George Keate.

British Museum, Add. MS. 30992, f. 14.—Thomas, pp. 617–18; Shelley, p. 274; Dapp, p. 51.

Dear Sir

It is very kind in you to enquire after my Welfare, & it is quite as Natural as it is kind. One great Man has told us that all is Vanity & Vexation. And another that it is all Labour & Sorrow when we come to four-score. Now when these two last Enemies reinforce the former; wch is the common Lot, there is no small cause to doubt whether all is well? But all is well that Nature appoints; & I think it to be so, & shall rejoice under it when I see you at Welwyn.

I recd your Present. You seem to make me a King by your annu[a]l Tribute. For two or three Months I shall lay it up in my Exchequer, of which I shall make my Cat Chancellor, otherwise the Rats will rebel & show that I have a very limited Monarchy over them: They are of Wilke's Party, & I wish they were as far off;[1] but I submit to my fate; for why shod Edwds Reign, be less be less [*sic*] disturbed than George's? And why shod Rats be more loyal than Men?

---

[1] John Wilkes (1727–97), now in voluntary exile in Paris, was at the moment still in trouble with Parliament over publication in his *North Briton* of No. 45, which had been declared a seditious libel. Perhaps the 'present' was a cheese.

And now what is this kind of writing? It may be call'd
the smile of the pen; to let you know, that its Master can
fight Age & Infirmity & endeavour with Anacreon

> Of little life the most to make
> And manage wisely the last stake[1]

Heaven aid us to be pleas'd with all things; for on no other
terms will heaven be pleased with us.

> I am, Dear Sir,
> > Your Affectionate Obliged
> > And faithful humble servant
> > > EYoung

Mrs Hallows begs her Comp[liment]s
Welwyn Feby 12th 1764.
Nandos[2] was my Coffee house
above three score Years agoe.

485. Welwyn, Herts. [Tu.] 13 March 1764. Duchess of Portland.

Longleat MSS. 288.—Bath, pp. 328–9; Shelley, pp. 274–6.

[In the hand of Mrs. Hallows]

May it please Your Grace
If gratitude is any virtue, I have great reason to be truly
consern'd upon your Graces indisposition; may a good
Providence soon remove it, & restore You to perfect health,
& a true relish of it; wch nothing can give us so effectually,
as a little taste of the contrary. Please to accept my humble
thanks for the great honour You Disign me; I have long
wished for it; for few pleasures are equal to seeing the face of
those whom we know to wish us well. The dancing Dutchess
woud scarce have so much pleasure in a well perform'd
Minuet; or the busie Duke in his political country-dance,

[1] Abraham Cowley, 'Age', *Anacreontiques: or, Some Copies of Verses translated paraphrastically out of Anacreon.*
[2] According to Bryant Lillywhite (*London Coffee Houses*, 1963, p. 382), Nando's, near Temple Bar in Fleet Street, was founded before 1696.

from the angry cabals of Town, to the learned banks of Cam. How vain the business, or amusements of Life, to those great things, which Infirmities, or Age will naturally, if not necessarily, bring to our thoughts! I bless God I am pretty well, & for me, to hope for more woud be folly, for miracles a[re] ceased.

Not being able thro the weakness of my sight to wait on Lord Bute, a pretty while ago I wrote to him, & recd a most obliging /[verso]/ Letter in answer, for which I thank Him and your Grace; but I do not thank him for raising the price of our provisions by his great hospitality. We are all very welcome if we please to indulge at his plentiful Table, but a Chicken will cost us very dear if we eat it at our own. He nobly entertains the Rich, & charitably relieves the Poor: And reads, I hope with christian patience, in the paper the great thanks which the publick Returns for those Virtues. I give Your Grace joy of being no polititian, for whoever turns hi[s] head that way at this time, might as good put it in the pillery, for he will be sure, to have dirt thrown at him, by some hand or another tho they stoop for it, into the kennel of nonsense, & ill will; yet some ears are so nailed to politicks that they are deaf to every thing else.

Madam, Your Grace has many that share your good wishes; I hope they are all well? And may they all contri-

bu[t]e to your happiness　^{till your happiness}　which must necessarily have its root in Earth /[conjugate leaf]/ shall arrive in its full bloom above. I am, Madam, with the most profound respect, & the warmest gratitude, your Graces

Most devoted,
And Obedient humble servant
EYoung.

Welwyn March 13nth 1764
Pray my best compliments to Mr Arshard.
Mrs Hallows hopes you will accept of her humble Duty.

Madam

Madam Your Grace says that you shall never forget that you are on the verge of fifty; if you shod live two fifties more, after all your experience, this woud be your last thought;

'What very, very trifles tis, all the World so pashionately persues? How great the Prize it so carelesly neglects! How inconceiveable must that Bliss be, which /[verso]/ cost the blood of God?['] These things force themselves on the thoughts of Age; But how much happier are they in the Day of enjoyment & streng[th] of Life? When the very Thought
then
is Virtue, since we must   fight our way through temptations to the Contrary to come at it. How very different the value of these thoughts in the fine walks of Bullstrode, & in the Melancholy chambers of languor or pain? These *Politicks* are a noble science, and too little studied by Country & Court; few Secretaries of State are made by them. Your Grace will pardon me for repeating to you your own words.

486. Welwyn, Herts. [Su.] 18 March 1764. George Keate.

Postmark: 19/MR.
British Museum, Add. MS. 30992, f. 15.—Thomas, p. 618; Dapp, pp. 52–3.

Dear Sir

from the verses
   Milton might possibly take his hint   which You was so kind to send me; but there is a great difference between the beauty of the Root, & the **Flower that** springs from it.

   You say this spring has produced nothing very considerable from the Press, every spring produces Daisie Authors, which true taste treds underfoot, but it is well if Genius, like the Aloes, vouchsafes to Blossom once in fifty Years.

   You say that your work has laid for some time Dorment by you, that is not amiss, for by that means, the fondness of a Parent, hardens into the impartiality of a Judge; /[verso]/ which is more a friend to the maturity of Composition; after a sound nap your Nertley [Netley] Abbey,[1] may gather strength, & Vivasity, and tho' it went to s[l]eep in perfect

---

[1] Keate's poem *Netley Abbey* was published in April.

health, yet shod I be glad to see what change is made in it,
for its Author shall be very welcome to, Dear Sir,

his Affectionate & faithful
humble servant
EYoung

Mrs Hallows
presents her
    Comp[liment]s

Welwyn March 18
  1764

487. Welwyn, Herts. [Th.] 22 March 1764. George Keate.

British Museum, Add. MS. 30992, f. 16.—Thomas, pp. 618–19; Dapp, p. 53.

Dear Sir

What you propose to prefix, is propper if not necessary.
I think all your alterations are for the better; my pen has
given a few hints, possibly all wrong, if so, pardon me. The
melancholy cast, & the Moral tendency of the Whole, &
your easie transition to the Ladies, have charms for me, &
probably will procure me many rivals; rivals (which is no
common case) in which I shall rejoice. I am

Dear Sir,
Your truly affectionate
& Obedient Servant
EYoung.

Welwyn March 22d,
  1764.

488. Welwyn, Herts. [Th.] 3 April 1764. George
Keate.

Postmark: WELLWYN.
British Museum, Add. MS. 30992, f. 17.—Thomas, p. 619; Shelley, p. 276;
Dapp, p. 54.

Dear Sir

I wish I could send you as much pleasure by the Post, as
you sent me by the Carrier. I take for granted that the hints
I gave you were wrong, however I shod be glad to dispute
with you on that point, or on any other provided Welwyn
be the field of Battle; the custom of which Place is, that the
Vanquished shall divide the smile with the Conquerer, & by
that means, tho' demolish'd, in some measure, to shine, like
your Netley Abby, in Ruins. I am, Dear Sir,

Very Affectionately Yours,

EYoung.

Welwyn April 3d,
1764.

489. Welwyn, Herts. [Sa.] 28 June 1764. Duchess of
Portland.

Longleat MSS. 290.

[In the hand of Mrs. Hallows]

May it please Your Grace,

Being disappointed in my hope, the spring far passed, &
the summer much advanced, my Letter is in great doubt,
where it shall find your Grace, whether in the always smoaky,
& now dusty Town, or in the delightful walks of Bullstrode,
where pleasant thoughts will meet you probably pleasant
thoughts, of more than the Town, or the World can give.
What a blessed Prospect have we before us! a prospect, wch
Multitudes now deceased, woud give a thousand Worlds to
enjoy. This is a Comfort to wch Crowns are trifles, & which
the malice of Fortune can never take from us. All our pains
arise from gazing on this World, & forgetting the next; but

that is not often forgotten in Solitude, especially in such a solitude where the richness of the scene, speaks the Bounties of Heaven And ^{it} speaks them so loud at Bullstrode, that I hear of them from many hands.

/[verso]/ But, Madam, wherever you are, please to give me leave to enquire after your welfare, & the welfare of those who are nearest to your heart: My duty is not the only Motive to this enquiery, for it woud give me the greatest sattisfaction, to hear that all is well; but if otherwise & your Graces indisposition, shod induce you to repeat your last summers Journey, that will bring you thro Welwyn, and if so, I cannot but heartily wish, that you woud look on it, as a point of Curiosity, to see one of the last Age, that is still alive, and whilst he lives, will think it his highest honour, as well as his greatest pleasure, to pay his Duty, where it is so greatly due.

The Nature of ^{a Letter} requires, that I shod now tell your Grace some news, but news is not the growth of the Country; indeed if I woud take example of the public papers, I need not be silent on this Head; but as ventureing on lies, woud be evidently, invading /[conjugate leaf]/ their peculiar property, I will content myself with the strictest truth, by assureing you, that I am with my whole heart,

Madam,

Your Graces ever devoted,

and most obedient humble servant

Edward Young.

Welwy[n] Hertfordshire
June 28th 1764.

490. Welwyn, Herts. [Tu.] 7 August 1764. Duchess of Portland.

Longleat MSS. 292.—Bath, p. 329; Shelley, p. 277.

[In the hand of Mrs. Hallows]

May it please Your Grace.

I greatly rejoice, that You have recoverd what is most valuable in Life, Health, &, Spirits; And that You have recoverd them by the most pleasant, as well as most Effectual Means, that is by driving away from Your Physitian as fast, & as far as You can; which is the most likely way of leaving Your disorder too behind You. As for my own health, wch Your Grace is so good as to ask after, I bless heaven that I suffer no severe pains, but I have little Appetite by day, & very indifferent Rest by night; & my Eyes grow worse, & worse, let Almighty God's most blessed Will be done.

I have not for a long time, either seen Mrs Montague, or heard from her, but I have heard often of her. Dr Monsey call'd on me a little while ago, & told me he was to wait on her, but could not be admitted, because my Lord Bath was dead:[1] And this last week, one Mr Keate of the Temple, an Author both in Prose, & Verse, favour'd me with a visit for two or three Days, and told me, that some little time ago he had the honour of dining with Mrs Montagu, with about ten more, all or most of them Writers; that the Entertainment was very Elegant, and that a celebrated Welch Harp added Musick to their Wit.

They are wise, who make this Life as happy as they can, since at the /[verso]/ the [*sic*] very happiest it will fall short of their desires, which blessed be God, are too large to be quite pleased, with anything below, and whilst by their Largen[ess] they give us some little disgust to this Life, they make rich amends for the disadvantage, by giving us at the same time, a strong assureance of a better.

---

[1] Messenger Monsey (1693–1788), physician, and William Pulteney (1684–1764), Earl of Bath, are said to have been rival suitors of Elizabeth Montagu. Bath had died on 7 July.

Please, Madam, to accept the most cordial good wishes
for Your welfare, from Your Graces

Most Devoted, and ever
Dutiful Humble Servant
EYoung.

Mrs Hallows pres[e]nts her humble Duty.
Pray my humble service to Mr Arshard,
if he is still with your Grace.

Welwyn, Augst 7th 1764.

491. [Th.] 23 August 1764. Thomas Percy.

Not traced.[1]

492. [Welwyn, Herts.]. [Su.] 7 October 1764. George Keate.

Postmark: 8/OC.
British Museum, Add. MS. 30992, f. 18.—Thomas, pp. 219–20; Shelley,
p. 278; Dapp, p. 57.

Dear Sir

On opening your Letter, I was pleas'd to find, that I
had still, one friend on this side the grave: of late I have lost

[1] The manuscript of this letter was offered for sale at Sotheby's on three occasions:
9 March 1870 as Lot 151, 24 April 1876 as Lot 396, and 27 July 1885 as Lot 1019.
It was described as 'A. L. s. 1 page 4to. Addressed to Rev. Thomas Percy. dated
Aug. 23, 1764. Expresses ignorance of the points mentioned, and forgetfulness as
regards the rest, sends his true regards to Mr Johnson'. This letter was in answer to
Percy's request for information about the *Spectator*, as is clear from a passage in his
letter to David Dalrymple, Lord Hailes of 21 August 1764 in which he wrote: 'Mr
Tonson and I are picking up anecdotes for our intended Edition of the Spectator;
we thank you for those you gave: should any more fall in your way, or be attainable
by your interest, we flatter ourselves you will be pleased not to forget us.—We had
just applied to Lord Bath, and been promised his assistance when he was taken ill
and died. At present we are pumping the Memory of Dr Young and other Literati
of the last age: but I am sorry to say that what is remembered, bears but a small
proportion to what is forgotten' (*The Percy Letters: The Correspondence of Thomas
Percy & David Dalrymple, Lord Hailes*, ed. A. F. Falconer, 1954, p. 86). Percy's
letter to Young must have been before 18 August as on that day Samuel Johnson,
who had been visiting him from 25 June, returned to London (*Boswell's Life of
Johnson*, ed. G. B. Hill, rev. L. F. Powell, 1934, i. 554).

so very many, that I began to doubt it. Poor Dodsley!
But why poor? Let us give him joy of his escape.

> None woud live past years again,
> Yet all hope pleasure, in what yet remain;
> And from the Dregs of Life, hope to receive
> What the first sprightly runnings could not give.
> I'm tired of waiting for this chimic gold,
> Which fools us Young, & beggars us when Old.
>   Dryden[2]

When Mrs Gataker,[3] told me that Dodsley [heavily crossed
through] had his doubts as to Xtianity, An Argument for it
occured to me, wch is not to be found, I think, in writers on
                       is
that subject as it   but short, & to me most convincing, I
will tell you what it is; first, such is the Nature of Xtianity
that the Plan of it coud not possibly have entered into the
Mind of Man. 2dy if it had enter'd, it coud not possibly have
/[verso]/ been recd by mankind, without a supernatural
interposition in its favour.

As for Voltaire, I have not seen what you mention, but as
long as there is fear, & pity, in the heart of Man, reading
a page in Shakespear, will be a sufficient reply, to what
Voltaire can urge against him. I heartily wish you had an
affecting tale under your hand; it woud give you great
pleasure in the Composition, & Your Fri[e]nds, in the
Perusal. Thus you see, Self interest, as usual, lies at the
bottom of our Civilities. Success attend You in all your
undertakings, & Fortitude Man you, against all the Defi-
ciencies of human Life.

                    I am
              Dear sir, Your Affectionate
              And Obedt Servant
                          EYoung.

Mrs Hallows
presents her
Compliments.
Octr 7th
  1764

---

[1] Robert Dodsley had died on 23 September while on a visit to Joseph Spence at
Durham.
[2] *Aureng Zebe*, IV. i. 39–44.   [3] i.e. wife of Dodsley's physician.

493. Welwyn, Herts. [Tu.] 19 February 1765. Duchess of Portland.

Longleat MSS. 293.—Bath, pp. 329–30; Shelley, p. 279.

[In the hand of Mrs. Hallows]

May it please your Grace

It is so long since I had the honour of writing to you that you may possibly look on This as a Letter from the dead; but I am still above ground, tho I can hardly venture to say that I am quite alive; the severe weather on Sunday night almost destroy'd me. My being so long silent was not occationed by disrespect, for I bear to your Grace the greatest, nor was it occationed by want of power, for I bless God I am pretty Well, nor was it occationd by want of Inclination, for I desire nothing more than to hear of your Graces Welfare. Whatever therefore was the Cause of it, I beg your Grace to permit me now, to enquire after your health, & the health of all those who have the happiness of being related to, or of being esteem'd by you. In the last Letter which I had the honour of receiving from your Grace, you was about to make a round of Visits to several entitled to one, or to both of the characters above. I hope you found & left them well and brought home at your return, an encrease of Health, & sattisfaction. Air, & Exercise, are not greater friends to the former, than the chearful smiles of those we love are to the latter; and when is it more Necessary to provide for our private Sattisfaction & peace, than at a time when that of the publick, seames to be in some hazard of being impaired, if /[verso]/ if [*sic*] not lost? But what have I to do with the publick affairs of this world? They are almost as foreign to me, as to those who wer[e] born before the Flood. My world is dead; to the present World I am quite a stranger, so very much a stranger, that I kno[w] but One Person in it, and that is Your Grace.

Please therefore, Madam, to accept the undivided regard, & Devotion, of Your Graces

Most obliged
and most Dutiful
humble Servant
E Young.

Wellwyn Feb 19 1765.

John Jones to Thomas Birch.[1] Welwyn, Herts. [Tu.]
2 April 1765.

Address: To / The Reverend Dr Birch / in Norfolk Street / in the Strand /
London. *Postmark*: 3/AP Welwyn.
British Museum, Add. MS. 4311.

Wellwyn 2d April 1765
Dear Sir
   I take the first opportunity after my return, of renewing
the assurances of my esteem & gratitude for the many civilities
you showed me during my short stay in Town. As soon as I
got home I inquired after Dr Young, & found that he had
gone through very great pains since the time when I left
him; and the pains return pretty frequently. Dr Cotton of
St Albans & Dr Yate of Hertford[2] meet at his house every
day on consultation: But whatever they may think of his
disorder, & the probable consequences, little or nothing as
yet transpires; only all that attend him constantly imagine
there is little or no hope of his doing well again. For my own
part, I judged so from the beginning. I find that opiates are
frequently administered to him; I suppose to render him the
less sensible of his pain. His intellects, I am told, are still
clear, tho' what effect the frequent use of opiates may by
degrees have upon him, I know not. I am pretty much of his
son's sentiments as to/[verso]/to [*sic*] this, viz. that those ingredients, if for some time longer continued, may have an ill
effect upon the brain. Having mentioned this young gentleman,[3] I would acquaint you next, that he came hither this
morning, having been sent for, as I am told, by the direction
of Mrs Hallows. Indeed she intimated to me as much Herself. And if this be so, I must say, that it is one of the most
prudent acts she ever did, or could have done in such a case

   [1] Historian and biographer (1705–66).
   [2] Nathaniel Cotton (1705–88), notable for his care of the poet William Cowper
(1731–1800) and a Thomas Yate, M.D., who is mentioned as a trustee of a Hertford
charity.
   [3] A certificate concerning Frederick Young is among the manuscripts in the
Houghton Library, Harvard University, MS. bMS AM 1631 (438), whose purpose
is unknown: 'Hertfordshire / To wit / This Day personally came before me, one of
his Majesties Justices of the peace for the County of Hertford, the Revd Edward
Young DCL & made oath, that Mr Frederick Young of Baliol College Oxford was
living on the Fifth Day of January now last past [signed] EYoung Sworn January
ye Fifth 1765 before me GTBisse'.

as this, as it may prove the means of preventing much confusion after ye Death of the Doctor. I have had some little discourse with the Son: He seems much affected, and I believe really is so. He earnestly wishes his Father might be pleased to ask after him. For you must know he has not yet done this, nor is, in my opinion, like to do it. And it has been said farther, that upon a late application made to him on the behalf of his Son, he desired that no more might be said to him about it. How true this may be, I cannot as yet be certain. All I shall say is, It seems not improbable. Mrs H. has fitted up a suitable apartment in the house for Mr Young; where I suppose he will continue till some farther event. I heartily wish the ancient Man's Heart may grow tender towards his son; tho' knowing him so well, I can scarce hope to hear such desireable news. He took to his bed yesterday about eleven in the forenoon, & hath not /[conjugate leaf]/ not [*sic*] been up since. I called soon after my coming home, but did not see him; he was in a doze. I imagine his farther stay upon earth, can be of no long duration. When that is over, I must, it seems, again emigrate. God knows whither. [The remainder of the letter concerns only Jones's affairs.]

Nathaniel Cotton to an Unnamed Correspondent [F. 5 April 1765].

Not traced.—*Various Pieces in Verse and Prose by the late Nathaniel Cotton*, 1791, vol. ii.

Dear Sir,

But alas! my dear friend, how little interesting are all these political points, when compared with the important scenes which I have been witness to this week! I refer to the sickness and dying couch of that great man Dr Young. It will never be my province to personate the statesman, or to move, even in the most subordinate sphere, relative to the administration of public affairs: but to act the part of a sick and expiring mortal, is an allotment which must soon be my portion; and God Almighty grant, that I may be enabled to sustain this character with patience, fortitude and faith.

In my last, I acquainted you that I was called to Welwyn.
When I arrived there, I found Dr Yate waiting for me. It
seems he had been sent for three or four days before my
assistance was desired. Dr Young's disorder was attended
with some obscurity. But on Tuesday matters wore a very
discouraging aspect; and on Wednesday, Yate and myself
gave up the case as lost. From that period to the present Dr
Young hath been dying. Whether the scene be closed this
evening I cannot take upon me to say; but this day, at noon,
the physicians took their leave. Dr. Young, although in his
eighty sixth year, had disputed every inch of ground with
death, from the strength of his constitution, never impaired
in early life by riot and debauchery. As I sat by his bedside,
how earnestly did I wish the vital knot untied! I humbly pray
God, that myself, and all who are connected with me,
whether by blood or friendship, may be favoured with an
easy transition out of this world into a better. For long and
painful agonizings of nature under her dissolution, appear
to me sufferings hardly inferior to some of the sweetest tor-
tures of martyrdom; and consequently trials which require
apostolic attainments and supernatural assistances to support our souls under them.

Your friendship will excuse the melancholy reflections,
for the sake of the object which suggested them. I was very
fond of Dr Young's company and greatly venerated his
mental abilities.

John Jones to Thomas Birch. Welwyn, Herts. [Sa.] 13 April 1765.

Address: To / The Reverend Dr Birch / in / Norfolk Street / in the Strand /
London. *Postmark*: 15/AP Welwyn.
British Museum, Add. MS. 4311, f. 216.—John Nichols, *Literary Anecdotes
of the Eighteenth Century*, 1812, i. 633-4.

Wellwyn, 13th of Apr
1765

Dear Sir

I have now the pleasure to acquaint you, that the late Dr
Young, tho' he had for many years kept his Son at a distance
from him, yet has now at last left him all his possessions,

after the payment of certain legacies.[1] So that the young gentleman, who bears a fair character and behaves well, as far as I can hear or see, will I hope soon enjoy & make a prudent use of a very handsome fortune.[2] The Father on his death-bed, and since my return from London, was applied to in the tenderest manner by one of his Physicians, and by another person, to admit the son into his presence, to make submission, intreat forgiveness, and obtain his blessing. As to an interview with his son, he intimated that he chose to decline it, as his spirits were then low, & his nerves weak. With regard to the next particular, he said, *I heartily forgive him*; and, upon mention of the last, he gently lifted up his hand, and, letting it gently fall, pronounced these words, *God bless him*. After about a fortnights illness, and enduring excessive pains, he expired a little before eleven of the clock at the night of good-friday last, the 5th instant, and was /[verso]/ was [*sic*] decently buried yesterday, about 6 in the afternoon, in the chancel of this church, close by the remains of his lady, under the communion-table; the Clergy who are the Trustees of his charity-school, and one or two more, attending the funeral, the last office at interment being performed by me.

I know it will give you pleasure to be farther informed, that he was pleased to make respectful mention of me in his will, expressing his satisfaction in my care of his parish, bequeathing to me a handsome legacy,[3] and appointing me to be one of his executors, next after his Sisters Son (a Clergyman of Hampshire) who this morning set out for London in order to prove the will at Doctors-Commons. So that, much according to my wishes, I shall have little or nothing to do in respect of executorship.

We hear that the name of the Clergyman who is to succeed Dr Young, is Bathurst,[4] Senr fellow of the college of All-

---

[1] Frederick's share of his father's estate amounted to £1,095. 3s. 6d. in cash and £10,500 in securities (records in the Gosling branch of Barclays Bank Ltd.) and presumably also ownership of the family home of Guessens.

[2] Except for a £100 life annuity, all cash and securities had been exhausted by 1780 when Frederick closed his account with Gosling's bank.

[3] Jones was left £200 and received full responsibility for executing Young's will as a result of the withdrawal of the nephew, Richard Harris (b. 1711), probably as a result of apparent irregularities in the document which made necessary the calling of Mary Hallows to London on the 25th of the month (see Appendix C).

[4] Thomas Bathurst (d. 1797) succeeded to the rectory 31 May 1765.

Souls in Oxford, & now living, I think, in Essex—Where
Providence will place me next, I know not.[1] I wait with
humble submission to the divine will; and am, dear sir, your
ever respectful affectionate & thankful servant.

J. Jones.

Mary Hallows to George Keate. Welwyn, Herts. [Su.] 28 April 1765.

British Museum, Add. MS. 30992, f. 19.—Thomas, pp. 620–1.

Sir   Welwyn April 28th 1765

I am favour'd with yours by Mrs Brown; and cant help
regreting with you, & every one, the loss of our most Valuable friend, the Great, & Good Docter Young.

The particulars you desire, will but add to your concern,
as every recollection does to mine; but I comply, in saying,
that the blessed Gentleman, passed a fortnight, in some
distressful circumstances, and expired on Good fryday
Night $\frac{1}{2}$ past Nine,[2] without a groan; excuse me further, my
tears prevent me, for which I will hope your pardon.

The good Dr, Sir, burnt most of his Manuscripts, long
before his death, & left orders that every thing of that
nature shod be destroyed,[3] wch I suppose you have by this
time seen in the publick papers, with some other (I believe)
genuine accounts. I hope, Sir, you enjoy Health & every
valuable blessing? & that they may be long continued to
you, for the best purposes, is the prayer of, Sir

Your Obliged
And Most Obedt humble servant
Mary Hallows

The good Dr
retained his
senses to the last.

---

[1] In April 1767 Jones was made Vicar of Shephall, Herts., five miles north of
Welwyn.   [2] 5 April.

[3] The last codicil to his will reads: 'To Mrs Hallows. It is my dying Request,
that You would see all Writings whatever, whether in *Papers*, or Books, (except my
Book of Accounts) burnt, & destroyd, as soon as I am dead. which will oblige yr
Deceasd Friend Ed: Young' (see Appendix C).

William Cowper[1] to Lady Harriet Hesketh. Huntingdon, Hunts. [F.] 12 July 1765.

Not traced.—William Hayley, *Life and Letters of William Cowper*, 1824, i. 44–5; Shelley, p. 280; Thomas Wright, ed., *Correspondence of William Cowper*, 1914, i. 33–5.

. . . Our mentioning Newton's treatise on the Prophecies[2] brings to my mind an anecdote of Dr. Young, who, you know, died lately at Welwyn. Dr. Cotton, who was intimate with him, paid him a visit about a fortnight before he was seized with his last illness. The old man was then in perfect health; the antiquity of his person, the gravity of his utterance, and the earnestness with which he discoursed about religion, gave him, in the doctor's eye, the appearance of a prophet. They had been delivering their sentiments upon this book of Newton, when Young closed the conference thus:—'My friend, there are two considerations upon which my faith in Christ is built as upon a rock: the fall of man, the redemption of man, and the resurrection of man—the three cardinal articles of our religion—are such as human ingenuity could never have invented; therefore they must be divine. The other argument is this: If the Prophecies have been fulfilled (of which there is abundant demonstration), the Scripture must be the word of God; and if the Scripture is the word of God, Christianity must be true. . . .'

[1] Cowper (1731–1800) had left the sanatorium of Dr. Cotton on 17 June, having been a patient there from December 1763.

[2] *Dissertations on the Prophecies, which have been remarkably fulfilled, and are at this time fulfilling in the world* (3 vols., 1754–8), by Thomas Newton (1704–82), later Bishop of Bristol.

APPENDIX A: PUBLISHING RECORDS

I

Record of Young's sale of copyright to the *Night-Thoughts*, parts 1–5, to Robert Dodsley for £168, 24 November 1743:

'. . . [Young] did on the 24th day of Novr 1743 in cons[iderati]on of £168 to him paid by Robert Dodsley bargain & sell unto the said Dodsley the 5 first parts (or Nights) of a Poem called Night Thoughts on life death & Immortality printed together in one Volume and the s[ai]d Dr Young did by a Rec[eip]t under his hand acknowledge to have rec[eive]d of the s[ai]d Dodsley 50 Guineas w[hi]ch with 110 Guineas before rec[eive]d was in full for the Sole right to him & his Heirs forever of the Copy of the s[ai]d 5 first parts (or Nights) of the s[ai]d Poem. . . .' Injunction awarded the plaintiffs against the defendant's 'vending selling or exposing to sale any more Copys of the s[ai]d Poems by the Def[endan]t already Printed or Caused to be printed. . . .' (Public Record Office, C33 Part 2 420/244: Case of Andrew Millar and James Dodsley against Alexander Donaldson; unpublished Crown Copyright material reproduced by permission of the Controller of H.M. Stationery Office.)

II

Receipt for Young's sale of copyright to the *Night-Thoughts*, part 6, to Robert Dodsley for £52. 10s, 26 January 1744/5:

'Jany 26th 1744/5 Rec[eive]d of Mr. Robt Dodsley fifty Guineas in Consideration of which I do assign to him his Heirs Executors Administrators or Assigns the sole Right of printing the Sixth Night of a Poem intituled the Complaint &c otherwise call'd the Infidel Reclaim'd, Part the First. Witness my Hand, /s/ Edward Young. John Spooner by I: T:' The receipt is endorsed: 'This Receipt was shown to George Hawkins at the time of his Examin[atio]n taken in Chancery on the part & behalf of Andrew Millar and James Dodsley Complainants ag[ains]t Robert Taylor Def[endan]t.' (Harvard University, Houghton MSS., fMS Eng 760.1; by permission of the Harvard College Library.)

597

Receipt for Young's sale of copyright to the *Night-Thoughts*, parts 7–9, and *A Paraphrase on Part of the Book of Job* to Andrew Millar for £63, 7 April 1749:

'Know all Men by these Presents that I Edward Young LLD. Rector of Welling in the County of Hertford for & in consideration of the Sum of Sixty three Pounds to me in hand paid by Andrew Millar of St. Mary le Strand in the County of Middlesex Bookseller the Receipt whereof is hereby acknowledged & myself therwith fully satisfied I the said Edward Young by these presents do bargain, sell, deliver, assign & set over all that my Title, Right & property in & to the Second Volume of a certain Book entitled The Complaint: or, Night Thoughts on Life, Death and Immortality: containing Night the Seventh, being the second part of the Infidel reclaimed, Night the Eighth, being Virtue's Apology, or the Man of the World answered; Night the Ninth and Last, being the Consolation; and a Paraphrase on Part of the Book of Job: Wrote by me the said Edward Young. Together with all Improvements, Additions or Alterations whatever which now are or hereafter shall at any time be made to the said Book. To Have and to Hold the said bargained Premises unto the said Andrew Millar his Executors, Administrators or Assigns for Ever, to the only proper Use and behoof of the said Andrew Millar his Ex[ecut]ors Ad[ministra]tors and Assigns. And I do hereby covenant with the said Andrew Millar his Ex[ecut]ors Adm[inistrat]ors & Assigns that I the said Edward Young the Author of the said bargained Premises have not at any time heretofore Done committed or suffered any Act or Thing whatsoever by means whereof the said bargained Premises or any part thereof is or shall be any way impeached or encumbered in anywise. And I the said Edward Young for myself, my Executors, Administrators & Assigns shall & will warrant and defend the said bargained Premises for Ever against all Persons whatsoever claiming under me; my Ex[ecut]ors Adm[inistrat]ors or Assigns

In Witness whereof I have hereunto set my hand and Seal this Seventh day of April, One thousand, seven hundred and forty nine /s/ EYoung   Signed Sealed & Delivered (being first duely stampt) by the within Named Edward Young the day and year above mentioned, in the presence of RSpavan'.

Endorsed: 'This Paper Writing was shewn to Robert Spavan at the time of his Examination taken in Chancery on the part and behalf of Andrew Millar & James Dodsley Complainants against Robert Taylor Defendant John Spooner by I: T:.' (Victoria and Albert Museum, Forster Collection, F. 9709.)

Receipt for Young's sale of copyright to *The Centaur not Fabulous* to Robert Dodsley for £200, 19 February 1755:

'Febry 19th 1755 / In consideration of the sum of two hundred Pounds to be paid six months after the date hereof, I do agree to assign, and do hereby assign over all my Right and Title to the Copy of a Book written by me & entituled The Centaur, in five Letters &c together with the Plate, to Mr Robt Dodsley his Heirs Executors Administrators & Assigns, in witness whereof I have hereunto set my hand the day above written. /s/ EYoung' (Somerville, New Jersey, Hyde Collection).

APPENDIX B: INSCRIPTIONS

Among the Jones papers in Dr. Williams's Library is the following record: 'Wellwyn—Motto's & Inscriptions, &c. In the Church-Yard on an Altar-Monument, erected at the Expence of Dr. Y. over a poor Day-Labourer. Here lies my Friend JAMES BARKER: Who was Poor in his Life, / But is Rich in his Death. E. Y. 1749. The Poetical Lines on the Side of this Tomb-Stone are effaced. Wellwyn—At Dr. Y. = *In the Hall*.—Under the Busts of *Sir Isaac Newton*: (in Bronze) *Hic Natura Clavis est* / Mr. *Locke*: (in Do) *Hic Hominis ostendit Tibi Te* / *Milton* (in Do) No Inscription / *Dryden* (in Do) None / *Demosthenes*: (In a Nich) *Pleni moderantem fraena Theatri* / *Lucretia* (Slab—in a nich) being herself No Motto / A Scaramuch-Face: Underneath *Ex Aegypto* / *Shakespear*: (Exactly as in Westmr Abby) The Cloud-clipt Towers, / The gorgeous Palaces, / The Solemn Temples, / The Great Globe itself / Yea: All which it inherit, / Shall Dissolve. / And like the baseless fabric of a Vision / Leave not a Wreck behind. / On the back of a Seat amongst the Shrubs in the Little-Island *Arbusta juvant humilesq Myrica*. *In the Garden*—South End of the Summer House *Ambulantes in Horto audiebant Vocem Dei* Underneath *Qui rede vivendi prorogat horam*, &c. Hor. On a small Pedestal (in the Field) *Eheu Fugaces*. Near the New Grove: *Neque harum quas colis Arborum*, &c. Hor. The sham delusive Summer House Under the Venetn Window: *Splendide Mendax*. Over the Door: *Invisibilia non Decipiunt*. *In the Chancel* On the North-Wall To the children of the Charity School Virginibus: *Increase in Wisdom & Stature* On the Opposite Wall: *Puerisque*: And in Favour with God & Man. Over the Charity-School (erected & maintained by Dr. Y.) *Virtus est Doctrinae Filia* / *O Matre Pulchra, Filia Pulchrior*. Upon the (sham) Dome near the great Road, under the statue of Trajan, standing on the Top. *Evescit ad Aethena Vi* . . . This on a rising Ground. In the Chancel Over the Communion Table, on a rich piece elegantly wrought by the Lady Betty Lee, these two sentences in capital letters of gold. *I am the Bread of Life* Underneath: *O Taste, and See How Gracious the Lord Is*. In a by-place, near the Stables (I suppose by another hand) 'Here lies interr'd the Widow, Miss; / If ever Dog was good, 'twas This. Died, Aged 20, 1752.'

APPENDIX C: YOUNG'S WILL[1]

In the name of God, & my most blessed Redeemer. Amen. I write this my last Will, with my own hand, Feby the 5th 1760, in ye manner following.

I give to ye *Communion table* all ye gilt Plate in the mahogany chest, the folio Bible, & Prayr-books, the Stoles, Cushions, Carpets, & all my usual furniture of it.

I give to my Successor One hundred pounds for repairs of ye Parsonage house, & ye Chancell.

I give to ye four poorest housekeepers of Wellwyn, who receive nothing from ye Parish, five pounds for each of them.

I give to each of my four Servants, ten pounds.

I give to my neighbours Mrs Ward, Mrs Battel, Mr Shotbolt, & to my friends Mr Saml Richardson, & Mr Alderman Gosling, Guinea = Rings; & to my friend Mr Henry Stevens Hatter at ye Temple Gate; & to Mr Bigg fellow of Winchester College.

I give to Allsouls Library in Oxford fifty pounds to buy Books.

I give to my dear nephew ye Revd Mr Richard Harris my Silver Bread basket, & fifty pounds.

I give to ye Revd, & worthy Mr Jones for his pious assistance in my Parish, Two hundred pounds.

I give to Mrs. Mary Hallows all ye wrought work for chairs &c: in my mahogany chest; and eight hundred pounds.

I appoint my Nephew Harris, & ye Revd Mr Jones to be my Executors; &, (in a particular manner,) desire of them, that all my manuscript writings, whether in Books, or Papers, immediately on my decease may be burnt; my *Book of Accounts* only excepted.

My Nephew Harris will find among his Fathers books, a *large Folio*, with a *chain* to it, belonging to Allsouls Library: This Book I desire him to send with ye *fifty pounds above =given, to that Library*, as soon as he, consistently, can.

I give to my friend Mr Henry Stevens, Hatter, at ye Temple Gate, Twenty Guineas.

[1] Young's will, as it is here reproduced from the original in Somerset House, differs in a number of important respects from the transcript published in Thomas (pp. 621–3).

I give to my two Cousin Youngs in St Martin's Lane, or to ye Survivor of them, Fifty pounds.

After ye payment of ye Legacies above I give all ye Residue of my Possessions to my Son.

In witness, & confirmation of this my Will I hereunto set my hand & seal, this 25th of April 1760.

Ed:Young

Signd, seald, & declad by ye Testator above mentiond, as his last Will, and Testament in ye presence of us whose names are at his request, & in his presence, & in ye presence of each other, here underwritten Robert Milward / Thomas Pentlow / Jno. Deards. [On wrapper sheet:] This is my Last Will Ed: Young Sept 17 1762 To Mrs Hallows. It is my dying Request, that You would see all Writings whatever, whether in *Papers* or Books, (except my Book of Accounts) burnt, & destroyd, as soon as I am dead. Which will oblige yr Dearest Friend Ed:Young. This I opened EYoung [new sheet] This is a Codicil to the last Will and Testament of me Edward Young Rector of Wellwyn in the County of Hertford, which Will I made and Published bearing Date the 21 of June 1760 and which ~~Will~~ I do hereby Ratify and Confirm, as I do also the Contents of this Codicil, that is to say; If the Assistance of an Additional Executor shall be found necessary towards the more safe and effectual Execution of my said Will and Codicil, I do hereby request Nominate and impower, the Revd Dr. Henry Yarborough, Rector of Tewing in the aforesaid County, to act in the Capacity of such an Assistant-Executor; relating both to my said Will and Codicil. And I do hereby Will and order, that all the necessary Charges and Expences of proving and executing my said Will and Codicil or any Way attending the same, shall be chargable upon and defrayed out of my Estate real and personal and be first and before all other Accounts, deducted and reimbursed out of the said Estate to my respective Executors nominated in my said Will and Codicil. Lastly I earnestly desire that there may be no Disputes or Lawsuits touching any of my testamentary Concerns after my Decease, and that none of my Legatees may give any unnecessary Trouble to my Executors in reference to any part either of my said Will or Codicil.

Furthermore, by this Codicil I give to Mrs Mary Hallows two hundred Pounds besides the Eight hundred given to Her in my Will; so as to make up ye Sum One thousand Pounds.

And I give Rings to ye following Persons (viz) My Nephew Big ye Ds. of Portland, Miss Nancy Richardson, Mr Boteler, Shallcross, Yarborough, North, Gardiner, & to my two Cousin Youngs.

Edward Young. Signed Sealed and published by the Testator and by him declared to be a Codicil to his last Will and Testament in the presence of us whose Names are underwritten and who at his request in his presence, and in the presence of each other do witness the same Robt Milward / Thos. Pentlow / Jno. Deards.

[new sheet] 25th April 1765 On which Day appeared personally Mary Hallows of the parish of Wellwyn in the County of Hertford Spinster and made Oath that she well knew and was acquainted with the Reverend Edward Young Doctor of Laws late Rector of Wellwyn in the County of Hertford decd and she further saith that the said Doctor Young did ~~sometime in the latter End of the Year 1762~~ [over-written] about Six Months before his Death/as she best remembers and believes the Time to be deliver to her this Dept. the original Will and Codicil hereunto annexed closely sealed up in the Envelope or Cover hereunto annexed (which had been sometime before in her Possession and afterwards opened by the Doctor) about Six months before his Death, desiring her to keep the same in her Custody till after his Decease and she further deposeth that in a few Days after the said Deceased's Death she deliver'd the same to ~~the Reverend Mr.~~ Frederick Young Esquire the Son of the said Deceased who then opened the said Cover in the presence of this Deponent and she lastly saith that the said Will and Codicil are now in the same plight State and Condition in all respects as When the same was so opened as aforesaid (save as to the Endorsements appearing to have been made at Doctors Commons) and that she is certain that the said Envelope had never been opened from the Time she last received the same from the Hands of the said Doctor Young ~~sealed up with wax~~ as aforesaid till the delivery thereof to his Son after his Decease as aforesaid. Mary Hallows / same day The said Mary Hallows Spinster was duly sworn to the Truth of the Premises before me Geo. Harris / surrogate / Present Hen: Major Not[ary] Public. [The following endorsement has been stricken through.] 15th April 1765. The Reverend Richard Harris Clerk the Nephew and one of the Executors withinnamed was duly sworn to the Truth of the within written Will and the Codicil thereto annexed, and the due Performance of the same Power reserved to [blank] before me Geo. Harris Surrogate / Major. [Further endorsements:] 25th April 1765 The Revd John Jones Clerk one of the Executors within named was duly sworn to this Will and Codicil & duly to administer the Effects before me Geo. Harris Surrogate. Major. The Revd Richard Harris Clerk the Nephew and other Executor within named hath renounced. datd 30th. The Revd Edward Young Doctor of Laws late Rector of Wellwyn in the County of Hertford died in the present Month. Proved at London with a Codicil the thirtieth Day of April

1765 before the Worshipful George Harris Doctor of Laws and Surrogate by the Oath of the Revd. John Jones Clerk one of the Extors to whom Admon was granted having been first sworn and duly to Admter the Revd. Richard Harris Clerk the Nephew of the decd and the other Extor named in the Will ~~when he~~ first renouncing.

INDEX OF CORRESPONDENTS

GENERAL INDEX

Abercorn, Lady, 577
Achard, John, Swiss secretary to Duke
of Portland, 95 and n. 1, 136, 146,
199, 233, 302, 369
Adderley, Robert, Fellow of All Souls
College, Oxford, 4 and n. 2
Addison, Joseph, 5 nn. 2 and 3, 7 n. 8,
8 nn. 2 and 4, 9 n. 1, 21 and nn. 2 and
3, 28 n. 4, 401, 450, 479 f., 482–3,
488, 490 ff., 499 ff., 521; Y. *and*, 6
and n. 1, 8 f.
Aix la Chapelle, Y.'s reported visit to,
73 n. 2; peace negotiations at (1748),
299 and n. 1, celebrations of Treaty
of, 312 and n. 1
Akenside, Mark, 428 n. 2
Aldworth, Revd. John, Rector of East
Lockinge, Berkshire, 66 n. 4
All Souls College, Oxford, 1 n. 4, 4, 49,
66 n. 4, 601; *and* living of Welwyn,
Herts., 66 n. 4, 402, 594–5; *and* Y.'s
portrait, 88 n. 2, 360 n. 2, 414 n. 1
Allen, Ralph, 499
Allestree, Richard, *The Whole Duty of
Man*, 314 n. 1
Amelia, Princess Dowager of Wales, Y.
Clerk of the Closet to, 523 n. 1, 524
n. 1, 540 n. 2, 541, 544
Amhurst, Nicholas, and *The Craftsman*,
53 n. 3
Andover Mary, *née* Finch, Lady, 137
and n. 1, 142 n. 2, 195, 199, 211 ff.,
295
Andover, William, Lord, 435 and n. 2
Anson, George, Baron Anson, 475 and
n. 1
Anstey, Revd. Dr., of Trumpington,
357 n. 2
Aquinas, Thomas, recommended to Y.
by Pope, 22 n. 2
Arbuthnot, Dr. John, and *Miscellanies
in Prose and Verse*, 55 and n. 4
Arnaud, Abbé François, with reference
to Richardson, 574 and n. 1

Atkinson, William, Fellow of the Queen's
College, Oxford, 58 and n. 3

Bacon, Francis, 450
Baltimore, Charles Calvert, sixth Baron,
56 and n. 7, 101 and n. 4 (possibly)
Banks, John, *The Unhappy Favourite*,
19 and n. 2
Baretti, Guiseppi Marc' Antonio, 392
and n. 2
Barker, Edward, of Hatton Garden,
London, 323 n. 3
Barnard, Sir John, Lord Mayor of
London, 79 n. 1, 80 n. 4
Barnet, Herts., The Mitre, 375 and
n. 2
Baskett, Thomas, bookbinder, 352 n. 1,
353
Bateman, Lady Anne, 144–5 and n. 1
Bath, William Pulteney, Earl of, 587
and n. 1, 588 n. 1; and *The Craftsman*,
53 and n. 3, 56
Bath, Somerset, Y. at, 74 n. 5, 463 ff.,
467 and n. 1, 468 and n. 1; Wade's-
passage, 466
Bathurst, Thomas, successor to Y. as
rector of Welwyn, 594 and n. 4, 595
Battell, Isabella, 273 and n. 1
Battell, Mrs., 601
Battell, Revd. Ralph, 423 and n. 3
Battell, Revd. William, Rector of Digs-
well, Herts., 273 n. 1
Beattie, James, 310 n. 4
Bedford, John Russell, fourth Duke of,
352 n. 2
Belenden, Margaret, of Beaconsfield,
Bucks., 358 and n. 1
Bennet, Mrs., 499
Bentinck, Edward Charles, 178 and
n. 1, 200. *See also* Portland, Duchess
of, children
Berkeley, Anne, *née* Forster, 517 n. 2
Berkeley, George, Bishop of Cloyne,
46 and n. 2, 517

Eeles, Luke, physician, of Holly Hall, Welwyn, 246 n. 2
Egmont, John Perceval, first Earl of, 144 and n. 2
Eliot, George, with reference to Y., xxxiii
Elphinston, James, 398 nn. 1 and 2, *Education*, 570 and n. 2. *See also* Index of Correspondents
Elstob, Elizabeth, 103 and n. 2, 105 n. 2, 106, 432 n. 1
Enfield Chase, 106 and n. 1
Eustace, *see under* Tickell
Evans, Abel, St. John's College, Oxford, 4 and n. 4, 6, 54 and n. 2
Exchange Alley, symbol of financial world, 57

Fayrer, James, Fellow of Magdalen College, Oxford, 21 and n. 1
Fénelon, François de Salignac de la Mothe-, mentioned, 70 and n. 6
Fenton, Elijah, *Mariamne*, 25 and n. 3
Fenton, Lavinia, 63–4 and n. 1
Fermor, Lady Juliana, 364 and n. 3
Fermor, Lady Louisa, 511 n. 1
Fielding, Henry, 311 n. 4, 377
Fielding, Sarah, *The Governess*, 337 and n. 4, 338
Fireworks, on Queen Caroline's birthday (1728), 63 and n. 1; on the Treaty of Aix-la-Chapelle (1749), 312 and n. 1
Fletcher, Ann, 435 and n. 3
Fletcher, John, ? allusion to *Philaster*, 140
Fletcher, William, 435 and n. 3
Fontenoy, battle of (1745), 200 and n. 1
Foote, Samuel, 277 and n. 4
Forester, Richard, Vicar of Ashwell, Herts., 429 and n. 2, 431
Forster, H. B., on Y.'s ordination, 38 n. 1
Foster, James, *Discourses on ... National Religion and Social Virtue*, 337 and n. 1
Frankland, Diana, *see* Litchfield
Freeman, Nathaniel, Rector of Ayot St. Peters, Herts., 513 n. 2, 521
Freind, Robert, Canon of Windsor and Headmaster of Westminster School, 132 n. 2
Freind, William, Rector of Witney, Oxfordshire, 132 n. 2

Freke, John, Richardson's physician, 275 and n. 3, 276
Frisching, Mr., 359 n. 1
'Frogmorton', *see* Throckmorton
Frowde, Philip, 'Verses on her Majesty's Birth-Day', 63 n. 1

G——, Lord, unidentified, 127
Gainsborough estate, Wickham, Hants, bought by J. Rashleigh, 57 n. 1
Galloni, or Galeni, dentist, 420 and n. 2, 430 and n. 1, 431
Gardiner, Bernard, Warden of All Souls, 39 and n. 2
Gardiner, 602
Garrard, Sir Samuel, of Wheathampstead, Herts., 179 and n. 2, 513 n. 2, 521
Garrick, David, 279 and n. 3, 344 n. 4, 382 and n. 3, 385 n. 1, 387 n. 1, 389 n. 1, 428 n. 2. *See also* Index of Correspondents
Gastrell, Francis, Bishop of Chester, 168 and n. 5
Gataker, Mrs., 589 and n. 3
Gay, John, *Beggar's Opera*, 61 and n. 5, 63–4 and n. 1, 437 n. 1; The *Captives*, 23 n. 1, 25 and n. 3; *Fables*, 54 and n. 4, 56
George I, *and* children of Prince of Wales, 16 n. 3
George II, 54 n. 4, 292 n. 2
Germany, Y.'s fame in, 499
Giffard, Lady Martha, *née* Temple, 16 n. 1, 18 n. 2, 517–18 and n. 1. *See also* Index of Correspondents
Gilbert, Miss, 136 and n. 1
Godscall, Nicholas, 80 and n. 3, 83, 85 f., 88, 90–1
Godscall, Sarah, 80 and n. 3, 88, 90–1
Godscall, Sarah, daughter, 80 and n. 4, 82
Godstone, Surrey, well of medicinal water at, 380 n. 1
Gore, Charles, M.P. for Hertfordshire, 290 and n. 1
Gosling, Sir Francis, 362 n. 1, 382 n. 1, 393, 506, 601
Gosling's Bank, 323 n. 1, 343 n. 3, 382 n. 3, 409 n. 1, 414 n. 1, 506 n. 2, 561 n. 1, 569 n. 3
Granville, Miss, 334 and n. 2, 351
Great Frogmore House, Windsor, 266 n. 1

YOUNG, EDWARD (*cont.*):
Vindication of Providence, A, 34 and
n. 2, 58 and n. 4, 62 and n. 2, 65
n. 2, 69 n. 1, 75 n. 2, 234 n. 1,
248 and n. 1, 562 n. 3
— Mottoes and Inscriptions in Welwyn
Church and churchyard, and in his
house and garden, Appendix B
— Portraits, 74 n. 3, 88 and n. 2, 360
n. 2, 414 n. 1
— *With reference to*: Andover, Lady,
137; Bolingbroke, 357; Cibber, Colley,
61, 208–9; Cole, Captain J. M.,
224–5; Donnellan, Anne, 123–4
and n. 2, 125; Dashwood, Catherine,
132–4; Fénelon, 70 and n. 6; Fenton,
Lavinia, 63–4; Hartley's *Observations
on Man,* 319 ff.; Montagu, Mrs.
Elizabeth, 131, 145, 209; Newton,
Isaac, 71 and n. 1; Parsons, Grace,
233, 258, 303; Pendarves, Mrs. 113–
15, 130–1; Portland, Duchess of, 147;
Swift, 53 and n. 2, 374 and n. 2;
Taylor, John, 163; Thomson, James,
52 n. 4, 58; Vertue George, 168;
Voltaire, 53 and n. 1, 58, 71; Whatley,
Rev. Mr., 234–5
    Affliction, 120–2, 136–7, 152–3,
414, 500; bishops, 268; Christianity,
589, 596; Church, the, 56; compassion, 240–1; *Craftsman, The,* 53, 56;
death, 183; disappointment, 324;
education, 278; equanimity, 222–3;
esteem, love of, 133–4; female sex,
231; Gay's *Fables,* 56; happiness,
87 f., 214–15, 556; Homer, 70;
Horace, 70 and n. 5; lawyers and
politicians, 176–7; London, 176 and
n. 2; lunacy, 241–2, 246–7; marriage,
494, 509, 512; newspapers, 586;
oddities (eccentrics), 277; old age,
237, 254–5, 517; pleasures, 57, 127–8,
152–3, 522; politics, 582 f.; preaching
and sermons, 150–1, 250; Providence,
152–3, 258; Royal Society, The, 57;
society, 108–9; Universities, the, 56;
virtue, 263; wit, 179
Young, Lady Elizabeth, formerly Lee,
56 n. 7, 74 and n. 2, 76 nn. 1–3, 77
and n. 1, 78 n. 1, 85, 87 and n. 1, 94
nn. 1 and 2, 301 n. 2, 359 n. 1, 492,
594
Young, Elizabeth, *née* Heysham, 323 n. 2
Young Frederick, 267 n. 2, 323 n. 2,
347 n. 2, 349 and n. 1, 372 n. 1, 382
n. 3, 478 and n. 1, 591 and n. 3,
592 ff., and nn. 1 and 2, 602 f.
Young, Judith, 1 n. 4, 2 and n. 3,
88 n. 2, 186 n. 1, 349 n. 2

Zincke, Christian Friederich, miniatur-
ist, 142 and n. 2